THE CAMBRIDGE HANDBOOK OF LAWYERING IN THE DIGITAL AGE

With increasing digitalization and the evolution of artificial intelligence, the legal profession is on the verge of being transformed by technology (legal tech). This handbook examines these developments and the changing legal landscape by providing perspectives from multiple interested parties, including practitioners, academics, and legal tech companies from different legal systems. Scrutinizing the real implications posed by legal tech, the book advocates for an unbiased, cautious approach for the engagement of technology in legal practice. It also carefully addresses the core question of how to balance fears of industry takeover by technology with the potential for using legal tech to expand services and create value for clients. Together, the chapters develop a framework for analyzing the costs and benefits of new technologies before they are implemented in legal practice. This interdisciplinary collection features contributions from lawyers, social scientists, institutional officials, technologists, and current developers of e-law platforms and services.

LARRY A. DIMATTEO is the Huber Hurst Professor of Contract Law at the Warrington College of Business and Levin College of Law, University of Florida. He was the Editor-in-Chief of the *American Business Law Journal*, a 2012 Fulbright Professor, and author of fourteen books. His most recent publications include *The Cambridge Handbook of Smart Contracts, Blockchain Technology and Digital Platforms* (with Michel Cannarsa and Cristina Poncibò, Cambridge, 2019) and *The Cambridge Handbook of Judicial Control of Arbitral Awards* (with Marta Infantino and Nathalie M-P Potin, Cambridge, 2021).

ANDRÉ JANSSEN is a chair for (European) Private Law professor at Radboud University, The Netherlands. He has held previous positions at multiple international institutions, including the Universities of Münster, Turin, and the City University of Hong Kong. Professor Janssen is also a member of several international research networks and has published more than 150 books and articles in the fields of private, European, comparative and international sales law, and artificial intelligence and law. He is the co-editor-in-chief of the *European Review of Private Law* (ERPL) and is a member of the editorial board of the *International Arbitration Law Review* (IALR).

PIETRO ORTOLANI is Professor of Digital Conflict Resolution at Radboud University, The Netherlands. Before joining Radboud University, he was a Senior Research Fellow at the Max Planck Institute Luxembourg for Procedural Law and a Law Research Associate at Queen Mary, University of London. In 2016, Pietro won the James Crawford Prize. He has also contributed to a European Parliament Study concerning the legal instruments and practice of arbitration in the EU.

FRANCISCO DE ELIZALDE is the Chair of Legal Studies at IE Law School, IE University (Spain). He focuses on Comparative Private Law, especially Contracts and the Law of Property. He is a Visiting Professor at Koç University (Turkey) and has lectured at the City University of Hong Kong and FGV Sao Paulo (Brazil). He is a member of the Madrid Bar Association, the American Society of Comparative Law and the European Law Institute. Professor Elizalde is also the head of the EU-financed Jean Monnet Module 'Liability of Robots: a European Vision for a New Legal Regime'.

MICHEL CANNARSA is Professor and Dean of Law at UCLy. His areas of research include product liability, law of new technologies, comparative law, consumer law and law of obligations. He has published recent books and articles on the interaction between law and technology, contract law and products liability law.

MATEJA DUROVIC is a Reader in Contract and Commercial Law and Deputy Director of the Centre for Technology, Ethics, Law and Society at King's College London. He had held previous positions at the City University of Hong Kong, the EUI, Italy, Stanford Law School, USA, and the Max Planck Institute of Private International and Comparative Law, Hamburg, Germany.

The Cambridge Handbook of Lawyering in the Digital Age

Edited by

LARRY A. DIMATTEO
University of Florida

ANDRÉ JANSSEN
Radboud University Nijmegen

PIETRO ORTOLANI
Radboud University Nijmegen

FRANCISCO DE ELIZALDE
IE University Madrid

MICHEL CANNARSA
Lyon Catholic University (UCLy)

MATEJA DUROVIC
King's College London

Shaftesbury Road, Cambridge CB2 8EA, United Kingdom

One Liberty Plaza, 20th Floor, New York, NY 10006, USA

477 Williamstown Road, Port Melbourne, VIC 3207, Australia

314–321, 3rd Floor, Plot 3, Splendor Forum, Jasola District Centre, New Delhi – 110025, India

103 Penang Road, #05–06/07, Visioncrest Commercial, Singapore 238467

Cambridge University Press is part of Cambridge University Press & Assessment, a department of the University of Cambridge.

We share the University's mission to contribute to society through the pursuit of education, learning and research at the highest international levels of excellence.

www.cambridge.org
Information on this title: www.cambridge.org/9781009295727

DOI: 10.1017/9781108936040

© Cambridge University Press & Assessment 2021

This publication is in copyright. Subject to statutory exception and to the provisions of relevant collective licensing agreements, no reproduction of any part may take place without the written permission of Cambridge University Press & Assessment.

First published 2021
First paperback edition 2023

A catalogue record for this publication is available from the British Library

Library of Congress Cataloging-in-Publication data
NAMES: Lawyers in the Digital Age (Conference) (2019 : Amsterdam, Netherlands) | DiMatteo, Larry A., editor. | Janssen, Andre, 1972- editor. | Ortolani, Pietro, editor. | Elizalde, Francisco de, editor. | Cannarsa, Michel, editor. | Durovic, Mateja, editor.
TITLE: The Cambridge handbook of lawyering in the digital age / edited by Larry A. DiMatteo, André Janssen, Radboud Universiteit Nijmegen; Pietro Ortolani, Radboud Universiteit Nijmegen; Francisco de Elizalde, IE University Madrid; Michel Cannarsa, Catholic Lyon University; Mateja Durovic, King's College London.
DESCRIPTION: Cambridge, United Kingdom ; New York, NY : Cambridge University Press, 2021. | Series: Cambridge law handbooks
IDENTIFIERS: LCCN 2021025008 (print) | LCCN 2021025009 (ebook) | ISBN 9781108837460 (hardback) | ISBN 9781108936040 (epub)
SUBJECTS: LCSH: Lawyers–Effect of technological innovations on–Congresses. | Legal services–Technological innovations–Congresses. | Practice of law–Technological innovations–Congresses. | LCGFT: Conference papers and proceedings.
CLASSIFICATION: LCC K120 .L395 2019 (print) | LCC K120 (ebook) | DDC 340.0285–dc23
LC record available at https://lccn.loc.gov/2021025008
LC ebook record available at https://lccn.loc.gov/2021025009

ISBN   978-1-108-83746-0   Hardback
ISBN   978-1-009-29572-7   Paperback

Cambridge University Press & Assessment has no responsibility for the persistence or accuracy of URLs for external or third-party internet websites referred to in this publication and does not guarantee that any content on such websites is, or will remain, accurate or appropriate.

Contents

Detailed Contents	*page* vii
List of Figures	xvii
List of Contributors	xix
Preface	xxv

1	**Lawyering in the Digital Age** Pietro Ortolani and Larry A. DiMatteo	1

PART I EFFECTS OF TECHNOLOGY ON LEGAL PRACTICE

2	**Disruptive Effects of Legal Tech** Jiaying Christine Jiang, Larry A. DiMatteo, and Robert E. Thomas	9
3	**The Effects of Technology on Legal Practice: From Punch Card to Artificial Intelligence?** André Janssen and Tom J. Vennmanns	38
4	**Legal Drafting and Automation** Benjamin Werthmann	57
5	**Emerging Rules on Artificial Intelligence: Trojan Horses of Ethics in the Realm of Law?** Florian Möslein and Maximilian Horn	77

PART II LEGAL TECH AND ADR

6	**Legal Tech in ADR** Mateja Durovic and Franciszek Lech	99
7	**A Blockchain-Based Smart Dispute Resolution Method** Alessandro Palombo, Raffaele Battaglini, and Luigi Cantisani	122
8	**Digital Dispute Resolution: Blurring the Boundaries of ADR** Pietro Ortolani	140

PART III LEGAL TECH IN CONSUMER RELATIONS AND SMALL CLAIMS

9 Legal Tech in Consumer Relations and Small-Value Claims: A Survey — 159
   Francisco de Elizalde

10 Regulation of Legal Services and Access to Justice in the Digital Age: A War Report — 179
   Jin Ho Verdonschot and Max Houben

11 Legal Tech and EU Consumer Law — 195
   Martin Ebers

12 The Two Faces of Legal Tech in B2C Relations — 220
   Eric Tjong Tjin Tai

PART IV LEGAL TECH AND PUBLIC LAW

13 Blockchain's Heterotopia: Technological Infrastructures and Lawyering in the Public Sector — 239
   Georgios Dimitropoulos

14 Fundamental Rights and the Use of Artificial Intelligence in Court — 257
   Jean-Marc van Gyseghem

15 Legal Tech in Public Administration: Prospects and Challenges — 272
   Antonios Kouroutakis

PART V LEGAL ETHICS AND SOCIETAL VALUES CONFRONT TECHNOLOGY

16 Ethics Guidelines for Trustworthy AI — 283
   Michel Cannarsa

17 Ethical Digital Lawyering: From Technical to Philosophical Insights — 298
   Mathieu Guillermin, Arnaud Billion, Carine Copain-Héritier, and Emmanuel de Vaujany

18 Law, Disintermediation and the Future of Trust — 312
   Christoph Kletzer

PART VI FATE OF THE LEGAL PROFESSIONS

19 Lawyering Somewhere between Computation and the Will to Act: A Digital Age Reflection — 327
   Jeffrey M. Lipshaw

20 Surviving the Digital Transformation: A Method for Lawyers to Approach Legal Tech — 358
   Paw Fruerlund and Sebastian Peters

21 Road Forward: Promise and Danger — 372
   Larry A. DiMatteo and Pietro Ortolani

Detailed Contents

1	**Lawyering in the Digital Age**	1
	1.1 Introduction	1
	1.2 Scope and Structure of the Book	2
	1.2.1 Effects of Technology on Legal Practice	3
	1.2.2 Legal Tech and Alternative Dispute Resolution	4
	1.2.3 Legal Tech in Consumer Relations and Small Claims	4
	1.2.4 Legal Tech and Public Law	5
	1.2.5 Legal Ethics and Societal Values Confront Technology	5
	1.2.6 Fate of the Legal Professions	6

PART I EFFECTS OF TECHNOLOGY ON LEGAL PRACTICE

2	**Disruptive Effects of Legal Tech**	9
	2.1 Introduction	9
	2.2 Legal Practice before the Age of Information	12
	2.2.1 Dawning of a New Era: Pre-1970s	12
	2.2.2 Advent of the Internet and the First Legal Databases	12
	2.3 Twenty-First Century: Interface of Legal Practice and Technology	14
	2.3.1 Baby Steps: E-Discovery and Early Staged Automation	15
	2.3.2 Legal Tech: Augmenting the Lawyers' Work	16
	2.3.2.1 Drafting Legal Documents	17
	2.3.2.2 Analyzing Legal Documents	17
	2.3.2.3 Measuring Legal Performance	18
	2.3.2.4 Structuring and Management of Legal Workflows	18
	2.3.2.5 Legal Research	19
	2.3.3 Technology as a Legal Substitute	20
	2.3.3.1 Online Pseudo-law Services	20
	2.3.3.2 Internet Courts and the Use of Tamper-Proof Evidence	21
	2.3.3.3 Notary Publics and the Blockchain	23
	2.3.3.4 Smart Contracts and the Challenges of Implementation	25
	2.4 Future of Legal Practice	26
	2.4.1 Advanced AI: Thinking and Performing like a Lawyer?	27

		2.4.2 Smart Contracts and the Blockchain: Executable Law?	28
		2.4.3 Future of Legal Ethics	28
	2.5	Co-opting Legal Tech	30
		2.5.1 Using Technology to Make Lawyering More Efficient	31
		2.5.2 Retaining the Human Dimension of Lawyering	33
		2.5.3 Reforming Legal Education	35
	2.6	Conclusion	37
3	**The Effects of Technology on Legal Practice: From Punch Card to Artificial Intelligence?**		38
	3.1	Introduction	38
	3.2	Law and Technology: Two Opposing Worlds Colliding?	39
		3.2.1 Traditional Character of Law as an 'Analogous' Field of Expertise	39
		3.2.2 Entrenched Working Methods, Unwillingness to Change and Scepticism: Prejudice or Real Phenomenon?	41
		3.2.3 Established Main Features of Working Methods and Methodology within Legal Practice: Lack of Formal Logic	42
		3.2.4 Expectations of a Lawyer in the Course of Time: Yesterday and Tomorrow	43
		3.2.4.1 Legal Practitioners and Law Firms	43
		3.2.4.2 State Courts, Arbitral Tribunals and Other Means of Private Dispute Resolution	44
	3.3	Artificial Intelligence: Lawyers in the Grip of Technological Change	46
		3.3.1 The Gradual Embedding of Technology in Legal Practice	46
		3.3.1.1 First Steps: Electronic Data Processing and Computing	46
		3.3.1.2 Big Data and Modern Telecommunication	48
		3.3.1.3 Artificial Intelligence, Algorithms and Automated Decision-Making (Legal Tech 3.0, ODR and Robo-judges)	49
	3.4	Some Problems and Threats Identified	49
		3.4.1 Lack of Legislative Will to Prepare Legal Practice for the Digital Age: The Example of Germany	49
		3.4.2 Failure to Make Full Use of the Existing Legal Possibilities	51
		3.4.3 Inequality of Arms: Disparities in Resources and Know-How for Investment in Digital Infrastructure	52
		3.4.4 Possible Consequences for the Legal Service Market: The Human Lawyer at Risk of Becoming a Discontinued Model?	53
	3.5	Outlook	55
4	**Legal Drafting and Automation**		57
	4.1	Introduction	57
		4.1.1 Automation and Legal Tech	57
		4.1.2 Automation in the Context of AI	58
		4.1.3 Automation and Blockchain	59
	4.2	Legal Drafting	60
		4.2.1 Drafting Background	60
		4.2.1.1 Document Purposes	60
		4.2.1.2 Expectations	60
		4.2.1.3 Contract Logic	61

	4.2.2	Quality Criteria for Contracts	61
		4.2.2.1 Legal Validity	61
		4.2.2.2 Transparency	62
		4.2.2.3 Consistency	63
	4.2.3	Internal Drafting Requirements	63
		4.2.3.1 Precise Language	63
		4.2.3.2 Clear Structure	63
		4.2.3.3 Compliance	64
		4.2.3.4 Velocity	65
	4.2.4	Contract Content	65
		4.2.4.1 Essential Rights and Obligations	65
		4.2.4.2 Ancillary Rights and Obligations	66
		4.2.4.3 Modifications and Business Logic	66
		4.2.4.4 Boilerplate Provisions	66
4.3	Automation	66
	4.3.1	Evolution of Contract Automation	67
		4.3.1.1 Use of Precedents and Templates	67
		4.3.1.2 Questionnaires and Annotations	68
		4.3.1.3 Automated Templates (Contract Generators)	68
		4.3.1.4 Robo-lawyers	69
	4.3.2	Document Automation Requirements	69
		4.3.2.1 Interface	69
		4.3.2.2 Logic	70
		4.3.2.3 Maintenance	70
		4.3.2.4 Compatibility	70
	4.3.3	Automation Instruments	71
		4.3.3.1 Expert Systems	71
		4.3.3.2 Artificial Intelligence and Blockchain	71
	4.3.4	Best Practices for Contract Automation	72
		4.3.4.1 Cost-Benefit Analysis (80/20 Rule)	72
		4.3.4.2 User-Centric Contract Design	73
		4.3.4.3 Open Source Practices	74
4.4	Conclusion and Outlook	75

5 **Emerging Rules on Artificial Intelligence: Trojan Horses of Ethics in the Realm of Law?** — 77

5.1	Introduction	77
5.2	Variety of Emerging Rules	79
	5.2.1 International Level	79
	5.2.2 European Level	80
	5.2.3 National Level	81
	5.2.4 Self-Regulation	82
5.3	Converging Substance of Emerging Rules	83
	5.3.1 Control and Controllability	84
	5.3.2 Disclosure	85
	5.3.3 Safeguarding Individual Rights	86
	5.3.4 Public Good Requirements	86

5.4	Legal Relevance	87
	5.4.1 Distinguishing between Law and Ethics	87
	5.4.2 Formal Classification	88
	5.4.3 Effective Impact	88
5.5	Fields of Application	89
	5.5.1 Company Law (Robo-directors)	89
	5.5.2 Securities Law (Robo-advisors)	91
	5.5.3 Rules of Professional Conduct (Robo-lawyers)	92
	5.5.3.1 Impact on Permissibility of Legal Tech	94
	5.5.3.2 Impact on Standards of Ethical Conduct	94
5.6	Conclusion	95

PART II LEGAL TECH AND ADR

6 Legal Tech in ADR — 99

6.1	Introduction	99
6.2	ODR, ADR, DR and Courts: Navigating the Terminological Minefield	101
6.3	Technology as a Key to Dissemination of Effective Justice	103
	6.3.1 Access to Justice	103
	6.3.2 Efficiency	108
	6.3.3 Blockchain: A Thorn in ADR's Side	110
	6.3.4 Technology: ADR's Saviour or Undertaker?	112
6.4	Technology in Practice: Examples of 'New' ADR	113
	6.4.1 Kleros	113
	6.4.2 Juris	115
	6.4.3 Mattereum	116
	6.4.4 JUR	116
	6.4.5 Jury Online	117
	6.4.6 Aragon	117
	6.4.7 RHUbarb	118
	6.4.8 Multi-signature Smart Contract	119
	6.4.9 Blockchain Arbitration Forum	119
	6.4.10 ClickNSettle and Others	120
6.5	Conclusion	120

7 A Blockchain-Based Smart Dispute Resolution Method — 122

7.1	Introduction	122
7.2	Arbitration and ADR: Current Status	122
	7.2.1 Scope of Arbitration and ADR	123
	7.2.2 Sovereign Jurisdictional Authority and Private Autonomy	123
	7.2.3 Existing Framework and International Conventions	124
	7.2.4 Advantages and Disadvantages of Arbitration and ADR	126
7.3	Advent of Blockchain-Based ODR	127
	7.3.1 Brief Introduction to Blockchain and Smart Contract	127
	7.3.2 Smart (Legal) Contracts and Their Inherent Limits	128
	7.3.3 Smart Dispute Resolution: State of the Art	129

		7.3.3.1 Kleros	130
		7.3.3.2 Mattereum	130
	7.3.4	Limitations of Oracles-Based SDR Systems	131
		7.3.4.1 Impartiality and Expertise of the Decision-Maker versus Economic Incentives Systems	131
		7.3.4.2 Due Process and Legal Validity of the Decision	131
	7.3.5	Advantages of the Oracles-Based SDR Systems	132
		7.3.5.1 Small Claims Courts	133
		7.3.5.2 Mediation	133
		7.3.5.3 Arbitration	133
	7.3.6	Summary of Oracle-Based SDR Systems	134
7.4	Proposal for Legally Binding SDR		134
	7.4.1	Designing Decentralized Smart Arbitration	135
	7.4.2	Economic Sustainability of the System	136
	7.4.3	Anti-corruption Measures and Reserve Account	136
	7.4.4	Preemptive Review on the Merits and Case Reassignment	137
7.5	Proposing a New *Lex Mercatoria* via Blockchain		137
	7.5.1	Fairness and Best Practices for Smart Arbitration and Trade	138
	7.5.2	Potential Benefits	138
7.6	Conclusion		138

8 Digital Dispute Resolution: Blurring the Boundaries of ADR   140

8.1	Introduction		140
8.2	Traditional Modes of Boundaries in ADR		142
	8.2.1	Quasi-monopoly to Delegation: Courts and Arbitration	142
	8.2.2	Enforceability without Adjudication: Rise of Mediation	144
	8.2.3	Bounded Autonomy: Judicial Intervention and Review as Boundary-Defining	145
8.3	Rise of New Forms of Digital Dispute Resolution		146
	8.3.1	Origins of Technology-Driven Self-Enforcement: Domain Name Dispute Resolution	147
	8.3.2	Platforms as Dispute Resolution Service Providers	148
	8.3.3	Smart Contracts and Settlement Agreements	150
	8.3.4	Smart Online Dispute Resolution	151
8.4	Increasing Porousness of Procedural Law in Times of Technological Acceleration		152
	8.4.1	Self-Enforcing Adjudication, Due Process and Judicial Review	153
	8.4.2	End of Finality?	154
	8.4.3	Public Policy and the Enforcement of Substantive Law	155
8.5	Conclusion		156

PART III LEGAL TECH IN CONSUMER RELATIONS AND SMALL CLAIMS

9 Legal Tech in Consumer Relations and Small-Value Claims: A Survey   159

9.1	Introduction	159
9.2	Survey	160
	9.2.1 Methodology	160

	9.2.2 Results	161
	9.2.2.1 Companies by Sector	161
	9.2.2.2 Self-Assessment of Automation	163
	9.2.2.3 Degrees of Automation and Control of the Self-Assessment Exercise: Technology and Success Rates in Court	163
	9.2.2.4 Applicable Law and Automation	166
9.3	A Qualitative Assessment of the Survey	167
	9.3.1 Classification of Companies by Degree of Automation	168
	9.3.2 Suitability of Law for Automation and Variations in Technological Efficiency	169
	9.3.3 How Law Determines Automation	171
	9.3.3.1 Air Carriage	171
	9.3.3.2 Banking	173
	9.3.3.3 Tenancy in Germany	176
	9.3.3.4 Telecommunications	177
9.4	Conclusion	178

10 Regulation of Legal Services and Access to Justice in the Digital Age: A War Report — 179

10.1	Introduction	179
	10.1.1 Global Access to Justice	179
	10.1.2 New Delivery Concepts	180
	10.1.3 What Now?	181
10.2	LegalZoom	181
10.3	LegalDutch	183
10.4	WenigerMiete	185
10.5	Doctrine	187
10.6	Demander Justice	189
10.7	Concluding Remarks	193

11 Legal Tech and EU Consumer Law — 195

11.1	Introduction	195
	11.1.1 Rise of LT in Consumer Markets	195
	11.1.2 Underlying Technology: From Hand-Coded to Data-Learned Knowledge	197
	11.1.3 Opportunities for Consumers	198
	11.1.4 Risks for Consumers	199
11.2	Current Regulatory Framework in a Nutshell	200
	11.2.1 The Interplay between Legal Services Regulation, EU Consumer and Data Protection Law	200
	11.2.2 Evaluation	201
11.3	Legal Services Regulations and LT	202
	11.3.1 Regulation of Legal Services in the EU	202
	11.3.2 LT as a Challenge for Legal Services Regulation	203
	11.3.3 Contract Generators as Unauthorized Practice of Law?	204
	11.3.4 Risks from Unregulated LT Providers	205
11.4	EU Consumer Law and LT	205
	11.4.1 Regulation of Consumer Law in the EU	205
	11.4.2 Applicability of EU Consumer Law to LT	206

	11.4.3 Prohibition of Unfair Commercial Practices	208
	11.4.4 Information Requirements and the Right of Withdrawal	208
	11.4.5 Quality of Service	209
	11.4.6 Legal Ethics and Fairness	210
	11.4.7 Further Gaps in Consumer Protection	212
	11.4.8 Summary	212
11.5	EU Data Protection Law and LT	213
	11.5.1 Legal Services Regulation and Data Protection Law	213
	11.5.2 LT and Data Protection under the GDPR	213
	11.5.3 Limits of the GDPR	214
	11.5.4 Summary	216
11.6	Outlook	216
	11.6.1 Unresolved Questions	216
	11.6.2 Current Approaches of Regulators	216
	11.6.3 Alternative Approaches: Regulatory Sandboxes	217
	11.6.4 The Future (European) Legal Framework	218

12 The Two Faces of Legal Tech in B2C Relations — 220

12.1	Introduction	220
12.2	The Promise of Legal Tech in B2C Relations	221
	12.2.1 General Considerations regarding Legal Tech in Businesses	221
	12.2.2 Customer Communications	221
	12.2.3 Business Protocols	222
	12.2.4 IT to Execute and Enforce Contracts	224
	12.2.5 Summary	224
12.3	Consequences of Legal Tech in B2C	224
12.4	Case of eBay	228
12.5	Traditional View of Regulation of Complaint Handling	230
12.6	Legal Regulation of B2C Relations: Bad Faith Insurance	231
12.7	Professional Diligence as Fundamental Principle for Legal Tech	233
12.8	Toward Developmental Diligence	234
12.9	Conclusion	235

PART IV LEGAL TECH AND PUBLIC LAW

13 Blockchain's Heterotopia: Technological Infrastructures and Lawyering in the Public Sector — 239

13.1	Introduction	239
13.2	Blockchain and the "Infrastructural Paradox" of Contemporary Public Law	242
	13.2.1 Conflicting Trends in Public Law	242
	13.2.2 Rise of Physical Infrastructure in Public Law	244
	13.2.3 Infrastructural Dimension of Blockchain	245
	13.2.3.1 Physical Manifestations	246
	13.2.3.2 Effects on the Individual and Society	247
	13.2.3.3 Blockchain as a Technological Infrastructure	248
13.3	Law and Lawyering in the Digital Age of Blockchain	248
	13.3.1 Law's Stance and Regulatory Reaction to the Rise of Blockchain	249

             13.3.2 Lawyering in the Digital Age: Reconciling Antitheses   251
                    13.3.2.1 Reconciling Innovation with Regulation   251
                    13.3.2.2 Reconciling Decentralization with Accountability   252
                    13.3.2.3 Reconciling the Coexistence of Multiple Infrastructures   254
      13.4 Conclusion   255

14 Fundamental Rights and the Use of Artificial Intelligence in Court   257
      14.1 Introduction   257
      14.2 Transparency   259
             14.2.1 Principles   259
             14.2.2 Transparency of AI   260
      14.3 Impartiality and Presumption of Innocence   265
             14.3.1 Principle   265
             14.3.2 Impartiality and Presumption of Innocence and AI   266
      14.4 Equal Access to Justice   269
      14.5 Further Processing   270
      14.6 Conclusion   271

15 Legal Tech in Public Administration: Prospects and Challenges   272
      15.1 Introduction   272
      15.2 The Prospect of Legal Tech in Public Administration   273
      15.3 Publictech Challenged: Concerns Coming from Case Law and Theory   277
      15.4 Preliminary Review and Scrutiny of Publictech   279
      15.5 Conclusion   280

      PART V LEGAL ETHICS AND SOCIETAL VALUES CONFRONT TECHNOLOGY

16 Ethics Guidelines for Trustworthy AI   283
      16.1 Introduction: Artificial Intelligence but Real Concerns   283
      16.2 Ethical Guidelines for Trustworthy AI: An Inflationary Trend   285
             16.2.1 Definition of Trustworthy AI   285
             16.2.2 Focus on Human Rights and Privacy   288
             16.2.3 Response Still under Construction   290
      16.3 Impact on the Law: Some Examples   293
             16.3.1 New Civil Liability Framework   293
             16.3.2 New Professional Framework   295
      16.4 Conclusion   296

17 Ethical Digital Lawyering: From Technical to Philosophical Insights   298
      17.1 Introduction   298
      17.2 Ethical Evaluation of New (Legal) Technologies: Need for Contextualization   299
             17.2.1 Insights from Technical Realities: Gain in (Economic) Efficiency?   300
             17.2.2 Gain in Objectivity, Rationality, or Neutrality?   301
      17.3 Influence of Theoretical Backgrounds and Debates   304
             17.3.1 Argument of Standardization   304
             17.3.2 Purging Subjectivity as a Gain in Rationality   307
      17.4 Conclusion   310

18 Law, Disintermediation and the Future of Trust 312

18.1 Introduction 312
18.2 Peer-to-Peer: Allure of Trustlessness 314
18.3 Limits of Smartness 317
18.4 Reliance, Kantian Trust and Human Nature 319
18.5 Trust and the Law 322
18.6 Conclusion 323

PART VI FATE OF THE LEGAL PROFESSIONS

19 Lawyering Somewhere between Computation and the Will to Act: A Digital Age Reflection 327

19.1 Introduction 327
19.2 Digital Capability and Lawyering 331
    19.2.1 Algorithmic Decision-Making Tools Generally 332
    19.2.2 State of the Art in Algorithmic Lawyering 333
        19.2.2.1 Well-Established Usages 333
        19.2.2.2 Cutting Edge 334
19.3 Ends, Thought, and Action 337
    19.3.1 Segue (or a Leap) from Algorithms (Machines) to Ends (Minds) 337
    19.3.2 Embodied *Telos* 339
        19.3.2.1 Evolution of Ends 339
        19.3.2.2 *Telos* of System 1 Thinking 343
    19.3.3 Intuition as More Than Mere Thought 345
    19.3.4 Insight 347
        19.3.4.1 Difference between Intuition and Insight 347
        19.3.4.2 Non-deliberation as Insight or Inspiration 349
    19.3.5 Action and Will 352
    19.3.6 Lawyering in the Face of Irreconcilable Complementarities 354
    19.3.7 Rest of the Caregiving Story (a Microcosm in Lawyering) 356
19.4 Conclusion 357

20 Surviving the Digital Transformation: A Method for Lawyers to Approach Legal Tech 358

20.1 Scope and Perspective 358
20.2 Buzzwords 360
    20.2.1 Fake Tech 360
    20.2.2 Hype Tech 361
    20.2.3 Actual Legal Tech 361
    20.2.4 Typical Lawyer 362
20.3 Developing or Adapting Legal Tech in a Law Firm 363
    20.3.1 Ideation 363
        20.3.1.1 Getting the Right People: Facilitator and the Participants 363
        20.3.1.2 Getting the Ideas 364
        20.3.1.3 Selecting the Good Ones 366
    20.3.2 Business Case 366
        20.3.2.1 Going from the Solution to the How 366

	20.3.3 Minimum Variable Product	367
	20.3.4 Sprinting!	368
	20.3.5 Implementation	369
	20.3.5.1 Inclusion from Beginning to End	369
	20.3.5.2 Right Users at the Right Time	369
	20.3.5.3 Implementation after Going Live	370
	20.3.5.4 Handoff to Operations and Maintenance	370
	20.4 Conclusion	370
21	**Road Forward: Promise and Danger**	372
	21.1 Introduction	372
	21.2 Law and Technology	373
	21.3 Legal Practice and Competition	373
	21.4 Consumers, Access to Justice, and Regulation	374
	21.5 Technology and ADR	377
	21.6 LT, Legal Education, and Legal Ethics	378
	21.6.1 Legal Education	378
	21.6.2 LT and Legal Ethics	378
	21.7 Conclusion	379

Figures

11.1 Interplay between legal services regulation, EU consumer and data protection law *page* 200
12.1 Opportunities for legal tech in the business process 225

Contributors

Raffaele Battaglini is founder of Battaglini-De Sabato Law Firm, acting as Chief Legal Officer at JUR A.G. He is a member of the "Blockchain Technology and Smart Contracts" working group at the European Law Institute and co-organizer of the Legal Hackers Torino Chapter.

Arnaud Billion leads an AI and IT Ethics initiative at IBM France Lab. Billion is a lawyer, specializing in international copyright law. His domains of interest encompass computable law, ethics of information technology, and the question of whether AI outputs can be copyright protected.

Michel Cannarsa is Dean of Law at Lyon Catholic University (UCLy). His areas of research are product liability, law of new technologies, comparative law, consumer law, and law of obligations. He has recent books and articles on the interaction between law and technology, contract, and products liability law including, "Civil Liability and New Technologies," in T. Tridimas and M. Durovic (eds.), *The Future of European Private Law* (Hart, 2021); *The Cambridge Handbook of Smart Contracts, Blockchain Technology and Digital Platforms*, co-edited with L. DiMatteo and C. Poncibò (Cambridge University Press, 2019); "Interpretation of Contracts and Smart Contracts: Smart Interpretation or Interpretation of Smart Contracts?" (2018) 26 (6) *European Review Private Law*, pp. 773–785; "Remedies and Damages," in L. DiMatteo and C. Lei (eds.), *Chinese Contract Law, Civil and Common Law Perspectives* (Cambridge University Press, 2017), pp. 377–403. He is regularly involved in European research projects and currently chairs the Notaries beyond Frontiers EU project (European Commission Justice Programme). He is a fellow of the European Law Institute and an elected member of UCLy's Scientific Committee.

Luigi Cantisani holds an LLM in international trade law, is a lawyer qualified to practice law in Italy, advising SMEs and start-ups in the field of corporate law, commercial contracts, and new technologies. Additionally, he works as an outsourced legal engineer for companies engaged in the development of LT platforms, including blockchain-based platforms for smart legal contracts and online dispute resolution.

Larry A. DiMatteo is the Huber Hurst Professor of Contract Law at the Warrington College of Business and Levin College of Law, University of Florida. He was the editor-in-chief of the *American Business Law Journal*, a 2012 Fulbright Professor, and author of fourteen books. His most recent publications include *The Cambridge Handbook of Smart Contracts, Blockchain Technology and Digital Platforms* (with Michel Cannarsa and Cristina Poncibò, Cambridge

University Press, 2019) and *The Cambridge Handbook of Judicial Control of Arbitral Awards* (with Marta Infantino and Nathalie M.-P. Potin, Cambridge University Press, 2021).

Georgios Dimitropoulos is an associate professor of Law at HBKU College of Law. He is also a research associate at the University College London Centre for Law, Economics and Society (UCL CLES) and the University College London Centre for Blockchain Technologies (UCL CBT). Georgios studied law at the University of Athens and holds an LLM from Yale Law School, as well as an LLM and a PhD summa cum laude from the University of Heidelberg. Before joining HBKU Law, he was a senior research fellow at the Max Planck Institute Luxembourg and a Hauser Research Scholar at New York University (NYU) School of Law. His work has appeared in journals such as the *Northwestern Journal of International Law & Business*, the *Journal of International Dispute Settlement*, the *Journal of World Investment & Trade*, *The Law and Practice of International Courts and Tribunals*, the *Journal of Law and Policy*, and the *Maastricht Journal of European and Comparative Law*. His coedited book *Regulating Blockchain: Techno-Social and Legal Challenges* was published by Oxford University Press in 2019.

Mateja Durovic is a reader in Contract and Commercial Law and Co-Director of the Centre for Technology, Ethics, Law and Society at King's College London. Previous to this, he was an assistant professor (2015–2017) at the School of Law, City University of Hong Kong. Dr. Mateja Durovic holds PhD and LLM degrees from the European University Institute, Italy, an LLM degree from the University of Cambridge, and an LLB degree from the University of Belgrade, Serbia where he graduated as the first and the best student of his class. Dr. Durovic was a postdoc research associate at the EUI, Italy (2014–2015), visiting scholar at Stanford Law School (2011) and at the Max Planck Institute of Private International and Comparative Law, Hamburg, Germany (2010). Dr. Durovic worked for the Legal Service of the European Commission, as well as a consultant for the European Commission, BEUC, GIZ, World Bank, and the United Nations. The work of Dr. Durovic has been published in leading law journals (*European Review of Private Law, European Review of Contract Law, Journal of Consumer Policy*) and by most prominent publishers (Oxford University Press, Cambridge University Press, Hart Publishing). He is a member of the European Law Institute, Society of Legal Scholars, and Society for European Contract Law.

Martin Ebers is Professor of IT Law at the University of Tartu, Estonia and Permanent Fellow (Privatdozent) at the law faculty of the Humboldt University of Berlin, Germany. He is cofounder and President of the Robotics & AI Law Society (RAILS). In addition to research and teaching, he has been active in the field of legal consulting for many years. His main areas of expertise and research are IT law, liability and insurance law, and European and comparative law. In 2016, he published the monograph *Rights, Remedies and Sanctions in EU Private Law*. (Mohr Siebeck). Most recently, he published *Algorithms and Law* (Cambridge University Press, 2020) and the *Rechtshandbuch Künstliche Intelligenz und Robotik* (C. H. Beck, 2020).

Francisco de Elizalde is the Chair of Legal Studies at IE Law School, IE University (Spain). He focuses on comparative private law, especially contracts and the law of property. He is a visiting professor at Koç University (Turkey) and has lectured at the City University of Hong Kong and FGV Sao Paulo (Brazil). He is a member of the Madrid Bar Association, the American Society of Comparative Law, and the European Law Institute. Professor Elizalde is also the head of the EU-financed Jean Monnet Module "Liability of Robots: A European Vision for a New Legal Regime."

Paw Fruerlund is a digitalization expert and a highly experienced litigator and arbitration practitioner with extensive expertise handling complex disputes within three areas: the technology sector, public decisions, and commercial matters. Paw assists in both major dispute resolution and counsels on matters within these fields, for example, regarding cutting-edge issues in technology and digitalization-related regulatory matters. In recent years, Paw has been in charge of extensive legal investigations into the legality of several public case management IT-systems. Further, Paw has headed several of the Law Firm Poul Schmith's LT endeavors, having headed the development and implementation of three sector-specific case management systems in the process. Finally, Paw is part of the firm's Digital Opportunity Board in charge of digitalization of the law firm and is a sought after lecturer on the matter of digitalization of the law industry.

Carine Copain-Héritier holds a PhD in criminal law. During her thesis, she studied the coercive powers of legal frameworks in French criminal procedure. Copain-Héritier is an associate professor at the Catholic University of Lyon. Since 2017, she is the Director of the "Digital Lawyer" university diploma. Her current research interests and teaching topics focus on the issue of data protection and on the impacts of new technologies upon legal professions.

Mathieu Guillermin holds a PhD in physics and a PhD in philosophy. He is an associate professor at the Catholic University of Lyon and belongs to the Group of Epistemology and Ethics of Science and Technology (a team of CONFLUENCE: Sciences and Humanities research unit). In this research team, he explores the articulations between ethics, scientific research, and technological developments. He focuses notably upon philosophical and ethical questions raised by new digital technologies (big data, artificial intelligence, robots, etc.).

Jean-Marc van Gyseghem has been working at the Research Centre on Information, Law and Society (www.crids.eu) at the University of Namur (Belgium) since December 2001, where he is now Director of Research after being head of the Research Unit "Liberties in the Information Society" from 2008 to 2016. He has also been a member of the bar of Brussels and partner at Rawlings Giles Law firm (www.rawlingsgiles.be) since 1997, and a member of an ethical committee in a Belgian hospital as well as an invited expert appointed by the Belgian Superior Health Council. He specializes in data protection, eHealth services and products, medical law (including civil liability), and insurance.

Maximilian Horn is Research Assistant at the Institute for Law and Regulation of Digitalisation and the Institute for Commercial and Economic Law at the Philipps University of Marburg. He was born in 1993 and graduated at the Philipps University of Marburg in 2018. He is currently writing his doctoral thesis in the field of digital and economic law. During his studies, he focused on banking and capital market law. His main fields of interest concern questions of the economic and legal implications caused by digitalization, particularly CorpTech, FinTech, and LegalTech. Horn has gained expertise in commercial arbitration as a participant and coach of the Willem C. Vis International Commercial Arbitration Moot Court.

Max Houben builds on his experience as a lawyer in the Netherlands and designs and develops legal tech solutions.

André Janssen is a chair for (European) Private Law professor at Radboud University Nijmegen, The Netherlands. Janssen was a visiting scholar/professor at the Universities of Leuven, Oxford, Turin, Lyon (Catholic University), Verona and at the Chinese University for Political Science and Law in Beijing and at the City University Hong Kong. He has taught and presented at international conferences on five continents, is a member of several international research networks, and published more than 150 books and articles in the field of private, European, comparative, and international sales law, and artificial intelligence and law. He is the Co-Chief Editor of the *European Review of Private Law* (ERPL) and a member of the editorial board of the *International Arbitration Law Review* (IALR).

Jiaying Christine Jiang is a Hauser Global Fellow at NYU Law. She is also the co-leader of the Central Bank Digital Currency project, cooperating with the China Center at Yale Law School, as well as a contributor of the RegTrax Initiative at the CodeX, Stanford Law School. Her research focuses on the interaction between law and technology, especially policies and regulations on emerging technologies, such as artificial intelligence, blockchain, and digital currencies. Her research interests also include computational law, comparative law, data rights, platform competition, and privacy issues. In addition, she has been admitted to the bar in China and the state of New York.

Christoph Kletzer is a reader in law at King's College London, having previously been a lecturer at the University of Cambridge and before that at the University of Durham. Dr. Kletzer's research is in the areas of legal, moral, and political philosophy. His main interests lie in German Idealism and the legal and political thought of the Weimar Republic. In recent years, he has also added an expertise in the intersection of law and technology with a special focus on cryptography and technologies of decentralization.

Antonios Kouroutakis is Assistant Professor at IE University in Madrid, Spain, where he teaches constitutional law and the regulation of new technologies and start-ups. Dr. Kouroutakis has taught a variety of law courses and conducted research at the City University of Hong Kong, the Free University of Berlin, FVG Sao Paolo, and Aristotle University of Thessaloniki. Dr. Kouroutakis received a DPhil in Law from the University of Oxford and an LLM from UCLA School of Law. Dr. Kouroutakis' research interests lie mainly in the field of constitutional engineering, public law, and regulation. In particular, Dr. Kouroutakis is interested in the concept of separation of powers, rule of law, emergency legislation, and the regulation of new technologies; he has published widely on these topics in international and peer-reviewed journals, and his work has been cited in numerous reports.

Franciszek M. Lech is a King's Undergraduate Research Fellow and a Dickson Poon Scholar at King's College, London.

Jeffrey M. Lipshaw is the author of *Beyond Legal Reasoning: A Critique of Pure Lawyering* (Routledge, 2017). He is presently Professor of Law at Suffolk University Law School in Boston, where he teaches contracts and courses in the business curriculum. Before becoming a full-time academic in 2007, Professor Lipshaw spent twenty-six years as a lawyer and business executive, most recently serving as Senior Vice President, General Counsel, and Secretary for Great Lakes Chemical Corporation. He began his career with the law firm of Dykema Gossett in Detroit, where he was a partner in the litigation and corporate groups, and served as the Vice President and General Counsel of AlliedSignal Automotive, a large auto parts manufacturer. Before coming to Suffolk, he was a visiting professor at the Wake Forest and Tulane law schools. He is a graduate of the University of Michigan and Stanford Law School.

Florian Möslein is Director of the Institute for Law and Regulation of Digitalisation (www.irdi.institute) and Professor of Law at the Philipps University of Marburg, where he teaches contract law, company law, and capital markets law. He previously held academic positions at the

Universities of Bremen, St. Gallen, and Berlin, and visiting fellowships in Italy (Florence, European University Institute), the United States (NYU, Stanford, and Berkeley), and Australia (University of Sydney). Having graduated from the Faculty of Law in Munich, he also holds academic degrees from the University of Paris-Assas (licence en droit) and London (LLM in International Business Law). Möslein has published three monographs and more than eighty articles and book chapters, and has edited seven books. His current research focus is on regulatory theory, corporate sustainability, and the legal challenges of the digital age.

Pietro Ortolani is a professor of Digital Conflict Resolution at Radboud University. He holds a law degree from the University of Pisa and a PhD in arbitration from LUISS Guido Carli University, Rome. Before joining Radboud University, he was a senior research fellow at the Max Planck Institute Luxembourg for Procedural Law, a research associate at the University of Pisa, and a law research associate at Queen Mary, University of London. Pietro is admitted to the bar in Italy. He has experience in both ad hoc and institutional arbitration. He has acted as an expert for the European Parliament and the European Commission. Pietro has published in many peer-reviewed international journals, including the *Oxford Journal of Legal Studies*, the *Journal of International Dispute Settlement*, and the *Leiden Journal of International Law*. He regularly acts as reviewer for a wide range of international journals and publishers. In 2016, Pietro won the James Crawford Prize, awarded by the Journal of International Dispute Settlement and Oxford University Press. In 2014, Pietro has contributed to a European Parliament Study concerning the legal instruments and practice of arbitration in the EU.

Alessandro Palombo is a tech entrepreneur with a legal background and the CEO and founder of JUR, whose goal is to provide anyone in more than 166 countries with access to open justice: fast, affordable, and 100 percent online. The vision of JUR is to ensure the same standard and quality worldwide for any civil and commercial disputes. Just like Uber experiences, JUR ensures the same standard on a global scale in New York, Rome, or Bangalore. Palombo is also an advisor for public and private entities such as Oxford University, Astana International Financial Center, San Marino Innovation, and Proriented. He is currently working on decentralized models applied to the justice sector.

Sebastian Peters acts as a digital product consultant based in Copenhagen, Denmark. Sebastian is trained as a lawyer, but now advises his clients on innovation and development processes when new products and businesses are being prepared. Sebastian's specialty is translating business needs into the language of software developers and implementing actionable plans. **Eric Tjong Tjin Tai** is Professor of Private Law at Tilburg University, where he teaches civil procedure and global tort law. His current research focuses on the interaction of IT and human labor in organizations and its consequences for private law, as well as the changes to private law necessary for dealing with new technologies.

Robert E. Thomas is Darden Restaurants Professor at the Warrington College of Business at the University of Florida. He is a former president of the Academy of Legal Studies in Business (ALSB) and Chair of the Department of Management. His research interests include balancing innovation incentives with access, e-commerce law, intellectual property policy, law and economics, managing technology, and patent law reform.

Emmanuel de Vaujany initially graduated in engineering (thermodynamics) and worked in the automobile industry. Through his interactions with lawyers in different projects, he became interested in juridical reasoning. He then studied law and obtained a PhD in history of law, with a thesis focused upon Roman Law. He is now associate professor at Lyon Catholic University's law faculty and Deputy Director of the "Digital Lawyer" university diploma. His teaching and research revolve around the topics of data protection and privacy. He is also interested in the impact of digital technologies on law.

Tom J. Vennmanns is a PhD student at Radboud University Nijmegen, the Netherlands. He studied European law (LLB), Dutch law (LLM) and European Law and Global Affairs (LLM) at Radboud University, and German law (LLM) at the University in Münster.

Jin Ho Verdonschot currently is Managing Director at Justix and HelloLaw. His work during the past two decades has focused on legal tech, online dispute resolution, and justice leadership. His experiences span Europe, North America, Asia, Africa, and Australia, where he worked with supreme courts, ministries of justice, legal services corporations, as well as local justice leaders to innovate justice and technology integration.

Benjamin Werthmann is a German-qualified lawyer and representative on the advisory board and lead of the legal tech group of the Robotics and AI Law Society (RAILS). He also organizes regular Tech & Law Camps for RAILS, which cater to students wishing to develop a better understanding of legal technology and innovation. He has a professional background in cross-border corporate and financial transactions as well as restructurings and holds a PhD in capital markets law. After six years with an international law firm, he co-founded a legal tech start-up in Germany and remains an active member of the German and international legal tech scene branching out into the machine learning and data science community. His current practice includes advice to start-ups and established companies on legal technology, innovation and agility, data protection, and related topics.

Preface

This book comprises the collected, revised, and expanded papers on the impact of the digital age (as captured by the term legal tech [LT]) on lawyering presented at a conference held in Amsterdam in October 2019. It should be noted that the editors equally contributed to this book project. The topics selected seek to present a range of perspectives on the rise of LT, from those who view it as highly disruptive and diminishing of the legal profession to those who argue that LT enhances the tasks of lawyers. As has long been the case, the effectiveness of legal practice, in terms of cost efficiency and competency, continues to be influenced by technology. This has already proven to be true, and currently we are witnessing the acceleration of legal technology. What the future holds for the practice of law can only be speculated upon. But, that speculation is worth theorizing about in order to plan for that future. This planning is needed in areas of legal education, investment in technological infrastructure, determining law firm staffing needs – both legal and nonlegal – and envisioning the mix of services that the lawyer of the future will provide. This book begins the process by providing a review of the core issues that lawyers and law firms will be forced to face.

Some of the issues discussed in the book include the following: How will digitalization and AI impact the practice of law? Will AI or machine learning replace or augment the work of lawyers? How has technology affected services provided to clients? How has technology altered policies and rules regarding the confidentiality of information? How will the use of new technologies affect legal ethics? Will LT expand or reduce cases of malpractice? What are the risks of overreliance on LT? How will AI aid arbitrators and mediators to perform their functions? Will smart dispute resolution platforms and robo-judges become alternatives to traditional arbitration and mediation? Will technology make public law more efficient? Can it make public law more just?

As editors of this book, we had the pleasure of working with a diverse group of academics, practitioners, and computer scientists from a dozen countries. We are in debt to all the contributors to this volume from whom we have learned and been enriched by regarding the evolving area of LT and its impact on lawyering.

We are also indebted to the sponsoring schools: IE University Madrid, King's College London, Lyon Catholic University (UCLy), Radboud University Nijmegen, and the University of Florida. Special thanks to the commissioning and editorial staff at Cambridge University Press, especially Matt Gallaway. Finally, we would like to thank the law firm of Allen & Overy for graciously hosting the Amsterdam conference.

1

Lawyering in the Digital Age

Pietro Ortolani and Larry A. DiMatteo

1.1 INTRODUCTION

Digitalization and the development of automated systems, as well as the evolution of artificial intelligence (AI), have radically changed the legal landscape and will continue to impact law at an accelerated pace. These developments have led to the creation of a new industry, legal tech (LT), which aims at creating technological applications specifically tailored for law and the legal market. LT includes a broad range of applications: some of the most prominent and recurrent examples include automation in the drafting of contracts, "mining" case-law, or the creation of smart dispute resolution systems not requiring human intervention. As a result, operations that were previously unthinkable, or that would demand an enormous amount of human resources, can now be readily done through numerous legal services available to lawyers, other professionals, and consumers.[1] The rise of LT has brought about various responses, from those who advocate the innovating potential of LT[2] to legal traditionalists that consider the replacement of human resources by technology to be highly disruptive.[3] In addition, there are those who

---

[1] From this point of view, debates concerning LT can be contextualized as part of a broader discourse concerning automation, work, and the prospect of a jobless future: M. Ford, *Rise of the Robots: Technology and the Threat of a Jobless Future* (New York: Basic Books, 2015); N. Srnicek and A. Williams, *Inventing the Future: Postcapitalism and a World without Work* (New York: Verso, 2015); D. Autor, "Why Are There Still So Many Jobs? The History and Future of Workplace Automation" (2015) 29(3) *Journal of Economic Perspectives* 3; M. Arntz, T. Gregory, and U. Zierahn, "The Risk of Automation for Jobs in OECD Countries: A Comparative Analysis," OECD Social, Employment and Migration Working Papers, No. 189 (2016); P. Frase, *Four Futures: Life after Capitalism* (New York: Verso, 2016); L. Willcocks and M. Lacity, *Service Automation Robots and the Future of Work* (Norcross: SB Publishing, 2016); M. Arntz, T. Gregory, and U. Zierahn, "Revisiting the Risk of Automation" (2017) 159 *Economic Letters* 157; A. Greenfield, *Radical Technologies: The Design of Everyday Life* (New York: Verso, 2017) 183–207; D. West, *The Future of Work: Robots, AI, and Automation* (Washington, DC: Brookings Institution, 2018); C. Estlund, "What Should We Do after Work? Automation and Employment Law" (2018–2019) 128 *Yale Law Journal* 254; A. Oppenheimer, *The Robots Are Coming! The Future of Jobs in the Age of Automation* (New York: Vintage Books, 2019).

[2] M. Fenwick and E. Vermeulen, "The Lawyer of the Future as 'Transaction Engineer': Digital Technologies and the Disruption of the Legal Profession" in M. Corrales, M. Fenwick, and H. Haapio (eds.), *Legal Tech, Smart Contracts and Blockchain* (New York: Springer, 2019) 253.

[3] F. Pasquale, "A Rule of Persons, Not Machines: The Limits of Legal Automation" (2019) 87 *George Washington Law Review* 1; G. Buchholtz, "Artificial Intelligence and Legal Tech: Challenges to the Rule of Law" in T. Wischmeyer and T. Rademacher (eds.), *Regulating Artificial Intelligence* (New York: Springer, 2019) 175. For an overview of this type of argument, see M. Hartung, "Thoughts on Legal Tech and Digitalization" in M. Hartung, M.-M. Bues, and G. Halbleib (eds.), *Legal Tech: A Practitioner's Guide* (London: Beck Hart Nomos, 2018) 3.

advocate for a level-headed distinction between "hype" and reality.[4] Nonetheless, it would be shortsighted not to see that the advancement of LT is going to have a profound impact on the legal sector, in a degree similar to that which industrialization had on manufacturing.

Despite the significant uncertainties surrounding LT, there is widespread belief that the legal professions are approaching a "tipping point" and that the legal services market is in need of new business models and talent procurement strategies.[5] It is estimated that 100 legal "roles" or tasks will be automated by 2036.[6] As law firms increasingly experiment with new technologies and organizational models, lawyers will progressively transition from being mere providers of legal services to more integrated and hybrid service providers.[7] Furthermore, the recent COVID-19 crisis acts as an additional catalyst for innovation: lockdowns and social distancing significantly hinder the traditional modes of "in-person" legal work, with digitalization of legal services and court proceedings gaining unprecedented momentum.[8] The effectiveness of legal practice, in terms of cost efficiency and competency, will continue to be highly influenced by LT in the years to come. What the future holds for the practice of law can only be speculated upon; but it would be prudent if lawyers and law firms begin theorizing about LT's impact in order to plan for that future. This planning is needed in areas of legal education, investment in technological infrastructure, determining staffing needs – both legal and non-legal – and envisioning the mix of services that the lawyer of the future will provide. This last element should be seen as an opportunity for the legal profession to expand the relevancy of lawyering into new areas of practice.

The aim of this book is to provide perspectives from different interested parties, such as practitioners, academics, and LT developers, across different legal systems, in order to assess the *real* implications posed by LT and to advocate for an unbiased, cautious approach for the engagement of technology in legal practice. It is important for the legal community to have a framework for analyzing the benefits and costs of new technologies before implementing them into legal practice. The costs of LT include potential legal and business risks, as well as ethical concerns and technological problems. The benefits and costs related to LT have profound consequences not only for lawyers but also for their clients, as well as the economy and legal system as a whole.

1.2 SCOPE AND STRUCTURE OF THE BOOK

In late 2019, a conference entitled "Lawyering in the Digital Age" was held in Amsterdam. The event presented an opportunity for an in-depth analysis of the intersection of law, legal practice, and technology. The presentations delivered during the conference, as well as the ensuing debates, form the backbone of this volume. Against the background of two days of productive discussions, a number of different approaches to investigating the idea of lawyering in the digital

---

[4] K. Low and E. Mik, "Pause the Blockchain Legal Revolution" (2020) 69(1) *International & Comparative Law Quarterly* 135.
[5] R. Susskind, *The End of Lawyers? Rethinking the Nature of Legal Services* (Oxford: Oxford University Press, 2010); R. Susskind, *Tomorrow's Lawyers: An Introduction to Your Future* (Oxford: Oxford University Press, 2013).
[6] Deloitte, "Future Trends for Legal Services: A Global Study," www2.deloitte.com/global/en/pages/legal/articles/deloitte-future-trends-for-legal-services.html (accessed July 16, 2020).
[7] J. Armour and M. Sako, "AI-Enabled Business Models in Legal Services: From Traditional Law Firms to Next-Generation Law Companies?" (2020) 7(1) *Journal of Professions and Organizations* 27.
[8] "Remote Courts" is an initiative mapping court digitalization around the world, https://remotecourts.org (accessed July 16, 2020). In general, on the digitalization of court proceedings, see R. Susskind, *Online Courts and the Future of Justice* (Oxford: Oxford University Press, 2019).

age were proposed. The book is broader in scope than the conference's coverage, as additional contributors were added in order to produce a more comprehensive and in-depth volume.

The core question discussed is how to balance the fear of industry takeover by technology and the need to change the business model of legal practice, using technology to expand services and create value for clients. This core question leads to many other questions yet to be resolved, involving the role of government regulation, judicial use of technology, the impact of digital technologies on specialized areas of the law, and the role of bar associations (legal ethics) in the management of technology in law. The chapters cover areas of both private and public law, as well as the legal and ethical implications of the use of technology in legal practice. The book proceeds in six parts, as set out below.

1.2.1 Effects of Technology on Legal Practice

Part I explores the general question whether LT is likely to enhance or disrupt legal practice in the near future. The American Bar Association amended its Model Rules of Professional Conduct to require lawyers to keep abreast of "the benefits and risks associated with relevant technology."[9] LT start-ups are founded with the purpose of either enhancing or disrupting the traditional legal market. In the area of disruptive technology, blockchain technologies have attracted enormous attention.[10] For example, the diffusion of distributed ledgers shared on peer-to-peer networks has the potential of replacing or diminishing the robust role that the European notary profession plays in legal systems. The blockchain has the ability to duplicate the tasks now performed by notaries, such as the secure procurement, indexing, storing, and time-stamping of legal documents. In legal practice, automated drafting software increasingly allows firms and companies to generate contracts with limited human input, thus marginalizing one of the most traditional roles of lawyers and progressively determining a shift in contract drafting, from "art" to "science."

The trend toward automation is visible in many fields: AI seeks to replicate certain functions of the human mind and is used to complete tasks that typically require human intelligence. Along similar lines, machine learning (ML) programs (algorithms) allow computers to analyze vast amounts of data to find patterns and insights that they then use to reprogram new searches (self- learning).[11] In the era of big data, AI-operated software can review large quantities of documents and "flag" the parts that are relevant to the case or problem at hand. ML can then search for other relevant documents. In the end, legal research and document reviews can be made more comprehensive and not subject to human time constraints and limited cognitive capabilities. AI can also analyze contracts in bulk to find clauses that pose risks to clients and then draft individual contracts. ML increasingly allows the development of software that gives automated legal advice or makes automated business decisions in a boardroom setting.

Part I offers a bird's eye view of these developments and the innovating potential of LT: Chapters 2 and 3 (respectively by DiMatteo, Jiaying and Thomas, and by Janssen and Vennmanns) set the scene by mapping the effects of technology on legal practice and predicting the future of lawyering. Against that background, Werthmann (Chapter 4) zooms in on the specific case-study of contract drafting automation, exploring how technology currently affects

---

[9] American Bar Association, "Text of the Model Rules of Professional Conduct," Rule 1.1(8), www.americanbar.org/groups/professional_responsibility/publications/model_rules_of_professional_conduct/rule_1_1_competence/comment_on_rule_1_1 (accessed July 16, 2020).

[10] For a comprehensive overview, see P. De Filippi and A. Wright, *Blockchain and the Law: The Rule of Code* (Cambridge, MA: Harvard University Press, 2018).

[11] See H. Surden, "Machine Learning and Law" (2014) 89 *Washington Law Review* 87 88.

legal practice, potentially eroding the traditional intellectual monopolies of law firms. Along similar lines, Möslein and Horn (Chapter 5) scrutinize the use of AI in the context of legal advice, financial advice, and fabricating corporate strategies, drawing important inferences from the law of liability and standards of ethical conduct.

1.2.2 Legal Tech and Alternative Dispute Resolution

For decades now, practitioners and academics have argued that court litigation, by itself, is not sufficient to ensure accessible and reliable dispute resolution. The complexity, costs and rigidity of court proceedings, often combined with significant backlogs, constitute serious obstacles to effective access to justice. Calls for widespread adoption of alternative dispute resolution (ADR) mechanisms have been steadily intensifying. However, despite the compelling arguments put forth by the ADR movement, procedures such as mediation and arbitration have also shown some crucial limitations in meeting the ever-growing demand for dispute resolution services. Technology, though, will soon change this state of affairs: digitalization holds exciting promises, not only in terms of cost-effectiveness and immediacy, but also because it opens new avenues for the creation of unprecedented, hybrid dispute resolution services and procedures.

Hybrid systems, many of them available online, will help individuals and small businesses, with disputes involving relatively modest damages, to pursue meritorious claims. Durovic and Lech (Chapter 6) survey dispute resolution possibilities by canvassing the current reality of online dispute resolution (ODR), as well as the use of LT in arbitration, mediation, and other ADR procedures. Against this background, Palombo, Battaglini, and Cantisani (Chapter 7) reports on the first-hand experience of a group of lawyers and technologists attempting to devise dispute resolution solutions based on blockchain technologies. In this context, the label of "smart ODR" is perceived as the procedural equivalent to the trend of creating substantive smart contracts. Finally, Pietro Ortolani (Chapter 8) takes stock of those experiences, reflecting on the changes that the traditional taxonomy of ADR will need to undergo as a consequence of the proliferation of new hybrid, technology-driven ADR mechanisms.

1.2.3 Legal Tech in Consumer Relations and Small Claims

The rise of the digital economy has triggered the development of a global network of commercial relations. Consumer transactions play a key role in this framework: digital platforms, for instance, act as global market-makers, enabling the conclusion of business-to-consumer (B2C) contracts at the click of a mouse. This development, however, also brings about new challenges: in the European Union, for instance, consumer law was largely developed before the emergence of the platform economy. New technological developments will likely highlight deficiencies in the current legal framework and the need for regulatory reforms.

In addition to digital platforms, other technological developments will also have important effects on consumers and on the ability of legal rules and protections to prevent consumer abuse. Notoriously, the enforcement of consumer law is undermined by the problem of plaintiff inaction, given the relatively low value disputes emanating from consumer transactions. Consumers are often unlikely to seek professional legal advice to assess whether their rights have been violated, or contemplate commencing litigation or arbitration against sellers and traders. In other words, consumer protection suffers from two interrelated Achilles' heels – insufficient access to legal information and assistance and, as a result, unsatisfactory enforcement of the law. In this respect, current technological developments hold the promise of allowing consumers to easily access the law (digitalization) and receive legal advice at limited or no cost. The gap between the "law in the books" and the "law in action" that favors those with bargaining power may be made more equitable in favor of weaker parties, such as consumers and small businesses. This prospect, however, also entails significant regulatory and ethical challenges, as LT innovators move into areas such as the giving of legal advice (by non-lawyers), potentially subject to regulatory penalties and claims of unauthorized practice of law.

To address this set of delicate challenges, Francisco de Elizalde considers the issue of small value, mass-volume claims, and the methods through which technology can help overcome the aforementioned problem of plaintiff inaction and effective enforcement of consumer law (Chapter 9). Subsequently, Verdonschot and Houben (Chapter 10) contextualize the analysis by adding a crucial regulatory perspective: the chapter reports on past attempts to operationalize LT (and specifically legal advice platforms) in consumer and small-value relations, and the subsequent reaction on the part of national regulators. Martin Ebers, in turn, provides a wide-ranging analysis of the relationship between LT and consumer law, covering both the regulatory and the consumer protection perspectives (Chapter 11). Finally, Tjong Tjin Tai (Chapter 12) investigates the way in which consumer law and technology can be merged and interconnected with each other so as to guarantee that the technological framework complies with some fundamental legal requirements. Through these investigations, it becomes possible to grasp the tensions currently existing at the boundaries of the legal professions.

1.2.4 Legal Tech and Public Law

LT opens up new possibilities for public administration and, as a consequence, for lawyering in the public sector. The use of technology in public administration (publictech) can help limit costs, enhance efficiency, and bring administrators closer to the citizens. Publictech also entails some significant risks, most notably, the adoption of automated decision-making by public agencies. The fear is that automated decisions may result in a dilution of due process guarantees that are traditionally associated with the exertion of public powers in democratic societies. These challenges fare examined through a comparative perspective.

Georgios Dimitropoulos (Chapter 13) unveils an interesting intellectual tension brought to light by the rise of LT in the public sector. On the one hand, technology increasingly enables global governance and the extraterritorial application of law. On the other hand, this development does not result in the annulment of physical distance. To the contrary, public law is currently characterized by a growing focus on the spatial dimension of regulation, especially given the strategic importance of the infrastructures on which our global, data-driven economy relies. In light of this, Dimitropoulos proposes a new approach to lawyering in the public sector, where lawyers are called to acknowledge and manage the apparent contradiction between the apparent delocalization of technology and the spatial dimension of public law. Subsequently, Jean-Marc van Gyseghem (Chapter 14) tackles the use of AI in court and its potential impact on fundamental rights. Finally, Antonios Kourotakis (Chapter 15) maps the rise of publictech and the impact of technology on public lawyering, providing a balanced overview of both benefits and risks and putting forth a normative argument for a phased, cautious implementation of LT in the public sector.

1.2.5 Legal Ethics and Societal Values Confront Technology

Part V examines the ethical implications of using LT, as lawyers will be responsible for the selection of LT products, as well as properly implementing and monitoring their use. LT will have a disruptive impact on the law and societal values. As noted above, "AI is best understood as a set of techniques aimed at approximately some aspect of human cognition using machines."[12] The increased functionality of ML has been impacted by faster computing speed and an enormous increase in available data. While the future of technology lies in the area of advanced AI or superintelligence, caution is required, and the law will need to anticipate potential harms. Lawmakers and lawyers will need to "jump" ahead of the technology at some point, to prevent harm to society before it is too late. The fear is that technology, including LT, may go too far by overreaching in such areas as privacy, fundamental rights, and the right of humans to be in control through their democratic institutions. Herbert Simon noted that it is the duty of people who study a new technology to offer their interpretations regarding its likely effects on society.[13] Will advanced AI enhance or harm humanity? How can technology be controlled so as not to hinder the pursuit of the public good? In order for the law to answer these questions effectively, lawyers in the digital age will need to deliberate on the ethical issues when implementing different types of LT. In the end, lawyers and law firms will ultimately do so if they implement LT products that result in breaches of their ethical duties of competence and confidentiality.

In Chapter 16, Michel Cannarsa focuses on trustworthy AI, scrutinizing the ethical guidelines currently being developed in this field and their relationship with the law. Against this background, Guillermin, Billion, Copain-Héritier and de Vaujany (Chapter 17) provide the criteria for distinguishing between the "technically feasible" and the "legally desirable." The authors argue that the philosophical and theoretical debates surrounding technology are often too abstract and, instead, should center on the concerns connected to actual policymaking. Christoph Kletzer (Chapter 18), in turn, explores the boundaries of legal automation by focusing on the relevance of the importance of trust in the legal profession and the human nature of the activities affecting society's reliance on lawyers.

1.2.6 Fate of the Legal Professions

Technology allows legal professionals to do their work more efficiently and provides opportunities for disruptive innovators to create value by doing things differently. This new reality demands a new breed of lawyers who can adapt to this new paradigm and understand the application of technology and the impact it has in the legal sphere. To succeed, lawyers must be customer-oriented, well-versed in management and strategy, tech-savvy, and innovative. This will require law schools to change their curricula in order incorporate LT, preferably in each course whose subject matter will be impacted by LT.

The final part on the "fate of the legal profession" formulates hypotheses on the future of legal practice. Jeffrey Lipshaw (Chapter 19) investigates the very nature of the intellectual activities at the core of the legal profession, distinguishing the type of thinking that can be replicated computationally from the inherently human aspects of lawyering, which involve non-replicable intuition, judgment, and creativity. Fruerlund and Peters (Chapter 20) provide a case study on the innovation and implementation of LT, sketching a roadmap for law firms to implement LT, as well as to develop their own LT solutions. They reveal the pitfalls they learned in developing proprietary LT solutions. Building on these insights, Chapter 21 presents a summary of the findings, and offers an outlook for a legal profession rooted in a mixture of traditional lawyering and technological enhancements.

---

[12] R. Calo, "Artificial Intelligence Policy: A Primer and a Roadmap" (2018) 3 *University of Bologna Law Review* 180 183; R. Calo, "Robotics and the Lessons from Cyberlaw" (2015) 130 *California Law Review* 513 532.

[13] H. Simon, *The Shape of Automation for Mean and Management* (New York: Harper & Row, 1965) vii.

PART I

Effects of Technology on Legal Practice

2

Disruptive Effects of Legal Tech

Jiaying Christine Jiang, Larry A. DiMatteo, and Robert E. Thomas

2.1 INTRODUCTION

Herbert Simon noted that it is the duty of people who study a new technology to offer their interpretations regarding its likely effects on society.[1]

The term "legal tech" (LT) refers to the use of technology and software to provide legal services. Although technology and legal practices have intertwined since the advent of the Internet, the term "legal tech" first appeared over the past few years and has become prevalent in the legal space. Since 2011, LT has evolved to become associated with technology start-ups, which disrupt legal practices by giving people access to online software that reduces or, in some cases, eliminates the need to consult a lawyer. LT can also connect people with lawyers more efficiently through online marketplaces and lawyer-matching websites.[2] Over the past few years, the LT industry has embraced more advanced versions of artificial intelligence (AI), allowing for greater automation in legal practices.

This chapter reviews the history of the digital revolution from the perspective of the legal profession. It then surveys the current state of LT focusing on its most common applications, including the advancements made in the use of AI.[3] A specific set of techniques known as machine learning has been the focus of recent advancements in LT. Machine learning is the idea that a computer system can be programmed to improve its performance over time.[4] The increased functionality of machine learning has been impacted by faster computer speed and the rise of big data. There are two types of AI: disembodied AI that acquires systems (outputs as data) and cyber-physical systems (robots).[5]

This chapter looks to the future practice of law including the paradigm shift of "thinking *and* programming like a lawyer," executable law, and the evolution of legal ethics to confront dilemmas posed by the use of LT in law practice. It concludes by suggesting that law firms need to co-opt LT in order to stay competitive with other law firms, in-house counsel departments, and nonlegal service providers. In order to do so, AI must be demystified, and legal

---

[1] Herbert Simon, *The Shape of Automation for Men and Management* (New York: Harper & Row, 1965) vii.
[2] B. Goodman and J. Harder, "Four Areas of Legal Ripe for Disruption by Smart Startups," American Bar Association, *Law Technology Today* (December 16, 2014), www.lawtechnologytoday.org/2014/12/smart-startups (accessed June 7, 2020).
[3] "AI is best understood as a set of techniques aimed at approximating some aspect of human cognition using machines." R. Calo, "Artificial Intelligence Policy: A Primer and a Roadmap" (2018) 3 *University of Bologna Law Review* 180 183.
[4] See H. Surden, "Machine Learning and Law" (2014) 89 *Washington Law Review* 87, 88.
[5] R. Calo, "Robotics and the Lessons from Cyberlaw" (2015) 130 *California Law Review* 513 532.

education will need to be retooled to provide future lawyers with the technical skill sets required in the age of the acceleration of technology. Failure to do so will cause a disconnect between traditional law firm practice and clients that embrace technological solutions.

The digitalization and development of automated systems and the evolution of AI have radically changed the legal landscape and will continue to impact law at an accelerated pace. In the words of McGinnis and Pearce, "the legal profession faces a great disruption."[6] These developments already have led to the creation of a completely new "branch" or area within the legal sector, namely, the LT industry. The wide range of different LT applications, including contract drafting software, case law mining programs, smart dispute resolution systems, and so forth, make operations and tasks possible that were previously unthinkable or would have demanded an enormous amount of resources. The aim of this chapter is to provide a review of the LT landscape.[7] It will scrutinize the *real* implications posed by LT and suggest an unbiased, but cautious, approach for the engagement of technology in legal practice.

The rise of LT has brought about various responses, from "legal tech believers" to legal traditionalists who consider the replacement of human resources by technology as "highly disruptive." Nonetheless, it would be shortsighted not to see that the advancement of LT is going to have an impact on the legal sector in a degree similar to that which industrialization had on manufacturing. It is important for the legal community to have a framework for analyzing the benefits and costs of new technology and computer programs before implementing them into legal practice. The costs of using new technologies include potential legal and business risks, as well as ethical concerns and technological problems arising from LT. In the end, the field of legal services is likely to expand, as lawyers become tech advisors in counseling their clients.

The most provocative question that can be asked is whether there is a danger of technology replacing lawyers. Such a question is good for dramatic effect, but it is the wrong question. Technology will never be able to fully replace a human lawyer because of the nuances of subjective judgment and counseling that only the human brain can provide; AI will be unable, for the foreseeable future, to fully mimic human intelligence. These shortcomings and the dangers of giving too much power to advanced AI systems results in a divergence problem, where the AI or lawyer robot makes a decision or an adjustment that it thinks is best for its human employer but is in fact different from that which the human would have made. The more practical, and important, issues currently facing us are how LT can enhance legal practice and what consequences there are for lawyers not using LT. Alternatively stated, LT will cause a massive disruption of traditional legal services but will not replace the need for lawyers. Failure to co-opt LT will decrease the competitiveness of law firms vis-à-vis one another and will allow non-lawyer entities – accounting firms and tech companies – to fill the void, decreasing the need for lawyers. The adoption of LT and how it is used is not purely a business decision. Lawyers must be alert to ethical considerations in the use of LT on behalf of clients and against an adversary. This is especially important given the acceleration of LT and the dangers represented by the lag in the adjustment of lawyer and judicial codes of ethics.

Finally, the continued hybridization of skill sets is expected. Lawyers will become technology advisers and providers to clients. Lawyers will need to more fully engage with technologists in providing such services as smart contracting. New types of positions will become common in

---

[6] J. McGinnis and R. Pearce, "The Great Disruption: How Machine Intelligence Will Transform the Role of Lawyers in the Delivery of Legal Services" (2014) 82 *Fordham Law Review* 3041.

[7] Legal Tech (LT) refers to the use of technology and software to provide or aid in providing legal services.

large law firms, including legal technologists, who develop innovative applications and manage the testing and implementation process for new software; legal analysts, who apply big data solutions to specific legal issues; legal process managers, who work to design workflows and optimize processes; legal designers, who transform the insights gained with LT into compelling graphics and visualizations; e-discovery practitioners; legal engineers, who are generalists and able to work in all areas of LT; and legal project managers, who coordinate the diverse projects of legal departments. In sum, law practice is no longer solely about lawyers; tech is no longer just about techies. The digital age will require cross-disciplinary collaboration.

As noted above, technology will have a disruptive impact on law practice – changing what lawyers do and how they do it. LT will enhance the practice by increasing efficiency and accuracy in producing lawyers' work products. Many manual processes, which are ripe for automation and digitization, will result in increased productivity and improved client experience, and show commitment to innovation.

LT is a personification of the age of acceleration, with the rate of new LT start-ups rapidly multiplying.[8] LT companies are generally start-ups founded with the purpose of disrupting the traditionally conservative legal market. New undertakings are providing tools for consumers and businesses to complete legal matters by themselves, obviating the need for a lawyer, providing tools to assist with immigration document preparation in lieu of hiring a lawyer and providing tools to in-house counsel to increase their areas of sophistication. LT has already resulted in an automation of legal writing and other substantive aspects of legal practice. Exponential growth in the volume of documents (mostly email) reviewed for litigation cases has led to the adoption of technology used in eDiscovery, with elements of machine language and AI being incorporated. Cloud-based services, platforms for succession planning and will writing, data and contract analytics, tools to connect clients with lawyers; and many other technologies are already being adopted by law firms.

In the end, LT can no longer be ignored by anti-tech traditionalists. Digital disruption has placed further upward pressure on the need to optimize legal operations. To remain relevant, traditional law firms must adapt and deliver more rapid and transparent services to clients. If lawyers do not provide the efficiency gains related to the use of technology, other entities will. The big accounting firms will continue to seriously challenge large law firms. The winners of this competition will be those firms (within law, between law and accounting, or tech companies) that can provide direct services to in-house counsel and that find the most creative solutions to the complicated problems clients face. Some law firms are already using data analytics, artificial intelligence to help build legal briefs, and blockchain-related technology in real estate transactions. Law firms will not have the option of ignoring LT, since legal practice standards will require a minimal level of technical expertise. For example, the American Bar Association amended the Model Rules of Professional Conduct to require lawyers to keep abreast of "the benefits and risks associated with relevant technology."

As a result of the use of LT, legal education will need to change more dramatically to provide law students with the technical skills needed for new models of the law firm. Technology today allows legal professionals to go beyond the legal sphere; it allows them to do their work more

---

[8] See, e.g., Ebrevia at https://ebrevia.com/#overview, which uses artificial intelligence, including machine learning and natural language processing technology, developed in partnership with Columbia University to extract data from contracts, bringing accuracy and speed to contract analytics, due diligence, and lease abstraction. See also Rocket Lawyer at www.rocketlawyer.com; CaseText at https://casetext.com; Shake Law at www.shakelaw.com; Priori at www.priorilegal.com; UpCounsel at www.upcounsel.com; LawDingo at www.lawdingo.com; Hire an Esquire at https://hireanesquire.com; Judicata at www.judicata.com; Kira Systems at https://kirasystems.com.

efficiently and provides opportunities for disruptive innovators to create value by doing things differently. This new reality demands a new breed of lawyer who can adapt to this new paradigm and understand the application of technology and the impact it has in the legal sphere. To succeed, lawyers must be customer-oriented, well-versed in management and strategy, tech-savvy, and innovative – skills that law schools traditionally don't offer their students. It is important to stress that law schools can only teach the LT in its current state. In the age of acceleration, lawyers will be in a constant state of learning new technical skills. For example, "machine intelligence is not a one-time event that lawyers will have to accommodate. Instead, it is an accelerating force that will invade ever-larger territory."[9]

The legal industry will need lawyers with an entirely new set of skills. Law schools have begun to launch LT classes in response to the growing availability of tech tools and the demand for more cost-effective services. In the process, they are redefining the future of legal practice. Law graduates of the future will need a fresh set of skills to meet the demands of the profession.

2.2 LEGAL PRACTICE BEFORE THE AGE OF INFORMATION

2.2.1 *Dawning of a New Era: Pre-1970s*

Before the 1970s, there was little difference between the technology used by law firms and that used in other business environments. Before 1950, typewriters and telephones dominated the legal landscape.[10] A few other technologies existed, such as the Autograph (to record dictation and conversations), the Voicecaster speaker phone, the Thermofax copier, and the Friden "automatic writing machine."[11] Most of these technologies posed no threat to the demand for lawyers' time or wisdom – they were largely concerned with expediting clerical work.

Early computers were of little help to legal work. They were used primarily for military purposes and had little commercial application.[12] Computers were used mainly to perform massive and complex mathematical calculations.[13] They proved their worth dramatically during World War II in the service of code breaking and in support of the development of advanced weaponry. The second generation of computers emerged in 1947 and relied on transistors for processing. Later, in 1951, the first computer intended for commercial use was introduced to the public. Over the next decade, more than 100 computer programming languages were developed, and computers acquired memory and operating systems.[14] However, there was still minimal interaction between computers and the work of lawyers, other than for data processing in non-numerical form.

2.2.2 *Advent of the Internet and the First Legal Databases*

The far-reaching impact of technology on the legal industry coincided with the advent of the Internet. The Internet profoundly changed the way lawyers work. In addition, increasingly powerful computers, with stronger data-processing capabilities, extended this impact, in ways exemplified by the establishment of the first legal databases.

---

[9] McGinnis and Pearce, n. 6 at 3043.
[10] J. B. Ruhl, "Legal Technology through the Ages – Why Didn't They Dread It Then?," Law2050 (October 8, 2015), https://law2050.com/?s=Legal+Technology+through+the+Ages&submit= (accessed March 2, 2021).
[11] Ibid.
[12] L. Freed and S. Ishida, *The History of Computers* (Emeryville: Ziff-Davis Press, 1995).
[13] R. Susskind, *The Future of Law: Facing the Challenges of Information Technology* (Oxford: Oxford University Press, 1996) 56.
[14] Freed and Ishida, n. 12.

The Internet traces its origins back to the late 1960s, when the United States Defense Department's Advanced Research Project Agency (ARPA) created the Advanced Research Projects Agency Network (ARPANET).[15] ARPANET arose from a desire to share information over great distances without the need of dedicated phone connections between computers in a network.[16] During its first decade, ARPANET led to numerous networking innovations, which in turn led to new applications and protocols. The first email program was one of the more successful outcomes. Later, in 1977, transmission-control protocol/Internet protocol (TCP/IP), a gateway between networks, which had the capacity to hand off data packets to other networks, was first tested on ARPANET. Eventually, the Internet evolved, consisting of a network of networks. By the late 1970s, a multitude of new networks had emerged, replacing ARPANET, which provided the foundations for the Internet. The term "Internet" was officially adopted in 1983.[17]

One of the significant impacts of such interconnected networks was the facilitation of instant communication via email, instant messaging, telephony (Voice over Internet protocol or VoIP), and two-way interactive video calls. Instant communication offered tremendous benefits to law firms, both internally and externally. It offered immediate and staggered feedback.[18] Suddenly, lawyers were able to communicate with colleagues, clients, expert witnesses, and court staff more efficiently.

Alongside the Internet, computers continued to evolve. In 1980, Microsoft Disk Operation System (MS-DOS) was created and IBM released its "personal computer" in 1981, the first widely sold desktop computer for ordinary business users.[19] Three years later, Apple introduced the Macintosh computer, with its icon-driven interface. By that time, computers had entered their third generation; they had become powerful enough to run more programs and were easier to use. Some lawyers learned word processing so they could type their own documents. Some used spreadsheets to calculate damages, negotiate settlements, or analyze securities trading patterns.[20]

As previously noted, early computers (first and second generation) had been devoted to the manipulation of numbers. As computers continued to evolve, there was widespread recognition of the extent to which the processing power of computers was also applicable to non-numerical data that could be represented in digital form. In the era of data processing, computer systems acquired the ability to perform tasks involving the capture, storage, retrieval, and manipulation of both numerical and non-numerical data.

The advent of legal databases resulted from the gradual development of more powerful data processing. In the legal space, 1973 was a pivotal year for technological evolution. Mead Data Central, Inc. introduced Lexis, an online legal database that provided computer-assisted legal research.[21] Lexis provided the full text of New York and Ohio codes and cases, the U.S. Code, and some federal case law. By the end of that year, Mead added the entire United States Code, as well as the United States Reports from 1938 through 1973.[22] The UBIQ terminal was

---

[15] K. Featherly, "ARPANET" (2016) *Britannica*, www.britannica.com/topic/ARPANET/A-packet-of-data.
[16] "Back to the Future: A History of Legal Technology," Prismlegal.com (2019), https://prismlegal.com/back_to_the_future-a-history-of-legal-technology (accessed June 6, 2020).
[17] Ibid.
[18] S. Migdal, "The Impact of Information Technology on Legal Education and Practice" (1998) 24 *Commonwealth Law Bulletin* 612.
[19] "Back to the Future," n. 16.
[20] Ibid.
[21] Lexisnexis.com (2019), www.lexisnexis.com/anniversary/30th_timeline_fulltxt.pdf (accessed June 6, 2020).
[22] C. Bourne and T. Hahn, *A History of Online Information Services, 1963–1976* (Cambridge, MA: MIT Press, 2003) 300–301,

introduced in 1979, and it placed Lexis directly on the desktops of attorneys.[23] In 1980, the Nexis service was added, providing access to *The Washington Post, Newsweek, The Economist, U.S. News and World Report, Dun's Review*, and the Reuters and Associated Press news wires.[24] By that time, the case law for all fifty states was accessible on the LexisNexis service. In 1975, West Publishing launched Westlaw. By the early 1980s, these search engines could execute over 90 percent of searches in less than five seconds, freeing up lawyers' time and allowing them to offer clients better service.

Although data processing (capture, store, retrieve, and reproduce data) was firmly established, the ability to use technology to help analyze, refine, and render more manageable the mass of data was limited. In the words of Richard Susskind, "We are great at getting information in but not so good at extracting the information that we want."[25] He characterizes this disparity as 'the Technology Lag" – the lag between data processing and knowledge processing. LexisNexis and Westlaw may hold vast quantities of data, but search techniques were not yet sufficiently adept at helping users to secure all relevant documents for their particular purposes. To address Susskind's lag problem, more advanced techniques were developed, such as conceptual retrieval, expert systems, and hypertext. These techniques were refined and applied successfully to help manage the difficulties of knowledge processing. In 1992, Microsoft released version 3.1 of Windows and eventually supplanted MS-DOS. By 1995, a range of legal applications for Windows were available to handle such tasks as case management, time management and billing, docketing, along with specialized tools for various practices, such as real estate and IP.

From 1990 onward, all branches of the legal profession awakened from their collective slumber and – with the advent of ever more powerful and networked personal computers – began to take technology from the back office to the front office. All of these advancements afforded more convenience to lawyers. On the other hand, they threatened to diminish the number of billable hours charged to clients. The profession was forced for the first time to reexamine itself and make sense of the possibility that tasks previously performed by lawyers were better performed by machines.

The first two decades of the twenty-first century have witnessed the beginning of a paradigm shift in legal practice. This transformation is due to the continued entry of technology into legal practice and legal institutions. The rise in recent decades of information technology (IT), legal online platforms, and specialized legal software has resulted in an acceleration of the use of technology in business, as well as technological applications related to law practice, government regulation, and the court systems.[26]

2.3 TWENTY-FIRST CENTURY: INTERFACE OF LEGAL PRACTICE AND TECHNOLOGY

The first decade of the twenty-first century witnessed the advent of e-discovery and the beginning of the automation of legal documents. The second decade has seen the rapid increase in advanced levels of automaton. Existing technologies, such as AI and its subfields, including robotics, natural language processing, and speech recognition, have presented more capability in process automation, project management, document review, and legal research. Newer

---

[23] "The LexisNexis Timeline," www.lexisnexis.com/anniversary/30th_timeline_fulltxt.pdf (accessed June 6, 2020).
[24] Ibid.
[25] Susskind, n. 13 at 58.
[26] T. Friedman, *Thank You for Being Late: An Optimist's Guide to Thriving in the Age of Accelerations* (New York: Farrar, Straus and Giroux, 2016).

technologies offer solutions to problems existing in legal practice. Technologies, such as blockchains and smart contracts, have begun to intertwine with legal practice. However, it would be an oversimplification to portray these technologies as applicable to a wide range of legal practice problems. So far, long-existing systems of traditional law practice remain the only viable options. Overall, the interface of technology and legal practices is a continuous but accelerating process.

2.3.1 Baby Steps: E-Discovery and Early Staged Automation

E-discovery is the electronic aspect of identifying, collecting, and producing electronically stored information (ESI) in response to requests for the production of information in a lawsuit or investigation.[27] ESI includes, but is not limited to, emails, electronically stored documents, presentations, databases, voicemail, audio and video files, social media, and websites.[28] The idea of e-discovery began with a landmark series of decisions beginning with *Zubulake* v. *USB Warburg*.[29] The ruling addresses both the scope of a litigant's duty to preserve electronic documents and the consequences for the failure to preserve documents that fall within the scope of that duty.[30] It also emphasizes the need to define new terms and concepts related to electronic preservation and discovery. In 2005, in order to address the lack of standards and guidelines in the e-discovery industry, lawyers Tom Gelbman and George Socha created the electronic discovery reference model (EDRM). Among EDRM's first projects was the creation of the EDRM diagram, which maps the stages of e-discovery, and it has since become an industry-wide standard for managing the e-discovery process.[31]

Although the e-discovery process has become clearer, properly managing each process is still challenging for lawyers. Challenges lie not only in the sheer volume of electronic data that lawyers need to review and process but in the technical skills that lawyers must have to understand and manage the process. Unlike hard copy evidence, electronic documents are more dynamic and often contain metadata, such as time–date stamps, author and recipient information, and file properties. These features cannot be easily understood and handled properly by the legal profession without technical training. In addition, preserving the original content and metadata for ESI is required to eliminate claims of spoliation or tampering with evidence later during litigation. This requirement increases the complexity of ESI processing in litigation.

These challenges resulted in the proliferation of start-up tech companies focused on e-discovery. EDRM uses computer-assisted review to reduce the number of documents required for review by lawyers and prioritizes the documents. Logikcull is a cloud-based system for managing the process of legal discovery. Utilizing Logikcull, lawyers can drag and drop files

---

[27] "The Basics: What Is e-Discovery?," *Complete Discovery Source*, https://cdslegal.com/knowledge/the-basics-what-is-e-discovery (accessed June 3, 2020).

[28] Ibid.

[29] 229 F.R.D. 422 (S.D.N.Y. 2004).

[30] Ibid. See also Adam I. Cohen and David J. Lender, *Electronic Discovery: Law and Practice*, 3rd ed. (Alphen aan den Rijn: Wolters Kluwer, 2019) §3.01 ("Unlike paper documents, electronic documents can be updated or changed without leaving an easily recognizable trace. Therefore, unique questions may arise as to the scope of a party's duty to preserve evidence in electronic form."). See, generally, "The Sedona Principles: Third Edition Best Practices, Recommendations and Principles for Addressing Electronic Document Discovery" (October 2017), https://thesedonaconference.org/publication/The_Sedona_Principles (Principle 5: "The obligation to preserve electronically stored information requires reasonable and good faith efforts to retain information that is expected to be relevant to claims or defenses in reasonably anticipated or pending litigation.").

[31] EDRM Model, www.edrm.net/frameworks-and-standards/edrm-model (accessed June 7, 2020).

as well as perform research and discovery tasks within a secure system. Onna is a platform for conducting real-time searches across multiple repositories, aiding e-discovery by finding high-value items across legal departments. Z-discovery is a cloud-based e-discovery suite that enables law firms to streamline their operations and fulfill compliance requirements. All these e-discovery technologies and tools facilitate and simplify a legal professional's work, reducing time and costs. They also help lawyers achieve the goal of e-discovery compliance.

In addition to e-discovery, automating legal documents became popular at the beginning of the twenty-first century. Early staged automation refers to the use of software to draft legal documents. The need for automation arises from traditional practices in which lawyers draft new documents or forms for every transaction, which is time consuming and prone to errors. Thus, it was recognized that a great deal of efficiency and accuracy gains could be achieved by converting frequently used documents and forms into templates. The templates could then be incorporated into automated workflows to produce types of documents that use similar language and formats, such as corporate formation documents, nondisclosure agreements (NDAs), wills, lease agreements, and deeds.

Document-automation companies emerged as a result including, LegalZoom and RocketLawyer. Founded in 2001, LegalZoom, the first online legal service provider, offered standardized documents and customizable legal forms at low costs. A few years later, RocketLawyer focused on providing individuals and small businesses with affordable legal documents. Thus, for simple documentation and standardized transactions (leases, establishing a business, sale contracts, lending, and divorce) these online services provided an alternative to hiring a lawyer. Document automation benefited individuals and small companies allowing them to receive easy access to affordable legal services online, without the need to hire a lawyer to complete simple tasks, such as forming a business or drafting a simple lease agreement.

Such automation for standardized transactions subsequently was adopted by law firms allowing them to be more competitive in the legal marketplace. Using document automation, law firms can reduce the errors, costs, and overall inefficiencies associated with traditional drafting methods. Efficient document formation also eases law firms' response to clients' cost-cutting demands.

2.3.2 Legal Tech: Augmenting the Lawyers' Work

If e-discovery tools and document automation were the earliest attempt to make law practice more efficient, the widespread emergence of LT companies in the twenty-first century has provided more sophisticated tools to augment lawyers' work. Some of the current areas where LT has impacted law practice includes practice management, due diligence, contract management, legal research, IP management, document services, lawyers' marketplace, and litigation analytics.[32] Another area that will gain in importance as lawyers switch to automation of services is cybersecurity in order to protect the ethical duty to keep client information confidential

The increase in LT start-ups in the legal domain has focused on streamlining interactions between lawyers and their clients.[33] Early leaders in this area include LawPal (project management tools), ViewABill (transparent billing management), and PlainLegal (document

---

[32] See K. Gresbrand, "Legal Tech: The Legal Profession Goes Digital: Greater Efficiency, Higher Quality, Novel Services: Digital Tools Are Changing the Way Lawyers Work," www2.deloitte.com/dl/en/pages/legal/articles/legal-tech-legal-department.html (accessed March 2, 2021).

[33] "Legal Tech Startups Have a Short History and a Bright Future," TechCrunch, https://techcrunch.com/2014/12/06/legal-tech-startups-have-a-short-history-and-a-bright-future/ (accessed June 14, 2020).

automation). Document review is being disrupted by machine-leaning tools, such as Diligence Engine and Ebrevia.

2.3.2.1 Drafting Legal Documents

In drafting legal documents, AI applications analyze previously signed legal documents and extract relevant information. "With legal tech's new document management tools, templates can automatically input contextual data, apply certain regional variations and generate related texts, actions or compliance-relevant queries." The advantages of such systems include reduced time needed to draft a document and a reduction in drafting errors. An example is Deloitte's intelligent contract lifecycle management system known as dTrax.[34] dTrax produces a first draft and allows negotiating parties to approve or disapprove its various provisions. In order to make negotiation easer, it offers an "integrated negotiation playbook." After an agreement is finalized, dTrak provides contract management tools, such as automatic alerts for specific milestones or expiration dates. Kira Systems provides software to perform accurate due diligence in the reviewing of contracts by searching, highlighting, and extracting relevant content.[35]

Legal Robot proactively helps the drafter write clearer documents. The software builds a legal language model from thousands of documents. This knowledge is used to score the contract based on language complexity, legal phrasing, and enforceability. It flags issues and provides suggestions for improving the contract's compliance, consistency, and readability by evaluating it on best practices, risk factors, and differences in jurisdictions. Judicata's software "Clerk" is capable of reading and analyzing legal briefs. It also evaluates their strengths and weaknesses and assigns a score for each brief based on arguments, drafting, and context. It helps reduce errors by identifying the quotations in a brief and cross checking them against the cited case to ensure the text is identical and the page numbers are correct.[36]

2.3.2.2 Analyzing Legal Documents

In the classifying and analyzing of legal documents, robot coworkers[37] allow for the intelligent, efficient analysis of large volumes of legal documents. One of the fundamental responsibilities of the legal profession, in addition to drafting legal texts, is reading and analyzing them. In technical terms, however, the vast majority of documents analyzed, such as contracts, ordinances, or pleadings, basically amount to unstructured data. Legal data is voluminous, including fact patterns, precedents, and case outcomes. Data analytics have the ability to process documents written in natural language and turn them into machine-readable texts that predictive analytics can search to uncover the most relevant precedents.

Predictive analytics, which use algorithms based on probabilities, produce a wide variety of analytical methods and applications. Data extraction, for example, enhances the lawyer's ability to perform legal due diligence in corporate takeovers. Buyers can examine the takeover target's existing agreements to identify problematic content such as change of control clauses. Results of the due diligence review can be uploaded as structured data into the buyer's ERP. eBrevia uses natural language processing and machine learning to extract relevant textual data from legal contracts and other documents to guide lawyers in analysis and due diligence. The lawyer

---

[34] See www2.deloitte.com/ca/en/pages/deloitte-analytics/articles/ai-factory-dtrax.html.html.
[35] Kira Systems at https://kirasystems.com.
[36] Currently only available in California.
[37] See, e.g., www2.deloitte.com/us/en/insights/focus/signals-for-strategists/cognitive-enterprise-robotic-process-automation.html.

customizes the type of information that is relevant to the task needed, the software converts it to searchable text and summarizes the findings in a report.[38]

For these systems to succeed, however, the software has to undergo targeted training up front. This preparation phase relies on human trainers to correct software errors, from case omissions to inaccurate assessments, using a rules-based process. Once properly trained, the software is capable of detecting 200 different types of information across all documents. One scholar-practitioner noted that 500 billable hours of document reviews can be performed in a few days using data analytics along with a single legal assistant. The process involves a lawyer familiar with the training data used to "teach" the computer to think, by coding and tagging a subset of documents. The computer software or search engine then produces the results of its review and predictions. The lawyer randomly samples the documents to determine the accuracy of the computer's output. This sampling is repeated a number of times. Once it is determined that the algorithm is producing accurate results then the computer program is left to finish the job.[39]

2.3.2.3 *Measuring Legal Performance*

Digital tools can make work easier for lawyers by eliminating "manual" tasks that are resource intensive. Automation can also provide new methods of measuring performance. LT gives legal departments the ability to calculate meaningful and realistic key performance indicators (KPIs), which can help them better manage resources. There are a number of useful metrics available in different areas of legal work. The system can automatically calculate the percentage of time saved during contract negotiations. It can record the number of contracts that have errors or inaccuracies, as well as distinguish between structured formatting and dynamic elements (for example, automatic alerts when a contract expires). It can track the productivity for each employee. Smokeball's cloud-based legal practice management tool automates the recording of time and activities by law firms.[40] One major feature of this tool is the capability to track all activities including emails that are valid for billing.

2.3.2.4 *Structuring and Management of Legal Workflows*

LT will play a huge role in reinventing how lawyers work in corporations and law firms. The demand for legal advice is growing, while regulatory requirements are becoming increasingly complex. The digital transformation in other fields has shown that automation can do more than improve efficiency. LT lightens the workload in certain areas of legal practice and frees up legal resources that can be channeled into more complex cases. LT has the potential to invent entirely new careers for people such as programmers and experts operating intelligent tools. Legal technologists will work across disciplines, combining legal skills with IT expertise and adding value to law firms and companies. General counsels will better be able to align the internal structure of their departments with the company's overall strategy.

In managing legal workflows, software programs can track and issue alerts for legal compliance. An example is Brexit Navigator,[41] which shows German companies how the UK withdrawal from the European Union will impact their operations – including personalized information that applies to individual cases.

---

[38] Ebrevia at https://ebrevia.com.
[39] M. Pistone, "Law Schools and Technology: Where We Are and Where We Are Heading" (2015) 64 *Journal of Legal Education* 586, citing M. Pistone and J. Hoeffner, "No Path but One: Law Schools in the Age of Disruptive Technology" (2013) 59 *Wayne Law Review* 193 249.
[40] See www.smokeball.com.
[41] See www2.deloitte.com/de/de/pages/strategy/articles/Deloitte-Brexit-Navigator.html.

2.3.2.5 *Legal Research*

Among all AI developments, its application in legal research most significantly augments lawyers' work. ROSS Intelligence (ROSS) is an online legal research tool built on its own AI framework (Legal Cortex) and combined with IBM's Watson cognitive computing technology. It offers a platform that allows for natural language searches, in order to quickly find relevant caselaw. Unlike traditional research platforms, which follow keyword searches, ROSS can understand input made in the form of a text or speech format. ROSS applies a new form of AI technology called natural-language understanding (NLU), which directly enables human–computer integration without the formalized syntax of computer languages and allows computers to communicate with humans. NLU is programmed to understand meaning despite common human errors such as mispronunciations or transposed letters or words. ROSS is intelligent in responding to a person's intent and the context of the query.

Unlike traditional methods, cases generated from keyword searches on Westlaw or LexisNexis, ROSS uses its machine-learning algorithms to retrieve the most relevant cases and then ranks those cases so that the first decision the reader sees is the most relevant.[42] ROSS is far more efficient and accurate, as it avoids the "general to specific" inverted research pyramid and takes one to the top of the pyramid. ROSS can also generate more comprehensive results, as it retrieves answers from the complete collections of US federal and state cases; federal statutes; selected state statutes and regulations; administrative decisions from the Trademark Trial and Appeal Board, the Patent Trial and Appeal Board, and the National Labor Relations Board; and decisions from state and federal specialty courts such as military and tribal courts.[43] ROSS eliminates the need for legal researchers to assemble groups of cases indexed based on the researcher's logic.[44]

In the legal research field, LexisNexis and Westlaw have historically had a duopoly on the market, but a number of LT start-ups offer a variety of research tools, including Casetext, Judicata, Lex Machina, and RaveLaw. Casetext allows lawyers to forecast an opposing counsel's arguments by finding opinions that were previously used by lawyers in similar cases. The system can also detect cases and arguments that have been negatively treated in subsequent cases and flag them as unreliable.[45]

The impact of the most recent AI developments has been monumental. In addition to benefits shared by automation systems (freeing up lawyers, reducing costs, and increasing efficiency), AI produces more accurate and higher-quality work. The AI contract-review platform LawGeex conducted a study where its AI solution competed against twenty top corporate lawyers in reviewing NDAs. They found that their AI tool achieved a "94% accuracy rate in detecting risks in NDAs compared to 85% for the lawyers."[46] AI can also boost revenues, profits, and employment.[47] A recent Accenture report on the future of the workplace stated that businesses committed to AI and investing in human–machine collaboration could see an estimated 38 percent revenue boost and increase employment levels by 10 percent between 2018 and 2022.[48]

---

[42] "How ROSS AI Turns Legal Research on Its Head," https://blog.rossintelligence.com/post/how-ross-ai-turns-legal-research-on-its-head (accessed June 3, 2020).
[43] See ROSS Intelligence, https://rossintelligence.com (accessed June 3, 2020).
[44] "How ROSS AI Turns Legal Research," n. 42.
[45] CaseText at https://casetext.com.
[46] S. Chang, "The Benefits of Using Artificial Intelligence in Law" at para. 4, https://blog.rossintelligence.com/post/benefits-ai-law (accessed March 2, 2021).
[47] "Future Workforce: Reworking the Revolution," Accenture, www.accenture.com/nl-en/company-reworking-the-revolution-future-workforce (accessed June 11, 2020).
[48] Ibid.

2.3.3 Technology as a Legal Substitute

With LT becoming more intelligent and sophisticated, concerns have been rising as to whether it will become an alternative to existing systems and whether it will displace the legal profession or disrupt the current model of delivering legal services. The value of LT in replacing work previously in the domain of the law firm depends on the perspective of the group doing the valuation. From the narrow perspective of lawyers, LT poses an existential threat to their livelihoods similar to the threat of blockchain technology to the European notary profession (see Section 2.3.3.3). From the perspective of society, businesses, and consumers, LT will be beneficial in lowering overhead costs and increasing access to justice. McGinnis and Pearce assert that LT can be leveraged to expand the services provided by the legal profession: "lawyers who can change their practice or organization to take advantage of lower cost inputs made available by machines will be able to serve an expanding market of legal services for middle-class individuals and small businesses, meeting previously unfulfilled legal needs."[49] The logic here is these groups currently ignore the use of legal services due to the high costs of lawyers. LT can lower the costs of legal services and expand the clientele served by lawyers. Sections 2.3.3.1–2.3.3.4 provide areas where LT is making inroads into the profession.

2.3.3.1 Online Pseudo-law Services

As previously noted, LegalZoom and RocketLawyer were the earliest online legal service providers. With nearly two decades of progress, LegalZoom expanded beyond automated legal documents to intellectual property protection services, such as trademark registration and patent application as well as prepaid legal plans that connect customers with lawyers regarding new legal matters for a monthly fee.[50] RocketLawyer offers its Document Defense service to connect customers with lawyers. They both can get users a personal lawyer with discounted representation fee rates.

The landscape of online legal services is growing. In addition to for-profit start-ups, such as LegalZoom and RocketLawyer, many government or court-sponsored information sites, not-for-profit legal services, and private legal information sites are increasing.[51] For instance, the California Courts Self-Help Center's website provides user guides on a variety of legal issues.[52] JustAnswer connects users one-on-one with legal experts who can answer legal questions online or by phone.[53] FindLaw.com is the most popular site for free legal information and has the largest online lawyer directory, with more than eleven million visitors each month.[54] New media, such as WeChat's public platforms, where lawyers and legal scholars can register their own accounts, publish articles addressing legal issues and offer expert opinions about specific legal issues. These resources allow ordinary people to find legal information and navigate the legal system to find solutions to their legal problems.[55]

---

[49] McGinnis and Pearce, n. 6 at 3042.
[50] "Prepaid Legal Plans – Affordable Legal Help for Your Family or Business," LegalZoom, www.legalzoom.com/attorneys/ (accessed June 10, 2020).
[51] M. Hagan, "The User Experience of the Internet as a Legal Help Service: Defining Standards for the Next Generation of User-Friendly Online Legal Services" (2016), https://papers.ssrn.com/abstract=2942478 (accessed June 10, 2020).
[52] Self-Help, www.courts.ca.gov/selfhelp.htm (accessed June 10, 2020).
[53] "Have Legal Questions?," JustAnswer, www.justanswer.com/law/ (accessed June 10, 2020).
[54] "FindLaw Corporate Information: Company Background," Findlaw, https://company.findlaw.com/company-history/findlaw-corporate-information-press-company-background.html (accessed June 10, 2020).
[55] J. Cabral et al., "Using Technology to Enhance Access to Justice" (2012) 26 *Harvard Journal of Law and Technology* 241 246–247.

Online legal products and services serve a need. They directly allow people and small businesses to find affordable legal help. Tech-enabled legal products and services also offer "an alternative source of affordable legal services [and can] help fill the gap left by overburdened and shrinking legal aid groups."[56] In addition, tech-based legal help offers many advantages over face-to-face service, including scalability for service providers and immediacy for customers.[57] However, most online pseudo-law services or alternative legal service providers (ALSPs) are not substitutes for traditional legal services. For instance, the Self-Represented Litigant Network surveyed the online experience for laypeople trying to find legal help and found that current online legal services were inadequate; court- and government-sponsored websites were often overloaded with information and provided no clear path to follow. In sum, consumers have difficulty finding specific legal information online[58]

Face-to-face consultations with lawyers remain the most reliable place to obtain legal information and advice. Clients find clarification about their legal issues and possible solutions in a shorter time without experiencing an overload of information. Law firms with a sound reputation are more structured with respect to their legal teams and resources to provide qualified legal services. They are also more capable of taking responsibility if things go wrong because of the standards set by the canon of ethics and malpractice rules. In contrast, users face higher risks of receiving inadequate legal help from online legal service sites.

Despite reliability issues, ALSPs are able to undercut the price of law firms for routine legal services. Routine legal services are those that do not rely on a high level of legal expertise, such as standardized transactions like leases, loans, simple contracts, wills and trusts, document review, and contract and IP management. Some legal industry observers see ALSPs as a threat to traditional law practice, others see the rise of the ALSP field as an opportunity if incorporated into traditional legal practice. Some law firms manage ALSPs for clients, establish partnerships with existing ALSPs, or create in-house ALSPs. Large law firms currently employ ALSPs in such areas as e-discovery, legal research, litigation and investigation support, and document review. Obviously, seeking partnerships with ALSPs to fill in any perceived gaps in technology, innovation, and process efficiency is the easier path for law firms.

Further, law firms "could reap further advantage in cost savings by learning from ALSPs how to better measure, document, and demonstrate to clients exactly how and where cost-savings are coming from."[59] In-firm ALSPs can be used for marketing purposes, offering practical information at the same time advertising the services offered by the firm. In the end, the idea of legal platforms or alternative sources for legal services is one that can be co-opted by law firms, either internally or by outsourcing.

2.3.3.2 Internet Courts and the Use of Tamper-Proof Evidence

In August 2017, China launched three internet courts in Hangzhou, Beijing, and Guangzhou. These internet courts are dedicated to resolving internet-related disputes through online litigation platforms. With internet courts, the entire litigation process is conducted online, including

---

[56] C. Johnson, "Leveraging Technology to Deliver Legal Services" (2009) 23 *Harvard Journal of Law and Technology* 259 281.
[57] N. Balmer, M. Smith, C. Denvir, and A. Patel, "Just a Phone Call Away: Is Telephone Advice Enough?" (2012) 34 *Journal of Social Welfare and Family Law*, 63.
[58] Hagan, n. 51.
[59] "Alternative Power Source: How Law Firms Are Leveraging ALSPs to Make Themselves Better, Faster, and Cheaper," www.legalexecutiveinstitute.com/wp-content/uploads/2019/06/Alternative-Power-Source_white-paper_05.10_FINAL.pdf (accessed June 8, 2020).

case filing, service of process, mediation, exchange of evidence, pretrial preparation, court hearings, verdict, and execution. China's Supreme People's Court published the *Provisions on Several Issues Concerning the Trial of Cases by the Internet Courts* (Provisions), clarifying the jurisdiction of these courts and regulating certain procedural issues.[60] According to the Provisions, the scope of jurisdiction is broad, covering disputes involving the online sale of goods and services, lending, copyright and neighboring rights ownership and infringement, domain disputes, infringement on personal rights or property rights via the Internet, product liability claims, internet public interest litigation brought by prosecutors, and online administrative disputes.[61]

Since the whole process takes place online, a prerequisite is be able to store evidence online. Scanning relevant materials and storing them on the platform is the first step to either filing a lawsuit or responding to a claim. The Supreme People's Court confirmed the legitimacy of using electronic evidence authenticated by electronic signatures, time stamps, hash value verification, blockchain, and other tamper-proof verification methods.[62]

The Hangzhou internet platform has a separate section for electronic evidence, which includes two subsections: judicial blockchain platform[63] and evidence storage platform.[64] The judicial blockchain platform focuses on generating, storing, transmitting, and verifying digital data. The goal of this platform is to build a credible chain of evidence using blockchain technology. Its application in the judicial sphere enhances credibility across all court procedures by using electronic data.[65] The evidence storage platform deals with access to electronic evidence. The platform links to evidence stored by third parties, including evidence authenticated by notary offices, produced by an unrelated third-party platform (such as, identify information stored in the database of police departments), obtained through court orders (attachment), and legally made by other departments, such as courts' verdicts and arbitral awards.

The appearance of internet courts and the use of technologies, especially tamper-proof technologies, to store and authenticate evidence benefits lawyers in two ways. The benefit of having trials online offers more flexibility in time and travel for lawyers. Another benefit is that using tamper-proof technologies to store and authenticate evidence reduces lawyers' burdens to prove the authenticity of electronic evidence. Pictures, texts, and transaction histories stored on the blockchain are tamper-proof. There is little need for lawyers to argue or cross-examine the other party regarding the characteristics of a transaction if the transaction has been recorded on the blockchain.

Concerns may exist regarding whether having internet courts or using tamper-proof evidence will affect or diminish lawyers' roles. A broad perspective view would see internet courts as simply moving offline trials to online platforms, with little change to the nature of lawyers' work – that is, advising clients, engaging in pre-litigation settlement discussions, drafting legal documents, presenting cases, and defending clients.

---

[60] 最高人民法院关于互联网法院审理案件若干问题的规定 – 中华人民共和国最高人民法院, www.court.gov.cn/zixun-xiangqing-116981.html (accessed November 6, 2018).
[61] 杭州互联网法院诉讼平台, www.netcourt.gov.cn/portal/main/domain/index.htm (accessed May 27, 2020).
[62] 最高人民法院关于互联网法院审理案件若干问题的规定 – 中华人民共和国最高人民法院, n. 60.
[63] 杭州互联网法院司法区块链, https://blockchain.netcourt.gov.cn/blockchain/index.htm (accessed May 22, 2020).
[64] 杭州互联网法院电子证据平台, http://evidence.netcourt.gov.cn/#/page (accessed November 7, 2018).
[65] D. Lee, "Hangzhou Internet Court Announces the Use of Blockchain Technology in Court Proceedings," Pandaily (2018), https://pandaily.com/hangzhou-Internet-court-announces-the-use-of-blockchain-technology-in-court-proceedings (accessed May 20, 2020).

Internet courts presently have limited scope, mostly limited to internet-related disputes. Although much evidence appears in electronic form, many other tangible sources of evidence are not electronic, such as physical evidence. These items still require investigation and verification from lawyers to assess their authenticity. For example, the ownership information of a house may be stored electronically, but information on the condition of the property would need to be physically verified.

However, the emergence of internet courts reduces the need for lawyers to some extent, and lawyers may not elect to take on some internet dispute cases because of their diminished roles. The most important benefit of online dispute platforms is that they provide access to justice for small claims and when hiring a lawyer is cost prohibitive. An online trader or consumer has the option to resolve disputes through a dispute resolution process provided by the digital platform or proceed to an internet court. The e-commence giant Taobao (721 million monthly users) manages common disputes online including, loss of items, delayed delivery, and defective product claims. Taobao streamlines these disputes through internal systems with various solutions, such as quickly refunding or replacing items. Ultimately, 95 percent of these disputes are resolved through internal processes, with the remainder going to Hangzhou Internet Court. The court provides litigants with automated legal documents, generating a complaint in seconds and simplifying the entire process without the need for a lawyer. If lawyers are used, the fees are capped. In cases involving less than 100,000 Yuan ($13,994), the lawyers are awarded a flat fee of 20,000 Yuan ($2,798.80). This keeps legal costs low for small claims, but may diminish the availability of representation or the quality of an attorney's work.

2.3.3.3 *Notary Publics and the Blockchain*

The hubris of technologists in seeing the widespread application of the blockchain as a way to eliminate the need for trusted third parties, resulting in the elimination of entire professions (commercial and central banks, lawyers, accountants, notaries) is somewhat illusory given the reality of the human component in these professions. The European notary is one profession that is most threatened by the blockchain coupled with AI. According to the National Notary Association,

> A Notary Public is an official of integrity appointed by state government – typically by the secretary of state – to serve the public as an impartial witness in performing a variety of official fraud-deterrent acts related to the signing of important documents. These official acts are called notarizations or notarial acts. Notaries are publicly commissioned as "ministerial" officials, meaning that they are expected to follow written rules without the exercise of significant personal discretion, as would otherwise be the case with a "judicial" official.[66]

The notary "screen[s] the signers of important documents for their true identity, their willingness to sign without duress or intimidation, and their awareness of the contents of the document or transaction."[67] Basically, a notary serves as an independent, even-handed witness who documents the presence or absence of certain facts.

Many of the functions of the notary – review of the legality of legal documents, providing advice for correcting mistakes to make documents conform to legal requirements, authenticating the parties to the document, certifying the date of execution – will be performable by LT and the blockchain in the near future. A blockchain as a distributed database system serves functions

---

[66] National Notary Association, "What Is a Notary Public?," www.nationalnotary.org/knowledge-center/about-notaries (accessed September 10, 2019).
[67] Ibid.

comparable to a notary. First, a blockchain is a ledger. This means data are stored in rigid structures called blocks, which are connected to each other in a chain. Each block includes a time stamp and a link to the previous block via a hash. Each block has a header with metadata and content, which includes the real transaction data. Every new piece of transaction data will be hashed and represented by a series of random numbers and letters. Second, it is a distributed ledger. This means every node (participants in the network) stores the same data and shares the same rights. Every node works independently but is simultaneously supervised by other nodes. Third, it is a fault-tolerant ledger. This means that even if one-third of the nodes are attacked, the system can still work normally. This function arises from the Byzantine generals' problem, wherein actors must agree on a concerted strategy to avoid catastrophic system failures when some of the actors are unreliable.[68] Essentially, a blockchain can record data and prove the existence of such data, provide traceability, transparency, and the time of the transaction or execution. Furthermore, AI programs can review documents to assess their compliance to legal requirements prior to them being placed on the blockchain. The combination of blockchain technology and AI can serve the core functions currently provided by human notaries.

However, the current state of technology is not sufficient to completely substitute for the integrity of notaries. First, data recorded on the blockchain via an oracle (third-party information source) cannot fully guarantee the authenticity of data.[69] Oracles have the sole function of supplying data to blockchains.[70] There is a chance that data sources from which oracles obtain information are not always credible. A remedy for this problem is to request data from multiple oracles and program a mechanism to select the single best source.[71] This may not be cost-effective due to the sheer volume of information available online. Second, the blockchain cannot determine whether the signature was procured through duress or intimidation.

Nonetheless, the blockchain may supplement the work of notaries. For instance, after the applicant signs and swears before a notary, the signed document can be placed on a blockchain to prevent subsequent fraudulent alterations. The recipient that receives the document can be confident that it is the same document that was witnessed by the notary. The evolution of such a system is seen in Luxembourg's establishment of the first European notary blockchain system.[72] The system allows the following: registering certain kinds of documents, ensuring their integrity, and providing a time stamp for the registration. It optimizes the security of notarization while reducing costs. If successful, it will demonstrate the potential for any system where the guarantee

---

[68] L. Lamport, R. Shostak, and M. Pease, "The Byzantine Generals Problem" (1982) 4 *Academy Transactions on Programming Language Systems* 382, https://people.eecs.berkeley.edu/~luca/cs174/byzantine.pdf. The "Byzantine generals' problem" states that no two computers on a decentralized network can entirely and irrefutably guarantee that they are displaying the same data. Assuming the network is unreliable, they can never be sure that the data they communicated have arrived. At its core, the Byzantine generals' problem is achieving a consensus across a distributed network of devices, some of which could be potentially faulty, while being wary of any attackers attempting to undermine the network.

[69] M. del Castillo, "Lawyers Be Damned: Andreas Antonopoulos Takes Aim at Arbitration with DAO Proposal," Coindesk, www.coindesk.com/damned-dao-andreas-antonopoulos-third-key (accessed May 26, 2016). See also M. Abramowicz, "Cryptocurrency-Based Law" (2016) 58 *Arizona Law Review* 359 (explains how blockchains can help facilitate peer-to-peer arbitration, which can lower transaction costs of commercial relationships and increase trust between parties).

[70] See A. Liu, "Smart Oracles: Building Business Logic with Smart Contracts," Ripple, https://ripple.com/insights/smartoracles-building-business-logic-with-smart-contracts (accessed July 16, 2014).

[71] B. Asolo, "Blockchain Oracles Explained," Mycryptopedia (2018), www.mycryptopedia.com/blockchain-oracles-explained/ (accessed June 11, 2020).

[72] "Luxembourg Launches First European Notary Blockchain System," Chronicle.lu, www.chronicle.lu/category/ict/28344-luxembourg-launches-first-european-notary-blockchain-system (accessed June 11, 2020).

of records' immutability is required. In the future, LT will transform notary services by limiting the roles of human notaries.

2.3.3.4 Smart Contracts and the Challenges of Implementation

Smart contracts are agreements whose execution is automated by computer codes that translate legal prose into an executable program.[73] The computer code (agreement) is then placed on a blockchain. They are designed to automatically ensure the performance of agreements without human involvement. Nick Szabo defined them as "a set of promises, specified in digital form, including protocols with which the parties perform on the other promises."[74] The protocols are usually implemented with programs on a computer network or in other digital forms. The basic idea of smart contracts is that human-readable contractual clauses (liens, bonding, delineation of property rights) are converted into executable computer code that can be run on a network. The contractual clauses, in the form of computer code, may thus be made partially or fully self-executing and self-enforcing. Smart contracts are essentially breachless contracts.[75]

Smart contracts have garnered attention because their automation avoids the costs of third-party intermediaries. For instance, smart contracts can automate compliance by digitalizing American Uniform Commercial Code filings and automating their renewal and release processes.[76] In the securities market, smart contracts can facilitate the automatic payment of dividends, stock splits, and liability management while reducing counterparty and operational risks.[77] In trade finance, smart contracts can facilitate the international transfers of goods through faster letters of credit and trade payment initiation while improving the liquidity of financial assets. Smart contracts have been proposed for various uses, such as in derivative contracts, government records, auto insurance, and supply chain management.

However, expanded use of smart contracts are still in the experimental phase. One of the technical limitations is the vulnerability of computer code. The infamous case of the "The DAO," where hackers exposed a loophole in the code and stole sixty million Ethers (cryptocurrency associated with Ethereum).[78] Another technical barrier is smart contracts' scalability – that is, the capability of processing transactions. While Visa can manage 1,667 transactions per second, Ethereum smart contracts can only process 20 transactions at a time. Some of these shortcomings can be minimized by the use of private blockchains but this would be at the cost of the anonymity and immutability provided by public blockchains.

In addition to technical barriers, legal challenges also impede the implementation of smart contracts. The first issue is the ambiguity of smart contracts' legitimacy. Assuming that a smart contract is used to execute a transaction, what is its legal effect in a given jurisdiction? Some US states, such as Delaware, Tennessee, and Arizona, have passed legislation recognizing the legal

---

[73] M. Raskin, 'The Law and Legality of Smart Contracts' (2017) 1 *Georgetown Law Technology Review* 305.

[74] "Smart Contracts Glossary," www.fon.hum.uva.nl/rob/Courses/InformationInSpeech/CDROM/Literature/LOTwinterschool2006/szabo.best.vwh.net/smart_contracts_glossary.html (accessed May 12, 2019).

[75] N. Szabo, "Smart Contracts: Building Blocks for Digital Markets," www.fon.hum.uva.nl/rob/Courses/InformationInSpeech/CDROM/Literature/LOTwinterschool2006/szabo.best.vwh.net/smart_contracts_2.html (accessed February 3, 2018).

[76] Chamber of Digital Commerce, "Smart Contracts – 12 Use Cases for Business and Beyond," www.the-blockchain.com/docs/Smart%20Contracts%20-%2012%20Use%20Cases%20for%20Business%20and%20Beyond%20-%20Chamber%20of%20Digital%20Commerce.pdf (accessed June 3, 2020).

[77] "Smart Contracts Glossary," n. 74.

[78] M. del Castillo, "The DAO Attacked: Code Issue Leads to $60 Million Ether Theft," Coindesk (2016), www.coindesk.com/dao-attacked-code-issue-leads-60-million-ether-theft (accessed June 1, 2020).

effects of smart contracts.[79] In 2017, Arizona amended the Arizona Electronic Transactions Act, which defines blockchain technology and smart contracts and further indicates that "data on the ledger that is protected with cryptography, is immutable and auditable and provides an uncensored truth."[80] Thus, Arizona recognizes the legally binding effects of smart contracts that are fully automated and executed on a blockchain. However, ambiguity as to their legality still exists in many other states and countries.

Several contract law scholars argue that smart contracts cannot offer a superior solution to many problems addressed by traditional contract law, such as contract validity and legality.[81] Max Raskin provides an overview of the classic stages of contract formation, performance, breach, and remedy, and poses a series of issues presented by smart contracts at each stage.[82] Scholars also correctly argue that smart contracts cannot replicate the relational context, which is essential for the day-to-day practice of contracting.[83] Another view is that smart contracts should not be analyzed through the lens of replacing the existing contract law system. Smart contracts should assume an instrumental role aimed at serving the current contract law system instead of being seen as an alternative to that system.[84] Embedding smart contracts within the current contract law system to function as a complementary tool enhances contract effectiveness.

In sum, smart contracts have the potential of establishing a parallel mechanism to the state-provided legal system for simplistic types of transactions (payment, title transfers) but will not be able to fully escape the legal system.[85] Considering all the technical limitations, such as the inability of complex or standard-like clauses to be converted into computer code, the widespread adoption and implementation of smart contracts in numerous legal and economic sectors will not likely take place anytime soon.

2.4 FUTURE OF LEGAL PRACTICE

Smart contracts, and the blockchain, along with advances in AI, are ushering in a new age of automation. The pace and extent of automation is accelerating continued technical progress, such as natural language processing, pattern recognition, deep learning, and data mining. In the future, in certain situations, machines will match and outperform humans in work requiring cognitive capabilities.[86] Equipped with cognitive capabilities, machines are likely to think or perform in similar ways to a lawyer. Sections 2.4.1–2.4.3 will examine three areas in which technological advancement is likely to impact legal practice – performing like a lawyer, executable law, and legal ethics.

---

[79] I. Shehata, "Smart Contracts and International Arbitration" (2018), https://papers.ssrn.com/abstract=3290026 (accessed June 5, 2020).
[80] Ibid. See also J. Bambara et al., *Blockchain: A Practical Guide to Developing Business, Law and Technology Solutions* (New York: McGraw-Hill, 2018) 103–104.
[81] H. Eenmaa-Dimitrieva and M. J. Schmidt-Kessen, "Regulation through Code as a Safeguard for Implementing Smart Contracts in No-Trust Environments" (2017), https://papers.ssrn.com/abstract=3100181 (accessed June 8, 2020).
[82] Raskin, n. 73.
[83] Eenmaa-Dimitrieva and Schmidt-Kessen, n. 81.
[84] J. Jiaying, "The Normative Role of Smart Contracts" (2018) 15 *US-China Law Review* 139.
[85] A. Wright and P. De Filipp, "Decentralized Blockchain Technology and the Rise of Lex Cryptographia" (2015), https://papers.ssrn.com/abstract=2580664 (accessed May 10, 2020). See generally, L. DiMatteo, M Cannarsa, and C. Poncibò (eds.), *Cambridge Handbook on Smart Contracts, Blockchain Technology and Digital Platforms* (New York: Cambridge University Press, 2020).
[86] "MGI: A Future That Works Executive Summary," https://www.mckinsey.com/~/media/mckinsey/featured%20insights/Digital%20Disruption/Harnessing%20automation%20for%20a%20future%20that%20works/MGI-A-future-that-works-Executive-summary.ashx (accessed June 6, 2020).

2.4.1 Advanced AI: Thinking and Performing like a Lawyer?

A great deal of law practice heavily relies on the ability to perform various mental activities most closely associated with problem solving. Cognitive computing is the term typically used to describe AI systems that aim to simulate human thought processes to assist humans in finding solutions to complex problems.[87] Human cognition involves a real-time analysis of the environment, context, and intent, among many other variables that inform a person's ability to solve problems. The goal of cognitive computing is to assist humans in their decision-making process. An example of a cognitive computing application is its use in assisting medical doctors in their treatment of disease.

In addition to cognitive computing, AI's other techniques, such as deep learning, machine learning, neutral networks, and natural language processing, are critical to helping machines think and perform like a human. In psychology, Woebot has functioned as a personal cognitive behavioral therapist[88] by tracking a person's mood and understanding her psyche over time through regular conversations. Woebot is capable of conducting productive conversations and offering helpful tips to reduce depression, anxiety, and other psychological problems.[89] This could also be the case in the legal space. Future AI-powered robots will communicate with lawyers and others by offering legal opinions to reduce legal risks such as regulatory noncompliance.

Elon Musk's brain–computer interface start-up, Neuralink, has pulled back the veil on its ambitions to implant chips in human brains.[90] The firm's goal is to use tiny electrodes implanted in the brain to cure diseases and "achieve a symbiosis with artificial intelligence."[91] Without such a symbiosis, Musk believes humans will not be able to prosper in technological advances of the future.[92] Neuralink has built an array of small and flexible electrode "threads," which a neurosurgical robot is capable of inserting six threads (192 electrodes) per minute into the brain.[93]

If this kind of integration between brains and threads is successful, robot lawyers could become a reality though the insertion of a chip into human brains. Any contemplated legal action or strategy would go through the robot's analysis regarding its legitimacy or potential legal risks. Before any action is made, the robot would alert the person of potential risks and consequences. Such an implantation could be attractive to businesspersons whose decisions have legal consequences and who require legal advice. It would also benefit society, since a person would immediately be warned by the robot of potential criminal aspects of their activities including, information on prison sentences and fines associated with the intended action. This could deter crimes *ex ante*, as well as eliminate the argument of innocent noncompliance.

---

[87] SearchEnterpriseAI, "What Is Cognitive Computing?," https://searchenterpriseai.techtarget.com/definition/cognitive-computing (accessed June 15, 2020).

[88] "Woebot – Your Charming Robot Friend Who Is Here For You, 24/7," https://woebot.io (accessed June 5, 2020).

[89] "Prepare Yourselves, Robots Will Soon Replace Doctors in Healthcare," www.forbes.com/sites/haroldstark/2017/07/10/prepare-yourselves-robots-will-soon-replace-doctors-in-healthcare/#74d1a27352b5 (accessed June 2, 2020).

[90] E. Lopatto, "Elon Musk Unveils Neuralink's Plans for Brain-Reading 'Threads' and a Robot to Insert Them" *The Verge* (2019), www.theverge.com/2019/7/16/20697123/elon-musk-neuralink-brain-reading-thread-robot (accessed June 6, 2020).

[91] K. Servick, "Elon Musk's Startup Eyes Human Testing for Brain-Computer Interface" *Science/AAAS* (2019), www.sciencemag.org/news/2019/07/elon-musk-s-startup-eyes-human-testing-brain-computer-interface (accessed June 19, 2020).

[92] Lopatto, n. 90.

[93] R. Robbins (STAT), "Neuralink White Paper," www.documentcloud.org/documents/6204648-Neuralink-White-Paper.html (accessed June 11, 2020).

2.4.2 Smart Contracts and the Blockchain: Executable Law?

The idea of executable law is illustrated in the following scenario. Assume two states have different laws with respect to the minimum drinking age: the legal age in State A is 16 and 18 in State B. Assume that a 16-year-old boy in State A is drinking, but then crosses the border into State B, violating State B's drinking-age law. The moment he crosses the state line, a ticket is automatically issued and a fine is automatically deducted from his bank account. At the moment of transfer, the enforcement process is completed – that is, the law has been executed.

How would this process work? The first step is to compose natural language provisions with ontological background and then place them into a smart contract. The purpose of using ontology is to have machine-readable language, which is a prerequisite for the execution of smart contracts. The legal database is the source of execution where a smart contract can retrieve a given person's age from the ID department's database, track the location of a person via GPS, and identify whether one is drinking via an AI analysis. The next step would be to set up "if ➔ then" rules to execute the smart contract. Once the condition "if" is met, the smart contract will immediately execute the "then." In the above scenario, if one is under 18, then a ticket is issued in the state with a drinking age below 18; secondly, if a ticket is issued, then a fine (with increased penalties for recidivism) is transferred from the violator's account to the state's account. The whole process could be done through a smartphone.

The idea of executable law refers to the situation where legal provisions can be converted into a machine-readable language and then executed on smart contracts. In the future, executable law could occur in numerous scenarios, such as the monitoring of driving violations, replacing physical land registries, and the execution of copyright transactions. The successful execution of law would rely on the accuracy of data guaranteed by the blockchain. The blockchain would guarantee the accuracy of the source (legal database) and the information in the database would be inputted into the smart contract by oracles.

In the future, technology may have the capability of interacting with various laws and executing actions according to those laws. Richard Susskind offers a simple example of executable law and the future of professionals:

> [I]nterest is developing in embedding legal requirements into our social and working lives, so that, for example, automatic compliance with health-and-safety regulations can be integrated into the design of buildings that can identify and respond when temperature levels are above some statutory level. In this way, human beings do not need to know the law and make a conscious decision to comply, and consequently, lawyers' direct involvement is not needed.[94]

Although it is likely that technology will be used to automate repetitive and lower-skilled legal tasks,[95] it is currently unclear whether technology will be able to think like a lawyer and perform complex legal jobs requiring higher levels of cognitive abilities.

2.4.3 Future of Legal Ethics

The work of technologists like Elon Musk and the idea of machine-generated executable law, remains in the realm of speculation; their realization is uncertain. Nonetheless, legal practice is currently facing new ethical challenges related to the use of technology, which will grow with

---

[94] Susskind, *Future of Law*, n. 13 at 71.
[95] B. Simpson, "Algorithms or Advocacy: Does the Legal Profession Have a Future in a Digital World?" (2016) 25 *Information Communications Tech Law* 50.

the creation of advanced AI and other emerging technologies. Lawyers need to comply with ethical duties, regardless of whether or not they use technology to perform their work. In this sense, the general standards and characteristics of the ethical duties of lawyers will remain constant in the digital age.[96] Simultaneously, as more information is being stored and transferred online and more legal work is being delegated to machines, lawyers face new risks and obstacles in upholding their professional responsibilities.[97]

The use of AI is a case in point. According to the American Bar Association's (ABA) Model Rules of Professional Conduct, lawyers have duties of competence and diligence. With AI, "one of the most notable issues is the 'black box' challenge, [where] a lawyer submits a query to an AI-powered tool, it goes into a 'black box,' and the AI-based program provides a solution."[98] To meet the requirements of competence and diligence, how much will a lawyer need to know about what goes on inside the box? How much work must a lawyer do to analyze the credibility of AI-driven tools? Is it appropriate to delegate certain types of work to such tools? Could such delegation constitute an unauthorized practice of law? While an AI-powered tool may only provide a single answer to a legal enquiry, lawyers often need to deal in nuance and use judgment in rendering an answer or decision in order to meet ethical standards.[99]

In addition to ethical issues caused by delegating legal work to AI-powered programs, lawyers also face the ethical dilemma of underutilizing AI and risk serving their clients less competently or efficiently: "In fact, given some of the psychological attributes commonly associated with lawyers – a focus on detail, a desire for control, an aversion to risk, and bias due to escalated commitment – the greater danger might very well be underutilization of, rather than over-reliance upon, artificial intelligence."[100] In sum, lawyers will bear the burden of understanding the benefits and risks associated with LT and decide when and how it should be used.

The exponential growth of relevant data and the risk of a data breach is another area that relates to lawyers' ethical obligations such as the lawyer's duty of confidentiality. The American Model Rules of Professional Conduct call attention to client confidentiality,[101] but does not provide guidance relating to the implications posed by the digital age. However, the facts show that more and more legal work is done online and clients' confidential information is being stored electronically. At the same time, data breaches have been proliferating.[102] This reality has put lawyers in a vulnerable position in maintaining client confidentiality.

The *American Bar Association Cybersecurity Handbook* acknowledges that: "[c]reating, using, communicating, and storing information in electronic form greatly increases the potential for unauthorized access, use, disclosure, and alteration, as well as the risk of loss or destruction."[103] ABA surveys and intelligence reports show an increase in cyber threats to law firms over the last five years, which most often take the form of third parties hacking a firms' network or database.[104]

---

[96] "The Ethical Implications of Artificial Intelligence," Above the Law, https://abovethelaw.com/law2020/the-ethical-implications-of-artificial-intelligence/ (accessed June 14, 2020).

[97] N. Babazadeh, "Legal Ethics and Cybersecurity: Managing Client Confidentiality in the Digital Age" (2018) 7 *Journal of Law and Cyber Warfare* 33.

[98] "Ethical Implications," n. 96.

[99] Although, truly advanced AI would provide the lawyer with a range of answers and provide context (if you value X more than Y, then A, or if Y is more important than X and Z then ...).

[100] Ibid.

[101] Rule 1.6: "Confidentiality of Information," www.americanbar.org/groups/professional_responsibility/publications/model_rules_of_professional_conduct/rule_1_6_confidentiality_of_information (accessed June 16, 2020).

[102] Babazadeh, n. 97.

[103] J. Rhodes and V. Polley, *The ABA Cybersecurity Handbook: A Resource for Attorneys, Law Firms, and Business Professionals* (Chicago: ABA Book Publishing, 2014).

[104] Babazadeh, n. 97.

A report on the extent to which law firms have experienced breaches shows that approximately 15 percent of all law firms and 25 percent of law firms with at least one hundred attorneys have been victims of data breaches due to a "hacker, website attack, break-in, or lost or stolen computer or smartphone."[105] Lastly, the ABA surveyed about 90,000 attorneys in private practices and found that about 60 percent had experienced a breach that caused significant disruptions or harm to their businesses, and 47 percent said their firms had no response plan in place to address security breaches.[106]

As noted above, the digital age poses new threats and risks to legal practice. For this reason, the rules of professional responsibility need to be updated in order provide clearer guidance in areas such as maintaining client confidentiality. It remains uncertain as to what constitutes proper practices and minimum safeguards to protect client information, ensure data security, and respond to data breaches : "We are navigating murky ethical areas where the law and rules haven't caught up yet with the technology and [w]e are trying to apply rules that were written based on certain ways of practicing law and now trying to apply them to very different ways of working."[107] In the future, fulfilling ethical obligations will become more complex and ambiguous, as newer technologies are incorporated into law practice.

2.5 CO-OPTING LEGAL TECH

It is important to note that technology not only threatens to disrupt the legal profession but other professions as well, such as the accounting and European notary professions. It is thus helpful to see how other professions are reacting to rapid technological advancement. In 2020, the American National Association of State Boards of Accountancy (NASBA) and the Institute of Certified Public Accountants (AICPA) established the "CPA Evolution Initiative."[108] The stated goal of the Initiative is to "transform the CPA profession and its licensure model in recognition of the need for rapidly changing CPA skills and competencies necessitated by constantly escalating technological disruption." The Guiding Principles recognizes the imperative to respond quickly to the technological disruptions represented by data analytics, robotics, and AI. The core response will focus on the education and licensing of future accountants: "entry into the profession, must be redesigned to attract individuals with technological and analytical expertise." Thus, the "future" of accounting licensure will require applicants to demonstrate minimum required technological competencies.

Given the current state of LT and its anticipated growth in the future, the legal profession faces a variety of challenges. The first and foremost is how do lawyers and bar associations confront technological change? Instead of worrying about being replaced by increasing levels of LT, the legal profession should embrace or co-opt new technologies. The goal is to categorize the parts of legal work (speed and accuracy) that can best be performed by LT, those that are best left to the legal mind, and those that require continuing human intervention, especially in the realm of AI. Specifically, lawyers should use technology to make lawyering more efficient and retain the human dimension in legal practice. An initial step in embracing technological change should start with legal education (see Section 2.5.3).

---

[105] Ibid. See also M. Maleske, "1 in 4 Law Firms are Victims of a Data Breach," Law360 (September 22, 2015), www.1aw360.com/articles/705657/1-in-4-lawfirms-are-victims-of-a-data-breach (accessed June 5, 2020).
[106] Ibid.
[107] "Ethical Implications," n. 96.
[108] See www.evolutionofcpa.org.

Clearly, law firms will need to develop strategies for incorporating LT into their legal practices. The Law Society has highlighted three types of innovation that will need to be considered by law firms in order for them to retain competitive advantages – product innovation, process innovation, and strategy innovation.[109] In the area of product innovation, law firms will have to decide whether to restructure in order provide specialized services to their clientele or offer broader services to fit all the needs of their particular clients. Process innovation relates to the specialization of labor involving the interface between humans and LT. Closely related to these two types of innovation is strategy innovation in which the law firm assesses "how innovation creates value for clients and how the firm captures a share of the value its innovations generate."[110] The pressure for law firms to show the value-added nature of its services will also come from in-house legal departments. LT is allowing in-house lawyers to do more of the work previously outsourced to law firms and deliver additional value to their companies.

Richard Susskind has asserted that LT will have internal and external impacts on the market for legal services, which he calls the "efficiency" and "collaboration" strategies.[111] The former is internal to the law firm and involves cutting the costs of its services. An efficiency strategy involves:

> the decomposition of legal work into component tasks, the more routine and repetitive of which should be undertaken in ways that are much more efficient than the methods of traditional ... charge by the hour practice. This leads us into a world of off-shoring, outsourcing, subcontracting, near-shoring, and computerizing the process-based and administrative work. In summary, this is the industrialization, digitization, and commoditization of legal service.

The "collaboration strategy" is client generated, where buyers of legal services create a co-op in order to reduce the overall costs of legal services. This would entail disaggregating common legal and compliance services and finding one legal supplier to create economies of scale for particular services.

In the end, disruptive technologies will lead to greater transparency in the pricing of legal services. In such an environment, law firms will need to demonstrate the value of the services they offer. In the past, law firms often determined their clients' legal needs. With the advent of LT, the focus will shift to the client's perspective of their needs. In this way, the process of innovating legal services is a full collaboration between lawyers and clients.

2.5.1 Using Technology to Make Lawyering More Efficient

Using technology to make lawyering more efficient requires (1) reassessment of the nature of legal practice, (2) open mind to embrace new technologies, (3) clear understanding of the capabilities of technology, and (4) humble and modest attitude to working with tech professionals.

To make lawyering more efficient, the first step is to reassess what lawyering means (nature of legal practice)? The International Association of Lawyers claims that lawyer's core mandate is to counsel, conciliate, represent and defend.[112]

---

[109] The Law Society, "Capturing Technological Innovation in Legal" (January 2017), www.lawsociety.org.uk/support-services/research-trends/capturing-technological-innovation-report (accessed June 24, 2020).
[110] Ibid. at 7.
[111] R. Susskind, "A Response to the More for Less Dilemma," 1 *The Practice* (2014), https://thepractice.law.harvard.edu/article/speakers-corner-richard-susskind (accessed June 18, 2020).
[112] International Association of Lawyers, *Core Principles of the Legal Profession* (2018), www.uianet.org/sites/default/files/core_principles_of_the_legal_profession_-_final_porto.pdf (accessed June 11, 2020).

> In a society founded on respect for the law and for justice, the lawyer advises the client on legal matters, examines the possibility and the appropriateness of finding amicable solutions or of choosing an alternative dispute resolution method, assists the client and represents the client in legal proceedings. The lawyer fulfils the lawyer's engagement in the interest of the client while respecting the rights of the parties and the rules of the profession, within the boundaries of the law.

A reassessment is important to determine the gap between lawyers and their clients' appreciation of the nature of legal practice. For instance, lawyers see legal problems differently than their clients:

> Typically, a client wants a quick and cost-effective way to solve a legal problem. On the other hand, lawyers hope that the legal problem will be challenging, and the law firm hopes that resolving the problem will be so challenging that it will [increase] billable hours. A client's view of a best outcome for a matter may differ from that of their lawyer. Where the client wants a solution that will advance their business interests, a lawyer, by training and by ego, will tend to see the best outcome as being a "win" in a case or transaction."[113]

The problem arising from such a gap is that lawyers and clients may approach technology differently. Lawyers are inclined to bill high hourly rates for lower-skilled work. If lawyering was meant to serve clients, any technology that benefits clients should be considered and applied. However, using technology to expedite the process goes directly against lawyers' perceived economic benefits. Therefore, it is necessary to reassess the nature of legal practice before approaching technology. Ethically, it would seem that decisions to use technology in legal practices should be based on the interests of clients. Ultimately, the decision to adopt LT will be made for many law firms due to competitive pressures.

Lawyers should keep an open mind toward embracing technology. Whatever the future holds for law and the legal profession, there is likely to be resistance to accepting radical transformations of the profession.[114] Lawyers are notoriously conservative because change affects their monopoly on power.[115] As Ivan Illich describes, "professionals assert secret knowledge about human nature, knowledge which only they have the right to dispense. They claim a monopoly over the definition of deviance and the remedies needed."[116] Thus, by nature, the legal profession is not inclined to change.

Lawyers' embrace of LT will be caused by external forces – that is, the unavoidable, disruptive impact of technology and the demand of their clients. First, new technologies have already disrupted entire industries. Often new technologies are disruptive across industries. The legal industry is no exception. Lawyers and law firms need to interact with clients in different industries that may have already incorporated new technologies in their processes and business models. Clients who have changed their businesses through the adoption of new technologies will expect the legal industry to adopt LT in order to better engage and network with their businesses.[117] Clients now have more flexibility in choosing lawyers and law firms, as well as alternative legal service companies. Sophisticated in-house counsels are far more demanding

---

[113] R. Susskind, *The End of Lawyers?: Rethinking the Nature of Legal Services* (Oxford: Oxford University Press, 2010).
[114] Simpson, n. 95.
[115] A. Sullivan, "Technology and the Law – New Opportunities for Lawyers and Their Clients" (2015), https://papers.ssrn.com/abstract=2648538 (accessed June 12, 2020).
[116] I. Illich et al., *Disabling Professions* (London: Marion Boyers Publishers, 2000).
[117] Goodman and Harder, n. 2.

than in decades past and carefully scrutinize legal bills. Their demand for lower costs and higher efficiency will require law firms to use LT.[118]

Firm-client fit will require lawyers to keep an open mind and proactively move toward the use of LT. Lawyers need to strategize how they can use technology to maintain a competitive edge in the legal marketplace, shifting some work to technology solutions, while seeking out new types of work. Staying current in LT developments will signal that lawyers or law firms are industry leaders, which will allow them to be the source of rulemaking in the digital age.

To adopt LT, lawyers will need to self-educate by interfacing with tech consultants as to the capabilities of different technologies. Technology can process specific and narrow tasks at much greater speeds than humans. Much legal work is repetitive and structured in a way that can be simplified – and improved – by new forms of technology.[119] The often-cited example is e-discovery software that can quickly scan and extract information from a voluminous set of documents: "If search robots armed with blisteringly fast and sophisticated algorithms can instantaneously scrutinize millions of pages of court evidence for the nugget that swings a case, why employ tens of thousands of junior lawyers to do the same?"[120] Thus, when dealing with tasks that have underlying patterns, it would be wise to adopt such technology to augment lawyers' work.

Again, the legal profession will need to engage on a deeper, collaborative level with tech professionals. This elite status of lawyers as part a self-regulating profession must not act as a barrier to embracing the expertise provided by technologists, while the tech community will need to recognize the important role of law in business and society and not something that can be ignored under the mantra that "code is law". This misunderstanding of the other's worldview has hindered collaborative efforts. The answer is that lawyers need to better understand what technologists do and technologists need to learn about law. Such a symbiotic relationship will enable lawyers to best utilize LT, determine appropriate regulation, and adjust the lawyer's codes of conduct. Technologists with a working knowledge of the law will be able to incorporate regulatory protections into new technologies. Simply put, members of the legal profession must approach technology with modesty and humility.[121]

2.5.2 Retaining the Human Dimension of Lawyering

The essence of lawyering is the human interaction between lawyers and clients. Legal technologies should be seen as instruments to better fulfill this integration. Technology is a means and not an end in a profession where human beings will remain dominant in lawyering. To retain the human dimension, the first question is to determine the areas in which humans outperform machines. What human properties are not replaceable by machines, at least not in the near future? Professor Burkhard Schafer highlights two areas where humans beat machines: creative endeavors and social interactions:

---

[118] "21st Century Legal Services? Lawyers and Law Students, You Can Learn These Skills," LegalTech Lever (2016), www.legaltechlever.com/2016/08/21st-century-legal-services-lawyers-law-students-can-learn-skills/ (accessed May 17, 2020).
[119] Simpson, n. 95.
[120] Ibid. See also M. Smith, "Threat of Ideas: How to Survive the Innovation Age" (January 2015) *Australian Finance Review* 2.
[121] "Ethical Implications," n. 96.

Creative endeavors: These include creative writing, entrepreneurship, and scientific discovery. These can be highly paid and rewarding jobs. There is no better time to be an entrepreneur with an insight than today, because you can use technology to leverage your invention. Social Interactions: Robots do not have the kinds of emotional intelligence that humans have. Motivated people who are sensitive to the needs of others make great managers, leaders, salespeople, negotiators, caretakers, nurses, and teachers. Consider, for example, the idea of a robot giving half-time pep talks to a high school football team. That would not be inspiring. Recent research makes clear that social skills are increasingly in demand.[122]

Other scholars see that empathy, storytelling, and creativity are the essence of lawyering and cannot be mastered by AI, at least not in the foreseeable future.[123] Technology is not capable of performing the creative, flexible analysis that legal argument requires.

Empathy is at the root of the uniquely powerful human ability to hear a story or observe an incident and react appropriately – to immediately assess the incident's essential elements, categorize it as a member of a particular class of legal problems, compare the elements to analogous cases we remember, and decide on how best to proceed. Lawyers go through this process without a second thought, and it's only when one stops and thinks how to get a machine to duplicate such a cascade of understanding, analysis, distillation, and analogizing that the complexity of human cognition stands out. While parts of this process may eventually get broken down into tasks AI can assist with, developing the ability to understand the relationships, emotions, facts, precedents, contingencies, and necessary decisions present in even the simplest client interview or legal strategy meeting is beyond AI's current horizon. In short, the nuanced and critical lawyering skills needed to form persuasive arguments are not likely to be susceptible to computerization.[124]

A lot of legal work is thought to involve much more judgement, evaluation, and flair, which are traits beyond the capacity of algorithms and machines to replicate.[125] These essential aspects of lawyering seem to be poor candidates for automation, as they involve "problem solving ... intuition, creativity and persuasion," as well as written and verbal communication.[126] Understanding areas where humans are superior than machines is the prerequisite to retaining the human element of lawyering.

Retaining the human dimension of lawyering requires lawyers to proactively seek opportunities. As a result of automation, legal jobs will disappear, especially those that "have an underlying pattern or structure susceptible to being turned into instructions that a computer can process."[127] Paralegals and junior associates are at risk of losing their jobs. However, other opportunities will appear as emerging technologies open the door to new types of legal work. As far as we can see, the widespread use of the Internet increases the need for cybersecurity and data-protection lawyers. In the future, as more technologies appear and advance, the need for

---

[122] The Inaugural Lecture of Professor Burkhard Schafer took place at the University of Edinburgh on March 26, 2018. The title of the lecture was "Who Needs Flesh and Blood(y) Lawyers? Legal AI, Following and Computational Creativity," https://media.ed.ac.uk/media/Inaugural+Lecture+of+Professor+Burkhard+Schafer/1_n3144wia/46112571.

[123] M. Love Koenig, J. Oseid, and A. Vorenberg, "Ok Google, Will Artificial Intelligence Replace Human Lawyering" (2018) *Marquette Law Review* 1269.

[124] Ibid. See also D. Remus and F. Levy, "Can Robots Be Lawyers? Computers, Lawyers, and the Practice of Law" (2017) 30 *Georgetown Journal of Legal Ethics* 501 519; M. Somers, "Emotion AI, Explained," *MIT Sloan School of Management* (March 8, 2019), https://mitsloan.mit.edu/ideas-made-to-matter/emotion-aiexplained or https://perma.cc/4FKH-BAHY.

[125] Simpson, n. 95.

[126] M. Markovic, "Rise of the Robot Lawyers?" (2019) 61 *Arizona Law Review* 26 27.

[127] Koenig, Oseid, and Vorenberg, n. 124.

lawyers will increase accordingly. Lawyers should actively seek and create opportunities to redefine the lawyer's role in the digital age.

2.5.3 Reforming Legal Education

Robert Stevens, a scholar of legal education stated that: "The Law student should learn, while in school, the art of legal practice."[128] The integration of law and LT must start in law schools, where future lawyers are first exposed to legal thought, knowledge, and training. Legal education requires reform to keep pace with the fast-changing LT environment of the twenty-first century. At minimum, legal education should incorporate tech courses into existing law school curricula. In addition, legal education should also emphasize creative thinking, problem-solving, sympathy, imagination, reasoning, persuasion, and the skills that are not easily replaceable by LT.

Law schools have begun to recognize that teaching tech skills is needed in order to make their students more marketable in an increasingly competitive legal job market. In the United States, according to a 2018 issue of *PreLaw Magazine*, some thirty law schools have redesigned curricula to address the latest technologies and have launched legal design labs to teach students how to use LT to solve legal problems.[129] Some law schools offer tech-related clinics and externships; some offer certificates, as well as LLM degrees in law and technology; and the number of law and technology journals continue to grow.[130]

An example of integrating law and technology in legal education is China's Tsinghua Law School's 2018 establishment of a two-year Computational-Law Masters Program.[131] The curriculum requires students to take basic law courses, such as constitutional, civil, and procedural law, jurisprudence, and training courses, such as moot court, negotiation, legal writing, and legal research. In the second year, students concentrate on computational law, such as AI, informatics research, big data algorithms, machine learning, data mining (theory and constructing algorithms), and computing linguistics. In addition to theoretical courses, students participate in law and tech salons, annual international computational-law forums, various student tech groups, and performing training projects with large internet companies and LT start-ups. Each student has two advisors: one from the law department and one from the computer-science department. Students complete the program by writing a thesis on law and technology.

Law firms have signaled the need for law graduates to be tech savvy. The global law firm Clifford Chance has encouraged its employees to use their training hours on developing

---

[128] R. Stevens, *Law School: Legal Education in America from the 1850s to the 1980s* (Union: The Lawbook Exchange, 1983, reprinted 2001) 156.

[129] *PreLaw Magazine* (Fall 2018) at 28, http://mydigitalpublication.com/publication/frame.php?i=531663&p=28&pn=&ver=html5 (accessed June 16, 2020).

[130] For instance, Chicago-Kent College of Law is one of the LT pioneers that became involved in document assembly in 1978 and that established the Center for Law and Computers to train students to use computers for tasks six years later. UC Berkeley School of Law started centers dedicated to law and technology more than twenty years ago, and it has one of the most extensive law and tech programs in the country. Also, its classes run the gamut from intellectual property to specialized courses dealing with space law, videogames, blockchains, and financial technology. There are many more new additions and new programs: Suffolk University offers students the chance to build expert systems, automate documents, and consider a new business model for legal works; Santa Clara Law unveiled a first-of-its-kind Privacy Law Certificate in 2014; Stanford Law School started CodeX; The Stanford Center for Legal Information is a multidisciplinary lab that brings together lawyers, researchers, entrepreneurs, and technologists to focus on computational law; and Northwestern Law unveiled its Innovation Lab, where law and computer science professors began to co-teach the interdisciplinary course from the spring of 2017.

[131] Information related to Tsinghua Law's Computational Master Program was obtained through an interview with the dean of Tsinghua Law School and the participation in Computational Law Summer Camp in June 2019.

technology-related skill sets, with the firm establishing a global training program focused on coding, blockchain, and cybersecurity.[132] Examples of courses related to LT in legal education include Harvard Law School's courses entitled "Computer Science for Lawyers" and "Programming for Lawyers." In the first course, "topics include algorithms, artificial intelligence, cloud computing, databases, networking, privacy, programming, scalability, security, and more, with a particular emphasis on understanding the work developers do and the technological solutions that can be employed that can impact clients."[133] The description for the second course states that students are taught:

> to be effective computer programmers, and therefore to deconstruct and understand the technologies they might encounter throughout their careers. Students learn basic computer programming skills using the programming language Python. We will then apply those skills to real-life legal scenarios drawn from the instructors' own legal and programming experience, such as data-driven lobbying and statutory analysis, mass litigation automation, and electronic discovery.[134]

The expectation is that these types of courses will become standard fare in all law schools. Again, integrating technology generally and LT in particular into legal education better prepares students with the knowledge and skills for twenty-first century law practice. Law schools that have strong technology programs place students in situations "where they must be flexible, creative and resilient while working in teams."[135] Hiring law graduates with technological skill sets "means significantly less training and costs for employers."[136]

Implementing tech courses and training in law schools also benefits society, as it increases access to justice. For instance, Chicago-Kent College of Law started the Center for Access to Justice and Technology to help students build web tools to assist legal-aid lawyers and pro bono volunteers.[137] Georgetown Law School offers courses that require students to design legal access applications to help address consumer needs for affordable legal services.[138] The Global Legal Technology Lab's – initiated by the University of Missouri, Kansas City School of Law, Queen Mary University, London, Brooklyn Law School, and MIT – stated purpose is to build new technologies and launch projects with a particular emphasis on "access to justice."[139] LT will make the legal and arbitral systems more accessible and efficient for the general public.

Legal education reform will include a heightened emphasis on imparting technical skills but not at the expense of de-emphasizing soft skills and emotional intelligence such as sympathy, reasoning, persuasion, problem-solving, and the comprehension of fairness and justice. Although some of these topics are currently the major focus of law school teaching, they have new implications and require new consideration in the digital age. For instance, algorithms are designed and written by humans, and humans are unavoidably biased when integrated into

---

[132] See www.thelawyer.com/clifford-chance-offers-coding-training-lawyers.
[133] See https://hls.harvard.edu/academics/curriculum/catalog/default.aspx?o=77017.
[134] See https://hls.harvard.edu/academics/curriculum/catalog/default.aspx?o=75487.
[135] "Some Law Schools Offer Tech Programs to Help Students Find Jobs, But Does It Work?," *ABA Journal*, www.abajournal.com/magazine/article/law-school-technology-programs (accessed June 16, 2020).
[136] Ibid.
[137] *PreLaw Magazine*, n. 130.
[138] K. Lee, "A Call for Law Schools to Link the Curricular Trends of Legal Tech and Mindfulness" (2017), https://papers.ssrn.com/abstract=2937721 (accessed June 5, 2020). See also T. Rostain, R. Skalbeck, and K. Mulcahy, "Thinking Like a Lawyer, Designing Like an Architect: Preparing Students for the 21st Century Practice" (2013) 88 *Chicago-Kent Law Review* 743 744–746.
[139] Ibid. See also Global Legal Technology Laboratory: Event Schedule, MIT Law, https://law.mit.edu/GLTL (accessed May 31, 2020).

social networks. How do we guarantee fairness and justice when human biases affect the development and application of LT? The results produced by algorithms need to be assessed for bias in their design, as well as the outcomes of their application.

2.6 CONCLUSION

The advent and acceleration of legal technology (LT) creates both opportunities and risks for lawyers and will transform lawyering as practiced today. LT is likely to end the reign of law firms and lawyers as exclusive providers of legal services. From a macro perspective, LT will provide "a benefit to society and clients as legal services become more transparent and affordable to consumers," making access to justice more widely available.[140] From a professional perspective, lawyers who marshal the capabilities of LT will become more effective practitioners and better positioned to exploit new opportunities and areas of practice as they arise. Just as online legal databases LexisNexis and Westlaw transformed legal research, almost every aspect of legal practice will be transformed or impacted by LT.

Lawyers who embrace change will certainly fare better than those who ignore the impact of LT. Certain legal services currently provided by lawyers and paralegals will be more effectively and efficiently performed by LT and other expert systems. Lawyers will need to reallocate their focus to activities that provide value to clients that are beyond the scope of LT. LT may result in the reduction in the overall number of lawyers and paralegals employed, however, LT will also encourage collaborations between lawyers and tech specialists, which will enable law firms to provide new and enhanced services. Such hybrid firms will spearhead creation, management, and monitoring of expert systems, such as the drafting of smart contracts. Some firms may, in addition to providing traditional counseling and representation, specialize in offering expert systems and other types of LT for clients who need day-to-day legal support in the running of their businesses.

The infusion of LT into legal services will necessitate the realignment and reallocation of responsibilities between law firms and in-house counsel. Some businesses will search for law firms that effectively exploit LT that may reduce the role of in-house counsel, or businesses may choose to expand the role of in-house counsel to manage and tailor LT to the specific needs of their businesses. The reallocation of duties, realignment of responsibilities, and reimagining the roles of lawyers will reduce the overall time needed by legal specialists to engage in repetitive activities such as document review, discovery, and other aspects of due diligence. Instead, lawyers will focus increasingly on tasks that cannot be replicated by AI – tasks that require human creativity, intuition, problem solving, and persuasion.

The only thing certain about the future is change; lawyers who actively work to manage the inevitability of change brought by the acceleration of LT and AI technologies will prosper. To prepare for this future, legal education must produce tech-savvy lawyers. Courses and the experiential learning provided in clinics and externships must increasingly integrate tech and legal training. Lawyers who are adept at working with informatics, big data algorithms, machine learning, and data mining will be in high demand. These changes should not be feared.

---

[140] McGinnis and Pearce, n. 6 at 3066.

3

The Effects of Technology on Legal Practice

From Punch Card to Artificial Intelligence?

André Janssen and Tom J. Vennmanns

3.1 INTRODUCTION

It is difficult to come up with any events after World War II that have led our entire global society to recognise that before *The Times They Are A-Changin'*[1] as clearly as today's global crisis has done. The COVID-19 pandemic and its aftermath have revealed that almost everything we once considered stable and sustainable is actually built on quite shaky ground. But the crisis has also brought out the best in our coexistence, seeing that societies in many countries have shown that they are capable of finding creative solutions to overcome the current challenges. Digital technologies have played a crucial role in the world's response to the COVID-19 crisis. Just think of modern methods of telecommunication such as video conferencing, which have made an immense contribution to maintaining the economy and work processes, or the various corona tracking apps, which try to help stopping the spread of the virus. It can be assumed that the harmful consequences of the pandemic would have grown even greater if those digital solutions had not been available. Just as almost every area of life is affected by the pandemic, so are the law itself and legal practice.

Immediate examples of the effects on legal practice can be found in the countless suspended litigations or arbitrations, or the fact that law firms were unable to conduct physical meetings with clients or other colleagues.[2] Digital solutions such as videoconferencing, which are practice-preserving in other areas, also helped in legal practice to maintain 'business (almost) as usual' throughout the crisis. However the digitisation of justice and legal practice has not progressed beyond approaches and pilot projects in some fields and jurisdictions.[3] For example, in some German federal states (Federal States of Bremen and Mecklenburg-Western Pomerania) there is not a single court that provides an official facility for video conferencing.[4] Also, digital file processing in litigation is beyond current technical capabilities in many jurisdictions around the world.[5] In general, old-fashioned means such as faxing are still

---

[1] Reference to Bob Dylan's 1964 third album with the same name.
[2] P. Schrader, 'Wie verändert sich die Arbeit des Anwalts durch die Corona-Krise?' (2020) *Neue Zeitschrift für Arbeitsrecht* 569 571.
[3] F. Zschieschack, 'Zivilverfahren in Zeiten des Coronavirus' in H. Schmidt (ed.), *COVID-19 – Rechtsfragen zur Corona-Krise* (Munich: C. H. Beck, 2020) para. 1.
[4] German judiciary, 'Overview per Federal State of Germany of the Locations with Video Conference Facilities at State Courts and Public Prosecutor's Offices', status 2 July 2020, https://justiz.de/verzeichnis/zwi_videokonferenz/videokonferenzanlagen.pdf.
[5] Zschieschack, n. 3.

dominating traditional court proceedings while they are hardly used anymore outside the courtroom. Therefore, it seems as if these very preliminary observations confirm the topicality of Luhmann's provocative statement, expressed half a century ago: 'Law and data processing have as much in common as cars and deer: Mostly nothing, but sometimes they collide.'[6]

Legal tech (LT) solutions in particular could offer a promising approach to making legal practice fit for the digital age. According to the simplest definition, LT comprises digital solutions that support or perform partly or entirely legal work.[7] Think, for example, of software and applications that support or could support the daily work of judges, arbitrators and legal practitioners. These include special programs for the creation of legal documents, special clouds allowing legal practitioners and their clients to share documents as well as tailor-made translation software for the legal environment. In addition, LT solutions exist for resolving disputes, such as Online Dispute Resolution (ODR) portals.[8] Take, for example, small claims or hundreds of thousands of consumers with scattered damages who have so far refrained from enforcing their rights in state courts because the costs, time and emotional hurdles were disproportionate to the damage suffered.[9] LT possibilities create a new dynamic structure within the legal sector: law firms suddenly face competition from LT startups, questioning the fundamental need for human legal professionals.[10]

This chapter will show how digital technology has influenced legal practice in the past, how it is changing the profession today, and how it will do so in the future. In a first step, Section 3.2 will examine the question of which challenges exist within the interplay of digital technologies and legal practice. How does legal practice actually differ from the function of technological processes, and can both worlds be brought together in a meaningful way? Section 3.3 analyses the different stages of development in the relationship between digital technology and legal practice. Questions regarding the evolving requirement profiles and sought-after qualities of lawyers[11] in the various professional groups will also be addressed. Section 3.4 deals with the problems that can arise from the bond of legal practice and the latest generation of digital technologies. How will the legal labour market change and will human service providers still be needed in the future, in a world possibly based on artificial intelligence (AI)? What is the position of the legislator and how can he influence future developments? The chapter concludes (Section 3.5) by shedding some light on the future of legal education in the digital age.

3.2 LAW AND TECHNOLOGY: TWO OPPOSING WORLDS COLLIDING?

3.2.1 Traditional Character of Law as an 'Analogous' Field of Expertise

Few people associate the legal profession with innovation or technical progress. In many law firms and courts worldwide, files still consist of paper and are still sent by regular post

---

[6] Cited in G. Buchholtz, 'Legal Tech – Chancen und Risiken der digitalen Rechtsanwendung' (2017) *Juristische Schulung* 955 955.
[7] B. Jakl, 'Das Recht der Künstlichen Intelligenz' (2019) *Multimedia und Recht* 711 712.
[8] S. Hähnchen, P. Schrader, F. Weiler and T. Wischmeyer, 'Legal Tech' (2020) *Juristische Schulung* 625 626.
[9] J. Keßler, 'Verbraucherschutz Reloaded – Auf dem Weg zu einer deutschen Kollektivklage?' (2016) *Zeitschrift für Rechtspolitik* 2 3.
[10] H. Hellwig and W. Ewer, 'Keine Angst vor Legal Tech' (2020) *Neue Juristische Wochenschrift* 1783 1783–1784.
[11] The term 'lawyer' is used here when all legal professionals such as judges, arbitrators and legal practitioners (like attorneys at law) are meant.

or fax.[12] Above all, it is certain conceptual aspects of legal practice that have for centuries required 'analogous' characteristics to form part of the profession. In this context, the term 'analogous' is understood to mean physical meetings of people or paper as an information carrier. The oral hearing is often considered the heart of litigation and the physical participation of the parties in the court has always been an important element of a fair trial. It serves among others the purpose of transparency and the possibility of reviewing the considerations of the judges. This applies in particular to criminal proceedings. For example, the procedural right to a fair trial under article 6 ECHR guarantees the accused the right to participate, the right to be heard and to follow the trial.[13] To this day, it refers primarily to *physical* participation. Participation via digital channels such as video conferencing is normally only permitted if it pursues a legitimate goal, as can be found for instance in connection with dangerous defendants or prisoners at risk of escape.[14]

There are other good reasons for shaping legal practice by use of these analogous and physical elements, which still remain indispensable today. In general, legal relationships are not simply static and do not serve mere financial interests; they affect emotions and can have a considerable reality-shaping influence on our lives, as is obvious in criminal proceedings. There can be no doubt that we perceive emotional connections and the needs of others most directly when we meet in person. This applies not only to proceedings in court but also to legal advice given by legal practitioners to their clients face to face. After all, we as social beings want to be perceived and appreciated comprehensively.[15] For many people seeking justice, a legal problem results in great uncertainty and sometimes even causes existential fears.[16] Digital technology cannot always meet social needs to the standard of physical connections. Generally speaking, it can be said that our primal need to experience empathy and to be understood is most directly satisfied by the pure physical experience. Above all, it is this human longing for physical connection that has contributed to the traditional dominance of analogous structures within legal practice.

Another essential reason for the aforementioned analogous structure is derived from the fact that the application of law is generally 'human work' and thus a social act.[17] In private law, abstract legal norms such as 'good faith' or 'fair dealing' need concretisation and application to the concrete case at hand, or more generally: law needs to be applied by humans. Also, the interpretation of the parties' conduct, oral or written statements or contracts is ultimately performed by human adjudicators. It is a particular feature of law that it is often ambiguous, that it can change in the course of time and that it is in need of interpretation. Buchholtz points to two central features of the application of law that arise from this social and methodological structure. The result of the application of law remains unpredictable to a certain extent, it is contingent on numerous factors and can thus vary.[18] At the same time, the interpretation of legal texts, language and cases depends on the individual abilities, motives, experience and knowledge of the lawyer at hand.[19]

---

[12] Buchholtz, n. 6 at 955.
[13] J. Meyer-Ladewig et al., 'Kommentar zu Art. 6 EMRK' in J. Meyer-Ladewig et al. (eds.), *Handkommentar zur Europäischen Menschenrechtskonvention*, 4th ed. (Baden-Baden: Nomos, 2017) no. 113.
[14] Ibid. at no. 118.
[15] C. Hommerich and M. Kilian, *Mandanten und ihre Anwälte* (Bonn: Anwaltsverlag, 2007) 107.
[16] M. Kilian, 'Die Zukunft der Juristen' (2017) *Neue Juristische Wochenschrift* 3043 3043.
[17] Buchholtz, n. 6 at 955.
[18] Ibid. at 957.
[19] Ibid.

Natural sciences, mathematical methodology and computer science form the evident contrast. They are based on reproducible, calculable and exclusively logic-based results. Social context, emotions and human abilities do not influence the result. Law is not about the technical-logical clarification of algorithmic yes-no questions, but the subsumption and evaluation of real-life situations in the light of abstract-general legal norms. Law, therefore, is not a matter of right or wrong but of achieving acceptable solutions.[20] A simple 'one and one equals two' just does not exist in law. Hence, another pillar of the analogous structure of law can be reconstructed by bearing in mind that law is a humanities discipline.

3.2.2 Entrenched Working Methods, Unwillingness to Change and Scepticism: Prejudice or Real Phenomenon?

Some years ago, Seligman, Verkuil and Kang showed that one of the most prominent characteristic of a lawyer is his pronounced pessimism.[21] They define pessimism not in the colloquial sense of 'seeing the glass as half empty instead of half full'. Under their definition, the pessimist will view bad events as unchangeable events while the optimist perceives setbacks as temporary.[22] Interestingly, the aforementioned authors are able to gain something positive from this finding, concluding that pessimists are better lawyers because their view of the world brings with it caution, scepticism and realism, which are important qualities for precise and accurate legal work.[23] Kilian therefore concludes from these observations that lawyers are rather anxious and worried when dealing with their contemporary existence or when daring to look into their future.[24] Other analyses of the lawyer as a psychological creature point to the problematic fact that it is not uncommon for lawyers to display an attitude of knowing everything better than everyone else.[25] One could find ample reasons in these properties alone to explain why the legal sector has traditionally shown great scepticism towards the advance of digitalisation,[26] while other areas such as production or logistics have made considerable and rapid advances through the use of digital tools.

Furthermore, the demographic of people working in legal practice must be pointed out. According to a study conducted by the Soldan Institute in 2017, the German lawyer has an average age of fifty years.[27] An empirical study by the American Federal Judicial Center shows that in 2017, American judges had an average age of almost seventy years.[28] This allows for the conclusion that the legal sector is increasingly shaped by people who grew up and went through legal education in a society that was mainly analogue. This may also explain the reluctance of some lawyers to embrace digital solutions.

Moreover, as far as the relationship of legal practice and digital technology is concerned, one must state the obvious: lawyers in general are simply not technicians, computer scientists or

---

[20] Hähnchen, Schrader, Weiler and Wischmeyer, n. 8 at 627.
[21] M. Seligman, P. Verkuil and T. Kang, 'Why Lawyers Are Unhappy' (2005) *Deakin Law Review* 49 55.
[22] Ibid. at 54–55.
[23] Ibid. at 55.
[24] Kilian, n. 17 at 3043.
[25] H. Dreier, *Rechtswissenschaft als Beruf* (Tübingen: Mohr Siebeck, 2018) 6.
[26] M. Fries, 'PayPal Law und Legal Tech – Was macht die Digitalisierung mit dem Privatrecht?' (2016) *Neue Juristische Wochenschrift* 2860 2865.
[27] M. Kilian, 'Die Altersstruktur der deutschen Anwaltschaft - Durchschnittsalter steigt' (2017) *Anwaltsblatt* 408 408.
[28] Federal Judicial Center, "Age and Experience of Judges 1789–2017, www.fjc.gov/history/exhibits/graphs-and-maps/age-and-experience-judges#_ftn7.

mathematicians – they are lawyers. Thus, their sceptical view towards any technological change is certainly also a result of the fact that they are judging something they do not really understand. Regarding examples of the connection between law and technology, as found in the LT sector, the key to success therefore lies, above all, in the interdisciplinary exchange between lawyers and technology specialists. First of all, the sceptical lawyer must therefore break away from the idea that he can solve all possible problems by himself. This requires trust and tolerance towards assistance and impulses from other professions.

3.2.3 Established Main Features of Working Methods and Methodology within Legal Practice: Lack of Formal Logic

A core method of legal work has always been a special form of translation work between everyday terms and legal terms.[29] Problems and situations arising in real life, as already pointed out above, have to be assessed and subsumed in the light of abstract legal norms. This working method results in problems when it comes to the latest technological developments. In numerous civil law traditions, the relevant legal norms are more than 100 years old (e.g., the German Civil Code [BGB] of 1900 or the Austrian Civil Code [ABGB] of 1812), meaning that originally the latest technological developments were not taken into account when the leading legal sources were established. And equally, the legal precedents of the common law world are regularly those of the pre-digital age.

Looking at the latest LT generations it is often difficult for lawyers to subsume these phenomena under the existing law(s). Is, for instance, a smart contract a traditional contract at all or must it be assigned to another legal construct?[30] This reveals the first problem encountered by established legal working methods in the digital age. While computer scientists can easily cope with new technological progress and new technology, lawyers are challenged by integrating the novel phenomena into their established working patterns.

A central method of legal work in both the court and in law firms can be found in valuation processes. Legal norms are based on conflicts of interest, as well as political, social, economic, but also psychological implications in general.[31] These influences must be assessed in the light of the specific case.[32] However, formal logic is not a method of applying law, even if some believe that the application of law is a purely logical process.[33] Data processing, on the other hand, is a correspondingly logical procedure in which the work pattern is limited to the comparison of values and numbers.[34] The result is either 'true' or 'false' (true/false or binary: zero/one). The further flow of the programme can be made dependent on this result. This results in a typical programme sequence following the scheme: 'if-then-else'.[35]

---

[29] M. Zwickel, 'Jurastudium 4.0? – Die Digitalisierung des juristischen Lehrens und Lernens' (2018) *Juristische Arbeitsblätter* 881 881.
[30] M. Durovic and A. Janssen, 'The Formation of Blockchain-Based Smart Contracts in the Light of Contract Law' (2018) *European Review of Private Law* 753 754 ff.; D. Paulus and R. Matzke, 'Smart Contracts und das BGB – Viel Lärm um nichts?' (2018) *Zeitschrift für die gesamte Privatrechtswissenschaft* 431 431.
[31] B. Rüthers et al., *Rechtstheorie*, 11th ed. (Munich: C. H. Beck, 2020) § 7.
[32] Needless to say, that also for the determination of the facts of a case it is necessary to perform an evaluation that transcends the simple formal logic of 'true' or 'false' questions.
[33] See, for further references, Hähnchen, Schrader, Weiler and Wischmeyer, n. 8 at 626.
[34] H. Gumm and M. Sommer, *Einführung in die Informatik* (Oldenbourg: De Gruyter, 2011) 424–425.
[35] Hähnchen, Schrader, Weiler and Wischmeyer, n. 8 at 626.

This brief comparison shows that legal working methods and the formal logical processes of information technology are fundamentally different. At first glance, this seems to result in a incompatibility and a necessary separation of the two sciences.

3.2.4 Expectations of a Lawyer in the Course of Time: Yesterday and Tomorrow

The lawyer of today is a being with many souls. A good lawyer must not only exhibit knowledge of the actual law itself. Regularly, he will also need to apply an essential understanding of business administration, deal with clients and other actors such as judges on a psychological level and, nowadays, demonstrate at least a minimum degree of technological understanding. Killian points out that in light of the change in the legal sector, the demands within the legal profession have to be redefined.[36] In order to understand how lawyers can fit into a technologised world and live up to these novel expectations, it is necessary to keep in mind the changing requirement profiles and dare to envision the lawyer of the future. In this spirit, let us take a look at legal practitioners and law firms, on the one hand, and state courts, arbitral tribunals and other forms of private dispute resolution, on the other.

3.2.4.1 Legal Practitioners and Law Firms

One driver behind the current changes in the legal services sector is the shift of supply and demand within the legal market itself.[37] In a report on the legal market, the US Legal Executive Institute noted that several factors contribute to a gradual decline in the profitability of law firms.[38] A steady demand for legal services, falling profit margins, falling productivity and competition from outside the profession are a number of examples.[39] Van Veenen and Schmaal point out that these trends are visible not only in the United States but also in Europe.[40] In general, the market share of law firms is in decline and although the demand for legal services within large legal departments of organisations is still increasing, the corresponding budget is not and, notably, the available funds are not necessarily spent on the legal profession any more.[41] In addition, businesses in particular are actively looking for more efficient means of dispute resolution than going through law firms. During the last ten years, several innovative legal services models have begun to offer corporate clients an alternative to big law lawyering. Clients are increasingly seeking alternate options to large multinational law firms that mainly provide legal services through the traditional partner-associate service model.[42] Alternative legal service providers (ALSPs) have turned to technology and process management to compete with law firms, promising cost reduction and alternative billing practices, moving away from the billable hours model.[43]

Because of these new players and business models, the legal services market must also submit to a phenomenon that is referred to as digital capitalism. Digital capitalism is the latest

---

[36] Kilian, n. 17 at 3045.
[37] J. van Veenen and J. Schmaal, 'Legal tech en de advocatuur' (2018) *Computerrecht* 77 77.
[38] Center for the Study of the Legal Profession at Georgetown University Law Center and Thomson Reuters Legal Executive Institute, '2018 Report on the State of the Legal Market: Transformation of Legal Services Market Is Accelerating – Are Law Firms Ready?', www.legalexecutiveinstitute.com/2018-legal-market-report.
[39] Veenen and Schmaal, n. 38 at 78.
[40] Ibid.
[41] Ibid.
[42] J. Dzienkowski, 'The Future of Big Law: Alternative Legal Service Providers to Corporate Clients' (2014) *Fordham Law Review* 2995 2996.
[43] R. Replogle, 'The Business of Law: Evolution of the Legal Services Market' (2017) *Michigan Business & Entrepreneurial Law Review* 287 297.

transformation of the economic system in which digital technologies constitute 'the central production and control apparatus of an increasingly supranational market system'.[44] In the legal sector, digital capitalism implies the introduction of profit-driven digital processes of outsourcing, automation, dispersion and commodification of the practice of law. Due to this increasingly competitive pressure, law firms and legal practitioners in general are forced to assert themselves in the legal service market through attractive price structures, constant availability for their clients and responsiveness as well as all-around carefree packages. Today and in the future, they must therefore be able to cut costs where necessary and develop economic strengths that distinguish them from other players within the legal services market.[45] The increasing competition also means that law firms and legal practitioners will have to make increasingly use of (lawful) advertising[46] and social media to promote their services to the public. This short list of illustrations suffices to show that legal practitioners of today and tomorrow are beings with several souls. There is a growing need for an understanding of digital technology and its application in the legal sector. This particular point will be discussed in Section 3.3 and in the outlook of this chapter (Section 3.5).

3.2.4.2 State Courts, Arbitral Tribunals and Other Means of Private Dispute Resolution

Not only has the requirement profile for law firms and legal practitioners changed considerably over time, but also for that of courts and their judges. A few centuries ago, courts and their jurisdiction were an expression of the absolutist power of the kings or emperors who were the highest judges in their empires. Jurisdiction to resolve conflicts was often an element of maintaining power, an expression of political will and ideology. Needless to say, those times have long gone and expectations towards dispute resolution have changed considerably. On an international level, as in any domestic legal system, respect and protection of the law and of individual rights can be guaranteed only by the availability of judicial remedies.[47] When the law is violated or a contract breached, access to justice is of fundamental importance and it is an essential component of the system of protection and enforcement of law.[48] From a qualified perspective, 'access to justice is used to signify the right of an individual not only to enter a court of law, but to have his or her case heard and adjudicated in accordance with substantive standards of fairness and justice'.[49] It can be deduced from this understanding that the resolution of legal disputes depends not only on the existence of courts, arbitral tribunals or other forms of dispute resolution as such (question of access), but also on the characteristics, construction and design of the procedures (question of accessibility). In Western industrialised countries, the question of access to justice in the sense of 'the right of an individual to enter a court of law'[50] is generally beyond question. However, the issue of accessibility has become increasingly important in recent times. Above all, it is the costs of the procedure, the time and the quality of conflict resolution, that are of decisive importance for the litigants.[51] Parties to a proceeding before state

---

[44] S. Caserta and M. Madsen, 'The Legal Profession in the Era of Digital Capitalism: Disruption or New Dawn?' (2019) *Laws* 1 2.
[45] Ibid. at 4.
[46] C. Menebröcker, 'Anwaltswerbung – Was ist erlaubt?' (2010) *Gewerblicher Rechtsschutz und Urheberrecht: Praxis im Immaterialgüter und Wettbewerbsrecht* 189 189.
[47] F. Francioni, *Access to Justice as a Human Right* (New York: Oxford University Press, 2007) 1.
[48] Ibid.
[49] Ibid.
[50] Ibid.
[51] Kamphorst, n. 9 at 175.

courts often incur significant costs for litigation itself and for legal representation. These costs are not always reimbursed to the winning party by means of an award on costs in favour of the losing party. Notably, the American Rule on attorneys' fees requires each party to pay its own legal costs, win or lose.[52]

The importance of an effective resolution of legal disputes is particularly evident in the phenomenon of 'rational apathy'. This term refers to the problem of injured parties often refraining from enforcing justified claims if the effort required to enforce these claims is disproportionate to the possible outcome.[53] Essentially, litigation costs, time and emotional barriers are the most likely factors to stand in the way of enforcing legitimate claims. Rational apathy is all the more frequent and blatant the smaller the claims and the less resources the parties have at their disposal to enforce them. Weighing up enforcement costs is not a new phenomenon; it is deeply rooted in the experience of litigation. This is already attested to by Lincoln who declared some 150 years ago that 'the winner of a lawsuit often is a real loser – in expenses, costs and waste of time'.[54]

Over the last few years, new digital possibilities were implemented in an effort to address rational apathy and the hurdles of law enforcement that are traditionally associated with proceedings before state courts. ODR-procedures such as Modria,[55] Smartsettle[56] and Resolver,[57] for instance, are mostly private dispute resolution portals on the Internet.[58] A digital forum is created via technological infrastructure in which, quite similar to a state court or regular arbitration procedure, legal disputes are resolved. ODR is often referred to as a particular form of Alternative Dispute Resolution (ADR) that takes advantage of the speed and convenience of the Internet as well as information and communications technology.[59] Therefore, ODR is a tool for enhancing the redress of consumer grievances, strengthening their trust in the market, widening access to justice and promoting the sustainable growth of e-commerce.[60] It creates an opportunity for the resolution of lesser-value and cross-border disputes that could otherwise not be resolved in such a simple manner.[61] ODR lowers the threshold for consumers to enforce their rights by allowing parties to participate in legal procedures from behind their personal computers at no or little cost.[62]

The emergence of these alternatives shows that dispute resolution mechanisms, whether public or private, are also increasingly competing with each other. It can be assumed that a large proportion of legal disputes is now resolved outside of courtrooms. The growing importance of mediation and arbitration has played an important role in this regard, and the

---

[52] G. Miller, 'The English versus the American Rule on Attorney Fees: An Empirical Study of Public Company Contracts' (2013) *Cornell Law Review* 327 327.
[53] A. Janssen, 'Auf dem Weg zu einer europäischen Sammelklage?' in Matthias Casper, André Janssen, Petra Pohlmann and Reiner Schulze (eds.), *Auf dem Weg zu einer europäischen Sammelklage?* (Munich: Sellier, 2009) 5.
[54] S. Sheppard, *The History of Legal Education in the United States: Commentaries and Primary Sources* (Clark: Lawbook Exchange, 2007) 489.
[55] www.tylertech.com/products/modria (accessed 2 August 2020).
[56] www.smartsettle.com (accessed 2 August 2020).
[57] www.theresolver.com (accessed 2 August 2020).
[58] P. Cortés, *Online Dispute Resolution for Consumers in the European Union* (Abington: Routledge, 2010) 2.
[59] P. Cortés, *Factsheet: What Should the Ideal ODR System for E-Commerce Consumers Look Like? The Hidden World of Consumer ADR: Redress and Behaviour* (Oxford: Centre for Socio-Legal Studies, 2011), www.law.ox.ac.uk/sites/files/oxlaw/dr_pablo_cortes.pdf.
[60] Ibid.
[61] Cortés, n. 59 at 2.
[62] Kamphorst, n. 9 at 175.

increasing possibilities offered by digitisation have had and continue to have a strong influence on the possibilities of resolving legal disputes.[63]

3.3 ARTIFICIAL INTELLIGENCE: LAWYERS IN THE GRIP OF TECHNOLOGICAL CHANGE

3.3.1 *The Gradual Embedding of Technology in Legal Practice*

Even though not all areas of legal work have been digitalised yet and modern technologies have not yet fully entered all legal workplaces, different development phases can be identified in which technological processes and legal practice have gradually grown together. Generally speaking, it can be said that, in one way or another, almost every lawyer uses digital tools to some extent – the use of computers, standard text editing software such as Word or the use of emails speaks volumes. And there are even some peculiarities in the relationship between law and technology that are linked exclusively to the legal sector. This concerns, for instance, the digital publication of legal documents. Almost all laws, judgements, legal journals and specialist legal literature are made available in digital form nowadays – though sometimes behind a paywall.[64] When talking about the use of digital technology in the legal sector, the already mentioned LT is currently on everyone's lips.[65] Even though the term 'legal tech' is a relatively recent neologism, digital solutions that support legal work have already existed for decades. The following will give an outline of the different development stages of the embedding of technology into the legal sector.

3.3.1.1 *First Steps: Electronic Data Processing and Computing*

The technological developments of the 1970s and 1980s have paved the way for legal practice to move from paper to digital documents. In the early 1970s, Wang Laboratories introduced the first word-processing computer, which quickly found its way into law firms and courts around the world.[66] These word processors were devices that provided for input, editing, formatting and output of text, often with some additional features.[67] The use of these systems enabled lawyers to achieve an unimagined increase in efficiency compared to working with typewriters or even handwritten documents.[68] By moving away from paper to magnetic cards or tapes, documents became reproducible, modifiable and easier to store.[69] Then, in the 1980s, word-processing programmes and computers also became easier to use.[70] Previously, law firms and courts had their own word-processing departments, which then gradually became obsolete. This held true also for the division of personnel, as legal practitioners and judges were increasingly entrusted with the preparation and processing of the texts themselves.[71] From then on, lawyers were not

---

[63] G. Vanderstichele, 'Het beslechten van geschillen in een digitale samenleving. Over rechters en algoritmes' (2015) *Computerrecht* 20 23.
[64] K. van Noortwijk and R. De Mulder, 'Het rijpingproces van juridische technologie' (2018) *Computerrecht* 58 59.
[65] V. Hoch and J. Hendricks, 'Das RDG und die Legal Tech-Debatte: Und wo bleibt das Unionsrecht?' (2020) *Verbraucher und Recht* 254 254.
[66] J. Peterson and M. Young, 'Using a Word Processing System in a Small Firm' (1974) *American Bar Association Journal* 613 613.
[67] S. Waterhouse, *Word Processing Fundamentals* (Alexandria: Canfield Press, 1979) 1.
[68] Peterson and Young, n. 67 at 617.
[69] Ibid. at 613.
[70] P. Everett-Nollkamper, *Fundamentals of Law Office Management* (Boston: Cengage Learning, 2013) 315.
[71] Ibid.

only the intellectual creators of the texts, which in earlier times were co-written or typed by secretaries, but also the administrators of the texts. Of course, secretaries are still essential in law firms today, but law firms generally do not see the need for word-processing departments anymore, since lawyers do most of the word processing and text editing themselves. Today, almost all lawyers work with digital tools for text processing in one way or another.

The use of digital solutions in the legal world became even more effective and accessible with the introduction of the personal computer (PC) by IBM in 1981.[72] Step by step, the PC became a standard tool in the industry, while the move into private households followed swiftly. This made data processing and data collection cheaper and easier to use, paving the way for new software possibilities. Previous computer systems were huge, stored behind closed doors and had to be constantly maintained and monitored by data-processing experts.[73] These demands changed the requirement profile for lawyers when asked to work with the PC. For the first time, lawyers became (if only to a minimal degree) 'amateur computer scientists'.

Not only has the lawyer's text work been affected by the technological change but also the task of document management. For a long time, law firms, courts and legal professionals understood document management as an exercise of populating paper files and keeping them within easy reach.[74] The case management system (CMS) introduced by Cone in the mid-1980s was the first off-the-shelf computerised case management system.[75] It enabled digital file and document management, the creation of reports, the insertion of client information and included an built-in calendar. In addition, the first information systems for consulting legal sources became available in the 1970s and 1980s. For example, the publisher Kluwer started offering a legal library filled with full text versions of judgements from case law journals as well as summaries of journal articles and books.[76] Its popularity increased in the mid-1980s when legal databases and libraries became available on CD-ROM.[77]

In light of the modern concept of LT, it must be conceded that some of these early manifestations of digital infrastructure already constituted 'legal tech' in its contemporary meaning. The simplest form of information technology and digital support for legal professions covers software for work and office organisation such as document management and accounting for legal professionals.[78] The legal databases and case management systems are in some way tailor-made for the needs of the legal profession. This first generation of LT solutions also includes information systems and databases that offer lawyers access to particular documents they need. LT is therefore not a phenomenon of the new millennium but rather looks back at a history of more than forty years. And even if new technological achievements have been accumulated over time, these first approaches have been maintained in legal practice. Online databases, file management systems and the PC as a workspace have remained an integral part of the profession to this day.

---

[72] P. Leith and A. Hoey, *The Computerised Lawyer: A Guide to the Use of Computers in the Legal Profession* (London: Springer, 1998) 1.
[73] Ibid.
[74] G. Cunningham and J. Montaña, *The Lawyer's Guide to Records Management and Retention* (Chicago: ABA Book Publishing, 2007) 8.
[75] A. Adkins, *The Lawyer's Guide to Practice Management Systems Software* (Chicago: ABA Book Publishing, 2009) 3.
[76] van Noortwijk and De Mulder, n. 65 at 59.
[77] Ibid.
[78] Hähnchen, Schrader, Weiler and Wischmeyer, n. 8 at 625.

3.3.1.2 Big Data and Modern Telecommunication

The next innovative leap for the legal profession must be seen in the establishment of big data and modern telecommunication channels. Big data is an information asset characterised by such a high volume, velocity and variety of data that it requires specific technology and analytical methods for its transformation into value.[79] This term is extremely broad but it has specific implications for legal work. The legal world often works with large amounts of information and, also, great amounts of relevant data are published. Just think of the countless judgements that are published worldwide every day and the amount of evidence that forms part of big lawsuit or large contracts, easily reaching the thickness of telephone directories, especially in the Anglo-Saxon tradition.[80] Kilian points out that legal work is essentially a matter of extracting information for the purpose of establishing the facts, offering assistance in the search for the proverbial needle in the haystack.[81]

New digital solutions, and especially LT solutions, have helped lawyers to evaluate the increasing amount of available legal materials in a faster and more efficient way.[82] The main focus lies on programmes and applications that make it possible to sift through big data in legal project management, especially during due diligence.[83] The technological basis for this process is mainly provided by the immensely advanced storage technology and the decentralisation of data in clouds. While decades ago a hard disk with a few megabits of storage was almost the size of a house, today storage media the size of a human hand can easily store several terabits of data. This progress drastically improved the problem of information accumulation in legal practice, since it erased the necessity for archives in courts and law firms, allowing for storage on a small object or on an external server.

In addition, the further development of telecommunication channels had a major impact on legal practice. This is due to the fact that language and communication are key competences in legal work. Whereas only a few years ago communication with clients and the court was mainly conducted via fax machines, via telephone and later via email, entire video conferences holding a large number of participants can now be held via easily accessible channels such as Zoom or Webex, to name just two. Also, services such as WhatsApp or Wechat allow for the exchange of messages and information within seconds. These developments make it possible to communicate in a more personal way in sound and vision, making detailed and near physical conversations possible even from a distance. This is of particular interest for law firms, not only because it might serve to maintain clients on the other side of the world, but also because it enables efficient communication channels within the law firm itself when physical meetings are not feasible. The COVID-19 crisis has confirmed the essential importance of these communication channels in maintaining legal practice.[84] Even if practitioners deplore the difficulties that come with the lack of face-to-face communication with their clients (e.g., concerning the sensitive task of determining what the client's actual goals are), the pandemic-related lack of alternatives remains apparent.[85] Again, it should be borne in mind that many law firms, and also some courts, have used video

---

[79] A. De Mauro, M. Greco and M. Grimaldi, 'A Formal Definition of Big Data Based on Its Essential Features' (2016) *Library Review* 122 131.
[80] Kilian, n. 17 at 3049.
[81] Ibid.
[82] M. Fenwick and E. Vermeulen, 'The Lawyer of the Future as "Transaction Engineer": Digital Technologies and the Disruption of the Legal Profession' in M. Corrales, M. Fenwick and H. Haapio (eds.), *Legal Tech, Smart Contracts and Blockchain: Perspectives in Law, Business and Innovation* (Singapore: Springer, 2019) 255.
[83] Kilian, n. 17 at 3049.
[84] Schrader, n. 2 at 572.
[85] Ibid. at 571.

conferencing during the pandemic to discuss internal matters such as strategic approaches to tackle the effects of the crisis. The use of videoconferencing and modern telecommunications in general has therefore become important, not only in relation to the client and the outside world, but also as an internal tool of communication.[86]

3.3.1.3 *Artificial Intelligence, Algorithms and Automated Decision-Making (Legal Tech 3.0, ODR and Robo-judges)*

The latest technological leap that has proven highly influential on legal practice can be seen in the extensive embedding and continuous further development of AI. This development is a true fire accelerant since it displays significant difference to the previous stages of technological development. AI can be defined as the technical ability (based on algorithmic creation) to solve problems arising in a human-social action context based on similar balancing processes as those carried out by humans.[87] Legal practice and AI come together in the latest generation of LT. The new digital solutions are able to perform various tasks in full autonomy and independence. This includes, for example, interactive and intelligent documents and interfaces, as well as self-learning systems, which, to a certain extent, also make independent decisions.[88] Some ODR-procedures include 'robo-judges' that independently analyse the facts of the case and come to their own conclusions.[89] These possibilities fundamentally challenge the legal profession since many of the standardised tasks performed by these systems no longer require any form of human intervention or, at least, to a much lesser extent than before.[90] Algorithms that predict the outcome of court decisions have attracted particular attention recently. Some have already concluded from the existence of such predictive algorithms that automated court decisions are waiting around the corner.[91]

This brief overview has shown quite plainly the rapid and far-reaching technological changes the last decades have brought about in the working structures of legal practice. The latest technical developments of LT, in particular, raise countless questions as to the future of the legal profession. New technical possibilities warrant an application in an appropriate and reasonable manner. This involves the creation of new legal standards, the adequate implementation of these standards and the emergence of a professional code of conduct for lawyers that allows the mutual growth of humans and technology in equal measure. In Section 3.4, a few selected problematic areas will be discussed in order to address these issues and gain inspiration for the concluding outlook on the future of lawyers in the digital age.

3.4 SOME PROBLEMS AND THREATS IDENTIFIED

3.4.1 *Lack of Legislative Will to Prepare Legal Practice for the Digital Age: The Example of Germany*

There are and will be various possibilities to technologise the legal profession and, in doing so, human intervention will increasingly fade from the spotlight. This development will create

---

[86] Ibid. at 572.
[87] Created from the following partial definitions, see S. Russell and P. Norvig, *Artificial Intelligence: A Modern Approach*, 2nd ed. (Boston: Addison Wesley, 2017) 3; Dartmouth Summer Research Project on Artificial Intelligence in 1956, S. Legg and M. Hutter, 'Universal Intelligence: A Definition of Machine Intelligence' (2007) *Minds & Machines* 391 391.
[88] van Noortwijk and De Mulder, n. 65 at 59.
[89] Ibid.
[90] M. Hartung, M. Bues and G. Halbleib, *Legal Tech* (Munich: C. H. Beck, 2018) 7 ff.
[91] H. Prakken, 'Komt de robotrechter er aan?' (2018) *Nederlands Juristenblad* 269 269.

problems since the lawyer is granted a particular privilege by law and the expansion of LT into legal practice is prevented (in part) by legal prohibitions. Therefore, the prophecy of the legal scientist Lessing that 'code is law'[92] cannot be fully affirmed as of now and maybe never will.

In some jurisdictions, the regulation of the legal services market is so conservative that the embedding of LT in the legal cosmos is considerably slowed down. At the outset, different 'mentalities' towards the use of LT can be detected. While an extensive embedding of the most modern means of LT and digital infrastructure in legal practice is taking place in Anglo-American jurisdictions with an emphasis on the vast array of new opportunities,[93] voices from Continental-European legal systems are often more critical, underlining potential risks. A good example can be found in the German legal system where, with the emergence of the latest LT business models, a debate has arisen on their admissibility, structure and regulation. The questions regularly concern the protection of the lawyers' monopoly that is meant to secure the quality of the legal services market, access to justice and until now effective enforcement of legal rights. Regrettably, the current German legal services market lacks an explicit regulation of marketed-orientated LT. In this context, market-oriented LT does not refer to applications that help *lawyers* in the execution of their particular work processes. Above all, it refers to those LT solutions that offer direct and automatic assistance to *legal-support seekers* with regard to their legal problems and the enforcement of their claims (such as online consumer applications flightright, bahnbuddy, refundrebel or weniger-miete[94] etc.).[95] In doing so, they have the potential to replace or at least compete with the classic legal assistance system in the particular legal service market identified by the market-oriented LT solutions.

Let us shed some more light on this matter. Generally speaking, lawyers in Germany have a monopoly for providing legal services in and out of court. Extrajudicial legal services are regulated by the Legal Services Act (Rechtsdienstleistungsgesetz/RDG). The RDG consists of a list of legal prohibitions subject to permission, meaning that extrajudicial legal services are generally prohibited unless they are expressly permitted (§ 3 RDG). The companies offering market-oriented LT are not traditional law firms; they are currently operating within a framework of legal uncertainty, as their precise legal status has not yet been fully clarified – neither by the legislator nor by the courts.[96] It is quite evident that this state of uncertainty slows down further developments of and investments in LT. For example, it is still disputed whether LT providers – especially those that offer legal assistance that is carried out entirely by a software program (LT 3.0) – provide a legal service at all[97] and whether a pure software application can be even considered a legal activity.[98] LT companies are often seeking access to the market through the acquisition of a license to operate as a debt collection agency (§ 2(2) RDG) as many of them (also) collect outstanding debts of the consumer (e.g., due to delayed or cancelled flights) against a company in one form or another. However, since the activities that are

---

[92] L. Lessing, *Code: Version 2.0* (New York: Basic Books, 2006) 1.
[93] Buchholtz, n. 6 at 955.
[94] See www.flightright.de, www.bahnbuddy.de, www.refundrebel.com or www.wenigermiete.de.
[95] It goes without saying that the exact business model of the LT companies can differ.
[96] See, however, the important *weniger-miete* decision of the German Federal Supreme Court from 27 November 2019 in (2020) Neue Juristische Wochenschrift 208 ff. Insightful on this also is Hoch and Hendricks, n. 66 at 256 ff. Insightful and with further case law, see also C.-M. Leeb, 'Update Legal Tech: So entscheiden die Gerichte', www.lto.de/recht/zukunft-digitales/l/update-legal-tech-rechtsprechung-urteile-uebersicht-2020-smartlaw-wenigermiete-inkasoerlaubnis-digitalisierung-kanzleien.
[97] M. Hartung, 'Legal Tech und anwaltliches Berufsrecht' (2018) *Legal Revolutionary* 137 137–139.
[98] J. Weberstaedt, 'Online-Rechts-Generatoren als erlaubnispflichtige Rechtsdienstleistung?' (2016) *Anwaltsblatt* 535 536.

performed often go considerably beyond offering pure debt collection services, it is argued that this 'flight to debt collection' is not permissible within the letter of the law and ultimately constitutes a violation of the lawyer's monopoly for legal services.[99] The RDG was created with the purpose of effectively protecting clients from false or incomplete legal advice and the opponents of LT argue that this purpose would be undermined by non-lawyer LT solutions. However, the German Federal Supreme Court took a much more liberal approach recently when it decided that the market-oriented LT solution offered by weniger-miete is admissible in principle under § 2(2) RDG.[100] Nevertheless, it remains to be seen whether this decision serves as an indication for the future direction of the Court's legal view with regard to all market-oriented LT solutions.[101] In the meantime also the German legislator realized that the RDG is not LT-ready. At the time the manuscript was finalized the proposal for a new RDG was still under revision.

The lack of a level playing field for LT entrepreneurs and lawyers is seen as a further threat to legal professionals since some legal systems prohibit law firms from entering into partnerships with experts from other professions and forbid the use of third-party funds – which is not the case for LT companies. Law firms thus find themselves in an uncomfortable situation. Digital infrastructure and the embedding of technology requires not only interdisciplinary know-how but also regular large-scale investments. Again, let us shortly focus on the German situation for further illustration. The German Federal Lawyers' Act (Bundesrechtsanwaltsordnung/BRAO) regulates the rights and duties that lawyers have to observe vis-à-vis clients and third parties as well as various other professional legal issues. Section 59e(3) BRAO contains a prohibition for law firms to raise capital from external sources (ban on external financing/*Fremdfinanzierungsverbot*). In addition, § 59a and § 59e(1) BRAO oblige law firms to ensure that the circle of partners is made up of lawyers (prohibition of partnerships/*Sozietätsverbot*). The interplay of these rules results in a structure that prevents lawyers and law firms from effectively entering the LT market.[102]

These observations underline the legislative difficulties in some countries in effectively allowing digital technology to access the legal services market. This shall not obscure the fact that there are also other examples, especially in the Anglo-American market. As an illustration, the legal services market in the United Kingdom has been greatly liberalised by the Legal Services Act 2007.[103] The introduction of Alternative Business Structures (ABS) has allowed law firms to be wholly owned by third parties and to fill management positions with non-lawyers. This admission of outside financing and social partnership promotes the development of LT, allowing the United Kingdom to become one of the LT hot spots in Europe.

3.4.2 Failure to Make Full Use of the Existing Legal Possibilities

Another problem in the relationship between legal practice and technology can be found in the failure of legal practice to make full and proper use of existing technical opportunities and legal possibilities. With regard to courts, it is striking that the legal possibilities for conducting

---

[99] German Bar Association (DAV), Statement from 26 April 2019, https://anwaltverein.de/de/newsroom/dav-kein-zusaetzlicher-regulierungsbedarf-fuer-legal-tech-angebote-rdg?page_n27=2.

[100] German Federal Supreme Court, judgement from 27 November 2019 in (2020) Neue Juristische Wochenschrift 208 ff.

[101] See for this aspect, Hoch and Hendricks, n. 66 at 257 ff.

[102] What remains possible is of course that law firms set up their own LT companies. On the question whether this ban on external financing is actually constitutional under German Law, see Federal Constitutional Court Germany (Bundesverfassungsgericht), judgement from 12 January 2016, BVerfGE 141, 82 ff. On the question whether the ban is violating EU-law see ECJ, case 342/14, *X-Steuerberatungsgesellschaft* [2015] ECLI:EU:T:2014:1084.

[103] Dzienkowski, n. 43 at 2995.

e-justice are not being (fully) exploited in some jurisdictions. The German law on intensifying the use of video conference technology in court and public prosecution proceedings of 2013 (Gesetz zur Intensivierung des Einsatzes von Videokonferenztechnik in gerichtlichen und staatsanwaltschaftlichen Verfahren) has enabled civil proceedings to take place by means of video and audio transmission. Section 128a(1) German Code of Civil Procedure (Zivilprozessordnung, ZPO) stipulates that the court may, upon application or ex officio, allow the parties, their representatives and advisers to remain out of court during an oral hearing and still perform procedural acts. However, after more than seven years, some courts and, as mentioned, even entire court systems within some German federal states, have not managed or considered it necessary to provide courtrooms with the appropriate technical infrastructure. As a result, especially during the COVID-19 crisis, courts were frequently not in a position to allow proceedings to continue by digital means. This is remarkable, especially when comparing the German status quo with the development in other countries. For the purpose of illustration, the Hangzhou Internet Court in China has been in existence since 2017 and is offering a fully online-based procedure, from document transfer to webcam-guided negotiations.[104] It shows that equipping legal practice for the digital age is not only a question of legislative effort, but also requires actors in the field to take advantage of existing opportunities. One of the reasons for the manifest lack of will to implement the existing possibilities (besides the omnipresent aspect of cost) probably lies in the scepticism felt by many lawyers towards digital technology as illustrated earlier.[105]

3.4.3 Inequality of Arms: Disparities in Resources and Know-How for Investment in Digital Infrastructure

Regardless of the legal system, the law firm landscape is characterised by fierce competition and an imbalance in the financial possibilities and the structural organisation of the players. The legal practice can thus be compared to a sea of big sharks and small fish. Under regular circumstances, legal practitioners are service providers in a competitive market, looking to make a profit. For law firms, it is therefore about cost reduction, effectiveness and turnover. State-of-the-art digital legal services and LT instruments are not simply created because progressive development offers new opportunities.[106] The efficiency of legal work has to be increased in order to gain economic advantages and to ultimately earn money. Often, large investments are necessary to integrate LT into the law firm's operations. This involves purchasing software licenses and corresponding hardware equipment.[107] Also, it is necessary to bear in mind that staff must be trained in the use of the acquired digital infrastructure.[108] Even larger sums must be made available if a law firm attempts to develop new LT software by itself and thus seeks to participate in the LT market.[109] A step towards a legal services market that allows for such investments is implementing regulation that allows for recruitment of outside capital, as is the case with the already mentioned example of the British ABS.[110]

---

[104] H. Jin, 'Research on the Mode of Online Administrative Litigation under the Background of "Internet +": A Case Study of Hangzhou Internet Court' (2019) *Big Data and Cloud Innovation* 31 31.
[105] See Section 3.2.2.
[106] Hähnchen, Schrader, Weiler and Wischmeyer, n. 8 at 630.
[107] Hellwig and Ewer, n. 11 at 1784.
[108] Referring to this aspect, see Hähnchen, Schrader, Weiler and Wischmeyer, n. 8 at 630.
[109] Hellwig and Ewer, n. 11 at 1784.
[110] M. Kilian, 'Alternative Business Structures ante portas?' (2014) *Neue Juristische Wochenschrift* 1766 1766.

However, since large law firms generally have greater financial capabilities than their smaller counterparts, it can be assumed that insurmountable trenches will emerge in the long run. It is questionable whether individual legal practitioners or small law firms have a perspective in a highly digitalised world of legal services. Nonetheless, it must be pointed out in this context that capital and manpower are not everything when it comes to the success of a venture in this market. LT startups in particular try to secure a share of the market by compensating for little capital with a lot of know-how. As an interim conclusion, it can be stated that these foreseeable problems regarding competition among law firms of different sizes will emerge in the future; it remains to be seen in what form and to what extent.

3.4.4 Possible Consequences for the Legal Service Market: The Human Lawyer at Risk of Becoming a Discontinued Model?

For many, the most interesting question in light of digitalisation and the expansion of LT is whether lawyers as we know them today will be needed in the future. In order to answer this question, it must again be pointed out at the outset that LT is essentially about increasing efficiency and taking on labour that is otherwise performed by humans. At all times, technological development has led to the reduction of the need for human labour, illustrated, for example, by the highly automated production facilities in the automotive industry, where robots are used, for example, for painting, welding and gluing work. It goes without saying that this process mainly concerned (and still concerns) simple and reproducible activities and that the loss of these jobs has created other more complex jobs elsewhere.

To a certain extent this development can also be predicted in the legal sector and is partly already ongoing. LT solutions are already at a level where they can take over large parts of simple, reproducible legal activities, meaning that human jurists (e.g., paralegals) have become superfluous here (e.g., AI-driven e-discovery). If one thinks further and imagines that those technologies could become more sophisticated and more widely used in the future, the question arises as to how the job market for lawyers will change. Susskind's prediction is quite scary for future jobseekers:

> 'My guess is – and I say this with some hesitation because it could easily be stripped from context by critics – that entire bodies of law and regulation will then be embedded in chips and networks that themselves will be implanted in our working practices or, eventually even, in or remotely accessible to our brains.'[111]

A Deloitte Insight Report foresaw in 2016 that over 100,000 lower-rung legal jobs – some 39 per cent – are likely to be replaced by automated systems over the next decade in the United Kingdom.[112] Various legal scholars equally estimate that there will be fewer human practitioners in the future because LT service providers will undercut them in price competition and in some cases outbid them in quality competition.[113] But will LT in general make the human lawyer redundant in the future? To give a straight answer to the question: No, human lawyers are not in

---

[111] R. Susskind, *Tomorrow's Lawyers: An Introduction to Your Future* (Oxford: Oxford University Press, 2013) 160.
[112] See https://legaltechnology.com/deloitte-insight-100000-legal-roles-to-be-automated.
[113] M. Fries, 'Rechtsberatung durch Inkassodienstleister' (2020) *Neue Juristische Wochenschrift* 193 195. In addition, the outsourcing of legal work plays a major role in a digitalised global world and endangers the legal labour market in some countries. Needless to say that not all legal services can be outsourced to another country due to the specific characteristics of the legal profession. However, one would be foolish to believe that not at least a chunk of the current legal work could be outsourced to another country in order to maximise profits.

danger of becoming a discontinued model. Thus, despite the predicted changes, they will remain a core element of the legal services market. This conclusion is based, first of all, on reasons that lie in the horizon of human-emotional needs referred to above. For many people, seeking justice or even legal problems as such lead to great uncertainty, sometimes even to existential fears.[114] They feel the need to experience counsel by someone who is empathetic, reassuring and can convincingly promise that the legal problem will be resolved.[115] Killian points out that LT solutions only solve the needs of those clients who approach their problems from a strictly rational perspective.[116] Empirical studies have shown that aspects such as the opportunity of a personal conversation with a legal expert and the ability to contact a real person at any time, are of considerable importance for the manner in which a legal problem and its solution are experienced, especially the satisfaction generated by the process of problem-solving.[117] Since technical solutions cannot comprehensively address these needs, human lawyers will continue to be in demand in the future and many clients in a digitalised world will be grateful for humans willing to listen to their concerns.

Besides that, law is not about the technical-logical clarification of algorithmic yes-no questions, but rather the subsumption and evaluation of real-life situations in the light of abstract-general norms. One can derive from this that the use of LT in legal practice will take place, above all, where legal questions can be reduced to a chain of simple yes-no questions. In the case of complex legal problems that require the interpretation of facts and the interpretation of vague concepts such as ordre public, contra bonos mores or good faith, human lawyers will continue to be indispensable since adequate solutions cannot yet be achieved technologically. With the law, it is not always a matter of right or wrong, black or white, yes or no, but about achieving acceptable solutions and adequately weighing interests.[118] Especially in complicated socio-cultural contexts, the capabilities of technology are exhausted at a certain point and human strengths come back into play. Humans, for example, outdo software, when they not only recognise text and translate it, but extract the exact meaning from the particular wording, comparing numerous possible translations and understanding it from a social perspective. Moreover, since each LT application is only a specialist in a certain field, the flexibility and omnipotence of human beings will remain an advantage in the long run.[119] All these conclusions suggest that the human lawyer is not an endangered species. It is however likely that fewer lawyers will be needed in the future and that the legal services market will change considerably. This will be the case especially with regard to simple and reproducible activities. That said, it can be assumed that the reduction of legal jobs involving less demanding and reproducible work will not remain the only and stand-alone change. It has already been pointed out at the beginning of this section that this process will be accompanied by the creation of (fewer) new and higher-skilled jobs. This is especially apparent for the LT developer scene, which requires a new kind of lawyer, namely, lawyers with a profound understanding of programming. Law firms as well will need more and more lawyers who can not only deal with complex legal issues beyond the capabilities of software, but can also use LT applications and have at least a general understanding of the technology behind it. The term e-lawyer is already in use as a job title for this new type of work profile. An e-lawyer is someone who combines legal skills with insights into

---

[114] Kilian, n. 17 at 3043.
[115] Caserta and Madsen, n. 45 at 2.
[116] Kilian, n. 17 at 3050.
[117] Hommerich and Kilian, n. 16 at 107 ff.
[118] Hähnchen, Schrader, Weiler and Wischmeyer, n. 8 at 627.
[119] Russell and Norvig, n. 88 at 51 ff.

new technologies, offering digital means of legal assistance by applying LT solutions.[120] Ultimately, LT must not be understood as a mere threat to the legal labour market, but equally as an opportunity for those (future) lawyers who are willing to familiarise themselves with digital technology in general and with programming in particular.[121]

3.5 OUTLOOK

This chapter has shown the multifaceted relationship between digital technology and legal practice. The basic functionality and the established working methods in legal practice are often fundamentally different from those in information technology and computer science. Law and its application are phenomena that depend on human abilities and on solutions that are open to (human) interpretation.[122] Digital processes, however, are purely logic-based mathematical procedures that function according to reproducible and predeterminable sequences. Nonetheless, since courts, law firms and legal practitioners in general are subject to growing competition in the market as well as the ever-increasing need for efficiency and cost reduction, the legal practice has not been able to turn a blind eye to the benefits of technical progress. While the introduction of technical infrastructure was centred around facilitating time-consuming and costly singular tasks in the 1970s and 1980s, today, with the use of LT, entire work processes can be carried out without or with hardly any human intervention. This development is not always considered as positive; technology has grown into a competitor for legal practitioners and judges.[123] It is thus foreseeable that fewer lawyers (especially legal practitioners) will be needed in the future and the lawyers who seek to assert themselves permanently will have to become more specialised, flexible and variant.[124] However, since the transformation of legal practice through digital technology also creates new work profiles, the main beneficiaries will be those lawyers who can acquire a profound understanding of digital technologies and LT. These specialised lawyers will be of particular interest for the labour market.

As a consequence of all this, the lawyer of the future will only succeed as a being with even more souls than he currently already has. His souls lingering outside his own profession in areas such as technical know-how will have to be further strengthened. Even though the lawyer of tomorrow will not have to be a computer scientist, he will be asked to display a basic understanding of the functionality of LT and AI processes, including coding. This evolution of requirements is necessary to make the best of contemporary technical possibilities, coordinate legal activities accordingly and identify and repair bugs within the LT applications in use.

Nobel Laureate Galsworthy once pointed out that 'if you do not think about the future, you cannot have one'.[125] Following this, the question arises as to how the legal world can prepare itself today for the expected challenges of tomorrow. As a first step, genuine thought must be devoted to future generations of lawyers and their necessary skills. In order to prepare future lawyers for the new challenges awaiting them, legal education and studies must be adapted. Newly designed content related to digital technology must be integrated into existing

---

[120] Caserta and Madsen, n. 45 at 7.
[121] Hellwig and Ewer, n. 11 at 1783.
[122] Buchholtz, n. 6 at 957.
[123] It can of course already be questioned whether a world with less lawyers is necessarily a bad one after all.
[124] Kilian, n. 17 at 3043.
[125] Ibid. at 3050.

educational structures. For the understanding of LT, it would most certainly be helpful if prospective lawyers themselves could acquire a basic understanding of programming LT applications.[126]

A suitable strategy for imparting such knowledge would be to transfer courses from computer science studies to the legal field.[127] This could be made possible by making LT a compulsory course or by integrating the relevant knowledge into established courses. It is to be welcomed that corresponding offers at universities worldwide have increased in recent years. In addition, the studies themselves must respond to the changing needs of practice. In many countries, there is a uniform education and the study of law regularly involves lengthy curricula and strict exams. For example, in Germany, the system of legal education, and above all the so-called Second State Examination, is focussed mainly on the particular legal knowledge required for becoming a *judge* – leaving almost completely aside the technological changes in the legal sector.[128] For students who are considering working in the LT sector, this qualification is routinely less relevant. It thus seems sensible to grant more versatile and practical opportunities to students who have a concrete vision of working in the LT sector, for example, a bachelor or master's course in LT. This would also help to create a level playing field for the LT sector. Many jurisdictions permit LT solutions offered by non-lawyers. However, since it seems appropriate that the LT market should be dominated by those who have solely an advanced understanding of the law, the legal world should not leave the field exclusively to players from outside the profession. It is time to direct an appeal at legal practice to promote an increased interdisciplinary exchange. In a changing legal world, communication with professionals from other fields will prove essential. No lawyer can delude himself into thinking that he will be capable of solving the challenges of the future on his own. In concrete terms, this means that more interdisciplinary forums for encounters of lawyers and computer scientists have to be created, hybrid courses of study should be offered and scepticism towards other professions within legal practice should be discarded. Only such an evolution will grant legal practice the incumbent preparation for the challenges of the digital age. The digital age will present a major challenge for the entire legal sector – but it will also create vast opportunities. It is up to us to make proper use of them.

---

[126] Zwickel, n. 30 at 882.
[127] Ibid.
[128] M. Fries, 'Staatsexamen für Roboteranwälte?' (2018) *Zeitschrift für Rechtspolitik* 161 165.

4

Legal Drafting and Automation

*Benjamin Werthmann**

4.1 INTRODUCTION

As the practice of law is heavily impacted by recent and ongoing advances in technology, it is difficult to provide an accurate picture of either the status quo or the future of the profession whilst focusing on details. Therefore, this chapter focuses on general principles as well as underlying developments and mechanics, rather than detailed accounts of which legal department, agency or law firm is using which techniques or technologies.

4.1.1 Automation and Legal Tech

The topic of legal drafting and automation is not a new one. It has, however, resurfaced as part of the emergence of legal tech (LT). LT has established itself as the term to describe the current push towards a digitalisation of the legal profession often fuelled by startup funding and methods.[1] However, this is not the first time that the practice of law has had to deal with digitalisation. The use of computers, email and data rooms, for example, has caused major changes to the way that law is practiced and the way in which lawyers work.

Another important aspect is that when it comes to the use of modern methods and technology, there is no consensus among legal practitioners. In some countries, the courts are very advanced; China, for instance, established an internet court.[2] In other countries – even leading industrial nations – courts are stuck with outdated equipment. Germany, unfortunately, belongs to the latter. Among others, electronic transmission of documents to courts was only introduced in Germany one year ago, with significant delays and technical problems in respect of security and usability.[3] The court of appeals in Berlin (Berliner Kammergericht) was hacked because it neglected basic requirements of IT security.[4] Various countries have state agencies, startups and lawyers that provide easy to use online services. The United Kingdom offers the possibility to

---

* For valuable contributions and the tedious task of proofreading, thanks are due to Tun de Jong, trainee lawyer in Bremen, Germany.
[1] https://en.wikipedia.org/wiki/Legal_technology (accessed 28 May 2020).
[2] G. Rühl, 'China's Innovative Internet Courts and Their Use of Blockchain Backed Evidence', Conflict of Laws (28 May 2019), https://conflictoflaws.net/2019/chinas-innovative-internet-courts-and-their-use-of-blockchain-backed-evidence (accessed 10 July 2020).
[3] See, for example, the statement of the CEO of the German lawyers' Association, https://anwaltsblatt.anwaltverein.de/de/news/das-beA-l%C3%A4uft-gl%C3%BCcklich-wer-Reno-hat (accessed 28 May 2020).
[4] www.zeit.de/digital/datenschutz/2020-01/kammergericht-berlin-hack-trojaner-datenverlust (accessed 28 May 2020).

challenge parking tickets online.[5] Singapore's Immigration Checkpoints Authority offers various online services.[6] Given the inconsistency of the use of technology even within the same country, the same sector or both, it is virtually impossible to make broad statements regarding the level of digitalisation even within such a narrow framework.

It may be for this reason that legal drafting and automation are not dominating the LT debate: they are not exciting new projects. Rather, a lot of technology has already been introduced but only mastered by few, who have adapted workflows and done a lot of 'homework' to make it work. Telling people that adopting new technology initially involves more work than it saves is, however, not a good pitch to make to those who feel left behind, as it involves swallowing bitter pills. It is more appealing to subscribe to new ground-breaking technology that does not necessitate hours if not weeks or months of homework by its intended user.

Consequently, these very important topics cannot possibly attract anywhere close to the attention that the following LT and general hot topics garner – artificial intelligence (AI) and blockchain. Currently, both topics have largely limited applications, despite the attention and funding sent their way. Both will not only require funding for development, but also more fundamental changes to current infrastructure. They do, however, also come with the promise of more revolutionary results in case of successful implementation. Legal drafting does not draw that kind of attention, let alone funding, and is rarely if ever mentioned outside of the context of automation, even though 'simple' automation might have the broadest scope of application in the short- to mid-term.

AI and blockchain are techniques that can serve the larger arc of automation. In that sense, they never develop a value of their own, unless they serve that particular goal. Unfortunately, way too often they are being used with the sole intention of being able to claim that one is using AI and blockchain. The pursuit of actual results will, however, require the groundwork of determining goals to be achieved, available techniques and resources and an honest cost-benefit analysis of it all.

4.1.2 Automation in the Context of AI

When AI was still in its infancy, automation was its twin sister. With the current AI-hype, automation feels more like an ugly little sister. It's worth remembering that in its early stages, AI was 'hard-coded'. So-called expert systems tried to build decision trees based on expert knowledge in several sectors.[7] For example, programmers would work with chess players to build algorithms for playing chess.[8]

Relatively recent advances in underlying technology and approaches[9] have sparked hope that automation in the legal sector could move on from expert systems to modern solutions that can be trained based on data.[10] One could imagine a system that would be provided with all available legal statutes and related court decisions to subsequently render judgement. This would also involve the ability of such a system to analyse the validity of contracts and potentially even draft

---

[5] www.nidirect.gov.uk/services/challenge-parking-ticket-penalty-charge-notice (accessed 28 May 2020).
[6] www.ica.gov.sg/eservicesandforms (accessed 28 May 2020).
[7] https://en.wikipedia.org/wiki/Expert_system (accessed 28 May 2020).
[8] https://en.wikipedia.org/wiki/Deep_Blue_(chess_computer) (accessed 28 May 2020).
[9] For a comprehensive and critical overview, see P. Moore, 'The Mirror for (Artificial) Intelligence: Working in Whose Reflection?' (2019) WZB Discussion Paper SP III 2019-30 at 7ff.
[10] H. Surden, 'Machine Learning and Law' (2014) 89(1) *Washington Law Review* 87 101ff.

them at some point, or at least answer related questions. If this sounds utterly ridiculous, one should bear in mind that there are already commercial offerings for AI to compose music.[11]

AI adds a facet to automation that is both exciting and scary. The scope of application for a machine with near human intelligence – to stay within the comfort zone of most humans – is almost infinite. As technology nears human-level intelligence, automation moves beyond freeing humans of tasks that are mundane or burdensome, or both; it is starting to replace humans, because it potentially eliminates the tasks that still require human action. Optimistically, this may lead to a utopia where humans do not work at all. Realistically, it has already led to many humans being relegated to doing the most mundane tasks of sifting through all kinds of data sets in order to sate the hunger to learn of an intelligent machine.[12]

From the perspective of lawyers, the obvious advantage of expert systems over neural networks is that the former requires a more intensive and continuous input from sector experts, that is, lawyers. Conversely, the latter is more attractive to those who have never been fans of the legal profession to begin with. The danger for lawyers is similar to that for all workers: obsolescence.

4.1.3 Automation and Blockchain

Blockchain is a collective term for technology intended to provide reliability and security, especially around transactions.[13] The most prominent example is Bitcoin, a digital currency. Various other digital currencies have emerged, as well as the infrastructures around them. Additionally, platforms such as Ethereum[14] provide a more flexible instrument to build infrastructure for any kind of automated transactions. On that basis, various startups have built their own hybrids of currencies, tokens and investment instruments and triggered a wave of ICOs (Initial Coin Offerings).[15]

It is apparent that blockchain has an inherent automation element. At its core, it facilitates the verification of data flowing through a network without involving a central authority.[16] Smart contracts constitute the most obvious link to the legal profession. These are essentially self-executing contracts.[17] Again, an optimistic lawyer may look at this development and see new opportunities for legal professionals to assist in building the underlying mechanics, providing ongoing support and assisting with further development. Pessimistic lawyers and frustrated clients, by contrast, may see another threat of or possibility for, respectively, the extinction of lawyers.

If one ignores marketing and fiction, the development of smart contracts can largely be seen as an exercise in legal drafting, in the light of the existing laws and the envisaged use of

---

[11] For example, AIVA, see www.aiva.ai (accessed 28 May 2020).
[12] H. Reese and N. Heath, 'Inside Amazon's Clickworker Platform: How Half a Million People Are Being Paid Pennies to Train AI', Tech Republic (16 December 2016), www.techrepublic.com/article/inside-amazons-clickworker-platform-how-half-a-million-people-are-training-ai-for-pennies-per-task (accessed 10 July 2020). For an example of a provider, see www.clickworker.com (accessed 28 May 2020).
[13] P. De Filippi and A. Wright, *Blockchain and the Law: The Rule of Code* (Cambridge, MA: Harvard University Press, 2018).
[14] https://ethereum.org/what-is-ethereum/ (accessed 28 May 2020).
[15] For more background and an overview on legal implications from a US perspective, see the SECs ICO website, www.sec.gov/ICO (accessed 28 May 2020); C. Catalini and J. Gans, 'Initial Coin Offerings and the Value of Crypto Tokens', MIT Sloan Research Paper No. 5347-18 (2018).
[16] A. Wright and P. De Filippi, 'Decentralized Blockchain Technology and the Rise of Lex Cryptographia' at 5ff., https://papers.ssrn.com/sol3/papers.cfm?abstract_id=2580664 (accessed 10 July 2020).
[17] https://en.wikipedia.org/wiki/Smart_contract (accessed 28 May 2020). For a definition from a legal perspective, see M. Raskin, 'The Law and Legality of Smart Contracts' (2017) 1 *Georgetown Law Technology Review* 304 309 ff.

precedent. An automated contract that is not powered by human- or superhuman-level intelligence must have built-in automated processes for all conceivable scenarios; there is no room for discretion. If the parties are presented with a scenario that has not been conceived and taken into account during the development of the smart contract, they will have to go back to the legal system they were trying to evade. Building a smart contract within the relevant legal frameworks or simply being aware of potential legal frameworks and reflecting all these eventualities requires the assistance of legal professionals, for better or for worse.

The fears of those lawyers that already feel left behind might, however, not be assuaged by this statement, as the breed of legal professionals needed to complete those development-related tasks is presumably not the one they already belong to. Hence, legal drafting is a key skill for any lawyer[18] going forward, which is why it is important to look at it in more detail.

4.2 LEGAL DRAFTING

Legal drafting can refer to a lot of tasks of a lawyer or legal professional. The writing of laws and regulations can be considered legal drafting, and so can the drafting of court rulings. Ancillary parts of what a lawyer does would also fit a broad definition of legal drafting: mandate letters, powers of attorney, bills, etc. Among the more sophisticated tasks of a lawyer, a distinction can be made between in-court and out-of-court work. In-court work revolves around case briefs and other correspondence with or within the courts. This chapter will, however, focus on the most economically significant form of drafting: the drafting of contracts. The German legal profession even has an archaic term for this, '*Kautelarjurisprudenz*'. This term refers to the part of the legal profession ('*Jurisprudenz*') that focuses on drafting contracts or referring to their constituting parts, clauses ('*Kautelen*').

4.2.1 Drafting Background

Principles of legal drafting should be driven by the purpose of the contract, the expectations of the parties, its underlying logic and generalised standards for quality.

4.2.1.1 Document Purposes

Among the examples of legal drafting referred to above, another distinction can be made between documents that involve a decision and documents that focus on prevention. The former predominantly deal with a problem that has already presented itself, while the latter seek to anticipate such problems and either avoid them or build mechanisms that can solve them with minimal effort and harm as they materialise.

Court and administrative decisions fall into the former category. In the private sector, they share that characteristic with one-sided transactions, such as notices, terminations, etc. On the other hand, laws and regulation share the prevention aspect with contracts in the private sector.

4.2.1.2 Expectations

In most cases, a contract is used to implement a transaction. From the perspective of a lawyer's client, the contract is solving a current problem or task, such as implementing the sale of a house

---

[18] E. Goldman, 'Integrating Contract Drafting Skills and Doctrine' (2006) 12 *Journal of the Legal Writing Institute* 209; T. Stark, 'Contract Drafting: A Prerequisite to Teaching Transactional Negotiation' (2011) 12 *Tennessee Journal of Business Law* 153.

or car. In this regard, it serves as a manual of what is to do, for example, payment and delivery details. But this manual has an inherent prognosis element. As a rule of thumb, parties that have a good working relationship do not need a written contract; they should not depend on a written contract to address problems in their business relationship. Consequently, a written contract is ultimately needed to provide protection in case the parties do not work together well in the future.[19] Most importantly, the client has no interest whatsoever in involving the lawyer at a later stage and paying the resulting fees.[20]

One might think that clients and lawyers should have more or less the same perspective, but that would ignore basic economic drivers: in one form or another, lawyers in all jurisdictions are bound to the client's interest by a fiduciary duty.[21] Despite what many clients may think, or what some TV shows and movies may suggest, most lawyers feel compelled to such duties beyond what is legally mandated by professional regulations. However, in a market economy, there is simply no room for a lawyer that invests more resources in a contract than what clients are willing to pay for its drafting. Just as the market creates the necessity of earning a fee, economic thinking also dictates that a lawyer will always try to avoid liability.[22] The underlying logic stays the same. No legal practice can survive if it produces more liability than it generates fees. Consequently, it may not pay for the lawyer to provide a very specific manual to his clients, as doing so might involve more work, increase the risk of liability and reduce the likelihood of follow-on business.

4.2.1.3 Contract Logic

In line with the idea of a manual for the client, contracts assign an outcome to an input.[23] One example is the payment of the purchase price. If the seller has delivered the goods, the buyer should pay the purchase price or vice versa. Another example is liability for defects. If the seller delivers an inferior product, the buyer should be entitled to reduce the purchase price accordingly and/or claim whatever damages resulted from this defect.

To serve its purpose, the contract needs to be sufficiently clear regarding both the input as well as the output. A sales contract needs to be specific regarding the goods to be delivered, including their quality; otherwise, the parties will end up having to go to court to determine the conformity of the goods. This could affect the obligation of the buyer to pay the full purchase price as well as the liability of the seller for damages.

4.2.2 Quality Criteria for Contracts

The overall quality criteria that can be distilled from the analysis carried out so far are

- legal validity,
- transparency and
- consistency.

4.2.2.1 Legal Validity

Obviously, a contract should be valid. As regards drafting, a lot of statutory validity requirements can be traced back to the ensuing requirements of transparency and consistency. For its very

---

[19] G. Triantis, 'Improving Contract Quality: Modularity, Technology, and Innovation in Contract Design' (2013) 18(2) *Stanford Journal of Law, Business and Finance* 4.
[20] S. Choi and G. Mitu Gulati, 'Contract as Statute' (2006) 104 *Michigan Law Review* 1129.
[21] G. Duhl, 'The Ethics of Contract Drafting' (2010) 14(3) *Lewis & Clark Law Review* 989 995ff. in respect of US law.
[22] Ibid. at 992 names uncertainty around liability as a difficulty of contract drafting.
[23] Triantis, n. 19.

formation, a contract requires a meeting of the minds. So, if the parties do not understand the meaning of contractual terms, this poses a risk to the formation of a binding contract.

Many other requirements relate to aspects outside of the drafting of a contract. This relates, for instance, to illegal means of manufacturing apparent but defective consent, such as fraud or duress. It may also refer to the illegality of the transaction itself, be it because it is generally forbidden (e.g., illegal drugs or weapons) or because it requires permits (e.g., banking, or even the practice of law in some jurisdictions). In this regard, a preamble in a contract may serve to provide background, to dispel concerns that a transaction was entered into due to duress or to illustrate the context of the contract, with respect to the scope of regulations requiring permits.

The requirements that are more relevant for the drafting of a contract and relate to transparency and consistency are those that relate to the fairness of the terms of a contract. This can be relevant for good faith arguments or for certain aspects concerning equitability. Generally, however, these will not be a concern where the stipulations of a contract are completely transparent and consistent. Most jurisdictions will recognise the validity of a contract where a party has willingly entered into unfavourable terms.

4.2.2.2 *Transparency*

If parties do not understand what a contract does, that should be considered a problem.[24] Nevertheless, there are various examples of contracts that are virtually illegible for parties without the assistance of lawyers. For this, however, lawyers are only partly to blame: clients and non-lawyers should also take more responsibility for contracts. Too often, it is considered the lawyers' task to make sure that a contract also reflects the business logic. This thought pattern can lead to serious issues: if the lawyer is not fully aware of the business rationale (and that is often the case) it is impossible to generate a working contract.[25] The result is uncertainty in the future and increased legal and business costs over the life cycle of the contract.[26] One solution can be life-cycle management by lawyers, which sounds profitable for lawyers but may not serve the client's interest. Another one is involving the users in the drafting of the contract and making sure that they understand it.

A crucial aspect is plain language.[27] One problem might be that people think that if they understand what a lawyer does for them, then there really was no need to ask them for advice in the first place. This belief, which the legal profession tries to uphold, is probably rooted in the wish to distinguish oneself from other economic sectors, in order to be able to charge more. While everyone knows how to farm or cook, we accept that there are people that we pay for those tasks so that we can focus on other tasks – in line with the principle of division of labour. However, what we are willing to pay for this service is limited, given that we assume that if we had the time or wanted to, we could complete those tasks ourselves. If, however, we feel like we could not complete a task ourselves, but we see the necessity of having it completed, we are willing to pay a lot more to someone who completes it for us. While from an economic perspective keeping this belief alive makes sense for lawyers, it is not entirely true. A puzzled look on a client's face is not a sign of superior legal quality, rather the opposite. A good lawyer

---

[24] S. Jacobsen, 'A Checklist for Drafting Good Contracts' (2008) 5 *Journal of the Association of Legal Writing Directors* 85.
[25] Stark, n. 18 at 163.
[26] A. Choi and G. Triantis, '*Strategic Vagueness in Contract Design: The Case of Corporate Acquisitions*' (2010) 119 *Yale Law Journal* 882.
[27] G. Berger-Walliser, T. Barton and H. Haapio, 'From Visualization to Legal Design: A Collaborative and Creative Process' (2017) 54(2) *American Business Law Journal* 347; Jacobsen, n. 24 at 108.

should be able to explain what he does in very simple terms, and complexity is often a disguise when lawyers themselves are unsure. Admitting such lack of faith in one's own work would, however, further depress prices. No one is willing to pay a mark-up for work done by someone who comments on it with the words: 'Honestly, I am also not entirely sure. We will have to make an educated guess.' So, lawyers are incentivised to say: 'This is very complicated and probably not worth explaining in detail. Just trust me because I am a very expensive professional.'

4.2.2.3 Consistency

Ultimately, a contract is a technical document. It assigns consequences to certain circumstances. Inconsistency in a contract can still cause problems, especially in long and complicated contracts, or when contracts interlink with each other. The most common inconsistencies revolve around the language used in a contract; this problem can present itself as variations in terms or phrases when the same meaning is intended, or identical terms or phrases even though different meanings are intended.[28]

While in a creative writing setting it is desirable to vary language to keep the reader engaged, the interpretation of a contract will be infinitely more difficult if language varies, as this could indicate that the parties wanted to indicate a different meaning when using different language, even if the different variations have the same meaning colloquially. Lawyers are often judged for being overly particular about the precise meaning of terms and phrases, but if one remembers that a contract is primarily a technical instruction, then this is critical. No one would want a manual for a technical device or a recipe to vary phrases unless a different meaning is intended. A contract that works is not supposed to be exciting, except maybe for lawyers that marvel at the beauty of the mechanics.

4.2.3 Internal Drafting Requirements

Internal drafting requirements concern characteristics that any organisation, whether a law firm or a company, should strive for when drafting standard documentation.

4.2.3.1 Precise Language

The main tool to ensure the preciseness of language is the use of defined terms.[29] This is very common in sophisticated UK and US transaction documents, for example, with regard to financial transactions: where a long document routinely refers to a term, a lawyer should ensure that this term always has the same meaning. There can be a trade-off with transparency, when definitions are used for each and every single term. Drafting a good contract requires striking a balance between the need for consistent meaning and an excessively long list of definitions. The task for the lawyer is to ascertain the importance of the relevant terms for the operation of the contract and the level of ambiguity associated with them. In many cases, this requires input from the client as well as (technical) experts.

4.2.3.2 Clear Structure

In order for a document to be easily understandable, it needs a clear structure.[30] Structure starts with meaningful and accurate headings and benefits from digestible paragraphs with respect to

---

[28] Choi and Mitu Gulati, n. 20 at 26; Jacobsen, n. 24 at 95.
[29] Jacobsen, n. 24 at 94; Triantis, n. 20 at 9–11 also addresses the need for a standardisation of contract terms.
[30] Jacobsen, n. 24 at 86–87. See Section 4.3.2.3 for the use of visualisation to make a documents structure more transparent.

both the message conveyed and the overall length.[31] This implies that the relevant content is included under the corresponding headings. The general structure of contract content[32] should be apparent when looking at any contract.

Links between documents can be equally important. A standard non-disclosure agreement (NDA) is essentially an independent confidentiality clause and often also reflects IT security needs. Changes to the standard confidentiality clause may also trigger changes to the standard NDA. If these documents are not connected, knowledge is bound to be stuck in one place, at the expense of overall quality,[33] unless the person in charge of each document or clause is the same, or there is an additional process in place to ensure conformity of drafting around similar topics in different documents or clauses. Managing these links is also based on understanding why specific parts of the relating documents are drafted as they are. This might seem simple, but in practice, more often than not, knowledge pertaining to the origin and purpose of clauses or even contracts, which are regularly used, is rather limited.

Any contract should begin with a preamble that can serve not only to provide the requisite structure within the document, but also to provide proper context.[34] Unfortunately, preambles are often considered either a tedious or a superfluous task, or both. Their importance can, however, not be overstated: they constitute a watershed moment. If a lawyer properly understands what a client is trying to achieve, it should not be a problem to draft a meaningful and helpful preamble. If a lawyer really cares about the quality of a contract, he will devote sufficient time to the preamble. A preamble explains the background of a transaction and gives the reader of a contract the information required to understand what the contract is trying to achieve. This is not only beneficial to the reader of the contract but can also serve as a test for the lawyer drafting the contract. Having drafted a clear preamble, it will be easier for him or her to discern whether the clause he or she is about to introduce into the contract actually serves its purpose.

Lawyers should care deeply about understanding the parties' needs and intentions and figuratively etching them into stone via the preamble for future reference. This is due to the fact that one of the main problems that contract users face over the life cycle of a contract is that it becomes difficult to reproduce the original intentions of the parties. Furthermore, in most jurisdictions, these intentions are the basis for an interpretation of specific clauses.[35] By including express language in the contract, a lawyer avoids problems of interpretation and pitfalls he may face in jurisdictions that limit the extent to which a judge may go beyond the stipulations of a contract to interpret its meaning. Only a cynical trial lawyer would be content to argue that a contract should be interpreted solely based on the contract language, even if the result were to stand in stark opposition to the will of the parties. In a well-drafted contract, the preamble provides the backdrop to the entire contract and everything that follows are properly structured mechanics that serve the purpose and goals established by the preamble.

4.2.3.3 *Compliance*

External compliance in respect of documents intended for the outside world, as opposed to internal documents, includes legal validity. The most sophisticated legal system of contract

---

[31] Jacobsen, n. 24 at 96–97.
[32] See Section 4.2.4.
[33] P. Lippe, D. M. Katz and D. Jackson, 'Legal by Design: A New Paradigm for Handling Complexity in Banking Regulation and Elsewhere in Law' (2015) 93(4) *Oregon Law Review* 842.
[34] Jacobsen, n. 24 at 91.
[35] Choi and Mitu Gulati, n. 20 at 22.

content control concerns general terms and conditions. In Germany, this principle also applies to business-to-business relationships. The consequence of a violation of this principle is the invalidity of either specific clauses or entire mechanisms. This might well alter the power dynamic within the contract. When drafting contracts, one can of course take a calculated risk that a particular clause might be invalid, especially if the law is not clear. But this implies that the user of a contract is always aware of the associated risks. Often, it can simply be good business practice not to draft clauses too aggressively.

Internal compliance is usually not a matter of validity. Rather, companies have internal guidelines that can take various forms and serve various purposes. Purely internal guidelines reflect business practice and policy decisions; however, compliance rules in regulated businesses promulgate regulatory requirements, for example, for financial institutions. While non-compliance does not necessarily result in invalidity, it can result in fines or unpleasant investigations and reputational problems. Drafting contracts in such an environment is difficult because the number of internal regulations as well as regulatory requirements has increased significantly.[36] Without a proper process and a high level of dedication, ensuring internal compliance is virtually impossible.

4.2.3.4 *Velocity*

Drafting is not free of constraints. Whether contracts are drafted by external lawyers or legal departments, speed with maximum impact is key. This constraint can be at odds with the requirements addressed above. All of those requirements involve attention to detail and time. Consequently, it is crucial for the drafters to be adequately prepared; otherwise, the choice is between a good contract and a bad contract delivered in time, so that it complies with the relevant business needs.

4.2.4 *Contract Content*

Doing the groundwork for contract drafting includes carving up contracts into blocks of content, depending on purpose and logic involved.

4.2.4.1 *Essential Rights and Obligations*

Essential rights and obligations define a contract. In a sales contract, that is the delivery of the purchased good and the payment of the purchase price. While this seems very simple, it can become quite complicated, for example, when the purchased good is difficult to describe or the nature of the contract is more obscure. Software, as an increasingly dominant product of the modern world, provides many challenges, the first of which concerns its categorisation as either a good or a service.

When describing a complicated 'good' such as software, it is common to include details in an annex. This makes perfect sense, as it keeps the overall contract readable; it can, however, make it more difficult to understand what the contract does without reading that annex. It often also disconnects lawyers from technical experts: lawyers look at the body of the contract, while technical experts focus on the annex. The risk that neither side makes sure that these parts of the contract are consistent with each other needs to be managed.

---

[36] Lippe, Katz and Jackson, n. 33 at 834.

4.2.4.2 *Ancillary Rights and Obligations*

Ancillary rights and obligations are not needed for the basic operation of the contract, but address further aspects of the contractual relationship. In some jurisdictions, such as Germany, they arise as a matter of law; for example, section 241 of the German Civil Code stipulates that the parties can be obliged to take account of the rights, legal interests and other interests of the other party, depending on the contents of the relating (essential) obligation.

A common ancillary provision is confidentiality. In line with the increasing attention to compliance, many ancillary provisions serve compliance needs of regulated industries, for example, when a borrower needs to provide information for know-your-customer checks to a bank. In software contracts, clauses around IT and cybersecurity are expanding.

4.2.4.3 *Modifications and Business Logic*

To the extent possible, it makes sense to separate contract content depending on whether it (1) repeats, clarifies or expands on mandatory law or default rules, or (2) modifies such rules. Additionally, one should keep track of the business logic of such clarifications, expansions and modifications, that is, the underlying commercial rationale. Otherwise, contracts can become bloated with clauses whose continued existence is owed to the fear of removing something important.

This applies specifically to operational provisions addressing governance between the parties in complicated or long-term transactions, or both. These provisions are often tailored to the specific needs of each transaction; understanding the needs that they address from a business perspective allows for clustering of aspects that translate to other transactions. Furthermore, this approach allows one to flag parts of the contract that may have been one-time concessions or outliers. To a lesser extent, this also applies to the parts of the contract that govern warranties, guarantees and the overall liability regime.

4.2.4.4 *Boilerplate Provisions*

Boilerplate provisions or clauses are reusable for a number of contracts and try to limit the need for lengthy negotiations of the parties.[37] This implies that they have no or only very limited dependencies with the essential parts of the contract. Making that distinction can be challenging. Common boilerplate provisions are clauses on confidentiality, third party rights, assignments, the form of amendments, governing law and jurisdiction. These are not exciting provisions, especially to non-lawyers. But the nature of the contract can have a bearing on them. A standard confidentiality clause may not be sufficient where a contractor has access to highly sensitive information. Written form may not suit all transactions. Certain parts of a business may give rise to disputes that are better solved by arbitration rather than courts, whilst others may not. Therefore, while boilerplate provisions should be the domain of lawyers, they also show the need for lawyers to understand the rationale of the business relationship.

4.3 AUTOMATION

In light of the abovementioned nature and inner workings of legal drafting, there is a clear case for automation and the use of technology to facilitate that automation. In practice, the main drivers that are pushing innovation in this area are the following:

---

[37] Choi and Mitu Gulati, n. 20 at 15.

- Client cost-consciousness: As even well-paying clients become more aware of what they are spending on legal services, all law firms must find ways to reduce the costs of their legal services. In particular, a move from hourly rates (loved by lawyers) to fixed pricing (loved by clients) can be a major incentive for automation in a transition from legal services to legal products.
- Internal budget ('more with less'): Legal departments as part of businesses are often faced with budget cuts or limitations that can drive automated document generation.
- Access2Justice/Minimum Values for Legal Departments: Bringing legal services to those that cannot usually afford them is traditionally filed under *pro bono* work. Automation can open business opportunities in these areas through the reduction of costs. Similarly, many companies save legal costs by using *de minimis* amounts to determine access to legal assistance. While this does make sense from an accounting perspective, it can create blind spots for the legal and compliance department. Furthermore, the value of a contract does not necessarily equal the potential for liability, neither contractually nor in terms of compliance.

4.3.1 Evolution of Contract Automation

None of the aforementioned drivers are particularly new, even if that does not always fit the narrative of digital transformation and disruption. They have already impacted legal drafting for decades.

4.3.1.1 Use of Precedents and Templates

The most basic approach in respect of contract automation is the use of precedents.[38] Even the most un-automated law practice will be making use of this approach. When drafting a sales contract, a practitioner will typically refer to the last sales contract they have drafted. But as any practice expands, this reliance on previous experience will become more and more complicated and require not just expert but ultimately legacy knowledge. This is evident in practices where a new lawyer or employee will not be able to be operational in a reasonable time frame, irrespective of skill level, because use of an extensive library of precedents requires knowledge of the history of each precedent. A highly skilled lawyer will of course be able to figure out the rationale of each clause at some point, but it is unlikely that he will be competitive when set up against a long-term employee at almost any skill level. Accordingly, one of the main problems when using precedents is that knowledge is locked up and does not scale.

Templates are a natural evolution of the precedent model. The most basic templates apply the 'fill in the blanks' approach. As certain use cases repeat themselves, it will become obvious that one can simply remove the parts specific to each individual case and substitute them with blanks to be filled in, depending on the requirements of future use cases. This makes the knowledge acquired by a law practice more accessible and scalable, but it assumes that the use cases are simple enough for it to work. Any use case that triggers a need for variations of clauses rather than different input to be taken from underlying facts is not suitable for such basic templates.

---

[38] S. Choi, G. Mitu Gulati and E. Posner, 'The Dynamics of Contract Evolution', University of Chicago Institute for Law & Economics Olin Research Paper No. 605; NYU Law and Economics Research Paper No. 12-162 (2012).

4.3.1.2 *Questionnaires and Annotations*

A template for a broader range of cases requires more variables. For simple purposes, blanks and boxes may suffice, if the user has sufficient intuition regarding the required input. As use cases become more complex, however, and the template more useful – in the sense that it can reduce the human element in the relevant task – comments on blanks and boxes will be required to make sure users can still operate the template. The context can be so complex that specific questions are required, which then point the user to the relevant alternative or guidance in respect of the required input.

To cover more demanding use cases, templates can be expanded to include (guided) questionnaires and annotations. The document would for instance ask for specific input, rather than just showing a blank and provide (anticipated) input to assist the user in choosing between variations of clauses, phrases or terms. This allows a legal practice to scale further and on board new team members more easily, at least in theory.

A practical problem is the amount of work required to produce proper questionnaires and annotations. This is why many larger law firms and legal departments have dedicated teams, devoted to general or specific knowledge management. Essentially, such templates are how a practice should manage knowledge. It's also what distinguishes actual practice from academic work: academics may be interested in a legal problem in the abstract, but for a practitioner the problem is only relevant in the context of a specific use case.

4.3.1.3 *Automated Templates (Contract Generators)*

In this chapter, the term 'automated templates' refers to templates that assemble a contract solely based on user input. All of the approaches mentioned so far work on paper. When considering how to scale a business model, however, technological automation is crucial. In evolutionary terms, the fully automated template is not that far advanced, in comparison to its predecessors: it simply combines the aforementioned techniques with digital tools for easier implementation.

In an ideal scenario, accumulated knowledge and digital tools propel each other towards better development. A digital solution that is supposed to constantly deliver superior results requires input of a lot of know-how. Expert systems, as the only tool that is currently operational, can produce such know-how independently. It follows that any practice or service provider needs to be smart about setting up a tool. The groundwork is predominantly legal work that requires a lot of practical experience. One of the reasons that we have not seen broad adoption of automated templates is that experts with the relevant skill and expertise were and still are often considered too valuable to use on know-how work.

In big firms, the ideal knowledge manager or knowledge support professional is either a lawyer with recent practical experience, or a lawyer that is still working in practice but has enough time to spare. It seems that big companies increasingly use in-house teams for such tasks to reduce internal and external costs. The fact that most law firms still generate a significant part of their fees from legal opinions suggests that a breakthrough has not happened yet, probably due to similar structural problems. Legal departments can get bogged down in day-to-day operations of assisting their corresponding business units. Devoting time to groundwork would come at the expense of the work that – by design – the business units are paying for. One should remember that legal department lawyers – as opposed to lawyers in law firms – do not generate fees, but costs. As a result, companies face the same dilemma as law firms: they have to invest rather heavily before seeing any tangible returns. With respect to the results, another problem can be that the impact of properly automated templates may not even be measurable at all. Who would be able to trace costs avoided due to better contract quality over the entire life cycle of a contract?

4.3.1.4 *Robo-lawyers*

Ultimately, there may be an evolution where a neural network or an even more sophisticated system takes over the drafting of contracts as well as other tasks of lawyers (see Section 4.3.3.2). For a while now, there has been talk of robo-lawyers,[39] which can take the form of very sophisticated systems replacing lawyers. To an external observer, these systems may present themselves as simple chatbots. In any event, however, current tools still have a long way to go, until the 'robo-lawyer' label will be anywhere close to being justified.[40]

4.3.2 *Document Automation Requirements*

The requirements for a proper automation of documents go well beyond (internal) requirements for contract drafting already touched upon. This section will expound on these further requirements, touching upon interface, logic, maintenance and compatibility.

4.3.2.1 *Interface*

Since users interact with automated templates or a contract generators' interface, a more intuitive interface design will produce better outcomes, as well as boosting acceptance of the tool at hand. Many legacy systems have interfaces that require the user to adapt to the system, rather than the system adapting to the user, thus contributing to frustration but also lock-in effects. If users have to invest a lot of time in order to learn how to interact with a tool, they will be less likely to transition to new tools in case of later advances in technology. Bad interfaces also present a business risk. The purpose of the interface is to make sure that the user ticks the right boxes and provides the necessary input; if this is not the case, all risks associated with inferior contracts are a consequence.

There are two interfaces that need to be addressed. One is the interface for the actual user of the contract generator. This is the person that receives the customised contract. If this user is not a lawyer, the interface needs to reflect that. Among other things, a lot of thought has to be put into the translation of necessary legal concepts into something digestible for non-lawyers. The other interface is the one for the operation of the contract generator. This interface is required to update automated templates when legal or other requirements change, or with a view to usability. If this requires the assistance of IT experts, that will dramatically increase the time necessary for updates and may trigger workarounds by frustrated users. In order to avoid these unwanted consequences, so-called no-code-solutions can allow for lawyers to directly maintain the system. They would only have to involve IT experts in case of malfunctions or fundamental changes.

One should also never underestimate that a 'fun' interface can additionally motivate people to stick to tasks that they might otherwise abandon in a hurry.

---

[39] R. Cellan-Jones, 'The Robot Lawyers Are Here – and They're Winning', BBC (1 November 2017), www.bbc.com/news/technology-41829534; J. Koebler, 'Rise of the Robolawyers: How Legal Representation Could Come to Resemble TurboTax', *The Atlantic* (April 2017), www.theatlantic.com/magazine/archive/2017/04/rise-of-the-robolawyers/517794.

[40] D. Freeman Engstrom and J. Gelbach, 'Legal Tech, Civil Procedure, and the Future of Adversarialism' (2020) 169 *University of Pennsylvania Law Review* 18.

4.3.2.2 *Logic*

Any tool should incorporate as much of the logic of a contract as possible. This is largely what separates approaches of 'fill in the blanks' from fully automated solutions. For example, if a system allows for the user to select the level of liability while providing helpful examples and background, this is already a good start. Ideally, however, and especially for non-lawyers, a contract generator should infer the required or desirable level of liability from other information that is easier for the user to provide.

This requires linking contract content to the purpose of the contract and the aspects of the business relationship that the contract is intended to govern and mapping out the dependencies.[41] If a certain part of the business is better served by (1) detailed warranties, (2) a stricter liability regime and (3) a clause that provides for arbitration, the interface should ask for the business sector and make consequential changes automatically. This would be much more helpful and less error prone than prompting the user to make a selection in each of the three cases. It can also extend the pool of potential users because of the more limited knowledge required to generate the contract.

4.3.2.3 *Maintenance*

An underrated factor is the maintenance of a contract generator. Putting a tool in place requires a lot of work, but contract content can be superseded rather quickly. Since having a system that is not maintained will quickly lead to diminishing returns, maintenance needs to be considered when building or selecting the system. This means not only making sure that maintenance is as easy as possible, but also setting aside the labour force, time and money to conduct the maintenance work ultimately required.

Furthermore, visualisation can be a powerful tool to assist maintenance. Leaving aside scientific debates, practical experience shows that humans work better when they have visual, or more specifically, spatial, aids.[42] A simple example of this are mind maps, or the mere fact that most modern offices have whiteboards. No-code-solutions already implement a lot of visual help. This is certainly an area where rather low-tech efforts could yield significant returns. This preference for spatial aids is by no means unique to the legal sector; it follows developments in other sectors (especially in the IT sector). In fact, maintaining a contract generator has a lot of parallels with maintaining software and IT infrastructure.

4.3.2.4 *Compatibility*

Finally, another underrated factor is compatibility. A system cannot be adopted without accounting for legacy systems around it. With respect to contract generators, Microsoft Word is an obvious problem. Within Word, a practical problem can be that the generated contract is not in line with document house style, since many law firms and companies have specific requirements in this regard.

Ideally, contract generators should also be able to draw information from other systems. This could relate to names and details of the parties, but also to annexes involving calculations. It might be impossible to have a perfect solution, but one should think about all of these practical implications and consider and ideally structure the relevant process around the generation of contracts, especially workarounds that may require specific training of users.

---

[41] Lippe, Katz and Jackson, n. 33 at 842.
[42] Berger-Walliser, Barton and Haapio, n. 27 at 31–52.

4.3.3 Automation Instruments

So, what are the instruments and tools available to implement fully automated templates? The inconvenient truth is that many have been available for some time, but were neglected due to an unwillingness to get familiar with them. Furthermore, the new tools on the market often appear to be easier to use but, ultimately, require the same devotion to groundwork.

4.3.3.1 Expert Systems

The term 'expert systems' refers to all systems that essentially copy already existing expertise in one form or another. One approach that has been around for a while in the legal sector is the decision tree. Like a tree, input and consequences are branching out, and a system built on this may appear very smart. As the designation expert systems suggests, this approach requires experts to build the decision tree and adapt it, whenever it becomes outdated.

The approach is agnostic with respect to the tool used to implement it. While this feature may not be widely known, even Word, the scalpel of any lawyer, has macros, which include very basic functions such as definition and attachment management. By using very simple functions, definitions and attachments can be tracked throughout a document. Ideally, an executed contract would be stored in a version that maintains that functionality, or at least be accompanied by a Word version. More sophisticated functions allow for the implementation of questionnaires and annotations to quite an astonishing level. The main drawback is the (lack of) user friendliness and the 'ugliness' of the resulting interfaces.

At the core of the process is a model of dependencies and workflows. The work that needs to be done is defining the input that is available and assigning the outcome, that is, the drafting that is desired depending on what the input is. This goes to the nature of a contract that is similar to computer code. For very simple documents, no separate modelling may be required. That is obvious where 'fill in the blanks' templates can be used.

It will, however, prove difficult to extract complex logic built into an automated form once it has been assembled, irrespective of the technical solution deployed. This will make it all the more difficult to fix deficiencies in the template, or update it in case the legal environment changes or when legal views or simply business processes change. Conversely, it is impossible to build a working template without mapping out these dependencies in advance.

The process also requires a lot of business logic, that is, (legal) sector-specific expert knowledge. Only someone that fully understands the entire process can differentiate core dependencies from subsequent dependencies. In fact, one of the most important decisions can be which form to use: for example, if a user wants to 'acquire' an asset, it is crucial to know whether he wants to purchase or lease it.

4.3.3.2 Artificial Intelligence and Blockchain

AI is a descriptive term that adds little value when used without proper context and detail. For example, spam filters used to be a nightmare that filtered out important email and failed to screen obvious scams. Nowadays, people rarely complain about spam, and would probably also not associate spam filters with AI. So, it is fair to assume that when people get excited about using AI to automate legal drafting, they refer to cutting edge technology. Nevertheless, service providers may use the term more loosely and refer to techniques that have been in use for ages.

New AI based on highly complex neural networks builds its own decision tree. However, like a child slowly learning to understand the world, this requires large amounts of data. People seem to forget that human intelligence is the result of years of learning, referring not only to schools or universities, but also to a child's constant struggle to master the simplest tasks, such as focusing eyesight, using its fingers, understanding and producing sounds and language, etc.

The required amount of data is simply not available for contracts. Accordingly, legal AI is restricted to very basic data analysis, especially in the context of e-discovery and compliance investigations.[43] In each case, the crucial factor is the availability of large data sets. Contract analysis is often done for larger companies that have the corresponding amounts of executed contracts, that is, precedents. AI ultimately learns from precedents (for example, by 'reading' all lease agreements of a property company), but it also has to be taught whether a contract is 'correct' or 'incorrect'.

Blockchain has the advantage of already following a prescribed logic rather than extracting such logic from data sets. The challenge for blockchain is finding use cases based on interfacing. Any blockchain solution requires accurate input and a finite output. The system is not flexible at all. A blockchain-based solution could, for example, digitalise letters of credit. It could also transfer payment when a good has been delivered. Both ends have to be digitalised and interfaced. Accordingly, blockchain is not something that helps with automated legal drafting. It could, however, be an add-on to an automated template if such templates have been designed to be compatible with a specific blockchain solution, for example, digital letters of credit.

4.3.4 Best Practices for Contract Automation

Automation in the context of legal drafting presents a lot of challenges, but also offers tremendous opportunities. Current success of LT startups is not based on revolutionary technologies – outside of marketing – but on smart strategies around covering large volumes with standardised documents and processes.

While this is not a new concept, implementing it through the use of and in the context of new technologies will be difficult without changing the mindset in the legal industry, or at least getting rid of bad habits that have been adopted in the past and sometimes even positively cultivated.

As AI is knocking on the door of the professional service industry, getting familiar with and taking full advantage of more simple and established tools is even more important. Best practices can help meet that challenge.

4.3.4.1 Cost-Benefit Analysis (80/20 Rule)

As lawyers take advantage of software at an increasing level, they should take a page out of the book of software development. There, the 'agile movement' has established an approach whereby development is conducted more flexibly and with a rigorous focus on finding out what actually works through trial and error. Lawyers, on the other hand, think big and are focused on getting everything right at the first attempt.

In trying to make software development more efficient, the '80/20 rule' based on the Pareto principle[44] is applied in various ways. One of them is an understanding that 80 per cent of the value of a product is in 20 per cent of the features.[45] Hence, in case of a 100 per cent solution, a lawyer would put in 80 per cent of its work to add just 20 per cent to the bottom line. The answer

---

[43] Lippe, Katz and Jackson, n. 33 at 847.
[44] https://en.wikipedia.org/wiki/Pareto_principle (accessed 28 May 2020).
[45] www.productplan.com/80-20-rule-agile/ (accessed 28 May 2020).

to this problem is iteration. Understanding this concept is not the difficult part; the real challenge is applying it in real life. Lawyers need to train themselves to think about smaller independent parts of larger solutions that can be implemented with minimum efforts, in order to test whether the result merits further work.

Traditionally, in the legal services industry, there is also no focus on being efficient. At first sight, this seems justified: when considering the essential services that the legal profession provides, such as defending those accused of criminal acts, it is difficult to think in terms of how much justice one is willing to invest. The danger for lawyers is that, based on that mindset, they over-commit to applying new technologies rather than those that make the most sense. The most cost-effective measure could turn out to be an online class on text processing or table calculations.

Based on modularised contract content,[46] automation could start with smaller projects, such as single modules of contracts, as well as less complex contracts, in order to gain valuable experience before committing too many resources. This also touches on the question of whether or not a contract will be used repeatedly or just once: obviously, automating a contract that is only used once does not makes sense. In this scenario, similarities with other contracts should be identified, and automation could focus on those parts of a contract that are common to a sufficiently large number of contracts.

As a precursor to actual automation, one could also cluster specifications for general use cases. For example, many companies do not only buy, but also sell items to conduct their business; since the contracts involved with these purchases and sales will follow the same structure, the use of a template can be expanded by tracking what versions of what parts of a contract one is looking for, depending on the role of the business (i.e., buyer or seller) in the contract.

Within groups of companies, individual companies conduct business with affiliates and external companies. Again, the overall structure of the relevant contracts is similar, even though the terms may change, because they will be more favourable within the group. If a legal department maps out what changes are required when turning a contract towards internal or external customers, the scope of the underlying contract expands. The same applies to companies that offer variations of the same product or service based on standard or premium terms or subscriptions, as is often the case for software solutions. It also applies when contracts are used for dealing with other businesses or consumers.

Experience is needed to understand or anticipate where a process will 'break'. Rather than forcing an automated template to always deliver an outcome no matter the circumstances, the system should know when it fails, or is about to fail. If the system is successful in the sense that it delivers a contract without frustrating the user, but that contract is likely to cause liability risks, then nothing has been gained, neither for the client nor the lawyer.

4.3.4.2 *User-Centric Contract Design*

Conducting a proper cost-benefit analysis and testing unfinished products requires something else that lawyers have come to neglect: user focus.[47] This is not because lawyers are more detached than other professionals; at least, there is little evidence supporting such a claim. The more plausible explanation is that the legal profession is a protected profession in many jurisdictions: privilege breeds complacency. Lawyers are not used to having to compete in an

---

[46] Triantis, n. 19 at 5, 11–14.
[47] Berger-Walliser, Barton and Haapio, n. 27 at 16–21, 26.

open environment. They are used to competing with other lawyers, who play by the exact same rules.

That is bound to change. Software can again be a good place to look to for guidance. In the hyper-competitive market of the app store, user-friendliness is key. Since users can switch from one solution to the next with ease and review functions, making their experience digestible for each new user, it is rewarding to make the user comfortable from the start. A lawyer, on the other hand, is used to something akin to a monopoly. Clients are to certain degree stuck with either the lawyer available, or the lawyer they have chosen, because it is difficult for them to judge the quality of lawyers, which makes it more burdensome to invest time and money in finding a new one. That allows a lawyer to relax and work on the basis of the assumption that the client will *ultimately* appreciate the quality of the overall outcome, even if the way to get there is painful. While this can be a good thing (for example, when it prevents the lawyer from applying superfluous solutions to appease an irrational client), it also takes away motivation to question whether the process makes sense.

Essentially, lawyers manage human conflict.[48] If they want to differentiate themselves from machines, they should focus on the human factor. Clients are not in a position to ascertain the accuracy of legal advice; they are looking to lawyers for comfort in a situation that is often accompanied by emotional turmoil, and they are confronted with a system they know little to nothing of. Hence, lawyers should primarily consider themselves as the human interface to the very complicated and cold-hearted area of law.

4.3.4.3 *Open Source Practices*

It does not really make sense to assume that protecting 'intellectual property' of lawyers' work provides proper incentive.[49] Lawyers are already legally bound by fiduciary duties to serve clients' interests. What protecting intellectual property does, in this case, is to incentivise lawyers to invest in obscuring their process.

Other tasks are hard enough. There will be plenty of room for lawyers to compete other than on nuances of clauses and made-up guesswork on potential rulings of courts. Putting the client back in focus should be the order of the day. Many clients complain that they do not understand why routine tasks require bespoke solutions. This is mainly because lawyers invest in secretive know-how concerning documents in an area that should be transparent, that is, the law.

More often than not, when two lawyers of two clients collide in what the clients would consider a routine transaction, the lawyers are approaching the transaction with different styles of documents. Often, they themselves do not know what particular clauses are supposed to achieve; they just know that they have always been using that clause. If that clause is questioned and the lawyer is billing by the hour, the client is actually paying the lawyer to familiarise himself with his own drafting. Insert the division of labour in larger firms between senior and junior lawyers, and the situation becomes even more problematic. For some time now, clients have also pushed for junior associates to be removed from bills, irritated by the idea of having to pay for their legal education.

If we look to the world of data science and encryption for guidance, the incredible advances made have been largely due to open-source philosophies. Data analytics is largely driven by libraries with functions to deal with specific types of data. These libraries are open source, because it does not pay for everyone to do the same work. They are maintained by people

---

[48] Ibid. at 28.
[49] Still the lack of protection is at times lamented, see Triantis, n. 19 at 17.

working 'for free'. Working on these libraries signals to potential employers and clients that the relevant person has desirable skills. Why should this not translate to the area of law?[50] In fact, academic work of practitioners is trying to achieve the same goal; in the area of law, however, the returns are diminished.

Many of these open source efforts are remarkable, even if they are still few:

- the incubator Y Combinator publishes standard documents for the financing of tech startups;[51]
- in Germany there is a similar initiative;[52]
- UNCITRAL has established the CLOUT database[53] for court cases on the CISG,[54] in which an international community of academics, students and practitioners provides free translations;
- a non-profit in Germany is building a database for German court cases that is already larger than the official one.[55]

Other worthwhile efforts to achieve broad standardisation hide behind paywalls for the general public, but at least provide a level playing field for a significant part of the legal sector. These are standard documents around financings from the Loan Market Association (LMA)[56] and standard documents for swaps published by the International Swaps and Derivatives Association (ISDA).[57]

4.4 CONCLUSION AND OUTLOOK

Overall, mastering the challenges around the automation of legal drafting is not rocket science. The necessary tools are available and lawyers, after their rigorous training at law school, bring a lot to the table in terms of thinking in abstract structures and concepts, not to forget the willingness to endure a lot of punishment on tasks that others may consider boring.

Effecting the necessary changes will, however, be infinitely more difficult, without direly needed changes to the training of lawyers. It should be a clear warning sign that, despite fundamental changes to the way that the world economy (including the social economy) works, it is difficult to identify similarly fundamental changes to legal education. Most jurisdictions still train lawyers to go through large amounts of data to find the correct statute, precedent, etc. As search algorithms become more sophisticated, the upside of that aspect of legal training will become even less plausible. The time devoted to that part of the training comes at the expense of training lawyers in the social skills that would set them apart of automated legal advisors. One should ask how much of legal training revolves around explaining legal concepts in basic terms to make them digestible for clients, or developing strategies reflecting business needs in case of legal uncertainties.

Many jurisdictions are also quite comfortable with lengthy legal educations that allow little time for anything else. If the future of law requires lawyers that are familiar with concepts of

---

[50] R. Susskind, *The End of Lawyers? Rethinking the Nature of Legal Services* (Oxford: Oxford University Press, 2008) 25ff.
[51] www.ycombinator.com/documents/ (accessed 28 May 2020).
[52] https://standardsinstitute.de/ (accessed 28 May 2020).
[53] www.uncitral.org/clout/ (accessed 28 May 2020).
[54] United Nations Convention on Contracts for the International Sale of Goods.
[55] https://openjur.de (accessed 28 May 2020).
[56] Loan Market Association, see www.lma.eu.com/documents-guidelines/documents (accessed 28 May 2020).
[57] International Swaps and Derivatives Association, Inc, see www.isda.org/book/complete-isda-documentation-package/ (accessed 28 May 2020). Choi and Mitu Gulati, n. 20 at 15–19.

project management, product design as well as technology and software, then many jurisdictions are training lawyers for the past rather than the future. At the moment, many lawyers and law students are open-minded about and relatively skilled in the realm of technology *in spite of*, not *because* of the education and training they have received. This is not sustainable.

Even when a new generation of lawyers with double degrees in law and software development or similar interdisciplinary skill sets emerges from universities, we need to take care that they not be met by a system of professional regulations designed to curtail their skills and creativity. Bar and other professional associations of lawyers need to make sure that they push for necessary reforms of the legal industry, rather than defending monopolies. Most importantly, regulations around professional secrecy should make it possible for lawyers to use state-of-the-art software solutions that are already used by their clients, rather than using outdated solutions for fear of breaching professional regulations. This would also make lawyers more compatible with other disciplines.

If anything, putting work into automated templates, specifically, and giving thought to automation in the legal sector in general, can be the ladder necessary for leaving the ivory tower every now and then and returning to the trenches to meet the common folk.

5

Emerging Rules on Artificial Intelligence

Trojan Horses of Ethics in the Realm of Law?

Florian Möslein and Maximilian Horn

5.1 INTRODUCTION

Given that artificial intelligence (AI) and machine learning (ML) count among the key technologies of the digital age, the debate on whether and how to regulate this technology raises some of the most fundamental current questions of lawyering in the digital age.[1] In fact, these issues are intensively debated and are particularly controversial. In Germany, for instance, two key institutional players have taken fundamentally different views. On the one hand, the influential 'Initiative D21', Germany's largest non-profit network, dedicated to a digital society and comprising key actors in business, politics, civil society, science and academia, prominently rejects the introduction of any new regulations for algorithms.[2] On the other hand, the Data Ethics Commission, a group of sixteen independent experts, created by the Federal Government, 'holds the view that regulation is necessary, and cannot be replaced by ethical principles'.[3] These positions seem to imply that an either-or decision needs to be taken with respect to AI – either ethical principles or legal regulation. At least, both the Initiative D21 and the report of the Data Ethics Commission are based on the understanding of ethical and legal rules as two entirely different categories, two categories that neither overlap nor interfere with one other. This chapter will query that understanding and argue that ethical guidelines and principles may in fact bring about significant legal implications, despite their ethical branding. If this is true, it seems misleading to disguise rules as purely ethical principles, thereby hiding their effective relevance and impact. The relevance of such a potential hardening of soft ethical principles cannot be overstated, given the current emergence of a multitude of such guidelines on AI, at various levels and by different players.

---

[1] For a recent comparative survey of the emerging regulatory and policy landscape in the field, see Law Library of Congress (ed.), 'Regulation of Artificial Intelligence in Selected Jurisdictions', www.loc.gov/law/help/artificial-intelligence/regulation-artificial-intelligence.pdf (accessed 14 February 2020); on conceptual questions, cf. also M. Scherer, 'Regulating Artificial Intelligence Systems: Risks, Challenges, Competencies and Strategies' (2016) 29 *Harvard Journal of Law & Technology* 353.

[2] Cf. Initiative D21, '#Algomon: 9 Leitlinien zum Ethischen Umgang mit Algorithmen-Monitoring', no. 5: 'Umfassende eigene gesetzliche Regelungen für algorithmische Systeme im Sinne einer eigenen Verordnung oder besonderen Gesetzes oder gar einer Änderung im Grundgesetz sind hingegen nicht zwingend erforderlich' (29 November 2019), https://initiatived21.de/app/uploads/2019/12/algomon_leitlinien_191216.pdf (accessed 14 February 2020).

[3] Data Ethics Commission, 'Opinion – Executive Summary' (October 2019) at 7, www.bmjv.de/SharedDocs/Downloads/DE/Themen/Fokusthemen/Gutachten_DEK_EN.pdf?__blob=publicationFile&v=1 (accessed 14 February 2020).

While all these rules concern AI, that subject matter is not very well defined.[4] There are only very few definitions of the term enshrined in legal provisions to date. In legal discourse, many other terms are used – robots, autonomous systems, machine learning, algorithms and artificial intelligence.[5] All these terms relate to technologies that are rapidly converging; they have similar meanings but are defined somewhat differently. One important element certainly concerns the distinction between algorithmic, deterministic behaviour, on the one hand, and autonomous behaviour, on the other.[6] The latter is enabled by ML and cannot be foreseen, so causation is difficult if not impossible to establish.[7] Given that it relates to causation, this distinction seems crucial from a legal perspective.[8] The very few legal definitions of AI, however, do not relate to this distinction: The legislation of New Jersey, for example, instead makes a comparison with human behaviour;[9] a recent bill that has been introduced in the US Senate is more explicit, but takes a very similar approach in substance.[10]

Even if there is no precise definition of the subject matter, our current economy and society increasingly face a multitude of applications of AI. Beyond Facebook, Google and Amazon's algorithms, robo-advisors take investment decisions, robo-lawyers give automated legal advice and robo-directors are in charge of business decisions in companies.[11] Of course, these robots have not yet replaced human advisors, lawyers and directors, but they are increasingly supporting and assisting human decision-making.[12] Decision-making in these fields has always been subject to various legal rules – in terms of securities and professional or company law. With the rise of AI, the question arises as to how these traditional, sector-specific legal rules can be applied, if

---

[4] See W. Barfield, 'Toward a Law of Artificial Intelligence' in W. Barfield and U. Pagallo (eds.), *Research Handbook on the Law of Artificial Intelligence* (Cheltenham: Edward Elgar Publishing, 2018) 2, 20–22 ('the problem with definitions').

[5] In a similar vein, for instance, European Group on Ethics in Science and New Technologies, 'Artificial Intelligence, Robotics and "Autonomous" Systems' (March 2018) (pertaining 'to a set of smart digital technologies that are rapidly converging and are often interrelated, connected or fully integrated, e.g. classical Artificial Intelligence, Machine Learning algorithms, Deep Learning and connectionist networks, generative adversarial networks, mechatronics and robotics'), http://ec.europa.eu/research/ege/pdf/ege_ai_statement_2018.pdf (accessed 14 February 2020). See n. 1.

[6] For a qualitative scale of algorithmic complexity, cf. A. Tutt, 'An FDA for Algorithms?' (2016) 69 *Administrative Law Review* 83 107.

[7] In more detail, for instance M. Hildebrandt, *Smart Technologies and the End(s) of Law* (Cheltenham: Edward Elgar Publishing, 2015) 22–27.

[8] F. Möslein, 'Regulating Robotic Conduct: On ESMA's New Guidelines and Beyond' in N. Aggarwal et al. (eds.), *Autonomous Systems and the Law* (Munich: Beck, Nomos, 2019) 48 (stating that 'this technological difference has an impact on the choice of a suitable regulatory design').

[9] Act concerning autonomous vehicles, NJ Senate No. 343, at no. 1 ('Artificial intelligence means the use of computers and related equipment to enable a machine to duplicate or mimic the behaviour of human beings.').

[10] Artificial Intelligence Initiative Act Draft Bill (S. 1558) sec 3 (1) ('The term "artificial intelligence" includes the following: (A) Any artificial system that performs tasks under varying and unpredictable circumstances without significant human oversight, or that can learn from experience and improve performance when exposed to data sets. (B) An artificial system developed in computer software, physical hardware, or other context that solves tasks requiring human-like perception, cognition, planning, learning, communication, or physical action. (C) An artificial system designed to think or act like a human, including cognitive architectures and neural networks. (D) A set of techniques, including machine learning, that is designed to approximate a cognitive task. (E) An artificial system designed to act rationally, including an intelligent software agent or embodied robot that achieves goals using perception, planning, reasoning, learning, communicating, decision making and acting.'), www.congress.gov/bill/116th-congress/senate-bill/1558 (accessed 14 February 2020).

[11] See, for instance, F. Möslein, 'Robots in the Boardroom: Artificial Intelligence and Corporate Law' in Barfield and Pagallo (eds.), n. 4 at 649; F. Möslein, 'Regulating Robotic Conduct: On ESMA's New Guidelines and Beyond' in Aggarwal et al. (eds.), n. 8 at 45.

[12] Information scientists usually distinguish between assisted, augmented and autonomous artificial intelligence, cf. A. Rao, 'AI Everywhere/Nowhere Part 3 – AI is AAAI (Assisted-Augmented-Autonomous Intelligence)' (2016), www.insurancethoughtleadership.com/ai-everywhere-and-nowhere-part-3/ (accessed 14 February 2020).

robots assist or even replace humans. For instance, how do rules specifying the duties of a director apply, if business decisions are not taken by human directors but decided by AI? So far, there is no respective case law on this question.[13] We lack any respective legal experience, simply because that technology is entirely new and disruptive. However, we will soon face new cases that will raise those precise, key questions in the different areas. In order to decide such cases, judges may think of following new guidelines that are currently about to develop, namely, rules on AI. These rules are not sector-specific, however, but technology-specific, and they are typically not enacted by the legislator but by various other rule-making bodies at different levels. The remainder of this chapter will give an overview, both on the variety of these rules (Section 5.2) and on their substance (Section 5.3), in order to discuss their legal relevance, both in general (Section 5.4) and with respect to specific fields of application (Section 5.5).

5.2 VARIETY OF EMERGING RULES

5.2.1 *International Level*

Different institutions and bodies are currently discussing and negotiating the need for regulation in the field of AI. At the international level, there are various AI-related initiatives of both the G7 and the G20, the United Nations and in particular the Organization for Economic Cooperation and Development (OECD). However, it has not been possible to establish generally accepted guidelines yet.

More specifically, a G7 ministerial conference issued a declaration on AI in March 2018.[14] This declaration served as the basis for a multi-stakeholder conference that tried to foster societal trust in AI and evolve a joint vision of a human-centred AI.[15] Moreover, Japan, the host country of the G20 meeting that took place in Osaka in June 2019, put AI on the agenda.[16] The United Nations, on the other hand, established an agency to monitor developments in the field of AI worldwide (UNICRI Centre for Artificial Intelligence and Robotics, based at The Hague).[17] Within the scope of the *AI for Good Global Summits*, they also analyse the potential of AI technologies with regard to global sustainability and develop strategies both to ensure a trustworthy, secure and integrative development of the relevant technologies and to safeguard equal access.[18] Despite these efforts, almost no specific regulations have emerged from these initiatives.[19]

A more specific regulatory instrument has recently been published by the OECD, namely, the Recommendation of the Council on Artificial Intelligence of 22 May 2019.[20] In fact, this

---

[13] For more detail on the challenges of AI for established law, cf. W. Barfield, 'Toward a Law of Artificial Intelligence' in Barfield and Pagallo (eds.), n. 4 at 2, 22–35.

[14] G7, 'G7 Ministers' Statement on Artificial Intelligence' (28 March 2018), www.g8.utoronto.ca/employment/2018-labour-annex-b-en.html (accessed 14 February 2020).

[15] G7, 'G7 Multistakeholder Conference on Artificial Intelligence: Final Summary Report' (6 December 2018), www.ic.gc.ca/eic/site/133.nsf/eng/00007.html (accessed 14 February 2020).

[16] See, for instance, Eric Johnston, 'With Six Months to Go until G20 Summit in Osaka, Japan Sets out Its Agenda' *Japan Times* (23 December 2018), www.japantimes.co.jp/news/2018/12/23/national/politics-diplomacy/six-months-go-g20-summit-osaka-japan-sets-agenda/.

[17] For more information, see www.unicri.it/topics/ai_robotics/centre/ (accessed 14 February 2020).

[18] Cf. 'Ensure trusted, safe and inclusive development of AI technologies and equitable access to their benefits', https://aiforgood.itu.int/ (accessed 14 February 2020).

[19] One of the few more specific claims concerns the prohibition of autonomous weapon systems, cf. https://news.un.org/en/story/2019/03/1035381 (accessed 14 February 2020).

[20] OECD, 'Recommendation of the Council on Artificial Intelligence' (22 May 2019), https://legalinstruments.oecd.org/en/instruments/OECD-LEGAL-0449 (accessed 14 January 2020).

recommendation establishes the first formal recognition of AI principles by a large number of governments: in addition to the thirty-six member states, six other states have also signed the recommendation.[21] Moreover, the final declaration of the Osaka Summit expresses an endorsement by all G20 member states.[22] In addition to the actual principles, the document incorporates five political recommendations, for example, to facilitate AI-related investments or to promote corresponding ecosystems. The principles have been developed since September 2018 and were drafted by a group of more than fifty experts, in part representatives from governments, in part exponents of business, labour, civil society and academia. Recommendations of the OECD are not legally binding, but in the past they have often formed the basis for the development of international standards, and have also served as guidelines for governments when drafting national legislations.[23] Due to the competence of the experts involved and formal governmental support, one can also expect the 2019 OECD AI recommendations to have a significant impact in the future, comparable with that of the 1999 OECD Corporate Governance Principles.[24]

5.2.2 *European Level*

At the European level, a High-Level Expert Group on AI, whose fifty-two members also represent a wide range of stakeholders, was established by the European Commission in June 2018.[25] Six months later, in December 2018, the group published a draft on ethics guidelines; after intensive consultation and exchange with representatives of the member states, these guidelines were released on 8 April 2019 in a revised version.[26] The guidelines are being evaluated in a piloting process.[27] In terms of content, they set out requirements for trustworthy AI. They also discuss various technical and non-technical options as to how these requirements could be implemented and evaluated, including questions of regulation, standardisation and certification. On the other hand, the drafters of the guidelines place the emphasis on the non-mandatory character of the guidelines and stress that they merely formulate ethical standards and requirements for the technical robustness of AI systems: 'The Guidelines do not explicitly

---

[21] Other countries beyond the OECD that have already adhered to the AI Principles include Argentina, Brazil, Colombia, Costa Rica, Peru and Romania.

[22] G20, 'G20 Ministerial Statement on Trade and Digital Economy' (9 June 2019) at 3ff and in the Annex, https://trade.ec.europa.eu/doclib/docs/2019/june/tradoc_157920.pdf (accessed 14 February 2020).

[23] See N. Bonucci, 'The Legal Status of an OECD Act and the Procedure for Its Adoption' at 1: 'Recommendations are not legally binding, but practice accords them great moral force as representing the political will of Member countries and there is an expectation that Member countries will do their utmost to fully implement a Recommendation', www.oecd.org/education/skills-beyond-school/31691605.pdf (accessed 14 February 2020).

[24] More intensively on the importance of that instrument, for instance, P. Hommelhoff, 'OECD-Principles on Corporate Governance' (2001) *Zeitschrift für Unternehmens- und Gesellschaftsrecht* 238 239ff.; K. Hopt, 'Vergleichende Corporate Governance' (2011) 175 *Zeitschrift für das gesamte Handels- und Wirtschaftsrecht* 444 455–461.

[25] Cf. Commission, 'Commission Appoints Expert Group on AI and Launches European AI Alliance' (14 June 2018), https://ec.europa.eu/digital-single-market/en/news/commission-appoints-expert-group-ai-and-launches-european-ai-alliance (accessed 14 February 2020); the starting point was Commission, 'Artificial Intelligence for Europe', (Communication) COM(2018) 237 final 17.

[26] Commission, 'Guidelines for Trustworthy AI' (8 April 2018) in both (draft and final) versions are available at https://ec.europa.eu/futurium/en/ai-alliance-consultation/guidelines#Top (accessed 14 February 2020). An additional review and update was planned for early 2020, cf. Commission, 'Building Trust in Human-Centric Artificial Intelligence' (Communication) COM(2019) 168 final 7.

[27] Commission, 'EU Artificial Intelligence Ethics Checklist Ready for Testing As New Policy Recommendations Are Published' (26 June 2019), https://ec.europa.eu/digital-single-market/en/news/eu-artificial-intelligence-ethics-checklist-ready-testing-new-policy-recommendations-are (accessed 14 February 2020).

deal with the first component of trustworthy AI (lawful AI), but instead aim to offer guidance on fostering and securing the second and third components (ethical and robust AI)'.[28] Like the OECD recommendation, it is nonetheless likely that the guidelines might have a significant impact on the legal assessment of artificial intelligence.

With its communication 'Building Trust in Human Centric Artificial Intelligence', published at the same time as the guidelines,[29] the European Commission underlined the guidelines' key requirements, albeit with partially abridged and revised wording.[30] Although the European Commission clarifies once again the non-binding character of the guidelines, it also assigns them an important role on the way 'towards international AI ethics guidelines'.[31] It even claims a 'leadership role in developing international AI guidelines', for instance with respect to 'relevant standardisation activities in international standards development organisations'.[32] The Commission clearly aims at developing international standards on how AI is used and developed. Against this background, the future impact of these guidelines – or at least of the (rephrased) key requirements as formulated in the Commission's communication – must not be underestimated.

5.2.3 National Level

At the national level, the German legislator has not yet provided any general sets of rules on AI, apart from technology- and industry-specific provisions. One specific provision of the German Securities Trading Act, for instance, concerns algorithms: Section 80 para 2 WpHG (formerly: Section 33 para 1a WpHG), introduced in 2013 by the Act on the Prevention of Risks and Abuse in High-Frequency Trading (High-Frequency Trading Act) and based on Art. 17 of the Directive on markets in financial instruments (MiFID II),[33] regulates algorithmic trading in financial instruments. It provides for a number of individual duties that investment service providers engaging in such trading have to follow.[34] Whether or not the rule also applies by analogy to robo-advice (or other 'robo cases') has been a matter of controversy.[35] At least, the organisational requirements that are laid down in this provision are comparable to those incorporated in the international and European AI guidelines: in order to comply with these requirements, investment service providers must ensure that the respective systems are designed in a technically reliable, that is, stable way. For example, the systems must provide precautionary measures in case of technical failure. Secondly, the systems must provide for permanent and effective arrangements against misuse, in order to ensure that no irregular trading takes place. Thirdly, investment service providers using such systems must be able to

---

[28] Commission, 'Guidelines for Trustworthy AI' (8 April 2018) at 6, https://ec.europa.eu/futurium/en/ai-alliance-consultation/guidelines#Top (accessed 14 February 2020).
[29] Commission, 'Building Trust in Human-Centric Artificial Intelligence' (Communication) COM(2019) 168 final.
[30] In more detail, for instance E. Gillen, 'Stets zu Diensten – EU-Kommission korrigiert die "Ethik-Leitlinien für eine vertrauenswürdige KI," die Experten in ihrem Auftrag ausgearbeitet haben', Frankfurter Allgemeine Zeitung (Frankfurt, 24 April 2019) 13.
[31] Commission, n. 29 at 9ff.
[32] Ibid. at 8ff.
[33] Directive 2014/65/EU of the European Parliament and of the Council of 15 May 2014 on markets in financial instruments and amending Directive 2002/92/EC and Directive 2011/61/EU, OJ L 173/2014 at 349.
[34] Cf. the commentaries on the section, for example Andreas Fuchs, 'Commentary on § 33' in Andreas Fuchs (ed.), *Wertpapierhandelsgesetz*, 2nd ed. (Munich: Beck, 2016) § 33, paras 144a–144m.
[35] See, for instance F. Möslein and A. Lordt, 'Rechtsfragen des Robo-Advice' (2017) *Zeitschrift für Wirtschaftsrecht* 793 803.

understand and control the respective algorithms. Finally, the provider must also document each individual modification.[36]

At a broader level, the Federal Government of Germany has recently announced future AI-specific regulatory initiatives in its Artificial Intelligence Strategy. For example, it indicated its intention to review the legal framework for regulatory gaps regarding algorithm- and AI-based decisions, services and products and, if necessary, to adapt certain rules to make them verifiable with regard to potential unlawful discrimination.[37] The Federal Government paid particular attention to including ethical standards in the entire development, testing and application process of AI systems (the so-called *ethics by, in and for design* approach); however it has yet to define specific standards.[38] That said, the government has at least revealed its general intentions by announcing that studies will be carried out to establish the transparency, traceability and verifiability of AI systems, in order to provide effective protection against distortions, discrimination, manipulation or other abuses, especially when algorithm-based forecasting and decision-making systems are used.[39] By this token, the German Federal Government's initiative takes the principles of European ethics guidelines into account.[40] In 2018, the German Federal Government had already appointed the Data Ethics Commission with the mission to provide recommendations for action and propose regulatory options.[41] In addition, technical and industry-specific sets of rules have been developed, such as the guidelines for programming automated driving systems, elaborated by the Ethics Commission for Automated and Networked Driving.[42]

5.2.4 Self-Regulation

In addition to these various state activities, a number of individual companies have developed sets of rules dealing with AI.[43] Business and other stakeholder associations are working on similar rulebooks. Recent examples of such regulatory activities include, for instance, the quality mark of the German Artificial Intelligence Association (Bundesverband Künstliche Intelligenz), the guidelines of the German Digital Economy Association (Bundesverband Digitale Wirtschaft)

---

[36] For more detail, see E. Jaskulla, 'Das deutsche Hochfrequenzhandelsgesetz – eine Herausforderung für Handelsteilnehmer, Börsen und Multilaterale Handelssysteme' (2013) *Zeitschrift für Bank- und Kapitalmarktrecht* 221 230ff.; J. Kindermann and B. Coridaß, 'Der rechtliche Rahmen des algorithmischen Handels inklusive des Hochfrequenzhandels' (2014) *Zeitschrift für Bankrecht und Bankwirtschaft* 178 180–183; T. Schultheiß, 'Die Neuerungen im Hochfrequenzhandel' (2013) *Zeitschrift für Wirtschafts- und Bankrecht* 596 601.

[37] Bundesregierung, 'Strategie Künstliche Intelligenz' (November 2018) at 38. The German version is available at www.bmbf.de/files/Nationale_KI-Strategie.pdf (accessed 14 February 2020). For a brief summary in English, cf. the press release 'Federal Government Adopts Artificial Intelligence Strategy', Berlin (16 November 2019), www.bmwi.de/Redaktion/EN/Pressemitteilungen/2018/20181116-federal-government-adopts-artificial-intelligence-strategy.html (accessed 14 February 2020).

[38] Bundesregierung, n. 37 at 16, 38 and 41. For the concepts themselves, see H. van der Loos, 'Ethics by Design: A Conceptual Approach to Personal and Service Robot Systems', *Proceedings of the IEEE Conference on Robotics and Automation, Workshop on Roboethics, Rome* (14 April 2007), https://pdfs.semanticscholar.org/7781/ce01265c04fcfab340493e331e5c8a06153d.pdf (accessed 14 February 2020); cf. also V. Dignum, 'Ethics in Artificial Intelligence' (2018) 20 *Ethics and Information Technology* 1 (and further contributions in the same issue).

[39] Bundesregierung, n. 37 at 39.

[40] Cf. ibid.

[41] See n. 3.

[42] These guidelines ('Leitlinien für die Programmierung automatisierter Fahrzeugsysteme' [June 2017]) are available at www.bmvi.de/SharedDocs/DE/Publikationen/DG/bericht-der-ethik-kommission.html (accessed 14 February 2020).

[43] See, for instance, the 'Guidelines for Artificial Intelligence' (2018) as elaborated by Deutsche Telekom, www.telekom.com/en/company/digital-responsibility/details/artificial-intelligence-ai-guideline-524366 (accessed 14 February 2020).

and, on an international level, the Global Policy Framework of the International Technology Law Association, all of them published in the spring of 2019.[44]

In summary, this overview of regulatory activities at various levels demonstrates an extremely dynamic development of standards and other normative measures. This process is resulting in a correspondingly wide range of different AI guidelines. The first steps towards a categorisation and systematisation of the various sets of rules have already been made: for example, the Berkman Klein Center for Internet and Society at Harvard University has begun to map a variety of regulatory approaches.[45] More specifically, both the OECD principles and the EU initiative can be regarded as attempts to recapture those ongoing regulatory dynamics in the field of AI, previously dominated by entrepreneurial self-regulation. It also attempts to steer rulemaking towards a more comprehensive approach, in terms of both content and scope but also towards a more official, sovereign character.[46]

5.3 CONVERGING SUBSTANCE OF EMERGING RULES

In order to describe the substantive content of these emerging regulatory regimes on the use of AI, it may suffice to consider solely the OECD principles and the EU initiative. Due to the political importance of their respective rule-makers, these two regimes are likely to gain the most significant influence in the future. Furthermore, in light of the considerable substantive similarities between these two regulations, they can be examined together, notwithstanding specific differences in detail. The key regulatory principles that are contained within these two regimes form, moreover, part of many other principles, as the mapping exercise of the Berkman Klein Center clearly illustrates.[47]

Already, the respective definitions of the term AI are similar in both sets of rules; they also define the substantive scope of application. In the preamble, the OECD principles describe AI systems as any 'machine-based system that can, for a given set of human-defined objectives, make predictions, recommendations, or decisions influencing real or virtual environments', regardless of the specific level of autonomy which may vary.[48] As the starting point of the EU initiative, the Commission defines the concept of AI quite similarly as 'systems that display intelligent behaviour by analysing their environment and taking actions – with some degree of autonomy – to achieve specific goals'; furthermore, it clarifies that these systems can be both software-based and embedded in hardware.[49] The more precise definition suggested by the expert group in its guidelines is even more in line with OECD principles.[50]

---

[44] Regarding these three instruments, see https://ki-verband.de/wp-content/uploads/2019/02/KIBV_Guetesiegel.pdf, www.bvdw.org/themen/publikationen/detail/artikel/bvdw-8-leitlinien-ki/ and www.itechlaw.org/ResponsibleAI (all accessed 14 February 2020).
[45] In detail and with a visual mapping, https://ai-hr.cyber.harvard.edu/ (accessed 14 February 2020).
[46] F. Möslein, 'Vertrauenswürdigkeit künstlicher Intelligenz und Corporate Governance' (2019) Issue II *Audit Committee Quarterly* 16.
[47] See 'Privacy, Accountability, Safety and Security, Transparency and Explainability, Fairness and Non-discrimination, Human Control of Technology, Professional Responsibility, Promotion of Human Values, Human Rights', differentiating between the categories, https://ai-hr.cyber.harvard.edu/images/primp-viz.pdf (accessed 14 February 2020).
[48] OECD, n. 20 at I., 1st indent.
[49] Commission, 'Artificial Intelligence for Europe', (Communication) COM(2018)237 final 1.
[50] Cf. High-Level Expert Group on Artificial Intelligence, 'A Definition of AI: Main Capabilities and Scientific Disciplines' (8 April 2019) at 6: 'Artificial intelligence (AI) systems are software (and possibly also hardware) systems designed by humans that, given a complex goal, act in the physical or digital dimension by perceiving their environment through data acquisition, interpreting the collected structured or unstructured data, reasoning on the knowledge, or processing the information, derived from this data and deciding the best action(s) to take to achieve the

Both definitions have several elements in common, including (1) the technical basis (machine-based or software-supported or embedded in hardware), (2) the finality (complex goals defined or determined by humans) and (3) the potential influence of the systems concerned (impact on the real or virtual environment or goal orientation). Additionally, both definitions (4) do not determine to which degree the respective systems must be able to act autonomously to meet the definition's requirements. However, since the wording of either definition requires a minimum degree of autonomy, deterministic systems are likely to be beyond the scope of applicability of the respective rules.[51] With regard to possible (5) forms of action, executed by artificial intelligence, the OECD principles list predictions, recommendations and decisions, whereas the EU Commission refers, in a less specific way, to analysis and action.

5.3.1 Control and Controllability

The first group of rules concerns the control and controllability of the technologies in use. These rules include the fundamental principle of granting priority to human action and supervision. Such a requirement of 'human agency and oversight' is particularly emphasised by the European Commission.[52] Likewise, although less emphatically, the OECD principles mention the requirement of human centricity.[53] This principle is particularly important because it defines the relationship between human and technical autonomy by subordinating the latter to the former, in order to give fundamental priority to human action and human values (including the rule of law, human rights and democratic values).[54] Depending on the respective circumstances, however, it will often be difficult to decide which degree of autonomous decisions relating to AI is in accordance with this principle: in order to comply, does each investment decision made by an AI-driven robo-advisor require human supervision? Or does that requirement depend on the amount of money at stake? Or is human involvement with the single, operative investment decision totally unnecessary and is it sufficient if humans decide on the fundamental investment strategy? The Commission distinguishes between the concepts of a 'human-in-the-loop', 'human-on-the-loop' and a 'human-in-command', each of which represents a different degree of human involvement in AI decision-making. This distinction tentatively signals that overall human control is, in general, sufficient.[55] If this were the case, a purely machine-based decision to reinvest a comparatively small dividend would, for instance, still be compatible with the basic principle, whereas a purely machine-controlled investment strategy would not comply.

The principle of technical robustness and safety can be conceptualised as the other side of the coin:[56] formulated almost identically in both sets of rules, it stipulates that there must not only be the possibility of human supervision, but that human actors are responsible for the respective technical systems, and that they are required to ensure the reliability of these systems. Basically, the principle obliges providers of AI technologies to take precautionary measures that protect the

---

given goal. AI systems can either use symbolic rules or learn a numeric model, and they can also adapt their behaviour by analysing how the environment is affected by their previous actions.' https://ec.europa.eu/digital-single-market/en/news/definition-artificial-intelligence-main-capabilities-and-scientific-disciplines (accessed 14 February 2020).

[51] See n. 7. It is nonetheless surprising that neither the OECD principles nor the European Commission explicitly refer to the key criterion of self-learning, as opposed to the definition of the European expert group.

[52] Commission, n. 29 at 4 (key requirement no. I).

[53] OECD, n. 20 at IV.1.2 ('Human-centred values and fairness').

[54] Explicitly, ibid. at IV.1.2.a.

[55] Commission, n. 29 at 4 (in particular n. 13: 'human intervention in every decision cycle of the system … in many cases … [is] neither possible nor desirable').

[56] Ibid. at 4ff. (key requirement no. II); OECD, n. 20 at IV.1.4.

systems in use against technical attacks or manipulation attempts, to install risk management systems including integrated protective measures and to adequately document technical safety. With regard to other high-risk technologies, comparable requirements concerning robustness and safety are well known and stipulated within legal guidelines, for instance, in legislation relating to nuclear energy.[57] As mentioned previously, the same applies to algorithmic trading. The conceivable consequences of a potential default or even crash of large computer systems are likely to be as far reaching as those stemming from other high-risk technologies.[58] On this basis, one can therefore argue in favour of the application of similar general guidelines for AI technologies.

5.3.2 Disclosure

Supporting the obligation to document technical processes for verifiability and traceability purposes, another set of requirements deals with issues concerning disclosure, including the principle of transparency and explainability of AI systems.[59] This principle requires providers not only to record and document algorithmic decision processes, but also to explain these processes to the persons involved in a comprehensive manner. According to the European Commission, the providers' duty to safeguard the explainability of the algorithmic decision-making process is meant to ensure 'not just data and system transparency, but also business model transparency'.[60] Taking the example of providers of robo-advice, an obligation of such disclosure entails far-reaching consequences, as it basically requires detailed explanations of the investment calculations and risk models that underly the robo-decisions. Such disclosure of business models would affect the providers' right to protect business and trade secrets. That right is not only of crucial importance to the competitive markets, especially in the financial sector; it is also expressly protected by the European Trade Secrets Directive.[61] It may be assumed that due to these conflicting legal provisions, the respective principle is limited to a duty to explain and thereby disclose processes merely 'to the extent possible', or as far as the information concerned is relevant and adequate.[62]

Accountability for AI systems, as defined by the OECD principles and the European Commission,[63] builds on disclosure but goes beyond this. It also requires providers to take responsibility for AI systems. Moreover, it necessitates their verifiability, for example, by involving internal and external inspections by auditors.[64] The principle specifically aims at evaluation,

---

[57] Cf., for instance, Gerald Spindler, *Unternehmensorganisationspflichten* (Cologne: Heymann, 2001) 17–41.
[58] On the dangers (also) of algorithmic trading, cf. T. Foucault and S. Moinas, 'Is Trading Fast Dangerous?' in W. Mattli (ed.), *Global Algorithmic Capital Markets* (Oxford: Oxford University Press, 2019) 9.
[59] Commission, n. 29 at 5 (key requirement no. IV); OECD, n. 20 at IV.1.3. In general, on explainability of algorithms, see Joshua A. Kroll et al., 'Accountable Algorithms' (2016–2017)165 *University of Pennsylvania Law Review* 633; P. Hacker et al., 'Explainable AI under Contract and Tort Law: legal Incentives and Technical Challenges' (2020) *Artificial Intelligence Law*, doi.org/10.1007/s10506–020-09260-6 (accessed 14 February 2020).
[60] Cf. again Commission, n. 29 at 5.
[61] Directive (EU) 2016/943 of the European Parliament and of the Council of 8 June 2016 on the protection of undisclosed know-how and business information (trade secrets) against their unlawful acquisition, use and disclosure [2016] OJ L 157/1; on the transposition in Germany, cf., for instance, A. Ohly, 'Das neue Geschäftsgeheimnisgesetz im Überblick' (2019) *Gewerblicher Rechtsschutz und Urheberrecht* 441; on the fundamental tension, see also W. Schön, 'Geheimnisschutz und Wettbewerb – eine Einführung' in W. Schön (ed.), *Rechnungslegung und Wettbewerbsschutz im deutschen und europäischen Recht* (Berlin: Springer, 2008) 1.
[62] Commission, n. 29 at 5 accordingly; OECD, n. 20 at IV.1.3.
[63] Commission, n. 29 at 6 (key requirement VII); OECD, n. 20 at IV.1.5.
[64] Commission, n. 29 at 6.

documentation and the minimisation of potential negative impacts of AI systems.[65] Accountability has, however, no specific, substantive content. It is rather an instrument to ensure the enforceability of other obligations, by serving as an effective procedural mechanism. In this vein, the EU Commission simply stresses that it aims at foreseeing 'accessible mechanisms ... that ensure adequate redress'.[66]

5.3.3 Safeguarding Individual Rights

As opposed to the aforementioned accountability principle, the requirements serving the purpose of protecting individual rights are of a more substantive nature. While the OECD principles enumerate 'freedom, dignity and autonomy, privacy and data protection, non-discrimination and equality, diversity, fairness, social justice and internationally recognised labour rights' in this respect,[67] the European Commission's communication solely focuses on 'privacy and data governance' and 'diversity, non-discrimination and fairness' when it comes to protecting individual rights.[68] Its communication, on the other hand, goes into much more detail regarding these two aspects. For example, it not only requires AI providers to act in accordance with data protection provisions, but also obliges them to guarantee the integrity of the data used. Furthermore, the communication deals with questions concerning regulation and control of access to data.[69] Such stipulations might imply far-reaching consequences for AI applications in practice, for instance, for robo-advisors, since they are likely to apply not only to customer data, but also to market data and information on investment instruments. Accordingly, providers must ensure that they do not rely on data that contains 'inaccuracies, errors and mistakes'.[70]

The diversity, non-discrimination and fairness requirement amount to a duty to avoid (unintentional) data-based distortions.[71] In the field of robo-advice, for instance, providers could infringe this principle if they coincidentally overemphasise domestic financial instruments or shares in a particular sector. By this token, the principle also interacts with the duty of loyalty of asset managers.[72] Similar effects may arise in company law, with respect to directors' duties. As a consequence, specific rules relating to AI and sector-specific provisions on equal treatment may overlap. They may even clash, if, for example, (only) the duty of loyalty of asset managers provides for exceptions in specific cases. Finally, the principle also concerns the internal organisation of AI providers, for example by calling for the formation of 'diverse design teams' and the establishment of 'mechanisms ensuring participation'.[73]

5.3.4 Public Good Requirements

Both sets of rules are not only aiming at guaranteeing individual rights, but also taking into account the potential societal and environmental impact of AI systems and providers.

---

[65] Ibid.
[66] Ibid.
[67] OECD, n. 20 at IV.1.2.a.
[68] Commission, n. 29 at 5ff. (key requirements III and V).
[69] In this vein, ibid. at 6 (key requirement III).
[70] Cf. ibid.
[71] Ibid. at 7 (key requirement V).
[72] For more specifically on this duty and in various fields of application, see F. Möslein, 'Kapitel 34 (Vermögensverwaltung)' in K. Langenbucher, D. Bliesener and G. Spindler (eds.), *Bankrechts-Kommentar*, 2nd ed. (Munich: Beck, 2016) paras 33–38.
[73] Commission, n. 29 at 6 (key requirement V).

The OECD principles, for example, state that stakeholders should 'proactively engage in responsible stewardship of trustworthy AI in pursuit of beneficial outcomes for people and the planet ... thus invigorating inclusive growth, sustainable development and well-being'.[74] Likewise, the EU Commission calls for the encouragement of the sustainability and ecological responsibility of AI systems as well as the consideration of their social impact.[75] The more vaguely these ideas are formulated, the more questionable and problematic their potential effects are with regard to specific questions, such as: Do these rules result in a duty to express a preference for sustainable corporate strategies or investment instruments to non-sustainable ones?[76] Are AI providers obliged to offer services to disadvantaged groups ('AI for Everyone')?[77] If the answer to these questions were positive, the consequences would be dramatic. For example, the requirement of a minimum investment, typically required by robo-advisors, would seem questionable in light of its social effects. Such a requirement would even be discriminatory in the sense that no such restrictions apply to traditional human (investment) advisors or corporate directors.

5.4 LEGAL RELEVANCE

5.4.1 Distinguishing between Law and Ethics

Against the background of these different, emerging AI rules and their substantive, potentially far-reaching and intrusive contents, the decisive, overarching question concerns the regulatory intensity of these rules: What is their legal relevance? More specifically, this question concerns the means of enforcement: if those guidelines were exclusively ethical standards, violations of their content might only result in social sanctions, such as loss of reputation. Legal sanctions such as judicial enforcement would, on the other hand, seem to be excluded.[78] Conversely, if these guidelines were formal and counted among the sources of law, violations could very well result in legal sanctions, either as a result of private lawsuits (private enforcement) or enforcement by state agencies (public enforcement).[79] For instance, if AI technologies violate non-discrimination rules, either a private party could claim damages, or public agencies could impose sanctions. Should such legal sanctions apply, the specific substantive questions of substantive law (such as whether the guidelines require advice to be given to disadvantaged investor groups) obviously gain tremendous relevance.

---

[74] OECD, n. 20 at IV.1.1.
[75] Commission, n. 29 at 7 (key requirement VI).
[76] In a similar vein, see Commission, 'Financing Sustainable Growth' (Action Plan) COM (2018) 97 final; in detail: F. Möslein and A. Mittwoch, 'Der Europäische Aktionsplan zur Finanzierung nachhaltigen Wachstums' (2019) *Zeitschrift für Wirtschafts- und Bankrecht* 481.
[77] Similar to claims of bank accounts for everybody (now laid down in Article 16 of Directive 2014/92/EU on the comparability of fees related to payment accounts, payment account switching and access to payment accounts with basic features, providing for a right of access to a payment account with basic features), for more detail, see T. Günther, 'Girokonto für jedermann?' (2014) *Zeitschrift für Wirtschafts- und Bankrecht* 1369.
[78] On the fundamental relationship between law and ethics, see, for instance, W. Bradley Wendel, *Ethics and Law – An Introduction* (Cambridge: Cambridge University Press, 2014) 62–66; cf. also D. von der Pfordten, 'Zur Differenzierung von Recht, Moral und Ethik' in J. Sandkühler (ed.), *Recht und Moral* (Hamburg: Meiner Verlag, 2010) 33; S. Vöneky, *Recht, Moral und Ethik*, (Tübingen: Mohr Siebeck, 2010).
[79] For a discussion of (the efficiency of) public and private enforcement, see W. Landes and R. Posner, 'The Private Enforcement of Law' (1975) 4 *Journal of Legal Studies* 1; cf. also D. Poelzig, 'Aufsichts- und zivilrechtliche Regeldurchsetzung – Abstimmung und Verzahnung am Beispiel von Kartell- und Kapitalmarktrecht' in F. Möslein (ed.), *Regelsetzung im Privatrecht* (Tübingen: Mohr Siebeck, 2019) 227; J. Forschner, *Wechselwirkungen von Aufsichtsrecht und Zivilrecht* (Tübingen: Mohr Siebeck, 2013) 63–80.

5.4.2 Formal Classification

From a formal perspective, the classification of these emerging rules on AI seems to be clear. The instruments in which these rules are implemented are of a non-binding character: both the OECD recommendations and the Ethics Guidelines of the High-Level Group of Experts – as well as the subsequent communication of the European Commission – have neither formal legal status nor direct, legally binding effect. The OECD cannot enact official legal acts with legal effects in its member states from the outset. Moreover, its guidelines on AI form part of a (non-binding) recommendation within the meaning of Article 5 lit. c of the OECD Convention.[80] The European Union, on the other hand, does in fact have the opportunity to adopt official legal acts, either as directly applicable regulations or in the form of directives that are addressed to the member states and require transposition (cf. Art. 288 TFEU).[81] The AI guidelines, however, are not incorporated into such a legislative act; they were merely issued in a communication of the European Commission. Communications have at best very limited legal effects; in any case, their content cannot be enforced. Due to their form alone, both guidelines are therefore not legally binding. Moreover, they do not claim to exert such effects by their wording. Rather, the EU Commission's communication expressly states that the guidelines drawn up by the High-Level Expert Group on AI are 'non-binding and as such do not create any new legal obligations'.[82] Similarly, the OECD instrument is only intended to be a recommendation for the signatory states to promote and transpose its principles; in addition, however, it 'calls on all AI actors to promote and implement' its principles 'according to their respective roles'.[83]

5.4.3 Effective Impact

However, the lack of formal legislative quality does not completely exclude certain, albeit limited, legal effects. In German legal theory, a distinction is made between sources of law and sources of legal knowledge (*Rechtsgeltungs- und Rechtserkenntnisquellen*): the second category includes all factors that are able to develop an influence on objective law, by contributing to the knowledge of the applicable law without exerting any legal effects themselves. Examples of such sources of legal knowledge are legal literature, administrative practice or general legal awareness (and in civil law countries, also case law).[84] In the future, the OECD recommendations and the Guidelines of the High-Level Expert Group could develop similar effects, because as ethical standards, they aim to shape the general sense of right and wrong. Indications of such legal effects can also be found in the wording of these texts. The communication of the European Commission, irrespective of its assertion of the non-binding character of the guidelines, states, for example, that 'when unjust adverse impact occurs, accessible mechanisms should be foreseen that ensure adequate redress'.[85]

---

[80] Cf. P. Carroll and A. Kellow, *The OECD: A Study of Organisational Adaption* (Cheltenham: Edward Elgar Publishing, 2011) 13: 'A recommendation is not binding but represents a policy commitment by governments, relying for its force upon peer group pressure and the adverse impact upon reputation that might follow if a country did not implement the recommendation.'

[81] For more detail on types of EU instruments (both binding and non-binding), see B. de Witte and B. Smulders, 'Sources of European Union Law' in P. Kuijper et al. (eds.), *The Law of the European Union*, 5th ed. (Deventer: Wolters Kluwer, 2018) 193, 198–221.

[82] Commission, n. 29 at 3.

[83] OECD, n. 20 at iii.

[84] See, for instance, B. Rüthers, C. Fischer and A. Birk, *Rechtstheorie*, 10th ed. (Munich: Beck, 2018) para 217; cf. also C.-W. Canaris, *Systemdenken und Systembegriff* (Berlin: Duncker & Humblot, 1983) 69–72.

[85] Commission, n. 29 at 6.

Certain legal obligations are therefore quite intentional, even if they are not directly established by the guidelines themselves ('as such').

The phenomenon of so-called soft law, having factual legal effects, is well-known in many other contexts and is often referred to as 'the hardening of soft law'.[86] Take corporate governance codes as an example: beyond the simple reputation mechanism, other forms of enforceability have been established or are being discussed, namely, the contestability of general meeting resolutions based on incorrect declarations of conformity, on the one hand, and the legal responsibility of company management for such declarations, on the other hand.[87] Accordingly, the discussion of the legal relevance of apparently non-binding AI rules must not stop with the determination of the lack of formal legal quality. Instead, the possible legal impact of such a codification, as a source of legal knowledge, needs to be explored: By what means can such apparently non-binding rules have an impact on applicable law and what are the possible gateways that indirectly allocate legal effects to these guidelines?

5.5 FIELDS OF APPLICATION

These effects and mechanisms can be analysed in all three different fields that have been mentioned earlier, namely, robo-advisors, robo-directors and robo-lawyers. The respective areas of law – in particular company law, securities law and rules of professional conduct – contain important gateways that make a legal hardening of AI ethical guidelines possible and in fact very likely.[88] Such a hardening will not even require any action by lawmakers, but it is likely to occur whenever courts have to decide new cases that involve specific actions of robo-advisors, robo-lawyers or robo-directors. The most important transmission belt by which ethical rules develop into legal obligations will relate to the respective duties – investment advisors' duties, directors' duties of care and loyalty and lawyers' duties. These duties are often of a very vague character: they are broad standards rather than concrete and precise rules.[89] This vagueness opens up opportunities for the implementation of extra-legal rules. Most of the aforementioned ethical standards are likely to evolve into legal obligations and requirements in this manner.

5.5.1 Company Law (Robo-directors)

In company law, the liability of board members who delegate business decisions to AI technologies depends largely on the scope and intensity of their duty to monitor. In most jurisdictions,

---

[86] Cf., for instance, R. Karmel and C. Kelly, 'The Hardening of Soft Law in Securities Regulation' (2009) 34 *Brooklyn Journal of International Law* 883.
[87] For an account of the intensive debate under German law, see P. Mülbert and A. Wilhelm, 'Grundfragen des deutschen Corporate Governance Kodex und der Entsprechenserklärung nach § 161 AktG' (2012) 176 *Zeitschrift für das gesamte Handels- und Wirtschaftsrecht* 286 291ff.; F. Möslein, 'Genuine Self-regulation in Germany – Drawing the Line' in H. Baum, M. Bälz and M. Dernauer (eds.), *Self-Regulation in Private Law in Japan and Germany*, Journal of Japanese Law, Special Issue 10 (Cologne: Heymann, 2018) 83, 100–105 (with further references).
[88] For more detail on the first two of these fields, see F. Möslein 'Leitlinien für den Einsatz künstlicher Intelligenz' in D. Linardatos (ed.), *Rechtshandbuch Robo-Advice* (Munich: Beck, Vahlen, 2020) 58; F. Möslein, 'Aktienrechtliche Leitungsverantwortung beim Einsatz künstlicher Intelligenz' in M. Kaulartz and T. Braegelmann, *Rechtshandbuch Artificial Intelligence und Machine Learning* (Munich: Beck, Vahlen, 2020); F. Möslein, 'Vertrauenswürdigkeit künstlicher Intelligenz und Corporate Governance' (2019) 2 *Audit Committee Quarterly* 2.
[89] On the fundamental distinction between rules and standards, see L. Kaplow, 'Rules versus Standards – an Economic Analysis' (1992) 42 *Duke Law Journal* 557.

however, this oversight duty is not very well-defined.[90] In German law, for instance, courts often refer succinctly to the circumstances of the individual case.[91] This approach is rightly criticised as being an empty formula.[92] Even the legal requirement of Section 91 (2) AktG, which obliges the board to take appropriate measures, in particular to set up a monitoring system in order to identify developments that could endanger the continued existence of the company at an early stage, provides nothing more than a vague indication.[93] At least, this type of provision creates an obligation to adequately provide against risks inherent in technology.[94] A more precise definition of the standard of care, however, requires the development of specific individual duties that must be followed when delegating entrepreneurial decision-making tasks to AI, in particular with respect to the necessary organisational precautions against erroneous AI decisions. Since AI is a new phenomenon, such obligations are not yet defined by legal provisions.

This regulatory gap can be bridged by two different approaches: on the one hand, analogies to legal rules concerning algorithmic decisions in other contexts may be considered. For example, the rule on algorithmic trading in financial instruments can be taken into account.[95] At least, it concerns similar types of decisions and stipulates responsibilities for such decisions, in order to protect potentially injured parties.[96] On the other hand, a recourse to extra-legal but generally accepted rules of conduct can also be considered. Due to the novelty of the technology, no market standard has developed yet, but emerging AI rules like the OECD principles, formally recognised by a large number of governments worldwide, can be taken into account. Both approaches – analogies to existing legal rules as well as reference to soft law guidelines – can help to develop several common principles that contribute to the development of AI-related corporate duties.

The variety of the OECD and EU guidelines raises the question, however, of the intensity of AI-related directors' duties. After all, the board enjoys broad entrepreneurial discretion, pursuant to the business judgment rule.[97] In particular, the board is, in principle, free to delegate decisions, including on AI technologies.[98] However, this discretion is limited in various respects, in particular by the duty to obey the law.[99] It is debatable, however, whether AI-related duties have similar effects, if they are not expressly stipulated in legal provisions, but (only) included in ethical guidelines or elaborated by analogy. The regulatory intensity is likely to vary gradually in

---

[90] With regard to US corporate law, cf., for instance, A. Tucker Nees, 'Who's the Boss? Unmasking Oversight Liability within the Corporate Power Puzzle' (2010) 35 *Delaware Journal of Corporate Law* 199; E. Pollman, 'Corporate Oversight and Disobedience' (2019) 72 *Vanderbilt Law Review* 2013.

[91] See, for instance, Federal Court of Justice (Bundesgerichtshof – BGH) in BGH NStZ 1986 at 34 ('hängt von den Umständen des Einzelfalles ab').

[92] J. Druey, 'Wo hört das Prüfen auf? Das Misstrauensprinzip – insbesondere im Gesellschaftsrecht' in Ernst A. Kramer and Wolfgang Schuhmacher (eds.), *Festschrift für Hans-Georg Koppensteiner* (Budapest: Orac, 2001) 8 ('Leerformel').

[93] For more detail, see D. Linardatos, 'Künstliche Intelligenz und Verantwortung' (2019) *Zeitschrift für Wirtschaftsrecht* 504 507.

[94] D. Zetzsche, 'Corporate Technologies – Zur Digitalisierung im Aktienrecht' (2019) *Die Aktiengesellschaft* 1 7ff.

[95] See nn. 33–35 (finance industry-specific law in Germany).

[96] For more detail, see F. Möslein, 'Aktienrechtliche Leitungsverantwortung beim Einsatz künstlicher Intelligenz' in Kaulartz and Braegelmann (eds.), n. 88; F. Möslein, 'Künstliche Intelligenz im Gesellschaftsrecht' in M. Ebers et al. (eds.), *Rechtshandbuch Künstliche Intelligenz und Robotik* (Munich: Beck, 2020) 472–480.

[97] In great detail, see D. Block, S. Radin and N. Barton, *The Business Judgment Rule: Fiduciary Duties of Corporate Directors*, 6th ed. (Riverwoods: Aspen, 2009); for a comparative account, see J. Armour, L. Enriques, H. Hansmann and R. Kraakman, 'The Basic Governance Structure' in R. Kraakman et al. (eds.), *The Anatomy of Corporate Law*, 3rd ed. (Oxford: Oxford University Press, 2017) 68–70.

[98] Möslein, n. 11 at 658–660.

[99] In more detail, with respect to German law, see F. Möslein, 'Aktienrechtliche Leitungsverantwortung beim Einsatz künstlicher Intelligenz' in Kaulartz and Braegelmann (eds.), n. 88; F. Möslein, 'Künstliche Intelligenz im Gesellschaftsrecht' in Ebers et al. (eds.), n. 96.

accordance with the respective normative basis. In contrast to unwritten principles of business ethics, however, the non-binding AI guidelines are based on a comparatively strong normative foundation: they are laid down in writing, they have a supranational, partly global, scope and they enjoy strong, multilateral support from state governments.[100] One can therefore expect them to develop quite a 'regulatory bite'.

5.5.2 Securities Law (Robo-advisors)

Similar legal developments are to be expected in securities law with respect to robo-advisors. In this field, however, both supervisory and civil law need to be taken into account. Many rules of supervisory law contain undefined legal terms that are subject to interpretation. As a consequence, AI-related guidelines can again serve as a source of legal knowledge: if, for example, the general principle of conduct in Art. 24 para. 1 MiFID II requires investment firms 'to act honestly, fairly and professionally in accordance with the best possible interests of its clients',[101] each of these requirements can potentially serve as a gateway to the development of AI-specific duties. Honesty can be understood as requiring data and system transparency, as well as transparency of the business model. Fairness may also include the avoidance of data-based distortions. Professional conduct can be understood to require the reliability of technical systems. Finally, the commitment to the best interests of clients may also include a requirement to ensure the integrity of the data used and to regulate and control access to data – and even respect for diversity, non-discrimination and fairness.[102] Some of these general obligations are specified in more detail in securities trading law. For example, the 'know your product' requirement provided for in Art. 25 para. 1 MiFID II may well call for comprehensive expertise in the technical functioning of the algorithms on which robo-advice is based.[103] This standard of conduct is likely to be considerably intensified, however, due to the AI guidelines at European and supranational level. Again, there are no specific rules on algorithms or AI in securities law, apart from the aforementioned provision on algorithmic trading.[104] Since it is unclear whether this provision can be applied by analogy to robo-advice, there is a considerable need for legal concretisation. AI-specific guidelines, even if not binding 'as such', can make a contribution as a source of legal knowledge.

On the other hand, these guidelines also have the potential to impact civil law. For example, a client might bring an action against robo-advice providers that have violated specific duties, such as the obligation to ensure the reliability of technical systems. If one takes the (debated) view that the rules of conduct under securities' trading law are to be qualified as both supervisory and civil law, the obligations of good conduct that have just been outlined are at the same time contractual obligations, so that respective violations amount to contractual breaches and justify corresponding claims.[105] On the other hand, a stricter position – as prominently taken, for instance, by the German Federal Court of Justice – claims that those duties of conduct are exclusively of a public law nature and have, in principle, no impact on the civil law contractual

---

[100] Möslein, n. 46 at 17.
[101] Extensively on this duty, for instance, M. Brenncke, 'Commentary on Art. 24' in M. Lehmann and C. Kumpan (eds.), *European Financial Services Law* (Munich: Beck, Hart, Nomos, 2019) Art. 24 paras 5–7.
[102] In more detail, F. Möslein, 'Leitlinien für den Einsatz künstlicher Intelligenz' in Linardatos (ed.), n. 88 at 58, 72ff.
[103] In a similar vein, T. Madel, *Robo Advice* (Baden-Baden: Nomos, 2019) 151–153.
[104] See nn. 34–42.
[105] In this vein, for instance, C. Benicke, *Wertpapiervermögensverwaltung* (Tübingen: Mohr Siebeck, 2006) 461–463, 473–486; P. Mülbert, 'Anlegerschutz bei Zertifikaten' (2007) *Zeitschrift für Wirtschafts- und Bankrecht* 1149 1157; R. Veil, 'Anlageberatung im Zeitalter der MiFID' (2007) *Zeitschrift für Wirtschafts- und Bankrecht* 1821 1825.

relationship between providers and their customers.[106] On the basis of this stricter view, contractual claims would still seem conceivable, albeit only on condition that the respective principles are not just laid down in supervisory law but are also an expression of widely recognised general legal principles. At least in this case, the latter can be taken into account in the interpretation of (implied) contractual declarations.[107] As a consequence, the principles in question determine the content of the contractual agreement, so that the client can clearly expect the service provider to comply with these obligations. Against this background, the legal impact of AI guidelines clearly depends on their general acceptance. In view of the largely identical formulation and the support of all G20 member states, but also in view of the development of numerous comparable principles by private and hybrid regulators, it can in fact be assumed that at least the 'lowest common denominator', that is, the core of these different sets of rules with identical content, is soon to be widely accepted.[108] Of course, such acceptance goes beyond written guidelines, even if adopted by supranational bodies and supported by numerous states. It rather requires a correspondingly widespread practice. For the time being, it is not foreseeable whether such practice will ultimately develop in the field of AI – but if it does, AI-related guidelines will accordingly have an impact on civil law, even on the basis of that stricter position.

5.5.3 Rules of Professional Conduct (Robo-lawyers)

Richard Susskind once asked whether digital innovation means 'The End of Lawyers'.[109] Since algorithms are not able to imitate general intelligence, they are still incapable of fully replacing human lawyers.[110] Nevertheless, legal technology, most often referred to as legal tech (LT), is rapidly changing the way legal services are provided.[111] This process is evidenced by a rising number of LT enterprises listed by the Stanford Center for Legal Informatics (CodeX)[112] but also by an increasing variety of accessible digital solutions. Besides applications that assist lawyers, such as databases or e-discovery systems,[113] there are others communicating directly with clients.[114] Beyond that, advances in so-called predictive analytics have led

---

[106] BGH NJW 2014, 2947 2950 at para 35.
[107] Ibid. at paras 36ff.
[108] F. Möslein, 'Leitlinien für den Einsatz künstlicher Intelligenz' in Linardatos (ed.), n. 88 at 58, 74ff.
[109] Richard Susskind, *The End of Lawyers? Rethinking the Nature of Legal Services* (Oxford: Oxford University Press, 2008).
[110] For further thoughts on 'super intelligent' systems, see Nick Bostrom, *Super Intelligence – Paths, Dangers, Strategies* (Oxford: Oxford University Press, 2014). For a crisp comparison of human and robotic capabilities regarding lawyering, cf. Dana Remus and Frank Levy, 'Can Robots Be Lawyers? Computers, Lawyers and the Practice of Law' (2017) 30 *Georgetown Journal of Legal Ethics* 501, 537ff. and 552ff.; cf. also E. C. Lashbrooke Jr, 'Legal Reasoning and Artificial Intelligence' (1988) 34 *Loyola Law Review* 287.
[111] See, e.g., Christian Veith et al. 'How Legal Technology Will Change the Business of Law' (2017), www.bucerius-education.de/fileadmin/content/pdf/studies_publications/Legal_Tech_Report_2016.pdf (accessed 17 February 2020); for a German perspective, cf. DAV, 'The Legal Services Market 2030' at 16, https://anwaltverein.de/de/anwaltspraxis/dav-zukunftsstudie (accessed 17 February 2020).
[112] The list comprised 1,284 companies at the time this chapter was written and is available at https://techindex.law.stanford.edu (accessed 14 February 2020).
[113] Interesting insights on the value of e-discovery are given by Rachel M. Zahorsky and William D. Henderson 'Who's Eating Law Firms Lunch: The Legal Service Providers, Law Schools and New Grads at the Table' (2013) 99 *American Bar Association Journal* 32 33ff.
[114] See, for example, the service provided by https://myflyright.com (accessed 14 February 2020), which is allowing for automatic enforcement of claims for compensation due to flight disruption on the basis of the Council Regulation (EC) No. 261/2004 of 11 February 2004 establishing common rules on compensation and assistance to passengers in the event of denied boarding and of cancellation or long delay of flights, and repealing Regulation (EEC) No. 295/91 [2004] OJ L46/1 and the Montreal Convention 1999.

to intelligent algorithms that are able to forecast outcomes of proceedings with a good degree of accuracy.[115]

These developments imply new legal questions, ranging from the permissibility of LTs under professional law,[116] to standards of ethical conduct that must be met by lawyers.[117] The complexity of these legal challenges depends on the degree of autonomy of the underlying technology. AI applications acting autonomously, such as chatbots,[118] are soon to prompt an urgent rethink of the standards of professional care that are applicable to lawyers offering AI-based legal solutions.

Rule-makers might have perceived these challenges but, as yet, there are no specific rules dealing with artificially intelligent LT applications. For example, the International Bar Association (IBA) asserted in April 2017 that 'intelligent software can also conquer the legal market and optimise work habits',[119] but it has refrained from establishing AI-specific regulations so far. At least, the Cyber Security Guidelines that have been elaborated by the IBA's Presidential Task Force on Cybersecurity can be viewed as a first step towards AI-specific professional rules.[120]

In the absence of any specific regulation, more general rules (as provided by the OECD and the EU guidelines) could be consulted by professionals and courts seeking orientation. In the field of professional conduct, however, soft law can face significant obstacles, particularly under German law. Since the 1920s, courts have referred to codes of self-regulatory nature for guidance on questions regarding the often vaguely formulated stipulations set out by German professional law.[121] This tradition came to an abrupt end in 1987, when the German Federal Constitutional Court in its *Bastille* decisions held that the regulations lacked democratic legitimation and, consequently, deprived them of their status as generally accepted supplementary tools for construing the German professional law for lawyers.[122] Legal professionals were then struggling to fill the resulting regulatory gap until the Berufsordnung für Rechtsanwälte (BORA) was set up by a newly established and democratically legitimated forum in 1997.[123]

Considering that the period of time that has passed since the constitutional court's groundbreaking decision is relatively short, it is likely that German courts will be hesitant to base their decisions expressly on the OECD and Commission guidelines in the field of lawyers' professional conduct. However, if regulatory gaps caused by technical evolution are left open by legislators, non-legislative sets of rules are nonetheless likely to affect the courts' findings indirectly – even if only as a source of inspiration.

---

[115] Cf., e.g., T. Sourding, 'Judge v Robot? Artificial Intelligence and Judicial Decision-Making' (2018) 41 *University of New South Wales Law Journal* 1114 1116ff.; M. Hatfield, 'Professionally Responsible Artificial Intelligence' (2019) 51 *Arizona State Law Journal* 1057 1066–1067.
[116] Cf. subsection a.
[117] Cf. subsection b.
[118] Cf., e.g., the chatbot of a German law firm, offering advice on questions regarding employment law, https://ratis.de/chatbot/ (accessed 14 February 2020).
[119] IBA, 'Artificial Intelligence and Robotics and Their Impact on the Workplace' (2017) at 34ff., www.ibanet.org/Press-Coverage-Robotics.aspx (accessed 14 February 2020).
[120] IBA, 'Cyber Security Guidelines' (2018), www.ibanet.org/Publications/publications_IBA_guides_and_free_materials.aspx (accessed 2 January 2020).
[121] Cf. M. Kilian and L. Koch, *Anwaltliches Berufsrecht*, 2nd ed. (Munich: Beck, 2018) 3ff.; Hanns Prütting in Martin Henssler and Matthias Prütting (eds.), *Kommentar zur Bundesrechtsanwaltsordnung*, 4th ed. (Munich: Beck, 2014) § 43 paras 7ff.
[122] BVerfG NJW 1988 191–197.
[123] Cf. M. Kilian and L. Koch, *Anwaltliches Berufsrecht*, 2nd ed. (Munich: Beck, 2018) 8.

5.5.3.1 Impact on Permissibility of Legal Tech

Both the OECD and the EU guidelines emphasise that member states should pursue an AI approach that contributes to general 'societal well-being'.[124] One of the most important societal goods concerns legal certainty and the rule of law. This good is obviously affected by the use of LT.[125] The AI guidelines are an invitation to legislators and state authorities to reconsider the consequences of LT for the system of justice.

One possible starting point for such a debate is the permissibility of different business models under national law. For example, under German professional law, basically solely lawyers are allowed to provide legal services.[126] Non-lawyers – such as many founders of LT startups – require exceptional permission in order to set up businesses, even if they merely intend to offer schematically structured legal services, such as debt collection services.[127] This very restrictive policy has led to an ongoing discussion about the possible societal benefits and risks associated with LTs among scholars and different stakeholders.[128] Recently, the debate culminated in the noteworthy *wenigermiete.de* decision by the German Federal Supreme Court, which was mainly concerned with interpreting the scope of § 10 para 1, no 1 of the German Act on Out-of-Court Legal Services (Rechtsdienstleistungsgesetz, RDG).[129] The provision expressly applies to debt collection services and allows them to perform their business. However, the court held that an online service platform, providing for a calculator that automatically compares the rent of the user with the maximum permitted rent in the relevant area and offering to enforce respective claims, also fulfils the prerequisites of said provisions.[130] More interesting than the specific details are the general considerations made by the court. The judges based their decision upon the general notion that the goal of professional law was to protect society from unqualified legal services, but also to lay the foundations for new legal business models. In so doing, the decision implicitly referred to the societal benefits of LT.[131]

This consideration directly affects the current and future task of legislators and legal professionals in dealing with AI. At the same time, it reveals the potential of the various AI guidelines. Requesting a thorough weighing up of individual and supra-individual interests, soft law on AI calls for case-by-case decisions regarding LT and offers orientation regarding a harmonised, international view on the implications that are evoked by it.

5.5.3.2 Impact on Standards of Ethical Conduct

Lawyering and AI raise numerous ethical questions, particularly in combination with one another. For instance, lawyers are to put their clients' interests first and to safeguard them in

---

[124] OECD, n. 20 at IV.1.1; Commission, n. 29 at 6 (key requirement VI).
[125] For detailed considerations regarding the societal impact of LT concerning legal systems and whether professional law is an adequate remedy for regulating technical innovations, cf. Dana Remus and Frank Levy, 'Can Robots Be Lawyers? Computers, Lawyers and the Practice of Law' (2017) 30 *Georgetown Journal of Legal Ethics* 501 545ff.
[126] This can be derived from § 3 Gesetz über außergerichtliche Rechtsdienstleistungen (RDG) in conjunction with § 3 Bundesrechtsanwaltsordnung (BRAO).
[127] § 10 Gesetz über außergerichtliche Rechtsdienstleistungen (RDG).
[128] Cf., e.g., Martin Henssler and Matthias Kilian, 'Rechtsinformationssysteme im Internet' (2001) *Computer und Recht* 682; Michael Stern, 'Rechtsberatung durch Computerprogramme – Software in vermeidbarem Konflikt mit dem Rechtsberatungsgesetz (RBerG) bzw. dem Steuerberatungsgesetz (StBerG)' (2004) *Computer und Recht* 561; Jakob Weberstaedt, 'Online-Rechts-Generatoren als erlaubnispflichtige Rechtsdienstleistung?' (2016) *Anwaltsblatt* 535; Frank R. Remmertz, 'Aktuelle Entwicklungen im RGD – In Dubio Pro Libertate?' (2018) *BRAK-Mitteilungen* 231; Michael Kleine-Cosack, 'Anfang vom Ende des Anwaltsmonopols des RGD' (2019) *Anwaltsblatt* 6, https://anwaltsblatt.anwaltverein.de/files/anwaltsblatt.de/anwaltsblatt-online/2019-006.pdf (accessed 14 February 2020).
[129] BGH, Urteil vom 27.11.2019 – VIII ZR 285/18, 1.
[130] Ibid. at VIII ZR 285/18, 3.
[131] Ibid. at VIII ZR 285/18, 1.

the most efficient way, without however disrespecting the law or endangering other clients' interests.[132] While the purpose of this fundamental principle seems to be clear, it puzzles practitioners on a daily basis. Professionals struggle to know the specific requirements they are to fulfil in a rapidly transforming reality, especially with regard to conflicts of interest, aspects of remuneration or advertising, as well as the application of new technologies.[133] As a consequence, lawyers will ask themselves whether or not they should apply AI in everyday practice. And if they apply it, in what way?[134]

These uncertainties are mainly due to a lack of clarity, caused by the stipulations set out in the respective legal acts dealing with professional conduct. Rule 1.1 of the American Bar Association's Rules of Professional Conduct, for example, states that '[a] lawyer shall provide competent representation to a client. Competent representation requires the legal knowledge, skill, thoroughness and preparation reasonably necessary for the representation'. ABA's comment on Rule 1.1 clarifies that '[to] maintain the requisite knowledge and skill, a lawyer should keep abreast of changes in the law and its practice, *including the benefits and risks associated with relevant technology*, engage in continuing study and education and comply with all continuing legal education requirements to which the lawyer is subject'.[135] Still, these rules will hardly guide legal professionals, supervisory authorities and courts through the challenges raised by AI. In this regard, non-legislative rules may serve as a supplementary tool for interpreting what has yet to be defined by the respective lawmakers. Thereby, recommendations and guidelines, such as those drafted by the OECD and the EU Commission, are likely to have an impact on the interpretation of professional law. Moreover, they may contribute to establishing the fundament of what could be considered as a 'Best Practice Guide on LT' in the future.

5.6 CONCLUSION

These examples in various fields of application – relating to rob-directors, robo-advisors and robo-lawyers – show that while legal and ethical rules are often considered as two different categories, the legal relevance of ethical AI rules must not be underestimated. These ethical rules may develop into standards that the law increasingly refers to, in particular where applicable legal rules are vague and experience with new technologies is still lacking. In that sense, the emerging ethical rules are similar to Trojan horses – while they claim to be purely ethical, they are not just a gift but imply official legal obligations. In that sense, the relevance of the recommendation to the Trojans still rings true today, even if more than 3,000 years old: 'Do not trust the horse, Trojans! Whatever it is, I fear the Greeks, even if they bring gifts'.[136] In the same vein, the ethical guidelines' claim that they are not legally binding should not be trusted. The opposite might soon be the case.

---

[132] See, e.g., § 43 BRAO (Germany); Art. 1 para 1 and 3 of the Legal Services Act 2007 (UK); Rule 1.1. of the ABA's Model Rules of Professional Conduct (US).
[133] Cf., e.g., Martin Henssler, 'Die Anwaltschaft zwischen Berufsethos und Kommerz' (2008) *Anwaltsblatt* 721 728.
[134] Cf. D. Remus and F. Levy, 'Can Robots Be Lawyers? Computers, Lawyers and the Practice of Law' (2017) 30 *Georgetown Journal of Legal Ethics* 501 555.
[135] Comment 8 to rule 1.1 of the ABA's Model Rules of Professional Conduct, emphasis added.
[136] Virgil, *Aeneid*, book ii. 48ff ('Equo ne credite, Teucri. Quidquid id est, timeo Danaos et dona ferentes').

PART II

Legal Tech and ADR

6

Legal Tech in ADR

Mateja Durovic and Franciszek Lech

6.1. INTRODUCTION

The justice system is infamously slow in adopting technology.[1] Although recent years saw an exponential increase in the role played by technology within the justice system,[2] the legal industry has not kept pace with technical advancements to the same extent as other sectors. As put by former Australian High Court Justice, Michael Kirby, a Dickensian lawyer would still feel at home in the court halls of the 1990s courts, while a Dickensian doctor would not comprehend a contemporaneous hospital due to immense modernisation that had taken place at the same time.[3] However, in the COVID-19 era, the courts and tribunals are forced to conduct remote hearings, which imposes a degree of technological awareness and proficiency on the justice system.

In England and Wales, the coronavirus legislation[4] sent a 'very clear message that [the legislature] expects the courts to continue to function ... safely by means of the increased use of technology to facilitate remote trials'.[5] This approach implies that the epidemiological situation will inevitably force the adjudicative bodies (including ADR entities) to open their embrace towards technology. Commentators have noted that 'the pandemic has necessitated an unexpected crash course in remote justice that the legal system did not want, but definitely needed'[6] and that the legal sector will have no choice but to 'leverag[e] tech-based solutions to keep the wheels of justice moving'.[7] Not only in the court system is COVID-19 precipitating an adoption of technology. Due to the pandemic, ICSID for example, made 'e-filing' its default procedure.[8]

---

[1] Tania Sourdin, Bin Li and Tony Bourke, 'Just, Quick and Cheap: Civil Dispute Resolution and Technology' (2019) 19 *Macquarie Law Journal* 17 30.
[2] Noam Ebner and John Zeleznikow, 'Fairness, Trust and Security in Online Dispute Resolution' (2015) 36(2) *Hamline University's School of Law's Journal of Public Law and Policy* 143 143.
[3] Michael Kirby, 'The Future of Courts – Do They Have One?' (1998) 9(2) *Journal of Law, Information and Science* 141 143–144.
[4] Namely, the Coronavirus Act 2020 and Health Protection (Coronavirus Restrictions) (England) Regulations 2020, S.I. No. 350.
[5] *Re One Blackfriars Limited* [2020] EWHC 845 (Ch), [23] (John Kimbell QC sitting as a Deputy High Court Judge).
[6] Saddie Whittam, 'Navigating the New Normal' (2020) 170(7889) *New Law Journal* 19 19.
[7] Suzanne Rab, 'Covid-19 & Virtual Mediation' (2020) 170(7891) *New Law Journal* 25 25.
[8] ICSID, 'ICSID Makes Electronic Filing its Default Procedure', ICSID News Release (13 March 2020), https://icsid.worldbank.org/en/Pages/News.aspx?CID=359 (accessed 22 June 2020).

Hence, it seems that reluctantly or not, the dispute resolution field is thrust into adopting technical and technologically advanced solutions by the exigent circumstances. In this context, the discussion of the impact of technology on the field of alternative dispute resolution (ADR) is highly pertinent, as the dispute resolution industry is about to undergo a significant technological leap forward.

The key trends that underpin the present discussion, and contribute to its importance are (1) the increase in the pressure exerted by the availability of technology, and (2) a concurrent increase in the significance played by ADR within the overall justice system. COVID-19 did not singlehandedly force dispute resolution (DR)[9] to adapt to advances made by technology. The legal sector is, after all, a part of the wider society, a society that lives increasingly on- rather than offline. As people become more integrated in the digital world – and increasingly aware and understanding of the technology making such interactions possible – they come to expect the same in the DR domain.[10] Hence, even a field as 'steeped in tradition' as the judicial system has to eventually adapt to and adopt technology.[11] The current situation may only accelerate the rate at which technology becomes embedded, but did not cause the process in the first place.

The second trend mentioned is the rise ADR's significance. This can be detected from judicial attitudes towards ADR methods. Recently, the Court of Appeal of England and Wales held that it could order parties to subject their dispute to ADR under CPR Rule 3.1(2)(m).[12] This power comes on top of its discretionary power to penalise a party for refusing to partake in ADR, at the assessment of costs stage.[13] This overt recognition of ADR's importance is not exclusive to England and Wales. In the European Union (EU) emphasis is laid on ADR primarily in the context of consumer disputes with the ADR Directive[14] and the complimentary[15] ODR Regulation.[16] Consequently, at the nexus of these two trends of technological advancement in ADR and growing importance of ADR lies the discussion of the impact of legal tech (LT) on ADR, which is precisely what this chapter concerns itself with.

So far we have used the term 'technology' rather cryptically. It is apposite at this point to specify what technology is actually being considered. In this chapter, we look at four discrete categories of technology. First, we look at 'supportive technology', consisting of e-filing technologies (file sharing, storing and digitalisation) and audio-visual links (Zoom, Microsoft Teams and Skype for Business seem to be the recent favourites), which together help to minimise costs and expedite the proceedings.[17] Secondly, we look at technology that facilitates the diffusion of legal expertise, in turn enabling 'self-help' and reducing the gap between experts

---

[9] Meaning broadly defined ADR and litigation together.
[10] Colin Rule, 'Technology and the Future of Dispute Resolution' (2015) *Dispute Resolution Magazine* 5 6.
[11] Jeremy Barnett and Philip Treleavan, 'Algorithmic Dispute Resolution – The Automation of Professional Dispute Resolution Using AI and Blockchain Technologies' (2018) 61(3) *The Computer Journal* 399 400.
[12] *Lomax v. Lomax* [2019] EWCA Civ 1467; [2019] 1 WLR 6527, [29]–[32] (Moylan LJ) (the case focused on Early Neutral Evaluation).
[13] *BXB v. Watch Tower and Bible Tract Society of Pennsylvania and another* [2020] EWHC 656 (QB), [6] (Chamberlain J).
[14] European Parliament and Council Directive 2013/11 on alternative dispute resolution for consumer disputes [2013] OJ L165/63 ('ADR Directive').
[15] Michael Bogdan, 'The New EU Regulation on Online Resolution for Consumer Disputes' (2015) 9(1) *Masaryk University Journal of Law & Technology* 155 156.
[16] European Parliament and Council Regulation 524/2013 on online dispute resolution for consumer disputes and amending Regulation (EC) No. 2006/2004 and Directive 2009/22/EC [2013] OJ L165/1 ('ODR Regulation').
[17] Lisa Toohey, Monique Moore, Katelane Dart and Dan Toohey, 'Meeting the Access to Civil Justice Challenge: Digital Inclusion, Algorithmic Justice, and Human-Centred Design' (2019) 19(1) *Macquarie Law Journal* 133 140.

and non-experts (here we can name LawHelp, Ask LOIS or Penda as examples).[18] Thirdly, we analyse the impact of AI, especially when it comes to evaluating the legal claims, catalysing settlement or expediting current ADR procedures. Fourthly, blockchain and distributed ledger technologies cannot escape scrutiny as they hold the most likely avenue for technological update of the ADR field. Lastly, automation and autonomous dispute resolution by a combination of all of the above-mentioned technologies is considered.[19]

The thesis of this chapter is that technological advance poses, in the words of Colin Rule – the co-founder of one of the first successful online dispute resolution (ODR) platforms, Modria.com – 'the biggest opportunity and the biggest challenge for the practice of dispute resolution'.[20] Technology will impact the ADR field by firstly increasing the access to adjudication for potential claimants previously deprived of access to traditional ADR channels. Secondly, technology will also streamline the process, in turn making it more desirable as a process for resolving low-cost high-volume disputes. Thirdly, it will also enable ADR to resolve disputes that originate through the use of new technologies, especially those that arise due to the expansion of blockchain technology and smart contracts. Fourthly, thanks to its relatively low rigidity, ADR will be first to adapt to the technological shift, which will result with it 'out-performing' traditional justice streams (i.e., municipal courts) in the digital domain. However, it is also posited that this technological shift, while changing the way that ADR is provided, will not remove the need for courts altogether.

In order to develop the argument sketched out above, it is first necessary to resolve terminological issues that may otherwise obfuscate the discussion (Section 6.2), before moving to evaluate the impact of technology (Section 6.3) and providing specific examples of platforms that are already bringing ADR processes into the twenty-first century (Section 6.4).

6.2 ODR, ADR, DR AND COURTS: NAVIGATING THE TERMINOLOGICAL MINEFIELD

Despite the fact that academic opinions seem to converge as to the potential impact of technology, they continue to diverge on the terminology used. There is a handful of notions that continue to be defined differently in various contributions whose meaning must be clarified before we embark on the analysis, such as ADR and ODR.

First, we look at the less elusive notion of ADR. It is best defined with a negative delineation: the method of settling disputes that is not the formal one of municipal courts.[21] Accordingly, it conventionally is said to include mediation, arbitration, negotiation and settlement. Unlike the courts, the ADR system is private and confident and focuses predominantly on resolving the disputes submitted to it, rather than on any goals of developing the law through producing precedent or serving the goals of distributive justice at the social scale,[22] though it is still in the business of dispensing justice.

Next is the idea of ODR, which continues to be defined differently. It has no 'generally-accepted definition',[23] and so is susceptible to being used to mean different things. To some,

---

[18] Ibid. at 141.
[19] Ibid. at 144.
[20] Rule, n 10 at 7.
[21] Ethan Katsh and Orna Rabinovich-Einy, 'Digital Justice: Reshaping Boundaries in an Online Dispute Resolution' (2014) 1(1) *International Journal of Online Dispute Resolution* 5 13.
[22] Ibid. at 13.
[23] Ebner and Zelznikow, n. 2 at 144.

ODR constitutes a part of the ADR field.[24] Barnett and Treleaven, for example, argued that ODR 'uses technology to facilitate' the provision of usual, traditional ADR (negotiation, mediation, arbitration).[25] This view, classifying ODR as a tool rather than a process continues to put this idea in different ways. For some, the constitutive elements include: (1) the claimant, (2) the respondent, (3) neutral third party and (4) technology-based intermediary.[26] For others still, ODR is a (1) virtual process of (2) ADR that is (3) technology-facilitated.[27]

The understanding of ODR as a mere method of ADR is not accepted by the pioneers in the field of jurisprudential study of ODR, Katsh and Rabinovich, who dispute this subservient position of ODR. They argue that the inclusion of technology as the 'fourth party' to the dispute means that ODR cannot be merely a *tool* of ADR – instead it generates 'completely new types of processes unimaginable in the face-to-face era'.[28] While they admit that ODR began as online ADR, they argue that the expansion of the cyber sphere has induced a paradigm shift, which places ODR in its own distinct category, a *way* of ADR on par with, say, arbitration or mediation, and not a tool for providing them.[29] Technological advances, specifically the ability to provide DR at a distance and utilising the 'intelligence of the machine'[30] separated ODR from its original genus. Following this argument, there was a 'first generation' ODR that centred on human beings resolving the dispute using technology as *equipment* (instant messaging, video and phone calls, etc.) but without any autonomy of the machines.[31] However, subsequently, ODR moved to the second generation where the technology is not only equipment but also as an 'autonomous agent' acting to resolve the dispute.[32]

Perhaps some of the disagreement on the terminology may be explained by a difference in emphasis. ODR can be read as *online dispute* resolution (i.e., a process of resolving disputes arising from online dealings, whether the actual process of resolving the dispute takes place on- or offline is irrelevant provided the underlying dispute arose online) or *online* dispute resolution, meaning a DR process taking place online regardless of how the underlying dispute arose.[33] UNCITRAL seemingly followed this latter path, defining ODR as a 'mechanism for resolving disputes *through the use of electronic communications* or other information and communication technology'.[34] This understanding of ODR sees it as substantially a way to provide ADR rather than a distinct concept – ODR is said to focus on facilitating the online provision of standard ADR procedures (such as negotiation, mediation, arbitration, conciliation, ombuds, etc.).[35] ODR, in the understanding of it as a tool and not a process, is not an exhaustive label either. Accordingly, the categorisation includes subcategories of online ADR (oADR), cyber ADR

---

[24] Katsh and Rabinovich-Einy, n. 21 at 25.
[25] Barnett and Treleaven, n. 11 at 400; Ebner and Zelznikow, n. 2 at 144.
[26] Emmy Latifah, Anis H Bajrektarevic and Moch Najib Imanullah, 'The Shifting of Alternative Dispute Resolution: From Traditional Form to the Online Dispute Resolution' (2019) 6(1) *Brawijaya Law Journal* 27 28.
[27] Gralf-Peter Calliess and Simon Johannes Heetkamp, 'Online Dispute Resolution: Conceptual and Regulatory Framework', Dickson Poon Transnational Law Institute, King's College London Research Paper Series, TLI Think! Paper 22/2019 (2019) at 2, https://papers.ssrn.com/sol3/papers.cfm?abstract_id=3505635 (accessed 22 June 2020).
[28] Katsh and Rabinovich-Einy, n. 21 at 32.
[29] Ibid. at 6.
[30] Ibid. at 21–22.
[31] Latifah et al., n. 26 at 32.
[32] Ibid. at 32.
[33] Koji Takahashi, 'Blockchain and ODR', Paper from the Workshop on the Use of Modern Technology for Dispute Resolution and Electronic Agreement Management Particularly Online Dispute Resolution Port Moresby, Papua New Guinea 3–4 March 2018 at 1, https://ssrn.com/abstract=3566676 (accessed 22 June 2020).
[34] UNCITRAL, 'Technical Notes on Online Dispute Resolution', UN (2017), Section V, [24] (emphasis supplied), www.uncitral.org/pdf/english/texts/odr/V1700382_English_Technical_Notes_on_ODR.pdf (accessed 22 June 2020).
[35] Calliess and Heetkamp, n. 27 at 4.

(cADR), electronic ADR (eADR) and electronic dispute resolution (eDR), which all together constitute ODR.[36] To that some add internet dispute resolution (IDR) and technology mediated dispute resolution (TMDR).[37]

The present chapter does not purport to clarify or reason away the discrepancies in the understanding of this jargon. Instead, we propose a simplified key to our discussion. It is understood that by adding technological components to ADR, such as video-conferencing tools, algorithmic discovery processes or blockchain-based enforcement, it would in any event fall into a category of ODR, since it would now be ADR dispensed with the help of technology, which satisfies most of the definitions looked at above. Accordingly, we find that trying to maintain the distinction between such 'new generation ADR' and ODR is somewhat artificial, and in any event not conducive to clarity nor brevity. Hence, we take ADR to mean the process of DR other than in courts, and 'traditional ADR' to mean ADR without the new technologies that form the focal point of our analysis.

6.3 TECHNOLOGY AS A KEY TO DISSEMINATION OF EFFECTIVE JUSTICE

The widespread assimilation of technology will have positive impacts on the availability of ADR. As such, it will greatly increase the access to justice with the corollary social and legal benefits that such a process brings, especially to those social groups who have previously been largely excluded from access to court justice or effective ADR (lower class individuals, SMEs). Evidently, this argument is premised on accepting ADR as dispensing 'justice'. The examination of the meaning of justice is not within the scope of this essay, but given that ADR is used to vindicate rights and protect interests of parties to legal agreements, it is seen as apposite to include access to ADR procedures as falling within the broader notion of access to justice.

Furthermore, the adoption of technology will serve to make the ADR process much more expedient and efficient, lowering the costs and increasing its availability even further. Additionally, the adoption of technology will enable ADR to effectively resolve disputes arising out of technologically advanced mechanisms, such as blockchain. We demonstrate why traditional litigation and ADR channels are inapposite to deal with blockchain disputes and how through the adoption of technology ADR can posit itself well enough to serve that ever-growing field. In the absence of such a technological advancement, ADR would be left squeezed for new work as new mechanisms would have to be designed to deal with such disputes. Lastly, technology-aided ADR will continue to challenge the traditional litigation domain harder than ever, constituting formidable competition for contentious work.

6.3.1 Access to Justice

Technology, when combined with ADR, has the potential to enhance the access to justice generally, but also for the currently disadvantaged groups specifically.[38] However, the concept of

---

[36] Latifah et al., n. 26 at 28.
[37] Sadiq O. Omoola and Umar A. Oseni, 'Towards an Effective Legal Framework for Online Dispute Resolution in E-Commerce Transactions: Trends, Traditions and Transitions' (2016) 24(1) *International Islamic University Malaysia Law Journal* 257 264.
[38] Michael Legg, 'The Future of Online Dispute Resolution: Online ADR and Online Courts' (2016) *University of New South Wales Faculty of Law Legal Studes Research Paper Series* 71 71.

'access to justice' remains somewhat 'nebulous',[39] and has to be defined before the argument can be developed. In a seminal Article, Cappelletti and Garth argued that access to justice is made up of two elements: (1) accessible justice system, where access is not contingent on financial means or legal expertise; and (2) ensuring individually and socially just results.[40] Technology will potentially support both limbs of this formulation in regard to ADR, by removing the financial and expertise barriers to justice, as well as removing biases of human adjudicators that have been present in some aspects of the ADR field.

Firstly, technology may contribute substantially to a greater diffusion of legal expertise and crucial legal information. Applications such as Penda or AskLOIS (pertaining to family violence) offer claimants legal, financial and safety information immediately and without the need to consult a legal expert. Similarly, US-based app DoNotPay, which markets itself as the world's 'first robot lawyer' allowing you to 'fight corporations, beat bureaucracy and sue anyone at the press of a button'.[41] The app was a brainchild of an eighteen-year-old who wanted to appeal his parking tickets, but today it relies on an AI-supported chatbot technology to offer instantaneous legal advice relating to a range of corporate practices such as subscription cancellations, airline consumer issues, parking tickets and more.[42] In the United Kingdom, Visrule allows users to build their legal decision trees by uploading facts and using their algorithmic software to get an overview of what their case would look like and what evidence is needed,[43] and AI-powered RobotLawyerLisa[44] utilises chatbot technology without actual lawyer intervention to provide cheap and quick legal advice in order to 'serve the many rather than the few by empowering the neglected 90% [of business and consumers who do not obtain legal representation for their case]'.[45]

The digital applications offering legal advice are likely to multiply exponentially, as disgruntled consumers and small businesses who could not afford traditional legal support turn to AI and algorithm-run programmes to inform themselves on their legal rights and procedures of enforcing them. Examples include JustFix.nyc,[46] which serves to inform tenants vis-à-vis neglectful landlords and RightsNOW,[47] which provides a 'conversational' access to law by providing legal answers through voice recognition software, allowing the customer to ask questions and obtain answers. Even where those apps do not outright resolve the legal questions, they may also facilitate the access to a legal practitioner in the first place. It will suffice to mention here BernieSez, which allows for several licensed lawyers to preliminarily review one's case and give their assessment as well as fees for continuing with it,[48] or any of the ubiquitous 'ask a lawyer' apps of which a quick Google search reveals hundreds.

Secondly, on top of diffusing information indispensable to concerned claimants, technology may also streamline the very process of ADR and make it more accessible to parties seeking justice. Algorithms can serve to personalise the DR process to the needs of individual parties.[49]

---

[39] Sourdin et al., n. 1 at 21.
[40] Mauro Cappelletti and Bryant Garth, 'Access to Justice: The Newest Wave in the Worldwide Movement to Make Rights Effective (1978) 27(2) *Buffalo Law Review* 181 182.
[41] DoNotPay.com, https://donotpay.com/learn/ (accessed 22 June 2020).
[42] Ebner and Zelznikow, n. 2 at 143, also see DoNotPay.com https://donotpay.com/.
[43] www.visirule.co.uk/decision-tree-flowcharts.
[44] Sourdin et al., n. 1 at 35.
[45] RobotLawyerLisa, https://robotlawyerlisa.com/ (accessed 22 June 2020).
[46] www.justfix.nyc/.
[47] www.rightsnowapp.com/.
[48] BernieSez, 'How Does It Work?', www.berniesez.com/how-it-works/ (accessed 22 June 2020).
[49] Latifah et al., n. 26 at 33.

Thanks to this, the procedure and elements of the legal process, so alienating to lay claimants, can be made more accessible and understandable, especially by parties who were previously disempowered.[50] This could in turn foster a growth of trust in the DR system, as well as increasing such groups' access to justice. Moreover, through translating the complex legalese and arduous legal process into simple language, they arm groups who have previously been excluded from DR channels with knowledge that can induce them to turn to ADR for their disputes.

As regards the procedural issues, AI and algorithms can help to draft legal documentation without the need for counsel, which in turn would have the effect of lowering costs, but also making the legal process (so alien to lay claimants) seem more accessible. Legal documentation assistants such as LawHelp[51] or A2J Author[52] allow claimants to create their own legal forms simply by filling in an online questionnaire.[53]

The technologies described above promise to open the doors to DR to claimants who would not have previously had the chance to do so. By lowering costs tremendously,[54] they cater to the 'low-value, high volume' disputes experienced predominantly by consumers or SMEs, where the legal costs may very well turn out to be higher than the amount at stake.[55] These disputes are insignificant at the individual level, but compound at the social level, creating inefficiency and endangering the collective rights of those groups. Hence, unlocking a viable dispute resolution method might be of paramount significance even outside the bounds of the DR field. Accordingly, the technological revolution in the ADR industry may well greatly open the access to justice.

However, this optimistic outlook is not broadly accepted. Despite the promises made to empower the 'many not the few' by these tech startups, the fact is that large law firms and corporate clients will continue to have the means to make the necessary investments to adopt such technologies.[56] Such clients are repeat players with the most at stake (in terms of the pecuniary value of their disputes), hence having the biggest incentives to streamline their process and meet the high initial costs of investment. Consequently, technology may disappoint in its role as the great equaliser in terms of access to justice.

To illustrate, Lex Machina, a big data project led by LexisNexis, promises to mine litigation data and provide clients with 'quantified insights into judicial behaviour, venues, opposing parties and opposing counsel to assist them to make better decisions about claim construction and case strategy'.[57] Access to such programmes, however, is costly and uneven, suggesting that technology will not only empower the previously disempowered, but rather provide everyone with speedier access to DR, leaving the disempowered in no more empowered a position.

Furthermore, there is the issue of digital exclusion, which means that those who most urgently need facilitated access to justice may not even have access to the digital technology that is supposedly giving them such access.[58] The Lloyds Bank UK Consumer Digital Index

---

[50] Ethan Katsh and Orna Rabinovich-Einy, 'Blockchain and the Inevitability of Disputes: The Role for Online Dispute Resolution' [2019] 2 *Journal of Dispute Resolution* 47 58.
[51] www.lawhelp.org/ (accessed 22 June 2020).
[52] A2J Author, 'Welcome to A2J Author', www.a2jauthor.org/ (accessed 22 June 2020).
[53] Toohey et al., n. 17 at 142.
[54] See Section 6.3.2.
[55] Calliess and Heetkamp, n. 27 at 9.
[56] Sourdin et al., n. 1 at 27.
[57] Ibid.
[58] Toohey et al., n. 17 at 145.

study of 2020, reveals that 9 million people (16 per cent of the UK population) 'struggle to get online by themselves'. Even today, 7 per cent of the population is still 'offline', of whom 96 per cent are older than sixty.[59] Of people aged 70+, 77 per cent have 'very low digital engagement'.[60] Age is the most obvious, but by far not the only, factor preventing digital inclusion. Other factors include disabilities (impairments reduce chances of full digital access by 25 per cent) and poverty. Individuals from households where annual household income (AHI) is below £17,499 are even 40 per cent less likely to have the basic digital skills as compared to those with AHI above £50,000; four in ten people on welfare benefits have very low digital engagement.[61] It seems then that it is precisely those who are most vulnerable and disadvantaged who have the least digital access. This fact casts doubt on technologically advanced–ADR's ability to bring genuinely accessible justice.

Some aspects of digital inclusivity may improve over time – it is clear that the world is trending towards more, rather than less, integration with the online world, and the younger generations are the perfect encapsulation of that trend. This supports the thesis that digital inclusivity trends will improve,[62] yet it does not dispute the fact that for the marginalised groups of today, a digital justice revolution does not necessarily imply readier access to justice. Hence, although there are high expectations for technology to improve the first limb of Cappelletti's and Garth's access to justice, there remains the second limb – namely, the ability to provide individually and socially just results – that has to be analysed.

Some see in algorithm- and AI-driven–DR systems the chance to solve the issues of systemic bias and discrimination, thus resulting in a fairer DR infrastructure. Morison and Harkens referred to those who 'may even think that robot judges could eliminate human biases – either accidentally or intentionally'.[63] This aspect of technological progress, however, is subject to serious scepticism, and there are three main objections that have to be raised: technical, legal and theoretical. Firstly, in terms of a technological obstacle, it must be stressed that technology is never truly 'neutral'. It always reflects the biases, assumptions and values of those who designed it,[64] which is why it is imperative that its use of algorithms and AI chatbots be made transparent. There is the danger of algorithmic bias, where one group is unfairly favoured or discriminated over another by the apparently impartial algorithms.[65] Such bias may be the result of the design of the algorithm or simply a glitch in its performance.[66] This is aggravated by the fact that unlike with human decisions, the algorithmic decision tree is not transparent, thus making it substantially more difficult to detect bias.[67] Transparency seems to be key, and without it we could have discriminatory (directly or indirectly) algorithms making significant decisions regarding human lives, all under the false pretence of being impartial and pure of any bias, only to inhibit the scrutiny of them.

---

[59] Lloyds Bank, 'UK Consumer Digital Index 2020' (2020), www.lloydsbank.com/assets/media/pdfs/banking_with_us/whats-happening/lb-consumer-digital-index-2020-report.pdf (accessed 22 June 2020).
[60] Ibid.
[61] Ibid.
[62] Toohey et al., n. 17 at 146.
[63] John Morison and Adam Harkens, 'Re-Engineering Justice? Robot Judges, Computerised Courts and (Semi) Automated Legal Decision-Making' (2019) 39(1) *Legal Studies* 618 619.
[64] Katsh and Rabinovich, n. 21 at 36.
[65] Toohey et al., n. 17 at 148.
[66] Ibid.
[67] See Mateja Durovic and Franciszek Lech, 'Global Big Data and Consumer Law' in Joe Cannataci, Valerina Falce and Oreste Pollicino (eds.), *Legal Challenges of Big Data* (Cheltenham: Edward Elgar, 2020) 154–173.

This technical objection may be addressed by a process of 'black box tinkering', which is essentially a disclosure of algorithms to the public for them to be scrutinised and analysed. Of course, the publishing of computer code and complex algorithms is not enough to permit meaningful scrutiny, and the information should be adapted to suit non-mathematicians and -computer scientists.[68] Another way to solve this issue is through human centred design, namely, designing the algorithms and the DR system they shall come to constitute with the end user (i.e., lay claimant) in mind, so that they clarify and facilitate rather than impede or obstruct access to justice.[69] Accordingly, the flaws identified in the ability of algorithms to solve the access to justice problems are not beyond the point of remedying, and instead should be addressed by careful design. If implemented correctly, they shall not only increase the access to justice, but also make the process significantly more efficient.

Secondly, as regards the legal barriers to AI-automated DR systems, it has to be mentioned that there are legal norms that prevent humans being subject to fully automated decision-making. In the EU, Art. 22 of the GDPR provides that the 'data subject shall have the right *not* to be subject to a decision based *solely* on automated processing, including profiling, which produces legal effects concerning him or her or similarly significantly affects him or her'.[70] This provision is also mirrored in England and Wales in section 49 of the Data Protection Act 2018.[71] Given that an arbitral award or a binding ADR resolution will inevitably have legal effects on the data subject, it seems to be at least plausible that a fully automated ADR system would fall foul of such provisions. However, these provisions allow the data subjects to consent to be subject to fully automated processing,[72] meaning that an autonomous AI DR mechanism could be compliant if it expressly notified the parties in the agreement to ADR that the process would be fully automated. This however only works when the data subjects are aware that the process is fully automated and does not solve the issue of a hybrid system (where some decisions may be fully automated) or where the parties do not know if their dispute is subject only to fully automated consideration.

Lastly, there is a theoretical objection to the ability of algorithms to take over the administration of law in an unbiased way. This is that law is permeated by other disciplines to a considerable extent. Many variables that are pertinent in the arbitral awards or other legal processes are not reflected overtly in the law as it is written down.[73]

> To create a system like this would require a complete instrumentalisation of all these social aspect of law into something that could be technologically calculated and predicted ... this would require an algorithmic actor identifying the issues and legal framework, establishing 'facts', evaluating the parties' interests, disaggregating issues, establishing positions, exchanging information, suggesting options for resolution, setting out a time frame for actions, seeking agreement and creating binding resolutions.[74]

---

[68] Toohey et al., n. 17 at 151.
[69] Ibid. at 152.
[70] Regulation (EU) 2016/679 of the European Parliament and of the Council of 27 April 2016 on the protection of natural persons with regard to the processing of personal data and on the free movement of such data, and repealing Directive 95/46/EC (General Data Protection Regulation), Art. 22(1) (emphasis supplied).
[71] Data Protection Act 2018, Art. 49: '(1) A controller may not take a significant decision based solely on automated processing unless that decision is required or authorised by law. (2) A decision is a "significant decision" for the purpose of this section if, in relation to a data subject, it – (a) produces an adverse legal effect concerning the data subject, or (b) significantly affects the data subject.'
[72] Art. 22(2)(c) GDPR and Art. 50(2) Data Protection Act 2018.
[73] Nicolas Lozada-Pimiento, 'AI Systems and Technology in Dispute Resolution' (2019) 24(2) *Uniform Law Review* 348 363.
[74] Ibid. at 631.

Accordingly, the ability to translate such factors to a 'if A – then B' logic of computer code may prove impossible, or at least highly difficult. If these aspects are not present in the automated DR system, then the ability of such technology to provide 'socially just results' may be heavily impaired thus reducing the ability of technology to increase access to justice.

6.3.2 *Efficiency*

The next effect that technology is likely to have in the field of ADR is that of increasing the overall efficiency of the process. This is obviously closely linked to the point made above pertaining to access to justice, after all 'justice delayed is justice denied'. Technology that can make vindication of rights both speedier and quicker is bound to also promote access to justice.[75] A typical high-stake arbitration may take anywhere from six months to a year,[76] an unforgivingly long time in the online, instantaneous world. Any technology capable of substantially reducing such delay is of incredible interest to potential claimants.

It may seem unexpected, but the pressure to adopt AI and algorithmic technologies to streamline the procedure comes from both high- and low-end claimants: litigants-in-person and SMEs want a cheaper, affordable service, while at the same time, corporate litigants see the benefits of an AI-streamlined process and want this new technology to allow lawyers to provide their services faster, cheaper and more reliably.[77] AI– and machine learning–based programs could even deal with disputes in parallel, and in seconds bring additional savings in terms of time and accompanying cost.[78] Compared to the costs of litigation or traditional ADR, the investment in technology supported–ADR is 'both value adding and cost saving'.[79] This provides paramount incentives to finance the technological shift.

This aspect can be seen in the fact that even the adoption of pretty unsophisticated technological elements (such as video conferencing, e-filing or other forms of remote communication), which, as an aside, shall in due time become universally accepted in the DR sector, thanks in no small part to COVID-19, has resulted in 'saved travel times and disbursement, whilst contributing to a faster [resolution] of disputes' when compared to litigation or old-school, rigorously face-to-face ADR.[80]

There are two essential levels at which this change may take place: the first is the ability of technology to expedite proceedings (or, in other words, aiding human decision-makers) by making the procedure more readily understandable and capable of being complied with from home. This has been described above in the context of bringing justice to one's doorstep. The next level is the ability of software to manage the DR process itself in a more efficient manner (but still just supporting the human adjudicator). It this context, that it is worth pointing out the already available AI tools that manage blind bids in negotiations.[81]

---

[75] Sourdin et al., n. 1 at 18.
[76] Law Times, 'AI May Help With Alternative Dispute Resolution', *Law Times* (3 June 2019), www.lawtimesnews.com/practice-areas/adr/ai-may-help-with-alternative-dispute-resolution/263579 (accessed 22 June 2020).
[77] Adrian Zuckerman, 'Artificial Intelligence – Implications for the Legal Profession, Adversarial Process and the Rule of Law' (2020) 136(2) *Law Quarterly Review* 427 427.
[78] Morison and Harkens, n. 63 at 619.
[79] Sourdin et al., n. 1 at 24.
[80] Ibid. at 26.
[81] See Section 6.4.10.

However, on top of such assistive improvements, there is the possibility that technology will take over the actual resolution of disputes (substituting itself for the human adjudicator). Examples of such technologies include AI and algorithms, but also by blockchain-based 'smart contracts'.[82] Such technologies can permit a total circumvention of the traditional channels of ADR. By inserting in the smart contract an 'oracle' that permits arbitration, or utilising a multi-signature scheme[83] a 'self-sufficient adjudication system' can be manufactured, one that, unlike traditional ADR, would not rely on the enforcement of awards by the state courts.[84]

This last point about the possible of automation of law is not subscribed to universally. Harkens and Morrison concede that there is something to be said about technology's capability 'to act mainly as a tool to assist in [ADR]' but suggest that the arguments of an 'autonomous system which can actually process, adjudicate or settle disputes independently' are premature.[85] They urge that the most that the technology can achieve is to 'disrupt current working patterns and flows' but not produce autonomous AI justice.[86]

However, it is argued that even by achieving 'merely' this efficiency, ADR would make a huge step towards actually serving a greater role in resolving the disputes that people have, and as such to bringing justice closer to its 'end-users', with all the social benefits that would accompany such a development. Even if a fully autonomous AI justice system is not a short-term possibility (though a blockchain-based system may be),[87] the impact in terms of efficiency that adopting such technologies would have is tremendous.

Another interesting facet of efficiency being introduced via technology is the oft-omitted aspect of dispute *prevention*. Algorithms can analyse the disputes submitted to ADR to 'learn about the sources of recurring disputes'.[88] Such insight will in turn enable adjudicators (human or machine) to focus on such factors inducing disputes and work at DR at the root, avoiding the conflict from arising in the first place. The ability to minimise the number of disputes arising, by resolving the issues apt to give rise to conflict, will circumvent the flood of repetitive cases in the ADR system, thus making it easier and faster to obtain a resolution for those with a genuinely complex dispute, while also keeping costs low.

It is interesting to note that perhaps the technological shift will not only *enable* but *require* a tremendous effort to streamline the procedure. This interesting point is linked to the argument presented above, that technology holds the key to allowing previously indisposed claimants to bring their complaints to ADR in the first place. Logically, if the access to justice is exponentially increased, without an accompanying increase in the efficiency of the ADR system, it would become clogged by the thousands of small value disputes, resulting in delays that would in any event defeat any advance made by adopting the technology in the first place.[89] Hence, the adoption of technology in ADR processes must focus on the ability to provide justice in a more expedient and cheaper way for it to have a meaningful impact outside the narrow scope of high-stakes corporate disputes.

---

[82] On smart contracts generally, see Mateja Durovic and André Janssen, 'Formation of Smart Contracts under Contract Law' in Larry A. DiMatteo, Michel Cannarsa and Cristina Poncibò (eds.), *The Cambridge Handbook of Smart Contracts, Blockchain Technology and Digital Platforms* (Cambridge: Cambridge University Press, 2019) 61.
[83] See Section 6.4.8.
[84] Pietro Ortolani, 'The Impact of Blockchain Technologies and Smart Contracts on Dispute Resolution: Arbitration and Court Litigation at the Crossroads' (2019) 24(2) *Uniform Law Review* 430 442.
[85] Morison and Harkens, n. 63 at 622.
[86] Ibid. at 631.
[87] See Section 6.3.3.
[88] Katsh and Rabinovich, n. 50 at 58.
[89] Omoola and Oseni, n. 37 at 262.

Academic literature is quick to point out that these benefits do not come for free. The cost of 'cheaper, faster, consistent' justice may be to permanently shift the status quo ante of the legal industry. The argument developed by Zuckerman runs as follows: with the streamlining of ADR procedures, and the increased access to digital, automated DR, which does not need lawyers, the legal profession will indubitably shrink. This will result in turn in a narrower social group from which we can recruit judges, and the remaining lawyers will have substantially narrower skill sets. As the justice system loses the 'human touch', there may appear a gulf 'between human conceptions of law and machine law', leading to a loss of legitimacy of the ADR system and damage to the rule of law, as well as permanent rupture of the social fabric.[90] There may even be a disparity in the ability to access a human lawyer – with rich clients having undisturbed access to a human expert, while those with slimmer budgets having no option but to rely on chatbots and machines.[91] This is not a novel argument, and a similar sentiment can be detected in responses to the news of a new industrial revolution with automation processes that will displace a lot of human employees. It is not in itself a rebuttal to the claim that technology can make justice systems more effective, but rather a warning about the dangers accompanying perhaps too haphazard a leap into the tech world.

It has been argued that technology can bring an immense streamlining of ADR procedures, lowering costs and lessening delays, and in turn aggravating the access to justice effect described above and genuinely contributing to the rise of ADR as a first instance DR channel. However, technology does not only promise solutions, it can also act to 'multipl[y] the number of disputes and their complexity',[92] for example, by the increased activity in the blockchain ecosystem that throws a challenge to the traditional forms of ADR. To that aspect we shall now turn.

6.3.3 Blockchain: A Thorn in ADR's Side

Much like AI and algorithms, 'blockchain' has also become a byword for the inevitable digitalisation of our lives. We can in fact draw a parallel between the development and public perception of blockchain with that of the Internet in the 1990s: strong distrust of regulation, and a belief that the new digital environment will be 'dispute free'.[93] In terms of ADR, it is true that an unprecedented growth of dealings conducted through the medium of blockchain-based smart contracts will require their own sui generis forms of ADR. It may even cause a rise of 'private, self-enforcing systems of arbitration', which can in turn marginalise litigation and traditional ADR.[94] Katsh and Rabinovich argue that as with the Internet, disputes initially arising online were difficult to resolve by traditional ADR or litigation agents who were initially incapable or unwilling to deal with such disputes, leaving the cyber sphere essentially without the means to resolve disputes, and thus annihilating user trust in the new technology. Subsequently, in order to elicit trust (and so attract users) e-commerce websites needed to provide a fair and effective DR and prevention system, which came to be known as ODR. By analogy, to increase trust in blockchain, an effective method for adjudication of disputes arising on chain will have to be provided.[95]

---

[90] Zuckerman, n. 77 at 428.
[91] Toohey et al., n. 17 at 147.
[92] Morison and Harkens, n. 63 at 619.
[93] Katsh and Rabinovich, n. 50 at 74.
[94] Ortolani, n. 84 at 430.
[95] Katsh and Rabinovich, n. 50 at 48.

This is particularly true as regards blockchain because, it is argued, the underlying technology makes it particularly difficult to resolve blockchain-related disputes within the traditional ADR method. Of course the conceptual background to such difficulties stems from the fact that smart contracts are seen as contracts in the *legal* sense, rather than just methods of contractual performance.[96] If one does not subscribe to the view that smart contracts can constitute *legal contracts*, then the problems that we lay out below do not arise, for (if such a view were true) no DR body would ever have to interpret or deal with a smart contract in the absence of an implied or express natural language contract.

Still, on the basis that computer-coded smart contracts may be contracts in the legal sense, it causes tremendous problems to their analysis by traditional ADR bodies. There are problems of interpretation of computer code as well as the application of traditional contract law principles, such as good faith, reasonable expectations, termination, frustration, etc., to smart contracts.[97] There also remains the issue of jurisdiction. One could argue that this is straightforward. For example, parties could insert a clause into their computer-code drafted smart contract that they desire to undertake non-binding negotiation or mediation if a dispute arises, and since these ADR techniques are non-binding, their outcomes would not have the need to be fed immediately back into the smart contract and executed automatically.[98] Scepticism should however be expressed as to the possibility of translating such a clause, relying as it does on the notion of good faith into a binary computer code, in a way that is actually meaningful and reflective of the parties' intentions.

In any case, these issues are on top of the other problems that hinder traditional ADR processes for disputes connected with smart contracts, such as the pseudonymity of the parties, automatic execution and irrevocability of the contractual codes.[99] Despite the apparent simplicity of computer code – binary, 'if-then' contracts, even for simple agreements – a lot of the parties' bargain cannot be reduced to code and continues to rely on open-textured notions such as good faith, reasonableness, etc.[100] Lastly, there is the issue of ideology. Proponents of blockchain technologies see traditional ADR and litigation as centralised systems that defeat the 'de-centralised' nature of blockchain and are consequently dissuaded from utilising traditional ADR channels.[101] We see that behind the notion of 'code as law', blockchain constitutes a platform that requires the parties (in order to foster trust that is a sine qua non for any commercial relations) to devise their own methods of DR,[102] rather than actually creating a frictionless utopia.

It is suggested that these elements make blockchain difficult to fit within the ADR framework without having to fundamentally rework it. In fact, a lot of blockchain-based startups have since undertaken the task of developing an ADR process precisely for on-chain disputes, motivated by the fact that, according to them, the existing channels are not only too slow and inefficient but also inapposite and lacking the necessary tools to deal with this kind of dispute.[103] Another key element that spurred the growth of blockchain-based DR startups is the fact that blockchains

---

[96] Mateja Durovic and Franciszek Lech, 'The Enforceability of Smart Contracts' (2019) 5(2) *Ital Law Journal* 493 494.
[97] Darcy W. E. Allen, Aaron M. Lane and Marta Poblet, 'The Governance of Blockchain Dispute Resolution' (2019) 25 (1) *Harvard Negotiation Law Review* 75 77.
[98] Ibid. at 82.
[99] Ibid. at 80.
[100] Ortolani, n. 84 at 438.
[101] Allen et al., n. 97 at 87.
[102] Ortolani, n. 84 at 433-434.
[103] James Metzger, 'The Current Landscape of Blockchain-Based, Crowdsourced Arbitration' (2019) 19(1) *Macquarie Law Journal* 81 82.

actually tend to be quite dispute prone: far from rendering dispute resolution obsolete, the recent wave of ICO has in turn generated many disputes,[104] which must be resolved by ordinary DR systems.

In any case, the permanent and irreversible aspect of smart contracts may aggravate disputes. Since traditional ADR is incapable of affecting the performance of a smart contract (which is final), it has to adapt in order to cater to the type of disputes that are likely to arise on chain. This is well illustrated by Ortolani: he gives the example of an anti-competitive smart contract – traditionally, under international law, a state may refuse to enforce an arbitration award that grants damages for a breach of an anti-competitive contract.[105] By contrast, if the arbitration is provided for a smart contract, and the arbitral award enforces the smart contract, it will self-perform without the ability of a state organ to intervene. Ortolani concludes that 'States, however, may have other possibilities of reaction' including by 'ordering that the sums of money automatically paid ... be paid back "off-chain"', noting, however, that it would be 'factually impracticable' if not simply impossible.[106] Hence, if states want to retain a gatekeeper function, or if ADR wants to continue to be relevant both to the parties and to the legal community at large, it has to adapt to be able to deal with such issues arising out of the technological nature of the smart contracts. That is precisely what a series of blockchain startups have been doing.

There are, however, some reservations for ADR to be able to effectively cater to the on-chain community. Firstly, a lot of the blockchain DR mechanisms are based on game theory ideas, which are to incentivise jurors to adjudicate disputes according to the perceived consensus majority. Secondly, a lot of these platforms require encoding into the original smart contracts, thus limiting the ability of the parties to be able to appoint a DR partner *ex post* of the dispute arising.[107] Still, it is argued that the ADR community is inherently more flexible and thus a lot more likely to adapt to the challenge posed by blockchain and thus capitalise on this emerging market, albeit at the cost of having to shift its approach.

6.3.4 Technology: ADR's Saviour or Undertaker?

Based on the points advanced in this chapter, one could argue that the cumulative effect of all the changes outlined here will be that ODR will completely supersede ADR, automating the DR system to the extent that traditional ADR will be useless and unnecessary.[108] Additionally, the effect that technology will have, in terms of radically lowering the cost of DR and reducing the time necessary for a dispute to be resolved, may replicate the very pressure that diverted case load from litigation to ADR in the first place.[109] This could mean that the trend will be repeated and there will be a massive exodus of cases from ADR towards ODR and similar dispute resolution methods.

Alternatively, the structure of ADR may remain the same, but be staffed exclusively by machines and automated decision-makers. This has already been the case with algorithmic DR mechanisms.[110] In a way, then, technology can help to rekindle the original spirit that was

---

[104] Ibid. at 430–431.
[105] UN 1958 New York Convention on the recognition and enforcement of foreign arbitral awards, Art. V(2)(b).
[106] Ortolani, n. 84 at 440.
[107] Katsh and Rabinovich, n. 50 at 72.
[108] Omoola and Oseni, n. 37 at 262.
[109] Sourdin et al., n. 1.
[110] See Section 6.4.10.

the foundation of ADR: 'simplicity, speed and cost efficiency'.[111] This process is already underway: over a million disputes are resolved exclusively online, and the growth is exponential – no longer a quirky tech-savvy vision, an automated and technology-dependent ADR is appearing more plausible day by day.[112]

The project of this tech-driven ADR is, however, still 'far from complete' and the fears of complete eradication of ADR and the practitioners in it are premature and exaggerated.[113] In order to pose a serious threat to traditional ADR, the technology-dependent process has to ignite the same dose of trust from the claimants. That is by no means obvious, and in fact trust in ODR, although rising, is not at optimal levels yet.[114] There are also the more abstract arguments: the proponents of complete automation of the process of law making and adjudication mistake the nature of law, interpreting it in the simplistic, Austinian notion of orders backed by threats, capable of being applied to a fact scenario. On the contrary, some point out that providing justice is not such a simple process – instead, it is a deeply social notion that cannot be mechanised, for machines, be it algorithm or AI, cannot reproduce the social nature of law.[115] There's also the point of mutual awareness of the identity of the two parties to the dispute that is somehow key to the process of dispensing justice.[116] A DR system that does not address this and is content at keeping the parties mutually unaware of each other's identity may not garner sufficient trust for it to be a successful endeavor.

Lastly, as will be demonstrated below, most of the DR programmes rely on game theory, Shelling Points, and incentive structures to ensure 'fair' results. If this is the future of ODR, which is said to eclipse ADR, it is subject to serious criticism. One is whether a group of dispersed individuals, stemming from different legal and cultural understandings of a particular dispute may even agree to a consensus decision.[117] These systems, if wanting to produce lasting change, must address this, as well as make sure that their software is immune to 'jurors' simply deciding the cases arbitrarily, or gaming the systems to reap awards that were supposed to incentivise them.[118] However, many of the new generation DR systems that were analysed already address such potential problems.

6.4 TECHNOLOGY IN PRACTICE: EXAMPLES OF 'NEW' ADR

6.4.1 *Kleros*

Kleros is a platform founded in 2017, and it offers what is described as 'crowdsourced ODR' – a justice mechanism at the nexus of crowdsourcing, blockchain and game theory'.[119] It has been hailed by some as the 'most ambitious' DR system to arise from the blockchain revolution.[120] It was created as an answer to the dearth of methods to adjudicate disputes arising from blockchain, and particularly aims to provide adjudication for smart contracts. It is described by its inventors as a 'decentralized application built on top of Ethereum that works as a decentralized

---

[111] Sam Karim QC, 'Artificial Intelligence: An Undiscovered Future of Arbitration' (2019) 22(2) *International Arbitration Law Review* 47 54.
[112] Ibid. at 55.
[113] Ibid.
[114] Ebner and Zelzinkow, n. 2 at 155.
[115] Morison and Harkens, n. 63 at 619.
[116] Katsh and Rabinovich, n. 21 at 73.
[117] Metzger, n. 103 at 100.
[118] Ibid. at 101.
[119] Allen et al., n. 97 at 86.
[120] Metzger, n. 103 at 99.

third party to arbitrate dispute' that utilises blockchain technology and game theory to supply dispute resolution in a 'fast, inexpensive, reliable and decentralized way'.[121] It works by way of an opt-in mechanism, whereby it has to be specified as the preferred DR method for the actual smart contract subject to the dispute.

Its process is as follows: potential jurors deposit Kleros' cryptocurrency (Pinakion – PNK) – the more they deposit the higher the chance of them being selected as a juror for a case.[122] Those selected are anonymous to each other.[123] This 'coin' (a skeuomorph evidencing a degree of nostalgia unexpected from the futurists of the Silicon Valley) was originally given for free to early users, but can now be purchased on the mainstream cryptocurrencies exchanges.[124] The indigenous Kleros coin is said to 'provide jurors with the incentive to vote honestly by making incoherent jurors pay part of their deposit to coherent ones'.[125] The reliance on 'coins' to incentivise the adjudicators is understandable, but it may also lead to some problems. Kleros requires an initial investment of 80,000 PNK in order to have a chance to become a juror,[126] which, as of June 2020, translated to $1,740 (~£1,390). Such a not negligible starting cost may act as a potential barrier to entry. An intelligent feature of the Kleros system is that it can freeze the performance of the smart contract (provided that Kleros' 'jurisdiction', for lack of a better term, was encoded into the original code), hence avoiding the DR being rendered futile by the self-executing nature of smart contracts.[127]

The jurors (three at first instance) then receive the evidence and decide the case. Each individual smart contract may provide for an idiosyncratic voting procedure as well as the possible remedies (be it transfer of tokenised assets, payment of cryptocurrency as 'damages', etc.).[128] Those judges who vote with the majority are rewarded by a proportional fraction of the sum of all deposited tokens, whereas the minority-voting jurors have the tokens taken away. This creates the incentive to vote consistently, fairly and honestly, according to Kleros. The underlying assumption seems to be that those jurors who did not agree with the majority either lacked the expertise, did not assess the evidence properly or did not attempt to reach an accurate decision (due to bribery, fraud or ill-will).[129] Following casting of the vote, the juror cannot change his or her mind, and other jurors do not see the way that their colleagues voted, all in order to prevent mutual influence.[130] The whole system relies on the notion of Shelling Points, or the idea that 'when a number of people with similar background and knowledge hear the same bit of information, they should all come to the same conclusion'.[131]

Parties can appeal from the first instance judgment and each appeal means doubling of the number of jurors plus one (if there were three initially, on appeal it would be seven, etc.); there is no cap on the number of appeals, though costs grow proportionally with each one, meaning that at some point it will make more economic sense for parties to settle amicably between themselves rather than pay so much for another chance at the adjudication.[132] The jurors who

---

[121] Clement Lesaege and Federico Ast, 'Kleros. Short Paper v1.05' (2018) at 1, https://kleros.io/ (accessed 22 June 2020).
[122] Ibid. at 3.
[123] Katsh and Rabinovich, n. 50 at 59.
[124] Metzger, n. 104 at 99–100.
[125] Lesaege and Ast, n. 121 at 4.
[126] Metzger, n. 104 at 100.
[127] Katsh and Rabinovich, n. 50 at 59.
[128] Ibid. at 60.
[129] Ibid.
[130] Allen et al., n. 97 at 82.
[131] Paul Keenan and Allen Taylor, 'Bringing Dispute Resolution to the Blockchain', *BlockchainTimes* (27 February 2018), https://blockchaintimes.io/2018/02/27/bringing-dispute-resolution-to-the-blockchain/ (accessed 22 June 2020).
[132] Katsh and Rabinovich, n. 50 at 60.

decided the judgment that is appealed are not paid, because the jurors are invited to explain their judgment, in a hope that a well-explained judgment is likely to disincentivise appeals, and so in case of an appeal punishing the juror is in place.[133] Klerors' inventors even foresee their platform development along the lines experienced by almost all developed national legal systems: into a grid of specialised courts, where the jurors would start in the general court and follow a path to a specific subcourt according to their skills, with each subcourt having specific features[134]. The verdict of the jurors may be communicated into the smart contracts through an 'oracle' (an encoded 'window' allowing real-world information to be fed to the on-chain smart contract).[135]

6.4.2 Juris

Similar in its nature to Kleros, the Juris system offers a DR system based on blockchain and Juris tokens (JRS).[136] Like Kleros, it has to be designated as the DR system in the underlying smart contract, preserving the consensual nature of ADR. It also provides an option to freeze the performance of the smart contract. It relies on Shelling Points and token incentives to promote coherent and consistent resolution.

What sets Juris apart is the multi-tiered system, which earned it the label of the 'most structured' of the blockchain dispute resolution systems"[137]. At first stage, the system provides a type of blockchain mediation, which it labels 'SELF Mediation'. It centres on consensual agreement between the parties.[138] This stage requires no tokens and so comes essentially free to the parties.[139] If this step proves insufficient to resolve the dispute, it then offers a process called 'SNAP Arbitration'. The catchy acronym stands for 'Simple Neutral Arbitrator Poll' and is just a complex way of saying that the dispute is then adjudicated by a pool of selected jurors who are anonymous and have to provide a short opinion explaining their judgment.[140] After this 'award', the parties can return to the mediation phase and settle. The decision can then again be reviewed with arbitrators, and legal advisors can be called to aid them in their deliberation, after which the arbitrators select of the available justifications and explain their reasoning.[141]

The level above that is the PANEL (Pre-emptory Agreement for Neutral Expert Litigation), where the experienced jurors (or 'High Jurists' in Juris-speak) adjudicate the dispute within thirty days, and the award is binding under the 1958 NY Convention.[142] The Juris White Paper argues that 'this panel will be selected by UN mandated rules, and convene virtually through the Juris Platform' as well as have power 'to hear additional arguments from the parties, request, collect, and review additional evidence' including by holding 'video-based hearings' before 'a presiding High Jurist will render a decision on behalf of the panel, which will be binding on the parties'.[143] The PANEL judgment rescinds the underlying smart contract and instead provides for the judgment to be automatically enforced.

---

[133] Lesaege and Ast, n. 121 at 8.
[134] Ibid. at 10.
[135] Allen et al., n. 97 at 86.
[136] Katsh and Rabinovich, n. 50 at 61.
[137] Metzger, n. 104 at 97.
[138] Katsh and Rabinovich, n. 50 at 61.
[139] Metzger, n. 104 at 98.
[140] Katsh and Rabinovich, n. 50 at 62.
[141] Ibid. at 61–62.
[142] Ibid. at 61.
[143] Metzger, n. 104 at 98.

6.4.3 Mattereum

Mattereum's primary mission is about 'creating digital identities for the world of physical goods',[144] to that goal it also provides a bespoke DR system. The system is based on the notion of a 'Ricardian Contract'. A Ricardian Contract is a method of collating a legal prose contract with a digital asset token to ensure certainty of transaction.[145] This is a method of converting a plain, natural language document into a digital, computer-readable code, which can be electronically signed by the parties on blockchain – which in turn allows it to retain its natural language format even on chain, helping to address some of the difficulties posed by smart contracts.[146]

Mattereum's platform also stands out for its 'automated custodian tool' – a real world asset's legal owner and registrar,[147] further collating the digital with the physical realities. In order to increase the certainty of the parties, it also provides arbitration by 'technically competent mediators' in a way that makes any awards legally binding under the 1958 New York Convention.[148] The arbitrators are said to be independent and provided by third body, either selected by the parties from the options suggested by Mattereum or any other mutually acceptable body.[149]

One can thus appreciate that the novel aspect of the platform is not in its ADR innovation, but rather in the fact that it attempts to use blockchain technology for off-chain assets. For the DR, it relies on the traditional model, providing for old school ADR rather than a token-incentivised, game theory–based, blockchain jury system.

6.4.4 JUR

JUR claims to 'allow anyone to build a jurisdiction on the blockchain to offer quick, affordable and fair dispute resolution'.[150] Its 'Court Layer' focuses on smart ADR worthy of the blockchain era.[151] Its internal mechanism resembles the mainstream with a 'decentralised voting system' that relies on game theory and tokenisation of impartial and anonymous jurors.[152] Those who vote with the majority are rewarded, though a more flexible approach as to structuring of the ADR process is provided, with users capable of regulating the voting procedure as well as voting rights.[153]

The cryptocurrency-based incentive system adopted by JUR differs from that of the other platforms discussed. In JUR's mechanism, it is those jurors whose votes actually constituted the majority that take over the tokens deposited by those who did not vote with the majority. This structure has as its goal ensuring that rational voters are supposed to vote only when they have a high degree of confidence in their ability to predict what the actual majority will select.[154] The jurors have an incentive to vote for the option they think will ultimately prevail, rather than just

---

[144] Mattereum, 'About' (2020), https://mattereum.com/about/ (accessed 22 June 2020).
[145] Allen et al., n. 97 at 84.
[146] Metzger, n. 104 at 88.
[147] Katsh and Rabinovich, n. 50 at 67.
[148] Allen et al., n. 97 at 84.
[149] Katsh and Rabinovich, n. 50 at 67.
[150] JUR, https://jur.io/ (accessed 22 June 2020).
[151] JUR, 'White Paper' (July 2019) at 27, https://jur.io/wp-content/uploads/2019/05/jur-whitepaper-v.2.0.2.pdf (accessed 22 June 2020).
[152] Katsh and Rabinovich, n. 50 at 63.
[153] Ibid. at 63.
[154] Ibid.

voting for whichever option has to most votes at the time of the vote to retain tokens, this is augmented by the ceiling on the gap between the votes obtained for each party (of 200 per cent by default).[155] To illustrate, if in a dispute of A v. B, 15 tokens were staked by the jurors, 10 in favour of A and 5 in favour of B, the 5 would be forfeit as B lost the dispute – they would be distributed to the 5.1 voters who first voted for A (since those 5.1 were the votes *necessary* for A to have majority).[156] All of those steps are required since the voting on JUR is transparent and visible to others.

6.4.5 Jury Online

Jury Online is predominantly a platform for promoting safe investments in cryptocurrency ICOs rather than a dedicated ADR tool. However, it has also provided for a dispute resolution mechanism, though it definitely did not comprise the platform's top priority, evidenced by the fact that it refers to its DR process as 'arbitration' and 'mediation' interchangeably, suggesting some confusion as to the nature and meaning of the ADR processes.[157]

The ADR tool works by including a dispute resolution clause in the original ICO agreement, hence providing the platform with jurisdiction in the event of a dispute arising. When the dispute does arise, a panel of jurors, or a judge or an arbitrator from a selected pool of expert arbitrators, is appointed.[158] The materials are provided to the arbitrators, or to the arbitrators and expert judge or solely to the judge who review it and anonymously make a decision, subject to appeal.[159] Each arbitrator is rated based on the decision they made. The higher the rating of the juror, the more likely he is to be staffed on decisions in the later stages of appeal.

6.4.6 Aragon

Aragon's mission is said to be not only to provide 'fast and fair' DR, but also to 'help communities protect shared resources'.[160] The company fairly points out that while 'traditional entities' (by which it seemingly understands real-world companies and organisations) can be 'managed optimistically' thanks to the 'social capital at stake' and 'reliable legal deterrents', while decentralised autonomous organisations (DAOs)[161] often lack the same protections when a managing member 'crosses a boundary they shouldn't'.[162] Hence, Aragon does not simply enforce the 'terms' of a contract between two parties, but can be programmed to enforce organisation's by-laws or statutes.[163]

Accordingly, Aragon provides an agreement that specifies Aragon as the designated forum for that particular DAO's disputes and thus gives it jurisdiction. If a dispute arises, a small number of jurors is randomly selected from the 'juror pool' to rule on the dispute; if any party (or, for that matter, an disinterested 'officious bystander'[164] outside the privity of the dispute, since everything on Aragon is transparent and public and everyone has the right to appeal) feels like the ruling

---

[155] Metzger, n. 104 at 97.
[156] Ibid. at 95.
[157] Ibid. at 92.
[158] Allen et al., n. 97 at 87.
[159] Katsh and Rabinovich, n. 50 at 69.
[160] Aragon Association, 'Court', https://aragon.org/court (accessed 22 June 2020).
[161] Organisations placed on a blockchain that are governed by coded, computer-readable rules.
[162] Aragon Association, n. 160).
[163] Metzger, n. 104 at 93.
[164] To borrow a classic phrase from MacKinnon LJ in *Shirlaw v. Southern Foundries (1926) Ltd.* [1939] 2 KB 206 227.

was deficient, they can pay a fee to have an appeal before a larger number of jurors, which process can be repeated until the dispute is being adjudicated by Aragon's *entire* juror pool.[165] The fees payable by the disputing parties would be a function of the overall reputation of the juror pool voting on the case,[166] and so one would expect it to be increasing proportionally with each appeal.

One could point out that the system is at least theoretically subject to serious shortcomings. If one was a malefactor towards the DAO that has its dispute adjudicated, it could appeal 'its' dispute forever, provided it had the funds for it. What is interesting, however, is that Aragon is planning to feed past juror rulings into an archive, to mimic a precedent system on chain, in an expectation that jurors would be familiar with such 'precedents' and thus rule consistently.[167] It is not stated if there would in fact be an obligation to support or reference a past decision in the ruling of the jurors.

6.4.7 RHUbarb

RHUbarb makes bold promises to provide the 'future of law' on blockchain as well as to 'decentralise' law.[168] They draw attention to the problem that traditional law is failing – it is 'highly centralised', 'excessively intermediated' and 'fails to address the unique needs of online, cross-border and emerging blockchain applications'.[169] They go on to point out that '60% of economic value goes to court costs, lawyers, expert witnesses, etc.', and that the law is 'unprepared to integrate ... ADR and rapidly-growing web and blockchain processes', all the while being prohibitively expensive ('fewer than 15% of Americans can afford a lawyer').[170]

The platform's answer is their own 'rapid distributed consensus mechanisms' (RDCMs),[171] though its precise technology is not described, and the website only argues that they help the platform to 'make dispute resolution faster, less costly and more democratic'.[172] RHUbarb has also partnered up (by virtue of being run by the same people) with PeopleClaim, the largest community ODR website, which handles 30,000 disputes, employs 3,000 arbitrators and adopts RHUcoin as their settlement currency.[173] PeopleClaim uses technology to suggest outcomes for disputing parties, using the wisdom of the crowd to resolve individual disputes.

Accordingly, RHUbarb's DR mechanism bases its process on PeopleClaim. Its first instance is in essence a community poll, similar to that conducted on PeopleClaim (i.e., asking the RHUcoin community for solutions and seeking a broad consensus), a RDCM jury verdict whereby again jurors supporting the minority decision forfeit their coins, with the possibility to actually make the outcome of this binding if such a clause is inserted into the initial contract.[174] At both levels there is a 'self-funding process' that allows jurors or community members to submit their own (previously unforeseen) solutions to the dispute and be rewarded

---

[165] Aragon Association, n. 160.
[166] Katsh and Rabinovich, n. 50 at 64.
[167] Ibid. at 64.
[168] RHUbarb powered by RHUcoin website, www.rhucoin.com/home.aspx#:~:text=Rhubarb%20was%20created%20by%20the,largest%20fully%2Ddistributed%20justice%20network.&text=This%20will%20be%20used%20to,where%20PeopleClaim%20has%20existing%20relationships (accessed 22 June 2020).
[169] Ibid.
[170] Ibid.
[171] Ibid.
[172] Ibid.
[173] Ibid.
[174] Katsh and Rabinovich, n. 50 at 68.

if that is the option that ends up being preferred.[175] Another very interesting aspect is what RHUbarb calls 'Interactive Class Action (ICA)' – allowing claimants with similar disputes to negotiate with a common defendant, or settle individually if they please,[176] thus bringing a staple of Anglo-Saxon judicial tradition on chain.

6.4.8 Multi-signature Smart Contract

This is not a separate platform advertising a given product, but it warrants analysis, inasmuch as it is a method of solving disputes online, especially those arising in connection with smart contracts concluded on a blockchain.

The process of multi-signature smart contracts provides a method for conducting self-enforcing arbitration on chain. This mechanism has been compared to a 'lock with two keyholes', every party has their own key, with the third one being given to a previously specified arbitrator or an ADR body.[177] In order to 'fulfill' the contract and release the asset tokens, two keys must be inserted into the smart contract, if the agreement goes to plan then each party inserts their 'key' and releases the exchange of goods, if, however, a dispute arises, then the arbitrator may assess the facts and decide whether to use their key (releasing the asset) or withhold their signature (thus in essence annulling the obligation to perform).

In 2019, 30 per cent of all bitcoin was stored on precisely this type of contract and there was a range of specialised websites dedicated to providing the arbitration for such disputes.[178] What is perhaps the most surprising is that traditional ADR providers have not seized on this opportunity and are not providing arbitration that could be linked in this method to the smart contract, though perhaps this apathy will not last long.[179]

Another related technical aspect is the mechanism of the so-called oracles. An oracle is essentially an 'external source of information' that a smart contract 'can refer to and draw inferences from'.[180] In this way, the smart contract will have a coded clause that gives a possibility for performance to be stopped or reversed if the designated outside world source gives a signal. The oracle could then communicate to the smart contract that an arbitral award was made and that performance ought to be halted. In other words, the 'external information retrieved [through the oracle] by the smart contract could be an arbitral award, and software script could be used to enforce the outcome of the procedure'.[181] This method is less secure than the multi-signature method because it does not make performance *conditional* on the assent of two parties, or the prevailing party and the arbitrator, but rather just allows the finality of the smart contract to be softened by virtue of a smart contract arbitration clause.

6.4.9 Blockchain Arbitration Forum

The Blockchain Arbitration Forum (BAF) was founded in 2018 in order to provide 'clear procedures and rules for fair play to arbitrate disputes' between companies 'deploying

---

[175] Ibid.
[176] RHUbarb, n. 168.
[177] Ortolani, n. 84 at 434.
[178] Ibid. at 435.
[179] Ibid. at 439.
[180] Ibid.
[181] Ibid.

smart-contract-based solutions'.[182] It provides a template for smart contracts that contains arbitration and mediation clauses. It must, however, be pointed out that on its website it only provides natural language formulations, suggesting that they are intended for the natural-language 'wrapper contract' around the actual smart contract, rather than to be inserted in computer code within the smart contract. It also provides a database of arbitrators with 'the necessary legal and technical background'.[183]

BAF also offers a Smart Contract Arbitration Library, which contains a set of coded rules based on UNCITRAL arbitration rules, which allow the parties to pause, resume, modify or terminate an on-chain smart contract.[184] A smart contract concluded with such rules in mind permits the party to utilise the 'pause and send to arbitrator' function on their dashboard, which halts the performance of the code and instead refers the dispute to the mediator or arbitrator, depending on what clause was inserted.[185]

6.4.10 ClickNSettle and Others

The next string of online platforms that are discussed are different from the ones discussed above by virtue of the fact that they do not centre on blockchain, but still implement technology to solve disputes in a faster and cheaper way than traditional ADR. The technology that is most prominently used by such fora are AI- and algorithm-supported 'blind-bidding' mechanisms for negotiations. The process of negotiation is and has been a type of ADR, but in this type of blind-bidding, an algorithm helps the parties to arrive at the optimal outcome by obtaining information from both disputants and their ranking of contentious points and combines those data points to suggest solutions.[186]

The main platform is Cybersettle.com, which is an online platform for insurance claims, and which is increasingly winning its place as a mainstream ADR provider, despite being one of the pioneers of ODR back in the 1990s. It utilises the 'patented' double blind negotiation mechanism to facilitate settlement.[187] It works by having the claimant and the respondent each submit their highest and lowest settlement figures that they are prepared to accept. Its algorithms then compare the offers confidentially and sees whether the parties are within the range of agreement. An offer of settlement is sent by the software to the other party, without disclosing the exact amount, allowing the other party to submit a counter-offer, and then again submitting an aggregate to the parties for acceptance or rejection.[188] It handled over 200,000 claims of combined value in excess of $1.6 billion,[189] indicating that despite being less technologically advanced than its blockchain-based older siblings it is still in high demand. This mechanism has been adopted by a range of providers such as Smartsettle.com, ClickNSettle, WeClaim and many more.

6.5 CONCLUSION

In conclusion, the argument advanced was that the technological revolution that is taking the ADR world by storm will have far-reaching impact on the way that ADR is provided. It shall also

---

[182] BAF, 'Dispute Resolution' (2020), http://blockchainarbitrationforum.org/dispute-resolution/ (accessed 22 June 2020).
[183] Ibid.
[184] Allen et al., n. 97 at 86–87.
[185] Ibid. at 87.
[186] Legg, n. 38 at 3.
[187] Cybersettle.com, http://cybersettle.com/ (accessed 22 June 2020).
[188] Omoola and Oseni, n. 37 at 271.
[189] Barnett and Treleaven, n. 11 at 404.

affect the fundamental principles that underpin the whole field. As frequently is the case with novelties, it is easy to fall into extreme optimism or pessimism about the impact of the technological change, though the truth as always lies somewhere in the middle.

It has been argued that technology has the profound possibility to increase access to justice, by allowing claimants, who were previously unable to utilise established ADR channels from submitting their disputes to the tech-aided ADR, by reducing costs and time delays. This in turn would make it even more accessible to consumer or SMEs claimants and enable ADR to concern itself with disputes arising from the new technologies such as blockchain, which have hitherto been considered outside the scope of traditional ADR or litigation. The possibility of complete automation of resolution of disputes is subject to serious reservations regarding the use of algorithms and game theory to the benefit of the claimants in a transparent and comprehensible way – as becomes apparent from the analysis of individual examples in Section 6.3; most if not all rely in some way or another on game theory, AI and algorithms, and if they cannot guarantee a safe and beneficial way of utilising such technologies, the positive impact will be in jeopardy.

Lastly, we argue that the technological advancements are already underway, but not established to the extent that some commentators claim. Robo-judges are not a reality yet, nor will they be in the next months, though it also is to be stressed that fundamental ODR technologies such as remote communication technologies will no doubt quickly permeate the ADR and litigation fields due to the COVID-19–related remote mode of dispensing justice. The fundamental shift will come when established ADR providers will turn to accommodate smart contract and online disputes.

7

A Blockchain-Based Smart Dispute Resolution Method

Alessandro Palombo, Raffaele Battaglini, and Luigi Cantisani

7.1 INTRODUCTION

Lex Mercatoria, Latin for 'merchant law,' is a very old concept that predates the rise of nation-states. During the medieval period, a body of legal conventions evolved through custom and commercial practice and was enforced by private courts along the merchant trade routes.[1] Modern nation-states came to replace this traditional method of resolving disputes with domestic courts. But the gradual increase in international commerce has encouraged nations to defer to international arbitration as a solution to complex cross-border business disputes, and various other alternatives to lawsuits brought in civil courts.

Now the blockchain, using distributed ledger technology, allows the programming of smart contracts and enables their use in business relationships. In response, various platforms are seeking to offer dispute resolution mechanisms specifically for smart contracts. These dispute resolution mechanisms may prove very useful for small disputes because, in those instances, it is essential to minimize costs and time required to achieve a resolution. Currently, the awards from this type of dispute resolution are generally not legally binding and hence are not suitable for disputes involving larger sums of money, nor can they render judgments that do more than merely move funds between parties.

This chapter describes, in general terms, a potential structure to deliver legally binding arbitration decisions using blockchain technology to improve on existing methods. This structure would support the development of a network of arbitration hubs, each with its own focus, leading to the evolution of a new system of naturally evolving *lex mercatoria*, where businesses can choose a virtual jurisdiction that is compliant with the laws of nations but is also designed to address their specific needs.

7.2 ARBITRATION AND ADR: CURRENT STATUS

This section of the chapter provides a brief summary of the existing framework for arbitration and other ADR mechanisms. An extensive body of literature already covers this subject matter,

---

[1] G. B. Born, *International Commercial Arbitration*, vol. 1 (Alphen aan den Rijn: Wolters Kluwer, 2014) 27; P. T. Leeson, 'One More Time with Feeling: The Law Merchant, Arbitration, and International Trade' (2007) *Indian Journal of Economics and Business*, https://ssrn.com/abstract=887170 (accessed May 19, 2020). See also P. Ortolani, 'The Judicialisation of Blockchain', (2020) *Social Science Research Network* 17, https://ssrn.com/abstract=3230880 (accessed May 19, 2020).

so this chapter will focus on some key points in order to better understand some of the weaknesses of such mechanisms and the problems that the current proposal aims to fix.

7.2.1 Scope of Arbitration and ADR

Arbitration is essentially a private system of adjudication, by means of which the parties involved in a legal dispute resolve disputes outside of the judicial system. For this purpose, the parties appoint one or more third-party arbitrators. The parties decide if the arbitral proceedings will be administered by an arbitral institution or by independent experts who are not related to any institution (ad hoc arbitration). The parties also choose the arbitration rules to be applied, the place of arbitration, and the language of the proceedings. The decision made by the arbitrator(s), namely, the arbitral award, is meant to be final, binding, and enforceable in a domestic court.[2]

Arbitration is a tool to manage and solve disputes that gives the parties substantial autonomy and control over the process. All the above-listed choices are made in writing by the parties through an arbitration agreement or an arbitration clause included in their contract. Arbitration clauses are common in international contracts, as the parties seek to avoid the risk being sued in a foreign jurisdiction: 'Partly to avoid some of these problems, arbitration is quite often chosen as the method of resolving disputes in international contracts, rather than leaving it to the courts.'[3] The arbitral body represents a neutral forum, administered by decision-makers who are specialists in business transactions and commercial practices, and where the rules can be tailored to the individual dispute.

Aside from arbitration, other dispute resolution mechanisms are available, usually referred to as alternative dispute resolution (ADR). Most of them do not provide for a final, binding, and enforceable decision; on the contrary, most of them result in settlement agreements. ADR refers to methods such as mediation, conciliation, and mini-trials, as well as to binding and hybrid methods such as last-offer arbitration, mediation-arbitration hybrids, and expert determinations. However, the term has a partially different meaning in each part of the world. In Europe, ADR does not include arbitration; in the United States, ADR means all dispute resolution mechanisms other than litigation, including arbitration. Such alternative methods arose out of the need for legal professionals to offer quicker and cheaper ways than arbitration to solve their clients' disputes, as well as a more predictable access to justice. The proposal put forth in this chapter is to improve upon the current models of arbitration with the aim of reducing costs, increasing accessibility, and reducing the duration of proceedings.

7.2.2 Sovereign Jurisdictional Authority and Private Autonomy

The rise of modern sovereign states in the eighteenth century made jurisdiction an expression of sovereignty. Hence, justice became an issue of public interest rather than a purely private affair. Nonetheless, in the field of trade and commerce, a model for private dispute resolution survived and evolved into the current paradigm for commercial arbitration. Moreover, due to the needs of international trade, the importance of arbitration has increased dramatically in the twentieth century, as reflected by the adoption of several international conventions (explored in Section

---

[2] See Section 7.3.3.
[3] 'Governing Law and Jurisdiction in International Contracts', Internationalcontracts.net (June 27, 2013), https://internationalcontracts.net/contract/blog/181-governing-law-and-jurisdiction-in-international-contracts (accessed May 19, 2020).

7.2.3) and by the rise of major arbitral institutions. In international trade disputes, businesspeople prefer the efficiency, confidentiality, and expertise offered by arbitration. Eventually, national laws evolved to support commercial arbitration as a preferred means of dispute resolution, especially in international transactions. This marked a shift from public to private justice.

This trend towards arbitration was inevitable and continues to accelerate, with international commercial arbitration growing at a rapid pace in Asia. The twenty-first century also marked the rise of online transactions. As a result, several online dispute resolution (ODR) mechanisms embedded in online platforms were created (such as, eBay and PayPal).[4] Such mechanisms provide traders and consumers easier access to justice and at little or no cost, but they suffer from three fundamental limitations:

(1) they do not have the same legal force as more sophisticated mechanisms capable of rendering legally binding and enforceable decisions;
(2) they are not supported by sophisticated technologies that allow for self-execution and self-enforcement, unlike the new blockchain-based models that are discussed in Section 7.3;
(3) each of them is designed around the platform of which they are a part, so they cannot serve as a universally applicable model for all types of microclaims.

The advent of blockchain technology has opened up new opportunities for the development of ODR mechanisms, but the ability of these mechanisms to fully address the needs of the parties is limited. A well designed ODR mechanism should enhance party autonomy and allow for the blossoming of a new *lex mercatoria*. If the contract is the maximum expression of the freedom of the parties, private arbitration, is its natural extension.[5] However, traditional arbitration's effectiveness still depends on state sovereign power. An arbitral award is effective, final, binding, and enforceable as long as it complies with the complex legal framework made of international treaties, guidelines, national procedural law, and public policy.[6] In other words, modern sovereign states permit arbitration as an exception to the jurisdiction of their courts, but only with some very functional 'safeguards'. Therefore, any new dispute resolution methods aiming to innovate within the ADR scenario, including ODR, have to be consistent with international and national rules of arbitration.

7.2.3 Existing Framework and International Conventions

There are five layers of rules that apply to the arbitration process. The arbitration agreement provides the first layer of rules governing private dispute resolution that is directly related to the parties. Additional rules allow for the expansion of the arbitration in terms of scope and the incorporation of other parties besides the parties to the contract.

The second layer is represented by the arbitration rules chosen by the contracting or disputing parties, such as the adoption of rules established by major arbitral institutions such as the London Court of International Arbitration (LCIA). Parties may choose the complete sets of

---

[4] C. Camion, 'Three Trade-Offs to Efficient Dispute Resolution' in K. Benyekhlef, J. Bailey, J. Burkell, and F. Gélinas (eds.), *eAccess to Justice* (Ottawa: University of Ottawa Press, 2016) 317.
[5] S. A. Fagbemi, 'The Doctrine of Party Autonomy in Commercial Arbitration: Myth or Reality?' (2015) *Journal of Sustainable Development Law and Policy* 223.
[6] L. A. DiMatteo, M. Infantino and N. Potin (eds.), *Cambridge Handbook of Judicial Control over Arbitral Awards* (Cambridge: Cambridge University Press, 2021).

arbitration rules or derogate from some by means of specifications written into their arbitration agreement. However, some types of derogations may not be permitted by the institution.[7]

The third layer consists of national laws, which include both the arbitration law of the seat of the arbitration (*lex arbitri*), as well as relevant substantive law. As regards *lex arbitri*, in order to achieve more uniformity for the benefit of business transactions, many countries have adopted the UNCITRAL Model Law on International Commercial Arbitration 1985, amended in 2006 (UNCITRAL Model Law).[8] It is worth noting that the UNCITRAL Model Law is not a binding international treaty; it acts as a guideline that countries elect to incorporate into their national laws to provide for more uniformity and harmonization among countries. Thus, the UNCITRAL Model Law's contents are directed at states, not at parties to a dispute, which means that if the parties choose, for instance, Japan's *lex arbitri*, they are automatically choosing the UNCITRAL Model Law, which is the *lex arbitri* of Japan, unless it is expressly excluded in the arbitration agreement. The second layer also includes substantive law, the national law chosen by the parties to interpret the contract and to decide on the merits of the dispute.

The fourth layer includes international arbitration practices, some of which have been codified as guidelines or additional rules governing proceedings.[9] Some are considered good practices that are merely known, shared, and applied within the relatively small arbitration community and act to provide more procedural coherence.

The fifth layer includes binding international treaties. The most relevant one is the United Nations Convention on the Recognition and Enforcement of Foreign Arbitral Awards, New York, 1958 (New York Convention), signed by over 160 state parties. It governs the recognition and enforcement of arbitration agreements and arbitral awards.

Other relevant treaties include:

- European Convention on International Commercial Arbitration, which supplements the New York Convention in terms of party's rights in arbitration, and reasons for refusing to recognize or enforce an arbitral award;
- Panama Convention, which has been adopted by seventeen countries including the United States, Mexico, and several Central and South American states, and it is similar to the New York Convention in terms of purpose;

---

[7] E.g., LCIA Rules, art. 17.1 ('The initial language of the arbitration shall be the language of the Arbitration Agreement, unless the parties have agreed in writing otherwise ....').

[8] UNCITRAL is the United Nations Commission on International Trade Law. Its mandate is to further the progressive harmonization and unification of the law of international trade. The following countries, territories, or states within the United States have adopted the UNCITRAL Model Law on International Commercial Arbitration: Armenia, Australia, Austria, Azerbaijan, Bahrain, Bangladesh, Belarus, Bulgaria, Cambodia, Canada, Chile, China (Hong Kong Special Administrative Region, Macau Special Administrative Region), Croatia, Cyprus, Denmark, Dominican Republic, Egypt, Estonia, Georgia, Germany, Greece, Guatemala, Honduras, Hungary, India, Iran (Islamic Republic of), Ireland, Japan, Jordan, Kenya, Lithuania, Madagascar, Malta, Mauritius, Mexico, New Zealand, Nicaragua, Nigeria, Norway, Oman, Paraguay, Peru, the Philippines, Poland, Republic of Korea, Russian Federation, Rwanda, Serbia, Singapore, Slovenia, Spain, Sri Lanka, Thailand, Tunisia, Turkey, Uganda, Ukraine, United Kingdom of Great Britain and Northern Ireland (Scotland; Bermuda, an overseas territory of the United Kingdom),United States of America (California, Connecticut, Florida, Illinois, Louisiana, Oregon and Texas), Venezuela, Zambia, and Zimbabwe, www.uncitral.org/uncitral/en/uncitral_texts/arbitration/1985Model_arbitration_status.html (accessed May 19, 2020).

[9] For example, the International Bar Association developed rules on the Taking of Evidence and on Rules of Ethics, as well as Guidelines on Conflicts of Interest for Arbitrators. UNCITRAL has produced Notes on Organizing Arbitral Proceedings, which, although not binding on the parties or the tribunal, serve to provide for more uniformity and harmonization.

- Washington Convention on the Settlement of Investment Disputes between States and Nationals of other States, promoted by the World Bank. This established the International Center for the Settlement of Investment Disputes, an arbitral institution that applies commercial arbitration mechanisms to investor-state disputes arising from measures adopted by states that damage investments made by a foreign company in that state, provided that the state that issued the measure and the state of incorporation of the damaged company are parties to the investment treaty.

7.2.4 Advantages and Disadvantages of Arbitration and ADR

An empirical study of why parties choose international arbitration to resolve disputes found that the two most significant reasons were the neutrality of the forum and the likelihood of obtaining enforcement under the New York Convention.[10] A report from the World Bank on the use of ADR (including arbitration) in Cambodia and its relevance for that state, explained that, in general, ADR's main advantages are that it is more flexible, simpler, cheaper, and quicker than conventional court proceedings.[11] A report from the OECD goes further and suggests other advantages including, flexibility in choice of decision-makers and process, ability to combine arbitration with other ADR mechanisms such as mediation (med-arb); detachment from a particular national legal order; and speed of process.[12]

Another advantage of ADR and arbitration is the high level of confidentiality covering the process, witnesses, and the award, found in most institutional rules. Many companies prefer confidential procedures in order to avoid disclosing information about business operations and to prevent a potentially negative outcome of a dispute from becoming public, resulting in negative reputation costs.

On the other hand, ADR and arbitration have some serious flaws. The OECD report notes that such procedures suffer from a lack of transparency[13] and lack of precedents. The latter derives from the confidentiality issue as well, since undisclosed or unreported arbitral awards prevent arbitral tribunals from establishing a coherent and predictable jurisprudence. Thus, one strength of arbitration – confidentiality – can also be a weakness. This reasoning also applies to flexibility, speed, and costs of arbitration: as commercial arbitrations have grown in number and in the amount of money at stake, parties have increasingly incorporated litigation-style tactics into the arbitration, which results in delays, longer duration of proceedings, higher costs, and an overall more conflict-ridden and complex process.[14] For example, law firms specializing in commercial arbitration charge extremely high fees for legal services. Other shortcomings of ADR and arbitration include the lack of a right of appeal and the lack of immediate enforceability, since arbitral awards can only be enforced by domestic courts.

---

[10] C. Bühring-Uhle, 'A Survey on Arbitration and Settlement in International Business Disputes' in C. R. Drahozal and R. W. Naimark (eds.), *Towards a Science of International Arbitration* (Alphen aan den Rijn: Kluwer Law International, 2005) 31.

[11] T. Mao and Michael Horn, 'Alternative Dispute Resolution: What It Is, and Why It Is Relevant to Cambodia' (2005) report no. 36824 vol. 1 *Business Issues Bulletin*, http://documents.worldbank.org/curated/en/815321468231847217/pdf/368240Alternation0BIB91Cam11PUBLIC1.pdf (accessed May 19, 2020).

[12] OECD, 'Hearings: Arbitration and Competition' (2010), www.oecd.org/daf/competition/abuse/49294392.pdf (accessed May 19, 2020) (competition disputes are among the most complex kind of disputes).

[13] The confidential nature of arbitration can be perceived as a method of concealing certain practices that the parties do not wish to be made public.

[14] M. L. Moses, 'Introduction to International Commercial Arbitration' in M. L. Moses (ed.), *The Principles and Practice of International Commercial Arbitration* (Cambridge: Cambridge University Press, 2012) 1–17.

Emerging technologies offer the possibility of designing new dispute resolution methods that can solve some of the shortcomings of traditional ADR noted above. Section 7.3 will investigate the development of blockchain-based ODR.

7.3 ADVENT OF BLOCKCHAIN-BASED ODR

The development of the blockchain is one of the most discussed of the new technologies. The potential of blockchain technology and smart contracts applied to dispute resolution has drawn the attention of legal professionals.[15] There is a wide-ranging debate about the development of new adjudication protocols to simplify the resolution of disputes between private actors and make it more efficient. Certain projects have arisen as a result of this debate and as a response to the flaws of current ADR mechanisms.

The purpose of this section is to provide a brief explanation of blockchain technology and smart contracts, illustrating how they can fit into an ADR scenario, and review the current projects committed to designing blockchain-based ADR systems as case studies. For the sake of simplicity, these systems will be referred to as 'smart dispute resolution' (SDR).

7.3.1 Brief Introduction to Blockchain and Smart Contract

A blockchain is a distributed ledger technology that involves a list of transactions that is shared across a numerous computers rather than being stored on a single centralized network or server. Although the notion of distributed ledger technology (DLT) is not new and not necessarily limited to blockchain technology, it became popular with the advent of Bitcoin, a digital currency that is traded digitally through the blockchain.[16] The main objective of Bitcoin was establishing a peer-to-peer transaction system, effectively eliminating the need for intermediaries.

Specifically, a blockchain is a network of computer devices, referred to as 'nodes', that operate in sync to process and store data contained in blocks, with no single point of ownership. Any data addition has to undergo a validating procedure referred to as a 'consensus mechanism', based on algorithms. Any unauthorized modification to an existing block triggers a warning to all the other nodes on the network. This ensures that the existing blocks are not tampered with and that any new data entered is stored only with the approval of the majority of the nodes to authenticate the modification (public blockchain) or approved by supernodes (often used in private blockchains). The integrity of a public blockchain is based on the need to gain majority consent of a large number of nodes, such as in the Bitcoin or Ethereum blockchains, making them less vulnerable to manipulation. In sum, they considered to be tamper-proof (consensus) and transparent (public).[17]

Smart contracts became popular owing to the Ethereum blockchain,[18] but the notion of smart contracts traces back to the writings of Nick Szabo in 1994, which asserted that a contract can be

---

[15] P. Ortolani, 'The Judicialisation of Blockchain' (2018) *Social Science Research Network* 31, https://ssrn.com/abstract=3230880 (accessed May 19, 2020).
[16] The idea of cryptocurrency was the first suggested by a researcher(s) under the pseudonym of Satoshi Nakamoto. S. Nakamoto, "Bitcoin: A Peer-to-Peer Electronic Cash System" (2008), https://bitcoin.org/bitcoin.pdf.
[17] Most of the blockchains are 'public', which, simply put, means that anyone can access the blockchain and view the recordings stored on the chain.
[18] For an in-depth analysis of Bitcoin as self-contained legal system and ODR platform, see P. Ortolani, 'Self-Enforcing Online Dispute Resolution: Lessons from Bitcoin' (2016) 36 (3) *Oxford Journal of Legal Studies* 608.

converted into computer code to ensure automatic enforcement. Szabo defined smart contracts as 'as a set of promises, specified in digital form, including protocols within which the parties perform'.[19] He also said that the smart contracts would enable a self-enforcing contract, where both parties could observe and verify the performance of the contract.

With the advent of blockchain technology, the use of smart contracts as grown at an accelerated rate. The first wave of smart contracts based on a decentralized computer network, allowed the issuing and transacting in digital currencies. The next step in the progression is placing other types of agreements on the blockchain, which is a way of securely storing documents in a tamper-proof way in a hashed form and creating automated transactions.

The creation of cryptocurriencies and smart contracts have posed a challenge to governments on how and when to regulate such activities. The existential question (death of courts or death of law) is whether the self-executing or breachless characteristic of smart contracts will allow private parties to escape the legal system?

7.3.2 Smart (Legal) Contracts and Their Inherent Limits

SDR systems based on smart contracts use automation to establish binding rules and achieve immediate execution. The initial issue becomes: are the smart contracts used in a SDR system legally valid contracts? The most plausible answer is if smart contracts are merely duplications of regular contracts through digitalization (compute coded natural language contracts), then they should be recognized as valid legal contracts (*facta concludentia*).

Obviously, many transactions are much more complex than simple monetary or currency transfers. One method to allow smart contracts to be used in more complex transactions is to allow them to rely on external sources during the performance stage. Oracles, namely, middleware meant to connect the smart contract to external sources of information in order to fill in the gaps in the smart contract. These gaps include fixing an open term or to take account of a change of circumstances subsequent to the formation of the smart contract.[20]

Despite the general legal validity of smart contracts and the ability to broaden their use through the use of oracles, this chapter goes in a different direction by assuming that:

(1) a smart contract is software and, generally speaking, is not a legal contract unless certain strict requirements are met;
(2) human intervention is the best oracle in those cases where the evaluation is subjective (such as, compliance with instructions provided by a customer).

Regarding the first point, it is fair to say that in the same way that the vending machine cannot be considered, in itself, a legal contract but only the material and automated transposition of the contract, similarly, a smart contract is only a means to automate.

Just as vending machines are subject to the application of contract law, smart contracts should be seen as an operational translation of proper legal contracts. In other words, one cannot ignore the need for an underlying traditional legal contract, just as one cannot ignore the need to

---

[19] N. Szabo, 'Smart Contracts Glossary' (1995), https://nakamotoinstitute.org/smart-contracts-glossary/. A vending machine has been seen as a simple form of a smart contract (the contract is purely mechanical: money is inserted and product is delivered).

[20] An 'oracle' on the blockchain is 'simply put, a translator for information provided by an outside platform'. This allows a decentralized application to receive data from the external world as explained in J. Buck, 'Blockchain Oracles, Explained', Cointelegraph (October 18, 2017), https://cointelegraph.com/explained/blockchain-oracles-explained (accessed May 19, 2020).

anchor that contract to a national governing law, which specifies the legal meaning of the transaction and provides a competent forum for disputes that cannot be resolved through automation.

This chapter embraces and pushes the importance of connecting traditional legal contracts to smart contracts for the purpose of having a solid legal basis empowered by automation, to achieve 'smart legal contracts'. This idea preceded the advent of the blockchain technology. The 'Ricardian contract' model, introduced by Ian Gregg in 1995, explained the idea of a hybrid model, meant as a conjunction between a traditional paper contract and a smart contract. It was defined as 'a form of digital documents that act as an agreement between the two parties on the terms and conditions for an interaction between the agreed parties'.[21] Modernizing this notion in the light of blockchain technology means that the parties to a transaction enter into a traditional legal, natural language contract that is machine-convertible. The implementation of a smart contract merely allows for the automatic execution of the legal contract via blockchain.

In its recently published consultation paper, the UK Jurisdiction Taskforce said: 'A smart contract may or may not have legal ramifications as it is merely computer code, whereas a 'smart legal contract' refers to a smart contract that either is, or is part of, a binding legal contract.'[22] That paper illustrates three models for smart contracts and smart legal contracts:

(1) 'Solely Code Model', that is, code standing by itself (without being a part or within the framework of a natural language contractual architecture);
(2) 'Internal Model' is a contract written in a document comprising natural language and code; and
(3) 'External Model' is a contract entirely in natural language but requires certain parts or purposes of the contract to be performed using an automated program.

The second point, the need for a human oracle, recognizes that the current state of technology is not sufficient to provide assessments of subjective elements, including fairness and good faith principles found in contract law. This may not be the case in the future with the evolution of advanced artificial intelligence. But for now, in order to broaden the use of smart contracts, smart contract designs will need to be based on ecosystems involving human oracles. These types of automated-human ecosystems are the genesis for the development of SDR.

7.3.3 Smart Dispute Resolution: State of the Art

This section provides an overview of new SDR systems in order to assess the potential of these emerging projects, if and how they relate to existing frameworks of arbitration and ADR, and to determine the value-added benefits of SDR compared to traditional forms of ADR. This section will also focus on the limitations of current SDR proposals, in order to offer suggestions for their improvement, as well as forwarding a vision of creating a new *lex mercatoria* via the blockchain.

Although these projects present case studies and scenarios, many of the features described by the start-ups examined below are still in development and their success is yet to be determined.[23]

---

[21] I. Grigg, 'Financial Cryptography in 7 Layers' (1998–2000), https://iang.org/papers/fc7.html; I. Grigg, 'The Ricardian Contract', https://iang.org/papers/ricardian_contract.html (both accessed May 19, 2020).
[22] UK Jurisdiction Taskforce of the LawTech Delivery Panel, Public Consultation, 'Consultation on the Status of Cryptoassets, Distributed Ledger Technology and Smart Contracts under English Private Law' (May 31, 2019), www.lawsociety.org.uk/news/documents/ukjt-consultation-cryptoassets-smart-contracts-may-2019/ (accessed May 19, 2020).
[23] For this reason and for informational purposes, this work relies solely on what is publicly available on the websites of these start-ups.

7.3.3.1 *Kleros*

The Kleros project started in 2017 as an open-source dispute resolution protocol that uses blockchain and crowdsourcing for adjudicating disputes. The idea is that the decision-making process is put in the hands of the community. Community members that decide disputes are referred to as jurors and are rewarded by means of economic incentives in the form of tokens named 'Pinakion',[24] and designed as a layer operating on the Ethereum blockchain.[25]

Parties choose the type of Kleros Court (specific for subject matter and experience) to resolve disputes arising from their smart contracts and the number of jurors. Kleros then randomly selects jurors within the selected court's jury pool who will initially be compensated for their availability by the counterparties.[26] The probability of being individually selected as a juror is proportional to the quantity of tokens held by the juror.[27] The jurors are entitled to collect further data from the 'real world' in order to make a decision on the merits. A verdict is issued based on the vote of a majority of the jurors, which automatically results in the transfer of a sum of money being held in escrow to the winning party.[28] Subsequently, Kleros compensates each juror in tokens if they voted with the majority or penalizes those jurors not voting with the majority. This incentive structure is based on game theory as illustrated in Kleros' White Paper.

It is worth noting that Kleros is intended to act as a multipurpose system that can be used for escrow, microtasking, as insurance or an oracle, and social networks.[29] Furthermore, the system is advertised as 'arbitration' even though the Short Paper, published in September 2019, fails to show a system that is a digital equivalent of *stricto sensu* commercial arbitration.

According to its annual report of April 6, 2020,[30] the Kleros project has currently implemented the following:

- SDR system known as 'Kleros Court';
- 'Escrow dApp', which allow users to conduct transactions empowered by escrow smart contracts, with embedded dispute resolution system;
- 'Oracle dApp' that allows users to select Kleros as arbitrator for oracle disputes.

7.3.3.2 *Mattereum*

Mattereum provides a platform for the creation of smart contracts that can solve a wide range of legal issues, with an initial focus on the legal transfer of rights and physical assets on a blockchain.[31] Mattereum uses a decentralized legal register called the 'Smart Property Register', which is an automated Ricardian contract that allows one to stake assets, ensure property rights, and transfer ownership. The system has been designed with a view toward avoiding disputes instead of resolving them, through the use of smart contracts for self-enforcement and an automated custodian.

In sum, the goals of Mattereum are to: (1) place titles or ownership rights of real-world assets on a blockchain and (2) remove the frictions deriving from seeking enforcement of arbitral

---

[24] The name Pinakion was inspired by the ancient Athenian token used to draw people to popular trials.
[25] Kleros, White Paper (September 19, 2019) subject to change, https://kleros.io/whitepaper.pdf (accessed May 19, 2020).
[26] Ibid.
[27] Ibid.
[28] Ibid.
[29] Ibid.
[30] Kleros, Annual Transparency Report (April 6, 2020), https://blog.kleros.io/kleros-annual-transparency-report-2020/ (accessed May 19, 2020).
[31] Mattereum, Summary White Paper (October 2018) subject to change, https://mattereum.com/wp-content/uploads/2020/02/mattereum-summary_white_paper.pdf (accessed May 19, 2020).

awards. It is not clear at this stage if and how cases that are based on traditional contracts rather than smart contracts will be managed and how Mattereum could prevent parties from resorting to traditional arbitration or litigation to reverse a Mattereum's verdict or award.[32]

7.3.4 Limitations of Oracles-Based SDR Systems

The projects examined above raise a number of doubts regarding the adequacy of the proposed SDR models for achieving effective justice. This section assesses competing approaches to determine which one is the most equitable. An oracle-based model is not suitable for making wide-ranging examinations of cases and for issuing decisions with proper legal value. The features of these projects do not fully ensure the rights to a fair hearing, cross-examination, and impartial judgement that are provided by traditional judicial and arbitration systems. SDR systems may successfully structure platforms that use economic modeling based on fairness variables and produce decisional outcomes through the self-execution of transfers guaranteed by smart contracts, but they have not risen to the level of traditional arbitration's expertise in conducting fair and sufficient proceedings and providing reasoned decisions.

The projects discussed above implement oracles-based solutions that include human activity, but the design choices of their oracle systems question the legal validity of these forms of ODR. Certainly, as ongoing projects, designs can be changed and improved. Nonetheless, they are in crucial stages of development that require identifying critical issues in order to make improvements to align the project outcome to its proposed criteria and goals.

7.3.4.1 Impartiality and Expertise of the Decision-Maker versus Economic Incentives Systems

As discussed above, oracles-based SDR systems do not fully comply with the impartiality criteria that govern the activities of arbitrators or other types of third-party decision-makers. The presence of economic incentives to vote with the majority devolves into decision-making based on prediction and not entirely based on the merits of the dispute. For, example, suppose one of the jurors is a notary, with a deep understanding of the principles and technology behind cryptocurrencies. Despite this expertise, instead of using her expertise to make an informed vote, she votes in a contrary way based on her assessment of anti-cryptocurrency bias of the uninformed majority of voters. Bias is antithetical to fair and impartial decision-making. Although bias exists at some level in all dispute resolution systems, it is likely to be amplified in groups of non-experts compared to systems that use expert judges or arbitrators.

The oracle-based models provide selection mechanisms that aim to obtain quality voters or jurors; however, they do not provide for direct control over the quality of the decisions and fairness of the underlying reasoning used to reach the decisions. This raises concerns as to whether these proposed SDR systems can be improved (redesigned) to ensure the expertise of the decision-makers and the quality of the decision-making process.

7.3.4.2 Due Process and Legal Validity of the Decision

The right to due process (proper notice and fair hearing) is the cornerstone for all reputable dispute resolution systems. It is important that any new ADR process, regardless of whether they are running on a blockchain or not, establish *ex ante* rules to manage the exchange and the flows

---

[32] It is worth noting that Ian Grigg, who theorized the Ricardian contract model, currently serves as a chief scientist at Mattereum.

of legal arguments and evidence, including safeguards such as time extensions for submitting defense arguments and documents when justified by the circumstances. The issue remains that an online system with adequate due process elements may not be sufficient to ensure legally valid decisions.

From a legal point of view, a decision made by an oracle-type system is potentially subject to being overridden by a domestic court at the request of either of the parties. Consider an example to clarify this idea. Suppose an online ADR system is marketed as specializing in resolving disputes in the range of 10,000 euros or less. A losing party appeals to a court on the basis that the platform wrongly advertised itself as 'online arbitration' since its decisions are not valid arbitration awards. Domestic courts have two options. First, they may recognize the decision as the equivalent of an arbitral award that lacks legally required elements, which would render the decision unenforceable, thus forcing the winning party to seek resolution of the dispute elsewhere. Second, they may recognize the decision rendered relying on the use of a smart contract as an equivalent to a settlement agreement, hence an agreement that modifies the contract in dispute arose. At that point, the domestic court would decide on the validity of the smart contract (settlement).

Courts may employ a number of analyses in rendering their decisions, such as, the conformity of the decision to existing legally recognized ADR frameworks and the validity of the self-execution nature of smart contracts. These types of analyses will be necessary when the losing party files an action with a domestic court to challenge the validity of the SDR decision. The court could recognize the validity of the online procedure but decide to fully review the decision on the merits or the court could declare the decision null and void because the online procedure is noncompliant with the legal framework governing ADR. Since the decision (transfer of funds) rendered by the blockchain-based platform will have already been executed by means of a smart contract, the losing party's only remedy is to obtain a court decision ordering the winning party to disgorge the funds received under the SDR. The setting aside of the decision defeats the purpose of SDR or ODR systems.

The overturning of a SDR award could be due to an error confined to the individual case and, therefore, is not a direct threat on the integrity of the system since it is easily correctable. However, if the error relates to a flaw in the design of the SDR or ODR platform the system may lose all its appeal and credibility.

The hypotheses listed above are just a glimpse of what may happen where the dispute resolution platform does not provide enough legal certainty and does not meet certain criteria set forth in alternative legal frameworks. In such cases, the SDR platform would become the cause of the event it was supposed to avoid complex litigation before domestic courts. Thus, ODR and SDR systems must be designed to comply with the legal prerequisites necessary for legal validity, such as measures to counter attempts to misuse the system by users.

7.3.5 Advantages of the Oracles-Based SDR Systems

The above discussion illustrates the potential shortcoming of the new SDR systems. But, despite these potential shortcomings, properly designed SDR systems offer important advantages over arbitration, traditional ADR systems, and current ODR systems that are integrated into digital platforms for platform-specific online transactions.[33] Sections 7.3.5.1–7.3.5.3 review the shortcomings of alternative dispute resolution options.

---

[33] For an analysis of ODR platforms in general, see Ortolani, n. 20 at 597.

7.3.5.1 *Small Claims Courts*

The first of these advantages is a reduction in costs and time required to resolve low-value disputes. Governments offer special small claims courts with streamlined procedures to resolve disputes over small money disputes, but a SDR system would less costly and may provide the only practical way to resolve such disputes, due to jurisdictional issues related to courts. For example, in the United States, bringing a suit in small claims court generally involves the investment of twenty hours or more and costs between $45 and $300 (filing and process serving fees). If a party seeks the advice of a lawyer, the costs escalate to an additional $500 for a two-hour consultation, and much more if the lawyer argues the case in court.[34]

7.3.5.2 *Mediation*

The costliness of small claims courts is also true of resolving disputes through mediation. Beyond the costs, although mediated settlement agreements are contractually binding, enforcement is especially problematic, especially in an international or transborder setting. There have been positive developments in the enforceability of mediated settlement agreements including the adoption of the Singapore Convention on Mediation[35] and the European Union Directive 2008/52/EC of the European Parliament and of the Council on Certain Aspects of Mediation in Civil and Commercial Matters. However, even if the Singapore Convention is widely adopted, which is likely to take decades, Article 5 allows parties to a mediation to opt out of the enforceability provision and Article 8 allows ratifying countries to provide that the Convention only effective when the parties to a mediation expressly agree to its application. Equally unfortunate, the EU framework on mediation does not envision the direct enforceability of mediation settlement agreements. In any case, outcomes of mediation largely depend on the relative bargaining power of the parties.[36] Unlike the current state of mediation, decentralized oracle systems offer enforceability by automatically moving money from escrow accounts. In sum, in comparison to small claims adjudication and mediation, SDR provides a viable option, offering lower costs and greater efficiency than these other 'low cost' forms of dispute resolution.

7.3.5.3 *Arbitration*

Arbitration if properly executed by filing recognized rules of arbitration are binding and generally enforceable under the New York Convention. Also, arbitration is considered a less costly alternative to litigation. Even if this is so, arbitration can be extremely costly. The cost of a half-day of arbitration for a FINRA case in the United States is $1,200.[37] The American

---

[34] L. Soskin, 'Cost of Small Claims Court vs. Mediation', Mediate.com (March 2013), www.mediate.com/articles/SoskinL1.cfm (accessed May 19, 2020).

[35] There have been some positive developments in international mediation. On December 20, 2018, the United Nations Convention on International Settlement Agreements Resulting from Mediation (Singapore Convention on Mediation) was adopted when it was signed by forty-six states, and has come into force in some countries beginning on May 11, 2020. The Convention provides a harmonized legal framework for enforcing settlement agreements. However, its importance will not be assured, as is the case of the New York Convention, until it is adopted by a substantial mass of countries. As of early 2021, only six countries have ratified the Convention (Belarus, Ecuador, Fiji, Qatar, Saudi Arabia, Singapore). See https://uncitral.un.org/en/texts/mediation/conventions/international_settlement_agreements/status.

[36] 'Mediation may not be effective if one of the parties is unwilling to cooperate or compromise. Mediation also may not be effective if one of the parties has a significant advantage in power over the other'. California Courts, the Judicial Branch of the State of California, 'ADR Types & Benefits', www.courts.ca.gov/3074.htm (accessed May 19, 2020).

[37] 'Is Arbitration Really Cheaper?', *Forbes* (July 14, 2009), www.forbes.com/2009/07/14/lipner-arbitration-litigation-intelligent-investing-cost.html#35ee9d3c4ed1 (accessed May 19, 2020).

Arbitration Association's minimum standard filing fee and final fee may add up to $1,725.[38] Thus, traditional arbitration is too costly for resolving 'microclaims'. It is likely that aggrieved parties with microclaims or larger, but modest claims, often simply give up rather than seek justice through methods that are not cost-effective. An oracle model using crowd wisdom holds the promise of providing access to justice for these types of claims.

This approach might not deliver standalone legally binding decisions, but the parties could agree to make escrow deposits and agree to apply a smart contract to govern the transfer of money between escrow accounts to satisfy an SDR judgment. In this way, self-execution becomes the method of enforceability.

7.3.6 Summary of Oracle-Based SDR Systems

As noted above, decentralized oracle-based SDR systems can use smart contract technology to enforce their decisions by moving funds in escrow and delivering swift, cost-effective resolution for disputes. Existing ODR systems are integrated into specific digital platforms for specified online transactions. SDR systems can be used more broadly by an unlimited user-base. These new systems can be used by parties to any transaction that is not subject to an ODR system managed by other digital platforms; outsourced to companies seeking to develop a dispute resolution (saving the costs of designing, operating, and maintaining its own proprietary platform); and for dApps (decentralized software applications based on blockchains) running on the same blockchain used by the SDR system. For example, an SDR based on Ethereum could be positioned as a reference point on the market for dApps running on Ethereum; a SDR based on VeChain could be positioned as a reference point for dApps running on VeChain.

SDR systems could overcome the limits of current embedded ODR platforms. New oracle-based SDR systems have the potential to replace current ODR systems and provide a complement to traditional ADR methods in cases involving small claims and microclaims; when their services are advertised correctly and accurately; provide deposit functions and automated transfer of sums through smart contracts; possess decision-making mechanisms that ensure fair decisions; offer minimal access costs for users or by use of reasonable tokenomic models; and have short decision-making process times.

The approach suggested here is to use the arbitration model and make it suitable for small and micro claims. Such an approach would implement, as far as possible, blockchain technology to reduce the time and cost of the proceedings; a design necessary to ensure compliance with the legal framework that governs commercial arbitration; and a modified oracle-based process in order to exclude features that are incompatible with the legal framework. Traditional arbitration, at least into the foreseeable future, will remain the preferred means to resolve disputes over large sums, but a redesign of arbitration model, based on SDR systems, can be implemented to optimize resolution of disputes involving smaller sums of money and lead to the development of a new *lex mercatoria*.

7.4 PROPOSAL FOR LEGALLY BINDING SDR

In light of the advantages and disadvantages of current commercial arbitration and the shortcomings in current SDR projects, this section investigates the possibility of designing a model of

---

[38] American Arbitration Association, 'Commercial Arbitration Rules and Mediation Procedures', effective as of May 1, 2018, www.adr.org/sites/default/files/Commercial_Arbitration_Fee_Schedule_1.pdf (accessed May 19, 2020).

dispute resolution that would combine the benefits of low cost and speedy resolutions through the use of blockchain technology.[39] The design would guarantee compliance with the existing legal framework (due process) and its underlying logic (fair decisions). Such a system would not be identical to traditional arbitration, but would include some of its key elements. From a theoretical perspective, this section proposes a new concept of dispute resolution, something that may be defined as 'smart arbitration (SA)'.

7.4.1 Designing Decentralized Smart Arbitration

A SA model should be designed in such a way as to reflect all the principles and rules suggested by the UNCITRAL Model Law,[40] which is the most widely accepted arbitration guideline in the world. The SA system would then be transposed in each country, by creating national 'arbitration hubs' with adjustments that take into account the national law of the hosting state (see Section 7.2, layers of the legal framework for arbitration).

More specifically, the rules of each hub would be designed to reflect the arbitration laws of the hosting state (*lex arbitri*). Such rules should include a mechanism for randomly selecting arbitrators from a group of legal experts, in order to meet the requirements of impartiality and quality. Impartiality, in particular, is a necessary requirement in order to ensure legally binding and enforceable online arbitral awards.

The platform on which the national hub is based should provide for a user interface and mechanisms that allow the parties to be heard and the rights of the defense to be exercised; for instance, through the submission of statements and documents, videoconferencing hearings, and other means to expand the adversarial part of the proceedings. The user interface should also allow for the cross-examination of the parties.

It is necessary to examine how decentralization *stricto sensu* can be implemented using the arbitration model. As explained in Section 7.3, relying on the concept of decentralization to aim only at providing economic incentives or disincentives for the arbitrators, thus reducing costs, is narrow-minded and antithetical to improve the quality of their decisions.

Therefore, the system should include a mechanism for decentralized peer review in order to guarantee the quality of the selected arbitrators. This goal could be reached by implementing anonymous peer review by three other arbitrators of similar competence selected from other hubs or arbitration chambers and institutions to rate the quality of arbitration decisions. This would entail the randomly selected external expert reviewers evaluating the quality of the provisional draft of the arbitral award written by the selected arbitrators. The peer-review mechanism purpose is to prevent an individual arbitrator from simply aligning her decision with that of other arbitrators: where the quality of the decision rendered serves as the sole criterion for evaluating each arbitrator, each arbitrator would be motivated to render their best judgment rather than simply following the others.

This proposed system combines the logic of the oracle-based mechanisms with a quality review process. The arbitrators will earn or lose reputation points according to the peer reviews. The reputation points would, in turn, be collected on a reputation board of each hub that allows users to view both the reputation points of each arbitrator and the average score of the roster of

---

[39] Much of the information in this section is based on the JUR project for which the authors are principals. JUR has released a decentralized oracle system and is in the process of developing an Open Justice platform. See JUR, White Paper, V2.0.2 (July 2019), http://bit.ly/jur-wp-v203 (accessed May 19, 2020).
[40] See n. 9 and accompanying text.

arbitrators used by the hub. This would ensure quality of decisions through an objective and decentralized ranking, not falsifiable by anyone. This process would create a SA ecosystem focused on the use of high-quality experts. The same peer review mechanism could be applied to expert witnesses appointed by the arbitral panel.

Instead of using a traditional centralized selection mechanism of arbitrators governed by the hub administrator, the hub could choose arbitrators through a decentralized selection method. The hub could list job openings for arbitrators and applications could be directly evaluated by all users of the ecosystem, that is, by anyone who owns valid tokens to interact with the smart arbitration system, through a binary voting system users would stake tokens to vote 'Yes' or 'No' on any application.

More technically, arbitrators would be randomly appointed to the dispute resolution panel according to an algorithm (decentralization principle), to ensure the highest level of impartiality. Thus, the anonymization of arbitrators would not only be used during the peer review process it would operate from the moment the arbitrators are appointed so that none of the parties to the dispute would be able to improperly influence any of the arbitrators.

In light of the above, the SA system, at first glance, would seem to be complex and costly due to the need to remunerate the arbitrators, peer reviewers, hub administrators, and possibly the costs of legal assistance. In sum, one might be concerned that the construction of such a system could increase the costs for end users instead of reducing them. Section 7.4.2 analyses the cost of SA.

7.4.2 Economic Sustainability of the System

Decentralization allows for the use of competing players with different roles, which the system allocates remuneration in such a way to minimize (but not entirely erasing) the costs for the end user. A good SA designer and manager that maintains the SA platform would avoid charging fees for use of the hub, instead, it would sell tokens that allow any player to interact with the SA system, in order to fragment and distribute the costs of the service among many 'buyers'.

If the platform chooses to rely on token sales and does not charge fees, the arbitration hub will not need to impose any additional cost above the normal costs of arbitration. The arbitral hub would reduce costs since arbitrators would not need to travel. The token should cover the compensation for the hub itself and the compensation for the arbitrators, who are also players within the SA. Peer reviewers would be compensated through a reward system using tokens. Peer reviewers could earn or lose tokens based on how closely their scores match the average score of all three peer reviewers. The logic behind the voting mechanism, and economic incentives and disincentives, is based on game theory. Sections 7.4.3–7.4.4 will explore other methods to make the SA system more efficient.

7.4.3 Anti-corruption Measures and Reserve Account

To minimize the risk of bias, corruption, and incompetence, the SA system hub could provide a reserve account to users. This reserve account would consist of a defined minimum number of tokens, instead of fiat currency, deposited in reserve equal to the amount of the dispute. This mechanism would also provide flexibility to hub operators to increase the amount of tokens held in reserve in order to host disputes of greater value. This design addresses the likely scenario in which new SA hubs may enter the industry cautiously and gradually with a minimal commitment, while institutions with a long history behind them, credibility in the market, and a roster of internationally renowned arbitrators at their disposal could make a greater initial investment to be able to host high-value disputes immediately.

The reserve account would cover the costs of anti-corruption complaints initiated by users. The complaint would be managed by a third-party hub, that is, a hub other than the one that hosted the corrupted dispute that uses the SA as well and so it is part of the same network. If successful in sustaining its complaint the plaintiff would be rewarded with tokens taken from the hosting hub's reserve account. This mechanism serves to encourage users to report corruption (improper influence or bribery of arbitrators); provide an efficient means to compensate the harmed party; and the risk of economic loss would motivate the hub administrator to scrutinize applicant arbitrators carefully and monitor their decisions.

7.4.4 Preemptive Review on the Merits and Case Reassignment

The current model of arbitration provides a right to appeal on very narrow grounds mostly related to process-related faults (arbitrator misconduct; jurisdiction over issues in dispute).[41] Would a process that allowed for merit-based, non-judicial review be an improvement? A SA system could offer a peer review conducted by randomly selected arbitrators to ensure that the procedures followed comply with the UNCITRAL Model Law and New York Convention, and that the judgment on the merits was reasonably fair. This would avoid the costs of judicial review and ensure high-quality unbiased judgments. The review process would use a separate pool of arbitrators and could be anonymized in an attempt to protect the confidentiality of the parties. In the alternative, a negative review of initial provisional drafts of the arbitral award, as discussed in Section 7.4.1, could trigger a reassignment of the case to another set of randomly selected arbitrators.

The appeal mechanism used to reverse awards based upon the merits would be problematic if judicial enforcement is needed. The presumption in law is that arbitral awards are final and binding. In traditional arbitration appeals, as noted above, are limited procedural issues and not a review of the merits of the dispute. Moreover, any such SA-based appeals process should be measured as to the degree it increases the costs of SA.

In sum, the better and most cost-effective check on unfair awards is external review while the case is still pending and case reassignment. This mechanism would not change the nature of a final and binding decision and it would remedy manifest incompetence or corruption at an earlier point in the process. The cost of the case reassignment, that is, the fees paid to the initial arbitrators would be reimbursed from the Hub's reserve account. Finally, the initial arbitrators could be purged from the pool of arbitrators-experts for corrupt behavior or incompetence (based on a number of negative reviews).

7.5 PROPOSING A NEW *LEX MERCATORIA* VIA BLOCKCHAIN

The proposal for a decentralized smart arbitration system, discussed above, is only a starting point for further discussion and investigation. Assuming that SA models provide decisions that conform to the New York Convention and are recognized as legally binding under national legal systems, is SA simply a way of making traditional commercial arbitration more efficient and accessible or does it change the current paradigm?

---

[41] See DiMatteo, et al., n. 7.

At the least, SA represents a system of private courts that could be connected through computer interface or APIs to software, rendering faster, cheaper, safer, and more impartial judgments, and allow immediate enforcement by the transfer of digital assets. This alone would be a major improvement over the current system. Further, such a SA model may lead to future evolutions, such as a new type of *lex mercatoria*.

7.5.1 Fairness and Best Practices for Smart Arbitration and Trade

If wide use of SA systems is implemented based on an arbitration clause that binds the judgment not to a specific legal system, but to general criteria of fairness, one might ask whether it is possible for that court to outline in more detail what fairness truly is? That could be achieved, for instance, by creating a collection of simplified rules for SA proceedings (perhaps varying according to the complexity and the value of the dispute), as well as guidelines for best practices and standards to be applied in deciding the merits of the dispute. Such a set of guidelines might also be helpful in other areas, such as the work by the UNCITRAL Arbitration and Conciliation-Dispute Settlement Workgroup is investigating how UNCITRAL might design a new set of rules for expedited arbitration to speed up the process while continuing to ensure fairness in the proceedings.[42] The Workgroup has yet to address the broader issue of fairness in the sense of best practices and standards for analyzing a dispute. The fairness criterion as the basis of SA could contribute to the development of fairness criteria to improve arbitration efficiency by replacing the complex definitions of fairness implicit in national laws.

7.5.2 Potential Benefits

This chapter presents a hypothetical scenario of evolution for legal systems with a *lex mercatoria* created using blockchain technology, designed by experts, applied for the purpose of delivering more efficient dispute resolution, and with internationally recognized as a form of binding arbitration.

This is the first proposal of its kind. Hence it is not meant to be a detailed and complete solution to the problem of inefficient dispute resolution. Further study is required in a number of areas including, (1) the creation of decentralized arbitration chambers with distinct pools of arbitrators to serve specialized industries, such as maritime, construction, engineering services and so forth. Each group could draft guidelines for analyzing cases on their merits, define fairness in the context of a particular industry, and develop merchant law over time based on principles revealed by their rulings. (2) improved efficiency, expanded services, newer frameworks would be driven by competition to deliver a higher level of performance. (3) improved transparency and reduction of the scope of judgment. This involves investigating if SA could make the scope of judgment, in many cases, more restricted and relegated to the evaluation of objective key performance indicators (KPIs), thus facilitating a uniformity of judgment according to predetermined parameters.

7.6 CONCLUSION

This chapter analyzes the current ADR scenario and in particular the arbitration system. It also finds that current projects using blockchain technology and smart contracts to resolve disputes

---

[42] United Nations Commission on International Trade Law, 'Report of Working Group II (Dispute Settlement) on the Work of Its Sixty-Ninth Session' (February 4–8, 2019), https://undocs.org/en/A/CN.9/969 (accessed May 19, 2020).

are, at this time, suitable to deliver a complete approach to making and interpreting legal agreements without human involvement and third-party decision-makers. It then discusses how blockchain technology and its features may address certain problems with arbitration, other traditional ADR mechanisms, and embedded ODR mechanisms, but do not yet provide clear complete and legally binding solutions.

This chapter discusses how oracle-based mechanisms that use incentives to choose a solution favored by a majority of jurors or arbitrators is the most popular model being used. Such a model provides an efficient access to justice for microclaims. This model, however, is not currently suitable for larger claims that require legally binding awards. Furthermore, these systems are ill-suited to render expert judgment in matters of great complexity and can only transfer money as the means of enforcement; they cannot deliver other outcomes, such as transfers of legal rights that are better addressed by traditional arbitration.

Due to the inability of current ODR systems to resolve complex cases and the potential unenforceability of their awards in national courts, an alternative model of blockchain-based arbitration is proposed. In the proposed system, decentralization does not impact the act of judgment, but rather the structure underlying the act of judgment, that is, selection of arbitrators and peer-review mechanisms to guarantee arbitrators' expertise and reliability. This system would work on a single platform that fully digitizes the flow of arbitral proceedings, complies with the existing legal framework for arbitration, and integrates anti-corruption measures.

This type of decentralized SDR system would be efficient and, where possible, legally binding and enforceable. The chapter speculates about the use of fairness criteria in the SDR process by stablishing guidelines containing simplified rules for deciding the outcome of a case. Such a fairness-based system would help establish a new *lex mercatoria* that uses the blockchain as its primary vehicle, with the hope of allowing more efficient national and international trade, supported by a dispute resolution method that is reliable, rapid, and predictable.

Such a scenario would represent a reimagination of the relation between sovereign jurisdictional authority and private autonomy, with an expansion of freedom of choice for individuals, who could select efficient online dispute systems recognized by nation-states. The realization of this scenario would infuse the *lex mercatoria* via the blockchain with a broadened view of private autonomy with respect to securing business relationships, whether offline, online, or blockchain-based, yielding greater freedom, efficiency, and security.

8

Digital Dispute Resolution

Blurring the Boundaries of ADR

Pietro Ortolani

8.1 INTRODUCTION

Any discussion of alternative dispute resolution (ADR) necessarily relies on some basic, shared notions, allowing us to identify those procedures that are considered an alternative to litigation in national courts. When legal scholars refer to arbitration or mediation, for instance, they often take it for granted that those linguistic labels are sufficient to designate a certain procedure. To be sure, none of these labels have a monolithic quality: the word 'arbitration', for instance, designates a family of private adjudication phenomena, which can differ in significant ways. Each ADR mechanism, hence, is best understood as a spectrum of procedures. Nevertheless, all of the instances falling within that spectrum must necessarily have some shared broad-stroke feature, so that they can all (with an unavoidable degree of simplification) be referred to as arbitration, mediation or another ADR mechanism. In other words, there must necessarily be some boundaries that lawyers heuristically deploy to build a rough yet shared taxonomy of ADR.

These boundaries are, by necessity, fuzzy; the Court of Justice of the European Union (CJEU), for instance, recognises the fact that some procedures may be formally named as 'arbitration' but do not actually qualify as arbitration from the perspective of EU law.[1] However, the porousness of those boundaries need not concern us. A different observation is relevant, instead, for the purposes of this chapter: for decades now, the criteria identifying different ADR mechanisms have remained relatively stable. More specifically, those criteria are stable enough for lawyers to intuitively identify different ADR procedures and attach different legal consequences (e.g., in terms of due process guarantees or enforceability of outcomes) to each of them. There are two interlocked reasons why these criteria have remained constant over time, despite their occasional haziness. A quick overview of these two reasons will help set the background against which the impact of technology in this field can be productively scrutinised.

First, those boundaries are largely defined by law. International and domestic lawmakers shape the aforementioned identifying criteria by enacting legislation that regulates different ADR mechanisms. By way of example, in setting forth a regime for the enforcement of arbitration clauses and the recognition and enforcement of arbitral awards, the 1958 New York

---

[1] *Merck Canada Inc. v. Accord Healthcare Ltd and Others*, C-555/13, ECLI:EU:C:2014:92; *Ascendi Beiras Litoral e Alta, Auto Estradas das Beiras Litoral e Alta SA v. Autoridade Tributária e Aduaneira*, C-377/13, ECLI:EU:C:2014:1754; for a comment, see P. Paschalidis, 'Arbitral Tribunals and Preliminary References to the EU Court of Justice' (2017) 33(4) *Arbitration International* 663.

Convention[2] implicitly provides criteria that a private procedure must comply with in order for it to result in an enforceable award for the purposes of the Convention.[3] The same largely holds true for the Singapore Convention, which ensures the enforceability of settlement agreements resulting from mediation, provided that the mediation procedure meets certain requirements.[4]

Second, legal practice has a strong incentive to comply with the criteria set forth in the law: by meeting those requirements, an ADR procedure can receive some crucial benefits. If, for instance, a private adjudication procedure complies with the requirements of the 1958 New York Convention, thus qualifying as 'arbitration' for the purposes of that instrument, it will have access to the friendly regime of recognition and enforcement contained in that Convention. This, in turn, brings about a transnational understanding of how arbitration should be conducted: given the presence of highly successful international conventions, as well as a high level of international harmonisation,[5] practitioners in different legal systems tend to converge towards a shared understanding of what the conceptual 'boundaries' of arbitration should be. This tendency is further amplified by the circumstance that ADR mechanisms such as arbitration and mediation are routinely used for cross-border cases, thus triggering the emergence of communities of transnational legal practitioners, which further refine such shared understandings by exporting practices across national borders[6] and developing transnational regulatory standards.[7]

---

[2] Convention on the Recognition and Enforcement of Foreign Arbitral Awards, New York, (10 June 1958).

[3] The problem of the legal qualification of a decision issued by an arbitral tribunal is notoriously relevant in the context of interim orders, formally labelled as 'awards', but potentially not meeting the applicability requirements of the New York Convention: see, e.g., the famous case *Resort Condominiums International Inc. v. Ray Bolwell and Resort Condominiums, Pty. Ltd.*, Supreme Court of Queensland, 389, 29 October 1993, in A. J. van den Berg (ed.), *Yearbook of Commercial Arbitration*, vol. XX (Deventer: Kluwer, 1995) 628. Recently, the problems connected with the characterisation of a certain procedure as 'arbitration' have gained practical relevance in connection with the emergency arbitration procedures set forth in the rules of many arbitral institutions: L. Markert and R. Rawal, 'Emergency Arbitration in Investment and Construction Disputes: An Uneasy Fit?' (2020) 37(1) *Journal of International Arbitration* 131; P. Shaughnessy, 'The Emergency Arbitrator' in P. Shaughnessy and S. Tung (eds.), *The Powers and Duties of an Arbitrator: Liber Amicorum Pierre A. Karrer* (Deventer: Kluwer, 2017) 339; S. Ramani Garimella and P. Sooksripaisarnkit, 'Emergency Arbitrator Awards: Addressing Enforceability Concerns through National Law and the New York Convention' in K. Fach Gomez and A. M. Lopez-Rodriguez (eds.), *60 Years of the New York Convention: Key Issues and Future Challenges* (Deventer: Kluwer, 2019) 67; R. Alnaber, 'Emergency Arbitration: Mere Innovation or Vast Improvement' (2019) 35(4) *Arbitration International* 441; M. Osadchiy, 'Emergency Relief in Investment Treaty Arbitration: A Word of Caution' (2017) 34(2) *Journal of International Arbitration* 239; B. Giaretta, 'The Practice of Emergency Arbitration' (2017) 1 *b-Arbitra – Belgian Review of Arbitration* 83; C. Müller and S. Pearson, 'Waiving the Green Flag to Emergency Arbitration under the Swiss Rules: The Sauber Saga' (2015) 33 *ASA Bulletin* 808; B. Baigel, 'The Emergency Arbitrator Procedure under the 2012 ICC Rules: A Juridical Analysis' (2014) 31(1) *Journal of International Arbitration* 1; P. Michaelson, 'When Speed and Cost Matter: Emergency and Expedited Arbitration' (2014) 218(4) *New Jersey Law Journal* 50.

[4] United Nations Convention on International Settlement Agreements Resulting from Mediation, New York (20 December 2018).

[5] A key example of harmonisation in the field of arbitration is the UNCITRAL Model Law on International Commercial Arbitration, which, at the time of writing, has served as a source of inspiration for the arbitration statutes of 83 states and a total of 116 jurisdictions.

[6] For decades now, sociologists have investigated the nature and practices of these transnational professional communities. The seminal work of Dezalay and Garth remains a key reference point: Y. Dezalay and B. G. Garth, *Dealing in Virtue: International Commercial Arbitration and the Construction of a Transnational Legal Order* (Chicago: University of Chicago Press, 1996). More recent sociologically oriented investigations include J. Karton, *The Culture of International Arbitration and The Evolution of Contract Law* (Oxford: Oxford University Press, 2013); T. Schultz and R. Kovacs, 'The Rise of a Third Generation of Arbitrators? Fifteen Years after Dezalay and Garth' (2012) 28(2) *Arbitration International* 161; E. Gaillard, 'Sociology of International Arbitration' (2015) 31(1) *Arbitration International* 1; M. Hirsch, 'The Sociological Dimension of International Arbitration: The Investment Arbitration Culture' in T. Schultz and F. Ortino, *Oxford Handbook of International Arbitration* (Oxford: Oxford University Press, 2020) 717–739.

[7] As a result of such cross-fertilisation among different legal traditions, practitioners operating in civil law countries now routinely act as counsels and arbitrators in arbitral proceedings that incorporate elements typical of the common law

The main thesis of this chapter is that digital technologies can have a disruptive effect on the boundaries that we routinely use to identify different ADR mechanisms. The introduction of technology in the field of ADR may bring about new hybrids, new understandings and new exercises in boundary drawing, which significantly diverge from the traditional criteria shaped by the interplay between law and practice, as pointed out in Section 8.1. In order to illustrate this argument, the remainder of this chapter proceeds as follows. Section 8.2 describes the traditional modes through which definitional boundaries are drawn in the field of ADR. Subsequently, Section 8.3 describes the emergence of new, technology-driven ADR phenomena (collectively referred to as 'digital dispute resolution'), which do not comport with the definitional boundaries described in Section 8.2. Section 8.4 then proceeds to draw some inferences, taking stock of the ways in which technology blurs the boundaries of ADR, and developing a normative argument. Finally, Section 8.5 concludes by providing a summary of the main findings.

8.2 TRADITIONAL MODES OF BOUNDARIES IN ADR

This section provides an overview of the criteria normally used to identify two of the most successful and widely used ADR mechanisms: arbitration and mediation. Having outlined the distinctive features of both, it will be possible to highlight how law and practice contribute to shaping the boundaries of ADR, especially through judicial intervention and review.

8.2.1 *Quasi-monopoly to Delegation: Courts and Arbitration*

The administration of justice is often portrayed as inextricably linked with an apparatus of state courts exercising public powers. Historically, one of the crucial steps in the rise of modern national states was precisely the establishment of jurisdiction as an expression of the state's sovereign power and the establishment of state courts as 'quasi-monopolists' in the exercise of that power.[8] However, despite the central role that courts have played for centuries in the resolution of civil and commercial disputes, phenomena of private adjudication (often predating the nation-state)[9] have survived. 'Arbitration', as a conceptual label, designates these phenomena, in which the rights and obligations of the disputing parties are determined not by state courts, but by (one or more) private adjudicator(s). The idea of the arbitrator as a 'private judge',[10] while not entirely correct at a technical level, does encapsulate the long-standing assumption of functional equivalence of arbitrators and judges:[11] arbitrators, like

---

tradition, such as the cross-examination of witnesses. These shared transnational understandings and practices are crystallised in instruments such as the IBA Rules on the Taking of Evidence in International Arbitration.

[8] For a brief summary of the historical construction of jurisdiction as one of the attributes of sovereignty and the consequences of the emergence of private technology-driven legal orders, see P. Ortolani, 'The Judicialization of the Blockchain' in P. Hacker, I. Lianos, G. Dimitropoulos and S. Eich (eds.), *Regulating Blockchain: Techno-Social and Legal Challenges* (Oxford: Oxford University Press, 2019) 296–299.

[9] F. Marrella and A. Mozzato, *Alle origini dell'arbitrato commerciale internazionale. L'arbitrato a Venezia tra Medioevo ed età moderna* (Padua: Cedam, 2001).

[10] For an extensive discussion of the tasks of arbitrators and their role as private judges, see T. Clay, *L'arbitre* (Paris: Dalloz, 2001).

[11] The question whether arbitral tribunals should be seen as functionally equivalent to national courts is often discussed in the context of debates concerning whether arbitrators should be allowed to refer preliminary questions to supranational courts such as the CJEU or to domestic constitutional courts. According to Basedow, for instance, arbitrators should be allowed to refer preliminary questions to the CJEU, because arbitral tribunals play a role that is comparable to the one of state courts: J. Basedow, 'EU Law in International Arbitration: Referrals to the European Court of Justice' (2015) 32(4) *Journal of International Arbitration* 367 384–385. On the relationship between

judges, have the task of resolving a dispute through an adversarial procedure in which substantive rules are applied to establish the rights and obligations of the litigants. Referring a dispute to private arbitrators, rather than to the courts of the state, has proven to be an attractive option for a wide range of parties, and for a host of different reasons, including speed,[12] expertise,[13] flexibility,[14] confidentiality[15] and enforceability.[16] Throughout the last decades, the use of arbitration has been steadily increasing, and the boundaries of arbitrability have been expanding.[17]

One of the features fostering the rise of arbitration has undoubtedly been the 'hands-off' approach that legislators and courts around the world have adopted vis-à-vis arbitral awards. The merits of a case decided by an arbitral tribunal cannot, in general, be relitigated in court. Awards can be annulled on a limited number of grounds, most of which revolve around due process, rather than (with some limited exceptions)[18] the substance of the decision issued by the arbitrators.[19] Importantly, analogous standards are applied by national courts in the context of the international recognition and enforcement of arbitral awards: the 1958 New York Convention, which at the time of writing counts 164 state parties, imposes an obligation to recognise and enforce foreign awards, with the limited exceptions listed in Article V,[20] which mostly revolve around procedural issues.

Over time, the idea of state courts as quasi-monopolists of adjudication has given way to a more nuanced approach in which private arbitrators administer justice alongside courts and, in some sectors, are in fact regarded as the prevailing dispute resolution method.[21] For some

---

commercial arbitral tribunals and the CJEU, see also Paschalidis, n. 1; G. Bermann, 'Navigating EU Law and the Law of International Arbitration' (2012) 28(3) *Arbitration International* 397. On the relationship between arbitral tribunals and constitutional courts, see P. Mayer, 'L'arbitre international et la hiérarchie des normes' (2011) 2 *Revue de l'Arbitrage* 361; J. Paulsson, 'Unlawful Laws and the Authority of International Tribunals' (2008) 23(2) *ICSID Review* 215.

[12] K. P. Berger, 'The Need for Speed in International Arbitration' (2008) 25(5) *Journal of International Arbitration* 595.

[13] M. Bühler, 'Technical Expertise: An Additional Means for Preventing or Settling Commercial Disputes' (1989) 6(1) *Journal of International Arbitration* 135.

[14] I. Hanefeld and J. Hombeck, 'International Arbitration between Standardization and Flexibility – Predictability and Flexibility Seen from a Client's Perspective' (2015) 13(1) *SchiedsVZ* 20.

[15] M. Hwang, K. Chung, S. Cheng Lim and M. Hui Wong, 'Defining the Indefinable: Practical Problems of Confidentiality in Arbitration (Second Kaplan Lecture, 17 November 2008)' in Hong Kong International Arbitration Centre (ed.), *International Arbitration: Issues, Perspectives and Practice: Liber Amicorum Neil Kaplan* (Deventer: Kluwer, 2018) 21.

[16] For recent discussions of the role played by the New York Convention in the international enforceability of arbitral awards, see K. Fach Gomez and A. M. Lopez-Rodriguez, *60 Years of the New York Convention: Key Issues and Future Challenges* (Deventer: Kluwer, 2019); M. Paulsson, *The New York Convention in Action* (Deventer: Kluwer, 2016).

[17] S. Brekoulakis, 'On Arbitrability: Persisting Misconceptions and New Areas of Concern' in L. Mistelis and S. Brekoulakis (eds.), *Arbitrability: International and Comparative Perspectives* (Deventer: Kluwer, 2009) 19.

[18] Even in legal systems where an appeal on point of law against arbitral awards is possible, this possibility is normally used in exceptional cases only: T. Dedezade, 'Are You In? Or Are You Out? An Analysis of Section 69 of the English Arbitration Act 1996: Appeals on a Question of Law' (2006) 2 *International Arbitration Law Review* 56.

[19] On judicial review and public policy, see also Section 8.4.3.

[20] More specifically, recognition and enforcement can be denied in case of incapacity of one of the parties or invalidity of the arbitration agreement, if one of the parties was not given proper notice of the appointment of the arbitrator or of the arbitration proceedings or was otherwise unable to present his case, if the award deals with matters falling outside of the agreement to arbitrate (*ultra petita*), if the composition of the tribunal or the procedure did not comply with the parties' agreement or with the law of the seat of arbitration, if the award has been set aside or suspended at the seat of arbitration, if the subject matter of the dispute is not arbitrable in the place where recognition and enforcement are sought (so-called requested state) or if recognition and enforcement would be contrary to the public policy of the requested state.

[21] Although the confidentiality of many commercial arbitrations hinders the retrieval of reliable and comprehensive statistical data, the widespread sense that arbitration has become the 'default' dispute resolution mechanism for

specific areas of law, the role of arbitration as a key vehicle for the enforcement of substantive law has been expressly acknowledged by state courts: in the case of competition law, for instance, both the US Supreme Court[22] and the CJEU[23] have confirmed the arbitrability of competition disputes, on the basis of the premise that arbitrators will apply mandatory provisions of competition law in a way that is comparable to what state courts would do in the absence of an agreement to arbitrate.[24]

In sum, the rise of arbitration has been made possible by the liberal attitude of lawmakers and courts, which progressively abandoned the view whereby state courts hold a monopoly over the adjudicative resolution of disputes. Instead, national legal systems adopted a supportive approach, ensuring the validity and enforceability of arbitral award, as long as the latter comply with some fundamental procedural requirements. In some areas, the task of enforcing substantive law has been even delegated by national courts to arbitrators, thus reinforcing the assumption that arbitration and court litigation are equivalent in terms of the function they perform. However, such support and delegation are not unconditional. Arbitration, in other words, does not enjoy unconstrained freedom: as already mentioned, arbitral tribunals must comply with certain basic requirements, set forth by the law, if their awards are to be valid and enforceable. For a relatively long time, hence, arbitration has been enjoying what is best described as a status of bounded autonomy. This state of affairs, however, may change in the near future because of the impact of digital technologies. Before scrutinising the effects of technology on arbitration, however, it is useful to observe how another widespread ADR mechanism, namely, mediation, has undergone a similar evolution.[25]

8.2.2 Enforceability without Adjudication: Rise of Mediation

Unlike arbitrators, mediators do not adjudicate disputes; the aim of mediation is not to exactly define the parties' rights and obligation, but to encourage and facilitate a settlement agreement between the disputants. Experienced mediators can help the parties to a dispute understand their respective positions, find common ground in a confidential environment and (if the procedure is successful) reach a new agreement, which may be more satisfactory than any

---

commercial disputes has prompted some authors to argue that the parties to a commercial contract should be legally presumed to have consented to arbitration, unless the contract contains a choice-of-court agreement: G. Cuniberti, *Rethinking International Commercial Arbitration: Towards Default Arbitration* (Cheltenham: Elgar, 2017); G. Cuniberti, 'Beyond Contract: The Case for Default Arbitration in International Commercial Disputes' (2008) 32 *Fordham International Law Journal* 417; P. Butler and C. Herbert, 'Access to Justice for Small and Medium Sized Enterprises: The Case for a Bilateral Arbitration Treaty' (2014) 26 *New Zealand Universities Law Review* 186; G. Born, 'BITS, BATS and Buts: Reflections on International Dispute Resolution', www.wilmerhale.com (accessed 8 July 2020). In some jurisdictions, the widespread use of arbitration in certain sectors (such as consumer contracts) has also sparked significant criticism; see, e.g., J. Resnik, 'Diffusing Disputes: The Public in the Private of Arbitration, the Private in Courts, and the Erasure of Rights' (2015) 124 *Yale Law Journal* 2804.

[22] *Mitsubishi Motors Corp. v. Soler Chrysler-Plymouth, Inc.*, 473 U.S. 614 (1985).
[23] *Eco Swiss China Time Ltd v. Benetton International NV*, C-126/97, ECLI:EU:C:1999:269.
[24] Ibid. at para 40.
[25] A focus on mediation is particularly desirable, considering that in some cultures (e.g., in Asia) interest-based conciliatory dispute resolution mechanisms are reported as being often preferred to their rights-based, adjudicatory counterparts: see, e.g., M. Woo, 'Law's Location in China's Countryside' (2011) 29(2) *Wisconsin International Law Journal* 101; F. Hualing and R. Cullen, 'From Mediatory to Adjudicatory Justice: The Limits of Civil Justice Reform in China' in M. Woo and M. Gallagher, *Chinese Justice: Civil Dispute Resolution in Contemporary China* (Cambridge: Cambridge University Press, 2011) 25.

solution imposed by a third-party adjudicator.[26] Because of this high degree of flexibility, and the central role of party autonomy, mediation has proven to be an attractive option for the resolution of civil and commercial disputes,[27] and it has been dubbed 'the fastest growing dispute resolution method'.[28]

Despite concerns that a wide-scale diffusion of settlement may hinder the enforcement and development of substantive law,[29] mediation has been widely embraced over the past few decades as an attractive alternative to court litigation and an efficient way to reduce the backlog of state courts. In the European Union, the Mediation Directive[30] requires all member states to encourage mediator training[31] and allows the disputing parties to agree that any settlement agreement reached through mediation will be enforceable, similarly to a court judgment.[32] Furthermore, the EU has adopted a Directive on ADR in consumer disputes[33] and a Regulation facilitating online dispute resolution in the same field.[34] Even more ambitiously, the recent United Nations Convention on International Settlement Agreements Resulting from Mediation (widely known as the 'Singapore Convention')[35] aims to create a harmonised regime for the enforcement of settlement agreements reached at the end of a mediation procedure. The main purpose of these legislative efforts is to eliminate one of the bottlenecks that have historically limited the attractiveness of mediation, that is, the need to resort to court litigation in order to obtain an enforceable title whenever one of the parties to the settlement agreement refuses to spontaneously comply with the terms of the latter. By ensuring enforceability without adjudication, lawmakers hope to further boost mediation as a consent-driven alternative to adjudicative procedures.

Mediation enjoys growing support from lawmakers around the world, but – similarly to arbitration – its autonomy is not unlimited. For instance, by attaching certain conditions to the enforceability of settlement agreements resulting from mediation, the Singapore Convention strongly incentivises mediators and parties to comply with those requirements. This tendency, in turn, contributes to shaping the overall boundaries of mediation as an ADR process. To further expound on this point, the Section 8.2.3 will focus on the role played by state courts in the definition of the distinctive characters of different ADR mechanisms.

8.2.3 Bounded Autonomy: Judicial Intervention and Review as Boundary-Defining

The analysis carried out in Sections 8.2.1 and 8.2.2 demonstrates that, while the rise of arbitration and mediation evinces the growing importance of party autonomy in the resolution of civil and

---

[26] T. Schultz, *Transnational Legality: Stateless Law and International Arbitration* (Oxford: Oxford University Press, 2014) 1–4 with reference to R. Mnookin, *Bargaining with the Devil: When to Negotiate, When to Fight* (New York: Simon & Schuster, 2010) 170.
[27] In the EU, for instance, the use of mediation has been incentivised with instruments such as the Mediation Directive (Directive 2008/52/EC of the European Parliament and of the Council of 21 May 2008 on certain aspects of mediation in civil and commercial matters, OJ L 136, 24.5.2008).
[28] P. Cortés, *Online Dispute Resolution for Consumers in the European Union* (Abingdon: Routledge, 2011) 144.
[29] O. Fiss, 'Against Settlement' (1983–1984) 93 *Yale Law Journal* 1073.
[30] See n. 27.
[31] Mediation Directive, n. 27 at Art. 4(2).
[32] Ibid. at Art. 6.
[33] Directive 2013/11/EU of the European Parliament and of the Council of 21 May 2013 on ADR for consumer disputes, OJ L 165, 18.6.2013.
[34] Regulation (EU) No. 524/2013 of the European Parliament and of the Council of 21 May 2013 on online dispute resolution for consumer disputes, OJ L 165, 18.6.2013.
[35] United Nations Convention on International Settlement Agreements Resulting from Mediation, New York (20 December 2018).

commercial disputes, such autonomy is not unconstrained, but rather bounded. In the case of arbitration, arbitral awards can have *res judicata* effects and be enforced (domestically and/or internationally), but only if the conditions set forth in (domestic and/or international) law are complied with. Along similar lines, settlement agreements resulting from mediation can in certain cases be enforced without the need for the creditor to initiate judicial proceedings, but it is up to (domestic and/or international) law to list the conditions under which those settlements will be regarded as valid enforceable titles. The state, in other words, holds the key to recognition and enforcement, and courts play a crucial gatekeeping role. Courts can, for instance, set an arbitral award aside, or decline recognition and enforcement thereof, if the arbitral procedure did not guarantee a sufficient level of due process. For the same reasons, the enforcement of a settlement agreement can be declined under the Singapore Convention if, for instance, the mediator committed a serious breach of the standards applicable to her or the mediation, and no settlement agreement would have been concluded without said breach.[36]

By acting as gatekeepers for the validity and enforceability of the outcomes resulting from different ADR procedures, state courts indirectly shape those procedures in a basic but fundamental fashion. Legal practitioners operating in the context of procedures such as arbitration and mediation have a strong incentive to respect the requirements and standards necessary to ensure validity and enforceability. This, in turn, triggers a phenomenon of homogenisation of ADR. For instance, in a wide range of sectors and jurisdictions, arbitration tends to be conducted in a certain, recognisable way (as confirmed by the countless similitudes among sets of institutional arbitration rules), precisely because that particular way of conducting arbitration ensures the validity and enforceability of the resulting awards. The same holds largely true for mediation, despite the relatively recent character of the Singapore Convention and of the other legislative efforts aimed at guaranteeing the enforceability of mediated settlement agreements. For these reasons, when lawyers use conceptual labels such as 'arbitration' or 'mediation', they can rely on a shared, predictable understanding of the features that a particular ADR procedure should have. The boundaries of ADR, hence, are relatively clear and predictable. The current state of affairs, however, may be significantly disrupted by technology, as Section 8.3 will argue.

8.3 RISE OF NEW FORMS OF DIGITAL DISPUTE RESOLUTION

This section will analyse the relationship between digital technologies and the emergence of new paradigms of ADR, which often fail to comply with the criteria traditionally used to identify a certain ADR procedure. For instance, it will become evident how technology enables forms of private, out-of-court adjudication that do not formally qualify as arbitration, but nonetheless lead to de facto enforceable outcomes. Along similar lines, the emergence of self-executing contracts allows the parties to a settlement agreement to achieve the goal of enforcement, even if the requirements set forth by national law and/or by the Singapore Convention for the enforcement of settlement agreements are not respected. In more general terms, this section will illustrate how technology can enable the coercive execution of ADR outcomes without relying on the traditional intermediation of the enforcement authorities of the state. As a result, the incentive for legal practitioners to respect the conceptual boundaries delimiting a particular ADR procedure, so as to meet the validity and enforceability conditions set forth in the law, may be progressively fading away.

---

[36] See Singapore Convention, n. 35 at Art 5(1)(e).

8.3.1 Origins of Technology-Driven Self-Enforcement: Domain Name Dispute Resolution

Domain name dispute resolution is by no means a new topic: since 1999, the Internet Corporation for Assigned Names and Numbers (ICANN) has been following a Uniform Domain-Name Dispute-Resolution Policy (UDRP). The purpose of the UDRP is to resolve certain trademark-based disputes concerning domain names. If, for instance, a party operating in bad faith registers a domain name referring to a trademark for the purpose of preventing the trademark owner from registering it (so-called cybersquatting), the UDRP sets forth rules allowing the trademark owner to file a complaint, ultimately obtaining either the cancellation or the transfer of the domain name.[37] ICANN does not handle UDRP complaints internally; to the contrary, it approves a list of external dispute resolution service providers, which administer the procedures.[38] In many respects, these procedures resemble arbitration: the parties exchange written defences,[39] the adjudicators (called 'panelists')[40] have a duty of impartiality and independence,[41] the procedure ensures the parties' right to present their case,[42] the decisions are rendered in writing and they provide the reasons on which they are based.[43] For these reasons, UDRP proceedings are sometimes referred to as a form of 'online (non-binding) arbitration'.[44] Despite these similarities, however, UDRP proceedings are not, strictly speaking, a form of arbitration: they produce no preclusive effects, nor do they lead to outcomes that can be recognised and enforced by national courts. The UDRP itself acknowledges that the disputants retain the right to submit the dispute to any national court having jurisdiction over the case, irrespective of whether UDPR proceedings have not been commenced yet, or have already been concluded.[45] In other words, nothing prevents the parties from relitigating the dispute de novo. However, it is relatively infrequent for the parties to a cybersquatting dispute to commence court litigation[46] because of a crucial feature of the ICANN framework: if a panel decides that a domain name registration should be cancelled or transferred, ICANN proceeds to implement the decision, cancelling the domain name or transferring it to the complainant. In other words, since the disputed assets (i.e., the domain names) are digital in nature and ICANN effectively exerts control over them, the enforcement of UDRP decisions is ensured by technological means, even though those decisions do not qualify as enforceable arbitral awards from the perspective of arbitration law.

To be sure, the enforcement brought about by ICANN is by no means final: as already mentioned, the parties remain free to relitigate the dispute, and any court having jurisdiction over the case can, in principle, modify or reverse the panelists' decision, ordering, for example, that a given domain name not be cancelled or transferred. For this reason, the implementation foreseen in the UDRP should be formally understood as a precarious allocation of disputed

---

[37] Uniform Domain Name Dispute Resolution Policy (UDRP), Art. 4(i), www.icann.org/resources/pages/policy-2012-02-25-en (accessed 24 June 2020).
[38] List of Approved Dispute Resolution Service Providers, www.icann.org/resources/pages/providers-6d-2012-02-25-en (accessed 24 June 2020).
[39] Rules for Uniform Domain Name Dispute Resolution Policy, Arts. 3 and 5, www.icann.org/resources/pages/udrp-rules-2015-03-11-en (accessed 24 June 2020).
[40] Ibid. at Art. 1.
[41] Ibid. at Art. 7.
[42] Ibid. at Art. 10.
[43] Ibid. at Art. 15.
[44] Cortés, n. 28 at 95.
[45] UDRP, n. 37 at Art. 4(k).
[46] E. G. Thornburg, 'Going Private: Technology, Due Process and Internet Dispute Resolution' (2000) 34 *UC Davis Law Review* 151 224.

resources, subject to future review and potential modification. In practice, however, UDRP decisions have a high level of finality; according to the available statistical evidence, it is relatively rare for the parties to relitigate the dispute.[47]

It is easy to grasp how UDRP dispute resolution may blur the boundaries of arbitration, clouding the conceptual criteria that lawyers traditionally deploy to identify arbitration, and distinguish it from other ADR procedures. If the parties can obtain enforcement without relying on the intermediation of the state and of recognition and enforcement procedures, all of the actors involved in UDRP disputes (including not only the parties, but also their counsels, the panelists and the dispute resolution service providers) lack a crucial incentive to comply with the requirements set forth in the law for the enforceability of arbitral awards. Inasmuch as ICANN is able to coercively allocate disputed resources (in this case, domain names), a private adjudicative decision can be enforced with the same ease as an arbitral award, or even with greater facility, even if it does not qualify as an arbitral award from the point of view of (domestic and international) law.[48] Furthermore, although relitigation is in principle possible, national courts have de facto very little opportunity to review the contents of that private decision. As a result, the definition of arbitration may progressively undergo a conceptual split: on the one hand, arbitration law gives us a 'top-down' definition of arbitration, setting the requirements that arbitral procedures and awards must meet, in order to enable the parties to obtain coercive enforcement through 'traditional' recognition and enforcement procedures. On the other hand, a 'bottom-up' definition of arbitration may potentially be shaping up, encompassing a broader range of private adjudication phenomena in which enforcement is ensured by technological means, rather than by the intermediation of the state and its system of courts.

While ICANN is an undoubtedly interesting case study, its relevance is by definition limited to a very specific type of asset: domain names. More recent technological developments, however, have triggered the same type of phenomenon well beyond the case of domain names. Sections 8.3.2–8.3.4 will scrutinise these more recent case studies.

8.3.2 *Platforms as Dispute Resolution Service Providers*

Over the past ten years, platforms have established themselves as market-makers, matching demand and offering of a wide range of goods and services, especially with respect to consumers. High-volume, low-value transactions unavoidably trigger a significant number of disputes: let us think, for instance, of disputes concerning the conformity of goods sold through platforms such as eBay and Amazon, or disputes relating to short-term rental agreements concluded via Airbnb. Needless to say, many of these disputes are not suitable for court litigation: given the typically low value in dispute and the significant costs that litigation would entail (especially in cases where the parties are located in different jurisdictions), it is unrealistic to think that consumers will seek judicial redress on a large scale. At the same time, however, it is important for platforms to ensure a relatively high level of consumer protection: the business model of a platform ultimately depends on the platform's ability to build trust

---

[47] See n. 46.
[48] For this reason, the ICANN framework (and the de facto delegation of public, quasi-sovereign powers to a private entity) has been subject to criticism from a constitutional law standpoint: A. M. Froomkin, 'Wrong Turn in Cyberspace: Using ICANN to Route Around the APA and the Constitution' (2000) 50 *Duke Law Journal* 17. On the other hand, other authors have highlighted how this sort of delegation is consistent with the logic of subsidiarity: L. R. Helfer and G. B. Dinwoodie, 'Designing Non-National Systems: The Case of the Uniform Domain Name Dispute Resolution Policy' (2001–2002) 43 *William and Mary Law Review* 141.

between contracting parties that would not have found and trusted each other outside of the platform. For this reason, most platforms now offer different forms of dispute prevention and resolution schemes and procedures, which are widely relied upon by users; according to scholarly estimates, for instance, eBay handles 60 million buyer-seller disputes annually.[49] Some platforms, such as eBay, have embraced their role of de facto dispute-managers for many years now.[50] Conversely, other platforms have initially tried to maintain a 'hands-off' approach, but they have progressively come to accept their role of trust-enhancers in the marketplace they aim to create. In the words of Airbnb's CEO, 'Ultimately, we're in the business of trust so we have to make … investments to protect our users'.[51] In light of this, it is unsurprising that platforms have been dubbed as informal 'courthouses' of consumer law,[52] and it has been argued that more stringent legal requirements should be imposed on them to ensure the respect of certain procedural minimum standards.[53]

To date, platform dispute resolution policies and procedures remain, at least partially, a black box. On a daily basis, platforms face an astounding number of (typically low-value) disputes, and the techniques they use to process those disputes often remain opaque.[54] Such opacity concerns, among other things, the question whether the platforms reaches its decisions through human intervention or by means of entirely automated decision-making.[55] Along similar lines, it is often unclear to what extent platforms aim at imposing an adjudicative solution on the disputing parties, or rather try to facilitate a settlement agreement between them.[56]

Given the significant uncertainties that surround platform-based dispute resolution, it is unlikely for the outcome of these procedures to be recognised and enforced by state courts. The procedures set forth in (domestic and international) law for the recognition and enforcement of arbitral awards and settlement agreements, for instance, are largely not accessible for the parties that have been involved in these new kinds of hybrid, platform-based dispute resolution schemes. Yet, the lack of state-mediated enforcement does not constitute a significant barrier against the widespread use of these new procedures: similarly to what happens with ICANN and UDRP procedures, platforms have some effective tools to ensure the implementation of dispute resolution outcomes, without the need to rely on state-intermediated enforcement procedures. In some cases, platform-based dispute resolution procedures are closely integrated with payment systems (think of PayPal), so that it may be possible to ensure the implementation of ADR outcome by forcing a payment in favour of the prevailing party.[57] In addition, and more generally, platforms can use their leverage on traders to induce compliance: the prospect of

---

[49] L. F. Del Duca, C. Rule and K. Rimpfel, 'eBay's De Facto Low Value High Volume Resolution Process: Lessons and Best Practices for ODR Systems Designers' (2014) *Arbitration Law Review* 204 205.

[50] Schultz, n. 26 at 140–143.

[51] J. Kastrenakes, 'Airbnb Intends to Verify All Listings following Shooting and Scam Report', *The Verge* (6 November 2019), www.theverge.com/2019/11/6/20951695/airbnb-100-percent-verified-listings-guest-guarantee (accessed 8 July 2020).

[52] R. Van Loo, 'The Corporation as Courthouse' (2016) 33(2) *Yale Journal on Regulation* 547.

[53] R. Van Loo, 'Federal Rules of Platforms Procedure' (2020) *University of Chicago Law Review*, https://papers.ssrn.com/sol3/papers.cfm?abstract_id=3576562&download=yes (accessed 8 July 2020).

[54] Van Loo, n. 52 at 578; E. Katsh and O. Rabinovich-Einy, *Digital Justice: Technology and the Internet of Disputes* (Oxford: Oxford University Press, 2017) 57–80.

[55] On the potential of automatic decision-making in the field of dispute resolution, see J. Barnett and P. Treleaven, 'Algorithmic Dispute Resolution: The Automation of Professional Dispute Resolution Using AI and Blockchain Technologies' (2018) 61(3) *The Computer Journal* 399.

[56] Van Loo, n. 52 at 566–568.

[57] P. Cortés, 'Online Dispute Resolution Services: A Selected Number of Case Studies' (2014) 20(6) *Computer and Telecommunications Law Review* 172 173–175.

reputational sanctions, for instance, may be enough for a trader to comply with the outcome of any platform-based dispute resolution procedure.[58]

The emergence of platform-based dispute resolution is likely to further blur the boundaries of ADR. The dispute resolution procedures carried out on platforms can hardly be subsumed within the conceptual boundaries of any single ADR procedure, such as arbitration, interest-based mediation or negotiation. Yet, those procedures lead to de facto enforceable outcomes. Since platforms have access to enforcement techniques (such as integration with payment systems or trader sanctions) that do not require the intermediation of the state, platform-based ADR has the possibility to evolve in unprecedented ways. In this field, the traditional conceptual criteria used by lawyers to identify different ADR procedures may prove largely ineffective.

8.3.3 Smart Contracts and Settlement Agreements

As Section 8.2.2 has already illustrated, domestic and international lawmakers have recently undertaken initiatives aimed at ensuring the enforceability of settlement agreements resulting from mediation. In so doing, these legislative proposals aim to cure mediation's traditional Achilles' heel, that is, the need for the creditor to initiate court proceedings in case of non-compliance, for the purpose of obtaining an enforceable title. By making enforcement easier (without the need to obtain a judicial enforceable title), such legislative initiatives change the pattern of incentives for the parties, rendering the breach of settlement agreements economically unattractive. Importantly, however, these laws subject the enforceability of settlement agreements to certain conditions. For instance, pursuant to Article 5 of the Singapore Convention, the enforcement of a settlement agreement resulting from mediation can be denied if the mediator influenced a party's choice to enter into the settlement agreement by breaching standards that were applicable to it or by failing to disclose circumstances raising doubts as to the mediator's independence and impartiality. As a result, not all settlement agreements resulting from mediation are automatically granted enforcement under the Singapore Convention, and national courts are given a powerful gatekeeping role, assessing whether the requirements for enforcement set forth in the Convention are met.

Although the Singapore Convention, as well as the domestic statutes facilitating the enforcement of settlement agreements, constitute a relatively new development,[59] they already may prove partially outdated in practice. As already noted, these instruments conceive of national courts as gatekeepers and intermediators for the enforcement of settlement agreements. New technologies such as smart contracts, however, may enable the parties to automate the execution of a settlement agreement, without relying on the intermediation of the state. It would be beyond the scope of this chapter to provide an exhaustive picture of the potential and limits of smart contracts;[60] nevertheless, an example may help clarify the possible impact of contract

---

[58] Van Loo, n. 52 at 569–571. The EU has recently taken action to ensure the authenticity of product reviews submitted by consumers: see Directive (EU) 2019/2161 of the European Parliament and of the Council of 27 November 2019, OJ L 328, 18.12.2019, Art. 3(4)(c), amending Directive 2005/29/EC.

[59] See Section 7.2.2.

[60] For an overview of smart contracts, see among others the contributions in L. DiMatteo, M. Cannarsa and C. Poncibò (eds.), *The Cambridge Handbook of Smart Contracts, Blockchain Technology and Digital Platforms* (Cambridge: Cambridge University Press, 2019); M. Finck, 'Grundlagen und Technologie von Smart Contracts' in M. Fries and B. Paal (eds.), *Smart Contracts* (Tübingen: Mohr Siebeck, 2019) 1; P. De Filippi and A. Wright, *Blockchain and the Law: The Rule of Code* (Cambridge, MA: Harvard University Press, 2018) 72–88; M. Durovic and A. Janssen, 'The Formation of Blockchain-Based Smart Contracts in the Light of Contract Law' (2018) 26(6) *European Review of Private Law* 753; M. Cannarsa, 'Interpretation of Contracts and Smart Contracts: Smart Interpretation or

automation in the field of settlement agreements. Suppose that two parties entered into a contract for the sale of goods. Upon delivery, a dispute arises as to the conformity of the goods, and the buyer requires a price reduction of 40 per cent. After a mediation procedure, the parties reach the following settlement agreement: the price will be reduced by 20 per cent, and the buyer will be given the possibility to pay the price in three instalments, at three-month intervals, rather than in a single solution. Let us now suppose that, after the first instalment, the buyer stops paying the reduced price. If the parties made no use of contract automation technologies, the seller could in some cases rely on the Singapore Convention, and/or on the applicable national mediation statues, to obtain the enforcement of the settlement agreement without having to commence court litigation against the buyer. Technology, however, may offer an alternative, frictionless avenue for the execution of the settlement agreement: the parties may use a smart contract to execute their agreement, ensuring that the instalment payments are automatically carried out every three months.

The use of contract automation technology can have a significant effect on the way in which mediation is conducted. If a mediator knows that any settlement agreement resulting from the mediation will be enforced automatically by technological means, she may have little incentive to comply with the requirements set forth by the law for the mediation agreement to be legally enforceable. Similarly to what Section 8.3.1 has argued with respect to arbitration, then, two different notions of mediation may be surfacing and potentially conflicting with each other. On the one hand, the laws creating a regime for the enforcement of settlement agreements embrace a 'top-down' notion of mediation, where the procedure is shaped by the minimum requirements ensuring enforceability. On the other hand, other forms of mediation may follow a different, 'bottom-up' model, where enforceability is ensured by technological means.

8.3.4 Smart Online Dispute Resolution

The potential of smart contracts is not limited to settlement agreements: contract automation technology can also be used in the context of adjudicative procedures. A good example is escrow mechanisms based on smart contracts and other similar arrangements routinely used by cryptocurrency users.[61] Let us go back to our example of a dispute arising out of the sale of allegedly non-conforming goods. When concluding the sales contract, it is possible for the parties to agree that the price (denominated in a cryptocurrency, such as Ether of Bitcoin) will be stored in an escrow wallet controlled by a smart contract, rather than being directly transferred from the wallet of the buyer to the wallet of the seller. An escrow wallet can be described (with an unavoidable degree of approximation) as the cryptocurrency equivalent of a bank account, where funds remain stored until two sets of keys (the equivalent of passwords) are used to unlock them. In the example above, buyer and seller are each provided with a key. As a result, whenever the transaction runs smoothly and no dispute arises, buyer and seller can agree to jointly use their keys, and the smart contract will unlock the price stored in the wallet, transferring it to the seller. Conversely, if a dispute arises, neither of the parties can unilaterally withdraw funds. Both parties, however, are given the possibility to initiate a dispute resolution procedure. At the end of

---

Interpretation of Smart Contracts?' (2018) 26(6) *European Review of Private Law* 773; N. Guggenheim, 'The Potentional of Blockchain for the Conclusion of Contracts' in R. Schulze, D. Staudenmeyer and S. Lohse (eds.), *Contracts for the Supply of Digital Content: Regulatory Challenges and Gaps* (Baden-Baden: Nomos, 2017) 83.

[61] For an in-depth description of these mechanisms, see P. Ortolani, 'The Three Challenges of Stateless Justice' (2016) 7 (3) *Journal of International Dispute Settlement* 596; P. Ortolani, 'Self-Enforcing Online Dispute Resolution: Lessons from Bitcoin' (2016) 36(3) *Oxford Journal of Legal Studies* 595.

this procedure, a decision will be issued as to which of the disputing parties should receive the funds stored in escrow. In our example, the buyer claiming nonconformity is likely to initiate the procedure and ask the repayment of at least a percentage of the price. If the buyer's claim is successful, the smart contract will automatically transfer the disputed funds back to her wallet. Once again, enforcement is attained by technological means, rather than through the intermediation of state courts.

The automatic enforcement of private adjudication outcomes through escrow mechanisms and smart contracts is far from being a merely theoretical prospect; to the contrary, the phenomenon is already widespread in practice. An early example of adoption of blockchain-based escrow arrangements can be found in darknet marketplaces, where private adjudication based on escrow mechanisms is used to enforce contracts contrary to public policy, which would not be upheld by national courts and would, in fact, in all likelihood trigger the parties' criminal liability.[62] Needless to say, this example speaks volumes about the potential dangers associated with the creation of dispute resolution systems that are largely self-sufficient and screened from the scrutiny of state courts.[63] Over the past few years, however, the idea of escrow-based ADR has extended beyond the darknet, having been embraced by startup companies looking for cost-efficient solutions to the problem of high-volume, low-value dispute resolution. The goal of these projects[64] is to create novel forms of ADR, in which the final outcome is automatically enforced by means of an escrow arrangement. Similarly to what has already happened with UDRP dispute resolution, these procedures do not fall within the 'top-down' definition of arbitration enshrined in the 1958 New York Convention and in national arbitration statutes; many of them, in fact, envisage the use of 'wisdom of the crowd' voting mechanisms, underpinned by game-theoretical incentives, which are clearly incompatible with arbitration law.[65] Technology, however, ensures the de facto enforceability of the final outcome. In terms of ease of enforcement, automatic payments via a smart contract may factually prove more efficient than the 'traditional' techniques of recognition and enforcement contained in domestic and international law. In other words, these dispute resolution mechanisms constitute an emerging form of enforceable, 'bottom-up' private adjudication, which does not fall within the traditional boundaries of arbitration, but can in practice ensure many of the advantages of that are typically associated with arbitration.

8.4 INCREASING POROUSNESS OF PROCEDURAL LAW IN TIMES OF TECHNOLOGICAL ACCELERATION

Section 8.3 has taken stock of the various ways in which technologies blur the boundaries of ADR. More specifically, technology fosters the emergence of new dispute resolution paradigms; these novel forms of ADR do not comport with the conceptual labels traditionally designating arbitration, mediation and other ADR procedures, yet operate in a functionally comparable

---

[62] M. Horton-Eddison and M. Di Cristofaro, 'Hard Interventions and Innovation in Crypto-Drug Markets: The Escrow Example', Policy Brief, www.swansea.ac.uk/media/Hard-Interventions-and-Innovation-in-CryptoDrug-Markets-The-escrow-example.pdf (accessed 8 July 2020). According to the authors, the adoption of escrow technologies in darknet marketplaces can at least partially be explained as an attempt of the users to screen their transactions against external scrutiny.

[63] Ortolani, n. 61 at 604–608.

[64] For a comparative overview, describing many of these projects, see the contribution of Durovic and Lech in this book (Chapter 6).

[65] For an in-depth analysis of these mechanisms, see the chapter of Palombo, Battaglini and Cantisani in this book (Chapter 7).

fashion, and they often ensure frictionless enforceability. What are the consequences of this increasing porousness of the conceptual boundaries of ADR? This section attempts to answer the question, drawing some normative inferences from the analysis carried out so far.

8.4.1 Self-Enforcing Adjudication, Due Process and Judicial Review

As illustrated by the analysis carried out so far, technology allows ADR procedures (be they adjudication- or settlement-oriented) to attain enforceable outcomes, without the need to rely on the intermediation of the state. For a long time, this type of intermediation has been operationalised through recognition and enforcement procedures, such as the ones set forth in the New York Convention for arbitration and in the Singapore Convention for mediation. In this traditional setting, the prospect of future judicial review (on pain of non-enforceability) helped specific ADR procedures to coalesce around coherent, state-sanctioned paradigms, traditionally encompassed under the labels of 'arbitration', 'mediation', etc. Now, however, things may rapidly change, as a variety of disputed assets can be coercively allocated without requiring the cooperation of courts, bailiffs and the enforcement apparatus of the state. As a consequence, the incentive to comply with the enforceability requirements set forth in the law, both at the domestic and at the international level, may be diminishing in the near future. In a world where private enforcement is widely available, new forms of 'bottom-up' ADR procedures become possible.

An evident consequence of the aforementioned technology-driven evolution of ADR is that the standards of due process, impartiality and independence traditionally required of particular ADR mechanisms may no longer be respected. An example may help clarify the practical impact of the phenomenon at hand. As already mentioned,[66] e-commerce platforms manage a high volume of disputes between traders and customers, and they can leverage powerful incentives (such as reputational sanctions) to convince a trader to reach a settlement agreement with a dissatisfied customer and respect the terms thereof. Platforms, however, may not always be independent and impartial mediators; a platform's business model, in fact, is likely to hinge on a high volume of retail customers and on the maintenance of a good level of consumer satisfaction. For this reason, a platform may encourage settlement solutions that are consumer-oriented, conversely minimising the economic and commercial interests of small-size businesses, which need uninterrupted access to the platform to remain solvent.[67] A settlement agreement encouraged by a mediator having this type of vested interest in the outcome of the dispute could, potentially, be declined enforcement under the Singapore Convention.[68] As already illustrated, however, the technological infrastructure within which the settlement agreement is reached

---

[66] See Section 7.3.2.
[67] Similar concerns regarding platform-to-business (P2B) relations have recently triggered a wide range of research and regulatory proposals, such as the European Law Institute Model Rules on Online Platforms, www.europeanlawinstitute.eu/projects-publications/completed-projects-old/online-platforms/ (accessed 8 July 2020); P. Alexiadis and A. de Streel, 'Designing an EU Intervention Standard for Digital Platforms', EUI Working Papers RSCAS 2020/14 (2020); C. Busch, 'Self-Regulation and Regulatory Intermediation in the Platform Economy' in M. Cantero Gamito and H. W. Micklitz (eds.), *The Role of the EU in Transnational Legal Ordering: Standards, Contracts and Codes* (Cheltenham: Elgar, 2019) 115; I. Graef, 'Differentiated Treatment in Platform-to-Business Relations: EU Competition Law and Economic Dependence' (2019) 38 *Yearbook of European Law* 448; M. Kenney, D. Bearson and J. Zysman, 'The Platform Economy Matures: Pervasive Power, Private Regulation, and Dependent Entrepreneurs', Berkeley Roundtable on the International Economy Working Paper 2019-11 (2019); C. Busch, H. Schulte-Nölke, A. Wiewiorowska-Domagalska and F. Zoll, 'The Rise of the Platform Economy: A New Challenge for EU Consumer Law?' (2016) 5(1) *Journal of European Consumer and Market Law* 3.
[68] See, in particular, Art. 5.

ensures enforceability, without the need to rely on the intermediation of the state. The same reasoning is even more obviously valid for private adjudicative decisions that may not offer sufficient procedural guarantees to qualify for recognition and enforcement under arbitration law, but that can de facto be coercively enforced.

To be sure, the rise of new 'bottom-up' paradigms of self-enforcing ADR presents not only risks, but also possibilities. The cost-effective attainment of enforceable results allows us to meet the demand for dispute resolution in a more granular way. By way of example, the traditional, state-sanctioned paradigm of arbitration is notoriously costly, and those costs largely derive from the need to comply with burdensome procedural requirements and guarantees (such as the exchange of written defences, an extensive taking of evidence, one or more oral hearings, etc.). Clearly, that paradigm is not suitable for all disputes, and certainly not for small-value ones. From this point of view, the blurring of boundaries brought about by technology can certainly facilitate the emergence of more flexible, suitable procedures, catering to disputes that cannot be effectively handled through traditional ADR.

On the other hand, sufficient attention should be paid to the risk that self-enforcing, technology-driven ADR will result in a problematic dilution of due process guarantees. In order to mitigate this risk, regulators may soon find it necessary to adopt a more 'hands-on' regulatory approach, imposing for instance minimum procedural standards that the new forms of ADR must comply with. In this sense, calls for a set of 'Federal Rules of Platform Procedure' have already been put forth in the United States, drawing inspiration from existing models of procedural oversight (such as credit card chargeback procedures).[69] However, the prospect of regulation at the transnational level should also be given serious consideration: given the inherently cross-border nature of the technologies that have fostered the emergence of these new forms of ADR, it would seem desirable to develop a transnational regulatory solution. Not only would a transnational approach level the playing field in an increasingly globalised digital economy; in addition, it would also limit compliance costs and ensure a productive cross-fertilisation among different legal traditions.

8.4.2 End of Finality?

Finality is one of the cornerstones of procedural law. The notion that the outcome of a dispute resolution procedure will produce *res judicata* effects is traditionally deemed to serve two interrelated purposes. First of all, this doctrine ensures certainty as to the parties' rights and obligations, preventing the relitigation of the same case and thus protecting the prevailing party against the risk of being repeatedly sued by its counterparty. Second, finality protects all of the disputing parties against the officiousness of courts, ensuring that public powers will not repetitively invade the parties' sphere of private autonomy.[70]

---

[69] Van Loo, n. 53 at 17–20; see also P. Cortés and T. Cole, 'Legislating for an Effective and Legitimate System of Online Consumer Arbitration' in M. Piers and C. Aschauer (eds.), *Arbitration in the Digital Age: The Brave New World of Arbitration* (Cambridge: Cambridge University Press, 2018) 209, proposing a set of guarantees for online consumer arbitration.

[70] A. Chizzini, *Pensiero e Azione nella Storia del Processo Civile* (Turin: UTET, 2013) 200–212. For a comparative overview of the notion of *res judicata* and its effects in a cross-border perspective, see J. van de Velden, *Finality in Litigation: The Law and Practice of Preclusion – Res Judicata (Merger and Estoppel), Abuse of Process and Recognition of Foreign Judgments* (Deventer: Kluwer, 2017); F. Ferrand, 'Lis pendens and *Res Judicata*: From National Law to a Possible European Harmonization?' in B. Hess, S. Kolmann, J. Adolphsen and U. Haas (eds.), *Festschrift für Peter Gottwald zum 70. Geburtstag* (Munich: Beck 2014) 144.

Given the importance of these functions, finality has been seen for a long time as a necessary consequence and attribute of adjudication and the natural outcome of the exertion of judicial powers. Over the past two decades, however, the set of guarantees associated with finality and *res judicata* have been progressively eroded on multiple fronts. Some of these developments are well-known and widely discussed in the literature. The CJEU, for instance, has held that it may, in some cases, be necessary to set aside national rules of *res judicata* in order to preserve the primacy and effectiveness of EU law.[71] Along partially similar lines, investment tribunals can de facto unravel the allocation of resources mandated by a national judgments, by ruling that said judgment constitutes a violation of an international investment agreement for which the investor must be compensated.[72] The erosion of finality, however, is not only a consequence of the interplay between domestic law and different international or supranational legal orders; to the contrary, the emergence of digital dispute resolution acts as an additional, understudied factor.

All of the forms of digital dispute resolution considered in this chapter (from UDRP adjudication to platform dispute resolution, from smart contracts to decentralised escrow mechanisms) share a common feature: the outcome of the procedure is technically enforceable, but not final. In the context of these new private adjudication paradigms, no rule prevents the litigants from continuing to pursue the dispute, relitigating it in different fora. For this reason, inasmuch as these new forms of technology-enabled dispute resolution gain traction, the traditional idea of finality may be further marginalised.

8.4.3 *Public Policy and the Enforcement of Substantive Law*

Procedural safeguards are not the only reason why the law subjects different forms of ADR to a modicum of judicial review; in a limited but crucial range of cases, the intermediation and control of state courts may also serve the purpose of enforcing certain substantive rules and policies. By way of example, under Article V(2)(b) of the New York Convention, the recognition and enforcement of an arbitral award may be declined if the award is incompatible with the public policy of the country of enforcement, and a similar provision is included in Article 5(2)(a) of the Singapore Convention, with reference to settlement agreements resulting from mediation.

Public policy clauses, such as the ones just mentioned, have been used by state courts to ensure that ADR procedures would not be used to circumvent the enforcement of certain important areas of substantive law. A good example, in this respect, is competition law: as already noted, both in the United States and in the EU, the circumstance that a contract between private parties may be contrary to competition law does not, per se, prevent the parties from submitting any disputes arising out of or in connection with that contract to arbitration.[73] However, with reference to the EU, the CJEU has stressed the need for the arbitrators to apply competition law: if an arbitral award violates provisions of competition law, its recognition and enforcement may be denied on grounds of public policy.[74] In other words, the CJEU sees

---

[71] *Ministero dell'Industria, del Commercio e dell'Artigianato v. Lucchini SpA*, C-119/05, ECLI:EU:C:2007:434; *Klausner Holz Niedersachsen GmbH v. Land Nordrhein-Westfalen*, C-505/14, ECLI:EU:C:2015:742; for a comment on this line of case-law, see X. Groussot and T. Minssen, 'Res Judicata in the ECJ Case Law: Balancing Legal Certainty with Legality?' (2007) 3 *European Constitutional Law Review* 385.

[72] More specifically, this type of finding is often possible in relation to fair and equitable treatment clauses contained in many investment treaties: V. Živković, 'Fair and Equitable Treatment between the International and National Rule of Law' (2019) 20(4) *Journal of World Investment & Trade* 513 546–551.

[73] See nn. 22 and 23 and accompanying text.

[74] *Eco Swiss*, n. 23.

commercial arbitral tribunals as enforcers of competition law, and allows national courts to perform a certain review of the contents of arbitral awards, to ensure that this task of enforcement of substantive law has not been disregarded by the arbitrators.[75]

This chapter has shown how technology facilitates the emergence of new ADR mechanisms, where the enforcement of outcomes is not mediated by the state and its courts. This development, in turn, minimises the possibility for state courts to review the contents of those outcomes, assessing whether they may be incompatible with public policy. In other words, whereas traditional ADR could be seen as subject to the control of state courts, so as to ensure the protection of some basic values norms and principles, the same may not hold true for the new, emerging paradigms of technology-enabled ADR. This development raises the question of how national and international regulators can safeguard the enforcement of key areas of substantive law, such as competition law. One partial solution to the problem at hand, of course, could be the strengthening of public enforcement: if private dispute resolution proves unreliable, a more active and pervasive role by public authorities may help ensure that the law is translated into actual practice. Public enforcement, however, can never entirely substitute the initiative of private parties. For this reason, it seems necessary to inject sufficient procedural guarantees into the new, emerging forms of ADR. The proposal put forth in this chapter, concerning transnational minimum procedural standards, could help ensure that private parties do not unwittingly end up waiving rights that the applicable substantive law confers upon them.

8.5 CONCLUSION

This chapter investigated the emergence of new forms of digital dispute resolution, where the enforcement of outcomes is ensured by technological means, rather than by relying on state-mediated procedures (such as the procedures for the recognition and enforcement of arbitral awards). To illustrate the phenomenon, different case studies have been presented, including ICANN's UDRP procedures, platform-based dispute resolution and smart escrow adjudication. An interesting consequence of this development is the blurring of the conceptual boundaries that lawyers traditionally use to identify and distinguish among different ADR procedures. For example, technology facilitates the creation of private adjudicative procedures that do not formally qualify as arbitration but do nevertheless lead to enforceable decisions in practice. On the one hand, frictionless enforcement can help private parties devise cost-effective dispute resolution mechanisms, thus potentially enabling a broader range of users to access dispute resolution services. On the other hand, however, the self-sufficient nature of these new digital dispute resolution paradigms also poses significant challenges. In this vein, this chapter has described the risk associated with the dilution of due process guarantees, the erosion of finality and the under-enforcement of substantive law. To mitigate these problems, this chapter has advocated in favour of the development of transnational procedural minimum standards.

---

[75] It is on these premises that the CJEU has drawn a distinction between commercial and investment arbitration, when ruling that only the latter is incompatible with EU law, in the context of intra-EU investment agreements: *Slowakische Republik v. Achmea BV*, C-284/16, ECLI:EU:C:2018:158, paras 54–55.

PART III

Legal Tech in Consumer Relations and Small Claims

9

Legal Tech in Consumer Relations and Small-Value Claims

A Survey

*Francisco de Elizalde**

9.1 INTRODUCTION

Legal tech (LT) companies operating in litigation predominantly address B2C relationships, which is odd against the overall LT backdrop where B2B solutions prevail.[1] A 'no win no fee' policy, whereby consumers are only charged for success, is popular among LT companies that manage claims.[2] Even though their contingency fees tend to be significant,[3] they attract consumers who would otherwise have abandoned a claim as a result of rational apathy due to its small value. The automated management of claims has impacted consumer access to justice as the activity of LT companies has led to an increase in redress for small value claims.[4]

Unlike the more individualised approach of traditional law firms, LT companies preselect the types of claims they handle. Specialisation makes the management of a large portfolio possible and suitable for automation.[5] The preselection of claims is also important in respect of access to justice as non-selected claims remain under-redressed.

The option that LT companies give for certain claims, with their corresponding applicable laws, could reveal important data on the relationship between law and automation. Some claims could be more suitable than others for automation depending on the laws applicable to them. In fact, the argument that this chapter makes is that legal rules in many cases do not meet the needs

---

* This chapter is an output of the EU Jean Monnet Module 'Liability of Robots: A European Vision for a New Legal Regime' and of the research project (Spain), DER 2017-84947-P. I would like to thank Eva Moral, Jorge Morell, Macarena Plaza and Pablo Rabanal for helping me to distribute the survey that was conducted for this chapter. Students and alumni from IE University contributed by translating the survey into five languages and distributing it, although I centralised receipt of responses. I am grateful to Sebastian Arnold, Aurora Dell'Elce, Bárbara Gómez Cortés and Elena Sabau for assisting with this task. Aurora and Elena also provided valuable research assistance. I thank Professor David Donald for comments on some of the arguments made here. The usual disclaimer applies. The survey is accessible at https://static.ie.edu/Legrob/Legal%20Tech%20Survey%E2%80%99.pdf.

[1] See M. Barendrecht et al., 'Charging For Justice, SDG 16.3 Trend Report 2020' at 87, www.hiil.org/wp-content/uploads/2020/04/HiiL-report-Charging-for-Justice-3.pdf (accessed 27 July 2020). A. Hook, 'The Use and Regulation of Technology in the Legal Sector beyond England and Wales', Research Paper for the Legal Services Board (2019) at 6, www.legalservicesboard.org.uk/wp-content/uploads/2019/07/International-AH-Report-VfP-4-Jul-2019.pdf (accessed 22 July 2020). See M. Ebers, Section 11.1.1.

[2] M. Hartung, 'The Digital Transformation' in M. Hartung, M.-M. Bues and G. Halbleib (eds.), *Legal Tech: How Technology Is Changing the Legal World. A Practitioner's Guide* (Munich: Beck-Hart-Nomos, 2018) 10.

[3] Ibid.

[4] C. Hipp, 'The Enforcement of Air Passenger Rights: An Analysis and Comparison of Claims Management Companies and Recently Established Conciliation Bodies' in M. Huseyin Bilgin et al. (eds.), *Eurasian Business Perspectives. Proceedings of the 22nd Eurasia Business and Economics Society Conference* (Cham: Springer, 2019) 342.

[5] Hartung, n. 2.

of automation and that the quality of the drafting of each law determines its fate vis-à-vis automation. This argument is made against the backdrop of litigation, a contextualisation that is relevant because it involves legal reasoning, which is probably one of the most difficult activities to automate.[6]

To achieve the aim of understanding the relationship between law and automation, it was deemed necessary to conduct a survey on LT companies involved in the litigation of small value claims. Information from participants in that market was relevant for the purpose of gathering data on the reasons underlying the selection of claims and on the impact of law on the automation of legal services. The main findings are presented in Section 9.2. A qualitative assessment of the data collected, with a focus on law and automation, is conducted in Section 9.3. The chapter ends with concluding remarks (Section 9.4).

9.2 SURVEY

9.2.1 Methodology

The survey was prepared for this book and the participants were informed of that intention. The target population of the survey comprised LT companies involved in litigation of consumer and small value claims. In the absence of a harmonised classification of LT companies,[7] the target population was limited to those platforms that are not traditional law firms or technologised versions of them and that, notwithstanding, represent clients vis-à-vis businesses out of court and before the courts. Due to this restriction, electronic marketplaces that enable clients to find a lawyer were discarded. For the same reason, the survey included neither mediation nor dispute resolution platforms. Companies that do not represent clients in court were not targeted.

Geographically, the target population included all LT companies in the defined field in France, Germany, Italy, Spain and the United Kingdom, which are the five largest markets for legal services in Europe.[8] It is important to recall that the purpose of the survey was to serve as a benchmark for the automation of legal services in respect of claims rather than to comprehensively map LT.[9] The survey was meant to gather data on how significant law is in the degree of automation of legal services in the area of claims/litigation. Therefore, it was considered appropriate to address different legal systems that hail from a variety of legal families (common law and civil law of Germanic and Romanistic traditions, with all the caveats applicable to this classification).[10] The selection of countries complies with these parameters.

The sampling frame of the survey (i.e., the sources from which the individuals in a sample are drawn)[11] was obtained from the available lists of LT companies from the target

---

[6] See C. Markou and S. Deakin, 'Ex Machina Lex: The Limits of Legal Computability', papers.ssrn.com/sol3/papers.cfm?abstract_id=3407856 (accessed 22 July 2020).

[7] See the variations among popular classifications such as those of the Tech Index of the CodeX Center for Legal Informatics at Stanford University (techindex.law.stanford.edu) and the Legal Geek Startup Map (www.legalgeek.co/startup-map) (accessed 29 June 2020). A simpler classification divides LT companies into those that provide automated legal advice products, electronic marketplaces, legal process outsourcing and e-Discovery and document review. The companies under analysis would be included in the first category. On this, see Hartung, n. 2 at 7–8. See also Ebers, n. 1.

[8] J. Leason, A. Connor and J. Vestbirk, 'Legal Tech Startup Report 2019: A Maturing Market' (2019), Thomson Reuters and LegalGeek at 4, https://blogs.thomsonreuters.com/legal-uk/2019/10/18/a-new-report-legaltech-startup-report-2019-a-maturing-market/ (accessed 10 July 2020).

[9] The participants were aware of this. Before the first question of the survey, it was stated: 'The following questions are meant to understand how your company interacts with technology'.

[10] See K. Zweigert and H. Kötz, *An Introduction to Comparative Law* (Oxford: Oxford University Press, 1998) 63–73.

[11] S. Diamond, 'Reference Guide on Survey Research' in National Research Council (US) (ed.), *Reference Manual on Scientific Evidence*, 3rd ed. (Washington, DC: National Research Council, 2011) 421.

population,[12] which was checked with requests to legal innovation centres.[13] The sampling frame was supplemented by a plethora of searches in internet search engines of the countries of residence of the targeted companies, in their own languages.

The sample of the survey was selected following stratification of the targeted companies, which were partitioned into subpopulations according to the sector in which they operate: air carriage, debt collection, employment, banking, telecommunications, insurance, tenancy and general claims platforms.

The survey data was collected through the Internet, complying with the GDPR.[14] Using the Internet as the mode of data collection was deemed optimal as the targeted companies are IT savvy. In this respect, the risk of noncoverage error (i.e., ignoring relevant populations whose responses the survey was designed to measure)[15] was trivial, if it existed at all. Companies in the sample received the survey in a corporate email, after agreeing to have it sent to them. The responses were anonymous, untracked, and the only corporate information that was requested from the participants was their country of residence. This information was considered necessary to link the data collected with a specific legal system in order to test the basic proposition of this chapter: that law could determine the fate of automation of legal services. Without country information it would have been impossible to conduct that assessment, which is expounded in Section 9.3 of this chapter.

The survey was drafted in clear and unambiguous language, which was pretested by a small sample of the targeted population.[16] All questions were close-ended except for one that was open-ended. In order to avoid bias arising from close-ended questions such as, for example, ignoring possible answers that a participant could have, the options presented to the participants were exhaustive. In several questions, participants could select more than one option and the option 'other' was recurrently offered, giving the possibility of a personalised answer. A concern raised when drafting the survey was the likelihood that participants would inflate their answers to present a better picture of themselves (in this context, of higher automation). To tackle that bias, control questions were frequent in the survey[17] and the websites of all companies of the target population were conscientiously scrutinised to understand how they operate.

9.2.2 Results

9.2.2.1 *Companies by Sector*

The classification of companies by sector and country is a precondition of the assessment of automation of legal services as it indicates the applicable legal framework for the claims that

---

[12] In addition to those mentioned in n. 7, the following lists were consulted: terminosycondiciones.es/2016/07/20/legaltech-espana-mucho, www.village-justice.com/articles/Les-start-up-droit,18224.html?secteur=Justice per cent20as per cent20service#annuaire-legaltech, lespepitestech.com/startup-collection/legaltech (accessed 25 May 2020).

[13] Forschungsstelle Legal Tech (Germany), Incubateur du Barreau de Paris (France) and IE Legal Tech Innovation Farm (Spain). I am grateful for their support.

[14] Regulation (EU) 2016/679 of the European Parliament and of the Council of 27 April 2016 on the protection of natural persons with regard to the processing of personal data and on the free movement of such data, and repealing Directive 95/46/EC (General Data Protection Regulation) [2018] OJ L119/1.

[15] Diamond, n. 11 at 407.

[16] A member of the targeted population in each of the countries involved was approached for this purpose.

[17] For example, to determine the degree of automation, Question # 3 asked about automation in general, Question # 4 about automation by sector and Questions # 5 and # 6 addressed specificities of automation such as the capacity of a company to determine if the client has a valid claim without the intervention of a lawyer and whether its IT system could autonomously calculate compensation. Additionally, Question # 15 aimed at determining the type of technology used. The direct questions supplemented with the control ones were intended to reduce the margin of error.

those companies manage. Only by matching LT companies with a specific substantive law is it possible to ponder the relationship between law and automation.

A website analysis of the target population determined the specific industry sectors in which the LT companies operate within the broader field of litigation. Participants were requested to select their own sectors among a list that had been drawn up from the website analysis. The questionnaire also allowed participants to include uncontemplated sectors.

The website analysis determined that, in the field of litigation, air carriage is the industry in which LT companies are clearly more numerous. Platforms that manage flight claims exclusively, including delay, cancellation and denied boarding amount to 44.44 per cent of the total. The figure is even larger if we also include those platforms that manage flight claims in addition to others.[18] The significant share of LT companies in air carriage claims, compared to other industries, is constant in the targeted countries with slight variations.[19]

Second in the numerosity rank of LT companies are general claims platforms, that is, those that do not focus on claims arising from a specific industry but, instead, deal with a broad spectrum of matters. They represent 13.33 per cent overall.[20] It is to be recalled that the sample excluded companies that do not represent clients in court.

The third level of companies by number is composed of those that claim employment rights, which amount to 8.89 per cent.[21] That group is followed by those LT companies that focus on debt collection in general (i.e., not sector specific), amounting to 6.67 per cent. They are spread equally between France, Italy and Spain.[22] The same share goes to companies that manage cumulatively air carriage and banking claims.[23] The subsequent level comprises companies that deal with train carriage or tenancy claims (in Germany). Each one represents 4.44 per cent overall.[24] The less frequented sectors are insurance, telecommunications, accidents and fines, as well as insurance and banking when handled by the same company.[25] Each type of business model represents 2.22 per cent overall, considering the targeted countries jointly.[26]

Participants were asked to explain why they had chosen those types of claims as the bases for their business models. They could select more than one option and, additionally, they could personalise their answer. Most respondents declared that the reason was the 'homogeneity of the applicable law (i.e., variations between cases being marginal or non-existent)'. An equally important number of answers justified their choice by the 'breadth of the potentially affected parties'. In third place, participants chose that '[t]hey are usual instances of non-claimed rights'. Personalised answers were seldom given.[27]

---

[18] Those companies amount to 6.67 per cent overall.

[19] France, 50 per cent; Germany, 52.38 per cent; Italy, 40 per cent; Spain, 50 per cent and the United Kingdom, 57.14 per cent. These shares include companies that manage flight claims in addition to others.

[20] In France they amount to 33.33 per cent, in Germany, 4.76 per cent, in Italy 20 per cent, and in the United Kingdom 28.57 per cent.

[21] LT companies that claim employment rights amount to 14.28 per cent in Germany and 16.66 per cent in Spain.

[22] I.e., 33 per cent of that figure in each country with no representation from Germany or the United Kingdom.

[23] The cumulative management of air carriage and banking claims was found in Spain (33.33 per cent of the overall companies) and in the United Kingdom (14.28 per cent).

[24] LT companies solely handling train claims were detected in Germany (9.52 per cent in that country). The same was detected in respect of tenancy claims (9.52 per cent in Germany).

[25] This type of business model was found in Spain only.

[26] The share at a national level of those companies is indicated next. In Spain, LT companies that deal with insurance and banking represent 16.66 per cent. In the United Kingdom, accident LT companies amount to 14.28 per cent. In Italy, LT companies that manage fines claims represent 20 per cent overall.

[27] The rates of each option were as follows: 78.57 per cent of respondents for the first and second ones, 57.14 per cent selected the third one, while personalised answers amounted to 21.43 per cent. Adjusted per mention (instead of per

Participants were also asked why they do not manage other consumer-related cases, beyond those that they currently handle. Those 'other' cases were exemplified with claims arising from car accidents or defective consumer goods. Participants could select more than one option and, additionally, they could personalise their answer. To this, 42.85 per cent of respondents declared that they do not manage those cases but that they would be able to do so without major changes to their business models. In contrast, 35.71 per cent of respondents justified not handling those types of claims on the grounds that the application of the law must be done on a case-by-case basis, which complicates automation. In a similar vein, 14.28 per cent of respondents explained the rejection of those other cases on the basis that they require the intervention of experts and, because of this, are more difficult to automate. A personalised answer was provided by 21.43 per cent of the surveyed companies.[28] Evidently, some respondents chose more than one answer.

9.2.2.2 Self-Assessment of Automation

After selecting the industries in which they operate, participants were asked to self-assess the degree of automation of their businesses. For this purpose, they were requested to inform to what extent they automate claims in general and, next, they had to answer a multiple-choice question on automation of claims (out of court) in the specific sectors in which they work. The survey did not provide a definition of automation; at this stage it was left open to the interpretation of participants. The companies' self-assessment was scrutinised with control questions, which will be explained in Sections 9.2.2.3 and 9.2.2.4.

The results of the self-assessment exercise do not follow a common pattern. There is great variation in the automation rate between businesses that operate in the same industry and offer comparable legal services. In the air carriage industry, there is a range of automation of activities starting with less than 50 per cent and reaching, in certain companies, 90–100 per cent. In banking, automation ranges from 50 to 90 per cent. In debt collection, telecommunications and employment claims, the range is 75–100 per cent. In insurance and general claims platforms, automation was self-assessed in less than 50 per cent in all cases.

If those results are organised according to the degree of automation, they show that this reaches its highest levels (90–100 per cent) in air carriage claims, debt collection, employment, telecommunications and, in Germany, tenancy. Whereas, it is weaker in general claims platforms and in insurance-related claims (less than 50 per cent). In turn, banking claim companies appear in between, as the highest levels of automation are in the range of 75–90 per cent.

9.2.2.3 Degrees of Automation and Control of the Self-Assessment Exercise: Technology and Success Rates in Court

The existing definitions of automation are broad and so include '[t]he use or introduction of automatic equipment in a manufacturing or other process or facility'.[29] From this it can be established that automation of a service could be high but not necessarily sophisticated. For example, automation of a vending machine is high as it requires little human intervention but, under current standards, it applies quite a simple mechanism. In contrast, an IT system that

---

respondent), the first and second options represent 33.33 per cent each, the third option amounts to 24.24 per cent and personalised answers make 9.09 per cent overall.

[28] The most extended personalised answer was related to specialisation in the type of claims.
[29] Oxford Dictionary, www.lexico.com (accessed 24 June 2020).

resorts to machine learning would be more sophisticated than a vending machine, allowing for smarter outcomes, although it could reach lower rates of automation if it required a more fluent interaction with humans.

Therefore, it could occur that the rates of automation arising from the self-assessment exercise that were presented in Section 9.2.2.2 paint an untrue picture of unequally sophisticated business models. To avoid that, the results of the self-assessment exercise were controlled with specific questions to obtain a more accurate picture of automation in the claims/litigation sector. With the same aim, those questions were supplemented with a website analysis of the targeted companies.

In LT, automation should be measured by the capacity of technology to operate autonomously, without the intervention of lawyers.[30] The more autonomous an IT system is, the less it requires the intervention of lawyers. If an IT system is fully autonomous, it is capable of replacing lawyers in the provision of legal services. This understanding of automation not only considers the extent to which a process is self-executed but also assesses the sophistication of automation as it relates it to the possibility of substituting lawyers. Against this backdrop, automation is deemed to be higher when the likelihood of technology operating without lawyers is also higher.

In litigation, automation in its compound meaning (i.e., autonomous operation that reduces or eliminates the intervention of lawyers) is benchmarked by the answers to two fundamental questions: first, whether an IT system can determine if a client has a plausible claim without the intervention of lawyers in the assessment of every single case; second, whether an IT system can autonomously calculate the exact compensation that is due. In both cases, of course, this needs to be done in a way that is likely to be confirmed in court. If an IT system is able to conduct a legal assessment on the plausibility of a claim and can determine the exact compensation that is due, automation is high, as technology would be substituting for lawyers in providing legal advice.

Automation is hindered if the claim has to be lodged with courts, as legal systems require the intervention of lawyers, of the parties themselves and, in some jurisdictions, of a lay representative. Moreover, in the evolution of courts into an online setting, the replacement of lawyers in court is forecasted to come in the final stage, if at all.[31] Even though LT companies have succeeded in automating their internal claims management, allowing them to handle a large portfolio,[32] physical interaction with courts is still required.

Therefore, the survey focused on the pre-contentious (out of court) phase of claims to determine the degree of automation of the targeted companies at that stage. The questions were drafted based on the notion of automation that was previously explained, that is, considering the extent to which technology can replace lawyers. Participants were asked to inform whether their IT systems could determine if a client has a plausible claim without the intervention of lawyers and, in a separate question, whether they could calculate the exact compensation due. In a third (control) question, participants were asked about their success rate in court in order to confirm the accuracy of their IT systems in conducting legal assessments. Later in the order of questions, companies were offered the possibility to indicate the technology they use. The purpose of that question was to frame the relationship of automation and technology.

---

[30] Hartung, n. 2 at 6. See Eric Tjong Tjin Tai, Section 12.2.1.
[31] R. Susskind, *Online Courts and the Future of Justice* (Oxford: Oxford University Press, 2019) 274.
[32] Interview with a LT company in Spain (anonymous).

The answers of participants to this section of the survey reflect the heterogeneity in automation. Comparable companies that deal with the same type of claims and in the same sector automate their clients' claims to a very different extent. For LT companies in the air carriage sector, the range goes from those that cannot determine whether a client has a plausible claim nor calculate compensation[33] to others whose IT systems can do both.[34] The same occurs in banking,[35] while in employment claims, all participants are able to automate the plausibility of the claim but diverge in their ability to autonomously calculate compensation.[36]

However, there is some homogeneity within certain sectors. In telecommunications, IT systems can autonomously assess claims but cannot estimate compensation. In general claims platforms, all LT companies have reported being unable to determine the plausibility of the claim and calculate compensation. In debt collection, IT systems cannot assess the claim, although they can estimate the compensation due.

The results can also be organised around the degrees of automation, taking into consideration the extent to which IT systems can operate autonomously without the intervention of lawyers in every case. The survey reveals that only in respect of four types of claims can IT systems determine the plausibility of claims and calculate the exact compensation due without lawyers: air carriage,[37] banking,[38] employment[39] and, in Germany, tenancy.[40] In telecommunications claims, IT systems can determine the plausibility of claims but not compensation.[41] In the general debt collection sector, they can determine compensation but not the plausibility of claims.[42] In general claims platforms, according to the data collected, IT systems do not establish the plausibility of claims nor determine compensation without the intervention of lawyers.[43]

As a further control question on automation, participants were requested to inform about the technology deployed in the service. Overall, the responses included the following: traditional coding (only),[44] blockchain,[45] predictive analytics,[46] natural language processing[47] and other forms of machine learning,[48] alone or combined.[49] By sector, traditional coding (only) is used in general claims platforms and debt collection.[50] Blockchain has been reported in air carriage.[51] Predictive analytics is used in air carriage, banking, insurance and employment claims.[52]

---

[33] 33 per cent of respondents.
[34] 50 per cent of respondents.
[35] 50 per cent of respondents on each side.
[36] 50 per cent on each side.
[37] 50 per cent of respondents.
[38] 50 per cent of respondents.
[39] 50 per cent of respondents.
[40] 100 per cent of respondents.
[41] 100 per cent of respondents.
[42] 100 per cent of respondents.
[43] 100 per cent of respondents.
[44] 28.57 per cent of respondents chose coding as the sole technology used.
[45] 7.14 per cent of respondents.
[46] 35.71 per cent of respondents.
[47] 21.43 per cent of respondents.
[48] 50 per cent of respondents.
[49] This is why the precedent figures add up to more than 100 per cent. Adjusted per mention, the figures are as follows: 20 per cent for coding only, 5 per cent for blockchain, 25 per cent for predictive analytics, 15 per cent for natural language processing and 35 per cent for other forms of machine learning.
[50] 100 per cent of the sample of each of those sectors uses coding only.
[51] 16.67 per cent of respondents.
[52] 50 per cent of respondents in air carriage, 50 per cent in banking, 100 per cent in insurance and 50 per cent in employment claims.

Natural language processing has been reported in air carriage and banking.[53] Other forms of machine learning are used in air carriage, telecommunications, employment, banking and tenancy claims (the latter in Germany).[54]

The survey additionally sought information on the success rates in court of the target population. The purpose of gathering that information was to further control for automation. It was stated before that automation in LT depends on the possibility for companies of assessing the plausibility of claims and determining compensation without the intervention of lawyers. The accuracy of the answers on that aspect should be benchmarked with the success rates in court of LT companies.

Respondents that declared to automate both the assessment of the claim and the calculation of compensation reported a success rate in court in the range of 75–100 per cent. Within those, participants in air carriage claims declared a success rate of 90–100 per cent. In banking, the rate is 90–95 per cent. In employment and, in Germany, tenancy, the success rate in court is in the range of 75–90 per cent.

Participants that automate the assessment of the claim but do not autonomously calculate compensation reported a success rate of 75–100 per cent. In contrast, companies that do not automate the assessment of the claim but calculate compensation reported a success rate of 25–100 per cent.

9.2.2.4 Applicable Law and Automation

As explained in the Methodology section,[55] the survey intended to gather data on the significance of law to the degree of automation of legal services in the area of claims/litigation. Therefore, a block of questions in the survey was designed for the express purpose of collecting information on the relationship between law and automation. The questions were aimed at determining whether the drafting of the applicable law has an impact on the automation of claims.

On this, it was assumed that laws can either be drafted to address the subtleties of individual situations or regulate them in a more homogeneous or standardised manner. For example, traditional rules on damages for breach of contract establish compensation on a case-by-case basis (individualised approach). In contrast, the European Flight Compensation Regulation (FCR) predetermines compensation based on the flight length – whether short, medium or long haul – among other non-individualised factors.[56] Section 9.3 delves into that. Participants were not informed of this distinction, although one question explicitly addressed homogeneity and individualisation in the drafting of law. Additionally, one question contained an example of homogeneity (compensation in air carriage) and another included an example of individualisation (damages exceeding the fixed amounts of compensation in flights).

Participants were asked whether homogeneity/standardisation of law is an important factor in the automation of their businesses. The options were as follows: essential, very important, important, not important and insignificant. Overall, 28.57 per cent of respondents chose the

---

[53] 50 per cent of respondents in air carriage and 50 per cent in banking.
[54] 66.67 per cent of respondents in air carriage, 100 per cent in telecommunications, 50 per cent in employment claims and 50 per cent in banking.
[55] Section 9.2.1.
[56] Regulation (EC) No 261/2004 of the European Parliament and of the Council of 11 February 2004 establishing common rules on compensation and assistance to passengers in the event of denied boarding and of cancellation or long delay of flights and repealing Regulation (EEC) No 295/91 [2004] OJ L46/1. See Section 9.3.3.1.

option 'essential', 64.28 per cent preferred 'very important', and 7.14 per cent went for 'insignificant'.

Companies were also required to justify the success rates in court that were presented in the previous section.[57] Several options were available to participants; they could select more than one and even personalise their answer. The results show that 78.57 per cent of respondents explain their success rate by the fact that 'the applicable law is homogeneous and it is possible to standardise with optimal results'. Second in preference, 42.86 per cent of respondents selected 'the law interacts with concrete facts which vary from case to case, making standardisation difficult'. The third most selected option (7.14 per cent) was 'the applicable law is not homogeneous but we are able to foresee an outcome based on predictive analytics'.[58] Evidently, some companies selected more than one option.

In a further question, participants were asked whether they claim individualised damages. There was no definition provided as to what 'individualised damages' meant. However, these were exemplified with compensation in air carriage beyond the fixed amounts of the FCR. On this, 35.71 per cent of respondents declared they do not claim individualised damages, whereas 64.29 per cent disclosed that they do. Those in the latter group were additionally asked if they automate individualised claims to the same extent as the non-individualised ones. A slight majority answered in the negative (55.56 per cent) over those that answered in the positive (44.44 per cent). All companies that manage flight claims gave a negative answer, whereas the positive answers came from a variety of sectors including telecommunications and employment and tenancy in Germany.

At the time of drafting the survey, it was considered that out-of-court settlements of claims could provide further clues about the relationship between law and automation. Settlements, especially if they occur on a large scale, could signal homogeneity in the claims. However, other unrelated factors could influence settlements, such as a concealed strategy of defendants not to settle in order to deter claims. Therefore, participants were asked about settlements, but the questions were drafted as stand-alone ones without an aim of controlling others. On this topic, the answers to the survey were varied. The rate of settlements covered the full range (i.e., 0–100 per cent), with over 70 per cent of respondents declaring that they settle in the range of 50–90 per cent.[59] Massive settlements were the most frequent in banking, followed by air carriage claims.[60]

9.3 A QUALITATIVE ASSESSMENT OF THE SURVEY

Following the presentation of the data that was collected under the survey, this section will assess it. The answers to the survey show heterogeneity in automation in LT companies operating in the claims/litigation sector. The lack of homogeneity permits a classification of companies to be drawn up according to the degree of automation (Section 9.3.1). It also calls for an explanation of

---

[57] Section 9.2.2.3.
[58] If the figures are adjusted per mention, the result is, correspondingly, as follows: 57.89 per cent, 31.58 per cent, 5.26 per cent. Personalised answers make up the rest.
[59] 14.28 per cent of respondents settle less than 25 per cent of their claims. 7.14 per cent of respondents declared a settlement rate of 25–50 per cent. 35.71 per cent of respondents settle 50–75 per cent of the claims they manage. Another 35.71 per cent of respondents settle 75–90 per cent of the claims. Finally, 7.14 per cent of respondents settle more than 90 per cent of their claims.
[60] 57.14 per cent of respondents selected banking; 21.43 per cent chose air carriage claims.

the causes of heterogeneity (Section 9.3.2), with a description of the relevant legal background of automated claims (Section 9.3.3).

9.3.1 Classification of Companies by Degree of Automation

As previously stated,[61] automation in LT should be measured by the capacity of technology to operate autonomously, without the intervention of lawyers. The more an IT system can operate without human intervention, the more automated the provision of legal services will be.

In the field of litigation, the service that lawyers provide to potential claimants can roughly be divided into four activities, two of them occur out of court and two in. First, lawyers assess the plausibility of claims, taking into consideration factual and legal materials. Second, they estimate the compensation that can be claimed in court. These two activities often require the support of non-legal experts, such as economists and engineers, depending on the nature of the claim. The assessment of claims and their estimation are the bases of the advice that lawyers provide clients to decide if they want to lodge a complaint in court. The other two activities are related to court: drafting and filing the complaint and representing clients before the courts.

The survey focused on the first two activities in order to frame automation: to establish whether an IT system can autonomously determine if clients have a plausible claim and calculate the exact compensation due. These predictive activities are central in the advice that litigation lawyers should provide.[62] As Oliver W. Holmes observed: 'The prophecies of what the courts will do in fact, and nothing more pretentious, are what I mean by law'.[63] Whether or not one agrees with this dogma of Legal Realism, predicting the likelihood of success of a case in court is very relevant in litigation.

The execution of legal advice in a case by drafting the complaint could also be automated but automation of that task is not particular to litigation. In fact, it is part of the more general automation of documents. Lastly, as stated, representation of clients in court is still a human activity that has not yet been automated, at least in the targeted countries. Therefore, both activities were not surveyed.

In respect of automation of the advice that clients should receive in litigation, companies can be classified into four groups depending on whether their IT systems can autonomously determine if clients have a plausible claim and can calculate the exact compensation due without the intervention of lawyers.

The first level of automation (*high degree of automation*) is occupied by those companies that can do both: assessment of the claim and calculation of compensation. In the second level (*medium-high degree of automation*) are those companies that can determine the plausibility of the claim but cannot determine compensation. In the third level (*medium-low degree of automation*) rank those companies that cannot determine the plausibility of the claim but can determine compensation. This level is lower than the previous one because compensation is normally based on information provided by clients and requires less sophisticated technology. The fourth level (*low degree of automation*) is occupied by those companies that can neither determine the plausibility of the claim nor calculate compensation without the intervention of a lawyer.

---

[61] Section 9.2.2.3.
[62] Susskind, n. 31 at 285.
[63] O. W. Holmes, 'The Path of the Law' (1897) 10 *Harvard Law Review* 457 461.

The survey reflects heterogeneity in automation between companies operating in the same sector, which can be attributable to different business models. However, when comparing companies with similar business models and technologies but operating in different sectors, heterogeneity in automation is still present. Hence, the sector in which the LT company operates, with its corresponding applicable law, impacts the degree of automation of legal services.

Only in respect of four types of claims (sectors) have participants reached a *high level of automation* (first level): air carriage, banking, employment and, in Germany, tenancy. In those sectors, IT systems of the best performing companies can autonomously determine if clients have a plausible claim and estimate compensation. The *medium-high level of automation* is reached by companies involved in telecommunications claims. They can determine the plausibility of claims but not compensation. Companies in the general debt collection sector can only determine compensation but not the plausibility of claims and so occupy the *medium-low level of automation*. Last, in the fourth level (*low degree of automation*) rank general claims platforms and insurance-related claims. They have reported not being able to establish the plausibility of claims nor determine compensation without the intervention of lawyers.[64]

This classification of companies by degree of automation and sector, according to their capacity to provide legal advice without lawyers, is largely consistent with the self-assessment exercise on automation that participants undertook.[65]

Importantly, the data collected under the survey shows that high levels of automation not only means executing tasks but also rigorous takeover of legal advice. Those companies that can determine the plausibility of claims (*high- and medium-high levels of automation*) obtain the best results in court and the range of their success rates is more stable (always above 75 per cent, reaching 100 per cent).[66] These data are key indicators of accuracy in the automated provision of pre-litigation legal advice.

9.3.2 *Suitability of Law for Automation: Variations in Technological Efficiency*

This section explores the reasons underlying heterogeneity in automation, which led to the classification of companies by degree of automation.

Heterogeneity in automation could derive from the particular business models of companies, whereby they have decided to automate the management of cases to a different extent. This is evident for LT companies operating in the same sector. For example, companies in air carriage claims have reported both high and low levels of automation, according to the categories defined in the previous section.[67] If reaching a high level of automation is possible, it can be assumed that not accomplishing it responds to a business decision, which is linked to a lower investment in technology. This is a fact that arose from the data collected.

However, diversity in business models seems insufficient to explain heterogeneity in automation across sectors. It is true that participants that report higher levels of automation use advanced technology including machine learning, natural language processing and predictive analytics, whereas those with lower degrees of automation tend to rely on simpler algorithms. The question when comparing extremes is whether the different investment in technology is a

---

[64] Section 9.2.2.3.
[65] Section 9.2.2.2.
[66] Section 9.2.2.3.
[67] The data collected is aggregated and anonymised so further breakdown cannot be provided. This applies to all data provided in this section except otherwise stated.

cost decision only or if the investment is unjustified because the company believes it would not lead to significant improvements in the degree of automation. For example, it would be pointless for general claims platforms, which rely on coding, to invest in a more sophisticated AI toolkit if, by doing so, they would still not be able to assess the plausibility of claims.

The insufficiency of the business model explanation becomes clear when comparing companies with similar business models and technologies but operating in different sectors: for example, when companies in air carriage claims (*high level of automation*) are compared with telecommunications claims platforms (*medium-high level of automation*), or when companies in banking (*high level of automation*) are contrasted with those dealing with insurance-related claims (*low level of automation*). Strikingly, this sometimes occurs within the same company if it manages claims in multiple sectors.

This particular data shows that the business model and the technology deployed are important but not determinant in the degree of automation of legal services. The relationship between technology and automation is direct, not proportional. A more sophisticated technology tends to improve automation, but the improvement does not depend on the investment in technology only. With the same technology, companies operating in different sectors reach varied degrees of automation.

This leads to an alternative explanation for heterogeneity in the automation of legal services in litigation. That explanation would exceed the scenario under analysis of private LT companies, as it purports to elucidate the reasons behind automation in the assessment of claims, which is a cornerstone in adjudication. On this, it is claimed here that law could determine the fate of automation and, more precisely, that the actual drafting of the law influences the possibilities of automation of legal services. The results of the survey support this hypothesis, as they show that sectors in which companies operate, with their corresponding applicable law, are key factors in automation. The variety in legal rules is central to the explanation of heterogeneity in the automation of legal services.

Therefrom, laws seem to be unequally fit for automation. Some lead to better results than others when used as an input to an IT system, leading to variations in the technical efficiency of the system (i.e., the effectiveness with which a given set of inputs is used to produce an output).[68] If instead of looking at the IT system, the focus is put on law and its suitability to interact with technology, it is possible to designate that fitness as the *technological efficiency* of law. This term is used here for the first time to describe that some legal rules are better inputs to IT systems than others, leading to higher levels of automation.

The technological efficiency of a legal rule seems highly dependent on how standardised and objectivised it is. In this context, standardisation refers to the applicability of a legal rule to numerous cases without variations. For example, compensation under the FCR is predetermined based on the flight length, among other non-individualised factors.[69] It is a more standardised rule than traditional compensation for damages, which requires a case-by-case assessment. In the same context, objectivisation of a legal rule describes its interaction with facts. A rule would be objectivised if its breach is not open to interpretation. For example, the rule that grants compensation for a delayed flight is more objectivised than compensation arising from a defective good, as delay follows a binary logic (yes/no or 1/0) whereas a defect could have multiple causes and even responsible parties. Of course, this does not mean that the airline

---

[68] www.economicshelp.org/blog/glossary/technical-efficiency/ (accessed 7 July 2020).
[69] Section 9.3.3.1.

would always be responsible for delays. It only implies that the breach and the remedies arising therefrom are more objectivised.

The technological efficiency of legal rules depends on their degree of standardisation and objectivisation because they lead to higher levels of automation, that is, an autonomous provision of legal services without the intervention of humans. As regards standardisation, it permits better predictability of outcomes. If the rule applies equally to all cases in the same situation, an IT system can predict more accurately their outcome without the need of a legal expert assessment in every single case. Objectivisation also allows for greater autonomy of an IT system, as it diminishes the need for human intervention. For example, blockchain technology can operate more autonomously with a rule such as the one that grants compensation for delayed flights than with the corresponding one that protects buyers from defective goods. Blockchain applies a conditional logic, for example, 'if the plane is late, then pay compensation'. The technology is able to determine the breach, that is, whether the plane arrived late or not, by using flight data, without human intervention. In contrast, in the case of goods, a human expert must establish whether and why the good is defective. The determination of the breach, in both cases, is an off-chain event but the latter is not computationally verifiable.[70]

The survey reflects the impact of standardisation and objectivisation of law in LT. When participants to the survey were asked to explain the selection of the sector in which they provide their services, the majority declared that the reason underlying the selection was the 'homogeneity of the applicable law (i.e., variations between cases being marginal or non-existent)'.[71] In the same vein, more than 90 per cent of respondents affirmed that homogeneity and standardisation of the law is either an essential or a very important factor for automation of their businesses.[72] This data reaffirms the relevance of law and its varied technological efficiency for the automation of legal services in litigation/claims management.

9.3.3 How Law Determines Automation

Standardisation and objectivisation in drafting legal rules determine the fate of automation. Rules that embrace those characteristics are technologically more efficient, as they serve as better inputs to IT systems, allowing them to reach higher levels of automation. The purpose of this section is to contrast this proposition with the applicable laws in the surveyed sectors to analyse if and to what extent they are standardised and objectivised. The assessment is restricted to sectors in which companies can reach high- or medium-high levels of automation.

9.3.3.1 *Air Carriage*

Nearly half of the target population of the survey are companies whose sole purpose is to seek redress from airlines under the FCR. The FCR applies to flights departing from the EU or incoming to the EU, in the latter case if the carrier is a 'Community carrier', that is, a company with a valid operating license granted by a member state.[73] It is a legislative instrument aimed at ensuring a high level of protection for consumers.[74]

---

[70] E. Mik, 'Smart Contracts: Terminology, Technical Limitations and Real World Complexity' (2017) 9 *Journal of Law, Innovation and Technology* 269 297–298.
[71] Section 9.2.2.1.
[72] Section 9.2.2.4.
[73] Arts 2(c) and 3(1) FCR.
[74] Recital (1) FCR.

The FCR grants redress for denied boarding, cancellation and delay of flights. Denied boarding is defined as 'a refusal to carry passengers on a flight',[75] typically in the event of overbooking. Cancellation is not defined. In respect of delay, the FCR establishes three layers to trigger redress: for flights of 1,500 km or less, a minimum of two hours of delay; for all intra-EU flights of more than 1,500 km and all other flights between 1,500 and 3,500 km, three hours; and for the remaining flights, four hours of delay. The remedies that the FCR grants to passengers include compensation, reimbursement of the ticket, re-routing and assistance (meals, refreshments, hotel accommodation, free phone calls and others).

Compensation under the FCR is flat-rated: EUR 250 is granted for all flights of 1,500 km or less; EUR 400 is the redress for all intra-EU flights of more than 1,500 km and all other flights between 1,500 and 3,500 km and passengers in all other flights receive compensation of EUR 600.[76] In the event of re-routing, the air carrier may reduce compensation by 50 per cent if pre-established thresholds of delays are not met.[77] These amounts are without prejudice to a passenger's right to further compensation[78] according to national law or the Montreal Convention. Although the FCR only foresees compensation for cancellation of flights and denied boarding,[79] the Court of Justice of the European Union (CJEU) extended the remedy to delays exceeding three hours.[80]

The redress of damages under the FCR is highly standardised and objectivised. Unlike compensation in contract law, the FCR enshrines fixed amounts that depend on the flight length, disregarding individual circumstances (*standardisation*). On this, the CJEU has pointed out that the FCR 'seeks to redress damage in an immediate and *standardised* manner'.[81] Additionally, breach of contract is objectivised as it is not open to interpretation. Delay is defined by a combination of time and flight distance. Denied boarding means a refusal to carry a passenger onboard for whatever reason. These, as well as the undefined 'cancellation' of a flight, are facts that are easy to assess without major controversy and largely rely on flight and weather data (*objectivisation*).

Air carriers can be exempted from liability arising from cancellation and delay in the event of 'extraordinary circumstances which could not have been avoided even if all reasonable measures had been taken'.[82] However, the CJEU has interpreted this exemption narrowly, in line with the protective character of the FCR.[83] Extraordinary circumstances should not be inherent to the normal exercise of the activity and must exceed the carrier's sphere of control.[84] For example,

---

[75] Art 2(j) FCR.
[76] Art 7(1) FCR.
[77] Art 7(2) FCR.
[78] Art 12(1) FCR.
[79] Arts 4(3) and 5(1)(c) FCR.
[80] Joined Cases C-401/07 and C-432/07, *Christopher Sturgeon, Gabriel Sturgeon and Alana Sturgeon v. Condor Flugdienst GmbH, and Stefan Böck and Cornelia Lepuschitz v Air France SA*, ECLI:EU:C:2009:716, para 61.
[81] Case C-354/18, *Radu Lucian Rusu and Oana Maria Rusu v. SC Blue Air - Airline Management Solutions SRL*, ECLI:EU:C:2019:637, para 28; Joined Cases C-402/07 and C-432/07, *Sturgeon*, para 51, and Case C-549/07, *Friederike Wallentin-Hermann v. Alitalia - Linee Aeree Italiane SpA*, ECLI:EU:C:2008:771, para 32. (emphasis added). See G. Hindriks, 'Bumped into Differences on the Possibility of the Air Passenger to Claim Further Compensation', (2020) 9 (3) *Journal of European Consumer and Market Law* 116 117; P. Markova, 'Consumer Protection while Travelling: Enforcement of Air Passenger Rights during "Extraordinary Circumstances" in Light of Regulation (EC) No 261/2004', (2019) 8(3) *Journal of European Consumer and Market Law* 114 114.
[82] Art 5(3) FCR. Case C-501/17, *Germanwings GmbH v. Wolfgang Pauels*, ECLI:EU:C:2019:288, para 31, and Joined Cases C-402/07 and C-432/07, *Sturgeon*, para 67.
[83] Markova, n. 81 at 115.
[84] Case C-315/15, *Marcela Pešková and Jiří Peška v. Travel Service a.s.*, ECLI:EU:C:2017: 342, para 22; Case C-549/07, *Wallentin-Hermann*, para 23.

technical problems are in principle not treated as extraordinary circumstances,[85] except if they are caused by foreign objects such as birds[86] or loose debris lying on a runway.[87] Moreover, the onus of proving extraordinary circumstances is on the air carrier seeking to rely on them, which must additionally have taken all the measures to avoid their occurrence.[88] The narrow interpretation of the exemption reinforces the objectivisation of the breach that triggers compensation.

Standardisation and objectivisation of compensation under the FCR make this regulation *technologically highly efficient*, as it is an excellent input for IT systems, improving their technical efficiency. Following data collected under the survey,[89] the best performing LT companies in this sector are able to autonomously assess the plausibility of the claim, that is, whether the plane arrived late, a passenger was denied boarding or a flight was cancelled (*objectivisation*). Additionally, the IT systems can calculate compensation without the intervention of experts. With fixed amounts of compensation, it is relatively easy to standardise. These two activities, which were traditionally carried out by lawyers with the support of non-legal experts, have been heavily automated. Consequently, the best performing companies in air carriage claims were classified as reaching a *high level of automation*.[90]

The FCR does not impede compensation of further, individual, damages.[91] However, among those companies that take care of individual damages, none of them automate those claims to the same extent as they do with the fixed amounts of the FCR.[92] Additionally, LT companies focus on compensation only, usually not dealing with the additional remedies foreseen in the FCR: reimbursement of the ticket, re-routing and assistance,[93] which are more dependent on a case-by-case assessment. These facts illustrate the importance of standardisation and objectivisation for the automation of legal services.

9.3.3.2 Banking

The best performing LT companies among those that manage banking claims can determine the plausibility of claims and estimate compensation without the intervention of lawyers or other human experts. Therefore, they also classify as companies that have reached a *high level of automation*.[94]

A website analysis of the target population in this stratum shows that a significant number of claims that LT companies manage have been litigated in court under the Unfair Contract Terms Directive (UCTD), an EU legislative instrument.[95] For example, floor clauses in loans, loans denominated in foreign currencies or convertible to them and mortgage expenses.

The UCTD controls unfair terms in non-negotiated B2C contracts, which are non-binding on the consumer.[96] It controls the substantive fairness of ancillary terms included in standard form

---

[85] Case C-257/14, *C. van der Lans v. Koninklijke Luchtvaart Maatschappij NV*, ECLI:EU:C:2015:618, paras 41 and 42.
[86] Case C-315/15, *Pešková and Peška*, para 24.
[87] Case C-501/17, *Germanwings*, para 26.
[88] Case C-315/15, *Pešková and Peška*, para 28.
[89] Section 9.2.2.3.
[90] Section 9.3.1.
[91] Art 12(1) FCR. Case C-354/18, *Rusu*, para 36. Hindriks, n. 81 at 117–119.
[92] Section 9.2.2.4.
[93] See Hipp, n. 4 at 347.
[94] Section 9.3.1.
[95] Council Directive 93/13/EEC of 5 April 1993 on unfair terms in consumer contracts [1993] OJ L95/29. This section is an adapted and updated presentation of the main features of the UCTD that were expounded in F. de Elizalde, 'Standardisation of Agreement in EU law. An Adieu to the Contracting Parties?' in T. Tridimas and M. Durovic (eds.) *New Directions in European Private Law* (Oxford: Hart Publishing, 2020) 42–46.
[96] Arts 3(1) and 6(1) UCTD.

contracts directly if grey-listed in the Annex of the Directive, which some member states have turned into blacklists, following the minimum harmonisation approach of the UCTD.[97] Ancillary terms can also be controlled when they reunite the characteristics of the general criteria set forth in Art 3(1) UCTD: contrary to good faith, the term causes a significant imbalance in the rights and obligations of the parties, to the detriment of the consumer.

The control of terms under the UCTD does not reach the essential obligations under the contract, namely, 'the definition of the main subject matter of the contract nor ... the adequacy of the price and remuneration, on the one hand, as against the services or goods supplied in exchange'.[98] However, those essential obligations under the contract can be controlled if they are not drafted in 'plain intelligible language',[99] which is the requirement of transparency, additionally set forth in Art 5 UCTD, for all terms (ancillary and main). The CJEU advanced the interpretation of the UCTD by defining that transparency has the same substantive meaning throughout the UCTD,[100] which exceeds mere grammatical control. Moreover, as consistently held by the CJEU, this substantive interpretation depends on the capacity of an 'average consumer' to understand the legal and economic implications of a term.[101] The 'average consumer' benchmark was developed by the CJEU and is already decades old.[102] It refers to a consumer who is 'reasonably well-informed, reasonably observant and circumspect'.[103] The average consumer is a legal standard.[104]

A special characteristic of EU consumer law is that the definition of 'consumer' is objective.[105] In the UCTD, it means 'any natural person who ... is acting for purposes which are outside his trade, business or profession'.[106] In *Costea*, the CJEU clarified that the category of consumer (and the protection arising therefrom under the UCTD) is to be determined solely by the purpose of the contract, the actual knowledge or expertise of the actual consumer being immaterial.[107] The claimant of the case was a commercial lawyer, who challenged the validity of a credit agreement into which he had entered for non-professional purposes. Therefore, under

---

[97] Civic Consulting (for the European Commission), 'Study for the Fitness Check of EU consumer and marketing law' (2017), ec.europa.eu/newsroom/just/item-detail.cfm?item_id=59332, 77–78 (accessed 23 July 2020).
[98] Art 4(2) UCTD.
[99] Ibid.
[100] Case C-621/17, *Gyula Kiss and CIB Bank Zrt. v. Emil Kiss and Gyuláné Kiss*, EU:C:2019:820, para 36; Joined Cases C-154, 307 & 308/15, *Francisco Gutiérrez Naranjo v. Cajasur Banco SAU; Ana María Palacios Martínez v. Banco Bilbao Vizcaya Argentaria SA (BBVA) and Banco Popular Español SA v. Emilio Irles López and Teresa Torres Andreu*, EU:C:2016:980, para 49; Case C-26/13, *Árpád Kásler, Hajnalka Káslerné Rábai v. OTP Jelzálogbank Zrt*, EU:C:2014:282, para 69; Case C-143/13, *Bogdan Matei and Ioana Ofelia Matei v. SC Volksbank România SA*, EU:C:2015:127, para 73.
[101] Case C-26/13, *Kásler*, paras 71–75.
[102] M. Durovic, *European Law on Unfair Commercial Practices and Contract Law* (Oxford: Hart Publishing, 2016)24 ff.; V. Mak, 'Standards of Protection: In Search of the "Average Consumer" of EU Law in the Proposal for a Consumer Rights Directive' (2010) 4(10) *TISCO Working Paper Series on Banking, Finance and Services* 4 ff.
[103] Case C-26/13, *Kásler*, para 74.
[104] Recital 18 of Directive 2005/29/EC of the European Parliament and of the Council of 11 May 2005 concerning unfair business-to-consumer commercial practices in the internal market and amending Council Directive 84/450/EEC, Directives 97/7/EC, 98/27/EC and 2002/65/EC of the European Parliament and of the Council and Regulation (EC) No 2006/2004 of the European Parliament and of the Council [2005] OJ L149/22 (UCPD). See V. Mak, 'Standards in European Private Law. A Model for European Private Law Pluralism' (2013) 15(20129) *Tilburg Law School Legal Studies Research Paper Series* 18. On the use of empirical evidence, see B. B. Duivenvoorde, *The Consumer Benchmarks in the Unfair Commercial Practices Directive* (Cham: Springer, 2015) 20 ff.
[105] E. Terryn, 'Consumers, by Definition, "Include Us All" ... but Not for Every Transaction' (2016) 24(2) *European Review of Private Law* 271 273–274.
[106] Art 2(b) UCTD.
[107] Case C-110/14, *Horațiu Ovidiu Costea v. SC Volksbank România SA*, EU:C:2015:538, para 21.

the UCTD, a consumer is treated and protected as such even if he or she is, in fact, a knowledgeable and experienced person.

Standardisation in the UCTD results from its homogeneous application to a multiplicity of cases, that is, to all parties bound by the same standard term. If a term is deemed unfair, it taints all standard form contracts that contain it, for example, when a term is considered to hinder the consumer's right to take legal action.[108] However, the extent of *res judicata* remains uncertain to some extent and, on occasion, the control of an unfair term can require further action.[109]

Standardisation is a characteristic of the UCTD for the purpose of controlling ancillary terms such as the one exemplified in the previous paragraph and to assess the lack of transparency of a term, even when it is a main one. This follows the objective definition of 'consumer' in the UCTD, whereby actual knowledge and expertise are immaterial, and the 'average consumer' is treated as a legal standard. Therefore, if a term is deemed non-transparent, it will taint all standard form contracts that contain it, even if a consumer does understand it. Standardisation of the UCTD makes it highly predictable and fit for automation.[110]

In respect of objectivisation in the UCTD, it is less evident than in the FCR. If a term is grey- or blacklisted, in some cases a breach can be determined objectively, for example, if it excludes liability of a seller for the death of a consumer.[111] In contrast, other unfair terms, including those affected by a lack of transparency, require an assessment of courts or other competent bodies. However, once a term is controlled and declared unfair, it will taint all standard form contracts that contain it without the need for a case-by-case assessment. Therefore, the breach (in this scenario, the unfairness) is only determined once.[112] Additionally, an unfair term contributes to the control of similar terms, which is a consequence of objectivisation and is a task that can be automated.[113]

LT companies that manage banking claims rely on the standardised character of the UCTD to predict outcomes in contracts that contain the same term as the one that has been deemed unfair. They normally collect claims only if a court or competent body has previously declared the term unfair. The prior declaration of unfairness justifies that those companies treat the breach as objective, in all contracts. This is how the best performing companies can determine the plausibility of claims. However, the need for a prior legal assessment of terms could explain why in the self-assessment exercise of the survey, respondents confirmed automation of banking claims to a lesser extent than air carriage claims.[114] As regards the estimation of compensation, an algorithm can calculate undue payments under the unfair term.

---

[108] Annex to the UCTD, 1(q).
[109] Joined Cases C-381 & 385/14, *Jorge Sales Sinués and Youssouf Drame Ba v. Caixabank SA and Catalunya Caixa SA (Catalunya Banc S.A.)*, EU:C:2016:252, paras 37, 39 and 43. Case C-472/10, *Nemzeti Fogyasztóvédelmi Hatóság v. Invitel Távközlési Zrt*, EU:C:2012:242, para 43. See C. Leskinen and F. de Elizalde, 'The Control of Terms That Define the Essential Obligations of the Parties under the Unfair Contract Terms Directive: Gutiérrez Naranjo' (2018) 55 *Common Market Law Review* 1595 1610; H. W. Micklitz and N. Reich, 'The Court and Sleeping Beauty: The Revival of the Unfair Contract Terms Directive (UCTD)' (2014) 51 *Common Market Law Review* 771 794–796.
[110] Predictability leads to very high success rates in court. For example, it has been reported in Spain that 96.32 per cent of floor clauses claims have been upheld, https://elpais.com/economia/2019/05/21/actualidad/1558460686_067476.html (accessed 17 July 2020).
[111] Annex to the UCTD, 1(a).
[112] Micklitz and Reich, n. 109 at 796.
[113] On this, see the project Claudette, http://claudette.eui.eu/.
[114] Section 9.2.2.2. 75–90 per cent v. 90–100 per cent.

9.3.3.3 *Tenancy in Germany*

LT companies that manage tenancy claims in Germany have been classified among those that reach a *high level of automation* as they are able to determine the plausibility of claims and calculate compensation without the intervention of lawyers.[115]

An assessment of the types of claims that those companies manage reflects that rental prices are a major source of cases. They are subject to control in Germany (*Mietpreisbremse*). In fact, in order to counteract the exponential rise of prices on the housing market in Germany, the Tenancy Law Amendment Act (*Mietrechtsnovellierungsgesetz*, MietNovG)[116] was enacted in 2015 and incorporated into the German Civil Code (BGB).[117] It coexists with other rent controls.

The MietNovG allows regional state governments (*Landesregierungen*) to designate areas with tight housing markets for a maximum period of five years.[118] Areas with strained housing markets exist when, under reasonable conditions, an adequate supply of rented housing in a municipality is at particular risk. This may be the case where: (1) rents rise significantly faster than the national average; (2) the average rental load of households clearly exceeds the nationwide average; (3) the resident population is growing without the necessary housing being created through new construction or (4) there is low vacancy with high demand.

Tenancy agreements concluded in an area with a tight housing market cannot specify at the beginning of the tenancy (i.e., a new lease) rent that exceeds the local comparative rent (*ortsübliche Vergleichsmiete*) by more than 10 per cent.[119] Any agreement that exceeds that cap is invalid and the landlord is obliged to compensate the tenant for overpaid rent according to the rules on unjustified enrichment.[120]

The local comparative rent 'is formed from the usual payments that have been agreed or that have been changed in the last four years in the municipality or in a comparable municipality for residential space that is comparable in type, size, furnishings, quality and location, including the energy systems and characteristics'. This local comparative rent forms the basis of the rent index (*Mietspiegel*).[121]

The scope of application of the rental break is subject to several exceptions. The rent cap of the MietNovG does not apply to pre-existing leases that, notwithstanding, are affected by other price limitations.[122] Neither does it apply to apartments that are used and rented for the first time since 1 October 2014,[123] or which were substantially renovated in the last three years before the beginning of the tenancy.[124] Moreover, if the last rent owed by the previous tenant exceeds the otherwise maximum rent, the landlord may agree to a new tenancy price up to the amount of this previous rent when re-letting (i.e., he/she does not have to adjust to the price cap).[125]

Rent control is a highly objectivised legal rule, as the breach can be determined by data, without human intervention. A rental price can be algorithmically benchmarked with the local comparative rent to establish whether it exceeds the 10 per cent cap. It is also highly

---

[115] Section 9.2.2.3.
[116] *Gesetzes zur Dämpfung des Mietanstiegs auf angespannten Wohnungsmärkten und zur Stärkung des Bestellerprinzips bei der Wohnungsvermittlung* (*Mietrechtsnovellierungsgesetz* – MietNovG), BGBl. 2015, Teil I Nr. 16, S. 610.
[117] §§ 556d–g BGB and other cross-referred sections.
[118] § 556d(2) BGB.
[119] § 556d(1) BGB.
[120] § 556g(1) BGB.
[121] § 558c BGB.
[122] §§ 557 ff. BGB.
[123] § 556f BGB.
[124] § 556e(2) BGB.
[125] § 556e(1) BGB.

standardised, as every tenant affected by a violation of the maximum rent has the same claim, that is, the amounts overpaid, with variations that can be easily calculated, also autonomously. However, the regulations on price control are certainly less standardised than compensation under the FCR. The peculiarities of the scope of application of the MietNovG, the exceptions to the application of the cap under the MietNovG and the coexistence with other rent controls may require an individualised assessment of facts. It comes as no surprise that in this sector fully automated claims management leads to lower success rates in court compared to those achieved in air carriage claims.[126]

9.3.3.4 *Telecommunications*

The management of telecommunications claims, among which nonconforming internet services stand out, has allowed the best performing LT companies to assess the plausibility of claims. However, they cannot determine autonomously the compensation due for such a nonconforming service. Therefore, they have been classified as *medium-high* in terms of automation.[127]

Regulation (EU) 2015/2120[128] ensures that the actual quality of internet services, especially regarding speed, matches that promised under a contract.[129] The breach is to be established by a monitoring mechanism certified by the national regulatory authority.[130] Nonconformity of performance triggers the remedies available to the consumer under national law, that is, they are not harmonised at an EU-level.[131]

Breach of contract under Regulation (EU) 2015/2120 is highly objectivised. The flawed provision of the promised internet speed can be determined without human intervention by speed tests, which, for the purposes of this legislative instrument, have to be certified by the national regulatory authority. Any stakeholder can easily determine the breach of an internet services contract by resorting to a speed test.

However, the second important element for automation, that is, standardisation of the legal rule, is absent. The remedies available to the consumer remain individualised and must be determined on a case-by-case basis. For example, compensation for a nonconforming service will depend on each contract and on the particular circumstances that surround it. Traditional rules for compensation will apply, taking the consumer protection framework into account.

Objectivisation in establishing a breach of contract explains that the IT systems of the best performing LT companies in this sector can autonomously assess the plausibility of claims. However, they cannot estimate compensation nor other available remedies under national law due to their individualised character. Current limitations on this aspect could be overcome if LT companies were to gain access to enough data on the resolution of telecommunications claims. If so, they would be able to predict compensation and the fate of other remedies. Nevertheless, even in that event, the lack of standardisation of Regulation (EU) 2015/2120 indicates that its technological efficiency as compared to the FCR, for example, will remain lower.

---

[126] Section 9.2.2.3. 75–90 per cent v. 95–100 per cent, in both cases taking into consideration the best performing companies.
[127] Section 9.3.1.
[128] Regulation (EU) 2015/2120 of the European Parliament and of the Council of 25 November 2015 laying down measures concerning open internet access and amending Directive 2002/22/EC on universal service and users' rights relating to electronic communications networks and services and Regulation (EU) No. 531/2012 on roaming on public mobile communications networks within the Union [2015] OJ L310/1.
[129] Art 4(4) Regulation 2015/2120.
[130] Ibid.
[131] Ibid.

9.4 CONCLUSION

This chapter purported to analyse the impact of law on the automation of legal services in litigation. The underlying hypothesis was that the drafting of law could determine automation. It was tested with data collected under a survey on LT companies that manage small value claims. It was then assessed against the backdrop of the laws applicable to the claims that participants to the survey handle.

The main finding of the chapter is that legal rules are unequally fit for automation. The way in which a legal rule is drafted determines its suitability for automation. This characteristic has been labelled here as 'technological efficiency'. The degree of standardisation and objectivisation of law contributes to its technological efficiency. Standardisation refers to the applicability of a legal rule to numerous cases without variations. Objectivisation of a legal rule describes its interaction with facts, whereby a rule would be objectivised if its breach is not open to interpretation.

A legal rule that is better in terms of technological efficiency serves as a better input to IT systems, leading to a higher technical efficiency. In LT, this means an increased automation, which leads to the substitution of lawyers in the provision of legal services. The best performing companies surveyed can determine the plausibility of claims and estimate compensation without the intervention of lawyers or other experts.

Business models and the technology deployed in a particular service are insufficient explanations for heterogeneity in the degree of automation of legal services. Variations in technological efficiency of law, which are determined by standardisation and objectivisation have a significant impact. These characteristics were assessed and detected in those types of claims that lead to higher levels of automation.

The unequal fitness of legal rules for automation is an issue that stretches beyond LT private companies. Taking this aspect into consideration would contribute to the task of building a framework for online justice, which could begin with those claims to which a highly technologically efficient rule applies. The key to success in automation seems not to be the amount of the claim but how the law is drafted. This approach to automation of law could impact legislators willing to draft laws that are suitable for automation. It could also determine success in the 'market' for law as has occurred to the common law in commercial transactions, for example, where a technological solution is foreseen. Parties would be more inclined to choose an applicable law to a contract that serves as a better input to IT systems.[132] The empirical and legal findings of this chapter would be reinforced if benchmarked with predictive analytics, a task that will hopefully be undertaken in the future.

---

[132] See, on the choice of law for smart contracts, G. Rühl, 'Smart (Legal) Contracts, or: Which (Contract) Law for Smart Contracts?' at 20, https://papers.ssrn.com/sol3/papers.cfm?abstract_id=3552004 (accessed 28 July 2020).

10

Regulation of Legal Services and Access to Justice in the Digital Age

A War Report*

Jin Ho Verdonschot and Max Houben

10.1 INTRODUCTION

The potential of digital solutions and legal tech (LT) for increasing access to justice is real. Although many LT developments focus on innovation of law practices, in several countries we see LT as champion of access to justice. These typically are new types of players in the market that provide legal services directly to the public. Even though practice-based evidence shows their positive impact, legal services regulations struggle to catch up and facilitate these developments. They, as a matter of fact, may actually hamper access to justice improvements. In that respect, it is illustrative that private investors acknowledge the potential of LT, but only dared to invest 2.8 per cent of their $1 billion total investments in 2018 in customer-facing services.[1]

This chapter presents some practice notes that show the challenges of innovators that took up the challenge to use digital technologies to improve access to justice with a business model behind it. It shows how companies who break open the access to justice market clearly meet justice needs, but often end up spending large parts of their precious funding on litigation against institutions and regulators.

10.1.1 *Global Access to Justice*

Organising access to justice is a major challenge across the globe. Governments traditionally face a hard time juggling their budgets to ensure a sufficient number of judges in courts and subsidies for legal aid to make legal services accessible to people with a low income. Economic hard times strongly amplify these challenges and require access to justice professionals to pave new paths.[2]

A good quality legal profession is essential for access to justice. The core values of the profession are as universal as self-evident: independence, integrity, expertise, confidentiality and partiality towards clients. These values are substantiated through rigid rules that regulate the legal profession, posing strict norms and strict monopolies.

---

* The manuscript for this chapter was finalized on 17 July 2020.
[1] M. Barendrecht et al., 'Charging for Justice, SDG 16.3 Trend Report 2020' at 87, www.hiil.org/wp-content/uploads/2020/04/HiiL-report-Charging-for-Justice-3.pdf (accessed 15 July 2020).
[2] D. Steven et al., 'Justice in a Pandemic – Briefing Two: Justice for All and the Economic Crisis', Pathfinders for Peaceful, Just and Inclusive Societies (2020), www.justice.sdg16.plus (accessed 15 July 2020).

One could argue that maintaining this status quo can be seen as an evidence-based approach: the current legal profession has proven to be solid, rather expensive, but delivering quality justice. The current set-up also provides evidence of flaws, especially where it does not enable new developments and possibilities to find their way to the public for the good. Our rules and underlying conceptions might not be ready for modern legal services in our digital age.[3]

Access to justice is essential for social, economic and personal development. It enables people to reach their full potential. It facilitates and protects investments in their professional and personal relationships, investments in their homes, businesses and other properties and investments in themselves. The business case for investing in justice is crystal clear, as recent reports again confirm.[4] But it remains a challenge to organise it for the masses. Estimations indicate that five billion people live outside the protection of the legal system for their legal problems of everyday life.[5] Every country struggles with this. No wonder that access to justice is part of the Sustainable Development Goals defined by the United Nations.[6] This is the best we can do.

10.1.2 New Delivery Concepts

The understanding of access to justice evolved over time. Initially, access to justice was seen as access to courts and access to lawyers. Many countries adopted legal aid schemes within this paradigm. The notion of access to justice, however, gradually changed into thinking about demystification of the law, access to fair solutions and prevention.[7] Several innovations illustrate this. Informational justice increases through court decisions in plain language[8] and empowers self-helpers with understandable and actionable guides and protocols.[9] Problem-solving legal facilitators like mediators and paralegals emerged across the globe as well.[10] They typically focus on early interventions, prevention and humanising the law.

The regulation of legal services delivery lags behind on the notion of justice as fair solutions. In a rigidly regulated country like the United States, the state of Washington, for example, started experimenting with limited license legal technicians. These professionals are non-lawyers and mostly cope with the high influx of self-represented litigants in many courts, especially in family law matters. They are allowed to provide basic information[11] and support people with filling in

---

[3] G. Hadfield, *Rules for a Flat World: Why Humans Invented Law and How to Reinvent It for a Complex Global Economy* (Oxford: Oxford University Press, 2016).

[4] Task Force on Justice, 'Justice for All – The Report on the Task Force on Justice' (2019), www.hiil.org/wp-content/uploads/2019/06/Justice-for-All-report-1.pdf (accessed 15 July 2020). See also G. Harley et al., 'A Tool for Justice: A Cost Benefit Analysis of Legal Aid' (2019), http://documents1.worldbank.org/curated/en/592901569218028553/pdf/A-Tool-for-Justice-The-Cost-Benefit-Analysis-of-Legal-Aid.pdf (accessed 15 July 2020).

[5] Steven et al., n. 2.

[6] United Nations, Goal 16: 'Promote peaceful and inclusive societies for sustainable development, provide access to justice for all and build effective, accountable and inclusive institutions at all levels', https://sustainabledevelopment.un.org/sdg16 (accessed 15 July 2020).

[7] R. McDonald, 'Access to Justice in 2003: Scope, Scale and Ambitions', Paper prepared for the Symposium on Access to Justice, Law Society of Upper Canada (2003).

[8] For example, The Netherlands judiciary has an annual award for clearest court decision, and the Swedish judiciary experiments with online enhanced, understandable court decisions.

[9] See, for example, the work of the Legal Education Foundation in England and Wales, which are pioneering countries in this respect, www.thelegaleducationfoundation.org (accessed 15 July 2020).

[10] Sometimes, they came forth out of the broader alternative dispute resolution movement that fundamentally criticises the legal system for its alienating effect on people and problems. However, in countries like the Netherlands, community mediators emphasise the importance of early interventions.

[11] Also see the seminal work by John Greacen on the distinction between legal advice and legal information, J. M. Greacen, 'No Legal Advice from Court Personnel – What Does That Mean?' (1995) *Judges' Journal* 10.

court documents and forms. Recently, the American Bar Association adopted a resolution calling for more innovation,[12] which may create some opportunities for modern legal services provision.

The overall innovation space for access to justice services, however, remains limited.[13] Law firms cannot benefit from outside investments that help them innovate user experiences and would enable them to catch up with their LT game.[14] In a time when investments in LT startups with consumer interfaces have reached an all-time high, access to justice misses an opportunity. Additionally, those other than registered lawyers are prevented from providing basic access to justice to the masses. Experiences in North America and Europe show the uphill battle access to justice startups may face and indicate lessons we can learn to enable access to justice improvements in the digital age.

10.1.3 What Now?

This chapter describes the experiences of five access to justice innovators. They have a few things in common that make them exemplary for the bridge between digital age solutions and outdated roles, regulations and frameworks. The examples also indicate the sometimes more hostile attitudes of conventional institutions towards these new kind of legal service providers.

Section 10.2 describes the events that LegalZoom was confronted with during their quest to make legal document creation more user-friendly and affordable in the United States. This example indicates how the distinction between 'legal advice' and 'legal information' is a grey area, and as such an instrument for protectors of the status quo. The experiences of LegalDutch are described in Section 10.3. LegalDutch is an online platform for people in the Netherlands who look for a lawyer. Its journey illustrates the difficulties of innovating business models in the realm of legal solution seeking. In Germany, WenigerMiete provides an example of how parts of the application of the law are 'computable', opening opportunities for better access to justice models. The opposition came from regulators of the legal profession, as is described in Section 10.4. When it comes to transparency of the law, basic algorithms come in effectively, but face resistance. The example of the French company Doctrine presented in Section 10.5 sketches the volatile response by some institutions. Also in France, the experiences of Demander Justice (Section 10.6) illustrate the fierce legal battle of a company that makes opening court procedures more parsimonious. Section 10.7 presents some insights on the mismatch on access to justice providers in the digital age and regulation that is not up to par.

10.2 LEGALZOOM

'The Internet is a perfect tool to make legal help more widely available to all Americans', was one of the insights that led to the first steps of what later became known as LegalZoom in 1999.[15] The company started to offer basic online legal document drafting in 2001 for issues as varied as

---

[12] American Bar Association, 'Resolution 115 – Encouraging Regulatory Innovation', www.americanbar.org/groups/centers_commissions/center-for-innovation/Resolution115/ (accessed 15 July 2020).

[13] For an overview of developments in the United States, see the Knowledge Center of the Institute for the Advancement of the American Legal System, https://iaals.du.edu/knowledge-center.

[14] Outside of England and Wales, some US states (California, Arizona and Utah) and Canada consider the introduction of so-called alternative business structures. See www.lawsitesblog.com/2019/10/arizona-task-force-calls-for-wide-ranging-practice-reforms-including-eliminating-ban-on-nonlawyer-ownership.html (accessed on 15 July 2020).

[15] LegalZoom, 'Our Story', www.legalzoom.com/about-us (accessed 15 July 2020).

estate planning, business formation and intellectual property protection.[16] A simple online survey enabled customers to assemble their document out of standardised clauses and document language.

Ever since, the company has managed to establish rapid growth, perhaps due to the fact that people could save a lot of time and money by using the do-it-yourself online tool. Ten years after its inception, LegalZoom pivoted to new business models and included basic legal advice that was provided through their 'independent attorney network'. Fifteen years after it was founded, the company built a base of 3.6 million customers, which shows the scalable impact an LT company can have, making conventional law firms look like a bit of a dwarf.[17]

Its success caught the attention of the North Carolina Bar Association. In 2003, it accused LegalZoom of 'unauthorized practice of law' and tried to restrain LegalZoom from operating in their state.[18] According to the Bar, the online document services of LegalZoom should be classified as legal advice. Since LegalZoom was a commercial company, not owned by a registered lawyer, it was not allowed to offer such services. LegalZoom's response to this accusation was that they did not deliver legal advice, but rather facilitated legal self-help. Indeed, their tools guided people to the appropriate clauses, much like a decision tree.

In 2003, the Authorized Practice Committee of the Bar (APC) opened an investigation on the services of LegalZoom. It concluded that the document services went further than merely providing self-help packages, since the result for customers were tailored documents, and no intervention of a lawyer was involved.[19] As such, these services were in the scope of 'legal advice', which is limited to registered lawyers. APC sent a letter with these conclusions to LegalZoom in 2003.[20] LegalZoom responded that in their opinion their document services were self-help services and not legal advice. In their opinion, the disclaimers on their website made sufficiently clear that the document service cannot be seen as legal advice. Their service merely provides the public a 'general understanding about the law'.[21] The APC ultimately dismissed the complaint after LegalZoom's reply.[22]

A few years later, in 2007, LegalZoom was again the subject of investigation by the APC.[23] Again, APC stated that LegalZoom was providing legal advice because it guided customers on which answers they would have to provide for their situation. For the document service, customers simply answer a number of multiple-choice questions. Their answers determine which clauses and language end up in the document. Their guidance on these questions make this legal advice, according to APC. LegalZoom received a cease-and-desist letter but took no action upon this.[24] The Bar additionally stated that the documents were checked by LegalZoom for errors after the user filled in the information. After LegalZoom denied that they were doing this, APC did not give any further response.[25]

---

[16] Ibid.
[17] Ibid.
[18] C. E. Brown, 'LegalZoom: Closing the Justice Gap or Unauthorized Practice of Law?' (2016) 17 *North Carolina Journal of Law & Technology* 219 221.
[19] Ibid. at 233.
[20] *LegalZoom.com v. N.C. State Bar*, No. 11 CVS 15111, 2011 WL 8424700 (N.C. Super. Ct. March 24, 2014). See also Brown, n. 18 at 233.
[21] Ibid.
[22] Ibid. at 234.
[23] *LegalZoom.com v. N.C. State Bar*, n. 20. Brown, n. 18 at 234.
[24] Ibid.
[25] *LegalZoom.com v. N.C. State Bar*, n. 20. Brown, n. 18 at 235.

In 2010, LegalZoom again pivoted their business model. Customers now could get unlimited consultations from external lawyers as part of a membership model. LegalZoom wanted to register its services at the Bar, but they were rejected since LegalZoom had received a cease-and-desist letter in the past from the APC.[26] In 2011, LegalZoom engaged in a legal action against the Bar. According to LegalZoom, the Bar never had the competence, based on the North Carolina Constitution, to send this cease-and-desist letter in the first place.[27] The Superior Court of North Carolina Business Court rejected the claim brought forward by LegalZoom.[28] The court stressed that the Bar did not exceed its powers, but remained silent about the alleged unauthorised practice of law.[29]

After almost a decade, the question whether LegalZoom was providing legal advice remained unclarified. Such uncertainty obviously is bad for business and also makes a company less attractive for investors. Rather than sitting still while they were being shaved, LegalZoom chose the counter-attack. In 2015, it launched an anti-trust case against the Bar:[30] it alleged that the actions of the Bar were 'anti-competitive and amounted to monopolizing the legal industry'.[31] It did not come to a judgement (unfortunately?) because LegalZoom and the Bar settled the situation. As part of this, LegalZoom agreed to refrain from filing the anti-trust lawsuit. Some other things they agreed upon were the following:

- LegalZoom is not providing 'legal advice' by personalising documents for their users, on the condition that a lawyer checks the documents before the user pays for the services.[32]
- The contact details for the lawyer are provided on the LegalZoom website.[33]
- LegalZoom provides a disclaimer that the documents cannot be regarded as 'legal advice'.[34]
- LegalZoom does not limit recovery damages.[35]
- Both parties support House Bill 436,[36] which clarifies the definition of 'practice of law' in the way that it was pending before the House Judiciary Committee at the time.[37]

Only after launching a counter-attack, LegalZoom (and the rest of the world) thus obtained clarity on the regulations concerning legal advice.

10.3 LEGALDUTCH

LegalDutch is an online platform in the Netherlands that enables companies that seek a lawyer to easily find one online. The business model of LegalDutch[38] is built around a form of remuneration from the lawyer for each lead they send to them. In the Netherlands, however,

---

[26] Brown, n. 18 at 235.
[27] Ibid. at 236.
[28] *LegalZoom.com, Inc. v. N.C. State Bar*, n. 20. Brown, n. 18 at 236.
[29] Ibid.
[30] T. Carter, 'LegalZoom Resolves $10.5 M Antitrust Suit against North Carolina State Bar', *ABA Journal*, 23 October 2015, www.abajournal.com/news/article/legalzoom_resolves_10.5m_antitrust_suit_against_north_carolina_state_bar (accessed 4 August 2020). See Brown, n. 18 at 238.
[31] Brown, n. 18 at 238.
[32] *LegalZoom.com, Inc. v. N.C. State Bar*, n. 20. Brown, n. 18 at 239.
[33] Brown, n. 18 at 239.
[34] Ibid.
[35] Ibid.
[36] H.B. 436, 2015–16 Gen. Assemb., Reg. Sess. (N.C. 2015).
[37] Brown, n. 18 at 239.
[38] LegalDutch, https://legaldutch.nl (accessed 15 July 2020).

the code of conduct for lawyers prohibited them to pay such a lead fee (the code of conduct is defined by the Dutch Bar Association [NOvA]). According to Article 2 paragraph 3 of the Code of Conduct, a lawyer cannot be granted remuneration for receiving a lead (case), unless the lawyer can prove that in doing so he is not acting *contrary to the core values and furthermore only the interest of the person seeking justice is decisive in this respect.*[39]

In the guidelines that accompany the Code of Conduct,[40] the NOvA stresses that although lawyers can engage with online legal platforms, the platforms can only (1) get their *fair share* if (2) they have a membership-based model. With a membership-based model, the lawyer is able to pay a fixed amount per month, and the amount is not related to the number of leads a lawyer receives. Paying per lead is forbidden for lawyers.[41]

Since this rule was an impediment to the business model of LegalDutch, and though there was no sufficient objective rationale for this rule, on 27 September 2017, it filed an enforcement request to the national competition authority (ACM). The argument was that the guidelines restricted their business model, and a pay-per-lead construction is the most desired business model in this sector.[42]

The ACM took this request into consideration and issued a statement on 14 December 2018:

- The ACM welcomes online legal platforms since they in general lower the transaction costs, make the offer more transparent for the customer and therefore create a better price/quality ratio.[43]
- The ACM also underwrites the fact that in order to make such a marketplace work, one needs to find a balance between offer (lawyers) and demand (clients). Because it would be difficult to let clients pay for the use of the platforms, the earning model has to focus on lawyers.[44]
- Based on the market research of the ACM there are two main business models for online legal platforms: (1) a membership-model where lawyers create a profile and pay a certain amount per month, and (2) a pay-per-lead-model where lawyers pay an amount for each lead they receive.[45]
- Based on the market research of the ACM, lawyers prefer the latter model, which is prohibited by the NOvA.
- Since it is not possible to use the second earning model, the ACM stated that this could lead to a 'distortion of competition among lawyers'.[46]

The ACM ordered the NOvA to adapt their guidelines to enable lawyers to pay per lead to online platforms, which it now has. Thus, currently, after intervention of the national competition authority, the pay-per-lead model is possible in the Netherlands for online legal platforms.[47]

---

[39] Nederlandse Orde van Advocaten, 'Gedragsregels Advocatuur', NOvA (2018), http://regelgeving.advocatenorde.nl/content/regel-2-onafhankelijkheid-partijdigheid-geen-provisie (accessed 15 July 2020).
[40] Ibid.
[41] Autoriteit Consument & Markt, Besluit op handhavingsverzoek Legal Dutch, ACM/17/012061, 14 December 2018 at [20].
[42] Ibid. at [18].
[43] Ibid. at [13].
[44] Ibid. at [15].
[45] Ibid. at [16–17].
[46] Ibid. at [20].
[47] Ibid. at [25].

10.4 WENIGERMIETE

WenigerMiete (MietRight GmbH) is a Berlin-based company, established in 2017. It offers a handful of products related to rental law. They assist customers (tenants) who are fighting for their rights related to rent increase, contract termination, renovations and repairs, defects in the apartment and rent price control (*Mietpreisbremse*).[48]

In June 2015, Germany adopted a law on *Mietpreisbremse*,[49] which is enforced in almost all states of Germany (except Saarland, Saxony and Saxony-Anhalt). The law stipulates that due to the high demand for rental housing, landlords are no longer allowed to ask for excessive rents but can only ask for a rent that is not more than 10 per cent higher than the rent index. If a tenant pays more, he/she can ask for a reduction. This is the process WenigerMiete supports.

If a tenant wants to know if his/her landlord asks for too much rent, he/she can do a free online survey that asks some questions about the rented object. The software behind the survey automatically checks if the tenant pays too much rent. If the tenant is overpaying, you can mandate WenigerMiete to take on your case.[50] The user only needs to pay after a successful trial and is not charged at any point during the process. The fee is not the sum of the billable hours – as a usual law firm charges its clients – but rather a one-time payment of four times the amount that the tenant will be saving each month (contingency fee).

According to the German Legal Services Act (RDG)[51] only lawyers registered at the bar associations are allowed to give legal advice. According to German law, 'legal advice' is defined *as any activity that requires a legal examination of the individual case.*

Other legal experts are able to provide legal advice only if they have a competence to do so. One of those competences – relevant for the case at hand – can be found in Subsection 2, Section 2 RDG, which reads as follows:

> the collection of third-party claims or claims assigned for the purpose of collection for the account of a third party is a legal service if the debt collection is conducted as a stand-alone business (collection service). Assigned claims are not regarded as third-party claims of the previous obligee.[52]

This means that debt collectors can give 'legal advice' regarding the subject of the matter on which they act. One of the questions brought forward in the case at hand was whether the 'legal advice' as laid down in Article 2 RDG, only deals with the advice in the field of debt collection, or whether a debt collector can also provide legal advice on the merits matter (i.e., rental law, labour law).

On 20 July 2017, the Berlin Bar Association (RAK) warned WenigerMiete to stop providing the legal services related to rental issues. RAK therefore ordered a cease-and-desist letter (*Unterlassungserklärung*).[53] If WenigerMiete would continue these services, the startup needed to pay an amount up to EUR 250,000 in fines to the RAK.[54]

---

[48] WenigerMiete (Conny GmbH), www.wenigermiete.de.
[49] §556d BGB.
[50] WenigerMiete, 'Miete senken per Mietpreisbremse', www.wenigermiete.de/mietpreisbremse (accessed 15 July 2020).
[51] Rechtsdienstleistungsgesetz vom 12. Dezember 2007 (BGBl. I S. 2840), das zuletzt durch Artikel 8 des Gesetzes vom 20. November 2019 (BGBl. I S. 1724) geändert worden ist.
[52] Rechtsdienstleistung ist, unabhängig vom Vorliegen der Voraussetzungen des Absatzes 1, die Einziehung fremder oder zum Zweck der Einziehung auf fremde Rechnung abgetretener Forderungen, wenn die Forderungseinziehung als eigenständiges Geschäft betrieben wird (Inkassodienstleistung). Abgetretene Forderungen gelten für den bisherigen Gläubiger nicht als fremd.
[53] *Urteil* LG Berlin 15. Zivilkammer, 15.01.2019, ECLI:DE:LGBE:2019:0115,15O60.18.00 at [3].
[54] Ibid. at [8].

It is not clear whether WenigerMiete complied or not with the cease-and-desist order, but on 17 March 2018, RAK started litigation.[55] The arguments presented by RAK can be summarised as follows:

- The automation software of the rental price control calculations can be seen as 'providing legal advice'. In this sense, this would be unlawful based on the RDG.[56]
- The fact that WenigerMiete had a debt-collection licence is not sufficient to support clients in out-of-court rental law settlements. Even though debt collection is seen as legal advice, the advice can only be given if it's related to the field of debt collection. No advice is allowed, according to RAK, on matters outside the realm of debt collection (i.e., rental law).[57]
- WenigerMiete promotes and advertises itself as a law firm both for its clients and counterparties when in fact they are only operating as a debt collector.[58]

The Berlin 15th Civil Chamber decided that:

- Regarding the allegation that WenigerMiete should not enforce the rental price control calculations because it is seen as legal advice, WenigerMiete was not acting in the realm of legal advice. It was rather doing a 'schematic and arithmetic operation' on which there is no legal examination.[59] WenigerMiete compared via a software the prices of other rental objects in the same area, based on the size, the year when the apartment was built and other criteria. This comparison, even though it is a precondition for the rental control according to § 556g (2) BGB does not need to be done by a lawyer.[60]
- Regarding the allegation that WenigerMiete is giving legal advice in out-of-court settlements while it has only a debt collection license, the Chamber decided that § 3 of the Legal Service Act (RDG) goes beyond only being a market access rule.[61] The decision explains that the debt collection permit allows the defendant to give legal advice also related to the merit matter, that is, rental law. A debt collection company can, according to the court, extensively examine the case in order to provide its clients with the best solution. Finally, the Chamber explains that the clients of a debt collection company are protected, especially with professional liability insurance.[62]
- On the representation towards third parties as a law firm, the Chamber decided that the defendant should cease the advertising activities, since it would be misleading, not only for its customers, but also for the counterparties (landlords).[63] The usage of sentences such as 'the existence of the proxy is insured by a lawyer' and 'in accordance with the Lawyers' Remuneration Act, the following disbursed costs have arisen' was also considered misleading.[64] Although it was created and run by lawyers, it would not change the fact that WenigerMiete was not a law firm, and the use of the term

---

[55] Ibid. at [7].
[56] Ibid. at [9–12].
[57] Ibid. at [15].
[58] Ibid. at [14].
[59] Ibid. at [46].
[60] Ibid. at [46–48].
[61] Ibid. at [36–41].
[62] Ibid. at [41].
[63] Ibid. at [67–75].
[64] Ibid. at [74].

'Rechtsdienstleistungsgesellschaft' (a legal services company) is not common, in the sense that it would be perceived as a law firm.[65]

WenigerMiete thus can operate as a debt collector, albeit WenigerMiete needs to adjust the website to be as transparent as possible for the consumers. Furthermore, MenigerMiete can provide legal advice on rental law in out-of-court proceedings and did not suffer a provisional penalty of EUR 250,000.

10.5 DOCTRINE

Doctrine is an online publishing company located in Paris. Legal experts can buy a membership that gives them access to legal information such as laws, court cases, academic articles, parliamentary documents, etc.

Case law is not generally publicly available in France. If a specific case is not open to the public, one can make a request to the court that issued the decision to obtain a copy. The rights for such requests are anchored in the Civil Procedure Code and in the Lemaire Act, which entered into force on 7 October 2016.[66] Based on Article 20 and 21 of this Act, court decisions – whether administrative or judicial – should be made available to the public free of charge. On 24 June 2014, an additional Order extended the scope by including the right to reuse legal databases.[67] This Order was adopted before the Lemaire Act. The Order says that the reuse of the existing public database is free, while the Lemaire Act provides that all case law should be made freely available online. In that way, the Lemaire Act extends the scope of the previously available database.

In order to enhance their product offer, Doctrine requested bulk access to court cases at the Tribunal de Grande Instance (Court of First Instance, TGI).[68] After collecting the requested cases, Doctrine wanted to anonymise the personal data and then offer it to its members. Based on the above, this should be a simple request on the right to access and reuse data. However, the TGI's clerk rejected the request based on 'material constraints of the service, mainly the move to a new courthouse, which did not allow them to acquire an additional consultant to support the workload'.[69]

After the rejection from the court's clerk, Doctrine addressed the matter to the Commission d'Accès aux Documents Administratifs (CADA), an administrative body that deals with access to administrative documents. CADA issued two opinions – the first on 7 September 2017[70] and the second one on 14 December 2017[71] – in favour of Doctrine. The Ministry of Justice raised the argument that the CADA would, as an organisation, not be admissible, however the CADA declared itself competent on the basis of Article L 342-1 of the Code of Relations between the Public and the Administration (CRPA).[72] The CADA underwrote once more that Doctrine had by law the right to access and to reuse the requested court cases.

---

[65] Ibid. at [65].
[66] Loi no. 2016-1321 du 7 octobre 2016 pour une République numérique, JORF n°0235, 8 October 2016.
[67] Arrête du 24 juin 2014 relatif à la gratuité de la réutilisation des bases de données juridiques et associatives de la direction de l'information légale et administrative, JORF n°0146, 26 June 2014.
[68] R. Letteron, 'L'accès aux décisions de justice, ou le dispositif 'Anti-Doctrine', Liberté, Libertés Chéries, 6 Janury 2019, http://libertescheries.blogspot.com/2019/01/lacces-aux-decisions-de-justice-ou-le.html.
[69] Ibid.
[70] CADA, Opinion 20171247 – Session of 7 September 2017.
[71] CADA, Opinion 20174865 – Session of 14 December 2017.
[72] Letteron, n. 68.

Even though the outcome of the CADA was positive for the Parisian company, the battle was not over. The Ministry appealed the clerk's opinion before the president of the TGI.[73] The TGI's president rejected access to the jurisprudence in a rather blurry decision on 6 October 2017, where the main focus was on procedural aspects of the law.[74]

Doctrine decided to appeal the decision from the TGI at the Court of Appeal in Paris, which handed its ruling on 18 December 2018.[75] The Court of Appeal stepped away from all the procedural hurdles in the beginning of the proceedings and focused mainly on the substantive part of this legal matter. The court stressed the following:

- The Court agreed with the reasoning of the two CADA-Opinions.
- The Court confirmed that the requested documents are open for disclosure for the public and that Doctrine has a right to reuse them.
- The ill-founded argument of the Ministry that they had to invest all their resources for moving into a new courthouse would also not hold anymore: the Court of Appeal simply stated that the move was complete and that the 'material obstacles' have disappeared.
- The Court demanded the TGI's clerk to provide Doctrine access to the documents 'under the same conditions as other authorised operators, provided that it makes use of them as authorised by law'.[76]

Interestingly enough, a part of the bulk request from Doctrine was already given to more 'old fashioned' publishers such as INPI.

Once Doctrine got its approval from the Court of Appeal to have a right to access and reuse the bulk documents, the legal saga still did not come to an end. Twenty-four hours after the ruling of the Court of Appeal – on 19 December 2019 – the Ministry published a *circulaire* (Appendix), which was applicable for all the registries dealing with access to document requests.[77] The *circulaire* was named 'Note on the processing of requests for copies of judicial decisions from third parties in the proceedings'. In this document it was stated that 'the dissemination of mass decisions responding to claims which does not clearly relate to specific cases … shall in principle be avoided'.[78]

This *circulaire* has the opposite *rationale* of the Court's decision. Some scholars even refer to it as the 'Anti-Doctrine System'.[79] In order to support the rather remarkable timing of the document, the Ministry explained its reasoning as follows:

---

[73] Tribunal de grande instance de Paris, Chambre des requêtes, 6 octobre 2017, no. 17/02017 [2017].
[74] Ibid.
[75] Cour d'appel de Paris, pôle 2 – ch. 1, 18 déc. 2018, no. 17/22211 [2018].
[76] 'Considérant dès lors qu'au regard de l'article 11-3 de la loi du 5 juillet 1972, de l'article L 111-13 du code de l'organisation judiciaire, modifié par l'article 21 de la loi du 7 octobre 2016 pour une République numérique, de l'article 1440 du code de procédure civile, de l'article 18 de la convention de la Haye du 25 octobre 1980, en vigueur depuis le 1er mai 1988, de l'avis de la CADA du 7 septembre et du 14 décembre 2017 que les décisions judiciaires publiques doivent être communiquées à tous requérants français ou étrangers, de sorte qu'il doit être enjoint au directeur des services de greffe judiciaires du tribunal de grande instance de Paris de communiquer au requérant, sous forme papier ou sous forme numérique ces décisions, à charge pour lui de les anonymiser, ou de le laisser accéder aux minutes dans les mêmes conditions que les autres opérateurs autorisés, à charge d'en faire un usage autorisé par la loi.' See also Letteron, n. 68.
[77] Relative à la communication de décisions judiciaires civiles et pénales aux tiers à l'instance, 19 December 2018, Bulletin officiel du ministère de la Justice n°2018-12, 31 December 2018.
[78] Ibid. 'La diffusion de décisions en masse répondant à des demandes dont il est manifeste qu'elles ne portent pas sur une ou plusieurs affaires en particulier mais sur la jurisprudence de la juridiction dans une ou plusieurs matières sera en principe évitée.'
[79] Letteron, n. 68.

- The Ministry added that the *circulaire* was necessary in order to enforce the 'proper administration of justice'. The new principle should protect the administration from disruption caused by large data requests.
- The Ministry furthermore wanted to safeguard the 'protection of personal data'. This motivation is also rather remarkable since the court cases would have been anonymised by the requesters before publishing them.

A simple circular therefore purports to obstruct the law and the principle of open data in court decisions that it sets out, as some scholars have stressed.[80]

A few months after the *circulaire*, the Minister of Justice requested the removal of the Paris Court of Appeal's decision of 18 December, which said that Doctrine should be provided with the case law.

The case was referred again to the Paris Court of Appeal, which, on 25 June, decided to retract its decision from 18 December. This decision rests on strange arguments and mostly avoids the legal discussion on the substantive matter. Doctrine decided to refer the case to the Cour de Cassation. The procedure is at the moment of writing ongoing.

In the meantime, a draft Decree on Open Data of case law[81] was published by the Ministry of Justice, which organises the future online publication of all case law from the judicial and administrative order. This Decree is much awaited since it was provided by the Lemaire Act of 2016. The publication of a draft tends to show that the litigation introduced by Doctrine against the TGI served to make it finally happen.

10.6 DEMANDER JUSTICE

Demander Justice (DJ)[82] was founded in 2012 and is one of the pioneers of the French LT industry. DJ operated from two different websites www.demanderjustice.com (dealing with general civil law issues) and www.saisirprudhommes.com (focusing on labour law issues). Later, www.litige.fr was added to their product offer. DJ has as its mission to simplify the access to justice for all French citizens.

DJ assumed that many French citizens refrained from going to court in order to get their rights. Possibly, many people do not know where and how to initiate a legal procedure, and they might have been afraid of the costs of such a legal trial. The result is that many people did not claim their rights in court, even though they might have had a valid legal case. In order to find a solution for this rising problem, DJ automated the first part of initiating a legal civil procedure:

- Via an online form a user can enter information about their problem. Via these questions, DJ can validate the problem and choose the correct legal document.
- Once the customer is done, DJ provides the user with the correct document that tries to solve the dispute without interference from a judge by means of a *mise en demeure* (formal notice).
- The documents will then be automatically sent via registered mail from their website to the counterparty. At this point two possibilities can occur, either the counterparty settles

---

[80] Ibid.
[81] Décret no. 2020-797 du 29 juin 2020 relatif à la mise à la disposition du public des décisions des juridictions judiciaires et administratives, JORF n°0160, 30 June 2020.
[82] Demander Justice, www.demanderjustice.com (accessed 15 July 2020).

the dispute out of court and the case is closed, or the counterparty does not react at all or comes with counter arguments. In the latter case the next step is triggered.
- DJ automatically sends the case to the competent court. The opponent will then be automatically summoned before a judge who will decide on the matter.

The complete process is automated and no lawyer is needed. DJ charges a fixed price for the sending and automation of the documents, so the customer always has transparency regarding the price. Since 2012, DJ has filed 983,048 cases via this automated process.[83]

By automating a part of the French civil process to initiate a case, DJ was sailing in the waters of the traditional French lawyers. The Conseil national des barreaux (National Bar Council [CNB]) and the Ordre des Avocats du Barreau de Paris (Paris Bar Association [PBA]) were not too fond of this innovative access to justice service. According to them, DJ was assisting and/or representing parties in justice without the capacity of a registered lawyer at the bar. With their service, DJ thus would provide unlawful legal assistance, which needed to be stopped in the eyes of the CNB and PBA. In order to do so, the CNB and the PBA came up with a rather aggressive legal strategy, which is summarised hereunder:[84]

- On 9 August 2012 and 19 February 2013, the President of the PBA presented two reports to the public prosecutor that gave rise to a preliminary criminal investigation addressed to 'Mr D X' (Jeremy Oinino, the CEO of DJ). The alleged accusation was that Mr D X assisted and represented parties, initiated proceedings and pleaded before different courts via the means of the websites www.demanderjustice.com and www.saisirprudhommes.com, without being duly registered at the bar.
- On 13 March 2014, the Tribunal Correctionnel de Paris (Paris Criminal Court) dismissed Mr D X for all the above-mentioned allegations.[85]
- The Cour d'Appel de Paris (Court of Appeal of Paris) later confirmed the judgement on 21 March 2016 and stressed that DJ had only a 'purely material role'.[86]
- On 21 March 2017, the Chambre Criminelle de la Cour de Cassation (Criminal Division of the Court of Cassation) dismissed once again all possible allegations that the appellants – PBA and CNB – brought up.[87]
- At the same time of the criminal proceedings on 8 December 2014, the CNB initiated a private litigation and summoned DJ to appear before the TGI in order to:
Cease all legal assistance provided by DJ;
Cease all legal representation provided by DJ;
Cease all legal advice provided by DJ;
Cease all drafting of procedural and/or legal documents provided by DJ;
Cease the operating disputed websites of DJ.

The judgement of the TGI was held on 11 January 2017 and the court, after declaring itself admissible, dismissed all the claims on the side of CNB and also dismissed the counter claims of DJ. In its ruling, it ordered *in solidum* that the CNB and the PBA were responsible for a sum of

---

[83] Ibid.
[84] See O. Dufour, 'Le feuilleton Demander Justice continue!', *Gazette du Palais*, 14 February 2017. See also L. Garnerie, 'Pour Demander Justice, ni fermeture, ni drapeau tricolore', *Gazette du Palais*, 9 November 2018. See also L. Garnerie, 'Demander justice obtient gain de cause devant la chambre criminelle', *Gazette du Palais*, 28 March 2017.
[85] Tribunal Correctionnel de Paris, 13 march 2014, no. 13248000544 [2014].
[86] Cour d'appel de Paris, 21 march 2016, no. 14/04307 [2016].
[87] Cour de Cassation, Chambre criminelle, 21 march 2017, 16-82.437 [2017].

EUR 5,000 under Article 700 of the Code of Civil Procedure (CCP) and the full costs of the proceedings.[88]

On 6 June 2017, the PBA appealed the decision of the TGI and requested DJ to:

- Cease all legal advice and drafting of legal documents, subject to a penalty payment of EUR 10,000 per day;
- Cease all legal assistance and representation activities;
- Cease all operating websites of DJ, subject to a penalty of EUR 10,000 a day;
- Pay the PBA a sum of EUR 30,000 based on Article 700 of the CCP;
- Make full payment of the process costs.[89]

On 18 June 2018, the CNB also appealed the TGI decision. The CNB asked:

- To reverse the judgement of the TGI, with the exception of the dismissal of the counter-claim of DJ;
- To rule that DJ unlawfully provides legal assistance and representation, legal advice and drafting of legal documents and/or 'services in legal nature';
- To rule that DJ is engaged in misleading commercial practices;
- To cease the activities on the operating websites of DJ, under a payment penalty of EUR 5,000 a day;
- To rule that DJ needs to pay a symbolic amount of EUR 1 to compensate the damage caused to the legal profession as a result of its actions;
- To dismiss all counter claims of DJ in the proceedings;
- To rule that DJ needs to pay an amount of EUR 30,000 on the basis of Article 700 CCP.[90]

On 7 June 2018 DJ asked the Paris Court of Appeal in a counter claim:

- To declare the grounds of the CNB and the PBA admissible but unfounded;
- To confirm the judgement of the TGI on 11 January 2017;
- To rule that CNB and PBA are liable for EUR 11,700,000 in respect for the loss of investment opportunities on the side of DJ;
- To pay a sum of EUR 5,000,000 for damage caused by reputational damage;
- To pay a sum of EUR 100,000 for immaterial damage;
- To pay a sum of EUR 10,000 for both the CNB and the PBA on the grounds of Article 700 CCP.[91]

The Court of Appeal ruled on the abovementioned grounds as follows in its judgement on 6 November 2018:[92]

- On the grounds that DJ was unlawfully providing legal assistance to its users, the Court stressed that the definition for 'legal advice' is a 'personalised intellectual service aimed, on a question raised, at providing an opinion or advice based on the application of a rule of law with a view to, in particular, possible decision-making'.[93] The Court points out that the activity of DJ is essentially not providing 'a syllogistic intellectual service' consisting in

---

[88] Tribunal de Grande Instance de Paris, 11 January 2017, no. 15/04207.
[89] Cour d'appel de Paris, 6 November 2018, no. 17/04957.
[90] Ibid.
[91] Ibid.
[92] Ibid.
[93] Ibid. 'une prestation intellectuelle personnalisée tendant, sur une question posée, à la fourniture d'un avis ou d'un conseil fondé sur l'application d'une règle de droit en vue, notamment d'une éventuelle prise de décision'.

analysing the personal factual situation of the litigant and then applying the corresponding abstract law rule to it.[94] Since the users from DJ who provide the advice by choosing from pre-selected models and templates offered by DJ, the 'intellectual' part of the definition is missing and therefore DJ is not providing legal advice in the eyes of the Court.

- The second argument from PBA and CNB, stressing that there was a phone number provided on the websites of DJ where customers could call in case they had questions could be seen as 'legal advice', was too hypothetical and did not bear sufficient evidence according to the Court.[95]
- The Court continued with the argument raised that drafting legal documents could be seen as providing 'legal advice'. After carefully analysing the process in which the documents are drafted, the Court noted that DJ solely provides a template for the document, which is not being finalised by DJ but by the user. Therefore, this in itself cannot be seen as 'drafting a legal act'.[96]
- As regards the alleged unlawful 'legal representation', the Court stressed that DJ never asked for a legal mandate, but that it solely sends – via a service provider – the tangible document to the right addressee (counterparty and court respectively). DJ does this by making use of an electronic signature. Furthermore, DJ warns the user that not all courts that could be seized accept this kind of signature, so that the user – in case the document is not accepted – needs to file the document in a manual process. All in all, the Court says, DJ is because of its actions not acting as a legal representative of the client but solely providing a material business service.[97]
- Regarding the claim of alleged 'misleading advertising', the Court ruled that since there are no illegal activities that were proven on the side of DJ, this argument does not need to be investigated further. The same goes for the request to cease the operating websites.[98]
- As regards the claims brought forward by DJ, that the CNB and the PBA have caused damages to the company that led to a loss in turnover, the Court ruled that these damages were not sufficiently reasoned, and it could not be proven that there was a causality between the legal actions of CNB and PBA alone and the potential loss in turnover.[99]
- Lastly, the appellants brought forward that DJ was using the three colours – red, white and blue – that represent the French flag. Because of that, they argued, the website(s) had the appearance to be a public/governmental website. This could cause confusion for the user. The Court also demanded to provide the user with a calculation of the 'success rate of 82%', which is stated on their website. The Court ruled that this could be indeed deceiving and ordered to change the coloured flag on the website on a provisional penalty from EUR 5,000 per day.[100]

After this ruling, the claimants brought forward two new legal actions:

- First of all, the claimants have informed DJ that they will bring the matter up to the French Supreme Court. In this way they hope to convince the Supreme Court that DJ is

---

[94] Ibid. 'l'assistance juridique, que seul un avocat peut apporter à son client, se manifeste essentiellement par ce qu'il est convenu d'appeler une prestation intellectuelle syllogistique consistant à analyser la situation de fait personnelle au justiciable pour y appliquer ensuite la règle de droit abstraite correspondante'.
[95] Ibid.
[96] Ibid.
[97] Ibid.
[98] Ibid.
[99] Ibid.
[100] Ibid.

providing legal advice or assistance and that the Court will squash the verdict of the November ruling of the Court of Appeals. The trail will probably commence in late 2020.
- Secondly, they brought a new case forward in front of the Juge de l'Exécution (JEX), which was held on 29 January 2020.[101] The reason for this judgement had something to do with the Appeal ruling. In this ruling, the Court stressed that DJ should change the colours of their tricoloured logo since it gives the appearance that it is a public website. Furthermore, DJ needed to demonstrate how their '82% success rate' is calculated. Both the decisions had as its objective to protect the consumer.
- After the judgement in 2018, DJ changed the white part in their logo to a grey colour.
- Secondly, DJ changed their website in such a way that one could click on the '82% success'– statement, which would give the user access to a marketing study.

The two above-mentioned actions were not enough in the eyes of the Bar and they brought up another lawsuit in front of the JEX. The Bar stressed that:

- The grey colour that DJ used in their new logo was too light and was hard to distinguish from the white colour they originally had.[102]
- The hyperlink that gives access to the marketing study is not clear enough for the user. The user could only 'discover' this study if they hover over the statement with their mouse.[103]

Because of that, the CNB and the PBA sued DJ once more with a EUR 2.5 million claim on 29 January 2020. The judge underwrote the importance of consumer protection and ruled in favour of the claimants by imposing a penalty payment of EUR 500,000 to DJ.[104]

At the moment of writing, DJ is struggling to suspend the provisional execution that could threaten the sustainability of the company. DJ has decided to appeal the judgement of the JEX later in 2020.

10.7 CONCLUDING REMARKS

The examples have shown that several new access to justice solutions have emerged in the digital age, all utilising technology. Although the market indicates there is a high demand for such modernised legal services, their emergence also comes with a lot of friction and fights.

Legal frameworks are not set up for these newer services. At best, they create grey areas that trigger uncertainty both for companies, regulators and customers. Legal regulations are mostly drafted by bar associations. Although bar associations play their important role in safeguarding and maintaining the quality of lawyers, they typically also have a wide variety of interests, which might include the continuity of the profession and its monopoly. Grey zones then easily turn into an arsenal to fight with, rather than to embrace these innovations.

---

[101] Tribunal Judiciaire de Paris, 29 January 2020, No. RG 19/82171.
[102] Ibid.
[103] Ibid.
[104] Ibid.

For as far as new providers enhance access to justice, it is important to create a level playing field. The examples described show how this is done through battle and bloodshed in court or through competition authorities. A better approach, which wastes less capital, would be to do this through a more deliberative form. By taking the needs of citizens and customers as a perspective. Some contemporary examples that involve the creation of regulatory sandboxes indicate how this can be done whilst also safeguarding the quality of these legal services.

11

Legal Tech and EU Consumer Law*

Martin Ebers

11.1 INTRODUCTION

Legal tech (LT) products and services automate certain tasks that lawyers usually perform. The use of these tools in business-to-consumer (B2C) markets create many opportunities for consumers and the justice system in general, but also raises concerns in terms of access to justice, choice and information, quality, fairness, redress, and representation (Sections 11.1.1–11.1.4). This chapter deals with the question of whether the current legal framework in the EU (Section 11.2) is fit to meet the challenge LT poses in consumer markets, focusing especially on (national) legal services regulation (Section 11.3), EU consumer law (Section 11.4), and EU data protection law (Section 11.5). It concludes that applying the current legal norms to LT creates the risk of both under-regulation and over-regulation and discusses possible regulatory options that should be taken into account at the national and EU level to strike the right balance between innovation and protection (Section 11.6).

11.1.1 Rise of LT in Consumer Markets

Large amounts of data, interconnectivity, and cheap, enormous processing power combined with intelligent automation and breakthroughs in what is commonly known as artificial intelligence (AI)[1] – especially machine learning (ML)[2] and natural language processing (NLP)[3] – have contributed to the rise of LT, that is, the use of information technology tools in legal practice and administration.

---

* This work was supported by Estonian Research Council grant no. PRG124.
[1] On the various definitions of AI, cf. S. Samoili, M. López Cobo, E. Gómez, G. De Prato, F. Martínez-Plumed, and B. Delipetrev, "AI Watch. Defining Artificial Intelligence: Towards an Operational Definition and Taxonomy of Artificial Intelligence," Joint Research Centre Technical Report JRC118163 (2020), doi:10.2760/382730.
[2] D. J. C. MacKay, *Information Theory, Inference and Learning Algorithms* (Cambridge: Cambridge University Press, 2003); E. Alpaydin, *Machine Learning* (Cambridge, MA: MIT Press, 2016).
[3] M. Z. Kurdi, *Natural Language Processing and Computational Linguistics: Speech, Morphology, and Syntax*, vol. 1 (London: ISTE-Wiley, 2016); M. Z. Kurdi, *Natural Language Processing and Computational Linguistics: Semantics, Discourse, and Applications*, vol. 2 (London: ISTE-Wiley, 2017); L. Deng and Y. Liu (eds.), *Deep Learning in Natural Language Processing* (Singapore: Springer, 2018).

Although the impact of LT has been felt predominantly in B2B markets,[4] technology also has great potential to impact consumer legal services.[5] More and more companies offer consumers and other end users the technical means to obtain (legal) information or advice; to draft contracts or review legal documents automatically;[6] to simplify complaint procedures, for example, by challenging speeding/parking tickets[7] or facilitating airfare refunds;[8] or to address complex legal problems from a consumer law perspective, such as tenancy[9] or employment issues,[10] divorce and child support,[11] immigration,[12] wills and succession;[13] and more. Some companies even provide citizens with automated dispute resolution and small claims services.[14]

LT applications come in different forms and shapes. Some are stand-alone technologies, such as legal chatbots, apps, and virtual assistants. Others are enablers of legal advice, such as automated drafting, legal document review and legal algorithms, as well as legal data analytics and predictors, whereas still other tools try to automate legal advice with smart contracts. Yet the underlying idea of most applications offered on consumer markets seems to be the same, that is, to provide a do-it-yourself (DIY) product or legal service, empowering the individual with the knowledge, expertise and the means to solve their legal problems wherever possible without reference to a lawyer.

Regarding the degree to which lawyers are replaced by technology, we can distinguish different – and partly overlapping – tools currently available on the market, namely, LT applications providing:

---

[4] Some authors estimate that LT businesses are operating about 80–90 percent in B2B markets; A. Hook, "The Use and Regulation of Technology in the Legal Sector beyond England and Wales," Research Paper for the Legal Services Board (2019) at 6, www.legalservicesboard.org.uk/our-work/current-work/lsb-technology-project/attachment/international-ah-report-vfp-4-jul-2019 (accessed June 9, 2020). According to a study conducted in the United Kingdom by The Law Society, LT in B2C markets "is less mature and much more fragmented across a greater number of, generally, smaller law firms"; The Law Society, "Lawtech Adoption Research," Law Society Research Report (February 2019) at 31. Others speak of "latent markets"; R. Susskind and D. Susskind, *The Future of the Professions: How Technology Will Transform the Work of Human Experts* (New York: Oxford University Press, 2015) 128 ff.

[5] Some commentators have argued that the term "legal tech" should be used only with regard to technological solutions created for lawyers, whereas the term "law tech" should be employed when automated legal services are provided to consumers or other customers; cf. The Law Society, "What Is Lawtech?," www.lawsociety.org.uk/support-services/lawtech/what-is-lawtech (accessed June 9, 2020); S. Navas, "The Provision of Legal Services to Consumers Using LawTech Tools: From 'Service' to 'Legal Product'" (2019) 7 *Open Journal of Social Sciences* 79 81. This chapter, however, only uses the term "legal tech." As Hook correctly points out, the use of two separate terms sets up a false dichotomy, whereas, in reality, the same software solutions might be used both by law firms and end users; Hook, n. 4 at 18.

[6] RobotLawyerLisa, https://robotlawyerlisa.com (accessed June 9, 2020); Docubot, https://aux.ai (accessed June 9, 2020); Clausehund, http://clausehound.com (accessed June 13, 2020).

[7] DoNotPay, https://donotpay.com (accessed June 9, 2020); Geblitzt.de, www.geblitzt.de (accessed June 9, 2020); Fixed, www.getfixed.me (accessed June 13, 2020).

[8] AirHelp, www.airhelp.com (accessed June 9, 2020); Flightright, www.flightright.com (accessed June 9, 2020); ClaimFlights, https://claimflights.com (accessed June 9, 2020).

[9] Wenigermiete.de, www.wenigermiete.de (accessed June 9, 2020); FlatLaws, www.flatlaw.ca (accessed June 13, 2020).

[10] Rightmart, https://rightmart.de/arbeitsrecht (accessed June 9, 2020); Gefeuert.de, www.gefeuert.de (accessed June 9, 2020).

[11] Wevorce, www.wevorce.com (accessed June 9, 2020); SupportPay, https://supportpay.com (accessed June 9, 2020); DivorceRight, www.divorceright.com.au (accessed June 9, 2020).

[12] RoadToStatus, www.roadtostatus.com (accessed June 9, 2020); Advisehub, http://advisehub.com (accessed June 9, 2020).

[13] Everplans, www.everplans.com (accessed June 9, 2020); Tomorrow, https://tomorrow.me (accessed June 9, 2020); AfterSteps, www.aftersteps.com (accessed June 13, 2020).

[14] FairClaims, www.fairclaims.com (accessed June 9, 2020); DemanderJustice, www.demanderjustice.com (accessed June 9, 2020); Swiftcourt, https://swiftcourt.com/en (accessed June 9, 2020); Pactanda https://pactanda.com (accessed June 9, 2020); JUR, https://jur.io (accessed June 9, 2020).

- infrastructure and marketplaces connecting clients with lawyers;
- legal information, providing consumers with general information about the law and legal processes, for example, outlining possible options for dealing with a legal problem or explaining legal procedures;
- automation of documents, helping consumers to draft or review legally relevant documents such as contracts;
- legal advice, applying the law to a specific situation, by interpreting and explaining how the law applies to someone's situation and/or recommending what steps someone should take and why;
- dispute resolution services and small claims services, helping consumers to enforce their claims; and
- algorithmic (automated) decision-making, where legally relevant decisions are fully automated.

11.1.2 Underlying Technology: From Hand-Coded to Data-Learned Knowledge

Another important distinction can be made with regard to the underlying technology of LT applications, specifically between *hand-coded knowledge*, on the one hand, and *data-learned knowledge*, on the other.[15]

In the past, most LT solutions consisted of legal expert systems relying on rule-based conditional logic operations.[16] Such systems typically break down complex human intellectual tasks into a set of computational steps or algorithms. In order to transform inputs (legal problems) into outputs (legal solutions), experts extract substantive legal knowledge from legal sources and convert it into a logical computational model using *symbolic rules* to represent and infer knowledge. Whereas expert systems have particular strengths in terms of transparency and interpretability, one major flaw is their limited capacity to deal with complex situations. Most expert systems are only useful for narrow applications and cannot cope with uncertainty well enough to be useful in practical applications.[17]

In contrast, the current wave of successful LT applications is based on *data-learned knowledge*, which does not rely so much on hand-coded human expertise, but on the knowledge learned from data. Instead of programming machines with specific instructions to accomplish particular tasks, ML algorithms enable computers to learn from "training data." Self-learning systems are not explicitly programmed; instead, they are trained by thousands and millions of examples, so that the system develops by learning from experience. For some legal tasks, such as document discovery, contract review, and legal prediction,[18] ML models have proven so

---

[15] J. Bennett, T. Miller, J. Webb, R. Bosua, A. Lodders, and S. Chamberlain, "Current State of Automated Legal Advice Tools" (2018) 1 *University of Melbourne Networked Society Institute Discussion Paper* 23.
[16] Cf., for example, R. Susskind, *Expert Systems in Law: A Jurisprudential Inquiry* (Oxford: Oxford University Press, 1987); P. Capper and R. Susskind, *Latent Damage Law: The Expert System* (London: Butterworths Law, 1988); T. Bench-Capon, *Knowledge-Based Systems and Legal Applications* (London: Academic Press, 1991).
[17] Cf. D. Kahneman and A. Tversky, "Variants of Uncertainty" (1982) 11(2) *Cognition* 143; D. Li and Y. Du, *Artificial Intelligence with Uncertainty*, 2nd ed. (New York: CRC Press, 2017); E. Brill and R. J. Mooney, "Empirical Natural Language Processing" (1997) 18(4) *AI Magazine* 13 16.
[18] Cf. D. M. Katz, "Quantitative Legal Prediction – or – How I Learned to Stop Worrying and Start Preparing for the Data-Driven Future of the Legal Services Industry" (2013) 62 *Emory Law Journal* 909 936; H. Surden, "Machine Learning and Law" (2014) 89 *Washington Law Review* 87.

successful that futurists predict that LT will replace lawyers entirely.[19] Others foresee that we are moving toward a "legal singularity,"[20] where technology eliminates all legal uncertainty, leading to a law that is "functionally complete." While such assumptions might very well belong to the realm of legal sci-fi,[21] it nevertheless seems evident that AI technology will dramatically change the entire legal sector.

11.1.3 Opportunities for Consumers

LT applications open up a number of advantages and opportunities for consumers, consumer organizations, and the justice system in general.

First of all, LT tools can increase the *consumer's awareness of legal problems*. Nowadays, many consumers have only limited knowledge and awareness of the legal system. LT can help to fill this knowledge gap. Many applications focus on problems rather than pure legal questions. Consumers are more likely to be reached with these "multidisciplinary" applications, especially where they know they have a problem but do not think of it as a legal issue.[22] LT software can also increase the ability to understand the law by helping consumers to independently analyze and prepare legal documents.[23]

Second, LT applications may give consumers a *wider choice*. DIY legal services are available twenty-four hours a day, seven days a week with no geographical restraint, providing consumers with self-help remedies for their legal problems.

In most cases, LT software will also come at a more *reasonable price* or even at no expense at all, because LT companies have lower operating expenses than traditional law firms. In addition, LT has a *higher price transparency* than traditional legal services. Instead of the traditional billable hours, LT companies often offer their products for fixed prices or flat rates.[24]

Furthermore, many commentators believe that LT applications might be of *better quality* than the legal advice of a human attorney. Whereas humans can err about facts, misrepresent precedent, or may be influenced by extraneous factors or bias, LT could provide the means to overcome human cognitive limitations through automation.[25] Legal advice might also be better matched to the respective case, especially where big data analysis of similar cases produces new insights.[26]

---

[19] See J. O. McGinnis and R. G. Pearce, "The Great Disruption: How Machine Intelligence Will Transform the Role of Lawyers in the Delivery of Legal Services" (2014) 82(6) *Fordham Law Review* 3041 3041; Susskind and Susskind, n. 4 at 202 ff. See also T. Meltzer, "Robot Doctors, Online Lawyers and Automated Architects: The Future of the Professions?," *The Guardian* (June 15, 2014), www.theguardian.com/technology/2014/jun/15/robot-doctors-online-lawyers-automated-architects-future-professionsjobs-technology.

[20] B. Alarie, "The Path of the Law: Towards Legal Singularity" (2016) 66(4) *University of Toronto Law Journal* 443 445; B. Alarie, A. Niblett, and A. H. Yoon, "Law in the Future" (2016) 66(4) *University of Toronto Law Journal* 423 427–428.

[21] Cf. F. Pasquale, "A Rule of Persons, Not Machines: The Limits of Legal Automation" (2019) 87(1) *The George Washington Law Review* 1; C. Markou and S. Deakin, "Ex Machina Lex: The Limits of Legal Computability" in S. Deakin and C. Markou (eds.), *Is Law Computable? Critical Perspectives on Law + Artificial Intelligence* (Oxford: Hart Publishing, 2020), https://papers.ssrn.com/sol3/papers.cfm?abstract_id=3407856.

[22] Hook, n. 4 at 7 and 26.

[23] M. Fries, "Man versus Machine: Using Legal Tech to Optimize the Rule of Law," Munich (2016) at 6 ff., https://ssrn.com/id=2842726 (accessed June 9, 2020).

[24] Susskind and Susskind, n. 4 at 206–207.

[25] F. Pasquale, "A Rule of Persons, Not Machines: The Limits of Legal Automation" (2019) 8(1) *The George Washington Law Review* 1 4.

[26] Companies like geblitzt.de, for example, can use their findings that some speed cameras have measurement errors for thousands of customers by challenging their speeding tickets.

Technology can also enhance *access to justice* by reducing existing cost barriers.[27] For example, companies such as Do-Not-Pay or Flightright help consumers at a large scale to enforce small claims that otherwise would not have been brought to court due to relatively high legal fees and the well-known problem of "rational apathy."

Consumer organizations and public watchdogs can also use LT services to monitor and enforce existing consumer law,[28] for instance, for detecting unfair contract terms in online contracts.[29]

As a result, LT offers the possibility to strengthen the rule of law, to reduce existing cost barriers, to open up latent markets, and create new areas of competition.

11.1.4 Risks for Consumers

On the other hand, LT might have considerable drawbacks for consumers in terms of access to justice, choice and information, quality, fairness, redress, and representation.

Regarding *access to legal services*, there is the risk that LT excludes consumers who lack IT literacy, digital equipment, or access to the Internet. As about 20 percent of consumers might not be able to access LT services at all,[30] there is a great potential for digital exclusion of analog or illiterate consumers. Furthermore, most LT companies use technology to decide which cases are taken on. It is therefore likely that companies will not attempt to enforce uneconomic or risky claims from the outset. A refusal to take on a case is particularly problematic if the reasons for such denial are flawed.

Second, consumers might face *choice and information problems*. Insofar as decisions are prepared or even taken by machines, the algorithmic choice may not always accurately reflect consumers' true preferences. Additionally, the use of LT applications can lead to a loss of transparency. In many countries, it is still unclear which types of LT services fall outside the traditional monopoly of lawyers.[31] Consequently, consumers might get confused over whether or not they are using a regulated service, and what protection they have. Additionally, many LT applications and their outcomes are hard to understand, especially when they are based on ML, because of the opacity of many AI technologies (black box effect).[32]

As to the *quality and fairness* of LT applications, a couple of questions arise: Who makes sure that law is accurately translated into code? How can consumers assess the accuracy of legal advice? How to deal with new power asymmetries between consumers and LT providers? How can we ensure that LT providers do not exploit consumers' data and their vulnerabilities?

Beyond these problems, there is the issue of *redress rights*: Do consumers have access to redress mechanisms when something goes wrong? Are LT providers liable to the same extent as lawyers? Are LT companies allowed to exclude their liability for errors in their general terms and

---

[27] R. H. Brescia, W. McCarthy, A. McDonald, K. Potts, and C. Rivais, "Embracing Disruption: How Technological Change in the Delivery of Legal Services Can Improve Access to Justice" (2014) 78 *Albany Law Review* 580.
[28] G. Contissa, F. Lagioia, M. Lippi, H.-W. Micklitz, P. Pałka, G. Sartor, and P. Torroni, "Towards Consumer-Empowering Artificial Intelligence," Proceedings of IJCAI Conference (2018) at 5150–5157.
[29] Claudette, http://claudette.eui.eu (accessed June 9, 2020).
[30] Cf. Legal Service Consumer Panel, "Regulation That Supports Lawtech and Protects Consumers," roundtable event, summary of the key points raised by the speakers (July 9, 2019), www.legalservicesconsumerpanel.org.uk/wp-content/uploads/2019/07/Summary-of-LSCP-Lawtech-roundtable.pdf (accessed June 9, 2020).
[31] See Sections 11.3.2–11.3.3.
[32] Cf. M. Ebers, "Regulating AI and Robotics: Ethical and Legal Challenges" in M. Ebers and S. Navas (eds.), *Algorithms and Law* (Cambridge: Cambridge University Press, 2020) 48ff.; J. Burrell, "How the Machine 'Thinks': Understanding Opacity in Machine Learning Algorithms" (January–June 2016) *Big Data & Society* 1.

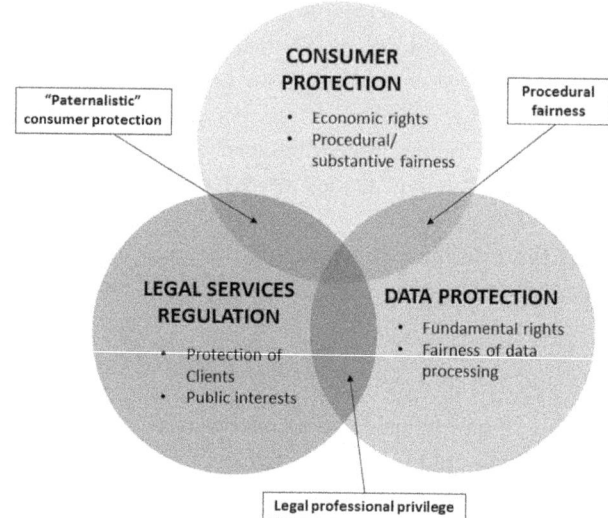

FIGURE 11.1 Interplay between legal services regulation, EU consumer and data protection law

conditions? Is the consumer entitled to lodge a formal complaint with the bar association? Do LT companies – just like lawyers – have to take out mandatory indemnity insurance? And: How to deal with cross-border situations where the LT provider is not in the consumer's country, but in a third state?

Finally, there is the problem of *representation* and the danger of a *hidden privatization* of decisions about public values. How can consumer groups get involved in the development, deployment, and evaluation of LT services? How can society make sure that LT systems – created by private companies – are aligned with the democratic and constitutional values that human rights are designed to serve?

11.2 CURRENT REGULATORY FRAMEWORK IN A NUTSHELL

11.2.1 *The Interplay between Legal Services Regulation, EU Consumer and Data Protection Law*

A first glance at the existing legal framework for legal services established in most countries reveals a disparate picture. Legal services regulation is fragmented and subdivided between various fields of law, especially legal services regulation, traditional consumer protection law, and data protection law. The interplay of these three main fields is illustrated in Figure 11.1.

The regulation of legal services serves different regulatory objectives. In most countries, the aim of this specific body of legislation is not only to protect public interests – such as the rule of law, an effective legal system, public confidence in the justice system – but also to promote the interests of "clients" or "consumers."[33] In this regard, *legal services regulation* is much

---

[33] In Germany, Sect. 1(1)(2) of the Out-of-Court Legal Services Act (Rechtsdienstleistungsgesetz, RDG) underlines that the Act "serves to protect the consumers of legal services, legal relations and the legal system from unqualified legal services." In the United Kingdom, Sect. 1 of the Legal Services Act 2007 defines eight regulatory objectives: protecting and promoting the public interest; supporting the constitutional principle of the rule of law; improving access to justice; protecting and promoting the interests of consumers of legal services; promoting competition in the provision

stricter – or more paternalistic – than traditional *EU consumer law*. While EU consumer law is largely based on a liberal consumer model that follows the "information rather than prohibition" principle,[34] the legal safeguards provided by legal services regulation go much further. They include professional standards regarding the quality, fairness, and ethics of legal services, strict quality controls of lawyers, the requirement to take out professional liability insurance, special redress mechanisms vis-à-vis the bar associations, and much more.

The relationship between *EU consumer law* and *data protection law* is also complex. Both fields of law are by no means congruent, but complementary. Admittedly, the two differ with regard to the protected groups (consumer vs. data subject) and the subject matter of protection (economic rights vs. fundamental rights of privacy). Differences also arise in that consumer law provides for mandatory law to ensure material fairness (e.g., by controlling unfair contract terms),[35] whereas data protection law is primarily concerned with the (procedural) fairness of data processing,[36] but not with the (material) result of data processing. Both areas of law, however, share the common goals of redressing imbalances of informational and market power, which have become more and more problematic with the rapid development and concentration of digital markets.[37] It is therefore precisely the interplay of consumer and data protection law that offers exciting opportunities for a more integrated vision of "data consumer law."[38]

On the relationship between *data protection law* and *legal service regulation*, on the other hand, it can be stated that legal services regulation provides – again – for a higher level of protection than EU data protection law, mainly because the legal professional privilege protects all communications between a professional legal adviser and his or her clients.

11.2.2 Evaluation

The preceding analysis shows that traditional legal services are subject to a high degree of regulation far above the level of protection provided by EU consumer and data protection law. Accordingly, the question arises as to whether LT applications also fall under the applicable national legal services legislation.

Under these circumstances, there is a risk of both over-regulation and under-regulation. If the existing legal services regulations are applied to LT companies, this could lead to overregulation of a market in which innovative tech services can be developed precisely because strict legislation is not yet in place, depriving consumers and the public of the benefits of innovation.[39]

---

of legal services; encouraging an independent, strong, diverse and effective legal profession; increasing public understanding of the citizen's legal rights and duties; promoting and maintaining adherence to the professional principles.

[34] This is the well-known "information paradigm," established by many judgments of the CJEU and EU consumer law; cf. M. Ebers, *Rechte, Rechtsbehelfe und Sanktionen im Unionsprivatrecht* (Tübingen: Mohr Siebeck, 2016) 799–802; G. Howells, "The Potential and Limits of Consumer Empowerment by Information" (2005) *Journal of Law and Society* 349.

[35] The main tool is the Unfair Contract Terms Directive 93/13, which "aims to replace the formal balance which the contract establishes between the rights and obligations of the parties with an effective balance which re-establishes equality between them"; case C-137/08 ECLI:EU:C:2010:659, [2010] ECR I-0847 [47].

[36] Cf. joined cases C-141/12 and C-372/12 YS. *and M and S* ECLI:EU:C:2014:2081; for more details, see Section 11.5.3.

[37] European Data Protection Supervisor (EDPS) Opinion 8/2018 on the legislative package "A New Deal for Consumers" (2018) at 8.

[38] N. Helberger, F. Zuiderveen Borgesius, and A. Reyna, "The Perfect Match? A Closer Look at the Relationship between EU Consumer Law and Data Protection Law" (2017) *Common Market Law Review* 1427.

[39] N. Semple, "Tending the Flame: Technological Innovation and the Legal Services Act Regime," a paper prepared for the Legal Services Board (August 6, 2019), https://ssrn.com/abstract_id=3616343.

If, on the other hand, legal services regulation does not apply to LT products at all, this could lead to gaps in consumer protection insofar as existing consumer and data protection laws are not able to compensate for this.

Against this background, the following observations focus in a first step on the latter risk of under-regulation, by explaining how difficult it is to apply legal services regulation to LT products (Section 11.3) and by analyzing the shortcomings of EU consumer law (Section 11.4) and EU data protection law (Section 11.5) regarding LT.

11.3 LEGAL SERVICES REGULATION AND LT

11.3.1 Regulation of Legal Services in the EU

Worldwide, there are notable differences in the way in which the activity of lawyers is regulated. As the UK Competition & Markets Authority (CMA) points out in one report, these differences include inter alia:[40]

- whether certain legal activities are reserved only to lawyers
- which types of activity are reserved to lawyers
- whether unregulated providers are allowed to operate in the legal services sector
- whether the regulation of lawyers is characterized by professional self-regulation
- whether non-lawyers can own and manage law firms
- whether non-lawyers can work alongside lawyers in a regulated entity, and
- whether lawyers are allowed to share their fees with clients.

The EU has not yet succeeded in harmonizing the professional rules for lawyers either. Admittedly, there are a number of directives[41] that have facilitated the mutual recognition of education requirements, the free movement of lawyers, and the possibility of providing cross-border services. In contrast, deontological rules in the individual member states continue to be unharmonized. Lawyers who provide cross-border legal services must observe the rules of professional conduct, without prejudice to their obligations in the member state where they are established, that is, their home member states.[42] Hence, a lawyer who provides services in another member state has to abide by two sets of rules: the rules of professional conduct of the host member state and those set by his home member state (so called double deontology or *Kumulationsprinzip*).

The E-Commerce Directive (ECD) 2000/31[43] has not changed this situation. Indeed, Art. 4(1) ECD 2000/31 requires the member states to ensure that the taking up and pursuit of the activity

---

[40] Competition & Markets Authority (CMA), "Legal Services Market Study," CMA final report, Appendix 1 (International Comparison) (2016) at 1.

[41] Council Directive 77/249/EEC of 22 March 1977 to facilitate the effective exercise by lawyers of freedom to provide services (Lawyers' Services Directive), OJ 1977 No. L 78, 26 March 1977; European Parliament and Council Directive 98/5/EC of 16 February 1998 to facilitate practice of the profession of lawyer on a permanent basis in a member state other than that in which the qualification was obtained (Lawyers' Establishment Directive), OJ 1998 No. L 77, 14 March 1998; European Parliament and Council Directive 2005/36/EC of 7 September 2005 on the recognition of professional qualifications (Professional Qualifications Directive), OJ 2005 No. L255, 30 September 2005; European Parliament and Council Directive 2006/123/EC of 12 December 2006 on services in the internal market (Services Directive), OJ 2006 No. L 376, 27 December 2006.

[42] Article 4 of the Lawyers' Services Dir 77/249/EEC, with a few exceptions, declares both home-country and host-country regulation to be applicable in parallel – the so-called Double Deontology (DD).

[43] European Parliament and Council Directive 2000/31/EC of 8 June 2000 on certain legal aspects of information society services, in particular electronic commerce, in the Internal Market (Directive on electronic commerce), OJ 2000 No. L 178, 17 July 2000.

of an information society service provider is not subject to prior authorization or any other requirement having equivalent effect. However, it does not follow from this that regulated legal services can no longer be subject to authorization solely because they are provided via an electronic medium.[44] According to the correct view,[45] Art. 4(1) ECD 2000/31 only applies to authorization requirements related to the (digital) way the service is provided. If, on the other hand, an authorization requirement – such as that for legal services – is triggered by the content of the service, the "no prior authorisation rule" of Art. 4(1) ECD 2000/31 is not applicable.

Differences in deontological rules across EU countries exist most notably with regard to the question of whether non-lawyers are allowed to provide out-of-court legal advice. In this respect, a study published by Claessens et al.[46] on the legal situation in the then twenty-seven member states is particularly revealing. According to this study, fifteen member states regard out-of-court "legal advice" as an activity that is reserved for lawyers. In the remaining twelve countries, on the other hand, "legal advice" per se does not seem to be subject to the legal services regulations.

11.3.2 LT as a Challenge for Legal Services Regulation

Most LT companies offer their products and services not as law firms but as regular tech companies, in order to escape the tight corset of legal services regulation that applies in many countries. Techies and lawyers consider the deontological rules as an obstacle to innovation and investment. This is especially true when these rules (1) restrict the possibility of non-lawyers becoming owner or manager, (2) limit the possibility of cooperation between lawyers and non-lawyers, (3) prohibit fee sharing, and/or (4) restrict advertising and other commercial activities.[47]

The key question, however, is whether LT companies can escape the rules of deontology at all. This issue is especially problematic in countries that regard "legal advice" as a regulated legal service. Typically, these jurisdictions distinguish between (unregulated) legal information and (regulated) legal advice.

Unregulated	Legal information	Standardized	Legal product
Regulated	Legal advice	Tailored	Legal service

Legal information can be understood as a public good that should be accessible to everyone.[48] Commonly, legal information is described "as generic, not addressing the particular circumstances of the individual," whereas legal advice "is more tailored and specific to the needs of the

---

[44] In this direction, however, see Wissenschaftlicher Dienst des deutschen Bundestages (Scientific Service of the German Bundestag), "Sachstand: Rechtsdienstleistungsgesetz und Legal Tech," WD 7-3000-111/19, 4 (July 9, 2019), www.bundestag.de/resource/blob/654316/ad2c5f4740d04d817ba6f7b6f18074cf/WD-7-111-19-pdf-data.pdf; C. Deckenbrock in C. Deckenbrock and M. Henssler (eds.), *Rechtsdienstleistungsgesetz*, 4th ed. (München: C. H. Beck, 2015) § 1, para. 44ff. According to this view, LT should be able to provide legal services abroad as long as they are entitled to do so under the law of their country of origin.

[45] BGH (German Federal Supreme Court), 05.10.2006, I ZR 7/04, NJW 2007, 596 597; B. Werthmann, in M. Ebers et al. (eds.), *Rechtshandbuch Künstliche Intelligenz und Robotik* (München: C. H. Beck, 2020) § 22, para. 76.

[46] S. J. F. J. Claessens et al., "Evaluation of the Legal Framework for the Free Movement of Lawyers," Zoetermeer Final Report (2012) at 40–42.

[47] M. Kilian, "Die Regulierung von Legal Tech: Risiken und Nebenwirkungen von Sonderregeln – Plädoyer für eine ganzheitliche Betrachtung" (2019) 1 Anwaltsblatt 24 26 ff.; B. Werthmann, "Legal Tech" in M. Ebers et al. (eds.), *Künstliche Intelligenz und Robotik – Rechtshandbuch* (München: C. H. Beck, 2020) § 22, paras. 44 ff.

[48] J. Bennett et al., "Current State of Automated Legal Advice Tools," University of Melbourne Networked Society Institute Discussion Paper 1/2018 (April 2018) at 16.

consumer."[49] Accordingly, printed legal materials, such as directions and how-to manuals, are generally not considered legal advice. The same applies to general instructions on how to file a lawsuit or explaining court requirements for documents requesting relief.[50] A non-lawyer may also publish and sell legal sample forms or DIY legal kits and provide general instructions for filling out forms, as long as no advice is given.[51]

Legal advice, on the other hand, is tailored to the individual circumstances and needs of the consumer. Typically, legal advice involves analysis of a set of facts and advising a person to take a specific course of action based on the applicable law. Examples of legal advice include (1) selecting, drafting, or completing legal forms, documents or agreements tailored to a person's particular situation; (2) representing a person before a court; (3) negotiating legal rights on behalf of a person; and (4) predicting the outcome of a legal dispute.[52]

Legal technology is disrupting these boundaries. The more sophisticated LT applications become, the more difficult it is to draw a sharp line between legal information and advice, between standardized and tailored forms of communication, and between products and services. As LT companies are increasingly likely to integrate AI-powered and other smart decision-making tools into their services, it becomes more and more likely that this may begin to cross into the territory of giving legal advice. In view of these developments, state bar associations and regulators all over the world have filed actions against LT companies for the "unauthorized practice of law."

11.3.3 Contract Generators as Unauthorized Practice of Law?

A good example of this is LegalZoom,[53] a leading legal document service in the United States, which provides customers with downloadable forms and internet-mediated walk-throughs of questionnaires and flow charts related to their legal problems. Although LegalZoom does not claim to be offering its users a lawyer, but instead "legal information" as a sophisticated series of forms and queries,[54] their business model led to the widespread concern that they engage in the unauthorized practice of law.[55] Whereas some US courts ruled that this was indeed the case,[56] other courts found that LegalZoom does not engage in the unauthorized practice of law.[57]

---

[49] J. Giddings and M. Robertson, "Informed Litigants with Nowhere to Go: Self-Help Legal Aid Services in Australia" (2001) 26(4) *Alternative Law Journal* 184.

[50] Cf. Judicial Council of California, "Legal Advice vs. Legal Information" (2003), www.courts.ca.gov/documents/mayihelpyou.pdf.

[51] D. A. Denckla, "Nonlawyers and the Unauthorized Practice of Law: An Overview of the Legal and Ethical Parameters" (1999) 67(5) *Fordham Law Review* 2581 2591.

[52] Bennett et al., n. 48 at 15.

[53] LegalZoom, www.legalzoom.com (accessed June 9, 2020).

[54] See L. Moxley, "Note, Zooming Past the Monopoly: A Consumer Rights Approach to Reforming the Lawyer's Monopoly and Improving Access to Justice" (2015) 9(2) *Harvard Law & Policy Review* 553 553–554; see also C. J. Lanctot, "Does Legalzoom Have First Amendment Rights? Some Thoughts about Freedom of Speech and the Unauthorized Practice of Law" (2011) 20(2) *Temple Political & Civil Rights Law Review* 255 257.

[55] See E. McClure, "LegalZoom and Online Legal Service Providers: Is the Development and Sale of Interactive Questionnaires That Generate Legal Documents the Unauthorized Practice of Law?"(2017) 105(3) *Kentucky Law Journal* article 5, https://uknowledge.uky.edu/klj/vol105/iss3/5 (accessed June 9, 2020); T. Spahn, "Is Your Artificial Intelligence Guilty of the Unauthorized Practice of Law? (2018) 24(4) *Richmond Journal of Law & Technology* 1.

[56] *Janson v. LegalZoom.com Inc* 802 F. Supp. 2d 1053, 1065 (W.D. Mo. 2011). LegalZoom settled that case; see Martin Bricketto, "LegalZoom Settles with Class over Legal Service Fees," Law360 (August 22, 2011), www.law360.com/articles/266603/legalzoom-settles-with-class-over-legal-service-fees; https://perma.cc/L9MV-586Z.

[57] *Medlock v. LegalZoom.com Inc* 2012-208067, 2013 S.C. LEXIS 362, 26–27 (S.C. 2013).

Similar developments can be observed elsewhere, for example, in Germany, where the Regional Court of Cologne[58] banned smartlaw,[59] an online contract/document generator that guides the user through a series of interview questions to customize a contract based on different templates. According to the Regional Court of Cologne, when drafting legally compliant contracts, it is usually necessary to clarify the relevant facts in cooperation with the client. As such a task cannot be provided by a computer, and so the court held that smartlaw engaged in unauthorized practice of law. Although this ruling was recently reversed by the Hamburg Higher Regional Court,[60] the legal dispute is – at the time of writing – ongoing.[61]

The above-mentioned examples nicely demonstrate that LT creates a set of new questions and challenges for regulators: At what point does LT move from information to advice? Does the distinction between (unregulated) information and (regulated) legal advice make sense at all? How can we justify the current regulatory monopoly of lawyers over legal advice in a technology-driven world?

11.3.4 Risks from Unregulated LT Providers

Whereas the application of legal services regulation to LT services clearly bears risks for innovation, the emergence of ever more sophisticated LT tools could also lead, on the other hand, to the growth of a large unregulated market. This is especially true for countries in which LT escapes the current professional regulation.[62]

Should this be the case, there are no longer minimum deontological standards regarding ethics, fairness, or quality, or rules concerning conflict of interest, mandatory insurance policies for LT providers, redress to the bar association, and much more.

Hence, the following observations focus on the question of to what extent existing EU consumer law can help to protect consumers from the particular risks of LT products/services.

11.4 EU CONSUMER LAW AND LT

11.4.1 Regulation of Consumer Law in the EU

Over the past thirty-five years, the EU has enacted a vast number of directives in order to protect the consumer,[63] who is commonly defined as a natural person acting for purposes that are outside his or her business, commercial, or trade activity.[64] Many directives establish the

---

[58] Landgericht Köln, judgment of 8 October 2019, 33 O 35/19, ECLI:DE:LGK:2019:1008.33O35.19.00.
[59] SmartLaw, www.smartlaw.com (accessed June 9, 2020).
[60] OLG Köln, judgment of 19 June 2020, 6 U 263/19, ECLI:DE:OLGK:2020:0619.6U263.19.00.
[61] The OLG Köln allowed an appeal to the Federal Court of Justice (BGH).
[62] The Temple report highlights that this risk is especially present in England and Wales, because the Legal Services Regulation (1) does not regard LT as special legal service, (2) does not directly apply to the technologies that providers use, or to the third parties who create those technologies (platforms!), and (3) does not apply to foreign legal services; Temple, n. 39 at 6ff., https://ssrn.com/abstract_id=3616343.
[63] On development of EU Consumer law, cf. Ebers, n. 34 at 737 ff.; G. Howells and T. Wilhelmsson, *EC Consumer Law* (Aldershot: Routledge, 1997) 9 ff.; J. Stuyck, "European Consumer Law after the Treaty of Amsterdam: Consumer Policy in or beyond the Internal Market?" (2000) *Common Market Law Review* 367 377 ff.; S. Weatherill, *EU Consumer Law and Policy*, 2nd ed. (Cheltenham: Elgar, 2005) 1 ff.
[64] For an overview of the various definitions of "consumer" in EU directives and the respective case law, cf. M. Ebers "The Notion of 'Consumer,'" in H. Schulte-Nölke, C. Twigg-Flesner and M. Ebers (eds.), *EC Consumer Law Compendium. The Consumer Acquis and its transposition in the Member States* (München: Sellier European Law Publishers, 2008) 453 ff.

precontractual duties of the business – by prohibiting unfair commercial practices, such as misleading advertisements or by establishing information duties – in order to allow the consumer to make an informed decision before concluding a contract. Other directives aim to protect consumers once a contract has been concluded by giving them certain *contractual rights* vis-à-vis the business as well as control mechanisms to ensure material *fairness ex post*, especially by providing a mechanism for reviewing unfair contract terms. Additionally, EU consumer law directives empower consumers and qualified entities (consumer agencies and consumer organizations) to *enforce* consumer rights. The "New Deal for Consumers"[65] aims to strengthen the enforcement mechanisms even further.[66]

With the recently adopted directives on digital contracts,[67] the European legislator has taken additional steps to adapt consumer law to the digital age by providing a *new legal framework* for digital content and services across EU borders.[68] Yet there are no special rules for the protection of consumers using LT products and services, which is completely in line with the principle of technology neutrality.[69]

Sections 11.4.2–11.4.8 analyze whether the existing EU instruments provide consumers with sufficient protection in the use of LT applications. The following directives are of particular relevance to LT: Unfair Commercial Practices Directive (UCPD) 2005/29,[70] E-Commerce Directive (ECD) 2000/31, Consumer Rights Directive (CRD) 2011/83,[71] Unfair Contract Terms Directive (UCTD) 93/13,[72] and Digital Content Directive (DCD) 2019/770.[73]

11.4.2 Applicability of EU Consumer Law to LT

One of the first questions is whether EU consumer law is applicable to LT applications at all. Regarding the personal scope, the CJEU highlighted in several judgments that EU Consumer Law Directives also cover contracts for legal services. In this vein, the CJEU stated in the case *Šiba* for the UCTD 93/13:[74]

---

[65] European Commission, "A New Deal for Consumers," COM (2018) at 183 final.
[66] Cf. S. Tommasi, "The 'New Deal' for Consumers: Towards More Effective Protection?" (2020) *European Review of Private Law* 309.
[67] European Parliament and Council Directive 2019/770/EU of 20 May 2019 on certain aspects concerning contracts for the supply of digital content and digital services (DCD), OJ 2019 no. L136, 22 May 2019; European Parliament and Council Directive 2019/771/EU of 20 May 2019 on certain aspects concerning contracts for the sale of goods (CSD), OJ 2019 no. L136, 22 May 2019.
[68] Cf. thereto D. Staudenmayer, "The Directives on Digital Contracts: First Steps towards the Private Law of the Digital Economy" (2020) *European Review of Private Law* 217.
[69] Cf. recital (10) of the DCD 2019/770: "Both the scope of this Directive and its substantive rules should be technologically neutral and future-proof." Moreover, cf. recital (15) GDPR.
[70] European Parliament and Council Directive 2005/29/EC of 11 May 2005 concerning unfair business-to-consumer commercial practices in the internal market and amending Council Directive 84/450/EEC, Directives 97/7/EC, 98/27/EC and 2002/65/EC of the European Parliament and of the Council and Regulation (EC) No. 2006/2004 of the European Parliament and of the Council ("Unfair Commercial Practices Directive"), OJ 2005 No. L 149, 11 June 2005.
[71] European Parliament and Council Directive 2011/83/EU of 25 October 2011 on consumer rights, amending Council Directive 93/13/EEC and Directive 1999/44/EC of the European Parliament and of the Council and repealing Council Directive 85/577/EEC and Directive 97/7/EC of the European Parliament and of the Council, OJ 2011 No. L 304, 22 November 2011.
[72] Council Directive 93/13/EEC of 5 April 1993 on unfair terms in consumer contracts, OJ 1993 No. L 95, 21 April 1993.
[73] European Parliament and Council Directive 2019/770 of 20 May 2019 on certain aspects concerning contracts for the supply of digital content and digital services, OJ 2019 No. L 136, 22 May 2019.
[74] Case C-537/13 *Šiba* ECLI:EU:C:2015:14 [23–24]. Cf. also case C-421/12 *Commission v. Belgium* ECLI:EU:C:2014:2064: According to the UCPD 2005/29, the notion of "trader" includes "liberal professions."

> As regards contracts for legal services ... there is, as a general rule, some inequality between "client-consumers" and lawyers owing in particular to the asymmetry of information between the parties. Lawyers display a high level of technical knowledge which consumers may not have and the latter therefore may find it difficult to judge the quality of the services provided to them.... Thus, a lawyer who, as in the case in the main proceedings, provides a legal service for a fee, in the course of his professional activities, to a natural person acting for private purposes is a "seller or supplier" within the meaning of Article 2(c) of Directive 93/13.

As a result, there can be no doubt that EU consumer law applies to the relationship between a consumer and an LT company. According to the CJEU, even lawyers can benefit as consumers from the protection rules, provided they are acting for personal purposes.[75] In contrast, if a lawyer or law firm uses LT services for professional purposes, he or she is not protected as a consumer.

Another issue is whether EU consumer law also applies to LT platforms. If a consumer and a business conclude their contract via an online platform, the platform is not usually party to this contract. Rather, in such a "triangular" situation, there are normally three different contractual relationships, that is, between the consumer and the business, the platform and the consumer, and the platform and the business. In such situations, it is unclear whether the legal relationship between the consumer and the platform falls within the scope of the current EU consumer law directives.[76]

Following the reasoning of the CJEU in its judgments *Uber Spain*,[77] *Uber France*,[78] and *Airbnb Ireland*,[79] one might argue that this depends on the degree to which the platform influences the service offered:[80] If the platform restricts itself to mere intermediation (i.e., matchmaking), it will be considered a mere information society service subject to the freedoms contained in ECD 2000/31. If, however, the platform also assumes decisive control over the substantive (legal) service the supply side provides (so that, in other words, the provision of that service is inherently linked to the use of the platform), the platform itself will become subject to the substantive rules governing the service it facilitates.

Finally, the question arises as to whether EU consumer law also applies to contracts that are offered "for free," in the sense that consumers do not pay a monetary price but only provide their personal data. For the ECD 2000/31, the CJEU has clarified in *Papasavvas*[81] and *Mc Fadden*[82] that the information society service ISS does not have to be paid by the recipient of the service (and can be free for him or her) but the service can be paid with income generated by advertisements.

The recently adopted DCD 2019/770 even contains a clarification. According to Art. 3(1), the Directive includes contracts entered for a monetary price as well as contracts in exchange for personal data. The application of the Directive is excluded only when personal data are (1)

---

[75] Case C-110/14 *Costea* ECLI:EU:C:2015:538.
[76] See C. Wendehorst, "Platform Intermediary Services and Duties under the E-Commerce Directive and the Consumer Rights Directive" (2016) *Journal of European Consumer and Market Law* 30; C. Busch et al., "The Rise of the Platform Economy: A New Challenge for EU Consumer Law?" (2016) *Journal of European Consumer and Market Law* 3.
[77] Case C-434/15 *Asociación Profesional Elite Taxi* ECLI:EU:C:2017:981.
[78] Case C-320/16 *Uber France* EU:C:2018:221 [22].
[79] Case C-390/18 *Airbnb Ireland* EU:C:2019:1112 [69].
[80] P. Hacker, "UberPop, UberBlack, and the Regulation of Digital Platforms after the Asociación Profesional Elite Taxi Judgment of the CJEU" (2018) 14(1) *European Review of Contract Law* 80 90.
[81] Case C-291/13 *Papasavvas* EU:C:2014:2209 [29–30].
[82] Case C-484/14 *Tobias McFadden v. Sony Music* EU:C:2016:689 [42–43].

exclusively processed by the trader for the purpose of supplying the digital content or digital service, or (2) for allowing the trader to comply with legal requirements to which the trader is subject, and the trader does not process those data for any other purpose. An almost identical text can now be found in Art. 3(1)(a) CRD 2011/83, as amended by Directive 2019/2161.[83]

11.4.3 Prohibition of Unfair Commercial Practices

The UCPD 2005/29 aims to establish European-wide safeguards against unfair commercial practices that contravene the requirements of professional diligence, mislead consumers, or expose them to aggressive commercial practices.

Applying these criteria to legal services, the Directive provides a high degree of protection. Examples of conduct that could infringe the provisions of the UCPD are:[84] (1) falsely claiming that the provider employs qualified lawyers, (2) creating the impression that the software provides the same service as a lawyer,[85] (3) failing to comply with recognized standards in the legal services industry/code of conduct, (4) failing to deal with complaints, (5) failing to provide consumers with full information on fees and charges, (6) pressuring a consumer to enter into a contract for the supply of a legal service, or (7) intimidating consumers into dropping complaints against the legal service provider.

What are currently missing, however, are safeguards against LT applications that are likely to harm consumers. The UCPD 2005/29 does not take into account the specific risks LT products or services might create, especially regarding access to LT services, transparency standards, quality, fairness, accountability, or redress. While it is true that the general clause of the UCPD with its criteria of "professional diligence"[86] could be concretized for LT, there is currently no guidance as to which "standards of special skill and care," "commensurate with honest market practice" may reasonably be expected.

11.4.4 Information Requirements and the Right of Withdrawal

Similarly, the information obligations and rights of withdrawal foreseen in directives do not contribute significantly to the protection of consumers using LT applications.

Most EU consumer law directives contain only standardized information requirements, in that the business is required to inform the consumer before or after conclusion of a contract in a clear and understandable manner about certain characteristics of the offered good or service, the price, specific rights and duties, and so on. They do not require, though, a consultation or recommendation (advice) that takes into account the informational needs of the individual consumer. Instead, information requirements are based on the fictional model of the average

---

[83] European Parliament and Council Directive 2019/2161 of 27 November 2019 amending Council Directive 93/13/EEC and Directives 98/6/EC, 2005/29/EC and 2011/83/EU of the European Parliament and of the Council as regards the better enforcement and modernization of Union consumer protection rules, OJ 2019 L 328, 18 December 2019.

[84] Cf. Competition & Markets Authority (CMA), n. 40, Appendix E (Overview of the Consumer Law Framework) at E5 ff.

[85] Cf. OLG Köln, judgment of 19 June 2020, 6 U 263/19, ECLI:DE:OLGK:2020:0619.6U263.19.00. In that case, Wolters Kluwer marketed their software smartlaw with terms such as "faster and quicker than a lawyer," "legal documents in lawyer quality." "more individual and safer than any template and chapter than a lawyer," and "legal documents in lawyer quality – in cooperation with our legal experts – all of them experts in their fields" – "we have developed the creation process to mimic the conversation with a lawyer." The court held that such statements are misleading to potential clients.

[86] Art. 5(2)(a), Art. 2(h) UCPD 2005/29.

consumer, who is, in the words of the CJEU, "reasonably well-informed and reasonably observant and circumspect."[87]

Similarly, withdrawal rights in EU consumer law are also standardized instruments applying in typical situations. Like precontractual information duties, withdrawal rights aim at enabling the consumer to make an informed decision for or against a contract.[88] To this end, they override the well-recognized principle of *pacta sunt servanda* by giving consumers the right to terminate an already concluded contract without giving reasons. Consequently, as the BGH ruled in Germany, a consumer-client can withdraw from a contract concluded with a lawyer without giving reasons if this contract was concluded by means of distance communication.[89]

EU consumer law, however, does grant consumers a general right to withdrawal, but only when they need this protection because of the type of contract[90] or because of the circumstances in which the contract was concluded.[91] On the other hand, the concrete circumstances of the individual case are irrelevant.[92] Accordingly, standardized withdrawal rights do not offer any *specific* protection against LT providers.

11.4.5 Quality of Service

Another problem is that EU consumer law does not provide for a quality control of LT products/services. For traditional legal services, the legal services regulation of the respective country usually determines particular lawyers' duties to the court and to clients, such as acting in accordance with the deontological rules and avoiding professional negligence.

Similar standards could follow from consumer law, at least if we assume that the DCD 2019/770 also applies to LT. Art. 3(5)(a) DCD 2019/770 excludes contracts regarding the provision of services other than digital services. Recital (27) DCD 2019/770 cites as examples inter alia legal services. However, as some commentators have pointed out correctly, the delineation criterion should be whether or not the main subject matter of the contract is the provision of professional

---

[87] Case C-210/96 *Gut Springenheide and Tusky* [1998] ECR I-4657 [31]. For details, see M. Ebers, "German Consumer Law 15 Years after the 'Recodification'" in M. Gramunt Fombuena and C. E. Florensa i Tomàs (eds.), *Codificación y Reequilibrio de la Asimetría Negocial* (Madrid: Dykinson, 2017) 151–174. The same benchmark of the average consumer is also used in secondary legislation; see European Parliament and Council Directive 2005/29/EC of 11 May 2005 on unfair business-to-consumer commercial practices in the internal market (UCPD), OJ 2005 No. L149/22, 11 June 2005, recital (18), and, thereto, case C-122/10 *Ving Sverige* ECLI:EU:C:2011:299, [2011] ECR I-3903 and case C-611/14 *Canal Digital Danmark* ECLI:EU:C:2016:800.
[88] Cf. Ebers, n. 34 at 856 ff.; M. Loos, "The Case for a Uniform and Efficient Right of Withdrawal from Consumer Contracts in European Contract Law" (2007) *Zeitschrift für Europäisches Privatrecht* 5.
[89] BGH, 23.11.17, IX ZR 204/16.
[90] This is the case with Article 14-15 of the Directive on credit agreements for consumers, European Parliament and Council Directive 2008/48/EC, OJ 2008 No. L133; Article 6-8 of the Directive on protection of consumers in respect of certain aspects of timeshare, European Parliament and Council Directive 2008/122/EC, OJ 2008 No. L33; Article 186 of the Directive on the taking-up and pursuit of the business of Insurance and Reinsurance (Solvency II) (formerly: Life Assurance Directive 2002/83), European Parliament and Council Directive 2009/138/EC, OJ 2009 No. L335. Cf. also case C-209/12 *Endress* ECLI:EU:C:2013:864 [29]: "[A]s insurance contracts are legally complex financial products, capable of differing considerably depending on the insurer offering those products and of involving significant and potentially very long-term financial commitments, the policy-holder is at a disadvantage vis-à-vis the insurer."
[91] This is the case with off premises and distance contracts; cf. Article 9 of the Directive on consumer rights, European Parliament and Council Directive 2011/83/EU, OJ 2011 No. L304; Art. 6-7 of the Directive concerning the distance marketing of consumer financial services, European Parliament and Council Directive 2002/65/EC, OJ 2002 No. L271.
[92] Cf. case C-423/97 *Travel Vac* [1999] ECR I-2195 [43]; case C-229/04 *Crailsheimer Volksbank* [2005] ECR I-9273 [44].

services that are performed personally by the trader as a human being.[93] Consequently, we might assume that any kind of LT service that is not provided only by a human being is covered, if provided to a consumer on a contractual basis.[94] On the basis of this interpretation, LT applications would have to meet both the subjective and objective requirements for conformity, in particular, the requirement that digital content or digital service shall "be fit for the purposes for which digital content or digital services of the same type would normally be used, taking into account, where applicable, any existing Union and national law, technical standards or, in the absence of such technical standards, applicable sector-specific industry codes of conduct" (Art. 8 (1)(a) DCD 2019/770).

It is far from clear, however, how these standards are to be put into practice: Who is translating the law into code that decides the output of advice? Do the persons have to be legally trained? Who assesses whether the law is accurately translated into code? Who ensures that the law contained within the LT application incorporates the latest legal developments and is up-to-date?

Additional questions arise with regard to LT application based on data-driven knowledge and the previously mentioned black box problem, that is, that automated legal decisions or predictions do not provide any reason or explanation for this decision or prediction.[95] The ability to give reasons is crucial for sophisticated advice by human lawyers. Does an LT company or a lawyer using LT applications need to understand how that technology works? How can we trace legal reasoning logic? What (legal) data has been considered and why? How did learning occur and were there any biases? What values are encoded into the logic? What conscious or unconscious assumptions have been made that are not explained?

For the time being, all of these questions remain unanswered. Hence, consumers are not protected from poor quality in services delivered by LT applications.

11.4.6 Legal Ethics and Fairness

Further issues emerge with regard to ethical standards and the fairness of contracts concluded with LT companies. Whereas lawyers are subject to legal ethics regulations (including, for example, the duty to act in the best interest of the client, the duty of confidentiality and to prevent legal conflict of interests), the same does not apply to services provided by regular companies.[96] Arguably, if the activity of LT companies is not regarded as a regulated legal service, they are not subjected to such ethical duties to their users.

In this vein, many LT companies include in their contract terms far-reaching disclaimers. LegalZoom, for instance, highlights in its general terms and conditions[97] that they are not a law firm and may not perform services performed by an attorney, stating moreover: "the legal information contained on the Site and Applications is not legal advice and is not guaranteed to be correct, complete or up-to-date .... This Site and Applications are not intended to create any attorney-client relationship, and your use of LegalZoom does not and will not create an attorney-client relationship between you and LegalZoom." Consequently, LegalZoom

---

[93] K. Sein and G. Spindler, "The New Directive on Contracts for the Supply of Digital Content and Digital Services – Scope of Application and Trader's Obligation to Supply – Part 1" (2019) *European Review of Contract Law* 257 265ff.
[94] Ibid. at 266. Differently, Navas, n. 9 at 84 ff.
[95] Cf. Bennett et al., n. 48 at 33.
[96] S. Fina, I. Ng, and R. Vogl, "Perspectives on the Growth of DIY Legal Services in the European Union" (2018) *Journal of European Consumer and Market Law* 241 241–242.
[97] LegalZoom, www.legalzoom.com/legal/general-terms/terms-of-use (accessed June 9, 2020).

"expressly disclaims all warranties of any kind, whether express or implied." Similarly, DoNotPay emphasizes in their terms[98] that the information they provide does not constitute legal advice and that they "do not review any information you provide us for legal accuracy or sufficiency, draw legal conclusions, provide opinions about your selection of forms, or apply the law to the facts of your situation." Therefore, DoNotPay "assumes no liability for any errors or omissions in the information contained in the Service and expressly disclaims any responsibility to update this information."

Whether such disclaimers can be regarded as "unfair" and "nonbinding" under the UCTD 93/13 is currently unclear. First, one might doubt whether such clauses can be controlled at all. Art. 4(2) UCTD 93/13 excludes contract terms from the fairness test if they define the "main subject-matter of the contract." LT companies could therefore argue that the decision of whether they offer legal advice belongs to the "very essence of the contractual relationship,"[99] which cannot be reviewed. Yet such a disclaimer only escapes the fairness test if it is made in plain and intelligible language.[100] In other words, clauses excluding legal advice are still subject to control, if the consumer gains the impression – based on the factual circumstances, taking into account advertisements – that the LT application is a DIY product substituting for a human lawyer.

In addition, LT companies can only rely on Art. 4(2) UCTD 93/13 to the extent that they exclude (in plain and intelligible language) legal *advice*. In contrast, clauses restricting liability for legal *information* should always be subject to control: Arguably, offering LT services to consumers necessarily implies that the company will provide consumers at least with basic legal information. Clauses restricting the liability for incorrect information are therefore not defining, but rather limiting the essential obligations of the contract.

A quite different question is under which conditions disclaimers can be considered unfair within the meaning of Art. 3 and Annex I of the UCTD 93/13. Clauses limiting or excluding liability are not per se unfair under EU law. According to Annex I, paragraph 1(b) UCTD 93/13, such clauses are only potentially unfair if they "inappropriately" exclude or limit the legal rights of the consumer. Consequently, the question arises as to when exactly such an exclusion or limitation of liability should be regarded as "inappropriate." This may depend largely on the applicable national law. On the other hand, it might also be that the CJEU establishes the respective criteria in the future. While the Court of Justice emphasized in earlier rulings that the list contained in the Annex to the directive is only of "indicative and illustrative value,"[101] the Court has underlined since the *Invitel* case[102] that the Annex is "an essential element on which the competent court may base its assessment." At the same time the CJEU has gradually specified, in a number of cases, the abstract criteria listed in the Annex for reviewing whether a term is unfair.[103]

---

[98] DoNotPay, https://donotpay.com/learn/terms-of-service-and-privacy-policy (accessed June 9, 2020).
[99] Cf. Case C-143/13 *Matei* ECLI:EU:C:2015:127 [54].
[100] Cf. thereto case C-96/14 *Van Hove* ECLI:EU:C:2015:262 [40–50].
[101] Case C-478/99 *Commission v. Sweden* ECLI:EU:C:2002:281, [2002] ECR I-4147 [22].
[102] Case C-472/10 *Invitel Távközlési* ECLI:EU:C:2012:242 [26]; confirmed by case C-488/11 *Asbeek Brusse and de Man Garabito* ECLI:EU:C:2013:341 [55]; case C-342/13 *Sebestyén* ECLI:EU:C:2014:1857 [32]. In Case C-143/13 *Matei* ECLI:EU:C:2015:127 [60] the Court refers to the Annex even as a "grey list."
[103] For more detail, cf. Ebers, n. 34 at 887 ff.; H.-W. Micklitz and N. Reich, "The Court and the Sleeping Beauty: The Rival of the Unfair Contract Terms Directive (UCTD)" (2014) 51 *Common Market Law Review* 771 789 (judge-made "grey list").

Accordingly, the CJEU could develop Europe-wide fairness requirements for LT applications. However, even such case law would not provide consumers with a level of protection comparable to that of traditional legal services.

11.4.7 *Further Gaps in Consumer Protection*

In addition to the points raised above, there are a number of other gaps in protection in the event that LT are not covered by the professional rules.

First of all, EU consumer law does not provide for any claims for damages.[104] In contrast, client-consumers of regular legal services provided by a human lawyer have additional redress options that go beyond civil law. If a client feels that the lawyer has breached his or her ethical duties, the client can lodge a formal complaint with the responsible bar association. Disciplinary tribunals of the bar associations may then impose penalties against lawyers, depending on the extent of their breach.

Second, according to legal services regulations, practicing lawyers are normally required to take out professional indemnity insurance. Thus, if there is professional negligence, both lawyers and clients are protected. LT companies, on the other hand, are not required to take out such insurance if they provide services that are outside the legal services regulation.

Third, EU consumer law does not provide for effective protection in relation to intelligent systems. The AI-based processing of consumer data raises new problems. The use of AI by companies may introduce further imbalances between traders and consumers, limit the autonomy of consumers and their ability to make an informed choice, and lead to discriminatory treatment of consumers.[105] At present, none of these problems has been solved – either at a European or national level.

Finally, yet importantly, EU consumer law does not foresee any special rules for (legal) chatbots.[106] EU consumer law is built on a text-based paradigm. Thus, for example, our current understanding of precontractual duties is based on the presumption that in order to be informed, the consumer should rather read, not listen to, the information. Chatbots, on the other hand, present novel challenges to consumer law. Spoken language is complicated to regulate[107] because it is ambiguous and neither race nor gender neutral because it reveals significant amounts of information about the person through its tone, choice of words, and semantic constructs.

11.4.8 *Summary*

Insofar as LT applications are not subject to the rules that apply to lawyers, consumers enjoy only limited protection. EU consumer law is not sufficiently equipped to deal with the specific problems of LT, especially with regard to access to justice, choice and information, quality, fairness, redress, and representation.

---

[104] In the past, there have been repeated attempts to enshrine a claim for damages in EU Consumer law directives. However, in view of the differences in the legal systems of the member states, no consensus could and cannot be reached at European level.

[105] Ebers, n. 32 at 70 ff.; G. Sartor, "New Aspects and Challenges in Consumer Protection: Digital Services and Artificial Intelligence," study requested by the IMCO committee of the European Parliament PE 648.790 (April 2020) at 24 ff.

[106] K. Sein, "Concluding Consumer Contracts via Smart Assistants: Mission Impossible under European Consumer Law?" (2018) *Journal of European Consumer and Market Law* 179.

[107] Cf. B. Subirana, R. Bivings, and S. Sarma, "Wake Neutrality of Artificial Intelligence Devices" in Ebers and Navas (eds.), n. 32 at 235–268.

A fundamental problem of EU consumer law is the standardization and typification of consumer protection instruments, which is reflected, in particular, in the (static) benchmark of the average consumer,[108] standardized information duties, and standardized rights of withdrawal. In the past, this regulatory approach made total sense: products and services that are offered in a standardized way for the purposes of mass consumption require, at the end of the day, a standardized response from law. With the spread of data-driven smart products and services, however, this is changing. AI-driven big data profiling techniques give companies the opportunity to gain superior knowledge about customers' personal circumstances, behavioral patterns, and personality, including future preferences.

The more companies target consumers with individual products and services, the more it becomes apparent that the current one-size-fits-all approach based on typification does not fit in the digital economy. Hence, modern consumer law should adapt to new market realities by providing flexible, tailor-made protection instruments, rather than standardized ones.[109]

11.5 EU DATA PROTECTION LAW AND LT

11.5.1 Legal Services Regulation and Data Protection Law

If LT is regarded as a legal service that is subject to the legal services regulation, the consumer-client benefits from extensive data protection, as the legal professional privilege protects all communications between the professional legal adviser and his or her clients from being disclosed without the permission of the client.

If, on the other hand, LT does not fall under this regime, consumers lose this kind of protection. The consumer would only be protected by data protection law, that is, in Europe by the General Data Protection Regulation 2016/679 (GDPR) and the Law Enforcement Directive 2016/618. In that case, the consumer would still be protected vis-à-vis private companies (particularly from using the information for other purposes). However, the consumer would lose his or her protection vis-à-vis the state because law-enforcement authorities would presumably be able to access the submitted information with a search warrant.[110]

11.5.2 LT and Data Protection under the GDPR

Insofar as personal data is involved, LT must be developed and deployed in conformity with the GDPR.[111] This is especially relevant for AI systems based on data-learned knowledge. As most of the data that drives AI systems is either directly linked to a person, or, if anonymized, at least identifiable by an algorithm,[112] the GDPR applies regularly both when AI is under development

---

[108] Critically, B. Duivenvoorde, "The Protection of Vulnerable Consumers under the Unfair Commercial Practices Directive" (2013) 2 *Journal of European Consumer and Market Law* 69. See also D. Leczykiewicz and S. Weatherhill (eds.), *The Images of the Consumer in EU Law* (Oxford: Hart Publishing, 2018).

[109] A. Porat and L. J. Strahilevitz, "Personalizing Default Rules and Disclosure with Big Data" (2014) 112 *Michigan Law Review* 1417; O. Ben-Shahar and A. Porat, "Personalizing Negligence Law" (2016) 91(3) *NYU Law Review* 627; P. Hacker, "Personalizing EU Private Law: From Disclosures to Nudges and Mandates" (2017) 25(3) *European Review of Private Law* 651. Moreover, see a special issue on "Personalized Law" (2019) 86(2) *University of Chicago Law Review*.

[110] Semple, n. 39 at 9.

[111] The GDPR applies to all personal data, meaning any information relating to an identified or identifiable natural person, Article 4(1) GDPR.

[112] In the era of big data, anonymous information can be de-anonymized by employing related and unrelated data about a person; S. Barocas and H. Nissenbaum, "Big Data's End Run around Anonymity and Consent" in Julia Lane et al.

(since it governs the collection and use of data in generating ML models) and also when it is used to analyze, predict, or reach decisions (because, also in that case, the system usually needs to process a consumer/data subject's personal data to apply the learned ML model and its prediction to a particular case).

For both stages, the training phase and the deployment phase, the GDPR provides specific safeguards – in particular, that personal data must be processed lawfully, fairly, and in a transparent manner (Art. 5(1)(a) GDPR), based on one of the legitimate grounds provided in Art. 6 GDPR. Additionally, the GDPR gives data subjects corresponding rights to information and explanation (Arts. 13–15), to rectify (Art. 16), erase (Art. 17), object to (Art. 21), or port (Art. 20) personal data.

The crucial question is, however, whether data protection law also applies to the ML model itself or at least to the data inferred from this model. Ultimately, it is the learned algorithmic model and the information created through deduction or reasoning that largely determines the outcome and quality of automated legal analyses and also the ability to understand the decision process itself.

If data protection law were applicable to the model itself or at least to the inferred data, this would trigger far-reaching data protection rights. In particular, data subjects would have rights to information and explanation, rectification and erasure, and much more.

This, at least, seems to be the position of the Article 29 Working Party (WP29).[113] According to WP29, where there is automated inference (profiling), data subjects have certain rights (especially the right to assess, correct, and erase) not only regarding the input data, but also regarding the (final or intermediate) conclusions automatically inferred from such data. Thus, WP29 appears to assume that data protection law gives data subjects not only control over how their data is collected and processed, but also how it is evaluated.

11.5.3 Limits of the GDPR

On closer examination, however, it is unlikely that the CJEU will follow this view.

First of all, it should be borne in mind that the ML model itself usually does not contain personal data, but only information about groups and classes of persons. The learned algorithmic model normally only links possible combinations of possible input values (predictors) to a corresponding likelihood of default (target). Since the correlations embedded in the algorithmic model apply to all individuals sharing similar characteristics, they cannot be seen as personal data.[114]

(eds.), *Privacy, Big Data and the Public Good* (Cambridge: Cambridge University Press, 2014) 49 ff.; L. Floridi, *The 4th Revolution* (New York: Oxford University Press, 2014) 110; I. S. Rubinstein and W. Hartzog, "Anonymization and Risk" (2016) 91(2) *Washington Law Review* 703 710.

[113] Article 29 Data Protection Working Party, "Guidelines on Automated Individual Decision-Making and Profiling for the Purposes of Regulation 2016/679" (2018) 17/EN WP 251rev.01 at 17–18, http://ec.europa.eu/newsroom/article29/document.cfm?doc_id=49826. Similarly, G. Sartor, "The Impact of the General Data Protection Regulation on Artificial Intelligence," study at the request of the Panel for the Future of Science and Technology (STOA) of the European Parliament PE 641.521(2000) at 6, 38.

[114] Models contain personal data only in exceptional cases. On the one hand, certain types of models, such as support vector machines (SVMs), might contain some key examples from the training data in order to help distinguish between new examples during deployment. In such cases, somewhere in the internal logic of the model, there will be a small set of individual examples; R. Bins, "Enabling Access, Erasure, and Rectification Rights in AI systems," ICO-Blog (October 15, 2019), https://ico.org.uk/about-the-ico/news-and-events/ai-blog-enabling-access-erasure-and-rectification-rights-in-ai-systems (accessed June 9, 2020). On the other hand, new forms of cyber attack might be able to reconstruct training data (or information about who was in the training set) in certain cases from the model; cf., in

Moreover, the CJEU has made it clear in a number of cases that data protection law is not intended to ensure the accuracy of decisions and the decision-making process.[115]

In joint cases C-141/12 and C-372/12,[116] the CJEU had to decide whether a third-country national who applied unsuccessfully for a residence permit has the right – under Art. 12 Data Protection Directive 95/46/EC – to access the legal analysis (minutes) explaining the reason for that administrative decision. The CJEU denied such a right on two grounds. First, the Court highlighted that the legal analysis, although it may contain personal data, does not in itself constitute personal data within the meaning of Art. 2(a) of Directive 95/46, because "such a legal analysis is not information relating to the applicant for a residence permit, but at most, in so far as it is not limited to a purely abstract interpretation of the law, is information about the assessment and application by the competent authority of that law to the applicant's situation."[117] Additionally, the CJEU pointed out that the purpose of data protection law is not to assess the accuracy of decision-making processes involving personal data. According to the CJEU, extending the right of access to the legal analysis itself would not "serve the directive's purpose of guaranteeing the protection of the applicant's right to privacy with regard to the processing of data relating to him, but would serve the purpose of guaranteeing him a right of access to administrative documents, which is not however covered by Directive 95/46."[118]

This view was later confirmed by the CJEU in case C-434/16. In that case, an exam candidate (Mr. Nowak) sought to exercise his right of access and "correction" in relation to his marked exam script. Although the CJEU determined this time that both the exam script and comments of the assessor were the candidate's personal data,[119] thereby contradicting the aforementioned judgment, the Court argued again that data subjects have only limited rights over assessments. According to the CJEU, the scope of the rights attached to personal data has to be interpreted both in line with the aims of data protection law and in the light of the purpose for which data was collected.[120] In the Court's view, this implies that the Data Protection Directive does not give exam candidates the right to rectify, a posteriori, answers that are incorrect.[121] The same applies to the comments and the exam questions.

Both rulings demonstrate the limited scope of data protection law when it comes to legal analysis. According to the CJEU, only the personal data contained or used within the legal analysis is subject to EU data protection rights. The legal analysis itself, in contrast, is not part of data protection rights.

---

particular, M. Veale, R. Binns, and L. Edwards, "Algorithms That Remember: Model Inversion Attacks and Data Protection Law" (2018) 376 (2133) *Philosophical Transactions of the Royal Society A*, http://dx.doi.org/10.1098/rsta.2018.0083 (accessed June 9, 2020).

[115] Cf. also the case law analysis by E. Brouwer and F. Zuiderveen Borgesius, "Access to Personal Data and the Right to Good Governance during Asylum Procedures after the CJEU's YS and M and S judgment (C-141/12 and C-372/12)" (2015) 17(2–3) *European Journal of Migration and Law* 259; S. Wachter and B. Mittelstadt, "A Right to Reasonable Inferences: Re-thinking Data Protection Law in the Age of Big Data and AI" (2019) 2 *Columbia Business Law Review* 494 521 ff.

[116] Joined cases C-141/12 and C-372/12 *YS and M and S* ECLI:EU:C:2014:2081.

[117] Ibid. at 2081 [40].

[118] Ibid. at 2081 [46].

[119] Case C-434/16 *Peter Novak* ECLI:EU:C:2017:994 [45].

[120] Case C-434/16 *Peter Novak* ECLI:EU:C:2017:994 [53].

[121] Case C-434/16 *Peter Novak* ECLI:EU:C:2017:994 [52].

11.5.4 Summary

EU data protection law grants consumers only limited protection with regard to LT applications. While it is true that data subjects have control over how their personal data is collected and processed, the CJEU has made clear that they have very little control over how this information is evaluated.

Ultimately, this reflects the different purposes of consumer law and data protection law. Whereas consumer law deals with fair contracting, data protection law is not so much concerned with fair results, but mainly with fair processing.[122]

11.6 OUTLOOK

11.6.1 Unresolved Questions

The previous analysis shows that there is as yet no sound legal framework for LT services – neither in Europe nor beyond. LT products challenge the legal services regulations in many jurisdictions. As technology enables new ways to deliver services and new business models, many questions arise:

- Is the scope of legal services regulation still right, in terms of what (and who) is being regulated?
- To what extent (if at all) is the distinction between (unregulated) legal information and (regulated) legal advice still useful?
- Is there a case for bringing "legal information" substantively into legal services regulation? Or, should LT generally be considered a service not covered by this kind of regulation?
- Does LT alter the ultimate purpose of legal services regulation? Are the objectives of this regulation still valid?
- Are the right rules in place, in the right form?
- Is there too much regulation of certain forms of legal service and under-regulation of others?
- How far can we stretch existing rules to fit new forms of delivery?
- Should (EU) consumer law be reformed to address the risks identified in the use of LT services (e.g., access to justice, choice and information, quality, fairness, redress and representation)?

11.6.2 Current Approaches of Regulators

Legal regulators around the world respond to these challenges in very different ways. Following the Hook report,[123] four different approaches can be observed.

"Wait and See": At present, regulators in many countries are not taking any special measures at all. This might be because the market for LT is still relatively small, or because regulators have only limited financial/human resources and lack the expertise to take effective action, or because they want to observe how the LT market develops.

---

[122] N. Helberger et al., "The Perfect Match? A Closer Look at the Relationship between EU Consumer Law and Data Protection Law" (2017) 54(5) *Common Market Law Review* 1427.
[123] Hook, n. 4 at 8.

Prohibition of LT: In other countries there is a tendency to subject LT companies to strict legal services regulation and to regard their activity as unauthorized practice of law or an ethics violation. This is especially the case in the United States as well as in Germany, where bar associations have been trying in many instances to take legal action against LT companies. In some cases, this has led LT companies to close down completely or to relaunch their services as law firms.[124]

Adaptation of LT: A third approach from regulators has been to seek ways of accommodating LT into existing rules. A classic example of this approach is the partnership between several US state bar associations, the American Bar Association, and the tech company Cloudlawyers, which aims to bring search engines into conformity with the ethical rules.[125]

Facilitating LT: The last category covers countries and/or regulators that have tried to facilitate the adoption of technology in the legal sector, especially by changing professional codes of conduct, by providing support and guidance to LT companies, by initiating dialog around the rules for business in the sector, or by setting up special task forces in order to identify possible regulatory changes to enhance LT services.[126]

11.6.3 Alternative Approaches: Regulatory Sandboxes

An alternative approach, which deserves special attention, is the introduction of regulatory sandboxes, which have emerged in recent years as ways of testing new types of financial services.[127] According to common definitions, a regulatory sandbox is a framework set up by a regulator that allows companies to test innovative business models or offer products or services in a controlled environment under a regulator's supervision.

Sandbox models are discussed not only for financial services, but also for LT.[128]

Following this approach, the United Kingdom announced in May 2020 that it was launching a LawTech Sandbox that will be delivered in collaboration with the Solicitors Regulatory Authority, the Legal Services Board, the Information Commissioner's Office, and the Ministry of Justice.[129] The Lawtech Sandbox will include (1) a Regulatory Response Unit bringing together relevant regulators and policymakers, (2) a Business Unit made up of experts and leaders from the business and legal community, and (3) an Ethics Unit to provide applied ethics input.

Comparable regulatory approaches also exist elsewhere. In May 2020, the State Bar of California's board of trustees supported forming a sandbox working group that will examine

---

[124] This happened, for example, with Avvo, a US-based legal marketplace, directory, and question and answer forum that connects individuals with lawyers. Between 2016 and 2018, the bar associations of eight US states issued ethics opinions that determined that participation by lawyers in the online legal services provider Avvo's services represented an ethics violation.

[125] See thereto Hook, n. 4 at 35, also with more examples.

[126] Ibid. at 36 ff.

[127] Cf. UK Financial Conduct Authority, "Regulatory Sandbox Lessons Learned" (2017), www.fca.org.uk/publications/research/regulatory-sandbox-lessons-learned-report (accessed June 14, 2020); D. Krimphove and K. Rohwetter, "Regulatory Sandbox – Sandkastenspiele auch für Deutschland? Zur Möglichkeit einer 'vereinfachten' aufsichtsrechtlichen Prüfung von FinTechs" (2018) *Bank- und Kapitalmarktrecht 494*.

[128] J. Gabriel Jiménez and M. Hagan, "A Regulatory Sandbox for the Industry of Law," *Stanford Law School Legal Design Lab White Paper* (2019), www-cdn.law.stanford.edu/wpcontent/uploads/2019/04/Regulatory-Sandbox-for-the-Industry-of-Law.pdf.

[129] LawtechUK collaborative initiative, https://technation.io/lawtechuk-vision/#the-lawtech-sandbox (accessed June 14, 2020).

permitting non-lawyer ownership of law firms and fee-sharing, among other rule changes.[130] In the same vein, Utah also announced proposals that could pave the way for non-lawyers to own or invest in law firms.[131]

11.6.4 The Future (European) Legal Framework

The discussion about the possible (European) legal framework is still in its initial phase. Applying the existing rules to LT services can either lead to innovation-hostile overregulation or to consumer-hostile under-regulation. Hence, reform proposals should seek to strike the right balance between innovation and protection, between the competing interests of consumers, the legal market, the legal profession, and access to justice.

One possibility to deal with the manifold problems discussed above is to *harmonize legal services regulations* at the European level. Such harmonization is, however, quite unlikely to happen any time soon. The existing differences between legal systems, legal education, and legal cultures are simply too great for a compromise to be reached.

Therefore, it is first of all up to the member states to start evaluating their legal services regulations, taking into account three aspects particularly:[132]

- Consistency: Is it appropriate to have different regimes for automated legal information on the one hand and legal advice on the other? Or should both be subject to the same regulation? What special rules should apply to LT companies?
- Purpose: Should future LT regulation enable access to lawyers (by protecting their monopoly) or rather provide access to law (by opening markets for tech companies)?
- Reach: Which matters should be regulated and to what extent? In particular: How can we ensure that law is accurately and transparently translated into code?

Another option at the European level is the *revision of the existing EU consumer law*. For the time being, though, the European Commission is focusing more on the regulation of AI systems rather than on LT. The White Paper on AI,[133] published in February 2020, does not mention LT applications at all. Instead, the Commission envisages new legislation specifically for so-called high-risk AI systems. LT applications would not necessarily fall within this category. According to the White Paper, applications should be regarded as "high risk" only if both the sector and the intended use involve significant risks.[134] This is not automatically the case with LT applications. The White Paper considers as "high-risk sector" only "parts of the public sector" such as the "judiciary."[135] Accordingly, LT services that are deployed out of court vis-à-vis consumers would not be covered. Apart from this, the Commission intends to develop new legislation solely for self-learning AI systems.[136] LT applications, however, can also be built on completely different

---

[130] L. Moran, "California Bar Gives Approval to Broad Aandbox Proposal," Abajournal (May 15, 2020), www.abajournal.com/news/article/california-bar-gives-approval-to-broad-sandbox-proposal (accessed June 15, 2020).
[131] L. Moran, "Utah's High Court Proposes Nonlawyer Ownership of Law Firms and Wide-Ranging Reforms," Abajournal (April 27, 2020), www.abajournal.com/news/article/utahs-high-court-proposes-wide-ranging-legal-industry-reforms (accessed June 15, 2020).
[132] Cf. in this sense also Bennett et al., n. 48 at 35.
[133] European Commission, "On Artificial Intelligence – a European Approach to Excellence and Trust," White Paper, COM (2020) at 65 final.
[134] Ibid. at 17.
[135] Ibid. with n. 50.
[136] The White Paper explicitly defines AI systems as products that "can act autonomously by perceiving their environment and without following a pre-determined set of instructions"; European Commission, n. 133 at 16.

technologies, such as rule-based expert systems or the blockchain technology, which are outside the White Paper's scope.

What is necessary, thus, is first and foremost a greater awareness across Europe of LT applications as well as additional research exploring, on the one hand, the opportunities of LT applications for law and legal practice and, on the other hand, the ethical and legal frameworks they require.

12

The Two Faces of Legal Tech in B2C Relations

Eric Tjong Tjin Tai

12.1 INTRODUCTION

In the blossoming field of legal tech (LT)[1] the majority of attention goes to the work of judges and advocates in the areas of dispute resolution, due diligence, and contract assessment.[2] Far less consideration is given to what LT might contribute to consumer relations for businesses, which is also referred to as B2C relations.[3] In this contribution, I would like to focus precisely on this area, as there are already developments underway that are legally relevant and may require legal intervention.

First, I will look at possible applications of LT in B2C relations (Section 12.2). Next, I will look at various consequences of those applications (Section 12.3). The principal danger is that LT in this area may be rather instrumental to corporate efficiency and profit maximization instead of to the promotion of justice. I will then examine why LT may or may not be subject to legal regulation. To do so, I will look into a modern example of dealing with customer complaints by eBay (Section 12.4), analyzing why complaint handling is usually not regulated (Section 12.5), and follow with an example of such regulation in the insurance industry (Section 12.6). My argument is that we need to use professional diligence as the fundamental basis of assessing LT (Section 12.7) but need to extend the requirements of diligence not only to actual behavior but also to the development of LT (Section 12.8). I will end with a brief conclusion (Section 12.9).

The focus of this chapter is on businesses involved in mass consumer relations, as these provide the best opportunities for large-scale application of LT. While my analysis will mainly presume corporations that contract themselves with consumers, I will also consider examples of platforms that intermediate between suppliers and consumers. Both kinds of corporations use similar techniques and encounter similar problems, while in practice the two kinds are not always clearly differentiated.[4]

---

[1] By which I provisionally mean the use of advanced IT to replace legal processes executed by humans.
[2] See the extensive overview provided by the contributions in M. Hartung, M.-M. Bues, and G. Halbleib, *Legal Tech: How Technology Is Changing the Legal World* (Munich: Beck, 2018). In the following, I will not look into LT for external legal service providers or courts.
[3] Some examples are found in Hartung, n. 2 at part 4 ("Legal Tech Goes Inhouse"). These mostly focus on contract drafting and contract management.
[4] A case in point is Amazon, which is both a webshop (selling to consumers) and a platform (for third-party sellers): both activities are seamlessly integrated on a single website.

12.2 THE PROMISE OF LEGAL TECH IN B2C RELATIONS

12.2.1 General Considerations regarding Legal Tech in Businesses

First of all, we need to have an understanding of what is meant by LT. A working definition is the use of information technology to take over tasks of lawyers and legal staff.[5] LT encroaches on territory that up to now was the exclusive domain of the lawyer because of his particular expertise. This evokes visions of robo-lawyers that are able to litigate, perform due diligence, and write court decisions.

However, in businesses the role of an in-house lawyer or corporate lawyer is far more diverse:[6] it may involve ensuring compliance with mandatory law, serving as internal counsel in case of (potential) claims, and advising on and setting internal policies. When dealing with consumer-business relations, a corporate lawyer may typically need to manage complaint procedures, devise strategies for minimizing risk, but also – if the dispute won't be settled easily – may need to step in to handle the dispute personally, like an advocate would. The lawyer or legal department may be consulted in case of specific disputes or questions that individual employees cannot resolve on their own or are uncertain about; for issues that come up regularly, the legal department may draft policies that are subsequently rolled out by management or by the legal department itself. As a result, LT goes beyond legal analysis and the drafting of legal documents: LT in business may also involve implementation and execution of legal policy. This area, the integration of legal policy and business policy by means of IT, is a potentially promising ground for corporate gains, while simultaneously being legally worrisome, as I will argue below.

To make the analysis tractable, I will sketch the business opportunities for LT with a broad brush. As far as B2C relations are concerned, the main areas of deployment of LT appear to be the following:

- Contracting
- Contractual performance
- Complaint handling
- Enforcement and debt handling

These are the areas in which, per the above overview, corporate lawyers may regularly be involved, either in specific cases or by setting policies.[7] For automation of the legal aspects of these areas, there are three kinds of IT that appear relevant: customer communication, business protocols, and automated execution and enforcement. I will explain each of these in turn.

12.2.2 Customer Communication

Communication with customers is part of the interface of the corporation with the outside world. Any business needs some way to conclude contracts and to handle complaints, which requires communication. Nowadays, businesses employ new forms of communication: besides websites and apps (which by now are almost traditional), customers may also contact a company through Twitter, Whatsapp, online fora, or smart devices. These technical media may come at

---

[5] This differentiates LT from normal business automation.
[6] A related example is D. Howarth, *Law as Engineering: Thinking about What Lawyers Do* (Cheltenham: Elgar Publishing, 2013), which sketches a far richer portrait of the lawyer's job than is often found in the literature.
[7] I will not discuss compliance with rules such as accounting rules or rules against money laundering, as that is only indirectly relevant to consumers. Compliance with consumer law will be discussed.

the expense of traditional human interaction: instead of being able to meet a customer representative face to face, or speak to a human on the phone, you may be forced to send in complaints via a web-based form that has limited options and a restricted amount of space for the complaint. The traditional legal approach to this area is to impose information obligations: corporate websites have to be vetted by the legal department to ensure that they abide by the applicable rules,[8] that terms and conditions are accepted, and that consent is ensured. In contrast to this, many companies are very interested in this area as they see this as an opportunity: they hire IT designers and social scientists to optimize the communication process.[9] Managers are increasingly aware that the "choice architecture"[10] or decision architecture may help to "nudge" consumers in a specific direction. This approach, which may be called consent design,[11] raises concerns from the viewpoint of GDPR rules on privacy consent. A related idea is the use of AI to make individualized offers and advice that tie in with the specific needs and characteristics of the individual customer.[12]

12.2.3 Business Protocols

The use of IT to communicate with customers has another side: communication is followed by some kind of response by the organization. If we consider traditional complaint handling, we envision a department of multiple employees, who answer the telephone, read letters, and answer questions and complaints. They can if necessary escalate to a manager of customer services or to "legal" (the in-house legal department) but are bound by policy and may have developed their own internal know-how from prior experience. Employees may know who are frequent complainers and may have their own jargon for certain categories of customers.

Once we have a digital communication channel, it becomes relatively easy to also automate the processing of consumer complaints and requests and interface with the internal business operation. For example, a complaint about a delivery can be dealt with immediately by sending it to the appropriate courier or, combined with delivery details, by confirming that a delivery failed for some reason. The receipt of a returned webshop purchase could automatically trigger a return payment. Part of the business logic is thereby taken out of the hands of humans and put

---

[8] Principally the Council Directive 2011/83/EU of 25 October 2011 on consumer rights [2011] OJ L 304/64 (Consumer Rights Directive) and the Council Directive 2019/770 of 20 May 2019 on certain aspects concerning contracts for the supply of digital content and digital services [2019] OJ L 136/1.

[9] See, from various other scientific disciplines, for example, B. Friedman, P. Lin, and J. K. Miller, "Informed Consent by Design" in L. Cranor and S. Garfinkel (eds.), *Security and Usability: Designing Secure Systems That People Can Use* (Sebastopol: O'Reilly, 2008) 477–504; E. Luger and T. Rodden, "Terms of Agreement: Rethinking Consent for Pervasive Computing" (2013) 25 *Interacting with Computers* 229.

[10] R. H. Thaler and C. R. Sunstein, *Nudge: Improving Decisions about Health, Wealth, and Happiness* (New Haven: Yale University Press, 2008).

[11] Cf. C. J. Hoofnagle, "Designing for Consent" (2018) 7 *Journal of European Consumer and Market Law* 162; J. Ryan, "GDPR Consent Design: How Granular Must Adtech Opt-ins Be?," https://pagefair.com/blog/2018/granular-gdpr-consent/.

[12] G. Helleringer, "Consumer Finance 3.0: Behavioural Insights, Big Data and Digital Technologies" in N. Aggarwal et al. (eds.), *Autonomous Systems and the Law* (Munich: Beck/Nomos, 2019) 51–54; L. Scholz, "Algorithmic Contracts" (2017) 20 *Stanford Technology Law Review* 128. There is further research into personalizing not merely contracts but legal rules as well: A. Porat and L. J. Strahilevitz, "Personalizing Default Rules and Disclosure with Big Data" (2014) 112 *Michigan Law Review* 1417; O. Ben-Shahar and A. Porat, "Personalizing Negligence Law" (2016) 91 *New York University Law Review* 627; P. Hacker, "Personalizing EU Private Law: From Disclosures to Nudges and Mandates" (2017) 25 *European Review of Private Law* 651; C. Busch and A. De Franceschi, "Granular Legal Norms: Big Data and the Personalization of Private Law" in V. Mak, Eric Tjong Tjin Tai, and A. Berlee (eds.), *Research Handbook in Data Science and Law* (Cheltenham: Elgar Publishing, 2018) 408–424.

into the computer. While a fairly traditional IT system can also do this, the use of AI and other advanced technology may improve complaint handling and contract performance, based on analysis of data patterns in consumer complaints. Similarly, the new forms of presentation and interaction of smartphone technology may give a business a competitive advantage. An app such as Uber can be considered an advanced form of processing that manages to perform most of the business operation (mediating between a consumer and a driver) automatically.

There are intrinsic relations between handling the operation and the legal aspects of a business. For example, a European web trader has to deal with the consumers' right to return.[13] There are legal aspects to the return process, for example, if the returned good is damaged. It appears that many businesses uphold a "no questions asked" return policy, as it is too costly to deal on an individual basis with "bad returns." However, customers who return too often may find some prerogatives revoked (such as the right to pay only on receipt). Furthermore, webshops attempt to ensure that customers only order goods that they want. It makes sense from a business perspective to optimize the business process in order to reduce return rates,[14] which may also benefit consumers who may be satisfied more often and do not need to expend effort to return goods. Data analytics could play a role in streamlining this returns process and the related complaints process.[15] When done right, it would prevent complaints: this has been called "online dispute prevention."[16]

A specific advantage of LT in this area is that the cases that are encountered are most likely very similar. In contrast to a court, which may be confronted with all kinds of cases, a business typically is confronted with a great number of similar issues, which opens up possibilities of efficiencies of scale. If we consider the kind of issues that may arise, some may be outside the scope of an easy solution and may need personal attention. For example, a claim based on mistake or misrepresentation may require an assessment of the individual details. Other issues that involve the core contractual obligations, such as alleged breach of contract and nonpayment, could in theory be handled by technology. An automated solution, possibly using AI, might filter the easy cases from the "hard" cases: process the easy cases and leave the hard cases to humans for further handling. To aid automated processing, customers may be required to enter their complaints in forms with limited options and categories. This is an extension of the current telephone "menus" that customers may have to navigate before they can speak to a human customer representative.

LT for complaints handling could simply involve a better designed automated complaints procedure. An extension would be that the underlying decision procedure is also improved and made more sophisticated by the use of AI techniques. As these systems would have to abide by the policies that are set out by the legal department, there is a legal side to it. The result of such forms of automation and LT would be a "protocolization" of the business operation, through which the most important categories of cases can be dealt with automatically. While

---

[13] Art. 9 of the Consumer Rights Directive, Council Directive 2011/83/EU of 25 October 2011 on consumer rights, OJ 2011 No. L304, 22 November 2011.
[14] M. van Rossum, "Heen en weer," *NRC Handelsblad* (September 14, 2019), on the efforts of Zalando, a clothing webshop. For general recommendations, see www.shopify.com/enterprise/ecommerce-returns.
[15] For scholarly work in this area, see, among others: T. Pfrang, "Behavioral Appeals to Influence Product Return Behavior – Theoretical Foundations and Experimental Applications," PhD thesis, University St. Gallen (2015); W. Zhou, O. Hinz, and A. Benlian, "The Impact of the Package Opening Process on Product Returns" (2018) 11 *Business Research* 279; S. Lee and Y. Yi, "'Retail Is Detail! Give Consumers a Gift Rather Than a Bundle': Promotion Framing and Consumer Product Returns" (2019) 36 *Psychology & Marketing* 15.
[16] E. Katsh and O. Rabinovich-Einy, *Digital Justice: Technology and the Internet of Disputes* (Oxford: Oxford University Press, 2017) 66, about AliBaba (based on AliBaba's own presentation, not on independent research).

traditional complaints departments have also used "protocols," which are usually called policies, LT may ensure that the policy is always observed, whereas humans may choose to deviate from the official policy.

12.2.4 IT to Execute and Enforce Contracts

A third form of technology is the use of IT to automate the execution and enforcement of contracts. This is not completely new: the automated bank transfer is a form of automated execution. However, the widespread use of digital means of communication and advances in technology allow more sophisticated decision procedures around performance and enforcement, which encroach on the terrain of lawyers, as this also means making decisions about whether execution and enforcement are allowed or can or should be withheld. A striking example is the use of smart contracts that can execute payments under complicated conditions and check the performance of obligations in the real world such as delivery of goods.[17] Such technologies cover payment as well as other forms of contract performance. Debt handling thereby also comes within the scope of LT. While there is reason to doubt whether smart contracts can fully replace the involvement of lawyers and contract law,[18] the availability of such instruments makes it necessary to ensure that decisions about the legally correct way of handling certain events are programmed into the system.

12.2.5 Summary

While the forms of LT that I have mentioned above are fairly well-known, they may not always be recognized as being *legal* in character, as they primarily seem to support the business operation. Nonetheless, they are forms of LT as they automate and implement legal decision procedures, policies, and considerations. They thereby take over part of the job of a corporate lawyer and the legal decision-making by other employees. If IT takes over more and more of the business organization, the law should also become part of IT: the tech has to become (partly) *legal* tech.

The three forms of IT discussed above may feed into each other, strengthen the process, and make it more efficient. Data obtained from one application can be used directly as input to another application. In all three techniques, AI may also be involved, as well as more traditional forms of data use and analysis. This is already happening: app-based business such as Uber have to a large extent integrated communication, business protocols, and contract execution (see Figure 12.1).

12.3 CONSEQUENCES OF LEGAL TECH IN B2C

At first sight, LT appears to be a force for good: it can produce results that are entirely beneficial. The prevention of needless returns of items is surely positive, as it reduces delivery costs and

---

[17] L. A. DiMatteo, M. Cannarsa, and C. Poncibò (eds.), *The Cambridge Handbook of Smart Contracts, Blockchain Technology and Digital Platforms* (Cambridge: Cambridge University Press, 2019).

[18] Eric Tjong Tjin Tai, "Challenges of Smart Contracts: Implementing Excuses" in DiMatteo et al. n. 17 at 80–100; E. Mik, "Smart Contracts: Terminology, Technical Limitations and Real World Complexity" (2017) 9 *Journal of Law, Innovation and Technology* 269; Mark Giancaspro, "Is a 'Smart Contract' Really a Smart Idea? Insights from a Legal Perspective" (2017) 33 *Computer Law & Security Review* 825; J. G. Allen, "Wrapped and Stacked: 'Smart Contracts' and the Interaction of Natural and Formal Language" (2018) 14 *European Review of Contract Law* 307.

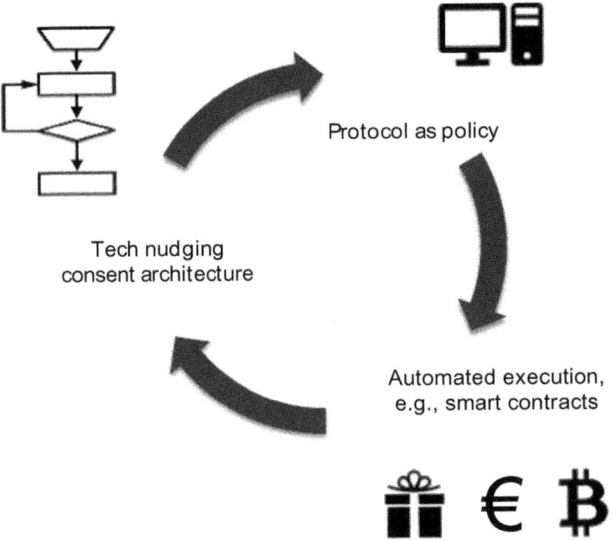

FIGURE 12.1 Opportunities for legal tech in the business process

energy consumption and increases consumer satisfaction. Similarly, the integration of legal know-how into the business process may increase the degree of compliance with regulation. Indeed, an important aim of automation is to increase efficiency, which in itself is also to the advantage of consumers and society at large, as it means a reduction in costs and time, which may allow lower prices and faster turnaround. Big data analysis may contribute to preventing common complaints by addressing these already in the business process, for example, by trying to prevent return of goods.

There may be other advantages as well: an automated system (including AI-based decision-making) may be more objective, lack personal partisanship, and act in a consistent manner.[19] Furthermore, technology may also help to shield employees from physically violent or verbally abusive customers.

However, we should not forget that in the strict capitalist view, customer interest is not the goal of improvements in business efficiency. The business itself would, if its directors subscribe to the notion of maximizing shareholder value, focus on maximizing profit.

A second category of consequences may invite hesitation toward the deployment of LT. These are unwittingly negative consequences. Broadly speaking, technological replacement of human processes is not a complete substitute, at least at the present state of technology. Indeed, technology may be fundamentally unable to substitute seamlessly for human interaction. As the technological process does not flawlessly mirror how humans interact, there is a gap between what the system allows and what humans want. At present, the tendency for businesses may be to streamline their operation and do away with human intermediaries, instead providing apps and other technical interfaces. In this way, they outsource the complicated business of dealing with specifics to the customer, who has to find someone willing and able to help him in dealing with the system. If a complaint form only allows restricted categories, the consumer may find himself unable to correctly communicate his complaint. An overloaded phone help desk may discourage consumers from complaining as they have to invest a lot of their own time to talk to a

---

[19] Of course, AI may also show bias if it has been trained by biased data.

consumer representative. Not having a telephone number available will be an obstacle for consumers who are not technologically savvy or do not have access to digital technology.

At this point, legal regulation is ambivalent. Art. 5(1)b Consumer Rights Directive[20] requires businesses that operate online to inform their customers of a telephone number where the business can be reached.[21] However, in its recent decision, Case-649/17 *BVV v. Amazon*,[22] the European Court of Justice (ECJ) decided that this obligation is not as strict as it appears and may be ignored by companies such as Amazon that operate chiefly online. While this decision may be applauded as showing an appreciation of the reality of modern online business, it can also be criticized for unthinkingly giving away the human need for communication with an actual human being.[23]

On the other hand, there is the decision in Case 673/17 *Planet49*,[24] in which the ECJ disapproved of a prechecked consent box: this shows awareness of the influence of choice architecture and nudging. Similarly, the German *Bundesgerichtshof* explained in a 2012 decision[25] (briefly put) that when ordering through an automated system the order should be interpreted according to human interpretation, not to how the system is programmed to execute it.[26] This clearly requires the business to make the technology match the human viewpoint.

Technology may go even further in forcing personnel to abide by a rule they find unjust. While LT allows stricter enforcement of customer policy than traditional paper policies, the consequence is also that it may disallow deviation in cases where humans would find this just and appropriate. If the computer has not been designed to take such cases into account or does not allow any individual discretion, the customer may find himself hindered by LT.[27] Although in theory the organization could strive to improve the system with more nuanced or detailed rules, or a discretionary option, it is possible that management does not sufficiently care as long as there are no directly measurable or negative consequences of inadequate customer treatment.[28]

Even if a company sincerely wants to improve its process and does not wish to hinder its customers, it may find itself unable to do so. The IT system may be developed by an independent contractor or may be based on a general framework that they cannot easily modify. If AI is involved, the system may be the result of a lengthy and costly training process that is nearly impossible to correct, at least in the short term.

Incidentally, the use of automated policies and rules may also open up potential for abuse. Any system invites abuse: with humans it is called fraud, for IT protocolization it is called

---

[20] Council Directive 2011/83/EU of 25 October 2011 on consumer rights [2011] OJ L304/64.
[21] The obligation was introduced earlier in Council Directive 99/44/EC of 25 May 1999 on certain aspects of the sale of consumer goods and associated guarantees [1999] OJ L171/12.
[22] CFI, 10 July 2019, ECLI:EU:C:2019:576.
[23] However, the ECJ decision may be outdated already as art. 4(4) Council Directive 2019/2161 of 27 November 2019 as regards the better enforcement and modernization of Union consumer protection rules [2019] OJ L 328/7 has changed art. 6(1)(c) Consumer Rights Directive to again explicitly require a telephone number. The ECJ decision was based on an earlier version of the Modernization Directive, which removed this requirement.
[24] CFI, 1 October 2019, ECLI:EU:C:2018:385.
[25] BGH, 16 October 2012, X ZR 37/12, BGHZ 195/126.
[26] A. C. van Schaick, *Digitalisering, vermogensrecht, de platformeconomie en grondrechten* (Deventer: Wolters Kluwer, 2019) 51.
[27] The issue of allowing discretion is also topic of research in application of administrative law. See two Dutch PhD theses: M. H. A. F. Lokin, *De wetgever als systeembeheerder* (Den Haag: Boom Juridische uitgevers, 2018); P. de Winter, *Tussen de regels* (Den Haag: Boom Juridische uitgevers, 2019).
[28] It is even possible that lack of attention to LT would increase short-term profits as it would entail that some justified complaints are not followed up and do not lead to payouts or returns. Of course, public opinion may differ, and the threat of loss of reputation may induce management to action.

hacking (and social hacking), or "gaming" the system. An example is the way in which Google tries to assess websites for ranking in its search results. The algorithm is kept secret, but specialized agencies claim to be able to hack the system in order to get your website higher in the ranking.

Finally, a third category of consequences appears even more worrying. Technology, as pointed out above, may not only be used to improve the efficiency of the business operation itself, but may also be put in the service of increasing profits by any means whatsoever. This may include behavior that is contrary to consumer interests. A few examples:[29]

- The data available on consumers and the technological know-how on nudging may provide companies with more power in their business interactions. This can be done by providing consumers with offers tailored to their profile, but also more worrying, by tailoring the presentation of information to subconsciously push them to make choices that they would not make with a more neutral or general presentation.
- The unavoidable obstacles inherent in tech use detailed in Section 12.3.2 may be exploited deliberately to discourage complaints. Policy protocols and complex consumer interfaces can be used to discourage consumers from effecting their rights. A complaints screen that is deliberately complex, requires lots of irrelevant information, and requires the user to reenter information even when a slight error is made, may easily discourage consumers in a way that an obtuse customer service representative would not. A human who refuses to listen to a complaint may rather incite anger and a firm conviction to take on the battle, while a cleverly designed discouraging interface will only be viewed as bad programming.

Such drawbacks may not even be a deliberate strategy. They may simply be the result of AI being trained to maximize profit. For instance, a complaint-handling AI that discourages valid claims will increase profits and will not take into account just claims if it has not been trained to recognize justice. Similarly, there was the case of Uber, where the algorithm hiked up prices when there was a sudden excessive demand following the June 2017 terrorist attack in London.[30]

A result of LT could be an improved understanding of issues and responses of consumers. This knowledge could either be used to sift the valid claims from the invalid, or to determine the way in which maximize profit, that is, minimize payout. An algorithm can take either road, it all depends on the way it is trained. Is it to find a way to "win" the complaint game no matter what, or should it use "fair play"? See by analogy the way in which algorithms "win" at arcade games: they may focus on "unconventional" ways that are not considered fair play by humans but cannot avoid the attraction of such "cheats": in technical parlance "it is hard for [AI] to escape from these local attractor states in policy space."[31]

Hence the employment of LT introduces two risks:

- restriction of consumer rights through inadequacies in the technology employed and
- deliberate abuse of technology to achieve results contrary to consumer interests.

---

[29] An interesting (hypothetical) example regarding bad faith insurance is the use of automated valuation of damage, deliberately set too low, see Douglas R. Richmond, "Defining and Confining Institutional Bad Faith in Insurance" (2010) 46 *Tort Trial & Insurance Practice Law Journal* 1 3–4 and 30–31.
[30] https://money.cnn.com/2017/06/04/technology/uber-london-attack-surge-pricing/index.html. Uber is apparently changing its system by having a centralized team of humans override system decisions on pricing, www.theverge.com/2018/9/25/17897836/uber-disaster-response-hurricane-price-cap.
[31] Patryk Chrabaszcz, Ilya Loshchilov, and Frank Hutter, "Back to Basics: Benchmarking Canonical Evolution Strategies for Playing Atari" at 5, https://arxiv.org/abs/1802.08842.

12.4 CASE OF EBAY

To give the above theoretical analysis a basis in actual fact, it may be instructive to examine an actual example: the dispute-handling process of eBay. eBay has become one of the dominant platforms for trading secondhand consumer goods.[32] Admittedly, eBay has a different position to that of traditional businesses as it is an intermediary between a seller and a consumer-buyer. The seller may be a large business but often is a private person who may simply wish to sell off some unwanted goods. The position of an intermediary is different from the usual cases of B2C interaction that are the topic of this chapter. Nonetheless, the case of eBay is useful as a reference point to see some consequences and drawbacks of large-scale policy if unchecked; for normal B2C companies it is harder to determine their specific policy.

eBay is reputed for having a strong buyer-protection policy.[33] If an item does not arrive, you are required to first contact the seller, but if that doesn't lead to a satisfactory resolution, eBay will step in and refund the money to the buyer.

This is similar to how credit card companies operate with buyer protection. However, a difference is that credit card companies only contract with commercial organizations or large organizations, while eBay sellers may often be private persons who are not operating commercially.

The way the eBay policy turns out often leads to unsatisfactory results. A search on the Internet leads to countless seller complaints over the years and to websites like www.screw-paypal.com.[34] *The Guardian* journalist Anna Tims has been writing critically about the eBay policy for a number of years.[35] Generally, the impression is that eBay tends to side automatically with the buyer, even when there are clear indications of fraud or abuse by the buyer. This is in itself to be expected given its "Buyer Guarantee" promise. However, a good faith seller who is the victim of a fraudulent buyer may thereby be left in the lurch. It is hard to prove who is correct in cases where the buyer claims he received a defective good or asserts that he returned the item as received, and eBay tends to be less than responsive to complaints from sellers. By now, eBay has implemented changes to create a more balanced form of seller protection.[36] For example, eBay now may require additional documentation in case of disputed claims.[37]

An alternative mechanism for preventing abuse is the reputation system, the feedback that sellers and buyers receive from earlier transactions.[38] However, it is by now well-known that this

---

[32] About the eBay dispute policy, see L. F. Del Duca, C. Rule, and K. Rimpfel, "eBay's De Facto Low Value High Volume Resolution Process: Lessons and Best Practices for ODR Systems Designers" (2014) 6 *Yearbook on Arbitration and Mediation* 204; C. Rule, "System: Lessons Learned from eBay" (2017) 13 *University of St. Thomas Law Journal* 354. See also the related analysis of P. M. P. Frenken, "ODR-Procedures bij platformen: Laagdrempelig voor consumenten, maar zonder waarborgen voor legaliteit en procedurele rechtvaardigheid" (2019) *Tijdschrift voor Consumentenrecht* 210, regarding the policy of PayPal.

[33] Referred to as "Buyer Protection," https://pages.ebay.com/cl/en-us/coverage/BuyerProtectionForBuyers.html, or "Money Back Guarantee," https://pages.ebay.com/ebay-money-back-guarantee/. A complication is that eBay also uses payment intermediary services of its subsidiary PayPal, which has a different kind of policy, including a "Seller Protection." See, for example, www.paypal.com/us/webapps/mpp/security/seller-protection. As this chapter is not the place for a detailed analysis of these policies, I will only provide a brief overview of the eBay policy.

[34] While PayPal is a different company, it is a subsidiary of the eBay conglomerate, and eBay sellers in certain countries are still required to use PayPal.

[35] See, for example, www.theguardian.com/money/2017/may/21/ebay-accused-failing-sellers-buyers-manipulate-system-protection; www.theguardian.com/money/2019/jan/13/ebay-sellers-scams-buyer-protection. Other media have also written critically, for instance, www.nytimes.com/2016/07/31/your-money/lesson-from-a-doughnut-fryer-debacle-let-the-ebay-seller-beware.html.

[36] See, for an overview, www.ecommercebytes.com/C/blog/blog.pl?/pl/2019/1/1546467519.html.

[37] Usually, digital photographs are used.

[38] H. Masum and M. Tovey (eds.), *The Reputation Society* (Cambridge, MA: MIT Press, 2011); C. Busch, "Crowdsourcing Consumer Confidence: How to Regulate Online Rating and Review Systems in the Collaborative

is not a complete substitute for a posteriori adjudication. Reputation mechanisms in e-commerce suffer from perverse effects and abuses such as manipulation and threats to leave negative feedback.[39] Similarly, eBay uses a variety of other mechanisms to discourage abuses, such as "loss of eBay Money Back Guarantee coverage, issuing warnings to buyers, blocking buyers from requesting returns or refunds on eBay, blocking buyers from opening claims, and account suspension."[40]

The case of eBay is interesting as eBay is, strictly speaking, impartial in a dispute between seller and buyer. Given the volume of transactions, eBay would be placed perfectly to employ advanced technology to fine-tune its complaints process and to investigate the actual behavior of sellers and buyers. An advantage of the platform and availability of data is that eBay can, if it wants, check whether a buyer shows a pattern of possible fraud. However, it appears that this data is not often used to adjudicate a dispute. Following up on a dispute would ultimately require eBay to perform a full investigation of the facts, which would be time-consuming and impractical. Without such an investigation, it is up to the word of the buyer and seller to determine in what condition an item really was; photographic evidence cannot conclusively prove this.

It could be argued that the eBay dispute resolution process need not strive for perfect just outcomes, as dissatisfied buyers and sellers can go to the courts.[41] However, court action is costly, and regardless of the possibility of court protection, eBay seems to "nudge" buyers and sellers toward a certain outcome by using its discretionary sanctions such as blocking accounts and withholding payments. It is in the interest of eBay to promote buyer confidence, which unavoidably means less protection for sellers. Hence, the process does not seem to promote a just resolution of disputes, it appears to be biased to increase buyer spending.

Incidentally, eBay was sued in a class action in California for perceived unfairness in its buyer policy.[42] The complaint, based inter alia on violation of a fiduciary duty of agency and violation of the California UCL (Unfair Competition Law), was dismissed.[43] While the judgment is comprehensible, given the lack of substantiation of the complaint and the relatively large freedom eBay should have in setting up its business and policies,[44] one may still wonder whether there should be some boundaries to ensure substantial evenhandedness in its treatment of buyers and sellers.[45]

Economy" in A. De Franceschi (ed.), *European Contract Law and the Digital Single Market: The Implications of the Digital Revolution* (Antwerp: Intersentia, 2016) 223–244; S. Ranchordás, "Online Reputation and the Regulation of Information Asymmetries in the Platform Economy" (2018) 5 *Critical Analysis of Law* 127, with further references. On the interaction of reputation and buyer protection, see X. Hui, M. Saeedi, Z. Shen, and N. Sundaresa, "Reputation and Regulations: Evidence from eBay" (2016) 62 *Management Science* 3604.

[39] Ranchordás, n. 38 at iii.
[40] See www.ebay.com/help/policies/ebay-money-back-guarantee-policy/ebay-money-back-guarantee-policy?id=4210 under "fraudulent claims and abusive buyer behavior."
[41] The policy of eBay does not seem to prohibit buyers and sellers suing each other in court.
[42] *Campbell v. eBay, Inc. and PayPal, Inc.*, No. 13-CV-2632 YGR, N.D. Calif.; 2013 U.S. Dist., see https://dockets.justia.com/docket/california/candce/5:2013cv02632/266982. A similar case is *Theo Chen v. eBay Inc., et al.*, No. 15-5048, N.D. Calif.; 2016 U.S. Dist.
[43] Order of September 5, 2013, in the case *Campbell v. eBay, Inc. and PayPal, Inc.*
[44] See generally on the positive effect of platforms having their own regulatory mechanisms C. Busch, "Self-Regulation and Regulatory Intermediation in the Platform Economy" in M. Cantero Gamito and H.-W. Micklitz (eds.), *The Role of the EU in Transnational Legal Ordering: Standards, Contracts and Codes* (Cheltenham: Edward Elgar, 2019) 115–134, https://ssrn.com/abstract=3309293; O. Lobel, "The Law of the Platform" (2016) 101 *Minnesota Law Review* 87.
[45] For an example of the requirement of fairness for ODR, see Noam Ebner and John Zeleznikow, "Fairness, Trust and Security in Online Dispute Resolution" (2015) 36 *Hamline Journal of Public Law & Policy* 143. This should be borne in mind when eBay's dispute resolution system is upheld as a model for state organized dispute resolution.

12.5 TRADITIONAL VIEW OF REGULATION OF COMPLAINT HANDLING

The argument so far makes a case for legal intervention and regulation of complaint handling and other customer interaction by businesses. However, at first sight there is very little regulatory activity in this area. This can be explained through a closer look at the position of customer interaction. Complaint handling (and therefore also the application of LT in this area), and by extension customer relations, seems to be viewed primarily as an internal business matter, relating to the way in which business is organized. As long as no particular laws are violated, businesses are free to arrange their affairs as they like. However, on closer inspection, there may be more at stake.

When we consider the way in which the law is perceived, there are two different positions that can be taken. First, you can consider the law as giving expression to the way in which persons should treat each other. You should strive to follow the law, meaning that you try to follow the purpose and intentions of the law. Second, you can see the law simply as a set of boundary conditions that may get you in trouble if you break them, but you can choose to ignore otherwise. You try to achieve your own aims while adhering strictly to the letter of the law. This is in essence the "bad man's" perspective of law.[46]

The organization of complaint handling can take either perspective of the law: justice as a goal, or law as a limitation. The objective can be to deal with cases in the same way that a court would, if a court decided on the matter. A business can refuse a complaint fairly if it is materially ungrounded, but would otherwise do its best to perform according to what is legally due. The main objective would be to organize matters efficiently and effectively.

Conversely, a business could also set up complaint handling to deny as many complaints as possible, only giving in when adjudication seems unavoidable. The purpose would arguably be to maximize profits. By doing so, the company would keep the money due or save costs in all cases where the customer was in the right but decided it was not worthwhile pressing his claim.

In practice, there are various reasons why the latter way of operating a business is not as common as might be expected at a time when maximizing shareholder value is paramount. Besides cases where the company culture genuinely is to adhere to the spirit of the law and to give customers their due, a business may be kept honest by the threat of loss of good reputation and consequent loss of business. A company may make a cost-benefit analysis and find that good complaint handling will save money over a stricter process.

Furthermore, the law provides protection if consumer rights are actually violated. Mass claims, for example, are defended as they provide an instrument whereby corporations do not get away with a policy that structurally causes small claims. Similarly, consumer rights organizations and supervisory agencies[47] may step in to force companies to improve their behavior – if it can be proven and if their behavior actually violates legal rules. Even if the behavior is not strictly illegal, a consumer rights organization could also try to raise bad PR, which could make a company give in.

To summarize: there are various incentives that may keep companies fair and honest.[48] Nonetheless, a business may deliberately take a different approach. Some companies are reputed

---

[46] As famously espoused by Oliver Wendell Holmes, "The Path of the Law" (1897) 10 *Harvard Law Review* 457.

[47] In the EU, there are various consumer protection agencies, see https://ec.europa.eu/info/policies/consumers/consumer-protection/our-partners-consumer-issues/national-consumer-organisations_en, for private and governmental bodies. In the United Kingdom, there is the Office of Fair Trading, in the United States, there is the Federal Trade Commission.

[48] There is also the point of view of individual employees, who may serve as whistle-blowers, or may advocate a more moderate approach as they may fear personal liability (such as in the case of Wells Fargo, see generally https://en.wikipedia.org/wiki/Wells_Fargo_account_fraud_scandal).

for their bad customer handling, but consumers still go to them because of aggressive pricing. Arguably, this shows that consumers may vote with their feet: some choose the risk of bad consumer handling and trade this off with lower prices, others make the opposite trade-off. This is just how a free market should operate, and there does not seem to be anything wrong with that. It should be borne in mind that companies are limited in how far they can go because of existing consumer protection law.

12.6 LEGAL REGULATION OF B2C RELATIONS: BAD FAITH INSURANCE

Nonetheless, the law does more than simply let the market run its course. In some instances, complaint handling is regulated more strictly. A specific example is the area of bad faith insurance claims policies. At the beginning of the twentieth century, many American insurance companies deliberately adopted the policy not (or not fully) to pay out valid claims by their customers, in order to increase profits, as many customers would eventually give up or settle for a lower payout than they were entitled to. Even if a few persistent customers would go to court, the total savings would still exceed what the insurance company rightfully would have had to pay out. As these practices became well known, legal activity started to eradicate them.

An insurance contract in common law has traditionally been qualified as a contract of *uberrimae fides*, utmost good faith. However, this qualification did not impose restrictions on payout practices by insurance companies. Instead, the doctrine of *uberrima fides* was primarily used to hold the insured to strict disclosure obligations on punishment of canceling the insurance.[49] In the English Insurance Act 2015, such disproportionate sanctions have been softened or outright abolished.[50]

Instead, an alternative doctrine was used.[51] In the landmark decision *Comunale* v. *Traders & General Ins Co*,[52] the California Supreme Court decided that the insurance company was liable for damages in excess of the policy limits. Its reasoning was based on the existence of an implied covenant of good faith and fair dealing in every contract, which for insurance companies implies that it needs to take into consideration the interests of the insured. The case involved an insurance policy for liability; because the insurance company refused to settle the case, the victims won an award of damages to the insured in excess of the policy limits. Because of the behavior of the insurance company in refusing to settle, the insured could claim payout in excess of the policy limits.[53] "It follows from what we have said that an insurer, who wrongfully declines to defend and who refuses to accept a reasonable settlement within the policy limits in violation

---

[49] Reuben Hasson, "The Special Nature of the Insurance Contract: A Comparison of the American and English Law of Insurance" (1984) 47 *Modern Law Review* 505; Francis Achampong, "Uberrima Fides in English and American Insurance Law: A Comparative Analysis" (1987) 36 *International & Comparative Law Quarterly* 329; and for Australian law, Catherine Larkin, "Uberrima Fides – Quo Vadis – Where to from Here" (1995) 7 *Bond Law Review* 18.

[50] For example, s. 14(1): "Any rule of law permitting a party to a contract of insurance to avoid the contract on the ground that the utmost good faith has not been observed by the other party is abolished." See further Attilio M. Costabel, "Utmost Good Faith in Marine Insurance: A Message on the State of the Dis-Union" (2017) 48 *Journal of Maritime Law & Commerce* 1.

[51] See, on developments before and after *Comunale*, Frank S. Hills and Richard J. Pivnicka, "Development and Direction of the California Bad Faith Insurance Doctrine or O Ye of Little Faith" (1973) 8 *University of San Francisco Law Review* 29; also S. S. Ashley, *Bad Faith Actions: Liability and Damages*, 2nd ed. (St. Paul: West Group, 1997).

[52] 50 Cal 2d 654 (1958).

[53] In this case the victims had obtained an assignment of all rights of the insured to the insurance company, which explains why the victims sued the insurance company.

of its duty to consider in good faith the interest of the insured in the settlement, is liable for the entire judgment against the insured even if it exceeds the policy limits."[54]

Thus, an action in tort based on bad faith was accepted.[55] This action has been extended to first-party insurance and investigation of a claim.[56] The developments in California were also adopted in other states. Subsequently, many states enacted statutes that established a prohibition of bad faith insurance and provided tort remedies.[57] There is not much case law about institutional bad faith.[58]

It should be noted that the tort of bad faith insurance is based in its argumentation on the implied covenant of good faith and fair dealing. From a civil law viewpoint, this sounds like the notion that all contracts have to be performed in good faith.[59] However, in a recent decision the US Supreme Court considered that US contract law does not recognize a general contractual duty of good faith as part of every contract, instead such a notion, when present, derives from specific state law that may impose such a duty outside of the general rules of contract law.[60] It is not entirely clear how this decision is to be interpreted, in the light of earlier state case law as well as the Restatement (Second) of Contracts § 205 (1981), which declares: "Every contract imposes upon each party a duty of good faith and fair dealing in its performance and its enforcement."[61] However, it is true that the literature shows considerable hesitation as to the meaning and consequences of such an implied covenant.[62]

The tort of bad faith insurance is particular to the United States and is not mirrored in other jurisdictions, possibly because insurance companies outside the United States behaved in a more acceptable manner.[63] This is not to say that there is no regulation at all. While an extensive

---

[54] *Comunale* v. *Traders*, para. 14.
[55] An action in tort has the advantage that tort remedies become available, such as an award of damages in excess of policy limits. Tort remedies are only rarely allowed for contractual cases. The exception for bad faith insurance was later to be based on the special relationship between insurer and insured: Matthew J. Barrett, "'Contort': Tortious Breach of the Implied Covenant of Good Faith and Fair Dealing in Noninsurance Commercial Contracts – Its Existence and Desirability" (1984–1985) 60 *Notre Dame Law Review* 510; also M. H. Cohen, "Reconstructing Breach of the Implied Covenant of Good Faith and Fair Dealing as a Tort" (1985) 73 *California Law Review* 1291.
[56] *Gruenberg* v. *Aetna Ins Co* 9 Cal 3d 566 (1973); *Egan* v. *Mutual of Omaha Ins Co* 24 Cal 3d 809 (1979).
[57] For instance, Georgia (OCGA § 33-4-6); California (Fair Claims Settlement Practices Regulations, based on Cal Ins Code § 790.03(h) and § 790.035). There is ample literature, mostly centered on specific states, such as Frank S. Hills and Richard J. Pivnicka, "Development and Direction of the California Bad Faith Insurance Doctrine or O Ye of Little Faith" (1973) 8 *University of San Francisco Law Review* 29; Rick Gibson, "Insurance Bad Faith in Mississippi" (1985) 55 *Mississippi Law Journal* 485; Gregory A. Bullman, "A Right without a Potent Remedy: Indiana's Bad Faith Insurance Doctrine Leaves Injured Third Parties without Full Redress" (2002) 77 *Indiana Law Journal* 787.
[58] Douglas R. Richmond, "Defining and Confining Institutional Bad Faith in Insurance" (2010) 46 *Tort Trial & Insurance Practice Law Journal* 1 4 n. 8 attributes this to settlement to avoid exposure and discovery.
[59] On this concept, see M. W. Hesselink, "The Concept of Good Faith" in A. Hartkamp et al. (eds.), *Towards a European Civil Code*, 4th ed. (Alphen aan den Rijn: Kluwer Law International, 2011) 619–649. Arguing for such a general duty in common law, in particular as a bulwark against exploitation: D. Markovits, "Good Faith as Contract's Core Value" in Gregory Klass, George Letsas, and Prince Saprai (eds.), *Philosophical Foundations of Contract Law* (Oxford: Oxford University Press, 2014) 272–293.
[60] See the US Supreme Court decision *Northwest* v. *Rabbi Ginsberg* 124 SCt 142 (2014), on which P. Goodrich, "The Wrecking Ball: Good Faith, Preemption and US Exceptionalism" in P. G. Monateri (ed.), *Comparative Contract Law* (Cheltenam: Elgar, 2017) 385–407.
[61] See also Uniform Commercial Code § 1–304 (2003).
[62] See earlier on this doctrine: H. Dubroff, "The Implied Covenant of Good Faith in Contract Interpretation and Gap-Filling: Reviling a Revered Relic" (2006) 80 *St. John's Law Review* 559; Monique C. Lillard, "Fifty Jurisdictions in Search of a Standard: The Covenant of Good Faith and Fair Dealing in the Employment Context" (1992) 57 *Missouri Law Review* 1233; P. MacMahon, "Good Faith and Fair Dealing as an Underenforced Legal Norm" (2015) 99 *Minnesota Law Review* 2051.
[63] Hasson, n. 49, points out that the stricter regulation in the United States was due to the excesses in behavior by US insurance companies, compared to UK insurers.

survey is outside the scope of the present chapter, a few examples may suffice.[64] In the Netherlands, insurance companies are subject to a form of sector-specific arbitration,[65] where the Dutch contractual duty of diligence (*zorgplicht*) is applied to make insurers treat their customers fairly.[66] In a recent case, an insurance company was held liable for slow claims handling.[67] In the United Kingdom, the Financial Conduct Authority supervises insurance claims handling in order to ensure fair treatment of consumers. The FCA handbook, chapter 8, is devoted exclusively to regulating the way in which insurance companies deal with claims.[68]

12.7 PROFESSIONAL DILIGENCE AS FUNDAMENTAL PRINCIPLE FOR LEGAL TECH

If we look at the two main drawbacks of LT in B2C relations (inadequate technology leading to restricted consumer interaction and actively abusing the consumer) the question becomes whether and how to discourage these effects.[69]

The best approach seems to be a mix of market pressure[70] and legal regulation against abuses.[71] Following the lead of the complaint handling rules we discussed in Section 12.6, the principal legal criterion appears to be good faith behavior. The strict approach to law in which only hard rules are followed and may act to the detriment of the customer seems to be prohibited. A corporation should at least partly take the interests of customers to heart. However, legal intervention on this basis seems to occur only in specific business domains.

Within the European Union, the concept of professional diligence seems the most relevant criterion to test questionable business practices. In art. 5(2) Unfair Commercial Practices Directive 2005/29,[72] this is the first criterion for disallowing certain practices, which may also cover consumer communication, protocols, and enforcement. This concept, I have argued elsewhere, requires that a business needs to take the consumer interest to heart, at least to some extent.[73] In several states in the United States, similar general good faith–based rules of protection against business practices are available.[74] More specifically, art. 6(1)(b) Unfair Commercial Practices Directive 2005/29 declares misleading practices giving false information regarding,

---

[64] For a comparative overview of the related issue of duties of care by banks, see D. Busch and C. van Dam, *A Bank's Duty of Care* (Oxford: Hart Publishing, 2017); and for financial services in Europe, V. Mak, "Financial Services and Consumer Protection" in C. Twigg-Flesner, *Research Handbook on EU Consumer and Contract Law* (Cheltenham: Elgar, 2016) 314–335.

[65] The KiFiD (Klachteninstituut Financiële Dienstverlening, the Institute for complaints regarding financial services).

[66] H. Wansink, N. van Tiggele-van der Velde, and F. R. Salomons, *Mr. C. Assers Handleiding tot de beoefening van het Nederlands Burgerlijk Recht. 7. Bijzondere overeenkomsten. Deel IX. Verzekering* (Deventer: Kluwer, 2015) 65–73. Furthermore, there is also governmental supervision on the behavior of insurance companies, partly based on EU legislation; this is outside the scope of the present chapter.

[67] Court of Appeal Arnhem-Leeuwarden 11 December 2018, ECLI:NL:GHARL:2018:10759, on which, see N. van Tiggele-Van de Velde, "Terug op de agenda: Het verlangen de verzekeraar te 'straffen' voor het verloop van de schadeafhandeling" (2019) 19 *Aansprakelijkheid, Verzekering & Schade* 77.

[68] www.handbook.fca.org.uk/handbook/ICOBS/8/?view=chapter.

[69] The following argument is based on the presumption that these effects are found undesirable.

[70] Which does not in itself require legal intervention except in cases of market dominance, which is the province of competition law.

[71] On which, see generally the contribution by M. Ebers, Chapter 11 in this book.

[72] Council Directive 2005/29/EC of 11 May 2005 concerning unfair business-to-consumer commercial practices in the internal market, OJ 2005 No. L149, 11 June 2005.

[73] Eric Tjong Tjin Tai, "Professional Diligence and the UCP Directive" (2016) 12 *European Review of Contract Law* 1.

[74] For example, the California Business & Professions Code §17200 prohibits any "unlawful, unfair or fraudulent business act or practice" and any "unfair, deceptive, untrue or misleading advertising." See also the Massachusetts Code, Chapter 93A, s 2(a) states "Unfair methods of competition and unfair or deceptive acts or practices in the

inter alia, "after-sale customer assistance and complaint handling." Hence, complaint handling is already within the domain of the professional diligence test.

However, the mere concept of professional diligence may be ineffective, considering the undermining effect that unjust LT can have. Current regulation still seems to assume a human organization, whereby management can direct the behavior of employees and the business is liable for any employee wrongdoing, on the basis of breach of contract or vicarious liability. Employees may furthermore have a moderating influence on the organization, thereby keeping it in line with social considerations of justice.[75] If the undesirable organizational behavior is the result of a combination of consent design, protocollization, and automatic enforcement, it is far from obvious that the existing ways of regulation will suffice.

The fundamental problem is that professional diligence assumes that if you know your customer and his vulnerabilities, you will protect him where he is vulnerable, while a technical AI-driven approach would use the knowledge of customer vulnerability to improve business operation, even if this comes at the expense of the customer's interests. Justice demands *protection* of the weak and vulnerable, while uncorrected technology quickly leads to *exploitation*.

12.8 TOWARD DEVELOPMENTAL DILIGENCE

To counteract a development toward exploitative LT, we need to stimulate the development of technology that abides by the demands of justice. This is not an easy task. How should we incentivize protocols and AI to operate in "good faith," as this is a concept primarily to be applied to humans, assuming a form of intention. Nonetheless, by extension this concept is also applied to organizations, as we saw in the case of insurance companies. By analogy, an algorithm may be said to operate in good faith if it behaves like a human acting in good faith would do. However, what if a corporation has hired an external consultancy to create an algorithm for its complaint handling? Is the corporation thereafter responsible for undesirable effects?

To my mind, we should accept that a corporation is indeed fully responsible for the actions of an algorithm, whether it wanted its behavior or not. This is an exact analogy of the liability of companies for undesirable employee behavior, which forms a powerful incentive to monitor and train employees. Such an organizational liability may provide a strong incentive to employ just AI. However, this is insufficient in itself as it does nothing to counteract the structural injustice that an inadequate form of LT can cause.

My suggestion would be that we also need to demand diligence of the company toward actually developing a proper form of LT. The company should be able to show that it actually did try to make its LT behave properly. This amounts to a "developmental" form of diligence.

To allow effective court supervision of such diligence, we can assume a variety of regulatory instruments, for example:

(1) Require a *documented effort* to implement justice in algorithms and other forms of LT. This may require keeping proof of how the algorithm has been developed.
(2) Require a company to prove that it makes a continual *good faith effort to correct systemic errors*: even if an incidental error may slip through in its tech, the company would at least be required to fix these errors.

---

conduct of any trade or commerce are hereby declared unlawful." However, in the *Campbell* v. *eBay* case mentioned in Section 12.4, an appeal to these rules was ineffective.

[75] See also Section 12.5. There is abundant research on the effects of culture on business operation, including the negative effects of "toxic" cultures, which presumes the possibility of opposite influences by benign corporate cultures.

These two suggestions would need to be complemented with a variety of disclosure obligations or reporting about the operation and content of its LT. One could imagine that investigating the compliance of such algorithms requires experts. Going one step further, one might suggest that some forms of LT may only be developed by trusted professions that have the aim of justice at heart. Indeed, this could form the basis of a new profession that investigates the legal compliance of algorithms, similar to how a lawyer may do a due diligence research. This would be the ultimate symbiosis of law and tech.

Besides the general suggestions sketched above, it is also feasible to use our current knowledge to impose a few more objective standards that can be used to prevent some of the possible shortcomings identified above. For example:

- Rules as to the quality and kind of communication, including restrictions on nudging and other forms of consent design. As this is a separate topic that requires more fundamental research, I will not elaborate on it here.
- A mandatory facility for humans to exercise some form of discretion in order to override the protocol embedded in technology.
- Mandatory disclosure of some characteristics of the operation of algorithms employed by a business. This would strengthen the countervailing power of market pressure. If consumers can easily inform themselves about the actual way in which consumer communication and complaints are handled (for example, number of complaints or consumer satisfaction), they can make an informed choice on whether to accept an unfriendly protocol because of lower prices.

These are only suggestions; I am hesitant to wholeheartedly recommend strict rules as these may impose undue regulatory burdens. It is vital that corporations have sufficient liberty to organize their business, as this allows for innovations and improvements in efficiency. Nonetheless, the specter of systemic injustice effected by LT in businesses requires some form of regulation.

12.9 CONCLUSION

I have argued that the employment of technology in businesses is not neutral in nature; it is often LT in essence, even if the legal character of a technological intervention is not consciously realized. Explaining the legal character of technology is important as technological systems may lead to circumvention of legal protection mechanisms.

The suggestions outlined in this chapter may move forward the discussion on how the law should respond to the power imbalance that may result from the wide-scale deployment of varieties of LT in B2C relations. Up to now, technology tends to drive out the law: we should ensure that tech in business really becomes *legal* tech.

PART IV

Legal Tech and Public Law

13

Blockchain's Heterotopia

Technological Infrastructures and Lawyering in the Public Sector

Georgios Dimitropoulos*

13.1 INTRODUCTION

New technologies are promising a new world. It has now become apparent that blockchain technology will have many more future uses than simply supporting cryptocurrencies and other cryptoassets.[1] Blockchain could support many new applications with a potentially disruptive impact on social life such as smart contracts, managing registers of assets, and the operation of autonomous agents. In addition, some governments intend to base essential government operations, such as land registries, on blockchain.[2] This may potentially lead to the law being of diminishing importance in the world.[3]

To some, these developments sound like a "utopia," namely, a "fundamentally unreal space" different from the tangible world, where everything would be possible.[4] Bitcoin and other cryptocurrencies have been supported by libertarians, anarchists, and other opponents of the global financial system in an effort to bypass the institutions of the financial markets, the central banks, and the commercial banks. This at least was the dream of Bitcoin founder, the

---

* I would like to thank Pietro Ortolani and the participants at the "Lawyering in the Digital Age" conference for their comments on a previous draft. All errors remain mine.
[1] See G. Dimitropoulos, "Blockchain Law: Between Public and Private, Transnational and Domestic" in T. Tridimas and M. Durovic (eds.), *The Future of European Private Law* (Oxford: Hart, 2020) 169–192.
[2] See generally World Government Summit, "Building the Hyperconnected Future on Blockchains" (2017); C. Mulligan, "Applications in Government, in Government Office for Science, Distributed Ledger Technology: Beyond Block Chain – A Report by the UK Government Chief Scientific Adviser" at 64.
[3] On the relationship between law and blockchain, see generally A. Walch, "The Bitcoin Blockchain as Financial Market Infrastructure: A Consideration of Operational Risk" (2015) 18 *NYU Journal of Legislation & Public Policy* 837; M. Abramowicz, "Cryptocurrency-Based Law" (2016) 58 *Arizona Law Review* 359; C. Reyes, "Conceptualizing Cryptolaw" (2017) 96 *Nebraska Law Review* 384; K. Werbach and N. Cornell, "Contracts Ex Machina" (2017) 67 *Duke Law Journal* 313; U. Rodrigues, "Law and the Blockchain" (2018) 104 *Iowa Law Review* 679; P. De Filippi and A. Wright, *Blockchain and The Law: The Rule of Code* (Cambridge, MA: Harvard University Press, 2018); M. Finck, *Blockchain Regulation and Governance in Europe* (Oxford: Oxford University Press, 2019); P. Hacker, I. Lianos, G. Dimitropoulos, and S. Eich (eds.), *Regulating Blockchain: Techno-Social and Legal Challenges* (Oxford: Oxford University Press, 2019); G. Dimitropoulos, "The Law of Blockchain" (2020) 95 *Washington Law Review* 1117. On the relationship between the state as space and law in modernity, see M. Meccarelli and M. J. Solla Sastre, "Spatial and Temporal Dimensions for Legal History: An Introduction" in M. Meccarelli and M. J. Solla Sastre (eds.), *Spatial and Temporal Dimensions for Legal History: Research Experiences and Itineraries* (Frankfurt am Main: Max Planck Institute for European Legal History, 2016) 3, 9, www.rg.mpg.de/gplh_volume_6; see also A. Agüero, "Local Law and Localization of Law Hispanic Legal Tradition and Colonial Culture (16th–18th Centuries)" in the same volume, at 101.
[4] M. Foucault, "Of Other Spaces" (1986) 16 *Diacritics* 22, at 24.

pseudonymous Satoshi Nakamoto, and the crypto-community.[5] Reality has – at least so far – turned out to be different. What it has offered is rather a "heterotopia": a place, according to Michel Foucault, different from the normal space but within the actual world, that can eventually be captured by it.[6] Lawrence Lessig has already remarked about cyberspace that "[y]ou are never *just* in cyberspace; you never just go there. You are always both in real space and in cyberspace at the same time."[7] This chapter discusses blockchain as a heterotopia of contemporary legal orders.

Two opposing trends may be observed in contemporary public law: a trend toward disintermediation, on the one side, and a simultaneous growth in importance of the notion of infrastructure, as well as the legislation and regulation of infrastructure and infrastructure development, on the other. Blockchain's primary goal has been to achieve disintermediation of transactions, whereby peers as "nodes" of the blockchain network operate online to verify transactions. The trend toward disintermediation may be interpreted to have the following two consequences: first, it depersonalizes transactions. This is reflected in the idea of pseudonymity of the participants as well as the transactions on the blockchain. Second, disintermediation also despatializes transactions. There is no need, for example, for physical banks and other financial institutions as long as the network of peers can operate online to verify transactions. Both claims are limited in their accuracy.[8] The development of blockchain technology has led to the emergence of new intermediaries to replace banks and other traditional financial institutions. Moreover, blockchain has a very obvious physical, personal, and spatial representation: these are the individuals and the computers behind the nodes of a blockchain network, as well as the servers that are used to store the data produced on the blockchain. New physical spaces are also created by governments, such as innovation hubs to host FinTech activities.

At the same time, there is a new trend that is in direct tension with the initial promise of the new technologies, and more specifically blockchain. The importance of physical infrastructure is rising.[9] There is an expanding practice to develop physical infrastructure, both within – but also across – national borders. An accompanying global trend for countries is to adopt legal frameworks for the development and regulation of infrastructure. These legislative instruments take two forms: screening mechanisms for foreign investors based on national security grounds and legislation identifying a separate category of "critical infrastructure."[10]

---

[5] S. Nakamoto, "Bitcoin: A Peer-to-Peer Electronic Cash System" (2008), https://bitcoin.org/bitcoin.pdf; see also P. De Filippi, "Bitcoin: A Regulatory Nightmare to a Libertarian Dream" (2014) 3 *Internet Policy Review* 1; cf. also P. Ortolani, "The Judicialization of the Blockchain" in Hacker, Lianos, Dimitropoulos, and Eich (eds.), n. 3 at 289, 292–296.

[6] Foucault, n. 4 at 24.

[7] L. Lessig, *Code and Other Laws of Cyberspace* (New York: Basic Books, 1999) 21.

[8] K. Low and E. Mik, "Pause the Blockchain Legal Revolution" (2020) 69 *International & Comparative Law Quarterly* 135.

[9] Infrastructure is becoming more important as a conceptual category for the analysis of all areas of law; see Brett M. Frischmann, *Infrastructure: The Social Value of Shared Resources* (Oxford: Oxford University Press, 2012); Benedict Kingsbury, "Infrastructure and InfraReg: On Rousing the International law 'Wizards of Is'" (2019) 8 *Cambridge International Law Journal* 171 (putting forward the idea of developing a conceptual framework for the understanding and analysis of international law in terms of "thinking infrastructurally"); see also the "Infrastructures as Regulation" (InfraReg) Project of the Institute for International Law and Justice at New York University School of Law; more information is available at www.iilj.org/infrareg (accessed March 30, 2020). In a similar vein, legal scholarship is rediscovering the importance of space in governance; see S. Blandy and D, Sibley, "Law, Boundaries and the Production of Space" (2010) 19 *Social & Legal Studies* 275; R. Hirschl and A. Shachar, "Spatial Statism" (2019) 17 *International Journal of Constitutional Law* 387 (as well as the other articles of the special issue).

[10] See Section 13.2.2.

The two opposing trends, namely, disintermediation, on the one side, and the growth in importance and regulation of infrastructure, on the other, may be called the "infrastructural paradox" of contemporary public law.[11] This chapter proposes an infrastructural reinterpretation of blockchain – as well as all new technologies and legal tech (LT). Even the less ardent proponents of cryptocurrencies praise Bitcoin for having brought to light and having made possible the broad use of its background blockchain technology, the reason being that it offers a new technological infrastructure for the conduct of multiple activities across the span of business and government.[12]

Almost all law is about the regulation of individual behavior and the space in which individuals live, work, and operate.[13] New technologies, and particularly blockchain, are bound to have an impact on law and lawyering in the digital age as well; however, will law lose its reason for existence? And, will lawyers accordingly lose their jobs? Using the example of blockchain technology, the response of this chapter is that this is not expected to be the case. Blockchain will always have a personal and spatial dimension, which can be called the "infrastructural dimension" of blockchain. Law, lawyers, and lawyering (in the public sector) will thus remain relevant.

By acknowledging the heterotopical and infrastructural dimension of new technologies, one highlights the importance of the law for their regulation, as well as the importance of government and government intervention in remedying new inequalities that new technologies bring with them. The heterotopical and infrastructural dimension of blockchain also reveals the main tasks for public lawyering in the digital age. Public lawyering in the digital age is about finding ways to reconcile antitheses and manage contradictions, with three standing out in particular: reconciling innovation with regulation, decentralization with accountability, and the coexistence of multiple infrastructures.

The present chapter is structured as follows: Section 13.2 discusses the "infrastructural paradox" of contemporary public law, namely, the conflicting trend of an effort to depersonalize and despatialize transactions in an era of simultaneous increase in the importance of physical infrastructure and legislation relating to infrastructure. It also discusses the infrastructural dimension of blockchain and presents blockchain as a new technological infrastructure. Blockchain is thus a heterotopia, not the unregulated utopia originally envisaged and promised by software developers and the crypto-community. Section 13.3 takes up the task of analyzing the effects of blockchain as a heterotopia for law and lawyering in the public sector and highlights the lessons for public lawyers in the age of blockchain.

---

[11] Blockchain is a technology that bears and creates a variety of paradoxes; see also V. Lehdonvirta, "The Blockchain Paradox: Why Distributed Ledger Technologies May Do Little to Transform the Economy" (November 21, 2016), www.oii.ox.ac.uk/blog/the-blockchain-paradox-why-distributed-ledger-technologies-may-do-little-to-transform-the-economy/ (accessed March 30, 2020); G. Dimitropoulos, "Global Currencies and Domestic Regulation: Embedding through Enabling?" in Philipp Hacker, Ioannis Lianos, Georgios Dimitropoulos, and Stefan Eich (eds.), *Regulating Blockchain: Techno-Social and Legal Challenges* (Oxford: Oxford University Press, 2019) 112.

[12] On the application of blockchain technology in the field of infrastructure, see J. Li, D. Greenwood, and M. Kassem, "Blockchain in the Built Environment: Analysing Current Applications and Developing an Emergent Framework" in M. Skibniewski and M. Hajdu (eds.), *Proceedings of the Creative Construction Conference 2018*, Ljubljana, Slovenia (June 30–July 3, 2018); see also J. Potts, E. Rennie, and J. Goldenfein, "Blockchains and the Crypto-City" (October 24, 2017), https://ssrn.com/abstract=2982885 (accessed March 30, 2020).

[13] On space as a value that is constitutive of a legal problem being addressed, as well as other relationships between law and space, see Meccarelli and Solla Sastre, n. 3 at 18.

13.2 BLOCKCHAIN AND THE "INFRASTRUCTURAL PARADOX" OF CONTEMPORARY PUBLIC LAW

Contemporary public law is torn between disintermediation and the increasing importance of infrastructure. The present section discusses the "infrastructural paradox" of contemporary public law and showcases how blockchain has developed into a technological infrastructure facilitating multiple uses in the private as well as the public sector.

13.2.1 *Conflicting Trends in Public Law*

Michel Foucault has identified our time as the era of anxiety for space.[14] There is indeed a special position in modern societies for land and land-based law. Initially, nearly all land was owned by the government. Property in land is referred to as *real* property or *real* estate.[15] The sale of land is also more complicated and lengthier than the sale of a chattel and there are land registries and records of land purchases in all countries.

It is said that the world has already entered the fourth industrial revolution.[16] The first revolution was that of industrialization. The main feature of industrialization was factorization.[17] Confirming Foucault's observation about modernity, the first industrial revolution had thus a distinct spatial and infrastructural nature. In a historically unprecedented urbanization spree, people moved from rural places to booming cities, and new spaces were created.[18] Already with the coming of the first industrial revolution, the law changed fundamentally. The law had to react to regulate the new spaces and the position of the individual in them.

The machine is coming back again, and this is raising multiple societal and legal questions. The new coming of the machine is being shaped to a large extent by blockchain technology and is associated with a move from physical power to knowledge-based work. While the machine replaced manual work and physical labor during industrialization, new technologies such as AI, machine learning, and blockchain are and will be replacing knowledge-based work. The fourth industrial revolution accordingly poses different challenges to law, regulation, and society at large.

Blockchain technology promises a new world: it promises the elimination, or rather the minimization, of the role of the individual as well as of space in society. This may potentially lead to the law diminishing in importance – at least in its traditional form.[19] Almost all law is about the regulation of individual behavior and the space in which individuals live, work, and operate; but blockchain is founded on an anonymous network of peers operating in a digital environment.[20] Accordingly, lawyers may become redundant as well.

---

[14] Foucault, n. 4.

[15] See Meccarelli and Solla Sastre, n. 3 at 15 (using the notion of "spatialization"); see also M. Meccarelli, "The Assumed Space: Pre-reflective Spatiality and Doctrinal Configurations in Juridical Experience" (2015) 23 *Rechtsgeschichte* 241.

[16] UNCTAD, "Development 4.0: Opportunities and Challenges for Accelerating Progress towards the Sustainable Development Goals in Asia and the Pacific" (2018), www.asia-pacific.undp.org/content/rbap/en/home/library/sustainable-development/Asia-Pacific-Development-40.html (accessed March 30, 2020).

[17] K. Polanyi, *The Great Transformation: The Political and Economic Origins of Our Time* (Boston: Beacon Press, 1944, 1957, 2001).

[18] Ibid.

[19] On the relationship between the state as space and law in modernity, see Meccarelli and Sastre, n. 3 at 3, 9.

[20] See ibid. at 18 (on space as a value that is constitutive of a legal problem being addressed, as well as other relationships between law and space).

Blockchains are digital ledgers that offer a record-keeping function. By sharing databases among multiple parties, blockchain's great aspiration was to remove the need for intermediaries who were previously required to act as trusted third parties to verify, record, and coordinate transactions;[21] blockchain's primary goal has been to achieve disintermediation of transactions, whereby peer nodes operate online to verify transactions on a blockchain in a self-governed way. The removal of the human or institutional third parties is a "core value proposition" of blockchain:[22] "Disintermediation is the technology's related promise. As a consequence of their very structure, blockchains are widely considered to decentralize and disintermediate economic relations."[23] When value is transferred through blockchain networks, the traditional human-based intermediaries responsible for verifying and validating transactions should become obsolete.[24] Disintermediation has a double effect: first, it tends to depersonalize transactions. This is reflected in the idea of pseudonymity.[25] Second, it tends to despatialize transactions. There should be, for example, no need for physical banks and other financial institutions so long as the network of peers can operate online.

Both claims are limited in their accuracy, however.[26] Rather than depersonalizing transactions, the development of blockchain technology has in fact led to the development of new intermediaries to replace banks and other traditional financial institutions. New intermediaries have arisen in the broader cryptoasset and blockchain environment. The cryptocurrency market has developed and most people will still rely on intermediaries when using cryptocurrencies,[27] such as trading platforms and exchanges of cryptocurrencies to fiat currencies, digital wallet service providers, payment systems and pricing indices, and other clearinghouses for cryptocurrency transactions.[28] New types of intermediaries are also being created. "Tumblers" or "mixers" offer services that obscure the origin of virtual currencies by allowing users to mix their coins, swap them, and change them from one address to another.[29] This achieves some further anonymity, but adds one more intermediary between the user and the token. Intermediary intervention can only be expected to increase as the proportion of cryptocurrencies and other cryptoassets in the global economy increases. The Bitcoin model of production of new currency, for example, presents an effort to replicate scarcity in the market. Late adopters and other interested individuals who have no capabilities in coding will not be able to produce new coins through mining; the Bitcoin economy will thus rely mostly on users buying Bitcoins with fiat currency through exchanges, namely, through the intervention of intermediaries.[30] Finally,

---

[21] J. Brito, H. Shadab, and A. Castillo, "Bitcoin Financial Regulation: Securities, Derivatives, Prediction Markets, and Gambling" (2014) 16 *Columbia Science and Technology Law Review* 144 216–218.

[22] Finck, n. 3 at 12.

[23] Ibid. at 18.

[24] M. Swan and P. de Filippi, "Toward a Philosophy of Blockchain: A Symposium: Introduction" (2017) 48 *Metaphilosophy* 604.

[25] Despite the usual misperception that blockchain anonymizes transactions, it does not. It only achieves pseudonymity of transactions, with the potential of the identification of the persons behind the transactions. In the Bitcoin blockchain, for example, Bitcoin users usually rely on intermediaries to purchase Bitcoins; these intermediaries often require identifying information to open an account. Authorities and/or hackers can potentially use this personal data to de-anonymize the user; see M. Möser, "Anonymity of Bitcoin Transactions," Münster Bitcoin Conference (2013), https://pdfs.semanticscholar.org/e1ae/d9296c3af9139f48d15e043e2e8beab55409.pdf (accessed March 30, 2020).

[26] Cf. also Low and Mik, n. 8.

[27] Ibid.

[28] See T. Moore and N. Christin, "Beware of the Middleman: Empirical Analysis of Bitcoin-Exchange Risk" in A.-R. Sadeghi (ed.), *Financial Cryptography and Data Security* (Berlin: Springer, 2013) 26.

[29] See https://bitcoinmagazine.com/guides/what-are-bitcoin-mixers (accessed July 15, 2020).

[30] A. Guadamuz and C. Marsden, "Blockchains and Bitcoin: Regulatory Responses to Cryptocurrencies" (2015) 20 *First Monday*, https://firstmonday.org/article/view/6198/5163.

existing payment intermediaries like PayPal have included Bitcoin and other cryptocurrencies in their services.[31]

In addition, blockchain has very obvious physical, personal and spatial representations, which are showcased in Section 13.2.3. At the same time, there is a new trend that is in direct confrontation with the initial promise of the new technologies, and more specifically blockchain technology: physical infrastructure is generally becoming more important. There is an expanding practice to develop physical infrastructure within national borders – but also across national borders. There is an accompanying global trend among governments to develop legal frameworks regarding infrastructure.

Two opposing trends may thus be observed in public law: disintermediation, on the one side, and a growth in importance of the notion of infrastructure, as well as the legislation and regulation of infrastructure and infrastructure development, on the other. This may be called the "infrastructural paradox" of public law.[32]

Section 13.2.2 discusses the trend of the rise of physical infrastructure in contemporary legal orders, and Section 13.2.3 turns to the infrastructural dimension of blockchain. Both moves contradict the original promise of blockchain technology.

13.2.2 Rise of Physical Infrastructure in Public Law

The anxiety of the epoch concerning land and space is now taking on a new dimension as anxiety for infrastructure. While blockchain has promised the diminishing presence of persons, space, and infrastructure through disintermediation, there is a newer trend that is in direct confrontation with this promise. The importance of physical infrastructure is rising. There is an expanding practice to develop physical infrastructure not only within national borders, but also across national borders. Most countries around the world are responding to this need by developing legal frameworks regulating infrastructure. These legislative efforts take two forms: screening mechanisms for foreign investors based on national security and legislation identifying a separate category of "critical infrastructure."

The United States has the oldest mechanism for the protection of domestic companies from foreign investment. Since 2008, the relevant framework has been developing in the direction of protecting critical infrastructure, critical technologies, and real estate.[33] Australia has also adopted the Foreign Acquisitions and Takeovers Act 1975 for the screening of foreign investment. This Act has a special focus on real estate and infrastructure.[34] The European Union in 2019 developed a framework for the screening of foreign direct investment in the European Union that specifically mentions investment in critical infrastructure and technologies, includ-

---

[31] See R. Mac, "PayPal Takes Baby Step toward Bitcoin, Partners with Cryptocurrency Processors," Forbes.com (September 23, 2014), www.forbes.com/sites/ryanmac/2014/09/23/paypal-takes-small-step-toward-bitcoinpartners-with-cryptocurrency-processors (accessed March 30, 2020).

[32] See also "The Blockchain Paradox: Why Distributed Ledger Technologies May Do Little to Transform the Economy," www.oii.ox.ac.uk/blog/the-blockchain-paradox-why-distributed-ledger-technologies-may-do-little-to-transform-the-economy/ (accessed March 30, 2020).

[33] See Section 721 of the Defense Production Act of 1950, 50 U.S.C. App. 2170, as amended by the Foreign Investment and National Security Act of 2007, and the Foreign Investment Risk Review Modernization Act of 2018 (FIRRMA).

[34] See Section 39 ("significant action"); Section 46 ("notifiable action"); Section 50 ("threshold test" and "change in control"); Section 80 ("Notice of notifiable actions and significant actions") of the Foreign Acquisitions and Takeovers Act 1975.

ing key enabling technologies.[35] Thus, the newest regulatory trend in investment screening laws has been to identify critical infrastructure and technologies as separate categories that may potentially raise issues of national security and allow government intervention to control investment in these areas.[36]

Apart from screening laws, various jurisdictions are developing separate regulatory frameworks for a new category of "critical infrastructure." This is also reflected in statutes on the protection of critical infrastructure and critical technologies that all discussed countries have developed alongside the investment screening laws. Already since 9/11 there has been an increased awareness in the United States regarding a separate category of critical infrastructure that needs to be protected.[37] In addition to the screening law, Australia has also adopted a law on the protection of critical infrastructure.[38] The European Union developed a framework for cross-border infrastructure long before the adoption of the FDI Screening Regulation.[39] The institutions administering critical infrastructure are often involved in the foreign investment screening process.[40]

13.2.3 Infrastructural Dimension of Blockchain

Blockchain technology initially promised a utopia of the digital world, an unreal space, different from the actual world, where everything would be possible.[41] Bitcoin and other cryptocurrencies have been developed by libertarians, anarchists, and other opponents of the global financial system in an overall effort to bypass the mainstream institutions of the financial markets.[42] The reality turned out to be different. What was offered was rather a "heterotopia," a place different from the normal space but within the actual world, that can eventually be captured by it.[43]

As explained above, modernity as well as modern law has a distinct spatial and, more recently, infrastructural quality. Blockchain also has a distinctly personal and spatial dimension, which

---

[35] Regulation (EU) 2019/452 of the European Parliament and of the Council of 19 March 2019 establishing a framework for the screening of foreign direct investments into the Union, L 79 I/1 (21.3.2019); see Article 4(1)(a) of the Regulation.

[36] The Russian Federation's legislation on foreign investment screening specifically mentions cryptographic services with a view to controlling foreign investment in companies working in the area of cryptography; see Federal Law No. 57-FZ "On the Procedures for Foreign Investments in Companies of Strategic Significance for National Defense and Security," dated April 29, 2008 (the "Strategic Companies Law").

[37] See Presidential Policy Directive 21 (PPD-21) – Critical Infrastructure Security and Resilience (February 12, 2013), https://obamawhitehouse.archives.gov/the-press-office/2013/02/12/presidential-policy-directive-critical-infrastructure-security-and-resil; see also PPD-21 under "Definitions": "The term 'critical infrastructure' has the meaning provided in Section 1016(e) of the USA Patriot Act of 2001 (42 U.S.C. 5195c(e)), namely systems and assets, whether physical or virtual, so vital to the United States that the incapacity or destruction of such systems and assets would have a debilitating impact on security, national economic security, national public health or safety, or any combination of those matters."

[38] See Security of Critical Infrastructure Act 2018, www.legislation.gov.au/Details/C2018A00029 (accessed March 30, 2020); see Section 9 ("Meaning of *critical infrastructure asset*"); Section 18 regarding Part 2 of the Act ("Register of Critical Infrastructure Assets" and "Obligation to give information and notify events"); Section 50 ("Declaration of assets by the Minister").

[39] Council Directive 2008/114/EC of 8 December 2008 on the identification and designation of European critical infrastructures and the assessment of the need to improve their protection.

[40] See Australian Government, Department of Home Affairs, "The Critical Infrastructure Centre and Foreign Investment," www.homeaffairs.gov.au/nationalsecurity/Documents/cic-factsheet-critical-infrastructure-centre-foreign-investment.pdf (accessed March 30, 2020).

[41] Foucault, n. 4 at 24.

[42] See n. 5.

[43] Foucault, n. 4 at 24.

may be termed the "infrastructural dimension" of blockchain. Blockchain has physical manifestations, as well as effects on the physical environment that are showcased in Section 13.2.3.1.

13.2.3.1 Physical Manifestations

Blockchain has its own distinct physical and spatial manifestations. First of all, individuals and computers compose the nodes of a blockchain; physical IT infrastructures in the form of servers are used to store the data produced on any blockchain. In addition, (data) mining conglomerates have been established and developed physical spaces in order to host miners and mining activities that are vital for the operation of blockchain.[44] Moreover, while the pseudonymity of the founder of Bitcoin worked toward reinforcing a nonpersonal imagery of blockchain, various blockchain leaders, such as the founders of Ethereum, have been very vocal about their technology and active in its promotion. While software developers were initially in the background, they have come into the foreground of the technology and into the public eye, further adding to a more express understanding of the infrastructural dimension of blockchain. Overall, blockchain technology has not eliminated the need for consensus by individuals.[45] One may even say that "those trusting the system ... don't, ultimately, trust numbers and mathematics but, rather, the humans behind them."[46]

In addition, new spaces such as innovation hubs are being created by governments to host activities relating to new technologies. Increasingly, countries around the world have started adopting policies directed toward the promotion of FinTech start-ups, prominently also including start-ups developing blockchain technology and cryptocurrencies. FinTech promotion policies include launching innovation hubs to help FinTech start-ups comply with the relevant laws and regulations and establishing regulatory sandboxes for new financial services participants – involving the lowering of licensing barriers for digital financial services participants reaching sometimes all the way to FinTech licensing exemptions.[47]

These policies allow businesses to test innovative products, services, business models, and delivery mechanisms in a more relaxed regulatory environment. Innovation hubs offer support to FinTech businesses that have innovation potential, namely, dedicated teams and contacts to help them understand the relevant regulatory framework and how it applies to them.[48] Since the United Kingdom took the lead in creating the UK Innovation Hub and a special regulatory regime for FinTech in 2015, many more countries, especially in the Asia Pacific region, such as Australia, Hong Kong, Malaysia, and Singapore, have followed its lead. The Australian Securities and Investment Commission (ASIC), for example, has launched an innovation hub to help FinTech start-ups on compliance matters.[49] The American Securities and Exchange Commission (SEC) has also launched its own Strategic Hub for Innovation and Financial Technology (FinHub).[50]

Finally, cryptoassets have an on-chain value that is endogenous to the token; this is, for example, the case with cryptocurrencies; sometimes tokens only represent an asset, in the form

---

[44] "Bitcoin Mining Centralization: The Market Is Fixing Itself," *Coin Brief* (June 19, 2018), https://99bitcoins.com/bitcoin-mining-free-market/ (accessed March 30, 2020).

[45] Finck, n. 3 at 6.

[46] Ibid. at 182.

[47] See generally P. Shoust, "Regulators and Fintech: Influence Is Mutual?," (undated), http://pubdocs.worldbank.org/en/770171476811898530/Session-4-Pavel-Shoust-Regulatory-Sandboxes-21-09-2016.pdf (accessed March 30, 2020).

[48] The UK FCA's "Project Innovate" is a very good example since it operates an innovation hub and a regulatory sandbox.

[49] See generally ASIC, "Testing Fintech Products and Services without Holding an AFS or Credit Licence," Regulatory Guide 257 (RG 257).

[50] More information can be found at www.sec.gov/finhub (accessed March 30, 2020).

of a product, service or entitlement, in the physical world.[51] There are thus very often gates from the digital to the physical world and the other way round. Smart contracts and DAOs have "exit-points" of interaction with the physical world using sensors that are called "oracles."[52] Oracles record and introduce information from the physical to the digital blockchain world.[53]

13.2.3.2 Effects on the Individual and Society

New technologies will also unavoidably have an effect on individuals and on the physical environment.[54] First, they create a sharp divide between those with access to the Internet and those without, or with poor connectivity. The digital divide is even more pronounced for blockchain.[55] Bitcoin was created as the currency of a specific community of people and is still very largely used by the same community. Cryptocurrencies may eventually turn out to be the currency of the privileged parts of the global population with access to the Internet. The same may apply to trade with cryptotokens. This brings us to the second physical manifestation of blockchain, namely, the divide between those who know how to code and those who do not. Bitcoin – and other cryptocurrencies – are peculiar in the production of new value in the system in that new Bitcoins are generated as a reward and at the same time as an incentive for the miners as the guardians of the system. Not everybody has the knowledge, capabilities, or the desire to code and become a miner; the production of new wealth is thus reserved either to the individuals that belong to the first community that established Bitcoin as a club privilege or to new mining companies that are involved in the business of producing new Bitcoins. The third possible manifestation is that caused by the geography as well as the natural and climatic conditions prevalent in a country.[56] Mining takes significant computing power. Greater computing power can generally be achieved in countries with a colder rather than a warmer climate. Huge parts of the world are by default excluded from the cryptocurrency map as a natural locus for mining, like the Middle East, parts of Latin America, Central Africa, and the Mediterranean. This creates new comparative advantages for the cooler countries in northern Europe and North America. Additionally, the verification process for blockchain, such as mining on the Bitcoin blockchain, is a very resource-intensive exercise. Mining and verification processes may have very adverse consequences on the environment that will eventually have to be mitigated.[57]

Finally, the rise of blockchain technology in the financial sector – currencies and transactions – has to some extent led to the strengthening of banks and other financial institutions.[58] While these institutions were meant to be bypassed, they have captured the field of development

---

[51] Finck, n. 3 at 10.
[52] "How Do Oracle Services Work under the Hood?," *Ethereum Stack Exchange*, https://ethereum.stackexchange.com/questions/11589/how-do-oracle-services-work-under-the-hood (accessed March 30, 2020); see also A. Egberts, "The Oracle Problem – an Analysis of How Blockchain Oracles Undermine the Advantages of Decentralized Ledger Systems" (December 12, 2017), https://ssrn.com/abstract=3382343 (accessed March 30, 2020).
[53] Oracles have a particular relevance for the "Internet of Things"; see P. De Filippi and S. Hassan, "Blockchain Technology as a Regulatory Technology: From Code Is Law to Law Is Code" (2016) 21 *First Monday* (special issue on "Reclaiming the Internet with distributed architectures").
[54] See Dimitropoulos, n. 3.
[55] UNDP, "Beyond Bitcoin: Using Blockchain to Advance the SDGs," https://feature.undp.org/beyond-bitcoin/ (accessed March 30, 2020) ("Then there is the digital divide: it is the most marginalized, the poor, rural populations, and the displaced who are the least likely to have access to reliable internet connections").
[56] Ibid.
[57] See J. Truby, "Decarbonizing Bitcoin: Law and Policy Choices for Reducing the Energy Consumption of Blockchain Technologies and Digital Currencies" (2018) 44 *Energy Research & Social Science* 399.
[58] See E. Ganne, *Can Blockchain Revolutionize International Trade?* (Geneva: World Trade Organization, 2018) 54.

of new technologies relating to blockchain, and they are now at the forefront of blockchain technology developments. This way, they may be bypassing certain restrictions that were imposed on them in the aftermath of the financial crisis.

13.2.3.3 *Blockchain as a Technological Infrastructure*

At the same time, blockchain as such is an infrastructure; a "nontraditional" or "intellectual infrastructure" that has a global outreach.[59] Blockchain provides the "infrastructure" of the global services industry. The sector-specific applications of blockchain can provide sectoral infrastructures for the facilitation of various activities in the relevant sectors. The Bitcoin blockchain, for example, operates as a "financial market infrastructure" for worldwide monetary transactions.[60] Blockchain could become the basis of the future "trade infrastructure," supporting transactions among logistics and transportation companies that constitute the backbone of international trade.[61]

What has been characterized as an "irony" given the origin of blockchain in the anarcho-libertarians of the digital world, the application of blockchain technology is fast transitioning from the private to the public sector as governments around the world do not want to be left behind when it comes to the use of technology.[62] Many government-related services could be provided without direct involvement of government – at least in the way that government is involved today. Some governments are more reluctant to relinquish their traditional trust-mediating role, while others are more open to new ways of delivery of government services. In some countries, like Estonia and Dubai in the United Arab Emirates, blockchain is being used as part of a broader approach to public service delivery, while in other countries, blockchains are used in more specific applications in the public sector such as the secure storage of healthcare-related data, attestation, or real estate transactions.[63] Blockchain is thus rapidly becoming a technological infrastructure for the facilitation of various functions in the public sector.

13.3 LAW AND LAWYERING IN THE DIGITAL AGE OF BLOCKCHAIN

The heterotopical nature of blockchain means that legal orders around the world have been able to capture blockchain and its uses. Different jurisdictions have responded in different ways to the rise of blockchain and cryptoassets; some have seen a need to control, while others seek to enable. Blockchain as an infrastructural heterotopia also means a different role for lawyers and public lawyering. Section 13.3.1 concludes with the regulatory reaction of the law to the rise of blockchain and the new role for lawyering in the digital age.

---

[59] Nontraditional and intellectual infrastructures are nontraditional infrastructure resources enabling, framing, and supporting a wide range of productive activities – mostly downstream – of economic and social nature in the lives of individuals; see Frischmann, n. 9 at 253.
[60] Walch, n. 3.
[61] See Ganne, n. 59 at 44.
[62] "Governments May Be Big Backers of the Blockchain," *The Economist* (June 1, 2017), www.economist.com/news/business/21722869-anti-establishment-technology-faces-ironic-turn-fortune-governments-may-be-big-backers (accessed March 30, 2020).
[63] Important public sector applications are identity management and attestation; the keeping of government records, such as land registration and corporate registration records; citizen services management in areas such as healthcare; the conduct of government activities, such as voting, taxation, customs, and public procurement; see J. Woods, "Blockchain: Public Sector Use Cases," CryptoOracle (October 2, 2018), https://medium.com/crypto-oracle/blockchain-public-sector-use-cases-49a2d74ad946 (accessed March 30, 2020).

13.3.1 Law's Stance and Regulatory Reaction to the Rise of Blockchain

The law is famously reactive.[64] It usually intervenes to regulate after the social facts that have led to the need for its existence have arisen. For this reason, the law typically has a negative stance toward the artificial and the appearance of new worlds such as the digital world of the blockchain. Even the more pragmatic Anglo-Saxon common law has had a negative stance toward the new and the artificial in the course of its development. This is reflected in the development of modern torts theory of strict liability. The modern theory of strict liability was advanced in the English decision *Rylands v. Fletcher*.[65] In *Rylands v. Fletcher*, there was an action against defendant mill owners who had built a large reservoir for the collection of water on their property. When the reservoir's barriers failed, impounded water flooded into the plaintiff's working mine shafts. The Exchequer Chamber found liability, imposing strict liability upon those who introduce a hazardous condition upon their property that, upon its escape, causes harm to another. The House of Lords added that liability should attach only if the activity was not typical, namely, "non-natural," to the land. This was the beginning of strict liability for abnormally dangerous activities and the subsequent creation of product liability.

Expectedly, various jurisdictions have reacted in the same way against the risks posed by cryptoassets and other applications of blockchain. Blockchain has faced a wave of regulatory backlash, with many countries around the world developing legal frameworks for the regulation of blockchain and cryptoassets such as cryptocurrencies. These are usually countries that have realized the potentially disruptive nature of cryptoassets functioning as currencies and have mainly pursued two approaches in their regulation: command and control and various intermediate interventions.[66] China has been the main example of a jurisdiction attempting a major ban on the use of cryptocurrencies.[67] Three main intermediate responses can be identified: First, cryptocurrencies have been subjected to related "neighboring" regulatory regimes and disciplines. For example, one of the first measures adopted in the United States with regard to cryptocurrencies was the imposition of an anti–money laundering regime.[68] Likewise, the SEC has successfully placed cryptoassets under its regulatory ambit by imposing sanctions on

---

[64] See generally on this point G. Dimitropoulos, "Compliance through Collegiality: Peer Review in International Law" (2016) 37 *Loyola of Los Angeles International and Comparative Law Review* 275; but see M. S. McDougal, "Law and Power" (1952) 46 *American Journal of International Law* 102 111 ("Law is not a frozen cake of doctrine designed only to protect interests in status quo"). According to Max Weber, law does not consist only of coercive rules, especially in the framework of the economy, but also of "legal empowerment rules" and "enabling laws"; see M. Weber, *Economy and Society*, Guenther Roth and Claus Wittich (eds.) (Berkeley: University of California Press, 1978 [1922]) 730–731; G. Dimitropoulos, "Global Administrative Law as 'Enabling Law': How to Monitor and Evaluate Indicator-Based Performance of Global Actors," IRPA Working Paper – GAL Series No. 7/2012 at 22–28.

[65] *Rylands v. Fletcher*, L.R. 1 Ex. 265 (1866).

[66] See generally Dimitropoulos, n. 11 at 116–120.

[67] The PBOC issued jointly with four other government agencies the "Notice on Precautions against the Risks of Bitcoins" disallowing banks and other financial and payment institutions from using and trading in Bitcoin; see People's Bank of China, Ministry of Industry and Information Technology, China Banking Regulatory Commission, China Securities Regulatory Commission and China Insurance Regulatory Commission, "Notice on Precautions against the Risks of Bitcoins" (2013), YIN FA, 2013, No. 289, www.miit.gov.cn/n1146295/n1652858/n1652930/n3757016/c3762245/content.html (March 30, 2020).

[68] FinCEN issued in 2013 a Guidance specifying that "decentralized" – i.e., based on public permissionless blockchains – virtual currencies should comply with money laundering regulations; see US Department of the Treasury, Financial Crimes Enforcement Network (FinCEN), "Application of FinCEN's Regulations to Persons Administering, Exchanging, or Using Virtual Currencies" FIN-2013-G001 (2013), www.fincen.gov/sites/default/files/shared/FIN-2013-G001.pdf (accessed March 30, 2020).

unauthorized traders operating securities online for cryptocurrencies like Bitcoin and Litecoin.[69] Second, domestic regulators, including the European Banking Authority (EBA) and the SEC, have issued warnings regarding cryptocurrencies.[70] Third, many countries have introduced various taxation schemes for cryptoassets.[71] The Internal Revenue Service (IRS) in the United States, for instance, issued a Notice clarifying that while virtual currencies are used by consumers in the same way as legal tender, the disposition of Bitcoin is – unlike cash – a taxable transaction to the consumer.[72]

Other countries have focused on the benefits of blockchain technology and have adopted more favorable approaches to the technology as well as cryptoassets, enabling their development and use. Governments may enable the adoption of cryptoassets and other blockchain applications in the private sector,[73] or even adopt blockchain for the provision of government services, as has been observed above.[74] Increasingly, countries around the world have started adopting policies directed toward the promotion of FinTech start-ups, also including start-ups working toward the development of blockchain technology and cryptoassets.[75]

Some of these enabling measures again showcase the distinct infrastructural dimension of blockchain. Countries, states, and cities alike are taking, for example, mining and mining activities or similar blockchain-based activities into account in their zoning and planning legislation and regulations. The state of New York has established a taskforce with the aim of studying the potential assignment of economic empowerment zones for the mining of cryptocurrencies.[76] The state of Arizona has taken private mining into account in its new regulatory package on blockchain. Arizona has passed a variety of measures along these lines making signatures, records, and contracts secured through blockchain technology legally valid.[77] Another Arizona law prohibits any county from disallowing individuals from "running a node on blockchain technology" in a residence.[78] Similar initiatives are bound to be adopted in the very near future elsewhere as well.

---

[69] See SEC, "SEC Sanctions Operator of Bitcoin-Related Stock Exchange for Registration Violations" (December 8, 2014), www.sec.gov/news/press-release/2014-273 (accessed March 30, 2020). The SEC issued a report in 2017 labeling the 2016 DAO tokens securities; see US Securities and Exchange Commission, "SEC Exposes Two Initial Coin Offerings Purportedly Backed by Real Estate and Diamonds" (September 29, 2017), www.sec.gov/news/press-release/2017-185-0 (accessed March 30, 2020); Complaint, *Securities and Exchange Commission v. Plexcorps, et al.*, CV17–7007, www.sec.gov/litigation/complaints/2017/comp-pr2017-219.pdf (accessed March 30, 2020). Order, *In re Minchee, Inc.*, (December 11, 2017), www.sec.gov/litigation/admin/2017/33-10445.pdf. FinHub, the innovation hub of the SEC, has published a framework for analyzing whether a digital asset is a security; see SEC FinHub, "Framework for 'Investment Contract' Analysis of Digital Assets," www.sec.gov/corpfin/framework-investment-contract-analysis-digital-assets (accessed March 30, 2020).

[70] See SEC, "Investor Alert: Bitcoin and Other Virtual Currency-Related Investments" (May 7, 2014), www.sec.gov/oiea/investor-alerts-bulletins/investoralertsia_bitcoin.html (accessed March 30, 2020); European Banking Authority, "EBA Warns Consumers on Virtual Currencies" (December 13, 2013), www.eba.europa.eu/-/eba-warns-consumers-on-virtual-currencies (accessed March 30, 2020).

[71] See generally O. Marian, "Are Cryptocurrencies Super Tax Havens?" (2013) 112 *Michigan Law Review First Impressions* 38.

[72] IRS, "Virtual Currency Guidance," IRS Notice 2014-21 (March 25, 2014), www.irs.gov/pub/irs-drop/n-14-21.pdf (accessed March 30, 2020); IRS, "IRS Reminds Taxpayers to Report Virtual Currency Transactions," IR-2018-71 (March 23, 2018).

[73] See Dimitropoulos, n. 11 at 126–128.

[74] See Section 13.2.3.3.

[75] See Section 13.2.3.1.

[76] Bill No. A09862 (Urban planning and cryptomining), https://nyassembly.gov/leg/?bn=A09862&term=2017.

[77] Arizona Statute § 44-7061. H.B. 2417, 53d Leg., 1st Reg. Sess. (Ariz. 2017).

[78] Arizona Statute § 11-269.22.

13.3.2 *Lawyering in the Digital Age: Reconciling Antitheses*

By acknowledging the heterotopical and infrastructural dimension of blockchain, one highlights the importance of the law for the framing of blockchain, as well as the importance of government intervention in order to remedy the new inequalities that blockchain – alongside other new technologies – bring with them.[79] The infrastructural reinterpretation of blockchain helps us better comprehend the potential development of the law in its interaction with blockchain technology – as well as other technologies – and learn certain lessons for the future of lawyering in the digital age.

While the previous version of globalization may have taught lawyers the lesson of hybridity in the sense of coming together of categories such as the domestic and the international, the public and the private,[80] the law of digital globalization teaches us a yet different lesson: multiple notions, concepts, categories, and paradigms coexist alongside multiple physical and virtual infrastructures. The task for (public) lawyers in the digital age of blockchain is to accommodate these differences. Public lawyering in the digital age becomes about reconciling antitheses and achieving interoperability of systems. One may thus expect not a diminishing, but rather a different, role for lawyers. Their primary task becomes contradiction management, namely, the management of different infrastructures and their interoperability.[81]

13.3.2.1 **Reconciling Innovation with Regulation**

One of the main advantages of the infrastructural reinterpretation of blockchain is that it helps public lawyers identify appropriate regulatory interventions. Acknowledging the personal and the spatial dimensions of new technologies may also point to the right locus for regulation.

Blockchain raises a regulatory dilemma.[82] Regulation of new technologies is sometimes difficult to justify; for example, cryptoassets rely on algorithm-generated trust.[83] Regulation might reduce trust in the technology and mathematics, which might eventually lead to distrust in the technology. Moreover, there is inherent uncertainty, as well as fundamental difficulties, when new technologies are regulated. Regulatory responses to cryptocurrencies threaten to increase the cost of compliance and/or slow the development or adoption of beneficial innovations.[84] Regulation may thus become an obstacle to innovation.[85] Government intervention in cryptoassets might stall a necessary wave of technological development and

---

[79] See also Dimitropoulos, n. 11; Dimitropoulos, n. 3.
[80] See generally G. Dimitropoulos, *Zertifizierung und Akkreditierung im Internationalen Verwaltungsverbund* (Tübingen: Mohr Siebeck, 2012).
[81] See also Dimitropoulos, n. 3.
[82] The same applies with other new technologies such as artificial intelligence; see "Elon Musk: Artificial Intelligence Is Our Biggest Existential Threat," *The Guardian* (2014), www.theguardian.com/technology/2014/oct/27/elon-musk-artificial-intelligence-ai-biggest-existential-threat (accessed March 30, 2020) ("I think we should be very careful about artificial intelligence. If I had to guess at what our biggest existential threat is, it's probably that . . . . I'm increasingly inclined to think there should be some regulatory oversight, maybe at the national and international level, just to make sure that we don't do something very foolish").
[83] See generally K. Werbach, *The Blockchain and the New Architecture of Trust* (Cambridge, MA: MIT Press, 2018).
[84] See with regard to artificial intelligence, Executive Office of the President, National Science and Technology Council Committee on Technology, "Preparing for the Future of Artificial Intelligence" (October 2016).
[85] See, e.g., OECD, "Regulatory Reform and Innovation," www.oecd.org/sti/inno/2102514.pdf; J. Pelkmans and A. Renda, "Does EU Regulation Hinder or Stimulate Innovation?," CEPS Special Report No. 96 (2014); L. Stewart, "The Impact of Regulation on Innovation in the United States: A Cross-Industry Literature Review" (2010), https://www.itif.org/files/2011-impact-regulation-innovation.pdf; K. Blind, "The Impact of Regulation on Innovation," Nesta Working Paper 12/02 (2012).

innovation that, through spillover effects, may benefit various sectors of the economy and, eventually, society at large.[86]

Taking into account the infrastructural dimension of blockchain, a way to reconcile innovation with the need for regulation is for regulatory efforts to address the physical manifestations of blockchain. One may want to look for and intervene in the physical manifestations, such as the intermediaries and their products.[87] During the first few years of existence of cryptocurrencies, intermediaries were left to self-regulate.[88] These new intermediaries can be subjected to traditional models of intermediary regulation, such as constraining regulation, while leaving the software developers unregulated.[89] This has already been the case in many countries around the world. In the United States, FinCEN has subjected certain cryptocurrency service providers to its regime as money transmitters[90] and the IRS requires certain cryptocurrency clearing organizations to provide information to the IRS and their service recipients.[91] The New York State Department of Financial Services has imposed separate licensing requirements on intermediary service providers of cryptocurrencies. The BitLicense framework creates a comprehensive licensing regime for a wide range of virtual currency intermediaries, including exchanges, wallets, dealers, and administrators.[92] The new rules require registration and licensing for certain cryptocurrency service providers. This seems to be the preferred approach in the United States, where a "Regulation of Virtual Currency Businesses Act" Committee has been established under the Uniform Law Commission in 2014. This Committee has proposed the regulation of virtual currencies in a manner similar to that which has already been adopted in New York.[93] In France, the Ministry of Finance has issued recommendations for regulation of cryptocurrencies, including obligations of intermediaries, such as limiting anonymity by making it mandatory for intermediaries and exchanges to require proof of identity upon opening an account and regulating platforms that exchange virtual currencies against official currencies at the European and international level.[94]

13.3.2.2 Reconciling Decentralization with Accountability

Decentralization is one of the main effects of the introduction of blockchain technology in social and bureaucratic organizations. With the introduction and increasing use of blockchain in government, decentralization is not only achieved for the private sector but also for the

---

[86] See T. Worstall, "Exactly What We Don't Need – Regulation of AI and Technology," *Forbes*, www.forbes.com/sites/timworstall/2016/10/12/exactly-what-we-dont-need-regulation-of-ai-and-technology/#4bc0361f5121 (accessed March 30, 2020) (with reference to the regulation of AI).

[87] The new intermediaries can be used as "regulatory agents"; see O. Marian, "A Conceptual Framework for the Regulation of Cryptocurrencies" (2015) 82 *University of Chicago Law Review Online* 53 66.

[88] L. Lam Pak Nian and D. Lee Kuo Chuen, "A Light Touch of Regulation for Virtual Currencies" in D. Lee Kuo Chuen (ed.), *Handbook of Digital Currency: Bitcoin, Innovation, Financial Instruments, and Big Data* (Amsterdam: Elsevier 2015) 309 315.

[89] On the politics of self-regulation, see P. De Filippi and B. Loveluck, "The Invisible Politics of Bitcoin: Governance Crisis of a Decentralised Infrastructure" (2016) 5 *Internet Policy Review*, https://policyreview.info/pdf/policyreview-2016-3-427.pdf.

[90] See Section 13.3.1.

[91] Ibid.

[92] New York Codes, Rules and Regulations (NYCRR), "Part 200 Virtual Currencies," www.dfs.ny.gov/legal/regulations/adoptions/dfsp200t.pdf (accessed March 30, 2020).

[93] For more information see Uniform Law Commission, www.uniformlaws.org/Committee.aspx?title=Regulation%20of%20Virtual%20Currency%20Businesses%20Act (accessed March 30, 2020).

[94] See Ministère des Finances et des Comptes Publics, Réguler les monnaies virtuelles, Recommendations 1 and 4 (2014).

administrative bureaucracy.[95] Another very important task for public lawyers in the digital age will thus be to cope with the consequences of social and legal decentralization – and, most significantly, to reconcile decentralization with accountability.

Administrative law developed in nineteenth-century France and spread quickly over the world;[96] it historically evolved as a body of law for the organization of the bureaucracy of the state[97] and then developed mechanisms to protect citizens from arbitrariness in the exercise of public power by keeping public administration within certain bounds.[98] This has been achieved through the institutionalization of procedures as well as the provision of procedural rights such as the duty to give reasons, the right to be heard, and the right of access to documents.

The administration is a bureaucratic organization that has internal operating procedures and governance structures and works based on a certain rationality aimed at taking into account the two basic functions of public administration developed in the previous paragraph. Along these lines, public administration is structured around the principle of hierarchy.[99] Hierarchy is an organizational principle of public administration, under which certain tasks are delegated to particular units of the administration in the sense of a "'vertical' division of labor."[100] This assumes as well as promotes a pyramidal structure within the administration.[101] Administrative hierarchy provides a procedure that determines who is to decide[102] and thus achieves unity of command.[103]

The very distinctive feature of administrative law as well as modern public administrations is government based on the principle of legality and due process. Accountability features as well as one of the most important principles in administrative law. Accountability in public administration takes the form of hierarchical accountability. Mechanisms of administrative supervision are usually put in place in order for one body to control the implementation of a policy or decision by another body.[104] The controlling body is more often than not a hierarchically superior body. Additional accountability lines have been developed from the public administration directly to the citizens through mechanisms of transparency and public participation that create the necessary link between the administration and the persons being governed.[105] This is very typical of US-style administrative law rationality.[106]

---

[95] See M. Atzori, "Blockchain Technology and Decentralized Governance: Is the State Still Necessary?" (December 1, 2015), https://ssrn.com/abstract=2709713 (accessed March 30, 2020).

[96] See, e.g., S. Cassese, *La construction du droit administrative* (Paris: Montchrestien, 2000).

[97] S. Cassese, "Global Administrative Law: The State of the Art" (2015) 13 *International Journal of Constitutional Law* 465 468.

[98] On the problems of describing administration as a conceptual category, see C. Möllers, "Globalisierte Verwaltungen zwischen Verselbständigung und Übervernetzung" (2008) 39 *Rechtstheorie* 217 219–220; on the historical development of the concept, see T. Groß, "Die öffentliche Verwaltung als normative Konstruktion" in Hans-Heinrich Trute et al. (eds.), *Allgemeines Verwaltungsrecht – zur Tragfähigkeit eines Konzepts* (Tübingen: Mohr Siebeck, 2008) 349.

[99] See H. Dreier, *Hierarchische Verwaltung im demokratischen Staat: Genese, aktuelle Bedeutung und funktionelle Grenzen eines Bauprinzips der Exekutive* (Tübingen: Mohr Siebeck, 1991).

[100] H. Simon, *Administrative Behavior*, 4th ed. (New York: The Free Press, 1997) 7.

[101] Ibid.

[102] Ibid. at 193.

[103] Ibid. at 191–197.

[104] V. Bekkers and V. Homburg, "Administrative Supervision and Information Relationships" (2002) 7 *Information Polity* 129.

[105] See, e.g., D. Esty, "Good Governance at the Supranational Scale: Global Administrative Law" (2006) 115 *Yale Law Journal* 1490.

[106] See generally R. Stewart, "U.S. Administrative Law: A Model for Global Administrative Law?" (2005) 68 *Law & Contemporary Problems* 63.

While the administrative law rationality requires the principle of hierarchy and command-and-control to prevail in decision-making as well as in achieving accountability for the public administration, the use of blockchain technology by the government and society at large means decentralizing traditionally hierarchically built social organizations. This presents a great challenge to public administration, administrative law, as well as administrative lawyers. The task for the public lawyer in the digital age of blockchain is to find ways to reconcile the traditional means of exercising sovereign power with the more contemporary ways of exercising public governance. Public lawyers will be called upon to resolve problems associated with losses in hierarchy as well as traditional forms of public accountability. Diffusion of responsibility and losses of accountability, alongside difficulties in judicial review, will need to be managed. New responses need to be found to the problems posed by blockchain through interpretative and other means, particularly in cases where the decentralized blockchain system fails to produce fair results. Cases of irreversibility of transactions pose great difficulties. A blockchain-based electronic ledger is tamper-proof, in the sense that transactions in blockchain are generally irreversible, which makes blockchain (almost) immutable.[107] Contemporary lawyers are tasked to find ways to make possible the reversal of transactions that would qualify as irregular under the ordinary legal system by using the tools of traditional law and existing legislative provisions such as civil codes, as well as financial and consumer law provisions.

13.3.2.3 Reconciling the Coexistence of Multiple Infrastructures

A broader task for public lawyers will be to reconcile the antitheses of the coexistence of multiple infrastructures, particularly when the antitheses are the result of the coexistence of traditional with digital blockchain infrastructures.

One of the major areas where this need arises is in the sphere of finance and the need to reconcile conventional finance with crypto-finance.[108] Since the global financial and economic crisis, there is a general tendency at the domestic as well as global level to constrain more conventional finance.[109] At the same time, Bitcoin made its appearance on the Internet and the global money market. This gave rise to a new type of regulation with the establishment of innovation hubs and regulatory sandboxes. These developments create the paradoxical situation of constraining conventional finance, while at the same time enabling blockchain technology and FinTech. Both conventional financial institutions and new start-ups now receive incentives from regulators around the world to work around conventional finance restrictions and develop new products that are potentially no less dangerous for consumers than conventional financial products.

The FinTech industry seems to be in a contradictory position where regulatory agencies insist that the world of finance has to be tightly regulated and constrained while simultaneously engaging in neo-mercantilist strategies of attracting investment in emerging FinTech hubs. The opposing tendencies between conventional finance and cryptofinance infrastructures are difficult to reconcile – this type of "infrastructural opposition" is expected to be characteristic of the field in the years to come. Public lawyers are called upon to reconcile and manage these antitheses with the overall goal of averting a situation whereby jurisdictions are eventually left with an overall less regulated field of finance.

---

[107] See Finck, n. 3 at 30 (using the term "tamper-evident").

[108] See generally C. Harvey, "Cryptofinance" (January 14, 2016), https://ssrn.com/abstract=2438299 (accessed March 30, 2020).

[109] K. Davis, "Regulatory Reform Post the Global Financial Crisis: An Overview," www.apec.org.au/docs/11_con_gfc/regulatory%20reform%20post%20gfc-%20overview%20paper.pdf (accessed March 30, 2020).

Another issue is agency clashes within single legal orders given the bureaucracy's lack of experience in dealing with multiple infrastructures. This goes to the very core of public governance and can again be exemplified by the case of cryptoassets; given their newness, cryptoassets may fall within the regulatory ambit of many regulators in one country.[110] This has already led to complicated regulatory scenarios involving regulatory interventions by multiple agencies. In the future, this situation might lead to a greater clash of agencies within some countries as to which regulator will regulate cryptoassets and what regulatory approach should be adopted. Different agencies may have different aims based on what infrastructure they depend on and the interests of the infrastructure they are designed to promote; ministries of economics and commerce departments may typically want to create economic hubs via enabling regulation. On the other side, ministries of finance, treasury departments, and central banks will have an interest in financial stability; the banking and financial supervision authorities may seek to minimize risks for market participants and consumers; anti–money laundering agencies will be willing to assume their powers to enforce the anti–money laundering legislation; commodities regulators might wish to enter the regulatory arena as well. The interplay between the various infrastructures is thus replayed within the government, for example, in a struggle for regulatory and deregulatory power and competence among different agencies. In the United States, for instance, several agencies have claimed jurisdiction over cryptoassets. The Derivabit Order of the CFTC classifies Bitcoin and other cryptocurrency derivatives as commodities. The IRS considers Bitcoin to be "property" for US federal tax purposes;[111] FinCEN treats virtual currency as "money" for purposes of the money services business (MSB) regulations.[112] The SEC has successfully argued that Bitcoin-denominated investments are "securities" that can be regulated under the US securities laws.[113]

This creates significant regulatory confusion, which may undermine the actual power of the state to regulate, as well as the "symbolic power" of the state;[114] namely, the perception of the state and its institutions in the eyes of its citizens, further impacting its capacity to regulate. This may have negative results especially in countries with less well-established institutions or when the authority of the state is also undermined by external factors such as an economic and financial crisis, national security emergencies, or a pandemic. Public lawyers are called upon to reconcile the antitheses that are brought about by the coexistence of various physical and nonphysical infrastructures, each bearing their own rationalities and implementation mechanisms.

13.4 CONCLUSION

The previous version of globalization taught a lesson of hybridity to lawyers, namely, the coming together of different categories: the domestic and the international, the public and the private. The law of digital globalization teaches us a different lesson: various infrastructures of the physical and the digital worlds coexist, each bearing their distinct rationalities and

---

[110] R. Leckow, "Virtual Currencies – the Regulatory Challenges" (2017) *Yale Journal on Regulation: Notice & Comment* 132.
[111] See Section 13.3.1.
[112] Ibid.
[113] Ibid.
[114] P. Bourdieu, Loic J. D. Wacquant, and Samar Farage, "Rethinking the State: Genesis and Structure of the Bureaucratic Field" (1994) 12 *Sociological Theory* 1.

implementation mechanisms. An additional lesson that is that there are no utopias, only physical and digital heterotopias. In this changing social environment, what is to be expected is not a diminishing, but rather a different, role for lawyers. The primary task for contemporary public lawyers becomes contradiction management, namely, the effective management of different – physical and digital – infrastructures. Public lawyering in the digital age is about reconciling antitheses.

14

Fundamental Rights and the Use of Artificial Intelligence in Court*

Jean-Marc van Gyseghem

14.1 INTRODUCTION

The modern world increasingly integrates information and communication technologies into more and more digital services. This involves the use of artificial intelligence (AI) and its algorithms with, necessarily, a transfer of data between various stakeholders, whether through networks or devices.

When introducing its report on algorithms and human rights, the Committee of Experts of the Council of Europe explained that:

> Automated data processing techniques, such as algorithms, do not only enable internet users to seek and access information, they are also increasingly used in decision-making processes, that were previously entirely in the remit of human beings. Algorithms may be used to prepare human decisions or to take them immediately through automated means. In fact, boundaries between human and automated decision-making are often blurred, resulting in the notion of "quasi- or semi-automated decision-making."[1]

The move from human to algorithmic justice implies multidisciplinary interactions between multiple actors processing data. It also involves new actors, such as the developers of software and algorithms. This multitude of stakeholders can make it difficult for citizens to have a real understanding of the algorithm or system beneath the AI. But what do we mean by AI?

The Council of Europe considers that "in the broadest sense, the term refers indistinctly to systems that are pure science fiction (so-called 'strong' AIs with a form of self-awareness) and systems that are already operational and capable of performing very complex tasks (face or voice recognition, vehicle driving – these systems are described as 'weak' or 'moderate')."[2] In other words, "algorithms need not be software: in the broadest sense, they are encoded procedures for transforming input data into a desired output, based on specified calculations. The procedures

---

[*] This work has been done with the financial support from the European Union's Horizon 2020 general MGA program under Grant Agreements no. 830892 (SPARTA) and FEDER dans le cadre du portefeuille de projets WAL-E-CITIES (2017–2020) pour la Région Wallonne This publication reflects the views only of the authors and the European Commission cannot be held responsible for any use which may be made of the information contained therein.

[1] Committee of Experts on Internet Intermediaries (MSI-NET – CoE), "Algorithms and Human Rights: Study on the Human Rights Dimensions of Automated Data Processing Techniques and Possible Regulatory Implications" at 3, https://edoc.coe.int/en/internet/7589-algorithms-and-human-rights-study-on-the-human-rights-dimensions-of-automated-data-processing-techniques-and-possible-regulatory-implications.html (accessed July 10, 2020).

[2] Council of Europe, "What's AI," www.coe.int/en/web/artificial-intelligence/what-is-ai (accessed July 10, 2020).

name both a problem and the steps by which it should be solved." Algorithms are thus perceived as "a series of steps undertaken in order to solve a particular problem or accomplish a defined outcome."[3]

Reading these two statements, the question arises whether the definition of "intelligence" as "the ability to learn, understand, and make judgments or have opinions that are *based on reason*" is still valid.[4] Obviously, AI needs humans to exist. Even if AI could develop itself autonomously by getting information and data, human intelligence is still needed to make it work. AI will either be an expert-level system receiving data and rules/models to deliver a response, or it will be a machine learning system receiving results and data and delivering rules/models, or both. But in each case, the human is at the base of the way in which AI operates. AI does what humans tell it to do, or use the knowledge provided at its creation, with all the potential biases that will be discussed in this chapter.

The use of algorithms in justice raises many questions, such as the ones about the transparency of data processing and decisions but also about further processing, impartiality/presumption of innocence, and equal access to justice. All these issues have a significant impact on fundamental rights, which states cannot divest themselves of. Citizens are entitled to dignity and respect, and the use of AI in court will necessarily have to take these rights into account. These questions will be addressed in this chapter.

The OECD stated in May 2019 that "AI systems should be designed in a way that respects the rule of law, human rights, democratic values and diversity, and they should include appropriate safeguards – for example, enabling human intervention where necessary – to ensure a fair and just society."[5] This summarizes the issues raised by the use of AI in any processing and, even more, when using it in the course of justice.

First, it is necessary to highlight the fact that technologies are more and more integrated in the professional world, in decision-making, and in the legal environment. AI does not change this paradigm, but triggers multidisciplinary interactions between computer scientists, lawyers, policy makers, sociologists, etc. In other words, AI is not only a technical tool, but it also involves legal and social issues.

With AI, decision-making is transformed from non-autonomous systems, characterized by full human control, to autonomous systems with no or very limited human control. The rise of algorithmic governance entails a lessening of human control and self-empowerment over matters that involve decision-making. Needless to say, this less human approach entails numerous legal and ethical dilemmas.

About the use of AI in a judicial context, the Committee of Experts on Internet intermediaries (MSI-NET) of the Council of Europe[6] highlights the fact that the use of AI in crime prevention and criminal justice might generate some benefits, such as facilitating the processing of large amounts of data faster. In the past, terrorist attacks have put the use of AI under the spotlight, as states asked social networks to use algorithms to track potential terrorists. However, AI is not harmless in terms of "freedom of expression, it also raises concerns for fair trial standards contained in Article 6 of the European Charter of Human Rights (ECHR), notably the

---

[3] T. Gillespie, "The Relevance of Algorithms" in T. Gillespie, P. Boczkowski, and K. Foot (eds.), *Media Technologies: Essays on Communication, Materiality, and Society* (Cambridge, MA: MIT Press, 2014) 167.
[4] Cambridge Dictionary, emphasis added, https://dictionary.cambridge.org/dictionary/english/intelligence (accessed July 10, 2020).
[5] OECD, *Shaping the Digital Transformation in Latin America* (Paris: OECD 2019) 92, with reference to the OECD Principles on Artificial Intelligence.
[6] MSI-NET – CoE, n. 1.

presumption of innocence, the right to be informed promptly of the cause and nature of an accusation, the right to a fair hearing and the right to defend oneself in person."[7]

This chapter will explore the use of AI as an actor/instrument of justice with respect to various fundamental rights and guarantees, such as the right to respect for private life and a fair trial, which might be significantly impacted by AI.

The division of this chapter in sections and subsections is obviously arbitrary and not an easy task. Indeed, the concepts analyzed are common to various fundamental rights. However, the chapter attempts to structure the analysis in a linear way.

14.2 TRANSPARENCY

14.2.1 *Principles*

We will analyze the concept of transparency from two perspectives, namely, the right to a fair trial and the right to data protection.[8] Transparency is a cornerstone of these two fundamental rights: is found it in the data protection legislation as well in Article 6 of the ECHR (in the case of the right to a fair trial). With reference to justice, it is an element of democracy; indeed, it makes it possible to differentiate between a democratic regime and a dictatorship.

The European Court of Human Rights (ECtHR) considers that the requirement of transparency and the right to information deriving from it are fundamental.[9] The lack of transparency may give rise to a violation of Article 8 of the ECHR, as the ECtHR stated in a judgment of January 17, 2019.[10] The case was about administrative proceedings in which a transgender Macedonian national, registered as female, had introduced a request of modification of the sex/gender marker on his birth certificate. After a diagnosis of transsexuality and an adequate hormonal treatment, he succeeded in modifying the first name to a clearly male one. However, the sex/gender marker and numerical personal code remained the same (female). The reason for this was that no official document showing the change of gender was produced. The applicant complained, with no success, of the absence of a regulatory framework for legal gender recognition and the arbitrary imposition of a requirement for genital surgery. The ECtHR considered that the lack of any regulatory framework led to a lack of transparency ensuring the right to respect for the applicant's private life. The ECtHR concluded that the "legal framework in [the former Yugoslav Republic of Macedonia] does not provide 'quick, transparent and accessible procedures' for changing gender on birth certificates for transgender people."[11]

The ECtHR's decision can be easily transposed to the framework of justice. Transparency is a fundamental right of every individual, which must be adequately protected even in the context of the administration of justice.

Brought to the field of justice, the right to transparency extends, among other things, to the reasoning of judicial decisions. In a judgment of November 16, 2010, the ECtHR had the opportunity to reiterate this principle in a case relating to a decision handed down by a Belgian assize court.[12]

---

[7] Ibid. at 10.
[8] This is linked with Article 8 ECHR.
[9] ECtHR (Grde Ch.), 17 October 2019, no. 1874/13 and 8567/13, *Lopez Ribalda and others* v. *Spain*, § 131. See also Jean Herveg and Jean-Marc Van Gyseghem, "La protection des données à caractère personnel en droit européen: chronique de jurisprudence 2019" (2020) 1 *Journal européen des droits de l'homme / European Journal of Human Rights* 30.
[10] ECtHR, 17 January 2019, *X* v. *the former Yugoslav Republic of Macedonia*, no. 29683/16.
[11] Ibid.
[12] ECtHR (grand chamber), *Taxquet* v. *Belgium*, no. 926/05, 16 November 2010.

The applicant had been convicted by the assize court in Liège of murder and attempted murder. At that time, sitting juries had to answer yes or no to questions asked by the president of the assize court. There was no reasoning for the decision, only an arithmetic calculation of the answers given to the various questions that lead to a decision of guilt or acquittal. The applicant therefore brought an action before the ECtHR on the ground that the judgment of the assize court violated Article 6 §§ 1 and 3 (d) of the ECHR, inter alia, on account of the failure to give a reasoned judgment. The ECtHR considered that "the questions, which were succinctly worded and were identical for all the defendants, did not refer to any precise and specific circumstances that could have enabled the applicant to understand why he was found guilty."[13] Prior to that, the ECtHR pointed out that "the national courts must indicate with sufficient clarity the grounds on which they base their decisions"[14] and that such a statement of reasons obliges "judges to base their reasoning on objective arguments, and also preserve the rights of the defence,"[15] "it must be clear from the decision that the essential issues of the case have been addressed."[16] It should be noted, however, that the ECtHR also made it clear that the absence of a statement of reasons does not automatically entail a violation of Article 6 ECHR. Indeed, it is also necessary to ascertain whether other elements of the procedure could make up for the lack of a statement of reasons.

Another aspect of transparency lies in the public nature of the hearing: the hearings before any court must be public – with some exceptions. This publicity "contributes to the achievement of the aim of Article 6(1) ECHR, namely a fair trial, the guarantee of which is one of the fundamental principles of any democratic society."[17]

Consequently, whether we are at the level of Article 6 or Article 8 ECHR, transparency is required.

14.2.2 Transparency and AI

It is necessary to question the compatibility of AI with the principle of transparency. While AI is basically the result of human creation, it subsequently develops its own knowledge. This development takes place using the algorithm that underlies its relative "intelligence," as we saw in Section 14.1. AI works in secret, and no one is able to assist in its internal "deliberations." How can such secrecy be compatible with the transparency required by both Article 6 and 8 of the ECHR? Furthermore, if it is not compatible, how can AI be used in court?

The OECD published a set of recommendations on the use of AI. One of them highlights the fact that AI actors commit to transparency regarding AI.[18] This being said, the question remains

---

[13] Ibid. at § 96.
[14] Ibid. at § 91. See also ECtHR, *Hadjianastassiou v. Greece*, no. 12945/87, 16 December 1992 at § 33.
[15] ECtHR, n. 12 at § 91.
[16] Ibid. See also *Boldea v. Romania*, no. 19997/02, § 30, 15 February 2007.
[17] ECtHR, "Guide on Article 6 of the European Convention on Human Rights (Criminal Limb)" (April 30, 2020) at 48. See also ECtHR, *Riepan v. Austria*, no. 35115/97, § 27; *Krestovskiy v. Russia*, no. 14040/03, § 24; *Sutter v. Switzerland*, no. 8209/78, § 26.
[18] OECD, "Recommendation of the Council on Artificial Intelligence," OECD/LEGAL/0449 (May 22, 2019, https://oecd.ai/assets/files/OECD-LEGAL-0449-en.pdf (accessed August 5, 2020). "AI Actors should commit to transparency and responsible disclosure regarding AI systems. To this end, they should provide meaningful information, appropriate to the context, and consistent with the state of art:

  (i) to foster a general understanding of AI systems,
  (ii) to make stakeholders aware of their interactions with AI systems, including in the workplace,
  (iii) to enable those affected by an AI system to understand the outcome, and,
  (iv) to enable those adversely affected by an AI system to challenge its outcome based on plain and easy-to-understand information on the factors, and the logic that served as the basis for the prediction, recommendation or decision."

whether the use of algorithms in the work of the judiciary meets the requirement of transparency at the level not only of decision-making, but also of the data processing that is carried out.

The European Commission for the Efficiency of Justice (CEPEJ) published the European Ethical Charter on the Use of Artificial Intelligence in Judicial Systems and their environment, in December 2018. The CEPEJ highlights that the lack of transparency might come from intellectual property issues. Indeed, and as already mentioned, the creation process behind each AI is likely to imply patents or copyright, trade secrets, etc. This situation leads to a protection of the creation (source code, etc.) that is likely to be in conflict with transparency. CEPEJ recommends that "a balance must be struck between the intellectual property of certain processing methods and the need for transparency (access to the design process), impartiality (absence of bias), fairness and intellectual integrity (prioritising the interests of justice) when tools are used that may have legal consequences or may significantly affect people's lives."[19] The Charter thus points out the issues raised by the tension between the use of AI and the duty of transparency required by fundamental rights.

There is a delicate balance to be struck between the right of the designer of the algorithm to keep his creation secret and the right to know what the algorithm hides. This is even more true when the right to a fair trial is at stake. This balance will not be easy to find, as the holder of the intellectual property right will be extremely reluctant to disclose the codes of the algorithms. In trying to find a solution, CEPEJ highlights options ranging from a total technical transparency to an audit of the system by independent authorities or a certification granted by public authorities with regular reviews.[20]

Calls for "open source" algorithms seem to be misleading: it is hard to imagine a developer making an algorithm completely transparent, after having invested time and money in its development. It also seems useless to demand such transparency, which clashes with other principles relating to intellectual property. Developers usually rely on intellectual property rights (IPR) or other legal and technical protections for their licensing strategy. Transparency may trigger tensions between the need to create new applications and the need to protect investments. However, such transparency might be reached when the public authority is the source of the algorithm (which is rarely the case).

It can be observed that many companies are not in favor of licensing their product under an open scheme such as open source. This trend finds its justification in the fact that innovation needs IP protection to remunerate investments. The reluctance seems even stronger when dealing with algorithms such as those used in the field of AI, where competition is strong. Indeed, such inventions are at the core of the business model of many companies. As discussed above, this reluctance to license under open schemes affects the transparency principle of privacy protection and a right to a fair trial.

Loomis v. *Wisconsin*[21] is an example of this lack of willingness to be transparent. In that case, the US Supreme Court refused to consider Mr. Loomis' appeal. Mr. Loomis applied to the US Supreme Court to gain access to the source code of the software named COMPAS, on fair trial grounds. Mr. Loomis had been sentenced to a prison term by the Supreme Court of Wisconsin, which had based its decision on the results of COMPAS. This software calculates the risk of a person reoffending within two years on the basis of 137 analytical criteria. Before the Wisconsin

---

[19] CEPEJ, "European Ethical Charter on the Use of Artificial Intelligence in Judicial Systems and Their Environment," adopted at the 31st plenary meeting, Strasbourg (December 3–4, 2018), https://rm.coe.int/ethical-charter-en-for-publication-4-december-2018/16808f699c (accessed July 13, 2020).

[20] Ibid. at 11.

[21] *Loomis* v. *Wisconsin*, cert. denied, 137 S.Ct. 2290 (2017).

Supreme Court, Mr. Loomis argued that "COMPAS reports provide data relevant only to particular groups and because the methodology used to make the reports is a trade secret" he "asserted that the court's use of the COMPAS assessment infringed on both his right to an individualized sentence and his right to be sentenced on accurate information."[22]

Furthermore, the lack of openness might also impact the availability of the results created by AI, and the availability of the data reduces the possibility to improve algorithms. Indeed, algorithms need to be fed with data to improve; if the amount of data is reduced, the evolution of algorithms is curtailed and, consequently, there could be a reduction in the quality of the results, as well as the competition between developers. This, in other words, could mean that only big companies would have the ability to improve algorithms; by reducing the competition, there is a high risk of creating a monopolistic position, with a reduction of the quality of services, rising costs, and so on. For these reasons, there are now growing demands for the use of open data (and not open source), which would allow smaller developers to create AI systems with fewer constraints. It should incidentally be noted that the European Union promotes open data as an instrument for research.[23]

While it seems unrealistic to demand open-source AI, it seems desirable to require more transparency on the way the algorithm works. In other words, the developer should provide the public with "key subsets of information about the algorithms ... for example which variables are in use, which goals the algorithms are being optimized for, the training data and average values and standard deviations of the results produced, or the amount and type of data being processed by the algorithm."[24] This would likely meet the requirement of transparency of Article 8 ECHR, as well as Regulation (EU) 2016/679 of 27 April 2016 on the protection of natural persons with regard to the processing of personal data and on the free movement of such data (GDPR hereafter) and Directive (EU) 2016/680 of 27 April 2016 on the protection of natural persons with regard to the processing of personal data by competent authorities for the purposes of the prevention, investigation, detection or prosecution of criminal offenses or the execution of criminal penalties, and on the free movement of such data (the Directive hereafter), and Article 6 ECHR.

There must be transparency about the source of the data, as implicitly demanded by both Article 6 and 8 ECHR. Indeed, Article 6 ECHR requires equality of arms, and respect for the adversarial process. This, in turn, implies that the data being processed must be subject to a contradictory control by the parties, as regards both the data's quality and lawfulness. This transparency of the source of the data is also required in terms of privacy. Thus, the transparency principle contributes to the guarantee of the informational self-determination of the data subject and acts as a control on the elements on which the judge bases the analysis of the case. This is concretized by an obligation to provide information, access, etc.

When considering the use of AI in the course of justice, substantial weight should be given to the risk of lack of fairness (including transparency concerns), but also the benefits that AI can bring about. Benefits include faster justice (speedier decisions) and more consistency across cases and decisions. These are the two major points highlighted by the various reports on the use of AI in the justice system. The Council of Europe states that

---

[22] *State v. Loomis*, 881 N.W.2d 749 (Wis. 2016) (2017) 130 Harvard Law Review 1530; see also Ellora Israni, "Algorithmic Due Process: Mistaken Accountability and Attribution in State v. Loomis," *Jolt Digest* (August 31, 2017), https://jolt.law.harvard.edu/digest/algorithmic-due-process-mistaken-accountability-and-attribution-in-state-v-loomis-1 (accessed May 5, 2020).

[23] See, e.g., the Health Programme Database, https://data.europa.eu/euodp/fr/data/dataset/health-programmes-database (accessed July 13, 2020).

[24] MSI-NET – CoE, n. 1 at 38.

the trend towards using automated processing techniques and algorithms in crime prevention and the criminal justice system is growing. Indeed, there may be some benefits in such use as massive data sets may be processed more speedily or flight risks assessed more accurately. Moreover, the use of automated processing techniques for the determination of the length of a prison sentence may allow more even approaches to comparable cases.[25]

However, any judgment is built around the elements brought by the parties, including the prosecutor and investigators, in compliance with the applicable legislation. The parties must respect the applicable legislation, including the one governing privacy. This means that the parties must have the opportunity to check the legality of the evidence and, more specifically, judges have to base their decisions on these elements combined, as the case may be, with his or her own perception of the elements. However, and as stated in the ECHR, "the question which must be answered is whether the proceedings as a whole, including the way in which the evidence was obtained, were fair. This involves an examination of the 'unlawfulness' in question and, where a violation of another Convention right is concerned, the nature of the violation found."[26] And the ECtHR added that: "In that context, regard must also be had to whether the rights of the defence have been respected, in particular whether the applicant was given the opportunity of challenging the authenticity of the evidence and of opposing its use, as well as the opportunity of examining any relevant witnesses."[27]

When it comes to AI, the algorithm may have access to a large amount of data available on the Internet, creating a "data lake." This brings us to the question of big data, which is typically summarized by reference to the so-called five V's:[28]

- Volume: the amount of data processed over an extremely short time is enormous;
- Velocity: the processing of data is extremely fast;
- Variety: the data is available in many different forms (structured, text, images, etc.);
- Truthfulness: this concerns the credibility or veracity of the data;
- Value: the data must bring an added value in regard to user-defined goals.

Antoinette Rouvroy points out some issues raised by big data from a privacy perspective. One of the issues that can impact the use of AI in the courts is that "in the context of Big Data, it is the exponential quantity, and not the quality of the processed data that makes automated processing potentially problematic for the rights and freedoms of individuals."[29] Rouvroy argues that big data focuses more on the quantity than on the quality and concludes that:

> by definition, big data are massive amounts of data, a phenomenon that is in direct opposition to the major European principles of data protection, including the principles of minimization (only data necessary for the purpose) and purpose (data only collected for an identified, declared

---

[25] Ibid. at 10.
[26] ECtHR, *Allan v. United Kingdom*, no. 48539/99, 5 November 2002 at §42.
[27] Ibid. at §43.
[28] The Council of Europe defines big data as "the growing technological ability to collect, process and extract new and predictive knowledge from great volume, velocity, and variety of data. In terms of data protection, the main issues do not only concern the volume, velocity, and variety of processed data, but also the analysis of the data using software to extract new and predictive knowledge for decision-making purposes regarding individuals or groups." CoE, "Guidelines on the Protection of Individuals with Regard to the Processing of Personal Data in a World of Big Data," T-PD(2017)1 at 2.
[29] A. Rouvroy, "Homo juridicus est-il soluble dans les données?" www.researchgate.net/publication/321193294_Homo_juridicus_est-il_soluble_dans_les_donnees (accessed July 13, 2020); see also A. Rouvroy, "Des données et des hommes: Droits et libertés fondamentaux à l'ère des données massives," Conseil de l'Europe, T-PD-BUR (2015) 09 REV, January 2016; and D. Gray and D. Keats Citron "The Right to Quantitative Privacy" (2013) 98 *Minnesota Law Review* 62.

and legitimate purpose), time limitation (data must be erased once the purpose has been achieved, and may not be used, with some exceptions, for other purposes than those initially declared).... Big Data, on the contrary of minimization, is the maximum collection, automatic, by default, and unlimited storage of everything that exists in digital form, without there necessarily being a purpose established a priori: the usefulness of the data only becomes apparent along the way, thanks to the statistical practices of data-mining, machine-learning, etc. A priori useless data may prove extremely useful in the long run for profiling purposes, for example, and become more useful as the data sets grow larger.[30]

In the context of justice, the two values of volume and truthfulness raise issues. The issue of volume was discussed above, the problem of truthfulness will be discussed here of data. Assuming that having mass data does not pose a problem, it is still necessary to have quality data, especially when such data is being used as a basis for a judicial decision – a decision that will necessarily have effects, positive or negative, on the concerned individual. "Data analysis algorithms are applied to large amounts of data to find patterns of correlation within datasets without necessarily making a statement on causation .... The use of data mining and pattern recognition without 'understanding' their correlation or causal relationships may lead to errors and raise concerns about data quality."[31] Is the data source reliable? Is the data continuously updated? These are the questions that must necessarily be asked when AI is used in the administration of justice. The quality of the data is also a question for the existing legal databases used by the algorithms. Let us imagine that Mr. X appears in court for assault and battery. He acknowledges the facts and will therefore be convicted with a moderate sentence due to his confession. However, the algorithm processed by AI finds, in the databases that it has access to, a previous judgment rendered in another country, convicting Mr. X based on similar facts. With this new element, the AI system could recommend the sentencing of Mr. X to a heavier penalty, on the grounds that he is a recidivist. However, it turns out that the judgment found by the algorithm and used to set the sentence had been overturned on appeal, but that decision was not accessible. In this scenario, the data had obviously not been updated. This example shows the need for the citizen to know where the data comes from and whether it is current. In sum, although AI has a large volume of data at its disposal, this does not mean the AI outcome is reliable. The AI can and should be, at most, only an aid to the decision, but not the decision-maker itself. It must, moreover, be accompanied by transparency.

The above hypothetical raises the issue of the integrity of automated decision-making. The AI will process data received or taken from databases and will deliver a decision (even under the form of a suggestion). Both the GDPR and the Directive address the issue of automated decisions by recognizing the principle of prohibition.

Automatic decision-making also includes profiling, which is defined as "any form of automated processing of personal data consisting of the use of personal data to evaluate certain personal aspects relating to a natural person, in particular to analyse or predict aspects concerning that natural person's performance at work, economic situation, health, personal preferences, interests, reliability, behaviour, location or movements."[32] Because of the dangers of profiling, the Directive prescribes a prohibition on automated decision-making, unless the member state establishes appropriate safeguards. The same holds true for the GDPR, which also lays down a principle of prohibition, with exceptions that must be interpreted restrictively.

---

[30] Rouvroy, n. 29.
[31] MSI-NET – CoE, n. 1 at 6.
[32] Art. 4(4) GDPR.

The rationale behind these two provisions is to prevent individuals from being profiled without their knowledge and without any rules to protect their data or, more generally, their privacy. From this point of view, we can link this principle to the notion of fairness in Article 6 ECHR.

It seems important to note that if AI is introduced in the context of court proceedings, it must remain under the control of the user who is, for the purposes of this contribution, the judge. The CEPEJ[33] expresses this concern stating that the AI must help the user to gain autonomy, instead of reducing it. This also means that a judge must be able to control the automatic decision, without being bound to it. However, as highlighted by the CEPEJ, this requires an education of the users with respect to legal tech (LT), so as to allow them to understand how to control the decisions generated by these technologies and the limits of AI. These arguments support the view that AI should be seen as a decision-making tool, but not as a decision-maker.

In order to guarantee transparency, the citizen and the parties must necessarily have access to the data that had been processed by AI, in order to have the opportunity to challenge its veracity and bring counterarguments. However, is it possible for the citizen or even his or her lawyer to analyze the large volume of data processed by AI? In order to reduce the amount of data to be challenged by the citizen, the judicial decision must be very clear about the elements that the judge used to arrive at that decision. Consequently, this means that the work performed by the AI must be clearly identified and controlled before a binding decision. In other words, a human (judge) must validate the AI processing, as requested is rendered by both the Directive and GDPR.

In sum, legislative initiatives will have to be taken to ensure a transparent and fair trial as required by Article 6 ECHR, and subsequently by the Directive and the GDPR, with respect to AI. These initiatives will need to ensure transparency by providing key subsets of information about the algorithms to the public, the source of the processed data, and how decisions are reached. Besides, the concept of empowerment requires that the data subject be given more control over the subject's personal data.

14.3 IMPARTIALITY AND PRESUMPTION OF INNOCENCE

14.3.1 Principle

Article 6(2) ECHR stated that "Everyone charged with a criminal offence shall be presumed innocent until proved guilty according to law." The ECtHR in various cases viewed that:

> as a procedural guarantee in the context of a criminal trial itself, the presumption of innocence imposes requirements in respect of, amongst others, the burden of proof (*Telfner* v. *Austria*, § 15); legal presumptions of fact and law (*Salabiaku* v. *France*, § 28; *Radio France and Others* v. *France*, § 24); the privilege against self-incrimination (*Saunders* v. *the United Kingdom*, § 68); pre-trial publicity (*G.C.P.* v. *Romania*, § 46); and premature expressions, by the trial court or by other public officials, of a defendant's guilt (*Allenet de Ribemont*, §§ 35–36, *Nešťák* v. *Slovakia*, § 88).[34]

In other words, the defendant is presumed innocent as long as no definitive conviction has been pronounced.

---

[33] CEPEJ, n. 19.
[34] ECtHR, n. 17 at 58.

The concept of impartiality is also a major element to the right to a fair trial as set by Article 6 (1) ECHR, providing that "in the determination of his civil rights and obligations or of any criminal charge against him, everyone is entitled to a fair and public hearing within a reasonable time by an independent and impartial tribunal established by law."

The ECtHR has stated in various decisions that:

> Article 6(1) ECHR requires a tribunal falling within its scope to be impartial. Impartiality normally denotes the absence of prejudice or bias and its existence or otherwise can be tested in various ways (*Wettstein* v. *Switzerland*, § 43; *Micallef* v. *Malta* [GC], § 93; *Nicholas* v. *Cyprus*, § 49). The concepts of independence and impartiality are closely linked and, depending on the circumstances, may require joint examination (*Ramos Nunes de Carvalho e Sá* v. *Portugal* [GC], §§ 150 and 152 – see also, as regards their close interrelationship, §§ 153–156; *Sacilor Lormines* v. *France*, § 62). The defects observed may or may not have been remedied during the subsequent stages of the proceedings (*Helle* v. *Finland*, § 46; *Denisov* v. *Ukraine* [GC], §§ 65, 67 and 72).[35]

14.3.2 Impartiality and Presumption of Innocence and AI

If, at first glance, AI gives the impression that it can only be fair given the absence of feelings; in fact, however, it remains a human creation. Behind all AI, there is human work. The Council of Europe has rightly pointed out that the "algorithms replicate the functions previously performed by human beings but involve a quantitatively and qualitatively different decision-making logic to much larger amounts of data input."[36] It also raised a major point about human intervention in the creation of the algorithm, by pointing out that:

> In the field of crime prevention, the main policy debates regarding the use of algorithms relate to predictive policing. This approach goes beyond the ability of human beings to draw conclusions from past offences to predict possible future patterns of crime. It includes developed automated systems that predict which individuals are likely to become involved in a crime, or are likely to become repeat offenders and therefore require more severe sentencing. It also includes systems meant to predict where crime is likely to take place at a given time which are then used for prioritizing police time for investigations and arrests. Such approaches may be highly prejudicial in terms of ethnic and racial backgrounds and therefore require scrupulous oversight and appropriate safeguards. Often the systems are based on existing police databases that intentionally or unintentionally reflect systemic biases.[37]

The question of bias is crucial because it can lead to discrimination grounded on, for instance, gender, race, ethnic or sexual orientation. This would bring justice back to the darkest years of the European continent, such as 1930–1945. The question is unfortunately not only theoretical, since situations of algorithms corrupted by bias have already been discovered. For example, the aforementioned COMPAS software has been criticized by authors[38] who found that some of the criteria taken into account by the algorithm were, albeit indirectly, linked to race. This, of course, opens the door to racial prejudice.

---

[35] Ibid. at 48.
[36] MSI-NET – CoE, n. 1 at 6.
[37] Ibid. at 11–12.
[38] J. Larson, S. Mattu, L. Kirchner, and J. Angwin, "How We Analyzed the COMPAS Recidivism Algorithm," Propublica (May 23, 2016), www.propublica.org/article/how-we-analyzed-the-compas-recidivism-algorithm (accessed August 21, 2021).

The stories that gave rise to the analysis by Issac and Lum[39] are as follows:

- An eighteen-year-old girl, who already had a criminal record for acts committed while a minor, was arrested for attempting to steal an unlocked bicycle and scooter worth $80 on the street with another teenager of the same age. Her data was entered into a computer program that determined that she was at high risk of re-offending.
- A forty-one-year-old man was arrested for stealing $86.35 worth of tools from a store. This man had previously been sentenced to five years in prison for armed robbery and attempted armed robbery. His data was encoded in a software program that determined that the risk of recidivism was low.

The results obtained are troubling given the criminal background of each of them. After analysis, it turned out that there was a difference between the two individuals – the color of their skin: the teenager was black, and the man was white. Ironically, a review of the records two years later showed that the teenager had not been charged with any new crimes, while the man was now serving an eight-year sentence for breaking into a warehouse and stealing thousands of dollars' worth of electronic equipment.

With reference to COMPAS, Larson, Mattu, Kirchner, and Angwin[40] reveal that "black defendants were often predicted to be at a higher risk of recidivism than they actually were."[41] A *contrario*, "white defendants were often predicted to be less risky than they were."[42] Their analysis also "showed that even when controlling for prior crimes, future recidivism, age, and gender, black defendants were 45 percent more likely to be assigned higher risk scores than white defendants."[43]

This confirms Kraemer, van Overveld, and Peterson's opinion that:

> some algorithms clearly produce genuine value-judgments. Consider, for example, algorithms used in decision support programs, i.e. systems that help decision makers to make better decisions by ranking a set of alternative actions with respect to some predefined criteria. A typical outcome of an algorithm used in such a program is a verdict like "Alternative X is the best option" or "Alternative X is better than alternative Y with respect to criterion Z." It would be pointless to deny that these sentences express genuine value-judgments.[44]

The authors conclude that "a strong case can be made for the claim that some algorithms are essentially value-laden. Some algorithms, such as those used for classifying cells as diseased or non-diseased, forces the designer of the algorithm to take a stand on controversial ethical issues, e.g. whether it is more desirable to prefer false positive errors over false negative ones."[45]

---

[39] William Issac and Kristian Lum, "To Predict and Serve? Significance," The Royal Statistical Society (October 10, 2016), http://onlinelibrary.wiley.com/doi/10.1111/j.1740-9713.2016.00960.x/epdf (accessed May 15, 2020).
[40] Larson, Mattu, Kirchner, and Angwin, n. 38.
[41] Ibid. The authors found that "black defendants who did not recidivate over a two-year period were nearly twice as likely to be misclassified as higher risk compared to their white counterparts (45 percent vs. 23 percent)."
[42] Ibid. The authors found that "white defendants who re-offended within the next two years were mistakenly labeled low risk almost twice as often as black re-offenders (48 percent vs. 28 percent)."
[43] Ibid. The authors found that "Black defendants were also twice as likely as white defendants to be misclassified as being a higher risk of violent recidivism. And white violent recidivists were 63 percent more likely to have been misclassified as a low risk of violent recidivism, compared with black violent recidivists" and that "the violent recidivism analysis also showed that even when controlling for prior crimes, future recidivism, age, and gender, black defendants were 77 percent more likely to be assigned higher risk scores than white defendants."
[44] F. Kraemer, K. van Overveld, and M. Peterson, "Is There an Ethics of Algorithms?" (2011) 13(3) *Information & Communications Technology Law* 251.
[45] Ibid.

The same type of bias can be encoded in relation to, for instance, ethnicity or geographical location (e.g., place of residence), in predictive criminal software. Unchecked, these biases can lead to unacceptable injustices in our democratic society. The risk of bias is high, and can lead to biased decisions that are not compliant with Article 6 ECHR. Indeed, these biases jeopardize the presumption of innocence: as mentioned above, the study by Larson, Mattu, Kirchner, and Angwin highlighted major violations. An AI – if created with bias, intentionally or not – might determine in advance that someone is at risk of committing a crime, on the basis of elements whose quality has not been demonstrated. This shows again the necessity of having human control over the way AI works.

Also in Europe, some jurisdictions make use of predictive software. Namely, this kind of software has been set up by the Durham police to predict the risk of an individual committing an offense within a certain period.[46] Whether or not the individual will be included in a reintegration program will depend on the result obtained from the process conducted by the software. The algorithm is supposed to predict an offending act based on thirty-four factors such as gender, criminal record, age, place of residence, etc. It should be noted that twenty-nine of these thirty-four factors are related to the individual's criminal record. Oswald, Grace, Urwin, and Barnes' analysis of the system concludes that "there is a sub-set of decisions around which there is too great an impact upon society and upon the welfare of individuals for them to be influenced by an emerging technology; to an extent, in fact, that they should be removed from the influence of algorithmic decision-making altogether."[47]

With respect to criminal justice, Leroux aptly points out that:

> criminal litigation encompasses diverse realities, not all of which are quantifiable or objectifiable. Thus, the reasoning followed by the judge in concluding the guilt or innocence of a suspect, while it is certainly based in a decisive manner on the objective elements revealed by the investigation and included in the file, can also be nourished by considerations that are not all likely to be brought together in an equation, because they are linked to feelings or emotions. In this respect, the calculation of probability delivered by analytical justice seems to us to be ill-suited to the decision-making process relating to the guilt or innocence of a suspect.[48]

Justice, in other words, is not a simple matter that can be dehumanized and entrusted exclusively to a software. Even in a "simple" traffic accident, the assessment of responsibilities can be delicate. Predictive software, hence, could be contrary to the principle of the presumption of innocence.

So far, we have analyzed software used in predictive analyses of recidivism, when the court is already seized of the accused's case file. However, the same type of software could also be developed to predict offenses by individuals who are not being accused and standing trial yet. In this "big brother" scenario, individual behavior would be analyzed outside of the context of criminal litigation, to predict any indictable offense. Needless to say, this use of the software would have an even greater impact on human rights, as well as privacy. In the worst-case scenario, an individual may be arrested and convicted not for what he or she did, but for what the AI claims he or she will do. If the presumption of innocence is already widely violated with software such as COMPAS and HART, this use of predictive technology is even more

---

[46] M. Oswald, J. Grace, S. Urwin, and G. Barnes, "Algorithmic Risk Assessment Policing Models: Lessons from the Durham HART Model and 'Experimental' Proportionality" (2018) 27(2) *Information & Communications Technology Law* 233.

[47] Ibid.

[48] O. Leroux, "Justice pénale et algorithme" in J. B. Hubin, H. Jacquemin, and B. Michaux (eds.), *Le juge et l'algorithme: Juges augmentés ou justice diminuée* (Brussels: Collection du Crids, 2019) 61 (loose translation).

problematic in predicting criminal acts. Furthermore, in light of the aforementioned risk of bias, entire categories of people would risk being charged with intent to offend, or being put under surveillance, even when they have nothing improper or illegal. In sum, the use of predictive software in criminal justice entail risks for the principle of fairness and presumption of innocence, which are difficult to accept in democratic societies.

14.4 EQUAL ACCESS TO JUSTICE

This section will consider legal analytics, that is, AI analyzing the jurisprudence of courts, or individual judges. This technology can be used by courts to reach a decision; the use of this type of software may entail gains in consistency of the case law and avoid disparity from one court to another. Many will see this as a major step forward in the search for an egalitarian justice. However, this development also entails risks. For instance, these analytical tools may be used not only by the courts, but also by individuals committing criminal acts, who would have an opportunity to adapt their criminal behavior based on decisions rendered in similar cases. Individuals, in other words, would be facilitated in their cost-benefit analysis, while undertaking criminal activities.

To be sure, legal analytics should not be prohibited; however, we need to be aware of the deviations to which it may be subject. Leroux points out that "these applications ... make it possible to determine which courts are likely to take a more favorable decision and, within these courts, which judges (identified by name) could be more lenient or stricter."[49] Leroux therefore notes that legal analytics may encourage a propensity to "forum shop". This raises not only ethical doubts, but also legal questions concerning equal access to justice: not all parties will have the same weapons, since the more affluent could benefit from the help of such software, to the detriment of the less affluent.

Indeed, the switch toward an algorithmic justice, autonomous from any human intervention, could create an effect of inequality of arms between parties. As Mougenot and Gérard point out, "it seems obvious that digital modes of dispute resolution are a priori accessible only to people who have the appropriate equipment and who are computer literate, i.e. who have sufficient skills to use these systems. Clearly, such a situation leads to a widening of the digital divide."[50] As a consequence, the switch from a human to algorithmic justice risks of marginalizing a whole category of litigants who are entitled to fair justice, as guaranteed by Article 6 ECHR. Moreover, the ECtHR considered that, based on Article 6 ECHR, governments should take positive measures to ensure access to justice, and the fulfillment this duty requires that countries undertake positive action to ensure that access to justice is effectively guaranteed. For these reasons, the ECtHR has held that litigants suffer a violation of their right of access to justice if the state fails to implement sufficient measures necessary for such access, such as the access to a lawyer.[51] We can, quite logically, draw a parallel between this case and the move from human justice to an algorithmic one. The use of AI as a means of "choosing" one's judge, or adopting one's criminal behavior to evade the justice system, could create a significant inequality of arms

---

[49] Ibid. at 58–59 (loose translation).
[50] D. Mougenot and L. Gérard "Justice robotisée et droits fondamentaux" in Hubin, Jacquemin, and Michaux (eds.), n. 48 at 41 (loose translation); see also B. Custers, K. La Fors, M. Jozwiak, E. Keymolen, D. Bachlechner, M. Friedewaldand, and S. Aguzzi, "Lists of Ethical, Legal, Societal and Economic Issues of Big Data Technologies," https://papers.ssrn.com/sol3/papers.cfm?abstract_id=3091018&download=yes (accessed July 13, 2020).
[51] ECtHR, *Airey v. Ireland*, no. 6289/73, 9.10.1979, para 25.

problems. Consequently, justice based on AI would not provide access to justice for all, which mean that governments would fail in their duty to take adequate measures to provide access to justice. A violation of Article 6 ECHR would therefore take place. The use of such software should be regulated by law, so that it can usefully assist judges and courts, rather than as a means to elude of the law.

14.5 FURTHER PROCESSING

Another aspect of AI is the further processing of personal data in the sense of the GDPR. Judicial actors, such as judges and attorneys, have at their disposal databases containing judicial decisions. These decisions might contain personal data, such as surnames, first names (parties, witnesses and judges) and, where appropriate, sensitive data such as health data, sexual life data, etc. Even when the data is apparently anonymized, the advent of big data might make re-identification possible. Anonymity thus might be illusory: research has demonstrated the possibility of re-identifying by using only fifteen attributes of an individual who had previously been anonymized.[52] In other words, the various elements contained in a decision may make it possible to identify the parties, as well as the witnesses or judges. As Mougenot and Gérard rightly point out, "the creation of databases of case law, their conservation and their subsequent use by artificial intelligence systems present a risk not only for the privacy of the litigants, but also for that of the members of the court and third parties."[53]

The data can thus be used for a new purpose: if the initial purpose being the rendering of justice, the new one is to create a database, often with a commercial objective. The question raised by this new purpose is its compatibility with the original one. The answer to this question depends on the obligations incumbent on the managers of these databases, who can be classified as data controllers in the sense of the GDPR. The GDPR adopts a principle of prohibition of further data processing for purposes not compatible with the first processing. De Terwangne reminds us that "the notion of 'compatible' use has given rise to many questions in practice and the authors of the GDPR have been concerned to further define it. Article 6(4) GDPR thus sets out a series of criteria for establishing whether the processing of data for another purpose is compatible with the purpose of the original collection or not."[54] These criteria include the link existing between the two purposes, so that it is possible to "admit all subsequent uses that are linked to, logical and consistent with the stated aims."[55] Besides this, "the context in which the personal data were collected, in particular with regard to the relationship between persons data subjects and the controller"[56] has to be taken into account. The nature of the data is also relevant, in light of "the increased risk of processing sensitive data"[57] together with the

---

[52] L. Rocher, J. Hendrickx and Y. A. de Montjoye, "Estimating the Success of Re-identifications in Incomplete Datasets Using Generative Models" (2019) 10 *Nature Communications* 3069.
[53] Mougenot and Gérard, n. 50 at 48 (loose translation).
[54] C. de Terwangne, "Les principes relatifs au traitement des données à caractère personnel et à sa licéité" in C. de Terwangne and C. Rosier (eds.), *Le Règlement général sur la protection des données (RGPD/GDPR: Analyse approfondie* (Brussels: Larcier, 2018) 97–98 (loose translation).
[55] Ibid.
[56] Ibid. at 97. The author states that "in order to be correctly identified and this criterion should be read in the light of the recital 50, which states: 'the context in which the data in question have been collected, in particular the reasonable expectations of the data subjects, depending on their relationship with the controller, as to the further use of such data.' This criterion of reasonable expectations of the data subject is particularly relevant, since limiting what is done with the data to this which enters into the forecasts of this subject, it allows the latter to retain controls the fate of its data." (loose translation).
[57] Ibid. at 97–98 (loose translation).

"possible consequences of the envisaged further processing for the persons concerned."[58] Furthermore, one must be careful to verify "the existence of appropriate safeguards, which may include encryption or pseudonymisation."[59]

There is no doubt that court decisions entail the processing of sensitive data (belonging to special categories), and that the processing of such data for purposes other than the rendering of justice may have an impact on the data subjects. Often, this makes further processing incompatible with the initial purpose, that is, the rendering of justice.

14.6 CONCLUSION

AI must be surrounded by the best safeguards to ensure that it does not infringe fundamental rights, especially in the area of justice. While triggering many questions, the rise of AI also offers new opportunities for the administration of justice. But does that mean that, in the future, AI will work autonomously in the place of a human judge? This is unlikely due to the problems noted by Irsani relating to the use of predictive software such as COMPAS in the field of criminal justice:

> morally troubling precisely because sentencing should not be easy. Actors in the criminal justice system should lose sleep over the fact that they are systemically depriving people of their life, liberty, and property. That should be hard. It is a serious, unimaginable thing. Anyone who has a hand in this system should have to grapple with the consequences of their work; as algorithms become a part of the criminal justice system, that 'anyone' should include technologists.[60]

If AI is used in the administration of justice, it must be under the supervision and control of the judge. Furthermore, any decision taken based on the results provided by such software must be motivated in comprehensible and clear words, to enable any litigant, whatever his or her level of education, to understand it. The judiciary cannot simply state that "it is the AI that made the decision," as this would be contrary to Article 6 ECHR.

In reality, the use of software could complicate judicial reasoning. Indeed, transparency should be provided on the following aspects of AI systems deployed in the administration of justice:

- key subsets of information about the algorithms;
- the way the algorithm works and how it arrives at the solution;
- the origin of the data;
- the quality of the data (e.g., reliability ratio).

Despite the benefit of using AI in terms of speed and amount of data processed, moving from human-made justice to AI-made justice raises many problems linked to the ECHR, the GDPR and Directive (EU) 2016/680 of 27 April 2016, which guarantee the respect of the fundamental rights of individuals. In conclusion, we should be in favor of the use of AI as an aid to decision-making, but certainly not as a judge itself.[61]

---

[58] Ibid.
[59] Ibid. at 98 (loose translation).
[60] Israni, n. 22.
[61] Mougenot and Gérard, n. 50 at 14.

15

Legal Tech in Public Administration

Prospects and Challenges

Antonios Kouroutakis

15.1 INTRODUCTION

Humanity always moves forward. From the agricultural revolution, which substantially increased productivity with new tools and methods, and on to the industrial revolution with an unprecedented improvement of manufacturing processes. Another step forward is the recent transition from the industrial revolution to the information revolution. The information revolution has accelerated due to the growing computational power in combination with network connectivity, which allows every type of device to be connected to the Internet, while collecting and processing masses of data. Interestingly, big data and the Internet of Things has providing a bridge between the newer information economy and more traditional industries.[1]

The information revolution affects every aspect of our life, such as communication, banking, learning and teaching, entertainment, and socializing, as well as in government and the administrative institutions. In some fields, the impact of the technology and information revolution is already apparent, as new kinds of value is created including, new forms of communication and marketing, the emergence of new business models in the financial industry (fintech), and the spread of social networks. Likewise, information, search, and predictive technologies have created opportunities, as well as disruption in the legal industry, with the emergence of legal tech (LT).[2]

In the field of public administration, the potential uses of new technologies have been primarily discussed in theory, but implementation has been slow, mostly in the form of experimental or pilot projects. As Section 15.2 will analyze the administrative use of technologies, at the experimental level, in a best-case scenario. A rapid shift, recently took place with economic and governmental lockdowns due to the COVID-19 pandemic. The pandemic is likely to have a

---

[1] "Adoption of standards brings credibility to technology advancements and facilitates an expanded interoperable marketplace." National Science and Technology Council, "The National Artificial Intelligence Research and Development Strategic Plan" (2016) at 32 ("potential for AI, resulting in strong industry growth and commercialization of AI approaches"), www.nitrd.gov/PUBS/national_ai_rd_strategic_plan.pdf (accessed March 1, 2021).

[2] According to Law Society of England and Wales, the professional association of the solicitors for the jurisdiction of England and Wales, lawtech is "technologies that aim to support, supplement or replace traditional methods for delivering legal services, or that improve the way the justice system operates. Lawtech covers a wide range of tools and processes, such as: document automation, advanced chatbots and practice management tools, predictive artificial intelligence, smart legal contracts, and knowledge management and research systems." See "What Is Lawtech?," www.lawsociety.org.uk/support-services/lawtech/what-is-lawtech/ (accessed July 14, 2020).

lasting effect in the fields of administration and public law, as it has spurred the implementation of the new technologies to perform many functions remotely.

Within this framework, the chapter will focus on the existing use of LT in public administration, referred to in this chapter as "publictech," and it will discuss the prospects of using new technologies to public sector efficiency, as well as the relationship between government administration and the citizens it is entrusted to serve. In addition, it will also discuss how new technologies may impact well-established principles of administrative law and procedure, such as due process, right to a fair hearing, transparency, and the protection of privacy.

Section 15.2 begins by describing recent projects to reform public administration, with a focus on the United Kingdom and the United States, that incorporate LT applications into public administration. Subsequently, the chapter focuses on the application of live chat services (chatbots), automated decision systems based on AI and machine learning, and the digitalization and virtualization of proceedings.

Section 15.3 will focus on the compatibility of such applications with the legal, constitutional, and administrative law values, such as due process and the right to a fair hearing, transparency, and right to privacy. It will analyze relevant case law and literature that considers the application of LT in public governance. Against this background, Section 15.4 will put forth a proposal. In particular, the chapter will argue that, before the employment of such innovative tools, a preliminarily stage would be necessary, to assess and review their application and to assess their compliance with the existing legal framework.

15.2 THE PROSPECT OF LEGAL TECH IN PUBLIC ADMINISTRATION

The acceleration of information technologies has played a disruptive role in reshaping a plethora of industries, from finance and banking to medicine and marketing. New business models have emerged, reshaping businesses and the global market economy. The disruption of technology has impacted the traditional practice of law. A number of LT projects based on cloud computing, automation, AI and/or machine learning aim to modernize law firms and legal practice.[3] With automated analysis of contracts, for instance, LT has revolutionized due diligence and contract review,[4] legal research,[5] and day-to-day tasks and operations in law firms.[6]

Initially, the role of government in the emergence of new technologies and AI mainly consisted in supporting research and development in these fields.[7] The application of these new technologies in the government sector has proved to be, in various ways, also an opportunity and a catalyst for reform. Kraemer explains that "the era of E-Government, which can be defined as the use of IT within government to achieve more efficient operations, better quality

---

[3] Susskind identifies a number of disruptive technologies in the legal field, e.g., automated document assembly, relentless connectivity, the electronic legal marketplace, e-learning, online legal guidance, legal open-sourcing, closed legal communities, workflow and project management, embedded legal knowledge, and online dispute resolution. For more details, see R. Susskind, *The End of Lawyers? Rethinking the Nature of Legal Services* (Oxford: Oxford University Press, 2008) 99–145.
[4] See, e.g., Diligen, offering contract review based on automation and machine learning, www.diligen.com (accessed July 14, 2020).
[5] See, for instance, Ross Intelligence, aiming at making legal research more effective and efficient, https://rossintelligence.com (accessed July 14, 2020).
[6] See, e.g., AbacusNext, a technology provider offering "practice management, payment processing, private cloud hosting, and document automation solutions," www.abacusnext.com.
[7] National Science and Technology Council, n. 1.

of service and easy public access to government information and services, is now underway."[8] As has long been predicted,[9] information technology and computing power can bring about significant improvements and advancements not only in the private sector, but also in the public one. Within this context, governments and public administration may benefit from the use of LT in multiple areas, from special tasks (such as public procurement) to more general and day-to-day business, such as ordinary administrative or clerical decisions.[10]

For instance, the UK government has adopted a transformation strategy with fifty major projects to employ new technologies in various aspects of the administration to improve public services, make governance more efficient, and improve relationships between citizen and state.[11] According to an estimate, the implementation of these projects will realize almost 50 billion pounds worth of benefits.[12]

In the private sector, data collection, processing, and profiling play a critical role in the modern marketplace. Companies compete over big data and metadata, in order to generate insights into people's preferences and create comparative advantages in the marketplace. Jack Ma, the founder of AliBaba, famously said that big data allows companies to see the invisible hand of the market.[13] A report by the US National Science and Technology Council states that "with the rising capabilities of 'data fusion,' which brings together disparate sources of data [data born digital, created specifically for digital use by a computer or data processing system, and data born analog, emanates from the physical world but increasingly convertible into digital format], big data can lead to some remarkable insights."[14]

In the area of public administration, the issue becomes how the government can best employ data collection and analysis to enhance administrative efficiency, gain insight into identifying people in need of assistance, and then tailor the delivery of services. In practice, in the public sector, data is critical in areas such as crime prevention. For instance, the US Defense Advanced Research Projects Agency (DARPA) uses geo tracking (the identification of current physical locations with GPS), in combination with AI and machine learning.[15] the Nexus 7 program processes data from satellites, helping commanders to "visualize how traffic flowed through road networks, making it easier to locate and destroy improvised explosive devices."[16] Likewise, geo tracking is employed by the police in the context of a program called Geographic Information Systems (GIS) to map crime.[17]

Interestingly, during the COVID-19 pandemic, geo tracking and facial recognition technology have been employed for the purposes of digital contact tracing, to stop the spread of the

---

[8] K. Kraemer and J. L. King, "Information Technology and Administrative Reform: Will e-Government Be Different?" August 2003 1 https://escholarship.org/uc/item/2rd511db (accessed August 21, 2021).

[9] H. Leavitt and T. Whisler, "Management in the 1980s" (1958) 36 *Harvard Business Review* 41; K. Laudon, *Computers and Bureaucratic Reform* (Hoboken: Wiley, 1974).

[10] On the benefits of governance based on new technologies, see W. Eggers, *Government 2.0: Using Technology to Improve Education, Cut Red Tape, Reduce Gridlock, and Enhance Democracy* (Lanham: Rowman 2004).

[11] "The 7 Lenses of Transformation," www.gov.uk/government/publications/7-lenses-of-transformation/the-7-lenses-of-transformation (accessed July 14, 2020).

[12] Ibid.

[13] Jack Ma, "Can Technology Plan Economies and Destroy Democracy?," *The Economist* (December 18, 2019), www.economist.com/christmas-specials/2019/12/18/can-technology-plan-economies-and-destroy-democracy (accessed August 21, 2021).

[14] National Science and Technology Council, n. 1.

[15] Ibid. at 6.

[16] Ibid.

[17] For more details, see Fahui Wang, "Why Police and Policing Need GIS: An Overview" (2012) 18 *Spatial Crime Analysis and Modeling* 159.

virus.[18] In particular, Apple and Google are designing the operative systems for mobile phone with Bluetooth technology to enable governments and health agencies in conducting contact tracing.[19] Singapore, United Kingdom, and Ireland employ apps to trace the contacts of a person who has contracted the virus.[20]

The most revolutionary application of LT in public administration is the incorporation of automated decision systems. As Pasquale explains, "critical decisions are made not on the basis of the data per se, but on the basis of data analyzed algorithmically, that is, in calculations coded in computer software."[21]

In the past, computers assisted public administrators in the decision-making process, nowadays AI and machine learning have replaced human decision-makers.[22] Automated decision systems are capable of delivering outcomes with minimum human intervention;[23] such systems are provided data and an algorithm to process the data. Examples include automated decision systems are used to terminate healthcare programs or to impose travel bans on travelers.[24] Such systems deliver faster decisions and consistent outcomes.[25]

In the United States, the administration has applied AI and machine learning analytics software at the Centers for Medicare and Medicaid Services, in order "to flag likely instances of reimbursement fraud before claims are paid."[26] This analytics software has enhanced the fraud prevention system and helped "identify the highest risk health care providers for fraud, waste and abuse in real time, and has already stopped, prevented or identified $115 million in fraudulent payments – saving $3 for every $1 spent in the program's first year."[27]

Another application with potential benefits for public administration is the use of "chatbots." Public Service Chatbots use live chat software with the ability to communicate with written and oral speech, also known as robo-advisers; they are widely used in the private sector in the banking, finance, travel and marketing industries, as well in the area of customer care services.[28] In public administration, chatbots are used to handle frequently asked questions and conduct transactions. This type of application has a number of benefits, including the easing of public servants and staff workloads, increase of productivity, cost savings, and improvement of citizens' satisfaction by substantially improving communications with government agencies.[29]

---

[18] K. Grind, R. McMillan, and A. Wilde Mathews, "To Track Virus, Governments Weigh Surveillance Tools That Push Privacy Limits," *The Wall Street Journal* (March 17, 2020), www.wsj.com/articles/to-track-virus-governments-weigh-surveillance-tools-that-push-privacy-limits-11584479841 (accessed August 21, 2021).

[19] "Apple Google Privacy-Preserving Contact Tracing," www.apple.com/covid19/contacttracing (accessed July 14, 2020).

[20] "Why Britain Is Ignoring the Google-Apple Protocol for Its Tracing App," *The Economist* (May 9, 2020), www.economist.com/britain/2020/05/09/why-britain-is-ignoring-the-google-apple-protocol-for-its-tracing-app (accessed July 14, 2020).

[21] F. Pasquale, *The Black Box Society: The Secret Algorithms That Control Money and Information* (Cambridge, MA: Harvard University Press, 2015) 21–22.

[22] D. Keats Citron, "Technological Due Process" (2008) 85 *Washington University Law Review* 1249 1252.

[23] Ibid. at 1260.

[24] Ibid. at 1252.

[25] Eggers, n. 10 at 113.

[26] Executive Office of the President, "Big Data: Seizing Opportunities Preserving Values" (2014) at 6, https://obamawhitehouse.archives.gov/sites/default/files/docs/big_data_privacy_report_may_1_2014.pdf (accessed August 21, 2021).

[27] Ibid.

[28] See, for instance, "The Chatbots in Banking Report: How Chatbots Can Transform Digital Banking," Business Insider, www.businessinsider.com/ the-chatbots-in-banking-report-how-chatbots-can-transform-digital-banking-2017-1 (accessed July 14, 2020).

[29] A. Androutsopoulou, N. Karacapilidis, E. Loukis, and Y. Charalabidis, "Transforming the Communication between Citizens and Government through AI-Guided Chatbots" (2019) 36 *Government Information Quarterly* 358 359.

In response to the pandemic and general lockdowns, public institutions such as courts and lawmaking bodies have gone online. The UK House of Commons amended standing orders and allowed the use of remote technology in core business, namely, scrutiny proceedings (such as questions to the ministers), substantive proceedings (presentation of bills), and by launching hybrid proceedings.[30] However, the use of hybrid proceedings were made temporary, subject to a sunset clause.[31] According to the hybrid proceedings order, the speaker is entrusted with the power to select the electronic means for the virtual session; in case of technical problems, the speaker has the power to interrupt and suspend the session.[32]

Even before the COVID-19 pandemic, court proceedings had begun to implement online tools.[33] In Britain, courts have accepted e-filing and online case management for some cases beginning in 2014.[34] In 2016, the HM Courts & Tribunal Service (HMCTS), an Executive Agency of the Ministry of Justice, allocated a £1 billion program to implement a pilot program to transform the justice system, introducing and testing an online dispute resolution platform.[35] The digital transformation with online cases and virtual hearings has made justice more accessible and more efficient with less delays, it frees judges from bureaucratic and time-consuming tasks, and increases the satisfaction of the parties with faster and more convenient proceedings.[36] In addition, due to the pandemic, most of the UK courts have started to conduct hearings via Skype, with all parties involved (including, solicitors, counsel, and witnesses) participating via videoconference and accessing electronic bundles.[37]

Despite these advantages, doubts persist as to whether virtual proceedings meet appropriate procedural and substantive standards. As stressed by Završnik, "a fair balance should be struck between the right to participate effectively in the trial, on the one hand, and the use of opaque AI systems designed to help judges arrive at more accurate assessments of the defendant's future conduct, on the other."[38] In particular, online courts may not be suitable for certain types of cases. For instance, during the COVID-19 period, a family dispute was brought before the family division court in the United Kingdom. The local authorities alleged that the mother of a seven-year-old child abused the child by fabricating or inducing illness. The issue was whether the hearing should, or should not, be conducted remotely via the Skype for Business platform.[39]

Sir Andrew McFarlane, the judge and president of the family division of the courts, ruled that this "category of cases [involves] a particular form of child abuse which requires exquisite sensitivity and skill on the part of the court"[40] and thus refused to allow the final hearing to take place via Skype. The judge explained his decision by clarifying that

---

[30] HC Orders Relating to Hybrid Proceedings – Addendum to Standing Orders (Public Business) (April 23, 2020).
[31] About the utility of sunset clauses, see A. Kouroutakis, *The Constitutional Value of Sunset Clauses* (Abingdon-on-Thames: Routledge, 2017).
[32] HC Orders, n. 30.
[33] A. Sela, "E-Nudging Justice: The Role of Digital Choice Architecture in Online Courts" (2019) *Journal of Dispute Resolution* 127.
[34] See e-filing, www.judiciary.uk/you-and-the-judiciary/going-to-court/high-court/the-rolls-building/e-filing/ (accessed July 14, 2020).
[35] "HMCTS Reform Programme Projects Explained" (June 20, 2018), www.gov.uk/guidance/hmcts-reform-programme-projects-explained (accessed July 14, 2020).
[36] https://publications.parliament.uk/pa/cm201919/cmselect/cmjust/190/190.pdf (accessed July 14, 2020).
[37] "Trial by Skype" (April 9, 2020), www.judiciary.uk/announcements/trial-by-skype/ (accessed July 14, 2020).
[38] A. Završnik, "Criminal Justice, Artificial Intelligence Systems, and Human Rights" (2020) 20 *ERA Forum* 567 577.
[39] *Re P (A child: remote hearing)* [2020] EWFC 32 (16 April 2020).
[40] Ibid. at 11.

it is a crucial element in the judge's analysis for the judge to be able to experience the behaviour of the parent who is the focus of the allegations throughout the oral court process; not only when they are in the witness box being examined in-chief and cross-examined, but equally when they are sitting in the well of the court and reacting, as they may or may not do, to the factual and expert evidence as it unfolds during the course of the hearing.[41]

Apart from remote hearings, the most challenging application of LT would be the automation of judicial decision-making. Some LT projects have already implemented autonomous dispute resolution mechanisms in the field of ADR. For instance, Cybersettle offers online settlements and payment solutions with minimal human intervention.[42] Currently, in the sphere of public courts, criminal courts in the United States use AI systems to assess the possibility of recidivism for those awaiting trial, as well as those petitioning for release on bail or parole.[43]

15.3 PUBLICTECH CHALLENGED: CONCERNS COMING FROM CASE LAW AND THEORY

The implementation of technological advancements has potential to substantially improve public administration, but there are challenges that should not be neglected. Guidance published by the UK government on the transformation of the public sector has stressed, among other concerns, that "rushing to action before there is sufficient clarity" or "proceeding with a vision which is either undeliverable or not sufficiently challenging of the current service model" may cause preventable harms to the public.[44]

From a legal point of view, new models and applications based on technology challenge a number of well-established norms of administrative law, such as the transparency and due process in the decision-making process, the lack of bias, and the protection of privacy. As Pasquale has stated, "credit raters, search engines, major banks, and the [Transport Security Administration] take in data about us and convert it into scores, rankings, risk calculations, and watch lists with vitally important consequences."[45] In particular, data collection and processing in the area of law enforcement create privacy and data protection. Law enforcement agencies using advanced technological means of surveillance and collection of data create new ways to profile citizens known as "dataveillance."[46] Privacy rights predates these advancements requiring courts to adapt "old doctrines to new facts."[47]

The relationship between a state and its citizens is based on the ideas of due process and fair hearing, allowing citizens access to the decision-making process and the ability to argue their

---

[41] Ibid. at 12.
[42] Cybersettle, www.cybersettle.com (accessed July 14, 2020). For more details, see A. Sela, "Can Computers Be Fair? How Automated and Human-Powered Online Dispute Resolution Affect Procedural Justice in Mediation and Arbitration" (2018) 33 *Ohio State Journal on Dispute Resolution* 91.
[43] According to Završnik, "the Arnold Foundation algorithm, which is being rolled out in 21 jurisdictions in the USA, uses 1.5 million criminal cases to predict defendants' behaviour in the pre-trial phase." Završnik, n. 38 at 570.
[44] "The 7 Lenses of Transformation," n. 11.
[45] Pasquale, n. 21 at 4.
[46] Dataveillance is defined as "the proactive surveillance of what effectively become suspect populations, using new technologies to identify "risky groups": M. Levi and D. Wall, "Technologies, Security, and Privacy in the Post-9/11 European Information Society" (2004) 31 *Journal of Law and Society* 194 200. See also L. Amoore and M. De Goede, "Governance, Risk and Dataveillance in the War on Terror" (2005) 43 *Crime, Law and Social Change* 149 151.
[47] A. Butler, "Symposium: Millions of Tiny Constables – Time to Set the Record Straight on the Fourth Amendment and Location-Data Privacy," www.scotusblog.com/2017/08/symposium-millions-tiny-constables-time-set-record-straight-fourth-amendment-location-data-privacy (accessed July 14, 2020).

positions and concerns.[48] These due process rights have been grounded in long recognized rationales. From a "consequentialist" perspective, fair hearings increase the chances of a fair outcome as decision-makers hear both sides before reaching a decision. The "deontological" perspective, according to which individuals affected by administrative decisions are be treated fairly from a procedural perspective, which again is likely to result in a just outcome.[49]

In practice, automated decision systems are often incompatible often with due process and fair hearing rights by not providing proper notice and an opportunity to be heard.[50] This tension or incompatibility was the focus of a challenge brought before the Wisconsin Supreme Court pertaining to the use of closed-source risk assessment software in sentencing.[51] The state of Wisconsin applies a Correctional Offender Management Profiling for Alternative Sanction software or COMPAS, which performs an algorithmic assessment to estimate the risk of recidivism. Mr. Loomis was sentenced to six years of imprisonment, with five years of extended supervision, on the basis of such an assessment. Loomis appealed the decision, claiming that use of algorithmic assessment software encroached upon his right to due process as it "violates a defendant's right to be sentenced based upon accurate information in part because the proprietary nature of COMPAS prevents him from assessing its accuracy; it violates a defendant's right to an individualized sentence; and it improperly uses gendered assessments in sentencing."[52] However, the Wisconsin Supreme Court held that COMPAS was not the decisive factor that led to the calculation of the sentence, and thus the due process rights of Loomis were not violated.[53]

The case at hand confirms that automated decision systems are allowed to assist decision-makers. However, it remains to be seen whether decisions exclusively and solely based on automated systems will comply with due process principles. Simply stated, automated decisions do not necessarily lead to fair outcomes. Simply put, searching big data may find a correlation but not a definitive causal link. The importance of finding causation is need before there can be reliance on an AI prediction or decision that have a serious impact on individuals.

Automated decision systems are equally problematic from a procedural point of view.[54] While public administrators provide the data to be processed by the algorithm, how algorithms operate in rendering decisions remains opaque. Because of this lack of transparency, automated systems allow for less human scrutiny. Such opacity means that citizens do not have access on how decisions are reached, thus limiting the possibility to hold the administration accountable for its actions and decisions.[55]

In the United States, the administrators have an obligation to reveal the content of the algorithm in detail, that is, how it operates, which factors are critical, and which specific data

---

[48] Levy and Shapiro discuss how the administrative state employs procedures that resemble court procedures. Thus, principles of justice implemented in the adversarial trials (such as *audiatur et altera pars*) have been modified to comply with the non-adversarial nature of the administrative procedure, and this gave rise to the right to due process. See R. Levy and S. Shapiro, "Administrative Procedure and the Decline of the Trial" (2003) 51 *Kansas Law Review* 473.

[49] Swati Jhaveri, "Right to a Fair Hearing in Administrative Law Cases" in *Max Planck Encyclopedia of Comparative Constitutional Law* (Oxford: Oxford University Press, 2016), n.p.

[50] P. Schwartz, "Data Processing and Government Administration: The Failure of the American Legal Response to the Computer" (1992) 43 *Hastings Law Journal* 1321 1343–1374; Keats Citron, n. 22 at 1281.

[51] *Loomis v. Wisconsin*, 881 N.W.2d 749 (Wis. 2016).

[52] Ibid. at 34.

[53] Ibid. at 104. Subsequently, the US Supreme Court declined to hear the case. *Loomis v. Wisconsin*, cert. denied, 137 S.Ct. 2290 (2017).

[54] A. Vermeule, "Deference and Due Process" (2016) 129 *Harvard Law Review* 1890.

[55] Keats Citron, n. 22 at 1254.

influenced its decision. In *Kansas v. Walls*,[56] the court reviewed the practice of criminal courts making decisions on probation, rehab, and imprisonment based on an automated decision system, the so called Level of Service Inventory-Revised (LSI-R) assessment. The LSI-R assessment is a diagnostic tool based on an algorithm that assesses a person's data from ten categories: criminal history, education/employment, financial, family/marital relationships, accommodation, leisure and recreation, companions, alcohol and drug use, emotional/personal, and attitudes/orientations.[57]

The Court allowed Walls, who was assessed as a high-risk, high-needs probation candidate to access and review a copy of the completed LSI-R report. The Court ruled that "Walls was denied access to the LSI-R, which necessarily denied him the opportunity to challenge the accuracy of the information upon which the court was required to rely in determining the conditions of his probation. We find the district court's decision to deny Walls access to the LSI-R violated his right to procedural due process."[58]

Transparency as to the way algorithms operate is necessary in the public sector. As Pasquale explains, "faulty data, invalid assumptions, and defective models can't be corrected when they are hidden."[59] If the data pool and algorithmic models are not properly monitored and made accessible then due process rights will be in danger.

At a theoretical level, there is the danger that algorithmic models based on misleading data will lead to automated bias and discrimination. Furthermore, automated bias and discrimination might be an unintended consequence of the design of the algorithm, irrespective of the quality of data that it processes.[60]

15.4 PRELIMINARY REVIEW AND SCRUTINY OF PUBLICTECH

Section 15.3 has shown cases where publictech (automated assistance and automated decision-making) was challenged successfully on a number of grounds before the courts, for due process violations and lack of transparency. Furthermore, a number of scholarly concerns were voiced, namely, regarding automated bias and discrimination. In order to minimize these concerns, policymakers should ensure that the adoption of publictech complies with existing norms and principles. To this end, policymakers should review and scrutinize, for example, automated decision systems before their implementation. Such pre-implementation scrutiny is not unknown in the public sector: for instance, a recent report from the European Data Protection Supervisor (EDPS) underlines "the responsibility of the legislator to assess the proportionality of a measure."[61] In a similar vein, the UK Parliament has instituted the practice of prelegislative scrutiny, which is an examination stage that takes place before the drafting of a bill that often includes public consultation.[62] The United Kingdom's Parliament also is

---

[56] *State of Kansas v. John Keith Walls*, 116,027, Court of Appeals of the State of Kansas (2017).
[57] S. Manchak, J. Skeem, K. Douglas, and M. Siranosian, "Does Gender Moderate the Predictive Utility of the Level of Service Inventory-Revised (LSI-R) for Serious Violent Offenders?" (2009) 36 *Criminal Justice and Behavior* 425 430.
[58] *Kansas v. Walls*, n. 58.
[59] Pasquale, n. 21 at 17.
[60] S. Barocas and A. Selbst, "Big Data's Disparate Impact" (2016) 104 *California Law Review* 671 674–675. See also, Androutsopoulou, Karacapilidis, Loukis, and Charalabidis, n. 30 at 359 (importance of data feeding to algorithms, regarding the development and building of the knowledge base of chatbots).
[61] European Data Protection Supervisor, "EDPS Guidelines on Assessing the Proportionality of Measures That Limit the Fundamental Rights to Privacy and to the Protection of Personal Data" (December 19, 2019), https://edps.europa.eu/sites/edp/files/publication/19-12-19_edps_proportionality_guidelines_en.pdf.
[62] See J. Smookler, "Making a Difference? The Effectiveness of Pre-Legislative Scrutiny" (2006) 59 *Parliamentary Affairs* 522.

obligated to review proposed new laws to make sure they are compatible with the Human Rights Act;[63] in France, acts of Parliament and other institutional acts may be referred to the Constitutional Council before their promulgation, or a review of their conformity with the Constitution.[64]

A preliminary review of publictech tools should first of all define the purpose of the planned initiative (enhancing the administration's responsiveness to questions from the citizens). Second, a review should seek to identify the appropriate tools to achieve the given purpose (such as, via the implementation of public service chatbots). Third, any new tools need to be assessed for compatibility with public law norms and policies, for instance, evaluating whether there is any risk of automation bias.

In between these steps, it would be necessary for policymakers to conduct consultations, draft impact assessments and perform compatibility checks. Stakeholder consultation (with the support of new technologies and crowdsourcing) is an essential instrument in reviewing a publictech proposal and to guarantee transparency. Although not determinative, such practices provide probative information that courts can use when assessing whether any proposed publictech application is compatible with the existing legal framework.

15.5 CONCLUSION

This chapter has examined publictech, that is, the use of legaltech (LT) in public administration. It has shown that a number of countries have adopted data processing, online platforms, AI, and machine learning technologies in a number of administrative sectors, such as automated decision systems, chatbots, and virtual proceedings before courts. A multitude of benefits arise from these technologies, such as more efficient procedures at lower costs. In particular, the COVID-19 pandemic has normalized and amplified the digitalization and virtualization of courts proceedings, which until recently was only at the experimental or pilot phase.

However, the use of publictech has also had negative consequences including undermining well-established public law norms and principles, such as due process and fair hearing rights, the right to privacy, nondiscrimination, and transparency. Within this framework, this chapter proposes a preliminary review before the implementation of publictech tools and human monitoring after implementation to ensure the technology's compliance with public law norms. Additionally, a feedback loop should be established in which feedback from public consultation is provided in order to improve the technology's function, make it more transparent, and enhance public support for LT in public administration.

---

[63] Human Rights Act 1998 c 42, section 19.
[64] Constitution of the French Republic, Article 61.

PART V

Legal Ethics and Societal Values Confront Technology

16

Ethics Guidelines for Trustworthy AI

Michel Cannarsa

16.1 INTRODUCTION: ARTIFICIAL INTELLIGENCE BUT REAL CONCERNS

Artificial intelligence (AI) is one of many digital technologies currently under development.[1] In recent years, it is having increasing repercussions in the field of law. These repercussions go beyond the traditional effect of an economic and industrial evolution. Indeed, the epochal industrial transformations and paradigmatic shifts it generates in many sectors have, from a legal perspective, a structural impact on legal rules and on legal practice. Moreover, the speed of these transformations also impacts on the regulatory response that a legislator is able to provide. In point of fact, rather than running the risk of new legislation rapidly becoming obsolete, regulators around the world have preferred so far to take their time to observe the changes unfolding in current technologies, and to assess their impacts from the legal point of view, before proposing any specific courses of action.

---

[1] AI is one example of a rather long list of 'new technologies' or 'emerging digital technologies'. The European Commission (EC) relies, in its various communications and reports dedicated to this area, on a quite broad and open-ended approach, based on the main examples of such technologies: 'the Internet of Things (IoT), Artificial Intelligence, advanced robotics and autonomous systems' (EC, 'Liability for Emerging Digital Technologies', Staff Working Document SWD (2018) 137 final at 2). More specifically, the EC High Level Expert Group on Artificial Intelligence (AIHLEG) states that '[a]rtificial intelligence . . . systems are software (and possibly also hardware) systems designed by humans that, given a complex goal, act in the physical or digital dimension by perceiving their environment through data acquisition, interpreting the collected structured or unstructured data, reasoning on the knowledge, or processing the information, derived from this data and deciding the best action(s) to take to achieve the given goal. AI systems can either use symbolic rules or learn a numeric model, and they can also adapt their behaviour by analysing how the environment is affected by their previous actions' ('Ethics Guidelines for Trustworthy AI' (8 April 2019) at 36, https://ec.europa.eu/digital-single-market/en/news/ethics-guidelines-trustworthy-ai. The key aspects of the said technologies are 'complexity, openness, autonomy, predictability, data-drivenness, and vulnerability' ('Liability for Artificial Intelligence and other emerging digital technologies', Report from the Expert Group on Liability and New Technologies – New Technologies Formation at 5, www.ec.europa.eu/transparency/regexpert/index.cfm?do=groupDetail.groupMeetingDoc&docid=36608. The EU institutions started their work in the field of AI in order to determine the adequate response to it in 2017. On 16 February 2017, the European Parliament passed a resolution on Civil Law Rules on Robotics (European Parliament resolution of 16 February 2017 with recommendations to the Commission on Civil Law Rules on Robotics), www.europarl.europa.eu/doceo/document/TA-8-2017-0051_EN.html#title1. The EC then published the Communication on Artificial Intelligence for Europe in April 2018 and the Communication 'Plan for Artificial Intelligence "Made in Europe"' in December 2018 COM (2018) 237 final, 25 April 2018, www.ec.europa.eu/transparency/regdoc/rep/1/2018/EN/COM-2018-237-F1-EN-MAIN-PART-1.PDF and COM (2018) 795 final, 7 December 2018, www.ec.europa.eu/knowledge4policy/publication/coordinated-plan-artificial-intelligence-com2018-795-final_en. See recently: Proposal for a Regulation of the European Parliament and the Council laying down harmonised rules on artificial intelligence (Artificial Intelligence Act) and amending certain Union legislative acts, COM(2021) 206 final, 21 April 2021.

Although legal experts, contrary to ethicists, have traditionally shown little interest in AI, algorithms, machine learning and so forth, it is now virtually impossible for them to ignore the impact of AI on the law, and more specifically, the question of whether actual legal rules and regulations can cope with the changes taking place in the economy and in the society, on one hand, and whether the use of AI tools in legal practice is compatible with the founding principles of our legal orders, on the other hand. If new rules are needed, lawyers will have to define their content and how to make sure they are suitable for the long term, in a context of rapidly changing technologies.

Regarding the new approaches to be taken, and in part considering the rapid pace of change, it seems that soft law approaches, instead of the traditional positivist one, could be more adapted to the societal and legal challenges raised by the development of AI. It is indeed fairly likely that one preferred course of action will be to put forward a number of general principles or even soft law instruments that the industry will have to progressively introduce as these technologies emerge. This is where the many recently issued ethical guidelines, principles or recommendations come into play. The multitude of these non-binding texts released in the past few months by many governments and governmental and non-governmental organisations seems to highlight a transition from one phase to another:[2] because AI is spreading fast in the economy and in the society, the need of rules for the development and the implementation of AI is increasingly pressing. This is not surprising, as previous rules were designed for an analogue era, structurally different from the emerging digital era. The legal answer to this phenomenon is still at a rather early stage, one reason for that being that much of what could be the impact of a widespread use of AI in our societies is uncertain.

Almost all of the current ethical guidelines dedicated to AI mention the risks and opportunities brought by it. Regarding the opportunities, it is not surprising that they reside mostly in gains of productivity. The major drivers of the undergoing industrial revolution, just like the previous ones, are the said gains of productivity. One of the differences with the previous industrial mutations, though, is that AI is mainly concerned with the services sector, including legal services, which was traditionally human intelligence–dependent. Another difference is of course the immaterial dimension of AI. Regarding the risks, most of the current ethical guidelines for the development of AI focus on fundamental rights. This should raise the level of concern about the balance between gains of productivity, on one hand, and fundamental rights, on the other hand. Considering almost daily examples, it would indeed be naive to think that AI could bring gains of productivity and spread harmoniously without hurting fundamental rights. This should also raise questions about the adequacy of legally non-binding guidelines, principles and recommendations, in order to mitigate the threats to fundamental rights.

The last and most recent recommendations released by the European Commission (EC) Independent High-Level Expert Group on Artificial Intelligence (AIHLEG) is an 'Assessment List for Trustworthy AI' (ALTAI), which provides a 'checklist for business and organisations to self-assess the trustworthiness of their AI systems under development'.[3] The various proposals, including their drafting process and major features, will be discussed in the present chapter. The international and evolutive features are among the most significant. Because AI developments are rather recent, global and disruptive, many countries have to experience the issues raised by the said developments simultaneously. Regulators do not have previous preconceptions about them and previous legal rules specifically designed to deal with them. There is therefore a

---

[2] It could also highlight a normative competition among countries and international organisations: see AIHLEG, 'The Assessment List for Trustworthy Artificial Intelligence (ALTAI) for Self Assessment'(17 July 2020) at 4, https://ec.europa.eu/digital-single-market/en/news/assessment-list-trustworthy-artificial-intelligence-altai-self-assessment: '[w]e believe that this will enable Europe and European organisations to position themselves as global leaders in cutting-edge AI worthy of our individual and collective trust'.

[3] Ibid.

challenging, almost unrealistic, opportunity to draft rules on an international scale. This approach would of course create a reliable economic environment for the development of AI. It would also and more importantly, drawing analogies with the human rights area, be based on a 'universal' approach. The said universal approach seems to be particularly needed considering the interests involved (fundamental rights and freedoms), but also the frequent immaterial nature of AI applications and usages, making it hard to lock them behind national borders.

Subsequently, the interaction between ethical guidelines in the field of AI and legal rules will be analysed more precisely, in order to determine whether the said ethical guidelines will frame the legal rules in the making. At the moment, it seems rather that legal rules, especially human rights, are influencing ethical guidelines for a trustworthy AI. One could therefore consider legal rules to be self-sufficient, without appealing to other disciplines, especially if new mandatory legal provisions, designed for the use of AI and its consequences, are drafted. The numerous ethical guidelines and other self-assessment tools for the harmonious development of AI would therefore be much ado about nothing. The reality is probably more complex. Prior to any regulation, and by analogy with the field of bioethics (an area in which technology has to deal with philosophical, religious, moral and political concerns), regulators generally rely not only on scientific, economic and legal studies and analysis, but also on public debates with a broad participation of stakeholders. This is part of a political process requiring governments to keep their finger on the civil society's pulse on such sensitive issues. The same seems to be the ongoing process with AI. However, the analogy with bioethics highlights one major concern about ethical guidelines for the development of AI. Binding legal rules generally precede new technological implementations in biology and medicine, whereas AI is already spreading fast in many different aspects of life without clear and efficient regulatory boundaries. What is more, the focus on ethical guidelines could be deceptive because it would be presently more effective to focus on the task of drafting and implementing an adapted mandatory regulatory framework, considering that the risks (and consequences for citizens' rights) of a widespread use of AI are already more than visible, with almost daily examples.

This chapter will therefore also critically assess current institutional trends and actions directed to AI developments. The multitude of guidelines for a trustworthy AI seem more to reflect concerns among the political, social and legal communities than establishing a clear and safe legal framework into which AI could be developed without putting at risk rights and freedoms. Moreover, ethical guidelines are a weak tool to handle evolutions that can have significant negative impacts on citizens' rights, their moral and physical integrity, but also on the functioning of legal orders. Instead, clear legal rules (hard law), adapted to new realities, are strongly needed in order to make sure that unlawful consequences of AI developments are not left without a legal response. This requires that legal rules renounce a speculative approach and focus on practical examples into which AI is already deployed and where it generates legal problems to be solved.

16.2 ETHICAL GUIDELINES FOR TRUSTWORTHY AI: AN INFLATIONARY TREND

16.2.1 Definition of Trustworthy AI

A recent study by Harvard's Berkman Klein Center for Internet and Society mapped out and analysed over thirty-six AI principles documents.[4] The study identified thematic trends,

---

[4] J. Fjeld, N. Achten, H. Hilligoss, A. C. Nagy and M. Srikumar, 'Principled Artificial Intelligence: Mapping Consensus in Ethical and Rights-Based Approaches to Principles for AI', Research Publication No. 2020-1,

normative guidance and sectoral norms.[5] The eight key identified themes in the said study are privacy, accountability, safety and security, transparency and explainability, fairness and non-discrimination, human control of technology, professional responsibility and promotion of human values.[6] Though this chapter focuses on the EU and the ethical guidelines issued by AIHLEG, there seems to be convergence of ideas and aims in this area.[7] The present analysis can therefore be taken as a global perspective on the phenomenon of promoting ethics guidelines for a trustworthy AI. Not surprisingly, as discussed in Section 16.2.2, the key themes in ethics guidelines are generally in relation with the protection of people's fundamental rights.[8]

The declared main objective of governmental and non-governmental organisations, but also of private organisations, in drafting, promoting or endorsing ethical guidelines in the field of AI is to build and maintain users' trust in AI systems. Trust is of course considered to be an essential condition for an ecosystem to develop around AI. AIHLEG phrases it in the following way: '[a] trustworthy approach is key to enabling "responsible competitiveness", by providing the foundation upon which all those using or affected by AI systems can trust that their design, development and use are lawful, ethical and robust'.[9] There are therefore three main components of a trustworthy AI as defined in the Ethics Guidelines for Trustworthy AI: lawful, ethical and robust.[10] Regarding the first component, lawfulness, it is simply described as the fact of

---

https://cyber.harvard.edu/publication/2020/principled-ai (accessed August 23, 2021). The authors note that '[i]n the past several years, seemingly every organization with a connection to technology policy has authored or endorsed a set of principles for AI. As guidelines for ethical, rights-respecting, and socially beneficial AI develop in tandem with – and as rapidly as – the underlying technology, there is an urgent need to understand them, individually and in context'. According to AIHLEG, 'Ethics Guidelines for Trustworthy AI', n. 1 at 9: 'AI ethics is a sub-field of applied ethics, focusing on the ethical issues raised by the development, deployment and use of AI. Its central concern is to identify how AI can advance or raise concerns to the good life of individuals, whether in terms of quality of life, or human autonomy and freedom necessary for a democratic society.' The following are the main examples of ethics guidelines for the development of AI used in the study by Harvard's Berkman Klein Center for Internet and Society: Council of Europe, European Commission for the Efficiency of Justice, 'European Ethical Charter on the Use of Artificial Intelligence in Judicial Systems and Their Environment' (2018), https://rm.coe.int/ethical-charter-en-for-publication-4-december-2018/16808f699c; AIHLEG, 'Ethics Guidelines for Trustworthy AI', n. 1; Google, 'AI at Google: Our Principles' (2018), www.blog.google/technology/ai/ai-principles/; IBM, 'IBM Everyday Ethics for AI' (2019), www.ibm.com/watson/assets/duo/pdf/everydayethics.pdf; Mission assigned by the French Prime Minister, 'For a Meaningful Artificial Intelligence: Toward a French and European Strategy' (2018), www.aiforhumanity.fr/pdfs/MissionVillani_Report_ENG-VF.pdf; Organisation for Economic Co-operation and Development, 'Recommendation of the Council on Artificial Intelligence' (2019), https://legalinstruments.oecd.org/en/instruments/OECD-LEGAL-0449; UK House of Lords, Select Committee on Artificial Intelligence, 'AI in the UK: Ready, Willing and Able?', Report of Session 2017-19 (2018), https://publications.parliament.uk/pa/ld201719/ldselect/ldai/100/100.pdf; United States Executive Office of the President, National Science and Technology Council Committee on Technology, 'Preparing for the Future of Artificial Intelligence' (2016), https://obamawhitehouse.archives.gov/sites/default/files/whitehouse_files/microsites/ostp/NSTC/preparing_for_the_future_of_ai.pdf (accessed August 23, 2021). University of Montreal, 'Montreal Declaration for a Responsible Development of Artificial Intelligence' (2018), www.montrealdeclaration-responsibleai.com/the-declaration (accessed August 23, 2021). Chinese National Governance Committee for the New Generation Artificial Intelligence, led by China's Ministry of Science and Technology, 'Governance Principles for a New Generation of Artificial Intelligence: Develop Responsible Artificial Intelligence' (2019), www.chinadaily.com.cn/a/201906/17/WS5d07486ba3103dbf14328ab7.html (accessed August 23, 2021).

[5] Fjeld et al., n. 4 at 3–4.
[6] Ibid. at 4–5.
[7] Ibid. at 5: 'the conversation around principled AI is beginning to converge, at least among the communities responsible for the development of these documents. Thus, these themes may represent the "normative core" of a principle-based approach to AI ethics and governance'.
[8] AIHLEG, 'Ethics Guidelines for Trustworthy AI' at n. 1: '[t]hese Guidelines articulate a framework for achieving Trustworthy AI based on fundamental rights as enshrined in the Charter of Fundamental Rights of the European Union (EU Charter), and in relevant international human rights law'.
[9] Ibid. at 4.
[10] Ibid. at 5.

'complying with all applicable laws and regulations'.[11] The drafters of the said guidelines willingly left out from their developments the lawfulness component and focused on the second and third components (ethical and robust AI). The reason given for that is that '[w]hile [ethical and robust AI components] are to a certain extent often already reflected in existing laws, their full realisation may go beyond existing legal obligations'.[12] It seems therefore assumed that the legal norms only partially respond to the need of regulation in this area. This phenomenon, if true, could be a transitionary one (i.e., actual legal rules are not adapted to AI developments, but could be updated and could fill in regulatory gaps) or could at the contrary inherently affect technology (i.e., no matter the regulatory effort, legal rules will not be sufficient to answer all the societal challenges raised by technological developments). As further developments will pretend to show, one of the reasons why there seems to be a need to promote principles of ethical and robust AI, beyond existing and allegedly lacunary legal rules, is the fact that existing legal rules are not fit yet for the purpose of framing AI developments. At the very least, a fitness check of the said legal rules (in all the potential impacted areas of law: contracts, torts, law of persons, criminal law, human rights, etc.) should be conducted in a systematic way for any use case of AI. This requires a titanic effort and a full commitment of the legal community.[13] This would be the only way to determine whether new legal rules for AI and digital technologies are needed and/or if existing legal rules can adapt, through interpretation, to new situations.

Leaving apart the legal dimension of trustworthy AI, the ethics guidelines therefore focus on ethical and technical concepts considered to foster trust. While trying to give operational tools to implement their ethical guidelines for trustworthy AI, the guidelines can be quite complex and technical on one side,[14] and quite broad and conceptual on the other side. Legal concepts, almost exclusively fundamental rights from which ethical recommendations derive, are mentioned quite frequently, but paradoxically, without the objective to address the practical consequences of applying legal rules to AI.[15] Instead, legal concepts are used as justifying sources of

---

[11] Ibid.
[12] Ibid. at 6.
[13] Regarding the 'use case' approach, the Faculty of Law at Lyon Catholic University has developed in recent years 'Future of Digital Technologies Law Clinics': these bring together students, academics, members of the judiciary, lawyers and representatives of the business world and task them with identifying and solving the problems posed by the development of new technologies. This involves choosing slightly futuristic scenarios (looking five to ten years ahead) to ensure that we continue to work on highly realistic future planning exercises. This method and our project have been selected by the Erasmus+ agency, and our clinic is now an EU consortium whose partners include various EU universities, as well as the bar associations of various European cities, and the worlds of business and legal tech (LT), so that these matters can be considered on a Europe-wide scale. Having this structure enables us to compare the various national legal systems and to evaluate their capacity to respond to the changes taking place. It also enables us to identify any European principles in this area that could be the subject of recommendations made to EU and national legislators. Ideally, we should be able to 'test' technologies that are being developed, before they are marketed. The 'sandbox' approach to ensure regulatory compliance is comparable to this method. It can be added that this 'fitness check', performed in light of the law before products are marketed, would appear to be one of the conditions governing the social acceptability of emerging technologies, or at least some of them.
[14] Deriving from the three components (lawful, ethical and robust), seven requirements for a trustworthy AI are subsequently developed: (1) human agency and oversight, (2) technical robustness and safety, (3) privacy and data governance, (4) transparency, (5) diversity, non-discrimination and fairness, (6) environmental and societal well-being and (7) accountability.
[15] AIHLEG, 'Ethics Guidelines for Trustworthy AI', n. 1, makes sure to state that '[n]othing in this document shall be construed or interpreted as providing legal advice or guidance concerning how compliance with any applicable existing legal norms and requirements can be achieved. Nothing in this document shall create legal rights nor impose legal obligations towards third parties. We however recall that it is the duty of any natural or legal person to comply with laws – whether applicable today or adopted in the future according to the development of AI. These Guidelines proceed on the assumption that all legal rights and obligations that apply to the processes and activities involved in developing, deploying and using AI systems remain mandatory and must be duly observed'. See also ibid.

ethical guidelines (as we'll see in Section 16.2.2 it is therefore a quite surprising cycle as one would assume that ethical reflections could pave the way to the enactment of new legal rules, not the contrary), considering that

> [a]chieving Trustworthy AI requires not only compliance with the law, which is but one of its three components. Laws are not always up to speed with technological developments, can at times be out of step with ethical norms or may simply not be well suited to addressing certain issues. For AI systems to be trustworthy, they should hence also be ethical, ensuring alignment with ethical norms.[16]

This assumption of the inherently lacunary dimension of legal rules looks rather like a bland statement and almost a surrender to soft law approaches, a reactive instead of a proactive regulatory approach. Instead of defining what we would like an ethical AI to be (considering the fact that AI has been used for several years in our daily lives, it could therefore be an anachronistic approach), why wouldn't we focus on stating what is unlawful on the basis of current legal rules (there are plenty of examples) and on identifying the need of new legal rules to frame AI developments in conformity with legal orders?

Without downplaying at all the importance of the ethical and technical dimensions of a trustworthy AI, there can be skepticism in understanding what the lawfulness component of it really means and why it is barely addressed in the ethics guidelines. It seems indeed too easy to assume the lacunary flaws of legal rules, without even trying at this point to assess their fitness and their exhaustiveness. Unless specific and adapted rules are designed to apply, in a transversal and systematic way to AI-enabled products, services, decisions, etc., no AI will be trustworthy as it will be, if not impossible, hard to determine whether an AI is lawful or not. It is therefore, beyond the mere invocation to fundamental rights, crucial to thoroughly address the legal dimension of the phenomenon and to build a consistent and comprehensive legal framework for AI so that people can trust it. Only once this epochal task is completed will AI be trustworthy.

16.2.2 Focus on Human Rights and Privacy

As stated in ALTAI, '[t]he assessment list is firmly grounded in the protection of people's fundamental rights' and a fundamental rights impact assessment of AI project is a prerequisite.[17] The expressions 'fundamental rights' or 'human rights' are indeed referred to quite heavily and the EU Charter of Fundamental Rights is at the center of the ethical guidelines. These rights materialise into 'human dignity',[18] 'freedom of the individual',[19] 'equality, non-discrimination

---

[16] Ibid. at 6–7.
[17] AIHLEG, n. 2 at 3: fundamental rights 'is the term used in the European Union to refer to human rights enshrined in the EU Treaties, the Charter of Fundamental Rights ... and international human rights Law'.
[18] Ibid. at 10: '[R]espect for human dignity entails that all people are treated with respect due to them as moral subjects, rather than merely as objects to be sifted, sorted, scored, herded, conditioned or manipulated. AI systems should hence be developed in a manner that respects, serves and protects humans' physical and mental integrity, personal and cultural sense of identity, and satisfaction of their essential needs'.
[19] Ibid.: 'In an AI context, freedom of the individual for instance requires mitigation of (in)direct illegitimate coercion, threats to mental autonomy and mental health, unjustified surveillance, deception and unfair manipulation. In fact, freedom of the individual means a commitment to enabling individuals to wield even higher control over their lives, including (among other rights) protection of the freedom to conduct a business, the freedom of the arts and science, freedom of expression, the right to private life and privacy, and freedom of assembly and association.'

and solidarity'[20] and 'citizens' rights'.[21] The ethics guidelines for trustworthy AI promote 'an approach to AI ethics based on the fundamental rights enshrined in the EU Treaties, the EU Charter and international human rights law. Respect for fundamental rights, within a framework of democracy and the rule of law, provides the most promising foundations for identifying abstract ethical principles and values, which can be operationalised in the context of AI'.[22] In the Berkman Klein Center's study, fairness and non-discrimination is identified as the 'most highly represented theme in [the] dataset',[23] and international human rights are considered as 'an appealingly well-established core set of concepts, against which emerging technologies can be judged'.[24] The assertion of the centrality of fundamental rights when assessing AI could sound redundant as fundamental rights are indeed supposed to be paramount in the legal orders. However, considering the focus on human rights, one could therefore assume that the said rights and technology are not intrinsically compatible. This suggests even more a very cautious approach in AI developments and the need to put into place formal and compulsory legal rules to handle the consequences of non-desirable effects of AI developments, especially considering the fact that guidelines of this kind are intended for self-evaluation purposes.

In reality, we might not necessarily understand the same things when fundamental rights are mentioned in the guidelines, at least not if we have a positivist perspective on these rights. Indeed, the drafters of the ethics guidelines for a trustworthy AI consider that 'fundamental rights can however also be understood as reflecting special moral entitlements of all individuals arising by virtue of their humanity, regardless of their legally binding status. In that sense, they hence also form part of the second component of trustworthy AI (ethical AI)'.[25] Their laudable aim is to go beyond the strict compliance with existing and binding fundamental rights and possibly set a new horizon for fundamental rights in the context of digital societies and economies.[26] There could, however, be a risk of diluting fundamental rights, instead of enhancing them, by blurring their boundaries and therefore their effectivity. If we consider that moral entitlements of individuals shall be enforced, then we should first check whether they are already encompassed in existing legally binding norms and then make sure that their effectivity is achieved through law enforcement tools. From that perspective, the example of privacy is quite useful.

Privacy and protection of personal data is quite frequently mentioned in the ethics guidelines for trustworthy AI. Protection of personal data is a fundamental right in the EU, enshrined in

---

[20] Ibid. at 11: 'Equal respect for the moral worth and dignity of all human beings must be ensured. This goes beyond non-discrimination, which tolerates the drawing of distinctions between dissimilar situations based on objective justifications. In an AI context, equality entails that the system's operations cannot generate unfairly biased outputs (e.g. the data used to train AI systems should be as inclusive as possible, representing different population groups). This also requires adequate respect for potentially vulnerable persons and groups, such as workers, women, persons with disabilities, ethnic minorities, children, consumers or others at risk of exclusion.'

[21] Ibid. (right to vote, right to good administration or access to public documents, and right to petition the administration): 'AI systems offer substantial potential to improve the scale and efficiency of government in the provision of public goods and services to society. At the same time, citizens' rights could also be negatively impacted by AI systems and should be safeguarded.'

[22] AIHLEG, 'Ethics Guidelines for Trustworthy AI', n. 1 at 9.

[23] Fjeld et al., n. 4 at 47.

[24] Ibid. at 64.

[25] AIHLEG, 'Ethics Guidelines for Trustworthy AI', n.1 at 7.

[26] Ibid. at 10: '[E]ven after compliance with legally enforceable fundamental rights has been achieved, ethical reflection can help us understand how the development, deployment and use of AI systems may implicate fundamental rights and their underlying values, and can help provide more fine-grained guidance when seeking to identify what we should do rather than what we (currently) can do with technology.'

Article 8 of the Charter of Fundamental Rights of the European Union,[27] and its implementation and effectivity are based on the GDPR.[28] Beyond the EU, privacy is 'enshrined in international human rights law and strengthened by a robust web of national and regional data protection laws and jurisprudence'.[29] As we all know, digital technologies and AI especially, have been and still are greedy for personal data. Laws like the GDPR have been specifically drafted in order to fight against uncontrolled exploitation of personal data, especially by free-riding business actors. It would be naive to think that, prior to the implementation of personal data protection laws, those business actors that were wrongly exploiting personal data without being much disturbed couldn't understand that their actions and business models were unethical. In other words, the issue of personal data protection can show quite well how ethical constraints are generally not effective for protecting individuals' fundamental rights unless they translate into laws. Even more, the risk of dilution mentioned earlier seems quite high: privacy and protection of personal data must not be based on individual voluntary self-commitment by organisations, companies, etc. The incentives to respect these fundamental rights must come from compulsory legal rules, whose sanctions are deterrent enough to convince various actors dealing with individuals' personal data to comply with the rules and respect natural persons' privacy.[30] The impression that the regulatory framework is incomplete comes certainly from the fact that the process of defining it is still ongoing, not necessarily in the right direction, as policy recommendations can show.

16.2.3 Response Still under Construction

In the European context, regulation of AI seems to be all the more pressing. Indeed, there are significant risks of market fragmentation if national legislators take isolated regulatory initiatives and, in the absence of a legal framework applicable to AI in most member states, there is a significant risk that these states will adopt their own divergent national rules. This scenario would lead to major disruption of the internal market. This is one of the reasons why the EU sees an opportunity to adopt a harmonised framework that would enable various objectives to be achieved: not only that of offering an environment that will be favourable to the development of AI in Europe, but also the objective to position the EU as a global leader in trustworthy AI. In that context, it seems dubious that soft rules would allow to reach a sufficient level of harmonisation, whereas legal rules could. In addition to ethics guidelines, a burgeoning of policy recommendations initiatives in the area of AI and governance can be observed, though at a less advanced level. In June 2019, AIHLEG released its 'Policy and Investment Recommendations for Trustworthy AI',[31] two months after its ethics guidelines. The recommendations focus on four

---

[27] '1. Everyone has the right to the protection of personal data concerning him or her. 2. Such data must be processed fairly for specified purposes and on the basis of the consent of the person concerned or some other legitimate basis laid down by law ….' Privacy is of course also protected under art 8 of the European Convention on Human Rights.

[28] Regulation (EU) 2016/679 of the European Parliament and of the Council of 27 April 2016 on the protection of natural persons with regard to the processing of personal data and on the free movement of such data, and repealing Directive 95/46/EC.

[29] Fjeld et al., n. 4 at 21: 'Fuelled by vast amounts of data, AI is used in surveillance, advertising, healthcare decision-making, and a multitude of other sensitive contexts. Privacy is not only implicated in prominent implementations of AI, but also behind the scenes, in the development and training of these systems.'

[30] See J. Bryson, 'My Comments/Critiques on the EU's High Level Expert Group on AI's "Ethical Guidelines"' (2019), https://joanna-bryson.blogspot.com/2019/02/my-commentscritiques-on-eus-high-level.html (accessed August 23, 2021).

[31] AIHLEG, 'Policy and Investment Recommendations for Trustworthy AI' (26 June 2019), https://ec.europa.eu/digital-single-market/en/high-level-expert-group-artificial-intelligence.

main areas³² and list the main 'enablers' to achieve beneficial impacts of AI, one of which being 'appropriate governance and regulation'.³³

Then, in February 2020, the EC published its white paper on AI with a report on the safety and liability implications of AI, the Internet of Things and robotics accompanying it,³⁴ whose purpose is to set out policy options on how to achieve the objectives of a trustworthy AI and to develop a single market for AI. The white paper was published along with an online survey, focusing in part on options for a future regulatory framework on AI and safety and liability aspects on AI.³⁵ The same day, the EC Communication 'A European Strategy for Data' was published.³⁶ The white paper and this communication are considered the first pillars of the new digital strategy of the EC, still in an emerging phase. The EC strategy relies on various principles such as awareness raising about AI, institutionalised dialogue between policymakers, developers and users of AI technology, an appropriate governance framework and a review of the adequacy of the current regulatory regime. Regarding the review process, the AIHLEG and the EC suggest a risk-based approach,³⁷ to use 'sandboxes' to set legal and ethical standards³⁸ and to take into account both individual and societal risks. At this stage, the EC suggests in its white paper to limit the introduction of new mandatory legal requirements to be imposed on the relevant actors to high-risk AI applications only.³⁹ These new mandatory legal requirements could be further specified through standards implementing 'key features': training data, data and record keeping, information to be provided, robustness and accuracy, human oversight and specific requirements for particular AI applications.⁴⁰ Among the many items included in the suggested review process are product safety, civil liability rules (to be discussed in Section 16.3.1), criminal liability, data protection rules, non-discrimination provisions, cybersecurity and

---

[32] Ibid. at 6: 'Humans and society at large (A) ... the private sector (B), the public sector (C) and Europe's research and academia (D)'.

[33] Ibid. The other 'enablers' are 'availability of data and infrastructure (E), skills and education (F), [and] funding and investment (H)'.

[34] EC, 'On Artificial Intelligence – a European Approach to Excellence and Trust', White Paper, COM (2020) 65 final (19 February 2020), https://ec.europa.eu/info/publications/white-paper-artificial-intelligence-european-approach-excellence-and-trust_en; EC, 'Report on the Safety and Liability Implications of Artificial Intelligence, the Internet of Things and Robotics', COM (2020) 64 final (19 February 2020), https://ec.europa.eu/info/publications/commission-report-safety-and-liability-implications-ai-internet-things-and-robotics-0_en.

[35] Available documents at https://ec.europa.eu/digital-single-market/en/news/white-paper-artificial-intelligence-public-consultation-towards-european-approach-excellence.

[36] Communication from the Commission, 'A European Strategy for Data', COM (2020) 66 final (19 February 2020), https://eur-lex.europa.eu/legal-content/EN/TXT/?qid=1593073685620&uri=CELEX%3A52020DC0066.

[37] 'Policy and Investment Recommendations for Trustworthy AI' at 26; ibid. at 37: '[t]he character, intensity and timing of regulatory intervention should be a function of the type of risk created by an AI system. In line with an approach based on the proportionality and precautionary principle, various risk classes should be distinguished as not all risks are equal. The higher the impact and/or probability of an AI-created risk, the stronger the appropriate regulatory response should be. "Risk" for this purpose is broadly defined to encompass adverse impacts of all kinds, both individual and societal'. See, however, the European Parliament study: 'Artificial Intelligence: From Ethics to Policy, Study Panel for the Future of Science and Technology', European Parliamentary Research Service (EPRS) (June 2020) at 18, https://epthinktank.eu/2020/06/30/artificial-intelligence-from-ethics-to-policy/: 'the idea of risk-assessment and cost-benefit analysis, however, has been criticised for a variety of reasons, namely "they deny uncertainty and ignorance; second they short-circuit the moral dimension of new technological developments; third, they do not address the need for profound (social) learning from, for example, errors and catastrophes"' (van de Poel I. An Ethical Framework for Evaluating Experimental Technology. Sci Eng Ethics. 2016 Jun 1; (22)3: 667–686)'. The EU proposal for an Artificial Intelligence Act (n.1) seems to rely on the risk-based approach.

[38] 'Policy and Investment Recommendations for Trustworthy AI', n. 37 at 27.

[39] EC, 'On Artificial Intelligence', n. 34 at 18: 'For AI applications that do not qualify as "high-risk" ... and that are therefore not subject to [new] mandatory requirements, an option would be, in addition to [already existing] applicable legislation, to establish a voluntary labelling scheme.' See also ibid. at 25.

[40] Ibid. at 19 ff.

competition rules.[41] The outcome of the review process will show the potential need for amendments and offer updated guidance on existing legislation, on one side, and the need for new regulation, on the other side. The EC is keen to ensure that any regulatory intervention is focused and proportionate,[42] which in other words means regulatory parsimony. A risks/advantages approach is likely to be put forward.

One of the interesting points in the current policy phase is that the EC seems to move beyond voluntary guidance and to favour mandatory regulatory approaches when needed. Due to the rapid technological change, though, it intends to foster a principle-based approach to regulation, outcome-based policies subject to monitoring and enforcement, and to avoid prescriptive regulation, requiring agile policy-making solutions such as the above-mentioned 'regulatory sandboxes'. Like the 2019 ethics guidelines, this second wave of publications containing policy recommendations and opening consultations on them go from rather technical tools to broad and far-reaching governance objectives and regulatory strategies. Regarding the technical tools, they concern the quality of data,[43] the development of mechanisms for the protection of personal data (technological implementation of the GDPR – privacy by design), the volume of data in the assessment of market power for the purpose of applying competition law rules, certification and auditing mechanisms, etc. As far as governance and regulatory strategies are concerned, apart from the review process and the principle-based approach mentioned above, the white paper proposes a framework for cooperation of national competent authorities, especially in the perspective of European-wide standardisation and certification of AI-enabled products and services.[44] The main objective here is to pool expertise and share best practices, to enable capacity to conduct continuous assessment of the regulatory framework, but also and especially to avoid fragmentation of the single market.

These attempts are just the first steps of a colossal agenda, with many difficulties lying ahead: little evidence is available to inform policy-making, technology is developing rapidly, more than regulators' capacity to understand it properly and to react, requiring a kind of continuous systematic stress-test for regulations and governance structures and institutions, enforcement agencies etc. At this stage, first results of the feedback process conducted by the EC show that 'while a number of the requirements are already reflected in existing legal or regulatory regimes, those regarding transparency, traceability and human oversight are not specifically covered under current legislation in many economic sectors'.[45] The answers to the EC white paper are currently analysed and a full report will be published later. The preliminary trends that can be observed are that a revision of the EU 2018 Coordinated Plan on AI[46] is desirable, that the circumscription of new mandatory legal requirements to high-risk applications is not convincing and that a revision of the existing product liability directive 'to cover particular risks engendered

---

[41] Ibid. at 38–39.
[42] Ibid. at 19.
[43] To this regard, a recent study by the European Parliament suggest the introduction of a 'data hygiene certificate', see 'Artificial intelligence', n. 37: 'AI/ML system developers are required to hold a data hygiene certificate (DHC) to be eligible so sell their solutions to government institutions and public administration bodies.'
[44] EC, 'On Artificial Intelligence', n. 34 at 24: '[a] European governance structure could have a variety of tasks, as a forum for a regular exchange of information and best practice, identifying emerging trends, advising on standardisation activity as well as on certification. It should also play a key role in facilitating the implementation of the legal framework, such as through issuing guidance, opinions and expertise'.
[45] Ibid. at 9.
[46] Communication from the Commission, 'Coordinated Plan on Artificial Intelligence', COM (2018) 795 final (7 December 2018).

by certain AI applications' is probably needed.[47] On the basis of the complete analysis of the public consultation and of an impact assessment, the EC presented its proposal of an Artificial Intelligence Act. Considering the systematic dimension of this policy initiative and the fact that it is expected to lay down the foundations of a single market for AI, it is quite encouraging that the proposal was published within a year after the consultation. Time is pressing considering the rapidity of AI developments and the economic, democratic and geopolitical challenges it raises. If high-risk AI applications and the security of users come first in the regulatory priorities, EU product safety and liability rules are definitely to be reviewed and updated as Section 16.3 will show.

16.3 IMPACT ON THE LAW: SOME EXAMPLES

16.3.1 New Civil Liability Framework

Legal certainty and security as well as effective redress and compensation avenues are common needs for both economic operators and citizens and consumers.[48] But, of course, their respective interests (competitiveness, on one side, physical and moral safety, protection of human and political rights, on the other side) are far from being 'naturally' convergent. Striking a balance in the field of AI, from the perspective of new or updated mandatory regulations, between economic operators and consumers, as existing experiences show, looks like a headache. In the field of civil liability, the features of AI are sometimes disruptive enough to potentially give rise to a paradigm shift. In fact, one of the main characteristics of the harm that may potentially be caused by new technologies is that it may not necessarily be the result of any wrongdoing on the part of a human agent or the result of any product defect (in the 'traditional' sense of the term). Machine learning develops the 'capability' of AI to perform its own analysis and actions that subsequently become far-removed from the initial settings put in place by the human developers of the said system. Evaluating the behaviour of these autonomous systems and considering that there was wrongdoing is not a straight process on the basis of actual civil liability and product liability rules in most legal systems.[49] Moreover, it will require a disproportionate time-consuming and costly technical assessment to identify the cause of the problem and to establish a causal link between the harm suffered and AI-enabled products and services. As neither consumers nor the legal system will be able to absorb the costs involved, the idea of covering the cost of harm caused by new technologies by using guaranty mechanisms that are separate from the rules governing civil liability is put forward.[50]

We know that, in the past when previous industrial mutations took place, existing rules, although they have not been changed, have been interpreted in new and sometimes bold ways by the courts, in order to meet victims' needs for compensation. Conversely, where the scale or

---

[47] https://ec.europa.eu/digital-single-market/en/news/white-paper-artificial-intelligence-public-consultation-towards-european-approach-excellence. On the topic of product liability, see Section 16.3.1.

[48] EC, 'Report on the Safety and Liability Implications of Artificial Intelligence', n. 34 at 1: 'A clear safety and liability framework is particularly important when new technologies like AI, the IoT and robotics emerge, both with a view to ensure consumer protection and legal certainty for businesses.'

[49] The major piece of civil liability within the EU is the Product Liability Directive: Council Directive 85/374/EEC of 25 July 1985 on the approximation of the laws, regulations and administrative provisions of the member states concerning liability for defective products. It was of course written, as other product safety regulations, prior to the emergence of digital technologies such as AI.

[50] M. Monot-Fouletier and M. Clément, 'Véhicule autonome: vers une autonomie du régime de responsabilité applicable?' (2018) 3 *Recueil Dalloz* 129.

nature of harm has so required, the legislators have adopted new legal rules (as was the case with accidents at work, road traffic accidents and, of course, damage caused by defective products). Such precedents seem to be valuable sources of reflection in the current process of reviewing the existing EU legal framework in the light of the impact of AI and of drafting the policy and regulatory options and proposals. Civil liability is in fact one of the priority areas in the ongoing review process conducted by the EC. Apart from the report on the safety and liability implications of AI, the Internet of Things and robotics accompanying the white paper on AI,[51] previous and subsequent studies tackle the main issues raised by AI in the area of civil liability.[52] This focus is partly justified because there is pressing need of action, and if single states were to legislate on these matters at national level, there would be a high risk of fragmentation of the single market. Such domestic regulations would constitute barriers to the free movement of AI-enabled products and services.[53] Several risks and needs related to AI are not covered yet in the existing EU product safety and liability legislation, such as human oversight in the context of AI self-learning products and systems, inclusion of mental health risks within the concept of product safety, opacity of systems based on algorithms, data dependency, etc.[54] In order to deal with the complexity of the products and systems and the risks that they expose their users to, the EC suggests to follow the risk-based approach mentioned above: 'Strict liability schemes could ensure that whenever that risk materialises, the victim is compensated regardless of fault. The impact of choosing who should be strictly liable for such operations on the development and uptake of AI would need to be carefully assessed and a risk-based approach be considered.'[55] It means therefore that for unacceptable risks, the revision of existing rules or the introduction of new regulation should definitely be considered.[56]

Within the EU, the rules governing civil liability resulting from defective products constitute a horizontal legal framework, which is designed primarily for tangible objects and does not apply to the liability of service providers. Traditional legal rules and categories could cope though, to a certain extent, with new situations relating to AI. However, the complexity of the technologies in question makes it costly, both in terms of time and of expertise, to apply the traditional legal conditions governing civil liability. Mechanisms involving insurance, or even dedicated warranty funds for the compensation of damages caused by AI, would take some of these issues out of courts. Such a step might also be regarded as a precondition for the social acceptance of new technologies and thus for their development. A regulatory intervention has been decided on at EU level, in the field of AI, coupling a horizontal and a sectoral approaches.[57] A horizontal instrument offers the benefit of striving to achieve coherence of the system and avoids treating

---

[51] See n. 34.
[52] EC, 'Liability for Emerging Digital Technologies', n. 1; AIHLEG, 'Liability for Artificial Intelligence and Other Emerging Digital Technologies', n. 1; A. Bertolini, 'Artificial Intelligence and Civil Liability', Study Requested by the Juri Committee, European Parliament (14 July 2020), www.europarl.europa.eu/RegData/etudes/STUD/2020/621926/IPOL_STU(2020)621926_EN.pdf.
[53] Dir 2019/770/EU of 20 May 2019 on certain aspects concerning contracts for the supply of digital content and digital services and 2019/771/EU of 20 May 2019 on certain aspects concerning contracts for the sale of goods, as far as contractual conformity and remedies are concerned, intend to 'meet the multiple challenges posed today by an increasingly technology-driven economy' (Dir 2019/771/EU, recital 1). A similar approach should be strongly considered regarding rules on civil liability.
[54] EC, 'Report on the Safety and Liability Implications of Artificial Intelligence', n. 34 at 8–9 and 16.
[55] Ibid. at 16.
[56] EC, 'Policy Recommendations', n. 37 at 55.
[57] Proposal for a Regulation on artificial intelligence (n.1), in conjunction with the proposal for a Regulation on machinery products, COM(2021) 202 final, 21 April 2021.

victims of defective products differently, but may also present the drawback of inadequacy if it is not sufficiently tailored to the specific circumstances of different situations. Sectorial instruments are usually tailored to the products and situations concerned, but they also have the effect of a 'siloed' approach, fragmenting the regulatory framework and presenting the risk of discrimination among victims. By their very nature, sectorial regulations also are 'technical' instruments and reflect how technology shapes the law. A combination of horizontal instruments with sectorial instruments will require reflection on how they will work together, probably on a basis of a *lex generalis/lex specialis* approach.

16.3.2 New Professional Framework

As stated in the Introduction, building a true and consistent legal framework on which AI developments will be based requires lawyers to have a sufficient command of this field, its terminology, the main possibilities, obstacles, unknown consequences, etc. This is even more necessary when lawyers (judges and legal practitioners) use AI-based technologies in providing legal services to the citizens and to their clients. It certainly requires going beyond traditional ethical and deontological professional rules. There is indeed a risk of a rush to the technology in order to remain competitive and to gain productivity, without taking sufficient time to analyse the use of AI tools in legal practice. As stated in the EC Policy Recommendations,

> in the future, AI systems will augment and complement human capabilities in hybrid work settings. Practitioners in all areas will need to be upskilled with digital competences to be enhanced in their roles. At the same time, the future workforce will have to be equipped with a new – human centric – set of skills that empowers them on a cognitive and a socio-cultural level to face the challenges ahead.[58]

As a minimum threshold, lawyers would be required to understand how these tools work, what is the data on which decisions and proposals are made, what are the risks of bias, how to correct them, what are the patterns, etc. The Council of Europe Commission for the Efficiency of Justice partly addressed these concerns and adopted, in December 2018, the European Ethical Charter on the use of AI in judicial systems and their environment.[59] Technology is developing and changing rapidly. The pace of change gives rise to levels of concern and incomprehension that cannot easily be resolved. Lawyers, in particular, like society as a whole, find it difficult to understand the technological changes taking place and thus to keep up with them. Legal practitioners will more and more face practical and ethical issues when confronting AI-enabled tools in their practice, and especially how they can advise on AI unless they have a sufficient knowledge of the technologies employed. One of the priorities listed in the EC white paper on AI are actions on skill development.[60] Existing and future lawyers should definitely be educated in AI broadly speaking, so that they can keep up their professional obligations and, even more importantly, promote legal values into the various organisations developing and using AI and shape future AI developments. This should materialise more and more and urgently in law curricula in the various law schools and in professional training programs. One could even think of a specific designation for lawyers who are experts in AI. Law has the capacity to shape technology, certainly more than ethics guidelines, but it requires lawyers to understand

---

[58] EC, 'Policy Recommendations' at 31.
[59] Available at https://rm.coe.int/ethical-charter-en-for-publication-4-december-2018/16808f699c.
[60] EC, 'On Artificial Intelligence', n. 34 at 6.

technology. If not, technology will invariably shape legal rules and legal practice, which is probably one of the biggest risks of an unregulated development of technology. AI developments must not result just from technical feasibility. Developers and engineers can generally endorse ethics guidelines in their activity, but they are generally not sufficiently aware of legal obligations and what would be infringements of particularly important rights, for the simple fact that it is not their job to do so. Lawyers must play this role and it is indeed important to increase the availability of legal and technical support to implement legally compliant AI solutions.

16.4 CONCLUSION

So far, the various reflections on what the developments of AI should be have been made at a rather abstract and quite speculative level. As stressed in the Berkman Klein Center's study, 'there's a wide and thorny gap between the articulation of these high-level concepts and their actual achievement in the real world'.[61] There is certainly a legal vacuum at the moment and it will take time to fill it in. Ethics guidelines are not an adequate and comprehensive answer to the challenges raised by AI.[62] The numerous references to fundamental rights in the various documents analysed should indicate clearly that we need a specific legal framework, as has happened with privacy and protection of personal data under the GDPR. Hard rules have been deemed necessary in order to protect personal data; the said protection being considered as a fundamental right. Regulators should therefore take the same protective path, otherwise human rights protection from undesirable AI developments will remain quite theoretical, notwithstanding the numerous ethics guidelines and principles. Indeed, without going through all prior cases of bad consequences produced by AI, the news offers almost every week examples of negative impacts of AI, with serious infringements of fundamental rights.[63] This shows that urgent and more proactive action is needed because the risks are far from remote. The actual crucial question is therefore 'how can we move ... to specific policy and legislation for governing AI?'[64] Leaving it to standards, self-regulation and voluntary commitments seems a far too soft approach. It is difficult to admit that AI developers should be in charge of conducting an assessment on questions as '[d]id you take measures that ensure that the AI system does not negatively impact democracy?' or '[d]oes the AI system respect the freedom of expression and information and/or freedom of assembly and association?' If we go that route, the trade-offs between fundamental rights and economic stakes will always be resolved in a negative way for individuals' rights.

---

[61] Fjeld et al., n. 4 at 66.
[62] H. Hilligoss, F. A. Raso and V. Krishnamurthy, quoted in ibid.: 'It's not enough for AI to be "ethical"; it must also be "rights respecting"', Berkman Klein Center Collection (October 2018), https://medium.com/berkman-klein-center/its-not-enough-for-ai-to-be-ethical-it-must-also-be-rights-respecting-b87f7e215b97 (accessed August 23, 2021).
[63] To take some very recent examples just to illustrate the risk frequency, the UK Court of Appeals ruled on 11 August 2020, in a case concerning the use of a facial recognition software used by South Wales police, that a plaintiff's right to privacy under Article 8 of the European convention on human rights had been breached, and that the force failed to properly investigate whether the software exhibited any race or gender bias, www.judiciary.uk/judgments/r-bridges-v-cc-south-wales/; in another area, a recent article detailed how Instagram 'censorship' of a black model's photo reignites claims of race bias, www.theguardian.com/technology/2020/aug/09/instagrams-censorship-of-black-models-photo-shoot-reignites-claims-of-race-bias-nyome-nicholas-williams; globally (accessed August 23, 2021). G. Soros recently expressed the view that 'AI Is Leaning towards and Giving Advantages to Closed Societies', *La Repubblica* (12 August 2020).
[64] See 'Artificial intelligence', n. 37. The study suggests to 'understand AI as a social experiment and to introduce experimental conditions for the real-world applications of AI'. One can be sceptical about doing 'experiences' when fundamental rights are one of the parameters. The main other interesting suggestions are a data hygiene certificate, an ethical technology assessment (eTA) prior to deployment of the AI system, showing clear goals for the AI/ML application and produce an 'accountability report' in response to the eTA.

Focusing on a legal response does not mean that ethical principles cannot inspire new and specific mandatory rules and help in interpreting fundamental rights in a consistent way as society evolves.[65] But principles remain rather abstract prescriptions. The question is not if a given AI-enabled product or service is good or bad. What matters is how to determine whether someone (a human) is liable and/or guilty and on which grounds. There is a need to find a way to operationalise legal compliance of AI, after the past period of a stand-by and wait-and-see posture. As previously mentioned, the speed of the technological innovations currently unfolding is a feature that needs to be taken into account. This factor seems to favour a legal approach and legal rules that are flexible enough (and are not rigid) to prevent a risk of rapid obsolescence. Moreover, this approach would be adapted to the absence of uniformity among technologies. Regarding design and implementations of AI in ways that are compliant with legal prescriptions, the standards should be formalised in mandatory, preventive, product-by-product sectorial regulations. In this perspective, a concept of 'ethical by design' could be translated into technical requirements. In their journey into the AI world, legal experts (practicing lawyers, judges, notaries, legal academics, etc.) have to acquire new skills and take relatively new approaches. The new skills in question are largely technical ones. Lawyers have to dip more into the world of computers, automation, algorithms, machine learning and AI, which requires a significant investment in time and effort. This trend is under way and is the only way to come alongside the current industrial revolution and bind it where legal principles are imposed to do so.[66]

---

[65] AIHLEG, 'Ethics Guidelines for Trustworthy AI', n. 1 at 11.
[66] See the 'Neurorights Initiative' of Professor R. Yuste at Columbia University, https://nri.ntc.columbia.edu/ (accessed August 23, 2021). The five proposed neurorights are the right to personal identity, the right to free-will, the right to mental privacy, the right to equal access to mental augmentation and right to protection from algorithmic bias.

17

Ethical Digital Lawyering

From Technical to Philosophical Insights

Mathieu Guillermin, Arnaud Billion, Carine Copain-Héritier, and Emmanuel de Vaujany

17.1 INTRODUCTION

Digitalization in the legal domain is an amazing example of the way information technology (IT) can displace or enrich typically human tasks. Fueled by the recent progress in artificial intelligence (AI) (big data, machine learning, natural language processing, etc.), this phenomenon of digitalization affects more and more legal tasks and functions. Effective examples of digitalization in the legal domain are very diverse, ranging from exploration of patent classifications[1] to prediction of legal cases' outcomes (e.g., anticipation of foreseeable damages from an action).[2] One can also mention e-discovery,[3] as well as the digitalization of the organization and review of legal documents.[4]

Despite these successes in digitalization, full automation of lawyering remains largely speculative. Some legal tasks or functions are well known for their resistance to formalization and digitalization. Let us give a few examples of such a resistance. First, it can be said of many norms that they have an open texture;[5] the example can be given of the prohibition of vehicles in a public park: it is not clear when reading the rule, if bicycles, or the commemorative tank of the last war, are encompassed in the field of application of the rule.[6] No sets of formal criteria can exhaust or fully capture the correct meaning of such a rule. Similarly, it has been shown that statements expressing fundamental rights can be a means neither to summarize all the rules that allegedly derive from them, nor to put their meanings in coherence.[7] In other words, the meaning of those norms is always in the course of being discovered, it is never fixed, and the dream of calculating them is senseless. Second, some rules explicitly aim at taking into account the subjective opinion of some individuals in certain circumstances. For instance, Article 121-3 of

---

[1] J. G. Conrad and K. L. Branting, "Introduction to the Special Issue on Legal Text Analytics" (2018) 26 *Artificial Intelligence and Law* 99.
[2] S. Ophir, *Moral Decisions by Robots by Calculating the Minimal Damages Using Verdict History* (Hybrid Worlds: Societal and Ethical Challenges, Clawar Association Ltd., 2019).
[3] D. Reiling, "Quelle place pour l'intelligence artificielle dans le processus de décision d'un juge?" (2019) 2 *Les Cahiers de la Justice* 221.
[4] H. Surden, "Machine Learning and Law" (2014) 89 *Washington Law Review* 87.
[5] R. Greenstein, *La langue, le discours et la culture en anglais du droit* (Paris: Publications de la Sorbonne, Langues et langages, 2005).
[6] M. Genesereth, *Computational Law: The Cop in the Backseat* (Stanford: CodeX—The Stanford Center for Legal Informatics, 2015).
[7] J.-C. Billier and A. Maryioli, *Histoire de la philosophie du droit* (Paris: Armand Colin, 2001) 269, explain that the project of summarizing legal rules through some high-level principles and fundamental rights is a utopia.

the French Penal Code states that there is no crime or offense without the intent to commit. Intent assessment seems particularly delicate to automatize. Third, it is widely acknowledged that sometimes judges change their practices regarding, for example, the definition of a legal wording. In the end of the nineteenth century, the French Cour de Cassation decided to apply the existing rule of compensation of damage to new situations caused by workplace accidents in the context of industrialization.[8] Such a decision is certainly not the consequence of a calculation that could somehow be computerized.

In this chapter, we restrict the scope of our discussion to effective digitalization in the legal domain. Notably, we avoid the speculative investigation of ethical issues raised by, say, full automation of lawyering or of justice administration. We will only consider effective and realistic developments of IT in the legal domain. However, setting aside the most speculative and radical perspectives does not mean that there are no ethical concerns remaining. It is true that some digital tools, such as contract review services,[9] do not seem to raise, at first sight, major ethical issues. As a side remark, one could nevertheless criticize the restriction of the scope of such an ethical judgment solely to the level of theoretical impact upon legal tasks and functions, while automation embeds in itself psychological and socio-professional consequences for the impacted workers as well as broader economic difficulties. In any case, ethical challenges for legal computing become more direct and pressing when it comes to other applications such as predictive justice or AI involvement in justice administration (for instance, when sentencing is assisted by automatized risk assessment of the re-offense of defendants).[10]

Therefore, it is quite clear that an ethical investigation is needed for steering the development of digital lawyering and associated AI techniques. The purpose of our contribution is to shed some light upon the manner in which such ethical investigation should or could be conducted, upon what seem to us to be core elements of such an investigation. We will start with some general comments about the form of ethical evaluation in the domain of IT. Then, we will insist upon the content with two key elements we think should be mobilized in ethical investigations of the sort discussed here: we will insist upon the importance of adequate insights about IT technical realities; then, we will show that fundamental (philosophical) background debates should be convoked.

17.2 ETHICAL EVALUATION OF NEW (LEGAL) TECHNOLOGIES: NEED FOR CONTEXTUALIZATION

To the extent that we need ethical evaluation of legal computing, one can wonder about the tools available for such an evaluation and also about the form the latter should take. Benefits one can expect from AI techniques – for instance in terms of business value, efficiency, speed, or quality – are often brought to the fore in response to such ethical questioning. The topics of efficiency, speed, or quality are peculiarly relevant for legal activity: for instance, the vice-president of French Conseil d'Etat noted that AI could foster the quality of justice by facilitating standardization (reduction of hazard and randomness in judgments).[11] Removing biases involved

---

[8] Cour de Cassation, civil chamber, June 16, 1896.
[9] An example of transformation impacting tasks linked to contract review is given by H. Surden, "Computable Contracts" (2012) 46 *UC Davis Law Review* 629.
[10] C. McKay, "Predicting Risk in Criminal Procedure: Actuarial Tools, Algorithms, AI, and Judicial Decision-Making" (2019) 19 *Sydney Law School Research Paper* 67.
[11] J.-M. Sauvé, "Le juge administratif et l'intelligence artificielle," Conseil d'Etat (2018), www.conseil-etat.fr/actualites/discours-et-interventions/le-juge-administratif-et-l-intelligence-artificielle (accessed February 24, 2020).

in human judgments may be the first step in the standardization journey.[12] These highlighted advantages of legal computing are in line with narratives about a broader societal transformation in which AI is considered as "one of the keys to the future."[13]

These are interesting elements that must be considered. But they cannot exhaust the ethical investigation without risking missing some crucial dimensions. As exemplified by diverse initiatives in the field of ethics of technological innovation,[14] ethical investigation requires a broad scope. One can, for instance, approach ethical issues raised by IT implementation by identifying, characterizing, and evaluating the societal transformations they induce. Such a framework leads one to wonder about the manner in which technological possibilities should be mobilized to maximize the ethical quality of outcomes. It provides a fruitful ground to ask questions such as the following: Which degree of automation is desirable? Where are humans in the loop? Where should they intervene? What does "good human intervention" mean and how to guarantee the quality of human intervention? What mediation devices may be necessary? Is there a need for specific training of stakeholders? What are the points of vigilance? To illustrate the relevance of this framework, we can draw upon the case exposed by Himanen et al. of a data-driven approach for discovering new materials.[15] As the authors explain, machine learning tools are mobilized as a supplementary step that complements the traditional approach (based on experimentation and theory or computation). Therefore, the implementation of this new approach cannot be ethically evaluated by simply presenting the advantages and drawbacks of technology in itself because, rather than operating in isolation, the new techniques generate an appended dimension of complexity within a preexisting situation.

In sum, a certain level of contextualization is necessary for ethical investigation. Among elements that could prove crucial for contextualization of ethical assessment of IT implementation in the legal domain, two deserve, it seems to us, dedicated mention and highlighting: ethical evaluation requires (1) key pieces of knowledge about technical realities and (2) explicit consideration of fundamental background debates (notably, insights from philosophy and the history of law). When, for instance, it is claimed that a gain in efficiency or in justice is to be expected from legal computing through standardization, one should notably scrutinize and evaluate these promises in light of these two dimensions.

17.2.1 Insights from Technical Realities: Gain in (Economic) Efficiency?

Gain in efficiency is one of the major and most common promises associated with the implementation of IT. Computers and their powerful algorithms can process more information than humans, they are faster, never go wrong, pause, or go on strike. Nevertheless, such promises or advantages need mitigation. Some costs and risks should not be understated, as digital solutions are often based on complex systems whose industrialization is in progress. Such systems

---

[12] C. Chambers Goodman, "AI/Esq.: Impacts of Artificial Intelligence in Lawyer-Client Relationships" (2019) 72 *Oklahoma Law Review* 149: "AI has great potential to assist lawyers, as well as the opportunity to replace (some) lawyers. It can identify and minimize bias in client intake and initial consultations."

[13] "The point is that from now on, artificial intelligence will play a much more important role than it has done so far. It is no longer merely a research field confined to laboratories or to a specific application. It will become one of the keys to the future." C. Villani, *For a Meaningful Artificial Intelligence: Towards a French and European Strategy* (Paris: AI for Humanity, 2018), www.aiforhumanity.fr/pdfs/MissionVillani_Report_ENG-VF.pdf (accessed February 24, 2020).

[14] S. O. Hansson, *The Ethics of Technology: Methods and Approaches* (London: Rowman & Littlefield International, 2017); S. Spiekermann, *Ethical IT Innovation: A Value-Based System Design Approach* (Abingdon: CRC Press, 2016).

[15] L. Himanen, A. Geurts, A. S. Foster, and P. Rinke, "Data-Driven Materials Science: Status, Challenges, and Perspectives" (2019) 6 *Advanced Science* 1900808.

are subject to bugs and require maintenance and monitoring (which means technical expertise). These pragmatic aspects (one could also talk about hardware and energy consumption) may constitute hidden costs that would reduce the effective gain in (economic) efficiency induced by the implementation of a given IT in lawyering. They thereby count as important insights for the ethical evaluation of such implementation.

Moreover, possible risks and hidden costs are not restricted to digital systems themselves or to their organizational environment: difficulties also emerge at a more global level. IT raises more and more ecological concerns linked to resource depletion and pollution. Though studies about this problem are currently in progress,[16] more specialized and previous works[17] provide few metrics that carry sufficient conviction on the environmental impact of IT: the energy consumption of IT increases by 9 percent per year, which means an increase of 8 percent in greenhouse gas (GHG) emissions. IT may represent 4 percent of global GHG emissions as of today, and far more in the next few years, increasing the absolute quantity of GHG in the atmosphere and the probability of severe consequences.[18] This would not be a big deal if IT acted merely as a tool for dematerialization, for transformation of brick and mortar GHG emissions into IT ones. This inverse correlation unfortunately seems dubious.[19] In addition to the topic of energy consumption, one should also take into account issues associated with other resources such as rare earth metals.[20] The exploitation of these indispensable components of IT comes with acute ecological, social, and geostrategic difficulties (work conditions, pollution and toxicity, depletion, geographic concentration of resources, etc.). Such issues at the global scale also deserve consideration when assessing the gain in efficiency one can expect from IT.

In sum, the point we want to make here is the following: the assessment of possible gains in (economic) efficiency requires adequate knowledge of technical and natural realities. One must integrate, in the framework of ethical evaluation, all costs to avoid externalities (costs for maintenance, energy and hardware, socio-ecological costs, etc.). One should also get a grip on the risks that IT comes with or even generates. With dependencies on specific resources such as rare earth metals, hardware costs may well brutally increase in the future, as certain countries almost have the monopoly on some elements. Coming back to the legal domain, effective gain in efficiency could prove self-undermining by triggering bouncing effects. For instance, would lawyering become more efficient, litigants could themselves become more demanding, notably through digital tools enabling them to submit more and more litigation.[21] In a nutshell, promises of increased (economic) efficiency of lawyering through IT have to be confirmed. Externalities, all of them, should ideally be weighted in the balance.

17.2.2 Gain in Objectivity, Rationality, or Neutrality?

We can now concentrate on another benefit often attributed to legal computing: it could help remove biases possibly displayed by human actors (e.g., implicit discrimination based on gender

---

[16] H. Ferredeboeuf, "Déployer la sobriété numérique – rapport intermédiaire," The Shift Project (2020), https://theshiftproject.org/article/rapport-intermediaire-deployer-sobriete-numerique/ (accessed February 24, 2020).

[17] I. Ahmad and S. Ranka, *Handbook of Energy-Aware and Green Computing* (Abingdon: Chapman & Hall, 2012).

[18] Ferredeboeuf, n. 16.

[19] Frédéric Bordage, "Empreinte environnementale du numérique mondial," GreenIT.fr (2019), www.greenit.fr/empreinte-environnementale-du-numerique-mondial/ (accessed February 24, 2020).

[20] H. Ferreboeuf, F. Berthoud, P. Bihouix, P. Fabre, D. Kaplan, L. Lefèvre et al., "Pour une sobriété numérique. Rapport du groupe de travail pour le think tank the Shift Project," Association Française pour le Développement (2018), https://theshiftproject.org/article/pour-une-sobriete-numerique-rapport-shift/ (accessed February 24, 2020).

[21] E.g., E. Jeuland, "Justice numérique, justice inique?" (2019) 2 *Les Cahiers de la Justice* 193.

or ethnicity).[22] Properly evaluating the real gain to be expected in this domain requires minimal acquaintance with AI. In particular, one needs to grasp the distinction between symbolic or cognitive rule-based approaches and machine learning techniques. The former class of programming offers some guarantees in terms of bias reduction because the algorithms it produces are exclusively programmed "by hand," by explicitly coding the rules of data processing. In such cases, the risk of propagating human biases in algorithms is low, for this would mean explicit coding of biased rules.[23] However, many new ways of computing law[24] are based on machine learning techniques or mobilize them in combination with rule-based approaches.[25] And when machine learning is involved, the guarantee of neutrality or of bias reduction is far weaker.

To properly understand the issue with machine learning, minimal technical knowledge is necessary. Broadly speaking, machine learning can be conceived of as automatic tuning of free parameters within algorithmic structures. The idea is the following: AI algorithms, like any computer programs, transform input data into output data in order to operate some tasks. When relying on cognitive or symbolic approaches, the programmer integrally determines the transformation, he "writes it by hand." But when targeted transformations are too complex for such "handwriting," one can try to write only an algorithmic architecture, that is to say, only classes of transformation whose details correspond to parameters that can vary. Then the programmer will write a second program, this one by hand, whose mission will be to optimize the free parameters in order to find a satisfying transformation. This is the learning process. In this simplified picture, one crucial element is nonetheless missing. The optimization or learning process needs guidance, the programmer must provide more material. Guidance can be obtained through reward functions ensuring iterative mathematical evaluation of sets of parameters proposed by the learning process (reinforcement learning). Guidance can also be provided through examples of results that the transformation should achieve (supervised learning). Learning processes can also aim at compressing and regenerating large input data sets with the highest fidelity possible (unsupervised learning through auto-encoder structures). Such techniques allow the elaboration of algorithms capable of extracting highly significant patterns in big data sets.

Although somewhat imprecise, this rapid exposition gives, we hope, correct intuitions about machine learning. This is crucial because it provides very important elements for ethical evaluation. Notably, one can now understand that machine learning techniques give no absolute guarantee of bias reduction or of increase in objectivity and neutrality, in comparison with processes involving human judgments. And this is for the good and simple reason that human choices and judgments are inevitably at play in the elaboration of machine learning algorithms. There is thus the need for enlightened human choices and judgments to make trustworthy learning processes capable of producing reliable algorithms, that is to say, algorithms able to adequately perform intended transformations of data (for example, to ensure specific

---

[22] D. L. Chen, "Machine Learning and Rule of Law" (2019) 27 *Computational Analysis of Law* 15.

[23] This claim, though intuitive, nonetheless deserves caution, for very often codes are extremely complex and no single actor perfectly understands them.

[24] L. Robaldo, S. Villata, A. Wyner, and M. Grabmair, "Introduction for Artificial Intelligence and Law: Special Issue 'Natural Language Processing for Legal Texts'" (2019) 27 *Artificial Intelligence Law Review* 113: "NLP methods and semantic technologies for automatically analyzing, indexing, and enriching big data … automate extraction of knowledge from legal documents; formalize legal data as ontologies; and represent an ontology as Linked Data in RDF … a range of NLP approaches applied to legal texts to address classification, knowledge representation, argument mining, information extraction, information retrieval, ontology population, and multilingualism in legal documents."

[25] D. L. Chen, "Judicial Analytics and the Great Transformation of American Law" (2019) 27 *Artificial Intelligence and Law* 15: "Predictive analytics can also be used in the first step of causal inference, where the features employed in the first step are exogenous to the case."

tasks such as classification of legal documents or prediction of judgments outcomes). One can distinguish several important loci where human choices and judgments are indispensable and critical.

First, there are choices and judgments to make about the type of algorithmic architecture. The programmer is free to allow any class of transformation he can encode and to let any parameter within it vary. But he has to find the correct balance between too low or too high flexibility. If the class of possible transformations he chooses is too restricted, the learning process will not succeed. It will be impossible to find parameters that sufficiently satisfy the constraints guiding optimization. Such problems, corresponding to underfitting, are nonetheless the lesser evil, for it will be easy to detect that the algorithm is not operating as intended. Trickier is the risk of overfitting, which occurs when the programmer deploys a too flexible algorithmic structure. In this case, constraints guiding the learning process may be perfectly fulfilled, while performance will dramatically fall with new data and real-life use of the produced algorithm. One can imagine that these constraints act as flashlights that only partially reveal the shape of the intended transformation and that the learning process tunes parameters of the available algorithmic structure to fit those unveiled partial shapes. Overfitting occurs when the lightened parts of the intended transformation are perfectly matched, while parts remaining in the dark are completely misrepresented. In sum, there is no a priori guarantee that the learning processes will produce meaningful and adequate transformations, firstly, because humans can make mistakes in the choice of the algorithmic structures to be trained (issues can also occur in the definition of the learning processes themselves with for instance erroneous choices of hyperparameters).

A second important set of indispensable and critical human choices and judgments concerns constraints guiding learning processes. There is no a priori guarantee that these constraints are suitable. Programmers are free to choose the reward functions they like and must wonder about the quality of these key parameters (in reinforcement learning). When using big data sets to optimize algorithmic structures (in supervised or unsupervised learning), the quality and representativeness of these databases are crucial for the success of learning. One needs to be sure that these datasets catch or contain meaningful patterns that the learning process will try to reproduce or approximate. If databases guiding learning processes are biased (for instance, criminal databases that could be discriminatory with respect to persons' origins, underrepresented minorities,[26] etc.), trained algorithms will reproduce those biases (to the extent that the learning process is "successful"). This risk is well identified and is recalled by Article 2 of the Council of Europe Commission Ethical Charter.[27] In other words, data that will be computed to train machine learning algorithms possess uncertain quality. Data can encompass misrepresentations or biased information, but they can also be unproperly structured or difficult to exploit.[28] There is no a priori guarantee that a data set provides valuable knowledge of a studied topic. Data sets are human constructs that are highly dependent on their context of elaboration. This human influence on data is pervasive. Sweeping it under the rug will not make it disappear.

---

[26] D. Kehl, P. Guo, and S. Kessler, "Algorithms in the Criminal Justice System: Assessing the Use of Risk Assessments in Sentencing," Responsive Communities Initiative, Berkman Klein Center for Internet & Society, Harvard Law School (2017), https://206.191.184.172/handle/1/33746041 (accessed February 24, 2020).

[27] Council of Europe Commission for the Efficiency of Justice, "European Ethical Charter on the Use of Artificial Intelligence in Judicial Systems and Their Environment" (2018): "Given the ability of these processing methods to reveal existing discrimination, through grouping or classifying data relating to individuals or groups of individuals, public and private stakeholders must ensure that the methods do not reproduce or aggravate such discrimination."

[28] Reiling, n. 3 even draws a relationship between unstructured data and meaningless ones.

A serious ethical danger lies in the temptation of letting machine learning conceal human and subjective biases in the technical tunings of trained algorithms. It seems ethically crucial to resist this temptation and to recognize the necessity of human judgment about data quality.

In light of the technical insights exposed here, one can become a little circumspect. The claim that legal computing based on AI is desirable because it leads to gains in efficiency, neutrality, or objectivity, may be valid. However, its validity cannot be assumed just by virtue of the replacement of humans and their subjectivity by neutral algorithms. There is no absolutely neutral algorithm or data. AI and machine learning do not allow purging human subjectivity from legal reasoning or processes. They merely displace it (at most). Human subjectivity, arguably removed from legal processes, is replaced by the subjectivity necessary to make technical and engineering choices. Replacing the subjectivity of people who have an opinion regarding law by the subjectivity of people who have an opinion about technology does not in itself mean improvement in the efficiency, neutrality, or objectivity of legal systems or reasoning. That is why it is often proposed that people possessing reliable opinions regarding law and its functioning should assist those with IT skills to foster the development of trustworthy algorithms for legal computing.[29]

Again, it appears that such technological insights are crucial for the ethical evaluation of legal computing, in particular to ensure the validity and relevance of its alleged benefits. Although they may not always be mobilized at first glance, such insights prove essential and need to be put at the service of the ethical questioning of concerned stakeholders. As we shall see in Section 17.3, the same applies to other elements that are sometimes overlooked in the framework of the ethical evaluation of IT, despite their high relevance.

17.3 INFLUENCE OF THEORETICAL BACKGROUNDS AND DEBATES

17.3.1 *Argument of Standardization*

As we saw, some actors argue that digitalization in the legal field is desirable because it will ensure a gain in standardization (in the sense of repeatability, objectivity, and exactitude). The content of Section 17.2 already shows that such a gain is not assured. But should this gain really be achieved, one may still profitably wonder about the ethical desirability of standardization itself. In order to evaluate legal computing, one could ask why it would be a good thing to increase standardization in the legal field, and to what extent.

Seeking increased standardization seems natural as it fits the way legal institutions are designed (or perceived): as formal systems with different codes and rules. This is especially true in the French context, where standardization (in the sense of unification of the interpretation of legal rules by all jurisdictions) is part of the mission statement of the Supreme Court.[30] Stability and universality in the application of law are arguably necessary for ensuring justice and for performing the socialization process: legal decision-making must, for example, be reliable and fast enough. What is more, standardization may be one of the necessary conditions for the existence of a public state, enabling human groups to gather as societies. Historically, the growth of human population called for the law to be applied more widely and efficiently. Formalization

---

[29] Council of Europe Commission for the Efficiency of Justice, n. 27 at art. 3.
[30] The statement claims the jurisdiction's unicity will enable the uniformization of rules' interpretations, and therefore the performativity of jurisprudence, see www.courdecassation.fr/institution_1/presentation_2845/r_cour_cassation_30989.html (accessed February 24, 2020).

then allowed a more universal application of law and faster legal decision-making. This movement of formalization can be traced back, in France, to at least the thirteenth century (with the harmonization of criminal law to reinforce the power of the king to the detriment of feudal lords), if not to antiquity with the passage to statutory law as a means to consolidate the centralized power of the Roman Empire.

It thus appears that harmonization has been, in a certain context, perceived as a useful lever for certain purposes. But this shows, at most, that a certain amount of uniformity is necessary and desirable in certain situations. It may be, in this sense, that nowadays the standardization of quantifiable litigation is suitable. Hopefully, this is the case, because it seems this is currently the first and foremost application of AI within law.[31] However, these findings hardly prove, in themselves, that uniformity and standardization have to be considered as absolute goals that need pursuing no matter the case and need deploying to the highest possible degree. Dedicated evaluation may be fruitful in this matter.

Uniform application through algorithms may be right when it comes to the legal processing of parking tickets or infringements of speed limits, but this is less clear for other topics such as more serious criminal cases[32] or the administration of judicial institutions.[33] Here we see that legal uniformity is sometimes arguably a good thing. It is even possible to present standardization as a way to favor a common understanding and application of legal rules, through visualization, for example.[34] Better predictability of judicial decisions counts as another putative benefit of standardization. But the desirability of standardization is nonetheless far from straightforward. It relies on certain implicit paradigms, such as background commitments about the way law will influence people's behavior,[35] or the way people react to information.[36]

Therefore, assessing whether a gain in standardization through legal computing is a good thing seems to mobilize, inevitably but not exclusively, a background debate about the desirability of uniformity itself in law performance and administration, and about the adequate dose of standardization to ensure justice.[37] The idea (one may say, the ideal) of "legal machinery" guaranteeing a fair application of law, based on mechanisms and objective processes to ensure uniformity and standardization, is an old one. Two prominent jurists, Montesquieu[38] and Beccaria,[39] made the point that judges should merely "apply" legal rules, without interpreting them.

---

[31] E. Buat-Ménard, "La justice dite prédictive: Prérequis, risques et attentes - l'expérience française" (2019) 2 Les Cahiers de la Justice 269.

[32] See Loomis v. Wisconsin, [2016] 881 N.W.2d 749 (Wis. 2016).

[33] According to Jeuland, n. 21, all online dispute resolution (ODR) failed in the United States, apart from Icann's and eBay's ones.

[34] A. Gonzalez Aguilar, "Visualisation interactive de la jurisprudence de la Cour de cassation" (2019) 2 Les Cahiers de la Justice 243gives the example of the "Vico" project, for the visualization of judicial decisions from open data.

[35] M. Hildebrandt, "Law as Computation in the Era of Artificial Legal Intelligence: Speaking Law to the Power of Statistic" (2018) 68 University of Toronto Law Journal 12: "Thinking of law in terms of a market of legal services aligns with an implicit adherence to the basic tenets of law and economics. The latter goes with an understanding of law as just one particular – and maybe even cumbersome – example of governmental regulation that should prove its worth in comparison to other types of regulation that may be more effective and/or efficient. The concomitant 'regulatory paradigm' thinks in terms of influencing the behavior of people, for which one could also use economic measures, techno-regulation, or various types of nudging, which may all prove more effective than legislation or adjudication."

[36] About the limits of the Input-Output model for charting the way people interact with the world, see J. Lassègue, "L'intelligence artificielle, technologie de la vision numérique du monde" (2019) 2 Les Cahiers de la Justice 205.

[37] Obviously, what "justice" means is itself a question in debate. Such a debate should be convoked in the ethical investigations about digital lawyering, which reinforces our point of the necessity to convoke theoretical background questions in these matters.

[38] C. de Secondat Montesquieu, De l'esprit des lois (Paris: Classiques Garnier, 2011) livre xi, ch. vi.

[39] C. Beccaria, Traité des délits et des peines (Philadelphia; Paris, 1766) §4.

Multiple debates about the validity of this idea can be found throughout history. One can take the example of the continuous tension between legal evidence and intimate conviction. With legal evidence, the value of proof is determined by law and the legislature (or according to customs). By contrast, the principle of intimate conviction attributes to judges or juries the role of freely appraising the value of proof. The old law in France was based on a system of legal evidence, with a hierarchy of forms of evidence that one could combine according to precise arithmetic rules. The highest, most reliable, form of evidence was the defendant confession, which led to the use of torture. Abuses of such a system had been denounced as early as the seventeenth century and the system was progressively discarded and finally abolished at the time of the French Revolution.[40] Intimate conviction then became the foundation of judicial truth.

Another illustration of the tension triggered by the ideal of a legal machinery can be found with the French codification within the Civil Code in 1804. The intention was to transform the perception of the volatility of legal rules under the Old Regime, bringing the steadiness and confidence that progressive systematization of legal disciplines could provide. In this process, historical empirical solutions were transformed into formal rules to ensure law would come from law and not from God,[41] jurisprudential solutions, or customs anymore. On top of this emerged the School of Exegesis to train judges to strictly apply legal rules,[42] with the will to purge judgments from any arbitrariness of the interpreter. This conception prevailed up to the late nineteenth century, when technical evolutions once again undercut the span of clarity, because it became obvious that many existing legal rules had not been written for regulating brand-new situations that appeared and therefore called for another way to make legal decisions. The field of interpretation extended once again, to the detriment of the one of mechanically applicable rules.

From these two historical examples, one could conclude that intimate conviction, and the instillation of subjectivity in the systemic functioning of law (subjectivity of the jurist, and also subjectivity of the defendant when it comes to paying attention to his past or personality), represent progress with regard to the system of legal evidence or the codification understood as a legal machinery. But this should not lead one to believe that the movement is or should be unidirectional. Indeed, acknowledging the indispensable role of intimate conviction and subjectivity in the practice of law does not imply that standardization and legal machinery are to be systematically rejected. Steadiness and uniformity also have their role in lawyering. Their excessive weakening can lead to abuses comparable to those of their excessive strengthening. *Le bon juge* (the "good judge") Magnaud made his reputation at the end of the nineteenth century, by deciding *contra legem*, on the ground of his feeling of what would be socially fair.[43]

This inquiry on the perception of the need for standardization in the history of law shows that opinions in this domain are largely influenced by contextual situations and representations. Moreover, in view of the extreme proliferation and diversification of legal rules between the Middle Ages and today, the claim that law has been standardized, for better justice, may be presumptuous. The best we can say here is that societies have often tried to standardize and harmonize legal rules and procedures. The current attractiveness of IT tools to ensure

---

[40] C. Gillieron, "L'évolution de la preuve pénale" (1946) *Revue pénale suisse* 197.

[41] Déclaration des droits de l'homme et du citoyen (1789), art. 6, which reads that law is the expression of general will.

[42] At least when those rules could be said to be clear, which is itself a profound question. Cf. in this matter. European Court of Justice, 6 Oct. 1982, no. 283/81, *Cilfit*.

[43] A.-D. Houte, "Le bon juge Magnaud et l'imaginaire de la magistrature à l'aube du XXe siècle" (2018) 5 *Déliberee* 38.

standardization (e.g., to try to reduce the "gap" between putative intrinsic meanings of legal rules[44] and socioeconomic data of trials) thus belongs to the long-standing historical tendency to bring mechanical reasoning into fuzzy and unforeseen situations.

This analysis is superficial but sufficient for our purpose. In fact, our goal here is not to dig deeper into these historical and philosophical debates. Rather, it is to demonstrate that the latter are relevant for ethically evaluating legal computing. Indeed, such an evaluation leads, through a reflection upon the desirability of standardization, to fundamental debates about law. In light of the societal stakes they relate to, it would be problematic to let such debates be settled by technological inertia or other pressures whose legitimacy can be questioned. We cannot go on considering them as mere philosophical debates to be addressed only in the academic context for theoretical purposes. The issue with the clarification of these theoretical backgrounds is nothing less than acquiring a conviction about the desirability of the effective digital transformation of the legal system.

17.3.2 Purging Subjectivity as a Gain in Rationality

There seems to be other fundamental backgrounds whose clarification may prove crucial for the ethical evaluation of digital lawyering. In fact, the tension exposed above between machinery and standardization, on the one side, and the irreducible need for intimate conviction, on the other side, reflects a concern regarding the influence of subjectivity in the practice of law.

In this respect, it may be that intimate conviction is merely tolerated in legal processes, as an indispensable mitigation of difficulties occurring in the course of the functioning of mechanistic legal systems. Following this idea, intimate conviction would be a lesser evil, a compromise with arbitrariness, abuse of power, and discretionary justice, waiting for the time when a complete and "objective" structuration of legal rules would become available. Can we then consider that purging subjectivity from lawyering is a desirable goal? It would be a strong argument in favor of legal computing techniques if they could help in that respect.

First a side remark: intimate conviction is not arbitrariness. The judge is asked to explain the basis, the grounds, and the rationale for his decision. This level of explanation, which can be said to be "contrastive, selective, and socially interactive,"[45] is, insightfully, in strong contrast with the logic of the functioning of machine learning algorithms, which is often quite opaque. In order to fight against subjectivity, we consider using algorithms that have encompassed subjectivity since their conception, and from which we would not expect a level of explanation for their decision as high as the one we expect from a human judge. This cannot really be considered as an improvement in rationality or objectivity. The addendum of explainability services on top of machine-learning treatment may be useful but will not modify our point. As we discussed above, machine learning algorithms mobilize irreducible human choices that are themselves in need of justification and evaluation.

Notwithstanding this side comment, there is more to say about the bewitching power of a machinery that could help in purging subjectivity pollution. This is a profound question. What lies in the background is the idea that subjectivity is necessarily a source of error, a kind of chaos that needs to be circumvented. Subjectivity would thus not be welcome in law because its

---

[44] According to J. Habermas, norms meanings are undetermined "from the origin," see J. van Meerbeck, "Penser par cas ... et par principes" (2014) 73 *Revue interdisciplinaire d'études juridiques* 3.

[45] B. Mittelstadt, C. Russell, and S. Wachter, "Explaining Explanations in AI" (2018), https://arxiv.org/pdf/1811.01439 (accessed February 24, 2020).

presence would induce a loss in rationality. The irrational human judgment would necessitate a digital prothesis. This deserves a closer look. Notably, one can reasonably state that law (that is, legal notions, rules, and methods) has been thought and formulated in consideration of the fact that subjective human people would make it work, rather than conceived as a system of deterministic or probabilistic cognitive tools that one day would be able to be operationalized in machines. Therefore, one might wonder whether this background case against subjectivity is really legitimate. Why such a ban on subjectivity? What are the reasons? This leads us to a broader debate about the relationships between subjectivity and rationality, a debate pertaining to philosophy and to epistemology.

Following this line of investigation, the idea that subjectivity is by principle opposed to rationality seems to be rooted in (or can at least be traced back to) Western modern philosophical and epistemological traditions associated with the Cartesian project of pure enquiry.[46] In this framework, rationality and objectivity are tightly linked to neutrality in the sense of the absence of any commitment or bias of any sort. For sure, according to this project, if one can arrive at a conclusion without at any step opting, judging, or choosing (let's say by relying exclusively on inevitable inferences and absolute foundations such as empirical data, formalization, logic, and mathematics), the conclusion would itself be inevitable! Our best instantiation of this ideal of pure enquiry is surely the scientific method, which, in its received understanding, stands on the firm ground of the inevitability of empirical observation and logical or mathematical computation.

According to this conception of rationality as neutrality, every contingent element in the processes of investigation, every element that could have been different, and every element of arbitrariness (in the sense of elements requesting arbitration) should be rejected. Admitting such elements would otherwise request from the inquirer to act as a subject, to choose or to judge. In turn, this eruption of subjectivity would mean that the results the inquirer arrives at are not inevitable. On this ground, subjectivity is clearly not welcome in the realm of rationality. Subjective biases or preferences, commitments or judgments can do nothing but undermine neutrality and rationality. Therefore, striving to eliminate subjectivity from legal process would be rational and legitimate. The more we purge subjectivity from judicial institutions and legal reasoning, the better.

Right? Maybe not . . . . It is worth mentioning that many insights from twentieth-century philosophy of science seem to paint a quite different picture. After the works of post-positivist thinkers such as Kuhn,[47] Quine,[48] and Duhem,[49] it becomes quite difficult to understand science as an instance of pure inquiry. Science includes indispensable choices and judgments. The inquirer must act as a subject to make these choices and judgments. One can further explicate this important epistemological point through the following illustration coming from physics. Presently, Einstein's theory of general relativity is recognized as our best available theory of gravitation. This is so because it has been experimentally demonstrated that its predecessor, basically Newton's theory of gravitation, was incorrect. The latter was notably unable to account

---

[46] B. Williams, *Descartes: The Project of Pure Enquiry* (Abingdon: Routledge, 2005).
[47] T. S. Kuhn, *The Structure of Scientific Revolutions*, 3rd ed. (Chicago: University of Chicago Press, 1996).
[48] W. V. Quine, "Main Trends in Recent Philosophy: Two Dogmas of Empiricism" (1951) 60 *The Philosophical Review* 20.
[49] P. Duhem, M. Maurice, P. P. Wiener, and J. Vuillemin, *The Aim and Structure of Physical Theory* (Princeton: Princeton University Press, 1991). See also K. Stanford, "Underdetermination of Scientific Theory" in Edward N. Zalta (ed.), *The Stanford Encyclopedia of Philosophy* (Stanford: Stanford University Press, 2017) https://plato.stanford.edu/archives/win2017/entries/scientific-underdetermination/ (accessed February 24, 2020).

for the observed deviation of light by massive bodies. For Newton, gravitational attraction is proportional to the product of interacting bodies' weights. Light being deprived of any mass, gravitational forces it undergoes should be null, which contradicts experimental findings. By describing gravitational forces through space-time deformations, Einstein's theory better fits experimental data. Here, one could think that the conception of rationality as neutrality applies. Newton's theory has been rejected according to pure inquiry through a decisive experiment. Unfortunately, things are not that simple. One could for instance claim that there are little demons that are completely unobservable, except through their action on light. And this action would be precisely to influence light to make it move just as predicted by Einstein's theory. Such an attempt at salvaging Newton's theory seems quite irrational. However, it cannot be discarded on the sole neutral ground of logic, mathematics, and experimental findings. Obviously, a physicist would reject such an attempt as unreasonable because it would violate the maxim of Ockham's razor or a similar principle of simplicity, stating that it is wrong, *ceteris paribus*, to add a dispensable hypothesis to a theory. But this is clearly a judgment, a choice. To reject the demon hypothesis, the inquirer needs to act as a subject, evaluating the balanced virtues of competing hypothesis.[50]

This illustration with Newton's and Einstein's theories highlights the point we want to make here: human subjectivity proves indispensable in the scientific method (our best-of-breed instance of rationality). At this point, we have a choice: either we claim that our best example of rationality is not rational, or we admit that rationality should not be conceived primarily through the lens of an absolute neutrality that requests the sacrifice of subjectivity. And this epistemological difficulty also occurs about basic empirical evidence. Can we really prove that it is true that it is the night when we see the dark outside? What can we answer if a sceptic argues that our claim is not certain, for we may well be victim of an elaborated hoax or even be living in an illusion (as in *The Matrix*)? We cannot absolutely or neutrally prove we are right. But this does not mean that we ought to treat our claim as really uncertain, that we must consider it as dubious as any other "weird" claim.... Here is a good clear case where subjective experience of evidence (or intimate subjective conviction) plays an indispensable role, unless one is ready to live in a really crazy world and to behave crazily accordingly.

There could be much more to say about the place of subjectivity in rationality, notably because the discussion above is not intended to claim that any subjective evidence is trustworthy. What we hope it shows, though, is that it is far from obvious that subjectivity is in principle a weakness in rational inquiry. It follows that systematically purging subjectivity from legal organizations and reasonings may not constitute a guarantee of increased rationality; at least, such a purge should not be taken as an absolute goal to be pursued as far as possible on principle. This reinforces the legitimacy of recommendations to keep human judgment "in the loop," at the right place within a computerized legal process. The difficulty is then to find the right place for legal subjectivity, the right place for technical subjectivity, and the right place for pure machinery.[51] In any case, we believe that ethical evaluation of digital lawyering could benefit from the type of philosophical or background insights proposed in this section.

---

[50] For instance, with the process of inference to the best explanation, see P. Lipton, *Inference to the Best Explanation*, 2nd ed. (Abingdon: Routledge, 2014).

[51] Apart from this methodological lesson from epistemology, there is a sound tactical reason, for people who believe in democracy, for saving subjectivity as a tool within rational enquiry, rather than considering it as a lack of rationality: giving even a small amount of credit to the pure enquiry conception, opens the door for an instrumentalization, where subjectivity can be seen as something that should be controlled and channeled, where individual freedom is only the ability to choose among predefined options. This would be, again, a very partial and restrictive understanding of law.

17.4 CONCLUSION

To ensure an ethical implementation of IT in the legal domain, we cannot afford to let technological inertia steer the deployment of legal computing. The blind reduction of the legally and societally desirable to the technically feasible must be fought with determination. In this fight, we need a kind of reflexive "procedure" or "recipe" for evaluating information technologies. In this chapter, we have proposed a broad account of ethical investigation of IT implementation in the legal field. Evaluating legal computing should include a global analysis of the transformations it induces. This would permit the determination of the degree of desirability of introducing a legal computing tool in a specific situation, as well as to reflect upon the best manner in which to implement it, notably to maximize the ethical quality of outcomes (What is the proper place for human intervention? Do we need mediation devices or specific training of stakeholders? What are the points of vigilance?).

We highlighted two key elements that seem to us indispensable to properly conduct such ethical investigation: sufficient technological insights and relevant background or philosophical debates. Concerning the first aspect, we showed that both general knowledge and also more precise information about IT and AI are necessary. Concerning the second one, mobilizing philosophical background debates might have thus appeared a priori as somehow counterintuitive, as some sterile speculative and theoretical sophistication. We nonetheless tried to prove that evaluation and steering of technological developments, at least in the domain of law, requires exploration and explication of implicit backgrounds (philosophical, common sense, systemic, etc.). These backgrounds exist, and they inevitably underlie our reasons and choices and influence our conclusions about what is good or not in terms of digital lawyering. Notably, we highlighted the relevance of debates about the role of subjectivity in legal processes as well as in rationality. We also discussed the role of debates about the status of objectives such as standardization or formalization. Deep philosophical debates and controversies of this type should be revived and openly reconsidered in the light of new technological developments, because they might not be pure theoretical matters anymore, or because they may have been settled in a given context and for reasons that may not hold as much in new digital context. It is not certain that Hans Kelsen, informed of IT capabilities to treat legal information, would further support his *pure theory of law*.[52] In the same vein, defending standardization and formalization as absolute goals to be pursued as much as possible may not imply the same consequences depending on the technological context. It may be seen as a sane regulative ideal when there is no other choice than having a human in the loop. But when technology becomes mature enough to effectively remove humans from more and more legal processes, such an ideal may deserve reconsideration.

Some other fundamental debates should probably be mobilized. One could wonder about the influence on legal computing evaluations of background commitments concerning, say, positivism about the law. There would also be much to say about the distinction between norms and rules (or technical norms), about the relationships between wisdom and technical effectuation in law administration, or about the question of whether law creates, stimulates, or merely puts words on social behaviors and values. One could also argue that socioeconomic debates about inequalities are relevant for the evaluation of legal technologies. In particular, it is often claimed that digitalizing justice contributes to compliance with the legal and political principle of access

---

[52] H. Kelsen, *Théorie pure du droit* (Paris-Bruxelles: LGDJ, Bruylant, 1999).

to justice.[53] At first sight, this is a very good reason to go forward, and a positive ethical outcome. But a closer look reveals that free access to justice, as a principle guaranteed by law and powered by IT, has totally different effects in a world where people can equitably introduce an action and be counseled, and in a situation where a few powerful actors have considerable means (including advanced IT tools and expertise) for gathering proof, introducing large amounts of litigations, and mobilizing, if not influencing, all the subtleties of legal systems.

Mobilizing such theoretical debates, specific to the field to be digitalized, may appear as a loss of time, as a sterile sophistication. But at the same time, most of the IT players strive to bring value to their customers, and at the same time intend to play a positive role in the world. They cannot escape these debates, which are not so much the reflection of ideological choices, as mere feedback from reality: the ways technologies, legal systems, and even societies, actually work matter when trying to transform lawyering through technology. We believe the reader who managed following us up to this point gets the idea: there is an urge to confront such fundamental background debates, notably because some have become very practical. It would be a very bad way of directing (or not directing) technological development to allow these debates to be settled through socio-technical inertia. Instead, for a suitable implementation of AI and digital technology, we must inject human collective and diverse intelligence into the legal domain.

In addition, we would like to conclude with an important consequence of the image we painted of ethical evaluation of IT for the digitalization of lawyering. Technological progress changes epistemological needs and renders some patterns of epistemological organization obsolete. In particular, the classical epistemological model we could name "in isolation" – within which scientific and technological developments are made in isolation by hard-science experts and engineers, while ethical and policy questions are treated separately – becomes dramatically insufficient. Some techniques lead to new questions that cannot be treated by single groups of actors taken separately. Some old questions, for instance, the one of positivism in law, are propelled into new contexts and communities where their treatment becomes indispensable. A proper evaluation of new IT for digital lawyering seems to require gathering information that is familiar to IT specialists, lawyers, or philosophers and rendering it available and understandable to relevant stakeholders. It requires building bridges. This is a key task for ethical evaluation, whose depth and complexity should not be underestimated.

---

[53] E.g., D. Salas, "Les défis de la justice numérique" (2019) 2 *Les Cahiers de la Justice* 201.

18

Law, Disintermediation and the Future of Trust

Christoph Kletzer

18.1 INTRODUCTION

In its 2020 survey, the Edelman Trust Barometer identified a paradox: 'despite a strong global economy and near full employment, none of the four societal institutions that the study measures – government, business, NGOs and media – is trusted'.[1] This is a rather grim sounding paradox. One can try to resolve it in a variety of ways. An obvious way would be to argue that when we measure trust, we are measuring a rather uninformative quantity. After all, trust can be considered good and a loss of trust would accordingly be bad only if and insofar as trust is placed in something or someone actually worthy of our trust. So, the true problem, one could argue, is not the loss of trust but the loss of trustworthiness – and this has not been measured.[2] Whether trust is a good proxy for trustworthiness has yet to be established.

But it seems that this line of argument does not get to the core of the issue since the way the Edelman Barometer presents its data suggests that we have a problem either way: either trust went down *because* trustworthiness decreased, or trust went down *despite* trustworthiness not decreasing. Both cases pose conceptually different yet significant problems: the former is bad because of the decrease of something good, namely, trustworthiness; the latter because of the decoupling of trust and trustworthiness. We face a similar situation in the relation of fear and crime rates. An increase of fear is certainly bad, but it may be bad for two different and unrelated reasons: either fear is increasing *because* crime rates go up, which is bad because increasing crime rates are bad. Or fear goes up *despite* crime rates not going up, which is bad because such a fear would be a sign of some kind of collective neuroticism.

Furthermore, as a form of social capital, trust does seem to be an important social good irrespective of the trustworthiness of the participants.[3] Even if the trustworthiness of people is lacking, a general openness, a preparedness to co-operate, and an optimism towards the working out of human interaction can be considered a value in itself and might in turn itself breed forms of trustworthiness.

---

[1] www.edelman.com/trustbarometer (accessed August 23, 2021).
[2] O. O'Neill, 'Linking Trust to Trustworthiness' (2018) 26(2) *International Journal of Philosophical Studies* 293.
[3] See F. Fukuyama, *Trust: The Social Virtues and the Creation of Prosperity* (New York: Free Press, 1995); R. D. Putnam, *Making Democracy Work: Civic Traditions in Modern Italy* (Princeton: Princeton University Press, 1993); J. S. Coleman, 'Social Capital in the Creation of Human Capital' Supplement: Organizations and Institutions: Sociological and Economic Approaches to the Analysis of Social Structure (1988) 94 *American Journal of Sociology* S95.

A better way to resolve the paradox is to distinguish trust and reliance: the smooth running of the economy and near full employment might not so much indicate the prevalence of trust in society, but simply the presence of mere reliance. People can rely on each other in business relations without trusting each other. According to this reading, the interesting and socially relevant category is reliance. Trust is but a moralised superstructure that can be indicative of reliability but does not truly track it. In any case, compared to actual reliance it is irrelevant.

This distinction between trust and reliability is, of course, of crucial importance and has been stressed under different headings since at least the twelfth century, when the newly discovered mode of hypothetical reasoning subverted the dominant universalistic thought and allowed for the opening up of a space of moral indifference. It is in this space of moral indifference, that is, of mere reliance rather than trust, that the modern capitalist state could emerge.[4] In a quite similar vein, Adam Smith famously argued that the great advantage of a functioning market economy is that in such a set-up, one does not have to *trust* the baker to supply one with bread, one does not need to appeal to his moral character, but can simply *rely* on his self-interest. This very welcome deflation of the moral character of social relations has been singled out as one of the defining features of capitalism. Capitalism rests on the invention and gradual expansion of this realm of moral indifference.

This deflationary reading of trust and a focus on reliance has also been stressed recently in the context of a discussion of the future of lawyering in the digital age.[5] In dealing with the common objection to automation and digital innovation, namely, that such digitisation would undermine trust, Richard and Daniel Susskind stress that 'our primary need is only for a reliable outcome'.[6] A reputation of trustworthiness, they argue, is first and foremost a proxy for reliability and not the other way around. What matters is not trust but mere confidence in reliability, or 'quasi-trust'.[7]

There is of course, an important truth in this assertion. In many cases mere reliance suffices for healthy economic relations and the deflation of substantive, morally charged, and thus ultimately contentious relations of trust can be seen as a requirement of some forms of doing business. Still, something seems to be amiss. First of all, trust as opposed to mere reliance backed up by a threat of legal sanction seems to be a driver of economic growth, and societies that abound in healthy forms of trust simply do better economically.[8] Conversely, where this trust is suddenly siphoned off, as was the case in the takeover of eighteenth-century Naples by the Spanish Habsburgs, despite the continuation of self-interest and threat of sanction, a deadly economic downward spiral is set in motion.[9]

In this chapter, however, I do not want to rely on the rich and developed literature on the economic importance of trust. Rather, I want to try to pursue a different course in order to demonstrate that whilst trust might not be sufficient to explain most economic relations, it is certainly necessary to explain some. I will try to do this by demonstrating that there are important cases, namely, cases of unsecured loans, which for principled rather than technological or practical reasons, cannot be fully automated. This indicates that they possess some quality that resists automation. This quality, it will turn out, is trust. In the present chapter, I will try to

---

[4] See K. Pribram, *A History of Economic Reasoning* (Baltimore: John Hopkins University Press, 1983).
[5] See R. Susskind, *Tomorrow's Lawyers: An Introduction to Your Future* (Oxford: Oxford University Press, 2013); R. Susskind and D. Susskind, *The Future of the Professions* (Oxford: Oxford University Press, 2015).
[6] Susskind and Susskind, n. 5 at 237.
[7] Ibid. at 238.
[8] Fukuyama, n. 3 at 26.
[9] A. Pagden, 'The Destruction of Trust and Its Economic Consequences in the Case of Eighteenth-Century Naples' in D. Gambetta (ed.), *Trust: Making and Breaking Cooperative Relations* (Oxford: Blackwell, 1999) 127–141.

explain, defend and explore the consequences of the claim that relations of trust cannot be fully automated. This exercise will help us understand better the nature of both trust and of automation systems like smart contracts.

In Section 18.2, I will briefly introduce these automation systems and analyse their relation to attempts to de-trust economic relations. I will argue that the ascent of distributed ledger technologies including smart contracts was energised by the attempt to de-trust, to de-intermediate digital relations and to enable truly peer-to-peer exchanges of values, rights and commitments in the digital realm.

In Section 18.3, I will introduce the unsecured loan as a form of contract that substantively resists automation and de-trusting. I will argue that the obstacle a possible automation of such contracts faces is a principled, not a technological one. This indicates that for certain relationships trust has to continue to play a role. Furthermore, unsecured loans do not only occur as free-standing contracts but are an element of many, if not most, social relations.

In Section 18.4, I want to find out what exactly it is in these relations that resits automation. This prompts a deeper analysis of the difference of trust and reliance and how trust relates to human nature. The chapter culminates in the suggestion that debt and trust relations are crucial to our self-understanding as human agents.

In Section 18.5, I elaborate the consequences of this distinction between trust and reliance on our understanding of the relation of law to blockchain technologies.

18.2 PEER-TO-PEER: ALLURE OF TRUSTLESSNESS

In the wake of the first wave of crypto and blockchain technology, it has become commonplace to think that minimising trust in interactions that transfer value from one person to another is a good thing and might be a goal in and of itself.[10] Insofar as trust involves risk and risk always comes at a cost, then the reduction of trust could be seen to simply be a cost-cutting exercise. This line of thinking, however, leaves entirely out of the picture the fact that many risks are merely the ancillary effect of expected rewards and one cannot have the latter without the former.

As a matter of fact, historically, de-trusting did not happen with the primary aim of reducing costs.[11] What was intended, rather, was to solve the problem of how to transfer value digitally, or, to be precise, how to transfer value over a communication channel. This, it turned out, was harder than one might have believed. To illustrate the problem, take a very simple case of the transfer of value: say, I hand over to you a nugget of gold. This simple action has two important features:

(1) After I have handed over the gold nugget to you, I cannot give it to someone else.
(2) I do not need a third party to monitor or confirm the handover for it to occur.

Now, these two features are rather straightforward in physical exchanges and are usually too trite to be noticed or deemed worthy of mentioning. However, they have two very important qualities:

---

[10] For a discussion, see K. Yeung, 'Regulation by Blockchain: The Emerging Battle for Supremacy between the Code of Law and Code as Law' (2019) 82 *Modern Law Review* 207 211; K. Werbach, 'Trust, but Verify: Why the Blockchain Needs the Law' (2018) 33 *Berkeley Technology Law Journal* 489; P. Paech, 'The Governance of Blockchain Financial Networks' (2017) 80 *MLR* 1073; S. Ammous, *The Bitcoin Standard: The Decentralized Alternative to Central Banking* (Hoboken: Wiley, 2018) 257 ff.

[11] See, for instance, the classic Bitcoin white paper, https://bitcoin.org/bitcoin.pdf or the forum debates in the early days of Bitcoin https://satoshi.nakamotoinstitute.org/posts/ (accessed August 23, 2021).

feature (1) makes sure that there is a value to be exchanged to begin with. If by some magic I could spend the same item that I have given you a second time, then I would have not really given it to you because the second person would have an equally valid claim to possessing it. Feature (2) makes sure that your possession of the thing really is non-reversible. If, conversely, a trusted party mediates the transfer of value between parties then this trusted party cannot avoid to also mediate disputes about the transfer: if two parties trust an intermediary to manage the transfer of value, then there must be some terms of this transfer that they trust the intermediary to observe. This, however, in turn means that the parties trust and thus authorise the intermediary to transfer funds according to these terms, which in turn means that the parties implicitly authorise the intermediary to authoritatively decide on the meaning of these terms and thus to mediate disputes about these terms. This mediation does not need to be formal or explicit. Not doing anything constitutes a decision in favour of one party who happens to have the value in his possession. A reversal of the funds is a more explicit decision of the intermediary mediating disputes. We can observe this difficulty with credit card providers, where payments can be reversed through chargebacks and where all payments are thus in principle reversible. The introduction of an intermediary thus does not only mean that parties have to trust the intermediary, but they also have to trust the other party not to initiate a payment reversal procedure *after* the payment has cleared. This, in turn, leads to a situation where merchants must become 'weary of their customers, hassling them for more information than they would otherwise need'.[12] In mediated relations the need of trust thus multiplies, setting off a vicious spiral of a need of trust.

Now, the problem is that whilst satisfying both conditions in the case of a physical handover is unproblematic, in the case of an attempted handover of value through a communication channel it seems impossible.

Feature (1) is impaired by the fact that in order to forestall double-spending of an item, this item has to be an original. It is simply impossible to double-spend actual gold nuggets, that is, to hand the same nugget over to two persons. In the realm of communication channels and in the digital world, conversely, there are no such things as originals. Any message and all digital content is inherently copiable.[13] It is thus futile to try to create a unique or singular digital representation, some kind of genuine token in the digital world. Exactly this, however, would be needed to guarantee requirement (1). One cannot do with an electronic representation, say, a picture, of a gold nugget, even if it had a series number or a watermark attached to it. All of these markers of originality need, in turn, to be communicated or digitally represented and could thus simply be copied together with the original they were supposed to certify, which would, in turn, allow one to hand out the supposedly valuable item as often as one wanted.

This means that in order to be able to *transfer* value in the digital realm one first has to find a way to *allocate* monetary value in the digital realm. As we have seen, allocating value by simply distributing some quantity of inherently valuable stuff does not work, so the only way to assign values is to keep track of value allocations, to keep a book, a ledger that records which quanta of value are assigned to which person or account. This, however, directly runs afoul of requirement (2).

In the digital world (1) and (2) thus seem incompatible.

---

[12] S. Nakamoto, 'Bitcoin: A Peer-to-Peer Electronic Cash System' at 1.

[13] This feature is not accidental but lies in the very nature of computation – any computational content is invariant to the specific organisation of its computationally neutral substrate. D. J. Chalmers, 'A Computational Foundation for the Study of Cognition' (2011) 12 *Journal of Cognitive Science* 325 339; D. C. Dennett, *Darwin's Dangerous Idea: Evolution and the Meanings of Life* (New York: Simon & Schuster, 1995) 50.

There is, of course, a solution to this quandary. This solution has been first presented in the famous Bitcoin white paper.[14] It presented the outlines of the architecture of a protocol that sets up a ledger that is not centrally administered but distributed throughout the network and which is kept authentic by a consensus mechanism. It thus does not require a trusted third party to allocate funds and thus does not require anyone in particular to act as an intermediary between the sender and the receiver of funds. Rather, participants can transfer value via the protocol peer-to-peer.

This inherent value of peer-to-peer relations can be analysed along three axes: complexity, confidentiality and authority.

(1) Peer-to-peer relations are different in kind from relations mediated by a third party as concerns their *inner complexity*. To get a sense of this, one can compare interpersonal relations with the physical forces at play between objects: if you want to understand the movements of and the forces between two objects you can simply represent their physical relation by a set of formulae that have a closed form and are solvable, that is, you can easily know where each object will be at a given time. As soon as a third body is introduced, however, the system changes into a dynamic and chaotic mode that does not possess stable or closed-form solutions any longer.[15] Moving from a two-place to a three-place relation thus represents not a mere quantitative but qualitative change with an infinite increase of complexity. Interpersonal relations are analogous to that. Say that you and I are in a relationship of whatever kind. If my relationship with you went sour and I know that I was not the problem, then I would immediately know who the problem was: it has to be you. As soon as a third is introduced, the situation changes fundamentally. Even if I knew that I was not the problem, I could not know whether you or the third or one of an infinite number of possible combinations of distributions of gradual faults between you and the third had caused the issue. A three-person relation thus has an infinite number of solutions. Moving from a peer-to-peer relation to a relation where interactions are mediated by a third party changes the relationship not merely in degree, but in kind.

(2) Relatedly, the nature of confidentiality is different in peer-to-peer relations. Peer-to-peer relations are private in a different sense than three- or *n*-person relations. Two's company, three's a crowd.

(3) Finally, the third party introduced in order to administer a ledger in a non-peer-to-peer relation is not merely a third party at eye level and on par with the sender and receiver of money. Rather, he stands in a hierarchical relationship with both of them, since this third party has authority to determine conclusively who owns which values.

Bitcoin managed the seemingly impossible task of automating or digitising the transfer of value. By doing that it has also innovated and allowed us to think about automating and digitising tasks that did not even exist before the invention of Bitcoin.[16] By using distributed ledger technologies we can now not only digitally hand over the equivalent of gold nuggets but we can also hand over promises, rights and commitments, or any combination thereof peer-to-peer without the interference of trusted intermediaries.

This promises to cut out a lot of middlemen: when someone buys a stock, for instance, he does not actually end up owning the stock. Rather, the legal ownership is mediated in a custodial

---

[14] Nakamoto, n. 12.
[15] J. Barrow-Green, 'The Three-Body Problem' in T. Gowers et al. (eds), *The Princeton Companion to Mathematics* (Princeton: Princeton University Press, 2008) 726–728.
[16] On the important distinction between automation and innovation, see Susskind and Susskind, n. 5 at 109; Susskind, n. 5 at 49.

chain of trusts where the legal owner is the custodian holding the global note (e.g., Cede & Co), the client holds equitable interest as beneficiary and investors thus have pro rata beneficial interest in the securities. Transferring stocks thus consists mainly in trading and clearing these beneficial interests via clearing houses as central counterparties. Since these custodial chains and clearing mechanism counterparties involve manifold and severe legal limitations, carrying over the holding and transfer of securities onto blockchains where they can be traded directly between holders without third parties mediating either the holding or the transfer of these securities has been widely commended.[17]

This extension of peer-to-peer transfer to complex and even programmable entities does indeed make the possibilities to rethink finance seemingly limitless, as the advances of decentralised finance (DeFi) illustrate. Whilst financial technology (FinTech) merely describes the employment of new digital techniques in old financial business models, DeFi allows for the direct, peer-to-peer exchange of complex financial products and entities (loans, derivatives, insurance) without any interference of a third party but rather through a protocol that sets the parameters of these peer-to-peer exchanges.

Most of these financial tools are provided to the public in the form of smart contracts, that is, digital automata that predictably, transparently and autonomously transfer funds given the fulfilment of certain conditions set in advance. For instance, a gambling site can quite easily be programmed into the Ethereum Virtual Machine which accepts funds and bets, say, on the level of the SPY: two parties both pay in 100 Ether and both enter their bets and after the contract has determined the level of the SPY on the next day, it automatically pays out 200 Ether to the address that was closer to that level. The point is that in such a way, one could allow for bets and other transactions in a purely peer-to-peer way, that is, without intermediaries. In principle, no one would have to know of this bet, yet the funds would still be paid automatically and without any way the parties could influence the payout (other than influencing the level of the SPY, of course).

All of this is rather promising and indeed quite exciting. Exchanging rights, claims and commitments like nuggets of gold between two persons and without any interference of a trusted third will certainly change the way we do and think about business. It will do so for the better, I believe, since it opens up transparent access to financial tools to everyone.

18.3 LIMITS OF SMARTNESS

Such great promise tempts one to overlook limitations. Now, these limits lie not so much in technological limitations like a possible over-complexity of code or in the lacking reliability of the oracles that feed real-world data into the smart contract. The problem is rather of a more principled nature. To get a sense of this problem, take the case of a smart contract that is trying to emulate an unsecured loan. Such a contract would be rather straightforward to programme into a smart contract language like Solidity.[18] Say that creditor C wants to lend 100 Ether to debtor D, who agreed to pay him back the principal after a year and also agrees to pay C an interest of 1 Ether every month. Such a contract would include the command to first transfer 100 Ether from an address of C to an address of D; then it would transfer 1 Ether every month from D to C and after a year it would transfer back the 100 Ether from D to C.

---

[17] See P. Paech, 'Securities, Intermediation and the Blockchain – an Inevitable Choice between Liquidity and Legal Certainty?' (2015) 21 *Uniform Law Review* 4; E. Micheler, 'Custody Chains and Asset Values: Why Crypto-Securities Are Worth Contemplating', (2015) 74 *The Cambridge Law Journal* 505.

[18] https://solidity.readthedocs.io/en/vo.6.8/ (accessed August 23, 2021).

The problem is, of course, that such a contract could not be implemented as a smart (automated and self-executing) contract. For the contract to be automated or self-executing it would have to be able to run independently of interference from the parties. If any of the repayments of D were conditional on acts of D, then the contract would not be a smart contract, but would rather be a classic contract that required performance by D, which could ultimately only be enforced via litigation. However, in the case of an unsecured loan, the actual repayments are always conditional on D keeping sufficient funds in his account for the contract to be able to execute. In case D were to clear his account and the contract then wanted to draw on D's account to transfer the interest each month or the principal after a year then the contract would not automatically execute but simply bounce. D can thus make the contract bounce and stop its execution by simply not funding his addresses. It thus remains for D to decide whether or not the contract can transfer the repayment from his account to C. Such a procedure is not automatic and the contract was not smart to begin with, since it depended on the goodwill and performance of D.

This is pretty straightforward. One simple way to solve this issue would be to lock the 100 Ether of principal and the 12 Ether of interest, thus 112 Ether, into the contract, to make sure it can then be automatically repaid. This however, would lead to a situation where D would need to lock 112 Ether in order to get out 100 Ether, effectively loosing 12 Ether of liquidity. Such a set-up is of course possible, but it would effectively turn an unsecured loan into a secured one.[19] Automating *secured* loans are indeed possible and examples of this do already abound in the DeFi world.[20] One can, for instance, stake one's Bitcoin in order to receive Ether as a loan. However, one usually has to put down a 1.5x margin to make sure the price swings are covered for. However, in case of unsecured loans we face the dilemma of either not having full automation or not having an unsecured loan to begin with. No third between these two horns of the dilemma is possible.

The dilemma is a logical one, it is a principled problem and not a mere technical obstacle. Unsecured loan contracts and thus any contract with an unsecured loan element are not fully automatable. The whole idea of an *unsecured automated loan* is in itself incoherent: the *unsecured* loan element requires the creditor to ultimately let go of the funds and fully cede control over them to the debtor, whereas the *automation* element makes it impossible for him to truly let go of the funds. The problem is not an underdevelopment of our programming technique that might be overcome in the future. As we have seen above, it is rather easy to programme the requisite transfer of funds. There is something else that is missing here. What is missing is, of course, trust. When lending out money without security the creditor does not expect automatic repayment, but he *trusts* that he will get it back. Insofar as the creditor by necessity has to let go of his funds, the debtor by necessity gains full control over them and thus is in principle free to do whatever he wants with the funds, which includes squandering them or just running away with them. As soon as this possibility is curtailed, which would be necessary to make the contract automatable, the loan would turn into a secured one. A loan agreement is thus an agreement that has to include trust, not just mere reliance. The creditor does not simply

---

[19] Since unsecured debt shares vary between 20 per cent (for small firms) and 75 per cent (for average sized firms going up to 87 per cent or more for the largest companies), it cannot be disregarded: C. Azariadis, L. Kaas and Y. Wen, 'Self-Fulfilling Credit Cycles', Federal Reserve Bank of St. Louis Working Paper Series, Working Paper 2015-005B, http://research.stlouisfed.org/wp/2016/2016-005.pdf (accessed August 23, 2021). C. Azariadis, 'Credit Cycles and Business Cycles' (2018) 100(1) First Quarter *Federal Reserve Bank of St. Louis Review* 1 45–71.

[20] Platforms such as, for instance, compound or Aave do that. See https://compound.finance and https://aave.com (accessed August 23, 2021).

rely on the debtor to pay back his money, but he *trusts* him to do so and whilst reliance is automatable, trust is not.[21]

To be sure, one good reason for entering such loan relations is the promise of some reward. The debtor offloads risk and the creditor accrues risk in exchange for a premium. But this risk trading is, I believe, not the sole reason why such unsecured loans are entered into. Hidden behind this profit motive there lies another, more speculative reason for why we are keen to enter into these kinds of trust relations with each other and this reason goes straight to the core of our humanity: trust relations allow us to mutually assure each other of our human nature as autonomous agents.

18.4 RELIANCE, KANTIAN TRUST AND HUMAN NATURE

In order to see this feature of trust more clearly, we have to look a bit closer at the exact difference between trust and reliance. It is not ungrammatical to use the term trust in a very wide sense to convey an attitude that might be more accurately described as an attitude of reliance. When someone says that he 'trusts' the bridge under him not to break down or that he trusts the weather will be good, we do understand what is meant, but might think that the attitude he is describing is better conveyed by the concept of reliance. He is not really *trusting* the bridge or the weather but he is relying on them. True trust is not placed in inanimate objects. But even when I place trust in animate objects, say, that I trust an avalanche dog to find my buried friend, this too does not yet represent true trust, but still mere reliance.

What, then, is missing in the bridge, the weather and the avalanche dog in order for it to deserve to be correctly described as instances of trust? It seems that true trust can only be directed at beings who are in principle responsive to reasons, that is, humans.[22] The fact that humans are responsive to reasons, however, does not mean that any reasonable action of a human is necessarily the object of trust. In not wantonly attacking me, the person sitting next to me on the tube is certainly acting reasonably and is thus responding to good reasons that apply to him. However, even though it would be grammatical to say that I trust him not to attack me, this relation still does not constitute true trust but mere reliance. In just sitting next to him I am in no way placing my trust in him. Some contemporary philosophers argue that true trust, that is, trust that goes beyond mere reliance, is defined by the fact the trusted party is taking into consideration the interests of the trustee. According to this definition, I would indeed not trust my co-traveller on the tube, since he is not at all concerned with my interests. Along this line, Russell Hardin, for instance, takes trust to be what he calls *encapsulated interest*:

---

[21] Aave recently announced its offering of 'peer-to-peer unsecured loans'. However, the system works via the mediation of a platform called OpenLaw, which provides legally binding contracts. This means that the system does not really provide an automated version of unsecured loans, which would be impossible, but simply provides a platform that allows participants to hand over money to other participants while also entering into a legally binding agreement with them. The monies handed out thus cannot be recouped automatically but only via traditional routes of litigation. Aave has also for a while now provided for *secured* loans, which do not require such legally binding contracts but where the technical payment automation via smart contract suffices for all the steps in the life cycle of the loan. This difference in treatment strongly supports the point made in this chapter that whilst secured loans (reliance) are automatable, unsecured loans (trust) are not. See http://aave.com and http://www.openlaw.io (accessed August 23, 2021).

[22] Humans, however, do not necessarily exhaust the category of beings that are responsive to reasons. If you are a believer, then God and angels belong to this category as well. It would certainly be right to say for a believer that he trusts God or his guardian angel and not merely relies on them. Similarly, if we ever had machines that were responsive not merely to input but to reasons, we could justifiably claim that we do not merely rely on them but that we trust them.

On this account, I trust you because I think it is in your interest to take my interests in the relevant matter seriously in the following sense: You value the continuation of our relationship, and you therefore have your own interests in taking my interests into account. That is, you encapsulate my interests in your own interests. My interests might come into conflict with other interests you have and that trump mine, and you might therefore not actually act in ways that fit my interests. Nevertheless, you at least have some interest in doing so.[23]

This definition might correctly exclude my relation to the co-traveler on the tube from constituting a relation of true trust, yet the attempt to capture the essence of true trust as encapsulated interest does not escape the above logic of the successive retreat of the concept of trust into ever narrower confines: after all, what Hardin describes does not really get us beyond mere reliance. According to this definition, trust might be a special form of reliance, but it is still reliance all the way down.

Another important tradition tries to distinguish trust from mere reliance by focusing on what kind of reasons trusting someone is supposed to give the trusted person. According to this line of thought, trust is a very special form of reliance where I expect that my expression of reliance on you gives you reason to act the way I rely on you and where, furthermore, this assumption that my reliance on you will give you reason to act as I rely on you to, gives me further reason to rely on you.[24]

In this attempt to distinguish trust from mere reliance, we have seen a successive retreat and narrowing of the concept of trust. However, we ended up with a situation where there seems to be no difference in principle between the case where I rely on the structural integrity of a bridge, on the good training and nature of a dog or on the disposition of a fellow human being. In all three cases, I make the assessment of qualities of the external world part of my calculation of how to act. So, it seems that whilst we do want to distinguish trust from mere reliance, we cannot. We want to define true trust as something that goes beyond mere reliance, yet any given case of trust, if looked at closely enough, reveals itself as being explicable in terms of mere reliance. So all we have found so far are different forms of reliance, some relating to a complex internal structure of encapsulation, others relating to the disposition to be moved by vulnerability. One way to solve this quandary would be to just throw out *true* trust and accept that trust is but a form of reliance. This, however, would be throwing out the baby with the bathwater. After all, each time we came to the conclusion that the phenomenon we were investigating did not constitute true trust, we did that by determining that something was missing. Trust is elusive, but there certainly was something we were chasing. What is that?

To answer this question, we must look at the relation of reliability and trustworthiness: a person is reliable if he is disposed to act in a way that I expect him to act. A truly trustworthy person, in contrast, is a person who is not only disposed to act in the way I expect him to act but someone who would also act this way *were he not so disposed*.

Now, to be sure, this concept of true trustworthiness is a pure concept or limit concept. We have arrived at it by chasing an elusive concept and simply extrapolated the chase to its logical limit. This means that we formulated the concept, that we can express what we mean by it without knowing whether it is actually instantiated anywhere, that is, we do not know if there ever has been or will ever be a truly trustworthy person.

---

[23] R. Hardin, *Trust and Trustworthiness* (New York: Russell Sage Foundation, 2002) 1.

[24] V. McGeer and P. Pettit, 'The Empowering Theory of Trust' in *The Philosophy of Trust* (Oxford: Oxford University Press, 2017) 15.

As a limit concept, the truly trustworthy person can be compared to the true friend in the Aristotelian sense or the truly moral person in the Kantian sense. A true friend, as opposed to a friend of utility (whom I merely exploit for my own purposes) or a friend of pleasure (whom I simply enjoy to be around), is a friend about whom I care not for my own sake but for his.[25] We can formulate such a concept of a true friend without knowing whether or not in human history there has ever been an instance of true friendship, since every suggested act of true friendship can be unpacked in terms of hidden interests that can explain these acts. In a similar vein, according to Kant, a truly moral act must not only conform with whatever an assumed moral law requires but it must happen *for the sake* of the moral law, since mere accidental conformity with a law would not speak to the moral nature of the agent but merely to the serendipity of circumstances. Now, the crux of the issue is that whenever we act in conformity with a law, we can in principle never know whether we acted for the sake of the law or from some kind of hidden motive. The problem is, famously, that we cannot 'prove by experience the nonexistence of a cause when all that experience teaches is that we do not perceive it'.[26] Thus we can never know empirically whether a moral act was truly moral or whether it did not actually happen for some ulterior selfish motive or disposition, like thirst for glory, fear of hell, cowardice or vanity. Morality is thus something we can have a concept of, but cannot empirically know if it exists or not.

A similar thing can be said about true trustworthiness. Any trust that relies on such a true trustworthiness can accordingly be called Kantian trust.[27] Now, a person can only really prove to be truly trustworthy in this Kantian sense if all his dispositions to be reliable have been taken away. This, however, means that ultimately, I can only ever truly trust an unreliable person. Insofar as I rely on you because I think you are a reliable person, I am not really trusting you, but I am merely relying on mechanisms in place that dispose you to do as I expect. When I am merely relying on you, however, I am, so to speak, treating you as a kind of machine, as a thing. Whether the mechanism in place that I rely on is the structural integrity of a bridge or the psychological disposition to honour promises is of no decisive importance.

It is in this sense that only by trusting you in a Kantian sense am I treating you as a human being and not a mere machine. It is for this reason that the increasing division of labour, which is ultimately a reliance system and not a trust system, has been charged with creating a very specific modern malaise: Durkheim called it anomy,[28] Weber, disenchantment.[29] It represents the pain of a very peculiar form of dehumanisation that emerges because our human nature is not directly accessible, is not an empirically available substance but always needs to be re-affirmed by mutual relations of Kantian trust: I trust that you are human and an autonomous, free agent rather than a mere desiring machine. I cannot rely on that fact, I need to trust, because it is empirically unavailable.

Now, it is in debt relations that we reveal our humanity to each other and thus ultimately to ourselves.[30] The unsecured loan is but a very technical and mundane example of this important

---

[25] Aristotle, *Nicomachean Ethics*, Book viii.3.
[26] I. Kant, *The Groundwork of the Metaphysics of Morals*, M. Gregor (trans.) (Cambridge: Cambridge University Press, 1997) 30.
[27] This coinage is done in order to stress the analogy between trustworthiness and a Kantian model of moral action. It is not supposed to refer to the way Kant actually treated trust. For a discussion of such a Kantian theory of trust, see E. Oluffa Pedersen, 'A Kantian Conception of Trust' (2012) 13 *Northern European Journal of Philosophy* 147.
[28] E. Durkheim, *The Division of Labour in Society*, W. D. Halls (trans.) (London: Macmillan, 1984) 291 ff.
[29] M. Weber, *The Sociology of Religion* (London: Methuen, 1971) 270.
[30] For a discussion of the constitutive function of this mutual trust and recognition, see R. R. Williams, *Hegel's Ethics of Recognition* (Berkeley: University of California Press, 1997).

relation. In the way people act when they owe us something we can see not merely how they are set up psychologically, how they are *disposed*, but also whether they possess this fleeting substance of true human autonomy. Whether they 'hold' as humans. The high metaphysical stakes involved in these seemingly mundane debt relations come to light in the extreme, visceral contempt that is and has been elicited by debt defaults in both ancient times and in contemporary unregulated relationships like the mafia. Someone who does not pay his debt is considered not to be 'good' in the most fundamental and intense sense of the word, he is considered to be subhuman. Nietzsche argued that most modern forms of normativity derive from this primordial relation of debt.[31] Our ubiquitous systems of reliance have, of course, luckily blunted the metaphysical edge of these trust relations and have, in most contexts, defused the explosively high stakes at play. Still, these debt relations do not only relate to the psychological make-up of our character but go to the heart of our understanding of being human.

18.5 TRUST AND THE LAW

There are entirely different stakes at play in reliance and trust. Whilst reliance is a mundane and technical issue, trust is a morally laden issue that potentially concerns our very human essence. This makes it crucial to keep these two concepts neatly separated. Failing to do so leads to a host of misunderstandings not only about trust and reliance itself but also about the relationship of technology and law.

In an influential paper on blockchain technologies and trust, Kevin Werbach, for instance, writes that 'the reason the blockchain needs law is that both the blockchain and the law are, at their core, mechanisms of trust'.[32] This view is illustrative of many discussions of the relationship between law and modern technologies. The problem is that in the light of the above analysis it is only half right: the blockchain is not a mechanism of trust but a mechanism of pure reliance; the law, conversely, is a hybrid mechanism of both reliance and true trust. The law and blockchain technology thus do overlap as providers of reliability but since the law touches the area of trust, whilst blockchain does not, they both ultimately inhabit different worlds.

As we have seen in our discussion of unsecured loans, the blockchain allows the automation of reliance, but does not allow the automation of trust, since true Kantian trust is not automatable.

The law, conversely, is not merely a mechanism of trust but a mechanism of both reliance and trust. On the one hand, the law is (1) a coercive mechanism; on the other, (2) it also addresses and thus presupposes the autonomous agent.

(1) Insofar as the law is a coercive apparatus it is a mechanism of reliance. When doing business with some stranger from the other end of the country, I do not need to trust him, but I can rely on him because ultimately I can rely on the law to influence his incentives in such a way that my interests are by and large protected. This alignment of incentives that the law effects works primarily through threatening the imposition of costs, that is, by coercive means.

(2) However, the law does not only coerce, it also summons our autonomous agency. It does so explicitly in codifications of fundamental rights, in human rights legislation or any rules or principles protecting civil liberties. It does so implicitly by employing terms like 'reasonable',

---

[31] F. Nietzsche, *On the Genealogy of Morality*, C. Diethe (trans.) (Cambridge: Cambridge University Press, 1994) 41ff.
[32] See Werbach, n. 10 at 494.

'best effort' or 'good faith' and by imposing fiduciary duties.[33] All these legal techniques ultimately rely on the elusive notion of human nature that we tried to sketch in Section 18.4. In all of these spaces of autonomous agency, true Kantian trust fills the gaps between the interests of the agents. But it is not only in the substantive sections of the law that autonomous agency and thus true trust plays an important role. For many legal philosophers, the law as such cannot exhaustively be described as a mere apparatus of coercion but also engages our moral core. This is certainly true for thinkers in the tradition of natural law.[34] However, even legal positivist like H. L. A. Hart and many legal philosophers writing in his tradition argue that law without coercion is conceivable and thus take the law to be in the business of setting standards and thus addressing itself to autonomous agents.[35]

The fact that the law and blockchain are *not*, at their core, similar mechanisms, means that they do not follow the same principles. This does not need to worry us, however, since it means that a potential conflict between the two is limited: in the field of reliance, the law and the blockchain do indeed compete, and in most cases a smart contract will provide better, cheaper, more direct, more transparent and more immediate reliability than the law ever can. In these fields, the law will likely be replaced by better mechanisms of automation where the law will only provide the regulatory framework or where regulators will directly employ technical fixes rather than relying on rules in a mode described by Roger Brownsword as law 3.0.[36] In the field of trust, however, the law cannot be replaced by automation, since trust cannot be automated. In these fields, the law does not have to fear to be replaced, but rather ever new areas where law is needed will emerge.[37]

18.6 CONCLUSION

This chapter illustrated the relation of law and automation by analysing the case of unsecured loans and came to the conclusion that these loans cannot be fully automated because they include an element of true trust. This logic, however, cannot only be found in explicit loan agreements. It is also present in the terms of many other contractual arrangements and certainly in the various modes of the fulfilment of contracts. Even in cases where performance upon counter-performance is agreed, it is usually necessary for one party to give advance payment or advance delivery, thus in fact, handing out an unsecured loan. The logic extends even further into our social and private relations, in which we all seem to do a rather good job at keeping track of the favours we have received and those that we have handed out and of whether we owe or are owed.

Finally, as concerns the relations we keep with our professions, there is, of course, an irreducible trust element too: one tends to require the services of an expert only in cases where

---

[33] See G. A. M. Ponzetto and N. Gennaioli, 'Optimally Vague Contracts and the Law', Working Papers of the Barcelona Graduate School of Economics (2015) at 747.
[34] See, for instance, J. Finnis, *Natural Law and Natural Rights* (Oxford: Oxford University Press, 1980); or more recently N. Simmonds, *Law as a Moral Idea* (Oxford: Oxford University Press, 2007).
[35] See H. L. A. Hart, *The Concept of Law*, 3rd ed. (Oxford: Clarendon, 2012). My own position on this important issue is that the law does all these morally relevant things (such as setting standards, demanding things, engaging our autonomy) *by means* of holding out the use of force. It has been worked out in detail in C. Kletzer, *The Idea of a Pure Theory of Law* (Oxford: Hart Publishing, 2018).
[36] See R Brownsword, *Law 3.0: Rules, Regulation, and Technology* (London: Routledge, 2020); 'Regulatory Fitness: Fintech, Funny Money, and Smart Contracts' (2019) 20 *European Business Organization Law Review* 5.
[37] An example of this is the OpenLaw project discussed in n. 21, which provides legally binding contracts through an online platform.

one lacks the expertise oneself. If one lacks the expertise, however, then one also lacks the fundamental tools to assess whether the putative expert actually is an expert. So before even being in a situation where we have to rely on the expert, we have to trust that the putative expert actually is an expert. So reliance is indeed very important, but contrary to Richard and Daniel Susskind's claim mentioned in the Introduction, it is certainly not enough and, as long as there are humans, trust will have a role to play.

PART VI

Fate of the Legal Professions

19

Lawyering Somewhere between Computation and the Will to Act

A Digital Age Reflection

*Jeffrey M. Lipshaw**

Until one is committed, there is hesitancy, the chance to draw back. Concerning all acts of initiative (and creation), there is one elementary truth, the ignorance of which kills countless ideas and splendid plans: that the moment one definitely commits oneself, then Providence moves too. All sorts of things occur to help one that would never otherwise have occurred. A whole stream of events issues from the decision, raising in one's favor all manner of unforeseen incidents and meetings and material assistance, which no man could have dreamed would have come his way. I have learned a deep respect for one of Goethe's couplet's: "Whatever you can do, or dream you can do, begin it. Boldness has genius, power, and magic in it."

William Hutchison Murray, often incorrectly attributed to Goethe[1]

19.1 INTRODUCTION

Increasingly capable machines will transform the work of human experts, including those I am most involved in educating: lawyers.[2] That strikes me as beyond any interesting debate, even if there is some segment of the law professoriate still bemoaning the obvious. At this point, the far more interesting subjects are the relative contributions of machine and human intelligence in making nuanced judgments and solving knotty problems. I borrow this definition of artificial intelligence (AI): machine computation that is capable of simulating some human-like cognitive processes, not merely limited to reasoning, strategizing, planning, and decision-making, but capable of processing symbols, context, language, spatial relations, and movement.[3] The AI development currently most relevant to lawyering is machine learning (ML), sometimes referred to functionally as "data mining."[4] This is "the analysis of (often large) observational data sets to

---

* Ashley Krezmien provided research on the state of the art in digital lawyering. Thanks also to the following for comments and criticisms: Michele DeStefano, David Haig, Paul Brest, Anne Tucker, and Larry DiMatteo.
[1] William Hutchison Murray, *The Scottish Himalayan Expedition* (s.n.: J. M. Dent, 1951). While widely attributed to Goethe, nothing in the quote turns out to have its source in Goethe, as finally concluded by the Goethe Society of North America in 1998. Hyde Flippo, "A Well Known Quote Attributed to Goethe May Not Be Actually Be [sic] His," www.thoughtco.com/goethe-quote-may-not-be-his-4070881 (accessed June 7, 2019).
[2] Richard Susskind and Daniel Susskind, *The Future of the Professions: How Technology Will Transform the Work of Human Experts* (Oxford: Oxford University Press, 2015) 2 n. 2.
[3] Harry Surden, "Artificial Intelligence and Law: An Overview" (2019) 35 *Georgia State University Law Review* 1305 1307. For a quick summary of the difference between science fiction like "general AI" and the more common and realistic "narrow AI," see ibid. at 1308–1310; Meredith Broussard, *Artificial Unintelligence: How Computers Misunderstand the World* (Cambridge, MA: MIT Press, 2019) 31–33.
[4] Harry Surden, "Machine Learning and Law" (2014) 89 *Washington Law Review* 87.

find unsuspected relationships and to summarize the data in ways that are both understandable and useful to the data owner."[5] Currently, these state-of-the-art computational tools (1) unleash processing power on vast stores of data to assess relevance in discovery or legal research, or (2) use logic and algorithms to undertake tasks involving complex computations like tax returns.[6] Just how powerful can these tools get? I agree with the characterization of a certain kind of thinking as the AI fallacy, "the mistaken supposition that the only way to develop systems that perform tasks at the level of experts or higher is to replicate the thinking processes of human specialists."[7] But some aspects of human judgment – the mental processes we experience as intuition, insight, creativity, and the will to act – still challenge the capability of the most sophisticated machines. The thesis here is that those qualities will be the contributions of human lawyering well into the digital age.[8]

Yet those qualities, if not under attack, are at least the subject of significant suspicion by some thoughtful scholars and teachers of lawyerly problem solving, decision-making, and professional judgment. I have in mind the comprehensive, masterful, and balanced treatise coauthored by Paul Brest and Linda Hamilton Krieger, one I admire enough to use (good-naturedly) as a foil throughout this essay.[9] Brest and Krieger enthusiastically take up the baton of another development coinciding with the advent of AI and ML: dual process theories of judgment and decision-making (often referred to as JDM, an abbreviation I adopt), particularly the System 1 and System 2 modes of "thinking fast and slow" in the behavioral psychology pioneered by Amos Tversky and Daniel Kahneman.[10] In his iconic *Thinking Fast and Slow*, Kahneman laid out the most influential body of work on the difference between fast, intuitive, heuristic System 1 thinking and slow, analytic, data-based, comprehensive System 2 thinking. Those involved in the research express a range of normative views about the pluses and minuses of System 1 thinking. Depending on where you stand in that discussion, there is something of holy or unholy synergy. If you see human judgment as subject systematically to non-deliberative heuristics and biases, then it ought to come as no surprise that deliberation is often viewed as the disciplined parent and *intuition* is the unruly and not-quite-respectable stepchild of the problem-solving family.[11] If we combine algorithmic intelligence with behavioral psychology, the holy synergy is, whenever

---

[5] Illhoi Yoo et al., "Data Mining in HealthCare and Biomedicine: A Survey of the Literature" (2012) 36 *Journal of Medical Systems* 2431 2432.

[6] Surden, n. 3 at 1305.

[7] Susskind and Susskind, n. 2 at 45. On the other hand, I am not going to rehash long-standing criticisms of the AI true believer camp. Hubert L. Dreyfus, Stuart E. Dreyfus, and Tom Athanasiou, *Mind over Machine: The Power of Human Intuition and Expertise in the Era of the Computer* (New York: Free Press, 1986).

[8] I *do* feel obliged to make a fine distinction regarding Professor Surden's gentle chiding of futurists on the subject of AI and lawyering. Surden, n. 3 at 1306 n. 3. I am interested, whether or not it qualifies as futuristic speculation, in the differences between machines and humans when it comes to deciding and to translating thought into action. That is a practical here and now issue. I also want gently to push back against a certain disciplinary tunnel vision I perceive among many legal academics, namely, that what we study is reducible a la physics, and therefore amenable to being wholly digitized.

[9] Paul Brest and Linda Hamilton Krieger, *Problem Solving, Decision Making, and Professional Judgment: A Guide for Lawyers and Policymakers* (Oxford: Oxford University Press, 2010).

[10] Daniel Kahneman, *Thinking Fast and Slow* (New York: Farrar, 2011). Michael Lewis, *The Undoing Project: A Friendship That Changed Our Minds* (New York: Norton, 2017) is a popular and readable telling of the Tversky and Kahneman story. Dual process theories of cognition distinguish between thinking that is "fast, automatic, and high capacity" versus that which is "slow, controlled, and low capacity." Tversky and Kahneman did not originate the concept nor are they the only theorists of it. Charlotte L. Doyle, "Creative Flow as a Unique Cognitive Process' (2017) 8 *Frontiers in Psychology* Article 1348 2. But Kahneman's work is popular.

[11] This is particularly true when one refers to intuition as "gut feelings." The former president of the United States has done many of us a disservice. When I refer to intuition, I do not mean to endorse it as a lazy alternative to digging into the details.

possible, to find an algorithm, a program, a machine that will take human heuristics and biases out of the problem-solving loop.[12]

Brest and Krieger focus on these tensions in their scholarly yet practical treatment of lawyering judgments. They treat System 2 "deliberation" (my shorthand for all reasoned manipulation of abstract symbols and empirical data), on one hand, and System 1 intuition, on the other, as "essentially two distinct but complementary, approaches to problem solving and decision making."[13] They are respectful of intuition, but in the same way I might be respectful of a useful but dangerous explosive. Indeed, they are inclined to metaphorical anthropomorphism. Deliberation is the hero. Like an honest person, deliberation is "transparent" to the decision maker.[14] Here are the verbs that the forms of deliberation bring to the party: "expands," "conceives," "critiques," "envisions," "troubleshoots," "fine tunes," "selects," "implements," "enables," "helps," and "inspires."[15] And deliberation is a good friend and teacher. It can be "informed by intuition at the same time it corrects for the limitations and biases of pure intuition."[16] If deliberation has any flaw, it is too slow for most of the decisions we are obliged to make. Then intuition, by necessity, takes over.[17]

By contrast, intuition is at best a flawed antihero, if not a villain. Brest and Krieger cast intuition as invidious and insidious, at least metaphorically. It is "opaque." It is shaped by hard-wired cognitive "schemas" that shape our perception without our being aware of them.[18] It is influenced by affect, "ranging from a 'faint whisper of emotion to strong feelings of fear and dread, to visceral drives such as hunger and sexual need.'"[19] It is merely an antihero and not a villain, however, because it has at least one key benefit: it is fast. Even then, however, going fast can lead to error by causing the decision maker to overlook aspects of the problem or considering "an impoverished set of potential solutions."[20] Not surprisingly, then, when it came time to assess the interaction of deliberation and intuition, Professors Brest and Krieger turned to the behavioral psychology of Tversky and Kahneman.[21] While Brest and Krieger give a fair account of intuition and creative thinking, Kahneman's own view of intuition is dark and only grudgingly sympathetic. If it does not endorse the superiority of machine intelligence, it certainly gives it a leg up. Kahneman's bottom line is "Whenever we can replace human judgment by a formula, we should at least consider it."[22]

My casual empiricism is that, when it comes to dual process theories of cognition, many law professors would echo the normative themes in the Brest and Krieger treatise. We are inclined to keep intuition at arm's length and inspiration on a short leash for all the reasons Kahneman

---

[12] Michael Livermore used just that phrase in contemplating the possibility of computationally self-executing legal rules, notwithstanding the famous jurisprudential debates about the "open texture" of language. Michael A. Livermore, "Rule by Rules" in Ryan Whalen (ed.), *Computational Legal Studies: The Promise and Challenge of Data-Driven Legal Research* (Cheltenham: Edward Elgar, 2020) 238–264.
[13] Brest and Krieger, n. 9 at 11.
[14] Ibid.
[15] Ibid. at 13–14.
[16] Ibid. at 11.
[17] Ibid. at 14.
[18] Ibid. at 17–18.
[19] Ibid. at 19, quoting Paul Slovic et al., "The Affect Heuristic" in Thomas Gilovich, Dale Griffin, and Daniel Kahneman (eds.) *Heuristics and Biases: The Psychology of Intuitive Judgment* (Cambridge: Cambridge University Press, 2002) 397–421.
[20] Brest and Krieger, n. 9 at 25.
[21] Ibid. at 21. Indeed, the final paragraph of their acknowledgments reads as follows: "The citations make evident our indebtedness to Amos Tversky, Daniel Kahneman, and many social psychologists who developed and expanded the lines of inquiry they began." Ibid. at xxviii.
[22] Kahneman, n. 10 at 233.

identifies and then a few more of our own. First, there is good science behind the Brest and Krieger inclination to get beyond mere good judgment in common parlance, and to "draw heavily on the field of social science known as [JDM], in which 'judgment' refers mainly to the processes of empiricism – how one ascertains facts and makes predictions about the physical and social world."[23] Lawyers are not immune to judgment errors arising from heuristics and biases; "[JDM] focuses particularly on the systematic errors made by intuitive decision makers – all of us, much of the time."[24] Second, intuition or inspiration as the basis for legal outcomes seems simply non-theoretical or antiscientific. Since Langdell's great dictum, law is supposed to have been "considered as a science" as to which "mastery ... as to be able to apply them with constant facility and certainty to the ever-tangled skein of human affairs, is what constitutes a true lawyer."[25] Scholarship not based in theory is, in the words of the respected and influential Columbia law professor and former University of Virginia Law School dean Robert Scott, "lazy thinking masquerading as theory" or, worse, mere brute ipse dixit of Dean Scott's bê̂te noir, the "wise man."[26] Third, in other areas of professional endeavor, the point has been, as Brest and Krieger suggest, to bring discipline, rigor, and data to decisions that are better made with the support of discipline, rigor, and data. The quality revolution in manufacturing, the "lean enterprise," has been based on the use of data to undermine the conventional wisdom about efficiency.[27] Evidence-based management is superior to making it up as one goes along.[28]

I worry, however, about the extent to which we, as scholars and scientists, are selling short the non-deliberative process of thought – not just intuition but other forms of non-deliberative judgment as well. This will hardly be a rejection of the behavioral insights. On the other hand, I do not think many serious people would suggest that machines will replace human lawyers. The question is what to emphasize, in education and practice, about human capabilities in the digital age. Should lawyering follow Kahneman's default rule and substitute formulas (particularly those capable of being translated into machine code) for human judgment wherever possible? If so, what is the best that algorithms and data science have so far offered lawyers for purposes of making their most sophisticated judgments? To the extent that making legal judgments and solving problems involve prediction and optimization, what do the tools of operations research, and processes like data mining, clustering, linear programming, decision trees, Bayesian updating, Markov models, Monte Carlo simulations, and the like bring to the party? And what are their limits? That is the subject of Section 19.2.

In Section 19.3, I jump to the far extreme of those qualities heretofore presumed to be reserved to humans. Over a forty-year professional career, in Kahneman's lexicon, my thinking has been both fast and slow. What that really means (with a nod to Ralph Nader) is that often I was unsure at any speed. At the same time, I made binary "go/no-go" decisions in the face of complexity and uncertainty. I have no doubt that much of what Brest and Krieger call deliberation can and will be replicated in machine thinking. But I am convinced, for the time being, that those machines

---

[23] Brest and Krieger, n. 9 at xxix.
[24] Ibid.
[25] C. C. Langdell, *Selection of Cases on the Law of Contracts*, vol. IV (Omaha: Legal Classics Library, 1983).
[26] Jeffrey M. Lipshaw, "Contract as Meaning: An Introduction to *Contract as Promise* at 30" (2012) 45 *Suffolk Law Review* 601 605–606.
[27] The classic exposition of the difference between lean production and mass production is James Womack, Daniel T. Jones, and Daniel Roos, *The Machine That Changed the World* (New York: Simon and Schuster, 1990) 21–69.
[28] Jeffrey Pfeffer and Robert I. Sutton, *Hard Facts, Dangerous Half-Truths and Total Nonsense: Profiting from Evidence-Based Management* (Brighton: HBR Press, 2006) 3–6(attributing Cisco's unusually successful track record in digesting acquired companies "without heartburn" to its "systematic examination of evidence about what went right and what went wrong in other companies' mergers").

can neither think inspirationally nor translate thought into action because they are not biological life-forms evolved to the point that they perceive themselves as having ends or purposes (*telos*). Even in a mundane lawyering exercise (my example will be Audrey and her problem with a neighbor's impending violation of the zoning ordinance in her pastoral township), effective legal caregiving draws on a wide continuum of capabilities, with computation and formal logic at one end and the ability to perceive and act in pursuit of human ends and purposes at the other.

The purest form of System 2 thinking can be modeled computationally, symbols reducible to machine code consisting of 0s and 1s that replicate some forms of human reasoning. As we move on the thinking continuum *away* from computation, we encounter human characteristics less amenable to such reduction: intuition, insight, decision, and judgment, and the perception of purposes and ends. Then, beyond the end of the mental continuum, there is action itself. I have simply encountered too many close decisions in which the data supports arguments either way but for which the course of action requires a leap into the unknown. We are charged with teaching students to think like lawyers, but thinking that way, at best, only takes you to the precipice. It does not impel you to act. Acting is an aspect of *being* in the world. We can act and *be* without thinking; we can think without acting; we can translate our thoughts into action; we can reflect on what we are and what we have done. But the dark and despairing lesson is that acting (not just deciding) in the face of uncertainty means confronting a world "where wildness lies in wait."[29]

Kahneman's heuristics and biases, the inspiration to solve problems, and the will to act stem from the same source: we are more than mere thinking machines. Trying to reconcile algorithmic calculations, at one extreme, and the will to act, at the other, leads to just the kinds of regress you would expect when trying to reconcile the fundamentally irreconcilable. To suggest that our goal, as lawyers or anyone else, is to cleanse our judgment making of anything but algorithmic rationality is like suggesting that we cleanse human reproduction of its dependence on sexual desires. Neither inspiration nor sex is going away any time soon. We will have to live with the complements of deliberation and that which is beyond it. And like all matters involving irreconcilable complements – position and momentum in quantum mechanics; completeness and consistency in formal axiomatic systems; objective experience and subjective qualia; or how a good God permits evil – the experts explain but their explanations merely orbit some physical or metaphysical singularity that, to paraphrase Kant, is the final but unreachable Unconditioned truth.

I am not hopeful about law school pedagogy on this topic. In the singular moment of acting upon judgment, the complementarities of slow System 2 deliberation, on one hand, and fast System 1 thinking, on the other, cannot be reconciled. They can only be managed. For practitioners, it means that action, if not insight as well, will always be a leap into the wildness of the unknown. For those professors charged with educating those practitioners, the most likely outcome is that we can merely offer examples, empathy, and solace. Or to say, "Whatever judgment you can make, borne somehow out of data, intuition, and inspiration, begin it."

19.2 DIGITAL CAPABILITY AND LAWYERING

To paraphrase Brest and Krieger, if the task requires lawyers to ascertain facts and make predictions about the physical and social world, what AI tools are available? There is now a significant body of literature for the nontechnical reader demystifying the claims of AI one sees,

---

[29] Peter L. Bernstein, *Against the Gods: The Remarkable Story of Risk* (New York: Wiley, 1998) 331

for example, on television commercials for IBM's Watson or for Microsoft's products. What follows is a baseline assessment of the state of the art in reducing real-life business and legal problems to computation.

19.2.1 Algorithmic Decision-Making Tools Generally

The term "artificial intelligence" is, at best, imprecise. Since World War II, the name for the discipline consisting of computational models for prediction and optimization in operational milieus like businesses, armies, or hospitals has been "operations research."[30] Its tools include linear regression forecasting, nonlinear and multiple regression, time series forecasting, linear programming, multi-period planning, integer programming, efficiency analysis, multi-goal and nonlinear programming, decision trees, Bayesian analysis, Markov models, queuing theory, Monte Carlo simulations, and stochastic risk optimization.[31] The tools provide mathematical solutions for problems of optimization like inventory management, railroad car placement, staff scheduling, investment risk management, television advertising sales, facilities placement, mail order catalog deliveries, human and machine waiting lines, and construction bidding.[32] When armed with computational logic and vast processing power, the tools outperform humans in generating relatively unambiguous answers when applying complex sets of constraints to equally complex circumstances.[33] Nevertheless, the key to effective use of the tools is knowing when and where their particular structure fits the problem to be solved.[34] In the sophisticated use of operations research tools to solve optimization problems, a human supplies the ends, namely, the specific quantity, the "objective," to be determined mathematically based on a finite set of input variables and constraints.[35]

Many of the tools of operations research now fall within AI, ML, or data mining, as I defined them above. The most important tool for lawyering is data mining, which has come "to include pattern recognition, database design, artificial intelligence, visualization, etc."[36] In contrast to other operations research optimization tools, "data mining, without a hypothesis, explores data that have been collected in advance, and discovers hidden patterns from data. In short, data mining is a process of producing the general (i.e., knowledge or an evidence-based hypothesis) from the specific (i.e., data)."[37] If there is an additional implication to ML beyond data mining, it is that ML involves "iterative adjustment of mathematical parameters, data retention, and error correction techniques" by which the "ML algorithms are said to automatically update (or "learn") through repeated exposure to data and optimise performance at various classification, prediction, and decision-making tasks."[38]

In ML, the programmer uses one or more of the above tools to create a model that predicts something. In every instance, the parameters of the model are reduction of something in the real

---

[30] Dreyfus, n. 7 at 170–177; Saul I. Gass and Arjang A. Assad, *An Annotated Timeline of Operations Research: An Informal History* (New York: Springer, 2005).

[31] Richard Bronson and Govindasami Naadimuthu, *Schaum's Outline of Theory and Problems of Operations Research*, 2nd ed. (New York: McGraw-Hill, 1982).

[32] Ibid.

[33] Surden, n. 3 at 1317–1318; Yoo, n. 5 at 2432–2433.

[34] Dreyfus, n. 7 at 191–192.

[35] Bronson and Naadimuthu, n. 31 at 1, 155, 169; Dreyfus, n. 7 at 171–172.

[36] Yoo, n. 5 at 2432.

[37] Ibid. at 2433.

[38] Christopher Markou and Simon Deakin, "Ex Machina Lex: The Limits of Legal Computability" (2019), https://papers.ssrn.com/sol3/papers.cfm?abstract_id=3407856 (accessed August 23, 2021).

world to a mathematical formula. In "supervised" or "predictive" learning, the programmer creates a model using tools like classification rules, regression, or time series analysis. Meredith Broussard's example is a model that will predict which credit card customers are likely to make late payments. The programmer feeds the model "training data," namely, vast amounts of information about customers who paid late and tests the model's predictions against results the programmer already knows. When satisfied with the model's accuracy, the programmer deploys it against the remaining data to generate predictive outputs. In "unsupervised" or "descriptive" learning, the programmer uses algorithms designed to spot hidden patterns in the data and thereby discover relationships between inputs and outputs previously not visible to the human programmer. The algorithmic tools consist of clustering, association, summarization, and sequence discovery.[39] As Harry Surden points out, "machine-learning systems are designed to learn and improve over time."[40] A good example is an email spam filter. It may begin as a supervised learning system with training data that the human programmer knows constitute either spam or desired email and can be supplemented with unsupervised learning that associated particular data with spam.[41]

19.2.2 State of the Art in Algorithmic Lawyering

I agree with Professor Surden's observation that current AI technology tends to work best for activities where the tools of ML are effective, which are also those aspects of thinking that suit System 2 deliberation. A significant asset of AI technologies is that they *are* less prone to System 1 heuristics and biases. The flip side is that they "work poorly, or not at all, in areas that are conceptual, abstract, value-laden, open-ended, policy- or judgment-oriented; require common sense or intuition; involve persuasion or arbitrary conversation; or involve engagement with the meaning of real-world humanistic concepts, such as societal norms, social constructs, or social institutions."[42] I confess that I view most of the algorithmic lawyering tools, while technically interesting, as unexciting. These tools perform statistical analysis with greater precision or unleash processing power on vast stores of data, far beyond the capacity (or patience) of a human being. I am far more interested in the state of the art in machine simulation of the most subtle and nuanced human judgments – outcome predictions in the face of uncertainty and outcome optimization when the factors to be juggled resist expression in a finite and accessible set of mathematical equations. Thus, what is the cutting edge, defined as those systems coming closest to simulating a practicing lawyer's most System 1 thinking?[43]

19.2.2.1 *Well-Established Usages*

Brest and Krieger offer almost 120 pages of superb text on lawyers' and policymakers' use of probability, statistics, regressions, and Bayesian analysis. The applications are primarily matters of proof – how to demonstrate that a particular foam insulation caused a particular rash outbreak;

---

[39] Broussard, n. 3 at 92–94. The Yoo article contains an extensive explanation of the algorithms used in supervised and unsupervised learning, including classification algorithms (naive Bayesian, neural network, decision tree, support vector machine, classification based on association [CBA], ensemble, and adaptive boosting), clustering algorithms (hierarchical and partitional), and association algorithms, along with guidelines for using them. Yoo, n. 5 at 2433–2441.
[40] Surden, n. 3 at 1313.
[41] Ibid. at 1312–1315.
[42] Ibid. at 1322.
[43] Because my concern here is about judgment and decision-making, I have not included the area of "smart" or "computable" contracts. Harry Surden, "Computable Contracts" (2012) 46 *UC Davis Law Review* 629; Jeffrey M. Lipshaw, "The Persistence of 'Dumb' Contracts" (2019) 2 *Stanford Journal of Blockchain Law & Policy* 1.

how to identify a cancer cluster; how to determine if an employer is engaged in wage-discrimination against certain classes of employees or that the death penalty is being imposed unduly based on race; and the correction of representativeness error in litigation (e.g., the "confusion of the inverse" in conditional probability manifested as the "'prosecutor's fallacy").[44]

The application of ML to the massive documents often collected in litigation discovery is now almost passé. The key is that lawyers are using supervised and unsupervised ML on text – statutes, cases, regulations, documents – rather than quantitative data. Such learning requires "reducing text to numeric data that can be quantitatively analyzed to identify and characterize patterns."[45] An example is "technology-assisted review" (TAR). A lawyer creates a set of training or "seed" data based on documents the lawyer knows are relevant or irrelevant to the case. Through this process, the software learns which documents are relevant and irrelevant and applies this analysis and coding to the overall data set, marking documents. The software becomes more adept at recognizing relevant documents because it learns from each training.[46] In litigation discovery, ML has fundamentally changed the game (although whether for better is still an open question) by routinely beating human trainers in retrieving relevant information.[47]

"Text as data" is also the basis for commercially available legal research platforms. In the most advanced versions, the system tries not just to retrieve cases but also to generate something approaching the text of the argument the lawyer wants to make.[48] The systems use natural language processing, that is, the application of the algorithmic tools of supervised and unsupervised learning to text, to assess the relevance of cases, statutes, and regulations. Neural nets update and revise the quantitative relationship among the variables relevant to the question posed by the researcher.[49] Examples include ROSS[50] and Casetext's CARA.[51]

19.2.2.2 *Cutting Edge*

Those are well-established or, at least, developing tools lawyers use to support their advocacy or policy positions, or to mine data revealing relationships that are helping in solving problems. Nobody would responsibly suggest that they are anything but tools to assist the human lawyer. Rather, "machine intelligence is used to augment human cognition in a competitive strategic environment."[52]

Far greater challenges for algorithmic solutions lie in those problems in which lawyers must assess business and legal outcomes in the face not just of risk but of great uncertainty. The great theorist of risk and uncertainty, Frank Knight, distinguished the two: "It will appear that a

---

[44] Brest and Krieger, n. 9 at 123–239.
[45] Michael A. Livermore and Daniel N. Rockmore, "Introduction: From Analogue to Digital Legal Scholarship" in Michael A. Livermore and Daniel N. Rockmore (eds.), *Law as Data: Computation, Text, and the Future of Legal Analytics* (Sante Fe: SFI Press, 2019) xx–xxi; Livermore and Rockmore, "Distant Reading the Law" in Livermore and Rockmore (eds.) at 3, 11.
[46] Thomson Reuters, "How to Make the E-Discovery Process More Efficient with Predictive Coding," https://legal.thomsonreuters.com/en/insights/articles/how-predictive-coding-makes-e-discovery-more-efficient (accessed July 8, 2019). Surden, n. 4 at 110–114; Livermore and Rockmore, n. 45 at xiv–xvi.
[47] Ibid. at xv.
[48] Dana Remus and Frank Levy, "Can Robots Be Lawyers? Computers, Lawyers, and the Practice of Law" (2017) 30 *Georgetown Journal of Legal Ethics* 501 521.
[49] Ibid. at 522.
[50] Kevin D. Ashley, *Artificial Intelligence and Legal Analytics: New Tools for Law Practice in the Digital Age* (Cambridge: Cambridge University Press, 2017) 351–352; ROSS, www.rossintelligence.com (accessed March 9, 2019).
[51] Casetext, https://casetext.com/product (accessed March 9, 2019).
[52] Livermore and Rockmore, n. 45 at xv; Remus and Levy, n. 48 at 523 (legal research systems like ROSS still require "substantial human role in defining and directing research").

measurable uncertainty, or 'risk' proper ... is so far different from an *unmeasurable* one that it is not in effect an uncertainty at all."[53] A lawyer confronts uncertainty in counseling on almost every aspect of the convergence of business imperatives and legal considerations. Does the prospectus and registration statement filed with the SEC comply with all of the disclosure requirements of the Securities Act of 1933? Does the acquisition of the Z Corporation not violate Section 7 of the Clayton Act because it does not tend to diminish competition?[54]

The prototypical prediction for a lawyer is the outcome of litigation. Some cases, like personal injury, repeat themselves sufficiently that lawyers can develop either databases or heuristics that assist in the valuation (i.e., prediction of the outcome).[55] Harry Surden has speculated whether a ML program in discrete areas of litigation, like workplace discrimination, might use data from previous lawsuits to assess outcomes in new cases.[56] Most business litigation, on the other hand, arising out of claims, for example, of contract breach, antitrust violation, or intellectual property infringement, are "one-off" in the sense of having so many variables, both substantive and procedural, as to resist measurable uncertainty (i.e., risk).[57] In other words, the machine-based predictive models must (a) be based on capturable data, (b) assess cases with similar pertinent features, (c) be able to avoid overfitting the data, and (d) avoid dealing with myriad extrinsic policy or other business imperatives.[58]

The accounting and legal professions long ago confronted each other on casting contingent liabilities in probabilistic terms.[59] Within GAAP, the United States mathematical model for financial accounting, uncertain liabilities are troublesome.[60] Under Statement of Financial Accounting Standards 5 (SFAS 5), a contingency is "an existing condition, situation, or set of circumstances involving uncertainty as to possible gain ... or loss (hereinafter a 'loss contingency') to an enterprise that will ultimately be resolved when one or more future events occur or fail to occur."[61] The accounting profession groups loss contingencies into three buckets: "probable," meaning that the future event is likely to occur; "reasonable possible," meaning that the chance of the event is more than remote but less than likely; and "remote," meaning the chance of the event is slight. SFAS 5 requires recording the loss contingency as a liability if (a) the present available information indicates the future event is "probable," and (b) the amount of loss can be reasonably estimated.[62] Suffice it to say that the decision to accrue or not to accrue a charge on the financial statements can be significant for the enterprise's management and equity owners.[63]

---

[53] Frank Knight, *Risk, Uncertainty and Profit* (Ithaca: Cornell University Press, 1964) 205, quoted in Bernstein, n. 29 at 219.
[54] Detlev F. Vagts, "Legal Opinions in Quantitative Terms: The Lawyer as Haruspex or Bookie?" (1979) 34 *Business Law* 421 423.
[55] Peter Toll Hoffman, "Valuation of Cases for Settlement: Theory and Practice" 1991 *Journal of Dispute Resolution* 1 6–7 (settlement value heuristic as a multiple of the special damages); Yun-chien Chang et al., "Pain and Suffering in Personal Injury Cases: An Empirical Study" (2017) 14 *Journal of Empirical Legal Studies* 199.
[56] Surden, n. 4 at 103–105.
[57] Vagts, n. 54 at 427 (contemplating action X, the client asks the lawyer [1] how likely will X be detected; [2] if detected, how likely is it to be challenged legally; [3] if challenged, what is the likely outcome; and [4] what is the likely cost of an adverse decision on point [3]).
[58] Surden, n. 4 at 105–107.
[59] Vagts, n. 54, 422–424.
[60] Karen M. Hennes, "Disclosure of Contingent Liabilities" (2014) 33 *Journal of Accounting & Public Policy* 32; Jamie L. Yarbrough, "Mind the GAAP: Moving beyond the Accountant-Attorney Treaty" (2014) 92 *Texas Law Review* 749.
[61] Financial Accounting Standards Board, "Financial Accounting Standards No. 5: Accounting for Contingencies" (March 1975) at 4.
[62] Ibid. at 4–5.
[63] R. Alexander Swidler, "Toeing the Line: The Delicate Balance Attorneys Must Maintain When Responding to Auditor Inquiry Request Letters" (2016) 50 *Indiana Law Review* 969.

Under generally accepted auditing standards, the auditors will request that a representative of the client (the chief financial officer or the controller) send a request to the client's lawyers who are representing it in any litigation that involves a loss contingency. The request will, among other things, ask the lawyer to opine on the loss contingency using the buckets set forth in SFAS 5. The form of the request and the response have been the subject of long-standing dialogue between the accounting and legal professions, with the latter's response set forth in a lengthy policy adopted by the American Bar Association. I can boil the message of the policy into one sentence. For many different reasons, "a lawyer should normally refrain from expressing judgments as to outcome except in those relatively few clear cases where it appears to the lawyer that an unfavorable outcome is either 'probable' or 'remote.'"[64] The ABA's reason for taking that position is that lawyers' relatively common usage of probabilistic terms has no meaningful predictive use. Thus, when a lawyer says to a client, "I think you have a 60–40 chance if we go to trial," that usage was "only undertaken in an effort to make meaningful, for limited purposes, a whole host of judgmental factors applicable at a particular time, without any intention to depict 'probability' in any statistical, scientific or empirically-grounded sense."[65]

To get a sense of how overwhelming this can be in the moment of decision, take a case in which I had some involvement and whose facts are on the public record.[66] Corporation A bought a business from Corporation B. After the deal closed, A discovered that the business is not nearly as profitable as it expected. In real life, A filed a lawsuit against B, claiming securities fraud, common law fraud, and breach of the representations and warranties in the acquisition agreement. But let us return, hypothetically, to the business and legal decision whether to file the lawsuit in the first place. In addition to all of the substantive and legal issues involved in the case, another uncertainty would have been the effect of the disclosure to the securities markets upon the filing the lawsuit that (a) the acquisition had been problematic, and (b) A's due diligence capabilities rather than any legal infirmity may have caused of the problem.

Presently, the tools that might have provided A's management with a mathematical answer to the question "what should we do?" are as undeveloped as the General AI of science fiction. In theory, data could be available to support regressions and therefore probability estimates for every factor involved in the decision. Clustering could assist in determining whether there were relationships among the factors not previously detected by management or its lawyers.[67] Decision trees could provide a logical structure for reaching a conclusion, with the probabilities at each juncture set by the previously discovered regressions and relationships. Neural networks could adjust those relationships as additional data came to light. Computational models of legal reasoning and legal analysis could be employed.[68]

Apart from the business factors in the decision, I suspect little has changed between 1979, when Harvard Professor Detlev Vagts assessed the prediction of litigation outcomes for purposes of SFAS 5, and 2017, when the Legal Analytics Lab of Georgia State University conducted its own empirical study. Vagts presciently contemplated the use of mathematical representations of

---

[64] Committee on Audit Inquiry Responses of the American Bar Association, "Statement of Policy Regarding Lawyers' Responses to Auditors' Requests for Information" (2003) at 8.

[65] Ibid. at 16.

[66] *Great Lakes Chemical Corp v. Monsanto Co* 96 F Supp 2d 376 (D Del 2000); *Great Lakes Chemical Corp v. Pharmacia Corp*, 788 A 2d 544 (Del Ch 2001). It did not go well for the good guys in either forum.

[67] Surden, n. 4 at 107–108. For a detailed assessment of the application of ML tools to the fair use doctrine in copyright law (i.e., opining whether a particular use was fair), Stephen McJohn and Ian McJohn, "Fair Use and Machine Learning" (2019) 12 *Northeastern Law Review* 99.

[68] Ashley, n. 50; Charlotte S. Alexander et al., "Using Text Analytics to Predict Litigation Outcomes" in Livermore and Rockmore (eds.), n. 45 at 275–311; Surden, n. 4 at 102–107.

outcomes by way of decision trees using probabilities of success at each node.[69] He concluded, however, that, except for recurring incidents in the insurance context, "that the precision called by such a representation is seldom likely to be present in legal situations."[70] The Georgia State researchers used the tools of ML on text in all employment law cases in the United States District Court for the Northern District of Georgia from 2010 to 2017 (5,111 cases, approximately 8,600 court documents, and 200,000 text entries from docket sheets).[71] Not to take anything away from the admirable work but, as the researchers concluded, general predictive models for lawsuit outcome, much less predictive models for one particular area like employment litigation, are a long way off: "It is too early to claim that litigation pathways are now predictable ... or that judges' decisions can be easily classified, forecast, or understood in bulk."[72] Moreover, even if researchers can refine the model, legal diagnoses (including predictions of litigation outcomes) will struggle with the same issue that medical researchers face in mining data in aid of clinical diagnoses: "garbage in, garbage out."[73] And even if the model can predict litigation outcomes, will it also assess the circum-litigation issues like those facing Corporation A when deciding whether to litigate at all?

Might legal AI software develop "intuitions" about legal outcomes in the same way that AlphaGo and AlphaGoZero seem to have developed intuitions about moves in the game of Go? The answer is that the AI "intuition" is in fact unsupervised ML on a vast amount of data, namely, the millions of games of Go that the machine plays with itself, and then the use of that learning to assess probabilities of success at each move.[74] I believe the issue is "garbage in, garbage out." Real life presents far more possibilities than even the complex strictures of AlphaGo. So perhaps someday something that looks like AI legal intuition will exist. But that still does not end the inquiry. AlphaGo "knows" that its job is to win the game. How did it learn or decide that? I thus turn to an assessment of less algorithmic or deliberative forms of judgment, decision-making, and action.

19.3 ENDS, THOUGHT, AND ACTION

19.3.1 Segue (or a Leap) from Algorithms (Machines) to Ends (Minds)

Only a fool or a Luddite would deny the impact and the value of both System 2 deliberation and algorithmic analysis in support of decision-making. Yet the distinguished theorist and practitioner of intuition, Gary Klein, has a profound assessment of the relative benefits of System 1 and System 2 thinking when it comes to insight. He correctly observes that the emphasis of the cognitive heuristics and biases (H&B) community is to use System 2 thinking to reduce the common errors produced by System 1 intuitions. He noted, however, "it is important to

---

[69] Vagts, n. 54 at 424–425.
[70] Ibid. at 428.
[71] Alexander, n. 68 at 276.
[72] Ibid. at 310. Other attempts to predict case outcomes have used relatively restricted data sets, including Canadian capital gains tax cases, Supreme Court of the United States opinions, trade secrets cases, and intellectual property cases. Ashley, n. 50 at 107–126. As Professor Ashley notes, humans still do most of the work determining the significant features of prediction, with ML more helpful in determining the weight to accord the feature. Ibid. at 125; Remus and Levy, n. 48 at 524–525 (automated legal analysis and strategy involving prediction of outcomes "[a]s of now ... can only be constructed for repetitive and fairly narrow tasks under specific bodies of law").
[73] Yoo, n. 5 at 2445.
[74] Vince Tabora, "Artificial Intuition and Reinforcement Learning, the Next Steps in Machine Learning" (2018) *Becoming Human: Artificial Intelligence Magazine*, https://becominghuman.ai/artificial-intuition-and-reinforcement-learning-the-next-steps-in-machine-learning-6f2abeb9926b (accessed March 9, 2020).

counterbalance this negative impression of System 1 with a sense of awe and appreciation about the insights we create and the discoveries we make."[75] My own sense of awe and appreciation also includes "our ends and purposes and our will to act based on them." I am a poor excuse for a futurist, but I will bet those will be the last aspects of our experience to be digitized. The tools of the digital age are still tools even if they may become more inscrutable. Tools will not be agents until and unless they learn to determine their own ends and purposes and the will to propel themselves in their pursuit.

The segue from algorithms to ends begins with a story. I spend the summers in northern Michigan. I am an alumnus of the University of Michigan, and our family has a significant connection with the University's medical school. The University's development office holds a large event in the area each summer, and we usually have a chance afterwards to attend a dinner with leaders of the med school. At one such event, Carol Bradford, the executive vice dean for academic affairs (the chief academic officer within the University's broader health system) gave her usual after-dinner talk about the school. Thinking about this essay, I asked her, at the end of the Q&A, about AI and medicine and what she thought the last thing about health care to be digitized would be. Like me, she lauded what AI would bring to the party. But after just a few seconds of thought, she answered "The interaction with the patient."

Later, I asked both her and myself why that seemed like a correct answer, and then proceeded to answer my own question. I had thought about something else she had discussed during the talk, Michigan's approach to its selection of incoming students (something close to 8,000 applications for about 170 spots). She noted that Michigan might have slipped in the *U.S. News* rankings because its admissions process emphasized certain goals perhaps at the expense of GPA and MCAT scores. It reflected something she had previously written: that the school's curriculum would have "at its core, the expectation that our students will be change agents who transform medicine and health care," that everyone in the community "share these expectations," and that students' voices "often have spurred adjustments to the proposed course of action."[76] The abstraction of "transformation" jumped out at me, evoking what the Greeks called *telos*, meaning purposes or ends, from which the word *teleology* derives. Aristotle observed, not just in human tendencies but in nature itself, what he called "final cause," or that "for the sake of which things happen."[77] That is, nature seems to present invariable sequences of events that seemingly occur not incidentally or by chance, but for a purpose. For example, animals grow teeth in regular patterns because such arrangements of teeth are good for the purpose or end of promoting the animal's survival.[78] Transformation is teleological. Dean Bradford's vision for the school rested on agents who perceived ends and purposes, who saw a need to change from what is now to what ought to be in the future. Caring for a patient is teleological. The provider and the patient each have a subjective end or purpose, and those ends have been fused or melded. And ends and purposes are what are least capable of being digitized.

This conversation followed on my own contemporaneous experience of providing care, albeit as a lawyer. I board a horse at a stable located on a 100-acre farm in an idyllic rural, pastoral township in northern Michigan. The owner of the stable (call her Audrey) approached me, concerned about a potential noisy and congested commercial use on a nearby farm and its effect

---

[75] Gary Klein, *Seeing What Others Don't: The Remarkable Ways We Gain Insights* (London: Public Affairs, 2013) 98

[76] Carol R. Bradford, "Our Voices of Change" (2017) *Medicine at Michigan* www.medicineatmichigan.org/news-research/2017/summer/our-voices-change (accessed August 23, 2021).

[77] Andrea Falcon, "Aristotle on Causality," *Stanford Encyclopedia of Philosophy* (2019), https://plato.stanford.edu/archives/spr2019/entries/aristotle-causality/ (accessed August 23, 2021).

[78] Aristotle, *Physics Book II* (Oxford: Clarendon, 2006) at §8.

on both the quality of the neighborhood generally and on the well-being of her equine charges specifically. Audrey asked if I would help her craft comments to the township supervisory board in opposition to the use. I said "Of course." Over the course of a long career, I have been involved in far more complex transactions where far more money was at stake. But this was legal caregiving in microcosm. I will return to the story after further consideration of ends and purposes, not to disparage the analytics in my lawyering on Audrey's behalf, but to observe what a small part they constituted of the entire legal caregiving relationship.

But now it is time for a leap, not just a segue. I consider it a mistake to assess human versus machine capability merely by focusing on the increasing capabilities of machines. It strikes me as more than plausible that human thought is "shaped crucially by the peculiarities of our human bodies, by the remarkable details of the neural structure of our brains, and by the specifics of our everyday functioning in the world."[79] I want to come at intuition and insight not to criticize their System 1 flaws or to explore their conceivable replication in digitized rationality, but to consider them as features of minds existing in a physical world.[80] What is it about our psychological natures and physical embodiments that produce non-deliberative thought, the desire to achieve an end, and the will to pursue the end? How might our hardwired tendency to infer purposes and ends even in mindless processes, our innate categorizations, and our ability to break or transpose those categories inform lawyerly judgment and decision-making beyond Kahneman's ideal of perfect rationality? And what does it mean to act rather than merely to think about acting?

My thesis is that ends, purposes, and the will to act are likely as critical to effective lawyering as thought. Even beyond intuition and insight, they will remain particularly human contributions to lawyering in the digital age. This is not merely a question of empirical judgment (i.e., science) but also one of philosophy. Bear with me as I deliberate about what the focus on deliberation and System 2 thinking leaves out.

19.3.2 *Embodied* Telos

19.3.2.1 *Evolution of Ends*

Before his early death, John von Neumann, widely considered one of the smartest people who lived in the twentieth (or any) century, began to develop a theory of both biological and machine automata.[81] What I mean by an automaton is a mechanical (artificial) or biological (natural) system that undertakes tasks toward the accomplishment of a purpose.[82] A Turing machine or its physical instantiation, a digital computer, is an automaton.[83] Von Neumann's

---

[79] George Lakoff and Mark Johnson, *Philosophy in the Flesh: The Embodied Mind and Its Challenge to Western Thought* (New York: Basic Books, 1999) 3–5.

[80] Dale Purves, "What Does AI's Success Playing Complex Board Games Tell Brain Scientists?" (2019) 116 *Proceedings of the National Academy of Sciences of the United States of America* 14785 14786 ("The presumption is that AI solves problems the way humans do, ignoring the fact that the way we solve problems is largely a mystery.").

[81] He never completed the work. His colleague, Arthur Burks, compiled part of it in John von Neumann, *Theory of Self-Reproducing Automata*, Arthur Burks (ed.) (1966), https://archive.org/details/theoryofselfreproovonn_0. Part of it consisted of manuscripts of the undelivered Silliman Lectures at Yale University, published posthumously as John von Neumann, *The Computer and the Brain*, 3rd ed. (New Haven: Yale University Press, 2012). Ray Kurzweil claims that of the five key ideas that underlie the information age, Von Neumann was responsible for three and contributed significantly to the fourth. Ray Kurzweil, "Forward to the Third Edition" in Von Neumann, *The Computer and the Brain* xi–xii. Melanie Mitchell, *Complexity: A Guided Tour* (Oxford: Oxford University Press, 2009) 123–126 is also helpful.

[82] Von Neumann, *The Computer and the Brain*, n. 81 at 70–71.

[83] Arthur Burks, "Editor's Introduction" in Von Neumann, *Theory of Self-Reproducing Automata*, n. 81 at 14.

broad, uncompleted project was to develop a formal, abstract (i.e., mathematical) complete model of automata "lying in the intermediate area between logic, communication theory, and physiology."[84] It was to be to all automata what the conception of the universal Turing machine was to computers, namely, a mathematical abstraction incorporating the essential elements of universality, constructability, self-reproduction, and evolution.[85]

Von Neumann thought the basis of comparison between mechanical and biological automata lay in *code*, "a system of logical instructions that an automaton can carry out and which causes the automaton to perform some organized task."[86] In biology, these instructions might involve "nerve pulses appearing on the appropriate axons, in fact anything that induces a digital logical system, like the nervous system, to function in a reproducible, purposive manner."[87] He speculated on the translation between *complete* codes (what we would call machine code) and *short* codes (what we would now call higher level programming languages) and their biological nervous system analogs.[88] But he died even before finishing his chapter on self-reproduction and evolution.[89] Nevertheless, he recognized that extension of a theory of self-producing automata to biological systems would be its most problematic aspect.[90] For example, computers are designed to stop when there is a single error so the engineer can find it and correct it. Not so in natural organisms. Von Neumann speculated:

> The fact that natural organisms have such a radically different attitude about errors and behave so differently when an error occurs is probably connected with some other traits of natural organisms, which are entirely absent from our automata. The ability of a natural organism to survive in spite of a high incidence of error (which our artificial automata are incapable of) probably requires a very high flexibility and ability of the automaton to watch itself and reorganize itself.

This is tantalizing.[91] Have we learned anything in the intervening sixty-plus years that bears on how a natural or digital automaton might come to be able to construct its own ends, to have its own teleology? I start with the bald assertion that we have subjective inner consciousness, the source of which is still difficult to explain, and that teleology is a by-product of that consciousness.[92] The key evolutionary step toward subjective and self-referential consciousness, under neuroscientist Michael Gazzaniga's thesis, was "semiotic closure," whereby living systems evolved a "self" capable of replication by way of symbols (e.g., patterns of DNA nucleotides) existing within the system itself.[93] Thus, a computer, even one capable of ML through neural nets, is not a closed semiotic system because the ultimate codemaker is a programmer who is not part of the system.[94] As Von Neumann observed and is still true, "The use of a modern computing machine is based on the user's ability to develop and formulate the necessary

---

[84] Von Neumann, *Theory of Self-Reproducing Automata*, n. 81 at 91.
[85] Ibid. at 91–93.
[86] Von Neumann, *The Computer and the Brain*, n. 81 at 70–71.
[87] Ibid. at 71.
[88] Ibid. at 71–83.
[89] Von Neumann, *Theory of Self-Reproducing Automata*, n. 81 at 93.
[90] Ibid. at 91.
[91] Particularly so, as Von Neumann died in February 1957 and Watson and Crick first announced their proposed structure for DNA in April 1953. J. D. Watson and F. H. C. Crick, "Molecular Structure of Nucleic Acids: A Structure for Deoxyribose Nucleic Acid" (1953) 171 *Nature* 737.
[92] A portion of the discussion that follows appears in Lipshaw, n. 43.
[93] Michael S. Gazzaniga, *The Consciousness Instinct: Unraveling the Mystery of How the Brain Makes the Mind* (New York: Farrar, 2018) 181–197.
[94] Ibid. at 188.

complete codes for any given problem that the machine is supposed to solve."⁹⁵ Thus, there are no non-natural self-reproducing automata, and semiotic closure continues to be a matter of biology rather than cybernetics.

There is an even more fundamental thesis about teleology as an inherent feature of evolved organisms, of which we humans are one of the most complex examples. Meaning descends and evolves both biologically and as a matter of thought. Kahneman derides the idea of simplified hindsight narratives of cause and effect – winners writing the history – masking the randomness of events in the world. But there is a plausible thesis that winning genes also write the history. The kind of interpretation that Kahneman thinks is misguided is at the very heart of the evolution of conscious life itself. The evolutionary biologist David Haig has reflected on the relationship of the randomness of natural selection and the powerful sense of evolution having an Aristotelian final cause.⁹⁶ As he observed about himself, there was no way to know which of his father's sperm would fertilize his mother's egg. And if his father's father, an ambulance driver in the First World War, had not survived the second battle of Villers-Bretonneux, there would have been no such sperm at all. Writes Haig:

> The point of this reductio ad absurdum is that, while all evolutionary processes are, in principle, reducible to physical causes, no feasible account can be causally complete. Every story needs a place to begin which leaves many things unsaid. So too, all scientific explanations include items that, for present purposes, are accepted without explanation.⁹⁷

Haig's fundamental point is that merely to look at evolutionary processes in terms of what Aristotle would have called "efficient cause," the explanatory of how things work, seems incomplete. What final cause supplies is meaning derived from an otherwise seemingly random process.⁹⁸ That meaning comes from interpreters. Outside interpreters (i.e., scientists and technicians) may derive meaning from particular information in DNA sequences to achieve their ends. Hence, a technician who reads T rather than A in the output of an automatic sequencer may infer that a fetus will express hemoglobin S. A geneticist may use selectively neutral single-nucleotide polymorphisms to isolate a disease-causing gene.⁹⁹

But interpretation of the code may occur within the organism itself. Genetic molecules interpret the text in other molecules and replicate by interpreting themselves. Texts and interpreters represent each other reciprocally. The same molecular text can mean different things to different interpreters. Reciprocal representation occurs between the strands of DNA, between DNA and the messenger RNA that transcribes it, between a protein and the mRNA from which it is translated, and between DNA and a protein. At increasing levels of complexity, from RNA polymerases to amino acids to proteins to cells to neurons to brains, "[l]ife is made meaningful by a multitude of mindless interpreters reinterpreting the molecular metaphors of other mindless interpreters."¹⁰⁰ Consistent with Gazzaniga's description of semiotic closure, Haig notes, "Organisms are self-constructed interpreters of genetic texts in environmental context."¹⁰¹ That is, environment interacts with such organic semiotics to produce natural selection, the "complex causal dependence between past environments and patterns and

---

⁹⁵ Von Neumann, *The Computer and the Brain*, n. 81 at 71.
⁹⁶ David Haig, "Fighting the Good Cause: Meaning, Purpose, Difference, and Choice" (2014) 29 *Biology & Philosophy* 675 695.
⁹⁷ Ibid. at 676.
⁹⁸ Ibid. at 677.
⁹⁹ Ibid. at 681.
¹⁰⁰ Ibid. at 682.
¹⁰¹ Ibid.

processes within cells."¹⁰² Even the passage of semiotic information is random, affected, for example, by culling or mutation.¹⁰³

Haig's thesis is that the winning genes and the winning organisms write the history. The evolutionary process takes on what appear to be ends and purposes because, in retrospect, it is the narrative of how the organism came to be, out of all the myriad possibilities, what it is *now*. Says Haig:

> There is a causal story behind each and every mutation, each and every chiasma, each and every choice of a mating partner, each and every union of gametes, each and every catastrophe that did not happen. But this story is untellable because of incomplete information, chaotic dynamics, and computational complexity. And if it could be told, the story would be incomprehensible. One must simplify to tell a tale, giving greater salience to some items and leaving loose ends.¹⁰⁴

Nevertheless, Haig's own interpretation of after-the-fact narrative building is significantly more optimistic than Kahneman's. Final cause, the imputation of ends or purposes by way of metaphor and narrative, has explanatory oomph. We explain how we got to here because we are here by the way we got here. "Natural selection is both a metaphor and a metaphorical process of recursive representation. It is a meaningless, purposeless, physical algorithm that produces things for which meaning and purpose are useful explanatory concepts."¹⁰⁵ That random process produces, among other things, ourselves, "rational agents, with beliefs and desires, pursuing conscious goals, exchanging truthful and deceptive information, who can delight in a meaningful life."¹⁰⁶

The theoretical biologist and complex systems researcher, Stuart Kauffman, has a similar thesis about final cause. In contrast to the systems modeled by physics, the biosphere as a whole is nonergodic. It is unpredictable yet not entirely random in its evolution. Unlike systems physics studies at the atomic level, the complex molecules of organic matter are not capable of visiting all possible states. In other words, the universe has created all of the possible stable atoms, but it is has not created all of the possible proteins.¹⁰⁷ In Aristotelian terms, biological organs and organisms have purposes, that is, final cause or reasons for existence, that are not reducible to the wholly efficient causes of physics.¹⁰⁸ Hearts, for example, *"exist in the nonergodic universe above the level of atoms by virtue of their functional role in abetting the survival of living, evolving organisms having such hearts."*¹⁰⁹

The punch line here is to distinguish our particular biological form of self-reproducing automata as uniquely conscious and capable of pursing ends and purposes. Michael Gazzaniga suggests that consciousness is an instinct, adopting William James' definition: "the faculty of acting in such a way as to produce certain ends, without foresight of the ends, and without previous education in the performance."¹¹⁰ Some instincts, like "anger, shyness, affection, jealousy, envy, rivalry, sociability, and so on," we share with other animals.¹¹¹ In the case of

---

¹⁰² Ibid.
¹⁰³ Ibid. at 688.
¹⁰⁴ Ibid. at 694.
¹⁰⁵ Ibid. at 695.
¹⁰⁶ Ibid.
¹⁰⁷ Stuart A. Kauffman, *A World beyond Physics: The Emergence & Evolution of Life* (Oxford: Oxford University Press, 2019) 2–4.
¹⁰⁸ Ibid. at 11–15.
¹⁰⁹ Ibid. at 7 (emphasis in original). Like Gazzaniga, Kauffman proposes a biological explanation – "constraint closure" – for the appearance of self-generated ends or purposes in closed biological systems such as cells. Ibid. at 27–31.
¹¹⁰ Gazzaniga, n. 93 at 232, quoting William James, "What Is an Instinct?" (1887) 1 *Scribner's Magazine* 355.
¹¹¹ Ibid. at 231–236.

humans, higher-level mental states that arise in the cerebral cortex interact with instincts arising in the sub-cortex to produce complex behaviors, all of which we perceive as consciousness, and its by-product, free will.[112] Not only do we have instinctive ends, but we can propel ourselves to act on them.[113] I am willing to compare myself with AlphaGo, the apparently intuitive game-playing machine. Even if it has a *telos* that is to win games of Go, a human gave it that purpose. I am pretty sure that AlphaGo has not achieved semiotic closure in which its ends might include continued self-replication, survival, beliefs, desires, or delighting in a meaningful life.

19.3.2.2 *Telos* of System 1 Thinking

Brest and Krieger focus on how lawyers and lawyer-educators should approach what they characterize as empirical judgments; "how one ascertains facts and makes predictions about the physical and social world."[114] Indeed, much of the debate about JDM is really about cause and effect, the relationship of everything that has happened up to the moment of judgment to everything that will occur after it. We do a pretty good job of teaching lawyers how to take stock of the past and use it rationally to assess the future. We are not as good about the problem of deciding in that moment what to do next, and then mustering the will to do it. I want to move the needle further away from Kahneman's skepticism even than the more balanced approach of Brest and Krieger, one I think still unduly privileges deliberation as the check on all thing non-deliberative. Getting better at educating the practice of deciding and acting entails understanding what Kahneman's influential behavioral psychology leaves out about getting from thought to action.

The point of turning to theoretical biologists like Gazzaniga, Haig, and Kauffman is this: ends and purposes are the difference between algorithmic, physics-like, computational processes and human thought. No being whose "thought" originates in ones and zeroes (like the tools of operations research) has ends beyond those supplied by another being with ends – and humans are the only such being yet extant. Kahneman's philosophy of judgment and decision-making privileges a particular conception of cause and effect that operates more like physics than biology. He measures human judgment against a purified and mathematical computation of risk. Human beings regularly and predictably perceive causal relationships in ways not supported by the mathematical probabilities an objective observer could demonstrate. What I am suggesting here is the connection between heuristics and biases, on one hand, and ends and purposes (*telos*), on the other, in human attributions of cause-and-effect.

To be clear, I am sympathetic to Kahneman's contempt for certain attributions of cause and effect. What he calls the "illusion of understanding" is otherwise known as hindsight bias, the tendency to say after the fact that the observer "knew it all along."[115] One of Kahneman's examples is my own bête noire: the willingness of so many observers to contend after the fact that they *knew* the 2008–2009 financial crisis was the inevitable bursting of a bubble.[116] What he calls the "illusion of validity" is in turn the elevation of the illusion of understanding into an unfounded confidence in one's ability to predict the future based on the past. And underlying both illusions is "our tendency to construct and believe coherent narratives of the past."[117]

---

[112] Ibid. at 232–235.
[113] Ibid. at 235.
[114] Brest and Krieger, n. 9 at xxix.
[115] Kahneman, n. 10 at 202–203.
[116] Ibid. at 201; Jeffrey M. Lipshaw, "The Financial Crisis of 2008–2009: Capitalism Didn't Fail, but the Metaphors Got a 'C'" (2011) 95 *Minnesota Law Review* 1532 1533–1534.
[117] Kahneman, n. 10 at 218.

But that is precisely what *telos* is. May we really dismiss it as nothing but an illusion? Thinkers at least as eminent as Kahneman have been more circumspect. Kant was likely as skeptical as Kahneman about the attribution of a narrative to causation in nature or human events. Kant saw no a priori reason to assume that nature had purposes as human beings have them. Instead, he thought it was an aspect of *human* nature, as minds observing the apparent order and design of the world, to infer purposiveness in nature from the fact of human purposiveness.[118] Like Kahneman, Kant was careful to distinguish what human beings could know (as opposed merely to believe) about cause and effect. Kahneman's contempt for those who claimed previous *knowledge* of the inevitability of the financial crisis is palpable and justified. They can only say now that they knew it *would* happen because it *did* happen. They may have thought or believed it would happen; that, however, is not the same as knowledge. And the import to Kahneman is the pernicious illusion "that the world is more knowable than it is."[119] Kant had a similar view; indeed, he considered "transcendental illusion" to be the mistaking of belief engendered by pure reason for empirical knowledge.[120] Kant acknowledged the power of the causal narrative at the same time he recognized proof or disproof of such purposes in nature to be beyond the capability of human knowledge.[121]

As I said, I am sympathetic to Kahneman's view that, when it comes to after-the-fact attribution of cause and effect, the winners write the history. Indeed, it is eerily consistent with Haig's evolutionary account, even down to the example from the randomness of fertilization. Those who reflect on it (i.e., employing their System 2 thinking) recognize that "reality emerges from the interactions of many different agents and forces, including blind luck, often producing large and unpredictable outcomes."[122] They are less inclined to explain the relationship of past and future by way of grand and coherent theories. They are skeptical of any image of the "march of history" that "implies order and direction." As Kahneman points out, there was a moment in time, just before an egg was fertilized, when there was fifty-fifty chance that embryo that became Hitler would be female (and thus presumably not likely to have lived a life like Hitler's).[123] Indeed, we *should* be skeptical of such grand attributions of order and direction between the past and future.

With all due respect to Kahneman, I suspect that teleology is more than mere illusion or cognitive error. To deride the illusion of understanding and validity as sources of the mistakes is to underestimate how those same illusions, when cast more favorably as teleology, foster creativity and initiative. Teleology, including the "illusions" of System 1, stem from the fact that we are biological life-forms that have evolved to perceive ourselves as having ends and purposes. Those ends and purposes bring something to the judgment and decision-making process that a machine (at least under present technologies) cannot. So merely to dismiss the creation of narrative as a distortion or oversimplification of the complexity of cause and effect is to ignore the adaptive benefits of choosing and acting in a way that goes beyond rational thought. To dismiss the illusions of understanding and validity is to dismiss their sources – our human ability to contemplate the *telos*.

Our goal ought not to be the containment of those evolved characteristics but encouraging their positive development for the benefit of lawyerly judgment. My thesis in the remainder of

---

[118] Immanuel Kant, *Critique of Judgment*, J. H. Bernard (trans.) (Mineola: Dover Publications, 2005) 153–154.
[119] Kahneman, n. 10 at 201–202.
[120] Immanuel Kant, *Critique of Pure Reason*, Paul Guyer and Allen W. Wood (trans.) (Cambridge: Cambridge University Press, 1999) 590.
[121] Kant, n. 118.
[122] Kahneman, n. 10 at 220.
[123] Ibid. at 218–221.

this essay is that to deride System 1 in favor of deliberative System 2 is to downplay just how important ends, purpose, and action are to the moment of judgment.

19.3.3 Intuition as More Than Mere Thought

When must less rational or reflective processes supplement or replace analytics in sophisticated judgment-making? The first such process is intuition. I define it as "an experienced-based process resulting in a spontaneous tendency toward a hunch or a hypothesis."[124] Brest and Krieger provide an example par excellence for lawyers. A young lawyer is trying her first case as lead counsel. She is about to make a legally warranted hearsay objection when the more experienced second-chair lawyer tugs at her sleeve and says to let it pass. Why? It is because the more experienced lawyer knows that the subject matter of the testimony is unimportant, that judges and juries get annoyed by lawyers who object too much, and the judge was communicating her increasing irritation.[125]

This is precisely the kind of professional intuition, borne of experience and cycles of learning, we respect. Kahneman quotes Herbert Simon: "The situation has provided a cue; this cue has given the expert access to information stored in memory, and the information provides the answer. Intuition is nothing more and nothing less than recognition."[126] While the "fast and frugal" (F&F) mental processes of intuition may lend themselves to the errors produced by heuristics and biases, they do not strike me as particularly mysterious. It may be harder to understand or identify its components than for System 2 deliberation. However, that form of intuition is still about using facts to make predictions about the physical and social world. And to the extent that intuition is merely very, very fast processing of many data inputs, it does not surprise me that AI as, say, in the case of AlphaGo, makes what appear to be intuitive judgments.[127]

Much of the debate about deliberation and intuition involves the substitution of the latter for the former when it comes to empirical judgments and predictions. How likely is it that something will occur? The core of Kahneman's work with Tversky is that cognitive H&B – primarily involving the availability and representativeness of information and the "anchors" or "frames" from which that information is observed – lead to predictable illusions or errors of judgment. In particular, subjective and intuitive assessments of probability vary from the results that would be predicted by the mathematics of probability and statistics.[128] The science of H&B theory largely turns on laboratory-style experiments in which subjects are asked to assess the probability of an event. The famous example is the "Linda experiment." Subjects are told that Linda is thirty-one years old, single, outspoken, and bright. As a student, she was deeply concerned about issues of discrimination and social justice and participated in antinuclear demonstrations. Subjects were then asked about the probability that Linda possessed series of possible characteristics. In the starkest form of the experiment, the question to the subjects was which of these two alternatives was more probable: (a) Linda is a bank teller, or (b) Linda is a bank teller and active in the feminist movement. Kahneman and Tversky reported that respondents consistently chose (b) overwhelmingly over (a). This was the case even though as a matter of

---

[124] Thea Zander, Michael Öllinger, and Kirsten G Volz, "Intuition and Insight: Two Processes That Build on Each Other or Fundamentally Differ?" (2016) 7 *Frontiers in Psychology* 1395.
[125] Brest and Krieger, n. 9 at 5.
[126] Kahneman, n. 10 at 11, quoting Herbert A. Simon, "What Is an Explanation of Behavior?" (1992) 3 *Psychological Science* 150 155.
[127] Purves, n. 80 at 14785–14786.
[128] Amos Tversky and Daniel Kahneman, "Judgment under Uncertainty: Heuristics and Biases" (1974) 185 *Science* 1124.

simple logic, all of (b) must be contained in the set of (a). Logically, (b) cannot be more probable than (a). Kahneman and Tversky called this the conjunction fallacy: people judge the conjunction of two events to be more probable than the probability of one of the events alone.[129]

While there is a contending school known as F&F that engages with the H&B theorists on the nature and the cognitive value of the heuristics themselves, their debates have turned largely on the results of psychological laboratory experiments and their interpretation.[130] I am more interested in the critiques that arise from the study of intuition in real-life applications. That is the work of Gary Klein, who has studied "how people use their experience to make decisions in field settings."[131] Klein observed what he has called "naturalistic"[132] or "intuitive"[133] decision-making.[134] Klein is no mystic; his view is that "intuition is based on accumulated and compiled experiences."[135] He acknowledges the need to balance intuition with rational analysis but contends that "rational analysis can never substitute for intuition."[136] What interests me most about Klein's work is his definition of intuition as *"the way we translate our experience into action,"*[137] something I suspect gets lost in the laboratory settings from which most of the H&B versus F&F debate arises. He recounts his first research project, studying how firefighters made quick life-or-death decisions in the face of the confusion and uncertainty of a disaster. The subject of the study, the firefighters themselves described it themselves as beyond thought: "they didn't really consider anything; they just acted."[138]

---

[129] Kahneman, n. 10 at 156–159.

[130] The most prominent F&F theorist is Gerd Gigerenzer. Gerd Gigerenzer, *Risk Savvy: How to Make Good Decisions* (New York: Penguin Books, 2014); Gerd Gigerenzer, *Gut Feelings: The Intelligence of the Unconscious* (New York: Penguin Books, 2007). In *Thinking Fast and Slow*, Kahneman characterizes Gigerenzer as his and Tversky's "most persistent critic" but only refers to him briefly and dismissively in three footnotes. Kahneman, n. 10 at 449, 457, 461. The central theme of Gigerenzer's critique is that the various heuristics are not violations of probability theory but only become problematic when H&B theorist adopt a "normative theory of probability." Gerd Gigerenzer, "How to Make Cognitive Illusions Disappear: Beyond 'Heuristics and Biases'" (1991) 2 *European Review of Social Psychology* 83 86–87. For example, there is something about the rules of language rather than logic that is supporting the respondents' intuition that Linda is both a bank teller and a feminist. That is, the rules that govern the meaning of the word "and" in formal logic do not necessarily transfer to conversations that take place in a context outside of the experiment. Gigerenzer, *Gut Feelings* at 93–99. Gigerenzer's other criticism of the H&B experiments lies in the difference between risk and uncertainty. Risk is calculable; uncertainty is not; heuristics can be helpful when the issue is one of the latter. Gigerenzer, *Risk Savvy* at 32–42. For a thorough review of the debate between the H&B and F&F schools, see Mark Kelman, *The Heuristics Debate* (Oxford: Oxford University Press, 2011).

[131] Gary Klein, *Sources of Power: How People Make Decisions* (Cambridge, MA: MIT Press 1998) 1. Brest and Krieger cite Klein's work extensively, conceding ultimately that "developing the systematic habits of thought inherent in deliberative decision making improves subsequent problem solving done at the intuitive end of the spectrum, or at least facilitates reflective monitoring of intuitive judgments." Brest and Krieger, n. 9 at 16–17, 28, 298–299, 632.

[132] Klein, n. 131 at 1.

[133] Gary Klein, *The Power of Intuition: How to Use Your Gut Feelings to Make Better Decision at Work* (New York: Currency, 2003) xiv–xv.

[134] In contrast to his dismissive treatment of Gigerenzer, Kahneman devoted an entire and respectful chapter in *Thinking Fast and Slow* to his differences with Klein, his "most satisfying and productive adversarial collaboration." Kahneman, n. 10 at 234–244. In 2009, Kahneman and Klein coauthored a remarkable article about their contending views. Their conclusion reflects a truth often lost in the vehemence of some academic debates, which is that reality is complex, and no particular model has the final word on something as nuanced as professional expertise. Kahneman, the HB spokesman, conceded that "a psychology of judgment and decision making that ignores intuitive skill is seriously blinkered"; Klein, the NDM spokesman, conceded that "a psychology of professional judgment that neglects predictable errors cannot be adequate." Daniel Kahneman and Gary Klein, "Conditions for Intuitive Expertise: A Failure to Disagree" (2009) 64 *American Psychology* 515 525; Klein, n. 133 at 7.

[135] Klein, n. 133 at 5.

[136] Ibid.

[137] Ibid. at xiv (italics in original).

[138] Ibid. at xiii.

On the question of lawyerly intuition in the digital age, part of being a great diagnostician is recognizing the symptoms of a particular disease, whether it be medical, legal, technological, or social. Nobody is suggesting that ML and the processing of big data will be anything less than transformational in identifying those patterns.[139] At the same time, nobody can be seriously suggesting that lawyers are to operate without using intuition, or that algorithms could seriously replace intuition even as to empirical matters of prediction or optimization. The key is to understand what kind of empirical judgment one is making, and to avoid all of the mistakes, whether the law of small numbers, the illusion of certainty, or the confusion of risk and uncertainty, and to use algorithms when it is appropriate to do so.[140] We will always have to make some decisions where there is insufficient data to avoid the law of small numbers or where the judgment truly is one of uncertainty rather than risk. Klein's assessments of intuitive decision-making arose out of field observations rather than laboratory tests of the effect of heuristics. Like the circumstances he observed, the setting for many lawyerly decisions involve "time pressure, high stakes, experienced decision makers, inadequate information ... ill-defined goals, poorly defined procedures, cue learning, context ... dynamic conditions, and team coordination."[141]

Nevertheless, the paradox of the judgment and decision-making debate is the infinite regress that requires an ultimate default to intuition rather than analytics. Brest and Krieger do not deny the importance of intuition and insight; they only contend that deliberation needs to be a check on it. But when the stuff hits the fan (so to speak) and the decider has to decide whether the conclusion just reached is an appropriate use of data and intuition or instead another instance of predictive error, the final call is something more approaching intuition than deliberation. Indeed, Kahneman himself despaired of his own ability to distinguish analytics and intuition when considering his own decisions. The best he could offer was good, if ultimately circular, advice. When the lonely actor feels the urge to act, test that urge against the advice of water cooler gossips and trusted critics.[142] When it comes to filtering out the noisy data that may cause judgment to be unreliable, look to algorithms whenever practical, except when not practical.[143] Klein's implicit conclusion about the regress is consistent with mine: even researchers who are skeptical about intuition rely on it themselves both in mind and body.[144] And the end of the regress in practice is not analysis but the translation of experience into action through intuitive judgment.[145]

19.3.4 Insight

19.3.4.1 Difference between Intuition and Insight

Lawyers who want to make judgments and predictions about the relationship of data, whether evidence or case law, ignore the tools described in Section 19.2 at their risk. It is deliberate

---

[139] As applied to diagnostics in medicine, I. Kononenko, "Machine Learning for Medical Diagnosis: History, State of the Art and Perspective" (2001) 23 *Artificial Intelligence in Medicine* 89; Yoo, n. 5.

[140] Ashley, n. 50 at 3 (predicting "a new kind of legal app, one that enables cognitive computing, a kind of collaborative activity between humans and computers in which each performs the kinds of intelligent activities that they can do best").

[141] Klein, n. 131 at 4.

[142] Kahneman, n. 10 at 417–418.

[143] Daniel Kahneman, Andrew M. Rosenfeld, Linnea Gandhi, and Tom Blaser, "Noise: How to Overcome the High, Hidden Cost of Inconsistent Decision Making" (2016) *Harvard Business Review* 39.

[144] Klein, n. 133 at 6–7.

[145] Ibid. at 20–21.

System 2 thinking par excellence. But nobody can seriously suggest that intuitive System 1 lawyering judgment is not and will not continue to be part of the lawyer's toolkit. Indeed, my reaction is that the move from algorithmic to seat-of-the-pants *predictive* or *empirical* judgments is not particularly interesting, at least when it comes to testing the bounds of machine and human contributions to the exercise of practical wisdom in the professional context. If intuition is, per Gary Klein, the result of accumulated and compiled experiences, it sounds like something ML *might* replicate. I am more than willing to categorize intuition as another means, albeit less amenable to scientific reconstruction, of making empirical predictions.

That still does not address setting the problem into a mode of solution. Brest and Krieger provide another apt example in lawyering. A small manufacturer in Southern California terminates all of its employees without prior notice in order to move its operation to Vietnam to take advantage of lower labor costs. The federal WARN Act does not apply to the layoffs, and the codified California "at-will" employment doctrine seemingly bars any relief in the form of severance pay. A commercial lawyer who volunteers pro bono for a legal services agency looks at the Labor Code provision permitting termination at will on "notice" to the other party. The lawyer knows that, under the Uniform Commercial Code, notice of termination of a continuing relationship would have to be "reasonable." Why isn't it the same for an employment contract?[146]

Consistent with Klein, Kahneman, and Herbert Simon, I view intuition "as tacit hunches or feelings that come to mind with little conscious awareness of processing."[147] What is important to me is that intuition is best thought of as a substitute for what we can know through other means of empiricism. Per Richard Brock, '[t]he experience of intuition, an explicit feeling of knowledge that is not fully articulable, bridges the boundary between the tacit and the explicit."[148] Insight, per Brock's summary of the literature, is different even if "it is related to, and often confused with intuition."[149] Insight is variously described as "the process by which a problem solver suddenly moves from a state of not knowing how to solve a problem to a state of knowing how to solve it";[150] as "pure Eureka events," insights in which the emergence of the new idea is "extremely fast," an existing idea is replaced by a new model and "the process is not explainable via normal reasoning processes";[151] or, in Brock's own summary, "an explicit awareness of novel relations between concepts that arrives with apparent suddenness and little conscious awareness of processing."[152]

I thus want to distinguish the non-deliberative processes of intuition and insight. While a machine might well functionally replace intuition as a matter of bringing past experience to bear on a problem, the digital replication of insight – the decision which algorithm to apply to the problem – will be a far tougher nut.[153]

---

[146] Brest and Krieger, n. 9 at 68–69.
[147] Richard Brock, "Intuition and Insight: Two Concepts That Illuminate the Tacit in Science Education" (2015) 51 *Studies in Science Education* 127 128.
[148] Ibid. at 131.
[149] Ibid. at 132.
[150] Ibid., quoting R. E. Mayer, "The Search for Insight: Grappling with Gestalt Psychology's Unanswered Questions" in Robert J. Sternberg and Janet E. Davidson (eds.), *The Nature of Insight* (Cambridge, MA: MIT Press, 1995) 3–32.
[151] Brock, n. 147 at 133, quoting J. J. Clement, *Creative Model Construction in Scientists and Students: The Role of Imagery, Analogy, and Mental Stimulation* (New York: Springer, 2008) 103–104.
[152] Ibid.
[153] For a doctrinal application of the difference between a machine's mere functional replication of human activity and more fundamental issues in human cognition, see Mala Chatterjee and Jeanne C. Fromer, "Minds, Machines, and the Law: The Case of Volition in Copyright Law" (2019) 119 *Columbia Law Review* 1886.

19.3.4.2 *Non-deliberation as Insight or Inspiration*

Consider the Brest and Krieger hypothetical in which it occurs to the lawyer to apply a concept from one area of the law to another. The noted philosopher of law, Susan Haack, described the literature on these lawyering "aha moments" as "luxuriant, to say the least – a steamy, tangled jungle in which it would be easy to get hopelessly lost."[154] I do not believe that insight derives from magic or divine gifts. Yet the infinite regress of problem setting, of deciding what you need to accomplish (your end or purpose) and only then selecting the tool or the algorithm or the app that is suitable, is among the most irreducible mysteries I have ever pondered.[155] The best I can do here is refer to others who have also confronted the mystery.

Categories and the evolution of meaning. Cognitive scientists George Lakoff, Mark Johnson, Gilles Fauconnier, and Mark Turner argue persuasively that much (if not all) of thought derives from "conceptual embodiment" – "[t]he idea that the properties of certain categories are a consequence of the nature of human biological capacities and of the experience of functioning in a physical and social environment."[156] Dean Bradford's use of the word "transformation" in health care is a prime example of the kind of conceptualization – a journey from here to there – Lakoff might say is a direct link from our physical being in the world to how our thoughts get shaped.

In his seminal work on categories, Lakoff rejected the metaphor of "mind as computer," merely undertaking disembodied and abstract symbol manipulation, and in which categories exist merely as the means of understanding the relationship of symbols independent of human experience.[157] Lakoff insisted instead that "human categorization is essentially a matter of both human experience and imagination – of perception, motor activity, and culture on the one hand, and of metaphor, metonymy, and mental imagery on the other."[158] As extended by Fauconnier and Turner, the theory holds that insight and imagination arise not from computation-like mental processes but from human conceptual systems originated in bodily experience, the ability to juxtapose categories, to break the accepted schema, or to transfer ideas from one domain to another[159] Their particular contribution was the concept of double-scope blending, in which we create a new conceptual frame that is different from its influences, not corresponding to either of them, but instead creating an entirely new meaning.[160] Indeed, they claimed that double-scope blending "is the mental capacity that makes human beings human, the one that separates them, and phylogenetically did separate them, from other species and

---

[154] Susan Haack, "On Logic in the Law: 'Something, but Not All'" (2007) 20 *Ratio Juris* 1 21.

[155] This capability is sometimes referred to as abductive reasoning. Jeffrey M. Lipshaw, *Beyond Legal Reasoning: A Critique of Pure Lawyering* (London: Routledge 2017) 34–40.

[156] George Lakoff, *Women, Fire, and Dangerous Things: What Categories Reveal about the Mind* (Chicago: The University of Chicago Press, 1987) 8, 338–343. Lakoff and his collaborator, Mark Johnson, assert that all thought derives from metaphors that our brains developed from the fact of their being embodied in human beings. Lakoff and Johnson, n. 79 at 3–5. Like Steven Pinker, I find their insights to be useful and persuasive without having to adopt the extreme view that any concept generated by thought derives from a metaphor of embodied physical experience. Steven Pinker, *The Stuff of Thought: Language as a Window into Human Nature* (New York: Penguin Books, 2007) 235-78. I have previously summarized this view. Lipshaw, n. 116.

[157] Lakoff, n. 156 at 8, 338–343.

[158] Ibid. at 8.

[159] Ibid. at xiv–xv; Mark Turner, *Cognitive Dimensions of Social Science: The Way We Think about Politics, Economics, Law, and Society* (Oxford: Oxford University Press, 2001).

[160] Turner, n. 159 at 11. For a detailed discussion, including examples, see Jeffrey M. Lipshaw, "The Venn Diagram of Business Lawyering Judgments: Toward a Theory of Practical Metadisciplinarity" (2011) 41 *Seton Hall Law Review* 1 58–63.

from earlier anatomically modern human beings."[161] Whether it also separates human from AI is probably an open question, although Turner's informed speculation is (a) that human meaning "descends" analogous to physical evolution, in the sense of "some meanings interact, in environments, to produce new meanings that inherit some of their aspects from the prior meanings but that have emergent meaning of their own that not contained in the prior meanings,"[162] and (b) that "partial" models of meaning, as in AI, "have problems 'scaling up' to include the 'rest' of the system."[163]

This latter point is evocative of Haig, Kauffman, and Gazzaniga. Human meaning is the product of a complex adaptive system, one that "cannot be partitioned into entirely separate modules, or into rudiments plus overlays."[164] Just as the biological semiotic closed system is its own interpreter and the creator of its own ends and purposes, human insight results from a cognitive system that interprets – that is, creates emergent meaning – and perceives its own ends and purposes. On the other hand, as Lakoff observed, the symbols being processed within a computational (i.e., AI) mind are meaningless unless someone or something outside the system supplies the basis for making those symbols represent a reality external to the system.[165] Moreover, algorithmic systems work by way of discrete rules that predictably process particular inputs into particular outputs. Human conceptual systems, like thought and language, do not work the same way. When we think or use language, we extend categories, engage in polysemy, or use idioms that are *motivated*. That is, those phenomena are neither arbitrary (i.e., simply random) nor are they necessarily predictable. And algorithmic systems have (and are likely to continue to have) a problem generally in replicating that kind of motivation.[166] Even in mathematics, that most formal and logical of disciplines, insights or breakthroughs are an aspect of the embodied human mind. Machine thinking is a simulation of human thinking. As the mathematician William Byers observed, "An algorithm cannot generate creativity. In fact [sic] the reverse is true – creativity is what produces algorithms."[167] In short, insight or inspiration, conceived of as the descent of unpredictable yet non-random, emergent, and heretofore unexpressed meaning, is still uniquely human.

Problem solving. Perhaps the iconic observer of the distinction between professionals' use of technology and setting the problem was Donald Schön.[168] Schön assessed the rise in the twentieth century of Technical Rationality, under which professional activity came to mean "instrumental problem solving made rigorous by the application of scientific theory and technique."[169] He saw the essential issue in Technical Rationality not as *problem solving* but *problem setting*. Thus, professional judgment mediates between, on one hand, the foundation of stable disciplines "grounded in systematic, fundamental knowledge, of which scientific knowledge is the prototype"[170] and, on the other, evoking Susan Haack's metaphor, the indeterminacy of the "swampy lowland where situations are confusing 'messes' incapable of technical

---

[161] Turner, n. 159 at 52.
[162] Ibid. at 140.
[163] Ibid. at 143.
[164] Ibid.
[165] Lakoff, n. 156 at 348–349.
[166] Ibid. at 346–348.
[167] William Byers, *Deep Thinking: What Mathematics Can Teach Us about the Mind* (Hackensack: World Scientific, 2015) ix–x.
[168] Donald A. Schön, *The Reflective Practitioner: How Professionals Think in Action* (New York: Basic Books, 1984).
[169] Ibid. at 21.
[170] Ibid. at 23.

solution."[171] How professionals mediated between the problems and the tools to solve them was "reflection-in-action": "the 'art' by which practitioners sometimes deal well with situations of uncertainty, instability, uniqueness, and value conflict."[172]

Gary Klein's field study is further evidence of the swamp of theory about insight. The stories he collected of discovery and invention persuaded him that the experience of insight defies easy reduction to theory and that "[t]he best we can do ... is to move the posts forward."[173] For example, the iconic "aha" moment might not be as sudden as others suggest. In his case studies, a slight majority of insights were sudden, but the rest were gradual.[174] Ultimately, he proposed an insight model that was a matrix of motivation, trigger, activity, and outcome. The reasons for wanting discovery or invention might arise from the observation of inconsistencies or contradictions, curiosity about connections or coincidence, or a desperate need to solve a problem. The result might be to reset the "anchors" of one's beliefs about the situation – either to reimagine the circumstances to eliminate the contradictions, to articulate a new foundation for belief, or to reject the basis of existing beliefs.[175]

At the far end of the thinking continuum furthest from computation is a concept called "flow," an experience in which actors in sports, games, occupations, rituals, and the arts have the "sense of having stepped out of the routines of everyday life into a different reality, clear goals every step of the way, immediate feedback, effortless attention, action and awareness merged, balanced between skill and challenge, time distortion, and spontaneity."[176] I confess I am a latecomer to the scholarly treatment of flow. When I first heard of it, I thought it was some brand of New Age mysticism. In fact, it is a serious treatment of a difficult subject – creative inspiration – taken seriously by serious people. The seminal theorist of flow is Mihaly Csikszentmihalyi, the former head of the department of psychology at the University of Chicago, whose scholarly and popular output on the subject is prodigious.[177] Among the serious people taking flow seriously are Kahneman himself. According to Kahneman, engaging in System 2 deliberation is more difficult than System 1 thinking, because the former requires the application of mental work and self-control. Flow, he acknowledges, is a state of effortless concentration on the task at hand.[178] And, as I now realize, I take it seriously because I experience it. On a regular basis, ideas pop into my head during the daily routine in which I walk the dog on the same circuit. I sit down at the computer to write, intending only to spend a few minutes, but look up and realize I have been at it for several hours. The point is the embodied subjective physicality of the endeavor, not that it is merely the product of disembodied thought.

Brest and Krieger devote an entire chapter, entitled "Generating Alternatives: Creativity in Legal and Policy Problem Solving" to what they call "divergent thinking" and what I would call

---

[171] Ibid. at 42.
[172] Ibid. at 50.
[173] Klein, n. 75 at 107.
[174] Ibid. at 92–93.
[175] Ibid. at 101–108.
[176] Doyle, n. 10 at 1.
[177] Mihaly Csikszentmihalyi, *Flow: The Psychology of Optimal Experience* (New York: Harper, 2008); Mihaly Csikszentmihalyi, *Creativity: Flow and the Psychology of Discovery and Invention* (New York: Harper, 2013).
[178] Kahneman, n. 10 at 40–41. Others include Brest and Krieger, n. 9 at 73, 79, and my friend and colleague Jessica Silbey in her work on the relationship of "eureka moments" to the law of intellectual property. Jessica Silbey, *The Eureka Myth: Creators, Innovators, and Everyday Intellectual Property* (Stanford: Stanford University Press, 2014) 35–36, 65–66.

insight.[179] As far as I can tell, however, they never really distinguish between, on one hand, intuition as a fast and frugal means of making an empirical or predictive judgment (Kahneman's bête noire) and, on the other, insight as the source of a new or different way of seeing the problem. For example, in the section headed "The Roles of Intuition and Analysis in Empirical Judgment," they cite two examples of unconscious judgment, one about assessing whether it is safe to cross a street with a car in the distance, and one about Kekulé's inspiration in a dream about the structure of benzene.[180]

I do not want to overstate the dichotomy. We have already seen the conception of intuition as a direct translation of experience into action without the intermediation of deliberate thought. Moreover, there are unconscious judgments, particularly creative ones, with aspects of both empirical intuition and inspiration. Mihaly Csikszentmihalyi's influential "system" model of creation (cited by Brest and Krieger)[181] demands, in addition to the creative insights of the individual creator, a domain of symbolic rules and procedures in which the creator works, and a field of other individuals who are the gatekeepers of the domain.[182] Nevertheless, there is research distinguishing intuition from insight. And tarring insight with the predictable errors one might find with intuitive empirical judgments is, in my view, a mistake.

19.3.5 Action and Will

Everything so far has to do with thought and how it might precede a decision or even action. Here I want to consider action itself. It is hard to argue with the proposition in Brest and Krieger that "developing the systematic habits of thought inherent in deliberative decision making improves subsequent problem solving done at the intuitive end of the spectrum, or at least facilitates reflective monitoring of intuition."[183] I am not in the least critical of their decision to conclude the volume on that note.[184] Nor do I think even they believe such deliberation ends the story of what lawyers bring to the party.[185] But *doing* differs from *thinking*, whether System 1 or 2. There needs to be an end not only to reflection, but an end to deciding itself in favor of acting on the decision.

Brest and Krieger offered not just tools for developing professional expertise in problem solving and decision-making, but an academic foundation for doing so. I want to focus on the link between academic theory in a discipline like lawyering and its practice in the field. On that very linkage in psychotherapy, Steven Cooper has written of the psychotherapist's "return of the repressed positivistic," the desire (conscious or not) to impose the science of the therapist's professional discipline on the patient's problem, whether or not that imposition is justified.[186] I have come to believe that the privileging (by Brest and Krieger, Kahneman, and others) of

---

[179] Brest and Krieger, n. 9 at 61–90. They discuss "divergent thinking" at 66–67, 74–76. They cite the work of Fauconnier and Turner on conceptual blending at 73.
[180] Ibid. at 119–120.
[181] Ibid. at 73, 79.
[182] Csikszentmihalyi, *Creativity*, n. 177 at 27–28; Brest and Krieger, n. 9 at 77–80.
[183] Brest and Krieger, n. 9 at 632.
[184] Ibid. at 637. ("The overarching hypothesis of this book is that academic study can lay the foundation for developing expertise in problem solving, decision making, and professional judgment on the job.").
[185] Elsewhere, Dean Brest wrote: "Solutions are often constrained or facilitated by the law, but finding the best solution – a solution that addresses all of the client's concerns – usually requires more than technical legal skill." Paul Brest, "Skeptical Thoughts: Integrating Problem-Solving into Legal Curriculum Faces Uphill Climb" (Summer 2000) *Dispute Resolution Magazine* 20 22.
[186] I have previously explored this topic in Lipshaw, n. 155 at 120–123 and Jeffrey M. Lipshaw, "What's Going On?: The Psychoanalysis Metaphor for Educating Lawyer-Counselors" (2013) 45 *Connecticut Law Review* 1355 1370–1381.

unadorned rationality, culminating in algorithmic thinking and embodied in AI, is the UN-*repressed* positivistic. What I mean is that such thinking insufficiently distinguishes between professional tools and their users, and the users' *choice* to use those particular tools in pursuit of an end.

I am hardly the originator of this critique. The philosophical existentialists were engaged in a similar reaction to the unadorned and exquisite rationality of science and technology long before I was born. Several of their insights help splash some cold water on the infatuation with AI-lawyering. If you were inclined to skip what follows, a pithy expression of that philosophy might be the epigraph to this essay or the adage, attributed to Woody Allen, that either eighty or ninety percent of either life or success is showing up.[187] The full quote, from Allen's co-writer, Marshall Brickman, is even more on point: "'Showing up is 80 percent of life.' Sometimes it's easier to hide home in bed. I've done both."[188]

I will hardly do justice to Heidegger, Sartre, and others, but here is the capsule.[189] The existentialists were dissatisfied with how positive and objective science came to terms with what was essential to a human being. The difference between tools (say, a saw) and me (a human) is that tools "are defined by the social practices in which they are employed, and their properties are established in relation to the norms of those practices." The difference between objects of "perpetual contemplation or scientific investigation" (say, a planet) and me (a human) is that the objects "are defined by the norms governing perceptual givenness or scientific theory-construction." The existentialist argument was that, unlike a saw or a planet, "[w]ho I am depends on what I make of my 'properties.'" I am more than my *facticity*, the physical or social properties a third person could observe about me. What makes me "me" is that I am capable of having an attitude about my own facticity, that I am engaged practically in the world, that I am an "agent ... oriented by the task at hand as something to be brought about through [my] own will or agency." The existentialists called this personal and subjective perspective "transcendence." And facticity and transcendence, even though they are an aspect of the same being, me, cannot be reduced to each other. They are complementary qualities of existence. As to facticity, I exist as matter of molecules built into proteins and organs. As to transcendence, I can make a difference in the facts of the world in which I exist. But transcendence is not "a function of anonymous forces (third-person or logical possibility) but a function of [my] *choice* and *decision*."

The will to act in pursuit of one's own subjective perception of ends and purposes is the key difference between a human lawyer and the most developed AI. The philosopher Steven Crowell notes Charles Taylor's phrase – humans "are 'self-interpreting' animals ... where the interpretation is constitutive of the interpreter."[190] Evolution, cybernetics, and philosophy converge on the same point. Human lawyers are self-reproducing automata. They have evolved through semiotic closure into beings capable of perceiving ends and purposes and having a will to act that cannot be reduced to mere third-party scientific explanation. They have intuition and insight, capabilities that resist scientific reduction because they seem to arise from both objective facticity and subjective transcendence. My conclusion is Heideggerian. He observed of cabinet-makers the following:

---

[187] William Safire, "On Language: The Elision Fields," *New York Times Magazine* (August 13, 1989).

[188] Susan Braudy, "He's Woody Allen's 1-1-Silent Partner," *New York Times* (August 21, 1977) at 83.

[189] I am relying on this excellent summary: Steven Crowell, "Existentialism," *Stanford Encyclopedia of Philosophy* (Winter 2007) https://plato.stanford.edu/archives/win2017/entries/existentialism/. The quoted material in this paragraph is from that unpaginated text. Brackets indicate my modifications and all emphases shown are in the original.

[190] Crowell, n. 189.

> His learning is not mere practice, to gain facility in the use of tools .... If he is to become a true cabinetmaker, he makes himself answer and respond above all to the different kinds of wood and to the shapes slumbering within wood ..... In fact, this relatedness to wood is what maintains the whole craft. Without that relatedness, the craft will never be anything but empty busywork, any occupation with it will be determined exclusively by business concerns.[191]

The programmer, not the machine, is still the cabinetmaker in the metaphor. In supervised learning, the programmer decides whether the training data supports the predictive algorithms. Even in unsupervised learning, if the machine responds to shapes slumbering in the data, it is because the programmer gave it the tools, the algorithms defining what constitutes a pattern, to do so.

I am not closing off the possibility that a Von Neumann of the future will successfully build a self-reproducing automaton capable of insight and action. If Sartre said of it as he did of a human being "condemned to be free: condemned because he did not create himself, yet nonetheless free, because once cast into the world, he is responsible for everything he does,"[192] it might as well be the cabinetmaker and not merely the tool. But that is still the stuff of science fiction or fantasy.

19.3.6 *Lawyering in the Face of Irreconcilable Complementarities*

The overarching meta-theme for those of us who lawyer (or educate lawyers) in the digital age is not to be seduced by the telic allure of Technical Rationality. The nature of *telos* is the inclination to seek order and coherence, ends and purposes perhaps when there are none. Explanations are troubling when they fail to cohere, whether they are inconsistencies in descriptive science (say, as between relativity and quantum mechanics) or normative attribution of blame (say, a lawyer's theory of the case that does not hang together). Not surprisingly, Karl Llewellyn's wisdom to new law students eighty years ago was that the work of a lawyer or judge in determining the law proceeds on the assumption "that all the cases everywhere can stand together. It is unquestionably the assumption you must make, at first. If they can be brought together, you must bring them."[193] Lawyering tools include rules and the logic it takes to apply them to circumstances. Those are fair game for sophisticated algorithmic analytics.

Kahneman was correct in observing the human desire for causal coherence; his primary concern was for the frequency with which humans appear to explain empirical events coherently but mistakenly. My sense is that he has merely substituted one form of coherent narrative for another. Granted, however, the substitution is warranted when the tasks at hand are predictions and risk assessments amenable to applications of mathematical models. When lawyers deal in those issues, they should turn to the tools set out in Brest and Krieger. But when facing uncertainty rather than mere risk, lawyers need to be circumspect in privileging deliberation (and its extreme in algorithms) over less deliberative aspects of thought, decision, and action. Some aspects of problem solving simply do not (and will never) cohere. When we think about reconciling what algorithmic and human lawyers bring to the party in the digital age, humans have it all over computers in dealing with those.

---

[191] Martin Heidegger, *What Is Called Thinking*, Fred D. Wieck and J. Glenn Gray (trans.) (New York: HarperCollins, 1963) 14.
[192] Jean-Paul Sartre, *Existentialism Is a Humanism*, Carol Macomber (trans.) (New Haven: Yale University Press, 1997) 29.
[193] K. N. Llewellyn, *The Bramble Bush: On Our Law and Its Study* (New Orleans: Quid Pro, 2012) 50.

Some things, like infinite regresses, complementarities, and asymptotic limits, by their very nature, will never hang together, or never be resolved conclusively. That is a hard pill to swallow for lawyerly minds committed to rationality. Fundamental non-coherence, indeed failure, of explanation is what the mathematician William Byers calls the blind spot, "things that are real but which the mind cannot grasp and thus cannot capture through words, symbols or equations."[194] The neuroscientist Michael Gazzaniga speculates that such a fundamental non-coherence is at the heart of our subjective consciousness in an objective world. While we still do not understand how the brain's neurons create our sense of personal consciousness, the answer is *not* going to lie in more and more granular reduction of biological processes to the deterministic assumptions of classical or quantum physics. Rather, the idea that needs to be borrowed from quantum physics is complementarity: some things "have complementary properties that cannot be measured, and thus known, at the same time."[195]

Non-coherence shows up in the struggles to explain intuition and insight. But the non-coherence most relevant to lawyering in the digital age has to do with things like showing up. The existentialists were on to something; nothing explains the transition from deliberating about a problem, even deciding what to do about the problem, and moving from mere subjective thought to doing in the physical world. When Audrey wanted me to go to the meeting, I was condemned to be free. I could (and did) come up with a dozen reasons why I was not really needed. Even so, I still went. That was more than mere decision; it was a commitment to action.

I am open to the possibility that someday, somewhere, somebody will proffer a reductive explanation of that freedom, but I am skeptical that either System 2 deliberation or AI will resolve it. In the meantime, I am open to suggestions about how to incorporate both non-coherence and the commitment to action into the law school curriculum. Some people are thinking about it. A prime example is the University of Miami's LawWithoutWalls, led by Professor Michele DeStefano.[196] One of Stuart Kauffman's interesting observations is the difference between the "adjacent possible" in physics, on one hand, and biology and, by extension, complex systems like economies, on the other. As to the models of the former type, consider chess or AlphaGo. There the adjacents possible – the possible next configurations of the board – are not only predictable but finite (albeit immense in number). As to the latter type, there are no laws by which anyone can deduce or "prestate" the adjacents possible – that is, new uses and new functions for biological characteristics or technological developments.[197] Those systems "explode in diversity," with each new species in biology or each new innovation in goods in service creating the possibility of even more creation.[198] Professor DeStefano's similar point for lawyering is that the world of evermore complex *becoming* is the one that business clients (at the very least) face every day.[199] The value of her insight is to cross the disjunction between mere thought and action: "What [business clients] really need, whether they want their lawyers to actually create innovations or not, is for their lawyers to learn *how* to innovate."[200] The problem,

---

[194] William Byers, *The Blind Spot: Science and the Crisis of Uncertainty* (Princeton: Princeton University Press, 2011) 1.
[195] Gazzaniga, n. 93 at 171.
[196] LawWithoutWalls, http://lawwithoutwalls.org (accessed March 10, 2020).
[197] Kauffman, n. 107 at 115–139.
[198] Ibid. at 106–107.
[199] Michele DeStefano, "Innovation: A New Key Discipline for Lawyers and Legal Education" in Michele DeStefano and Guenther Dobrauz (eds.), *New Suits: Appetite for Disruption in the Legal World* (Bern: Stampfli Verlag, 2018) 90. Professor DeStefano offers some practical suggestions for leaps in lawyering to the discontinuous adjacent possible in Michele DeStefano, *Legal Upheaval: A Guide to Creativity, Collaboration, and Innovation in Law* (Washington, DC: American Bar Association, 2018) 98–100.
[200] Ibid.

Professor DeStefano suggests, is that lawyers, by inclination and training, have trouble leaping from the possible to the adjacent possible in dealing with that complex *becoming*.[201]

I would only amend that slightly. Kauffman's core thesis is that the adjacents possible of physics (and all computational intelligence) are defined by the rules that permit the transformation of one state into another. They are thus capable of being "prestated" or predicted. But the adjacents possible of innovation are not so capable of prestatement or prediction.[202] For the digital age, it is not that lawyering by deliberation or algorithm will fail to see *any* adjacent possible. It *will* predict the predictable. But dealing with uncertainty, disruption, and non-coherence – the non-algorithmic adjacents possible – is likely to be the province of the human lawyer armed with intuition, insight, and the will to translate thought into action.

19.3.7 *Rest of the Caregiving Story (a Microcosm of Lawyering)*

How did the aspects of lawyering beyond deliberation affect my work on Audrey's problem? I used a digital tool. In less than ten minutes on Westlaw, (a) I was able to see the series of "if-then" propositions that established the impermissibility of the use (the area was zoned agricultural and the proposed use was not listed as one permitted as of right or one of the limited uses available by special approval of the planning commission), and (b) I found several Michigan Court of Appeals cases barring precisely that commercial use under identical zoning ordinances in other townships. Indeed, I found them in the Michigan state and federal cases database by entering only three search terms: "agricultural," "zoning," and the name of the particular objectionable use at issue. By some accounts, AI technology like ROSS can already use ML in the process of converting a natural language narrative into an assessment of the legal outcome.[203]

But what else was involved? First, there was some element of insight. Audrey was under the impression that her task was to oppose a special approval of the commercial use. It quickly became clear to me that her legal position was far stronger than that; one of the cases stood for the proposition that the township had no authority even to grant an approval because the use was not on the list. Second, intuition (rightly or wrongly) intervened. The neighbor had already invested a significant amount of money in construction. Would that affect the outcome, given that the logic of the law seemed to require the forfeiture of the investment? I was aware from experience in other areas that courts rarely favor forfeitures. I am not a land use lawyer, but one of my best friends is. I called him to ask and he responded that the issue of wasted money ought not to be a factor in a township's or a court's treatment of the impermissible use. Finally, there was action. I helped craft comments that Audrey would be comfortable reciting in public (her style of speaking not mine), attended the meeting to provide her moral support, discussed a united effort with a number of the neighbors, schmoozed township officials before the meeting, wrote a letter on behalf of the neighbors to the planning commission, calmed Audrey when developments agitated her, assessed the competencies of and interviewed several local lawyers who would take over the work when I left at the end of the summer, and anticipated possible next moves (including responding to any proposed change to the zoning).

To their credit, Brest and Krieger capture much of what I experienced in this vignette. A problem occurs when "the world we would like varies from the world as it is."[204] And solving

---

[201] Ibid. at 100.
[202] Kauffman, n. 107 at 133–134.
[203] Steve Lohr, "A.I. Is Doing Legal Work. But It Won't Replace Lawyers, Yet," *New York Times* (March 20, 2017), www.nytimes.com/2017/03/19/technology/lawyers-artificial-intelligence.html.
[204] Brest and Krieger, n. 9 at 8.

the problem has a metaphoric physicality: "to navigate through the problem space – through the virtual area between the actual or potential unsatisfactory space and the desired state."[205] Here is what the privileging of deliberation misses, however. Brest and Krieger acknowledge the role of lawyerly intuition. They grapple with the mysterious aspect of insight. Still, they do not capture the fullest extent to which effective lawyering is more than just an exercise in analytic thought; considering the adjacents possible and then doing something about them requires every mental and physical tool we have at our disposal.

When I contemplated Audrey's ends and purposes as a matter of facticity, they became my ends and purposes as a matter of transcendence. It was not enough merely to think about the problem. Rather, I became the agent, through my choice and my decision, of the change from the world as it was to the one it should be, and the captain, as it were, in the navigation of the problem space. Would that I could only have been a dispassionate third-party observer of the problem, dispensing wise counsel and moving on to other concerns. No, as Sartre noted, I was condemned to be free, cast into the world, and responsible. It made me effective. It also kept me up at night; I attribute that to the existential despair that I might *not* be effective. And, as Sartre also noted, '[D]espair means that we must limit ourselves to reckoning with only those things that depend on our will, or on the set of probabilities that enable action."[206] The despair fuels something – call it passion, persistence, or compulsiveness – that, even if not borne of noble causes, is still an aspect of action that is beyond rational thought. Does the AI really care?

19.4 CONCLUSION

The digital age portends two trends for lawyering having a real synergy: (a) the privileging of System 2 deliberative thinking, with its aspirations to pure rationality uncompromised by the heuristics and biases observed in System 1 thinking, and (b) the pervasiveness of *computational* deliberation – AI or ML – substituting for human cogitation in more and more of a lawyer's professional functions. Human lawyers will, however, still bring something to the party. Unlike even their most sophisticated digital counterparts, human lawyers are and will continue to be self-reproducing automata. They are and will be beings who can perceive ends and purposes and have a will to act in their pursuit, characteristics that resist easy scientific explanations. Their subjective "transcendence" – intuition, insight, creativity, and the will to change the objective world – means they will continue to respond to clients' problems as Heidegger's metaphorical cabinetmaker responds to the shapes slumbering in the wood. And the machines will never be capable of being anything other than tools in that craft. Intuition, insight, creativity and the will to act are as much a part of our System 1 inclinations as the heuristics and biases that can cloud our empirical judgments. As we saw in even the response to Audrey's mundane problem for lawyering, we need to be circumspect in privileging System 2-like deliberation (particularly that which can be replicated computationally) over those uniquely *human* contributions to effective lawyering.

---

[205] Ibid. at 9.
[206] Sartre, n. 192 at 34–35.

20

Surviving the Digital Transformation

A Method for Lawyers to Approach Legal Tech

Paw Fruerlund and Sebastian Peters

20.1 SCOPE AND PERSPECTIVE

Today, during the fourth industrial revolution, law firms are navigating in a somewhat changing landscape. Traditional legal practice and the ways of doing business in providing legal services is under pressure to change. The pressure comes from other law firms and increasingly self-sufficient in-house counsels who are gradually handling more and more legal matters internally. Companies and their in-house counsels are demanding more specialized services and alternative pricing structures other than the traditional practice of billing by the hour. This demand is one consequence of the fourth industrialization that includes the evolution of various forms of digitization, automation, machine learning, AI, and other technologies. As any other business, law firms are not exempt from the effects of such technologies. If anything, law firms will experience significant disruptive effects on how they do business and the types of services they provide. This is mostly due to the impact of emerging technologies on changing business models, as well as the content of the demand and needs of clients, in ways that were unthinkable twenty years ago.

In recent years, terms such as legal tech (LT), contract automation, artificial intelligence (AI), and smart contracts have been used increasingly inside and outside the legal industry. According to GoogleTrends,[1] over the last ten years daily searches for these words have increased as follows: (1) "legal tech" by 117 percent; (2) "contract automation" by 161 percent; (3) "artificial intelligence" by 174 percent; and (4) "smart contracts" by 422 percent. Within the same time frame, the number of LT start-ups, such as Legal Geek[2] or Iltacon[3] (and their number of participations),[4] and LT conferences has skyrocketed. The term "legal tech," short for "legal technologies," is widely used as a buzzword in the legal industry.

The impact of technology on lawyering dates back to the times of Hammurabi. More recently, Microsoft Word was one of the first digital LT products. However, even though LT has been around for quite some time, the speed and method of implementing technology in the legal industry has increased considerably in recent years. Technological developments have created new ways of working and the legal profession has become increasingly ready to adapt to these developments. LT start-ups have been proliferating and large tech companies are investing

---

[1] See GoogleTrends, https://trends.google.com/trends/ (accessed February 13, 2020).
[2] See Legal Geek, www.legalgeek.co/about-us/ (accessed February 26, 2020).
[3] See Iltacon, https://www.iltacon.org/ (accessed February 26, 2020).
[4] See, e.g., Legal Geek has doubled the number of participants every year the last three years, cf. www.legalgeek.co/about-us.

heavily in LT projects. These projects are not (directly) the focus of this chapter. Many of these projects focus either on replacing lawyers (to some degree or entirely), in certain services (bots giving legal advice and document automation tools), or enhancing the work of lawyers (other document automation, knowledge gathering and prediction indicator tools).

A practicing lawyer may approach these technological developments in several ways. One way would be to believe that LT is a passing fade. If so, you would be joining a group of people who made similar predictions about the telephone, the computer, and the Internet. You may believe that LT is overhyped and that there is a bubble in the LT investment market as was the case with the dot.com bubble. To a certain extent this may be true, such as in area of document automation, where the sheer number of LT products on the market is overwhelming and unsustainable. However, the LT companies and products that survive will change drastically the way lawyers work by reducing costs and minimizing errors.

A practicing lawyer who accepts technological development as a part of the future of lawyering will gain competitive advantages over those who ignore LT. Law firms that take this approach will greatly improve their chances of surviving the digital transformations taking place. Applying this approach can be done in many ways – ranging from buying point-specific standard solutions that solve isolated business needs (document automation, template solutions) to buying end-to-end highly configurable standard solutions (core back office systems covering almost all business processes such as business intake, case management, document management, finance). More aggressive law firms will integrate and configure several different standard solutions to support business needs, such as DMS from one vendor, creating a client platform from another vendor, and using a third vendor to create a system for handling the onboarding of clients, handling budgets, and time registry tasks. Another system may be employed to perform invoicing and another for developing or co-creating solutions to specific or more unique types of needs. The two approaches used by the law firm of Poul Schmith will be explored in this chapter as a case study on the implementation of LT.

From the beginning, a law firm's embrace of LT brings new kinds of issues and conflicts. Some of them stem from quite tangible differences between the culture of law firms and the culture in IT companies. Lawyers and LT developers use different working methods, communication styles, expectations, pace; clashes in approach are unavoidable. The purpose of this chapter is to share the experience and findings of a particular law firm's incorporating of LT into its practice. Mistakes were made and a number of pitfalls could have been avoided. For law firms that follow, they should begin by asking three fundamental questions. First, should the firm adopt LT in the first place? Second, if the decision is in the affirmative, what should lawyers be aware of in the process of choosing and developing LT into their practices? Third, what can the traditional law practice learn from the development process?

This chapter focuses on the Poul Schmith law firm's creation and implementation of a digitization agenda, led by a partner, Paw Fruerlund, and a digital consultant, Sebastian Peters. Poul Schmith acquired knowledge and experience from working in the LT sphere for a number of years. Making many mistakes and misjudgments, but also learning a great deal. Paw Fruerlund was actively involved in the digitalization of firm services including assisting clients with digitalization and developing several digital legal solutions. The in-house development of digital solutions stemmed from his investigation into the legality of different IT systems, namely, case management solutions such as the Danish tax department's debt collection system.[5] This

---

[5] The report has been published on the Danish parliament's webpage, http://new.folketingsbilag.dk/files/1544634.pdf (accessed June 12, 2020) and on the tax department's webpage www.skm.dk/media/1263547/Kammeradvokatens-legalitetsanalyse.pdf (accessed June 12, 2020).

led to assisting clients with creating compliant IT solutions using agile methods. Fruerlund's experience and perspective on LT comes from his work as a product owner, a project manager, steering committee chair, as well as partaking in the law firm's assessment of third-party solutions and advising LT start-ups. His projects have included development of case management solutions including The Insolvency Portal,[6] Caseview,[7] and eArbitration.[8]

20.2 BUZZWORDS

As a preliminary note, it is important to be aware of the existence and role of buzzwords in the LT industry. These buzzwords are used by IT consultants, so lawyers considering the use of LT should know the meaning of these words. Secondly, LT terminology is foreboding to those with a legal education and may act as a barrier to lawyers trained in traditional legal practice. Full understanding of words such as "legal tech," "scrum," "agile," "smart contracts," "ideation," "change management," and so forth takes a great deal of time and patience. Understanding their meanings and functions is vital in order for lawyers to separate the valuable and useful from the inferior or worthless. In short, there are three identifiable kinds or iterations of LT: "fake tech," "hype tech," and "actual legal tech," which are explained below.

20.2.1 *Fake Tech*

Fake tech relates to tech solutions that claim to solve a problem through technical means, when in fact the solution is not novel in any way. Examples include solutions that mainly consist of a landing page and a form that the client fills out. When the form is completed and submitted, the recipient (a lawyer, a secretary, or a clerk) receives an email with the enclosed information and begins to process the matter. How is this different from the practice where the client sends an email describing the problem? The fill-in form method may look innovative, and it may serve to assist the client in providing the right information,[9] but it does not change the way a lawyer works, or the speed or cost or the quality of the work.

While such solutions may provide a better client experience, their function may vary between mere branding to having a real purpose and effect. Such a tech solution can, however, also act as a prototype, a "minimal viable product" (MVP) (see Section 20.3.3),[10] for testing the commercial viability of an LT solution, by determining whether people would be interested in a proposed tech product based on interactions online through a chatbot. However, it takes time and resources to design a comprehensive bot. An alternative is having a physical person pose as

---

[6] See www.konkursportalen.dk/en (accessed June 17, 2020).
[7] See www.caseview.dk/en (accessed June 17, 2020).
[8] See www.eArbitration.dk (accessed June 17, 2020).
[9] When developing the Insolvency Portal, a module for filing claims against the bankruptcy estate was made. A part of this module was a claim submission form on the Internet (www.konkursportalen.dk) by which creditors could file their claims. The form instructs the creditor about the information necessary for changing the proof that the creditor previously lodged. This change of procedure saves a small amount of time and work for both the law firm and the creditor, which accumulates into rather substantial amounts of time and money. Also lodging the relevant proof through a submission form makes it possible for the law firm to access the data at the data point that makes the data easily measurable, but also allows the law firm to avoid making mistakes when registering the data in the back office systems handling the register of debts and claims.
[10] MVP is a technological solution that is narrow and targeted. It is a solution that can be developed quickly and at moderate costs. It also means that in selecting a provider-developer, the best provider is the one that will be faster to fail.

the bot.[11] Once testing has been completed, you will not only have a proof of concept about the prototype, you will have created your first data set.

20.2.2 *Hype Tech*

Hype tech are solutions claiming to use certain technologies but, in reality, the product does not use or uses only tangentially the advertised technology. At the beginning of 2020, makers of tech products claimed their products used machine learning (ML) or AI. Claims that a technology is "smart" or "intelligent" implies that the intelligence is achieved through the use of ML or AI when, in fact, the products simply use a long string of logical IF → THEN → ELSE statements giving the user the impression that the product is acting "intelligently."

Again, that is not to say that such tech products do not add value. It is simply a recognition that ML and AI, expressed or implied, may be a marketing ploy and is not an accurate description of certain products. True ML or AI needs data to predict and produce results (data is used to train the algorithm). This also means that output changes as the training data changes. If there is no such training, then the product is not based on ML or AI. If the product incorporates ML or AI, then the issue, not discussed here, becomes the quality and selection of training data and the effects it has on the outcomes. This issue in the future will need to be decided by law and ethics based on societal values.

20.2.3 *Actual Legal Tech*

So, what is actual LT? The Law Society of England & Wales defines LT as "technologies that aim to support, supplement or replace traditional methods for delivering legal services, or that improve the way the justice system operates." It also provided a list of LT tools and processes, including "document automation; advanced chatbots and practice management tools; predictive AI; smart legal contracts; and knowledge management and research systems." Further, it describes the LT sector as consisting "of law firms delivering legal services through technology, and the vendors that develop and supply technology solutions for those firms."[12] The scope of this chapter encompasses technology within the meaning of the above definition of LT. In practical terms, LT covers technical solutions that change the way lawyers work, and impact the speed, the cost, or the quality of their work.

An example is found in arbitration where LT can help lawyers write memoranda based on prior work, giving lawyers suggestions for content. A respondent's memorandum can be drafted based on the memorandum submitted by the claimant, as well as information taken from a database containing memoranda from past cases and arguments taken from published legal sources. Such a use of LT speeds up the process of drafting memoranda and ensures that it covers all the key issues in the dispute, along with citing appropriate sources. Other tools help lawyers navigate the arbitration process by providing an online platform for the automated filing of claims, instituting arbitration proceedings, and uploading and sharing case files during the arbitration.

---

[11] This method is also known as "The Wizard of Oz," see Fiona Harwood "Wizard of Oz Testing – a Method of Testing a System That Does Not Yet Exist," www.simpleusability.com/inspiration/2018/08/wizard-of-oz-testing-a-method-of-testing-a-system-that-does-not-yet-exist/ (accessed February 27, 2020).

[12] The Law Society, www.lawsociety.org.uk/support-services/lawtech/what-is-lawtech (accessed January 13, 2020).

20.2.4 Typical Lawyer

When selecting and adopting LT, cognizance should be made of some characteristics commonly found in lawyers. The study of law as well as the practice of law generally require a focus on detail. The skillful lawyer must examine the details of law and facts. The lawyer also expands analyses to include hypothetical factual scenarios. Law school encourages and rewards students with personality traits supporting this way of thinking. After law school, lawyers start practicing law where other skill sets are explored and developed. However, the dedicated dissection of law and facts at a very granular level is rewarded, especially in such areas as the drafting of documents or crafting flawless arguments in litigation or arbitration. Although important, these personality traits, as represented by the Myers-Briggs Type Indicator (MBTI) personality traits "thinking" and "judging," are heavily overrepresented.[13] According to Larry Richards: "Thinkers make decisions in a detached, objective and logical manner. They employ syllogistic thinking and make a conscious effort not to let their personal preferences get in the way of making a 'right' decision."[14]

Another important aspect of legal practice is the billing methodology used by lawyers. The predominant billing practice in the legal profession is structured around hourly rates. A great deal of pressure is placed on lawyers, especially in large law firms, to produce billable hours. This incentive structure places the focus on solving cases and charging billable hours rather than on investing, exploring, and experimenting with new ways of working. At the same time, clients expect round the clock availability through smartphones and emails. This is a situation that can hopefully be changed by technology.

The reason that lawyer and law practice characteristics are relevant can be illustrated by some examples. In developing the Insolvency Portal, wireframes (screen blueprint) were presented to a group of lawyers for the purpose of getting feedback on proposed functionality and design in respect to usability and expediency. The wireframe contained numerous elements in order to extract data on difference issues related to insolvency, including income and expense, mortgages, progress bars, and creditor information, as well as a text piece focusing on a specific asset, such as a piece of real estate. The feedback showed more than 50 percent of the initial time spent by the lawyers was related to identifying errors or irregularities in the mock data found in the budgets, bars, and texts. This created no value to the project and frustrated the developers. This led to the idea of using "Lorem Ipsum"[15] as a placeholder text to make sure that the numeric data seem realistic.

The authors' LT product auto-produces a bundle of documents and information that can be submitted to the court to meet recurring statutory deadlines in certain types of cases. The bundle is automatically produced based on information recorded during the winding up procedure in insolvency proceeding based on a draft version (80 percent complete), which would then have to be manually checked and completed. However, the idea of an 80 percent complete document or an 80 percent solution leaves most lawyers uneasy. As a result, the decision was made to use

---

[13] One survey showed that 78 percent of lawyers perceived representation as thinking over feeling and 63 percent thought of representation as judging over perceiving. See L. Richard, "The Lawyer Types" (1993) *ABA Journal* 77; A. Hammer, "Introduction to Type and Careers," CPP (1996), https://leavinglaw.wordpress.com/2010/12/01/more-on-the-lawyer-personality (accessed May 10, 2020). See also https://abovethelaw.com/2014/05/deviations-from-the-norm-the-lawyer-type-and-legal-hiring (accessed June 25, 2020).

[14] Further, "Judgers like to have a sense of control over their environment, and so tend to be methodical." Hammer, n. 13 at 77.

[15] See https://en.wikipedia.org/wiki/Lorem_ipsum (accessed February 20, 2020).

the new product to produce document bundles in some cases, while continuing to produce the bundles in specific situations manually as had been the practice. Ultimately, many pilot users reported back that the product solution should not be implemented. The pushback meant substantial delays and excessive use of time and effort by the development and implementation teams. The frustration was rather natural when considering the additional capacity needed for learning a new tool (which does not fully support your needs yet) in a hectic working environment. The above examples demonstrate the challenge of developing LT products for law practice and the legal mind.

20.3 DEVELOPING OR ADAPTING LEGAL TECH IN A LAW FIRM

This section examines the process of developing LT within a law firm, from ideation to valuation to narrowing the technology project to the MVP to accelerating the creation of the product through "sprinting," and finally, implementation.

20.3.1 Ideation

All projects start with an idea. A spark of innovation that in some way can change the cost and time and improve the quality of an existing process. At times, LT creates brand new products or types of services that lawyers may offer their clients. Ideation is a process that helps you get that spark of innovation. Basically, it is a form of brainstorming, but with a more structured approach. Books and consultants provide advice on methods for stimulating ideation. The next subsections provide the method used by the authors.

20.3.1.1 Getting the Right People: Facilitator and the Participants

First, and most important in starting an LT development project is getting the right people into a room and making sure they are prepared, motivated, and focused on the process.[16] One or two facilitators are then selected to lead the participants through workshops and encourage the group members to be creative. A facilitator needs to have experience with the process and a high level of energy to lead the ideation process. It is also beneficial if one of the facilitators is a lawyer or has extensive experience in practicing law in a law firm. This helps to reduce the skepticism of lawyers since the lawyer-facilitator gains a broader, more accurate, perspective of the project.

The facilitator must have a strong "yes-and" mentality in order to create an environment where the word "no" is not a permitted response to a proposed idea. No matter the content of the idea being presented, the response should be one that further develops the idea, pivots it into something different, or expands on it. Negative responses ("that is not possible," "you cannot do it that way," "it has to be done in X manner," and so forth) are counterproductive to the ideation process. A proposed solution may be faulty, but it should not be summarily rejected. Simply acknowledging the idea by writing it down on an idea board gives the ideation process a positive and inviting context that looks for possibilities and not limitations. Being able to withhold judgment is a key tenet of the development process. What is possible or legal at this stage is irrelevant. There is plenty of time and opportunity to vet an idea.

---

[16] For instance, it is now an established practice in the firm that first year young lawyers take an ideation workshop to discuss what could be changed to make the law firm better.

In selecting the participants, relevant diversity is the key and includes finding people from throughout the organization that have different types of job functions and excel at different ways of thinking – lawyers of different seniority or backgrounds, clerks, communication managers, and secretaries bring a broad range of perspectives to a problem. The only qualifying factor is that everybody should be motivated and excited about the process of working toward a solution.

Finally, the facilitator must create a horizontal organizational structure, within a law firm, which has a highly hierarchical management structure. All ideas, no matter the source, are equally important at the early stage of the process. Therefore, the goal is to create an environment where all ideas and experiences are welcome and considered. Some junior personnel may be reluctant in presenting ideas during the ideation process when senior partners are present. This reluctance can be alleviated by having the senior partner actively present and also by encouraging participants to present less than thoroughly thought-out ideas.

20.3.1.2 *Getting the Ideas*

In order to generate ideas, it is best practice to limit the scope of ideas. Counterintuitively, constraints are necessary for people to be creative. Constraints include the selection of topics or problems for which solutions are sought. The problems are gathered from interviews with a diverse range of people inside and outside the firm (clients, business partners, court personnel, arbitrators). The initial constraints provide the framework for the ideation session. The next step includes placing additional constraints and stimuli to encourage the creation of possible solutions. For this purpose, hundreds of techniques and exercises have been developed to provide the right stimuli. These include setting a tight deadline, about two minutes for the first exercise where participants offer as many ideas as possible. This creates an environment of quantity over quality, based on the assumption that it is beneficial to get a whole bunch of ideas in a given exercise rather than have people fuss about whether an idea is good or not. This encourages the participants to set aside critical analytical thinking in order to generate many ideas including those that may seem a bit crazy, which can later be refined to something not so crazy. Lowering the stress of needing to suggest "great" ideas aims at creating a judgment-free environment.

The next exercise entails giving each participant several major brand names and posing the hypothetical of how such a company would solve the problem, such as, How would Apple or Tesla go about selling legal services? This encourages the application of principles taken from successful businesses in order to get the participants to think in a different manner. For example, a McDonald's mindset would focus on how services could be commodified and sold directly to the average consumer at low margins.

Next, participants are asked to provide their most silly or terrible solutions to the problem. The hidden value in this exercise is that it tests the underlying assumptions of what makes an idea bad or silly. For example, one idea would be to try to sell high-end legal services by approaching random strangers in the street. This is a silly idea, but it can be reframed to a strategy of showing up unannounced at the offices of clients and asking for a meeting with anyone at C level to hear about what problems they are facing on a daily basis. This is not such a crazy idea, but it is still inappropriate, which leads to the question of how we make this socially acceptable? The goal of the exercise is to change our fundamental assumptions about the topic.

The next step is to directly challenge assumptions about how things are and have to be. In this exercise, the participants are asked to make statements about the problem and challenge all the assumptions founding or underlying their statements. For example, "We need to be more transparent in our work for clients." The participants then go through the statement word by word, like this:

We = Who else could do this? Could a third party do this for us? Can we make existing clients help us with this?
need = Why do we need this? What goal are we trying to achieve? Could there be other routes to achieve the stated purpose?
to be more = What do we mean by "more"? How it be measured?
transparent = How do we define transparent? What part of the process is the client most interested in obtaining greater transparency?
in our work = Is it a process of creating work or is it about the billing of the work?
for clients = Who are the clients? Do we have clients that are not clients in the traditional sense of the word? Could the public or local authorities be considered clients?

After going through the problem word by word, the answers to the individual questions allow for a rephrasing of the statement to something that hits a core need of the firm and increases the likelihood of seeing a clearer path to achieving a solution. For example, the statement may end up being changed to: "Lawyers at the director level deliver detailed information about the billing and follow up with a short questionnaire to the client about how transparent the firm is perceived to be." The client feedback may point toward a need to implement a more precise time registration system that automatically creates billing reports.

In the same line of testing assumptions, participants are asked to try to come up with a solution that is impossible to do. Then we ask the participants to challenge the impossibility of the solution. Have them examine the "why?" of the assumption of impossibility. If the solution really is impossible then we ask for a new statement that may be doable. This may provide the foundation for a moon shot project. While such projects may be outside the scope of development goals due to costs or risk factors, they can provide pieces that can be used to develop a MVP (see Section 20.3.3). A case in point is contract automation solutions, which in the beginning of LT were considered moon shot projects, but contract automation has been broken down into smaller value MVPs onto which more comprehensive solutions can subsequently be built.

At the other end of the spectrum, participants are asked to try and come up with the easiest solution to the problem: "Why cannot we just do that?" This exercise is especially well-suited for finding beneficial MVP solutions (see Section 20.3.3). Sometimes the simple solution can be the perfect way to start. For instance, to test the potential market for an AI-driven chatbot to handle common inquiries could entail the investment of large amounts of time and money. A market study may show that it would be cheaper to hire a call center in India. Thus, the market potential for the development of the chatbot may be relatively low.

Another approach is to ask the participants to describe what a 1-star solution (awful) to a problem, a 2-star solution, then a 3-star and so on up to developing a 10-star experience (extraordinary). Typically, solutions in the 5–7-star range pass a value-cost analysis. At around 4-stars, the proposed solution (product) delivers the promised result on time at the agreed cost with the client. A 6-star solution would be beyond what was promised or solves a problem that the client did not realize existed. At 8-stars, the solution or product provides a full package that allows it to be branded and marketed to other clients. The move from an 8-star to a 10-star solution may be one of diminishing returns, that is, it may not be doable or desirable, especially if core features are available in the 8-star solution.

20.3.1.3 *Selecting the Good Ones*

The final step in the ideation process involves selecting the ideas for further development. Each participant is asked to pick three ideas and prepare a one-minute presentation promoting their preferred ideas. After the presentations, the participants cast three votes on the presented ideas. The top three ideas are then selected and move forward to the making-a-business-case phase.

20.3.2 *Business Case*

A business case analysis acts as a stress test for the ideas. This section discusses the focal points that lawyers find particularly challenging during this part of the process.

20.3.2.1 *Going from the Solution to the How*

The first task is to assess the way the project moves from proposed solution to desired result. A software solution requires early involvement of the IT department or with software development partners. Through discussions with IT experts, a list of the potential risks and gains is developed for the following: (1) Expected results, (2) yield from results, (3) time needed, (4) cost, (5) quality of the delivered result, (6) people and other resources needed, and (7) overall risk of the project. The first hurdle is to overcome lawyers' worst-case scenario mindsets, as noted previously, lawyers often take a risk-focused approach that looks only for flaws. Looking for flaws is a necessary part of the assessment process, however, not all risks can or should be mitigated at this point.

First, the focus should be on finding asymmetrical risks. The closer the costs of development are to the value of the result the lesser the margin of error. Alternatively, the wider the distance between costs and value, the greater the number of intermittent failures that can be suffered in developing the solution. We often see opportunities for asymmetrical risk when a solution tries to improve internal manual processes. For example, solutions that can reduce the workload for a secretary by ten minutes per day for the cost of a €10,000 investment in LT, with forty-five secretaries equates to roughly a year's worth of work, which makes the €10,000 investment a good one. But this savings can only be captured if the number of secretaries is reduced by one or by assigning additional, more valuable tasks to fill the secretaries' time freed by the solution.

Even when presented with an opportunity for asymmetrical risk, there is a lot of anxiety about the potential downside. At this stage, fear-setting is a useful tool as a proponent for relevant risk mitigation. Risk mitigation starts by listing worst-case outcomes. This is followed by a vetting process that asks if the event occurs what the likely damage will be and how long it would take to repair. This allows for taking preventive steps or a realization that the approach is unsustainable at the moment. Another feature of the intense focus on flaws in a lawyer's work is a culture in law firms that does not allow for mistakes – a so-called zero margin of error culture. This means that at times there can be too deep of an aversion to making an error, resulting in an unproductive focus on achieving perfection on the first try. These qualities are appropriate when lawyers are handling cases that affect core aspects of a client's business, but they are less constructive in the development of a prototype solution and it is therefore undesirable to overemphasize this aversion to overcome deep-seated preconceptions that developing LT is a waste of time and money.

In order to reduce failures and lost investments, the developer should seek solutions with high asymmetrical risk-reward ratios. Development projects based on such ratios are more likely to succeed and the lower costs allow for intermittent failures on the road to success. This approach is endemic to the concept of developing LT gradually through creating MVPs (see Section 20.3.3). However, even with the asymmetrical risk–MVP approach, the owner-developer must be alert to not doubling down on sunk costs. Another best practice is to establish a steering committee to oversee the project and evaluate its progress from a business value perspective. This also may lead to the determination that projected costs were underestimated, which may require a reassessment of the feasibility of continuing the endeavor.

In order to avoid high opportunity costs (projects not funded), the project team needs to determine what types of projects are uniquely good.[17] This self-awareness will increase chances of success and lower opportunity costs. It grounds individual team members in the knowledge that they are not experts in all fields – law, technology, and business. This realization enlightens the members of the team to the fact that focused collaboration across disciplinary or professional lines is the key to success. The other factor to be considered is the relative quality of competitors working in the same area. If the goal is to market the LT product or to differentiate the firm from its legal competitors, then the project's goals should be to create something that would be market leading, which diminishes the external risks and opportunity costs posed by competitors. The idea of being a market leader was one of the reasons Poul Schmith decided to develop The Insolvency Portal and Caseview (a platform for handling and following litigation and arbitration cases). It gives the project developer a unique insight and leverage in a specific field of law and thereby reduces potential opportunity costs.

20.3.3 Minimum Viable Product

In choosing a developer or a provider of LT, the focus should be on the MVP, which designates that the best provider is the one that will be faster to fail. As lawyers, our focus is on not failing. Rather, it is doing everything right from the beginning: from contract to dispute resolution. Instead, in LT development, it is imperative to understand who is better at arriving at failure fastest, as modern-day development accepts the fact that everything cannot be sufficiently known or thought through before the development process begins. Therefore, it is accepted that during the process choices will be made, which will have to be revisited and changed. Starting small, release of the product to a sample of users, collecting feedback and building from there greatly improves the chance of reaching a successful conclusion in a faster period of time. Identifying the MVP proceeds in four steps.

First, the owner-developer must assess its most essential needs. One very common need in law firms is collecting billable hours. This requires the MVP to ensure that all hourly reports are made in a manner ensuring that time is registered and ensure that registrations are in sync with the budgets communicated to the client, which allows budgets to be revised in a timely manner. The success criteria for a new product could be set at a goal to increase billable hours by 5 percent, increase the accuracy of budgets by 50 percent, and make budgets revisions 40 percent faster. Second, the developer maps out the user journeys. This would involve looking at the employees, the way budgets are made, the way billable hours are reported, and how they are conveyed to clients. Third, the developer identifies the problems and obstacles (costs and risks) expressed in the user journeys. This begins with identifying where the lawyers, administrative employees, and clients find problems during the targeted process. One problem is allocating billable hours appropriately after a long day of work. Another problem is when clients find a billing statement to be too generic, providing insufficient detail as to what he or she is paying for.

---

[17] A simple definition of opportunity cost is the loss of potential gain from other alternatives when one alternative is chosen.

Fourth, the developer refocuses on the problems and decides which ones to solve in determining the scope of the MVP. One way of prioritizing is by scoring each problem solution's impact and urgency. An example would be a proposed product that collects information from a lawyer's phone and cross-references it with previous time recordings and other data, and on that basis, suggest time recording entries. It would also have a feature that sends alerts when billable hours exceed the parameters of proposed budgets and suggests a new budget by proposing staffing and task changes. However, such a product would have a long development time, be too costly, and have a much higher risk of failure. Once the project is narrowed to a modest number of features, the scope of the MVP can be determined. The goal is to make the MVP as limited as possible.

20.3.4 *Sprinting!*

The typical lawyer's work day focuses on a specific task, such as representing a client in an arbitration. The lawyer will meet with the client, draft memoranda in her office, and then send the memoranda to the client for comments and approval. The next step includes the submission to the arbitrators, interviewing witnesses, reviewing expert witness statements, followed by preparation and presentation of oral arguments. During the process much of the work is done by the lawyer or a team of lawyers. However, there are parts of this work schedule where IT enhancements or solutions can be used. The waterfall methodology starts with a requirements analysis, followed by a design phase, a development phase, a testing phase, and finally a maintenance phase. The waterfall methodology is best applied in development projects where all the requirements are clear from the initiation of the project. Oftentimes such projects are small in scope with clear specifications and little or no change after initiation. Making changes can be problematic. There is little or no involvement of the future user of the product increasing the risk of a misalignment between the developer and user. LT solutions often allow for a new process of collaboration, with the lawyer working together with clients in co-drafting the memoranda. One of the outcomes or benefits in developing LT has been the creation of synergy between lawyers and their clients through greater collaboration.

Developers often work in scrum teams. Scrum methodology is an agile approach for managing projects. Its working methodology focuses on delivering small results through working "sprints" that create short feedback loops, allowing the project to move agilely toward its goal. The methodology is suitable for complex projects and projects that are not clearly specified from the onset or that are subject to change during development. In a scrum team, the scrum master is responsible for managing a team of no more than nine members. The product owner has the vision and provides guidance in each sprint. The project collects all the desired features in a backlog. The backlog contains everyone's ideas for features, called user stories. The user stories are groomed and revised on a list as you build the project, collect experiences, and learn. Each user story is measured or valuated based on how many points (based on the amount of work/complexity) it entails.

In order for a user story to be built, it has to be moved to the sprint backlog by the scrum master. At this point, it is imperative that the user story contains a definition of when it is expected to be completed, along with a definition of when completion is deemed to have been reached. The definition of completion is something the scrum team agrees upon, a sort of contract of when a component can be considered to be delivered. Most often, the definition of completion entails that the component has gone through a series of processes, which could look something like the following:

Developed ➔ Peer reviewed ➔ Developer test ➔ Documentation created ➔ User acceptance test

In this process, the development phase is the one that takes the most time during a sprint. A sprint is a period of time where the scrum team seeks to develop and deliver components to the project. The sprint can range in duration from one to eight weeks. The sprint often starts with a kickoff called sprint planning, where the sprint backlog who-is-doing-what is defined. Then there are daily standups where the team and the scrum master get a picture of the status of whether things are progressing as planned. At the end of the sprint, a review is written. Finally, there is a retrospective on the sprint. During the sprint the developers will note the tasks that they had worked on and how far along they progressed (developing, testing, completion).

This methodology requires the product owner to be highly involved in the process. A role that the lawyer is often unaccustomed to. The importance of this role cannot be stressed enough. Without a good, available, accessible, involved and cooperative product owner, the development project will likely fail. Many projects have failed due to the lack of common understanding between owners, developers, and users. From a law firm perspective, this means not entirely turning the development project over to the technologists. Firm lawyers need to partake in the process by working together with the developers on the scrum team.

20.3.5 Implementation

The task of implementing new LT products is often overshadowed by the task of creating the software. However, the software is worthless if it isn't used. Implementation, and the change management that it entails, is as important as the development of the product itself. Lawyers often have strong opinions and may resist the change that LT presents unless it seems reasonable. Therefore, the process of implementation must be well-thought-out and focus on getting the large majority of firm lawyers to accept and use the new "thing."

20.3.5.1 Inclusion from Beginning to End

Due to lawyers' busy schedules, they are often excluded in the development process. This is not the right approach; firm lawyers should be involved from the beginning. By doing so, the developers are optimizing the degree and ease of acceptance once the product is created. Simply stated, development and implementation are intimately connected. One approach is to create a "superuser corps" made up of different types of users to obtain input on different features of the product. In this way the product can be tailored to user needs and increase the ease of functionality from their perspective. End user insights during development produces a roadmap, in order to ensure the delivery of some of the most sought-after features. When facilitating change in a law firm, such as the use of LT, it is vital that the users feel a sense of ownership of the change. When the users feel that their needs have been seen, heard, and prioritized, they are much more likely to adopt and promote the use of thee LT product.

20.3.5.2 Right Users at the Right Time

The selection of users to help with implementation has to be representative of the organization and the functions being affected by the product. This will often be a combination of administrative personnel, secretaries, junior associates, junior lawyers, and partners. Some personnel will be fast followers (early adopters) and others will be reluctant and slow in using the new tech tool. Innovators and fast followers are employees that love change, technology, and new ways of thinking. The fast followers mimic the examples of the early adopters.

Others will resist, when their habits and way of working has been consistent over a long period of time. Some of these naysayers are also responding to the challenge of learning a new way of working.[18] For this reason, it is important to include them in the process and get their needs incorporated in the development of the product. Regular meetings with demonstrations of the new tech product is important, as well as recording observations of the audience. An effort to show features of the product made based on the users' input is good practice. This practice will help accelerate the implementation process.

20.3.5.3 *Implementation after Going Live*

After the product is live in production, the next step is its implementation as a tool to be used firm wide. There are classic methods of implementation, beginning with the establishment of test groups that will use the software for a period of time and give feedback. Once the feedback is obtained, the test groups can be gradually expanded until all employees are using the program. The testing process should include the distribution of manuals, video guides, in-person courses and personal support to the extent necessary. Users that feel an ownership interest in the process are much more likely to engage and fully implement the new technology. Management engagement and heavy end-user involvement are crucial for successful implementation.

It is imperative that upper management communicate the importance of LT and tech products to the firm. Management's vision and goals for the implementation of new software should be made clear. Implementation must be followed by an assessment of the value created by the new technology. Users who are employees can be forces to implement the solution (technology) but that does not necessarily mean that value has been added by applying the solution. For example, a new business intelligence software solution might be able to process large amounts of data, but if it does not generate sufficient revenue or lower costs its success has limited consequences.

20.3.5.4 *Handoff to Operations and Maintenance*

Once implemented, the product and its use enter the maintenance phase. The software must be managed by an IT department. The project leader will have the obligation of facilitating cooperation between the scrum team and the IT department. The IT department will typically need documentation for the software, such as guides regarding troubleshooting, infrastructure, primary uses, and known bugs. The process of handing off to the IT department is not to be underestimated as the future success of the software relies on good maintenance and support. It is a good investment to involve the IT department in the early stages of development, as they will provide valuable input to how the product can be made easier to maintain and support.

20.4 CONCLUSION

Much can be learned by lawyers taking part in the process of developing new technology. This chapter provided insights mostly based on learning from the authors' mistakes in developing LT products. The road to success requires lawyers to challenge the assumptions that underlie the law firm's delivery of services to clients by questioning the way they work. There are increasing numbers of cases where traditional services are complemented by LT. In order to grow their

---

[18] The normal amount of late majority and laggards being 50 percent, see A. Vishwanath and G. Barnett (eds.), *The Diffusion of Innovations: A Communication Science Perspective* (New York: Peter Lang, 2011).

business, lawyers will need to embrace LT that allows lawyers to better collaborate with clients in finding creative solutions for the client's business problems.

In the future, law firms will look to existing LT market solutions to supplement their expertise. The menu of LT solutions will accelerate given the rise of start-ups and the number of law firms taking on the role of developer. One question all law firms will need to consider is whether they will act as developers and owners of LT. To do so strays from the core business of lawyers and entails a number of risks as described in this chapter. Law firms that develop IT are aided by the fact that lawyers and law firms have unique insight into their own failings and the nuances of serving particular clients. In the end, lawyers will have to collaborate with technologists at a deeper level to improve the success of LT undertakings. So, lawyers will need to rise to the challenges of being product developers and owners.

21

Road Forward

Promise and Danger

Larry A. DiMatteo and Pietro Ortolani

> *By 2020 law firms will be faced with a "tipping point" for a new talent strategy. Now is the time for all law firms to commit to becoming AI-ready by embracing a growth mindset, set aside the fear of failure and begin to develop internal AI practices.*[1]
>
> *A robust and ethical legal profession respects the flexibility and subtlety of legal language as a prerequisite for a just and accountable social order. It ensures a rule of persons, not machines.*[2]

21.1 INTRODUCTION

The intent of this book is to explore the impact of the evolution and acceleration of legal tech (LT) on the practice of law. It discusses the multifaceted relationship between LT or digital technology and legal practice. The book examines the intersection of technology with legal practice from a positive perspective (enhancement of lawyering) and a negative perspective (disruption of traditional law practice). There is no doubt that LT has disrupted legal practice and the disruption will intensify in the years to come, as LT start-ups continue to multiply. Some law firms have moved more rapidly than others in embracing the time and cost efficiencies provided by LT. Some law firms have resisted what they perceive as a threat to their livelihoods. This is likely the result of a distorted perception of what LT brings to the table. This distortion is due to a lack of due diligence, fear of new things, the technology-averse view of traditional lawyers, and the premature assessment that LT may be cost prohibitive, especially from the small firm perspective.

This chapter discusses the findings of the book in order to provide a more accurate view of the pros and cons of LT. It answers the following questions: Does the implementation of LT necessarily mean the diminishment of the need for lawyers? Does such a diminishment mean law firms will need fewer lawyers? Will new types of "law" jobs be created as a result of LT? What does LT mean for legal education? What should be the demarcation between tasks that should be reserved for the human mind and those handed over to LT, especially in the burgeoning area of artificial intelligence (AI)? How does LT impact the liability and ethical duties of lawyers?

---

[1] Bernard Marr, "How AI and Machine Learning Are Transforming Law Firms and the Legal Sector," *Forbes* (May 23, 2018), www.forbes.com/sites/bernardmarr/2018/05/23/how-ai-and-machine-learning-are-transforming-law-firms-and-the-legal-sector/#2c4acabf32c3.

[2] Frank Pasquale, "Rule of Persons, Not Machines: The Limits of Legal Automation" (2019) 87 *George Washington University Law Review* 1 1.

The essence of LT is captured in the following definition of automated decision system: "a computational process, including one derived from machine learning, statistics, or other data processing or AI techniques that makes a decision or facilitates human decision making."[3] A proposed US law, "Algorithmic Accountability Act of 2019" sketches the areas of regulatory concern encompassing the "development process, including the design and training data of the automated decision system, for impacts on accuracy, fairness, bias, discrimination, privacy, and security." These are some of the many issues discussed in this book.

21.2 LAW AND TECHNOLOGY

Expectations of the services provided by lawyers will change over time. This change will impact legal practitioners and law firms, as well as the dispute resolution process (litigation and arbitration). Courts and arbitral proceedings will continue to be digitalized and much of their business will be done online. We are at the beginning of the age of AI's impact on lawyering, and of discussions as to how professional and government regulations will need to change.

Currently, law firms can afford a gradual approach to incorporating technology into their law practices. In the era of big data, the first step is often the need to employ electronic data processing and computing systems. This is necessitated by the lawyer's tasks of due diligence involving the review of thousands of pages of documents. AI applications can search a vast amount of data in relevant materials in an astonishingly short amount of time. Furthermore, AI can do the task more accurately and see patterns that are unlikely to be seen by the human mind. The use of AI applications has already made a mark in legal research and e-discovery.

Of course, the quality of AI and algorithmic searching is dependent on the quality of human beings in creating algorithms at the beginning. One danger is that the biases of creators and programmers may be replicated in technologies. A counterweight is seen in machine learning capabilities allowing for programs to refine searches without the intervention of human beings. LT 3.0 will see advancements in AI and automated decision-making. The area of online dispute resolution, especially for small sized transactions, will be dominated by internet courts (with human judges) and the use of robo-judges. In the view of Karl Llewellyn, the "is" becomes the "should." The advance of LT and its benefits will overtake the ability of lawyers to choose whether or not to embrace it.

21.3 LEGAL PRACTICE AND COMPETITION

The earliest use of technology, dating back to the 1970s, centered around facilitating time-consuming and singular tasks. Today, with the use of LT, entire work processes can be carried out without or with hardly any human intervention. This development is not always considered as positive; technology has grown into a competitor for legal practitioners and judges. It is thus foreseeable that fewer lawyers (especially legal practitioners) will be needed in the future and lawyers have to become more specialized, flexible, and adaptive.[4] However, the transformation of legal practice through LT also creates new work profiles, and the main beneficiaries will be those lawyers who can acquire a profound understanding of digital technologies and LT. These specialized lawyers will no doubt be in particularly demand in the labor market, in view of their unique skills.

---

[3] US Senate Bill, OLL19293 (116th Congress), "Algorithmic Accountability Act of 2019."
[4] M. Kilian, "Die Zukunft der Juristen" (2017) *Neue Juristische Wochenschrift* 3043 3043.

The imbalances in the competition to provide legal services will be complicated from within and outside of the profession. Externally, if law firms are slow to adopt LT, they will create openings for nontraditional law firms, such as accounting firms, to capture a share of the legal market. Internally, LT will have contradictory impacts on the competition between law firms. One view is that the imbalance between large and small law firms will grow, as larger firms have the resources to enable them to more easily transition to an LT-based practice. Another perspective sees LT as the great equalizer. It will allow smaller firms to overcome resource disparities with larger firms. With LT reducing the needs to have a large group of lawyers perform numerous time-consuming tasks – regulatory due diligence, discovery of evidence, and legal research – lawyers may focus on the core elements of human lawyering, such as counseling, strategizing, and customize services for individual clients. More broadly, law firms (large or small) that innovate and create their own propriety LT may gain competitive advantages in providing services at lower costs and in expanding the menu of services that they can offer clients. Finally, an increased use of technology on the part of business firms requires law firms to incorporate technology as well, in order to efficiently interface with their clients.

LT will decrease the traditional revenue streams of law firms, as billable hours based purely on time will decrease. This is likely to result in different formats for billing legal services, with fixed or task-oriented billing replacing hourly billing. Also, through the use of LT, business firms are likely to keep more work to be performed by in-house lawyers and non-lawyers. In order to offset efficiency-related losses, law firms will need to expand the range of services they can provide. Technology is the vehicle for expanding those services. This will require the creation of new job types within law firms at the intersection of law and technology, such as lawyers expert in computer coding and the greater use of technologists. Lawyers will continue to be needed, due to their value as providers of experienced human judgment in business decision-making, critical thinking skills, and as advocates. The issue is to what extent LT will have disruptive effects on the size of law firms, on competition from nontraditional service providers, as well as the ethical ramifications of the lawyers' use of technology (and failing to use such technology). It will create new liabilities in the designing and implementing of LT systems, such as liability for AI-generated decisions.

As a first step, serious thought must be devoted to the role of future generations of lawyers and the types of skills they will need to possess. In order to prepare future lawyers for the new challenges awaiting them, legal education and studies must be adapted. Newly designed content related to digital technology must be integrated into existing educational structures. For the understanding of LT, it would most certainly be helpful if prospective lawyers themselves could acquire a basic understanding of programming LT applications.[5] For traditional lawyers, there will need to be a serious commitment to expand skill sets through continuing legal education.

21.4 CONSUMERS, ACCESS TO JUSTICE, AND REGULATION

The book presents empirical evidence (namely, the results of a survey) in the area of LT and dispute resolution. The survey selected the five largest markets for legal services in Europe (France, Germany, Italy, Spain, and the United Kingdom), which represent different legal traditions (common law and civil law, including the Germanistic and Romanistic families of the

---

[5] M. Zwickel, "Jurastudium 4.0? – Die Digitalisierung des juristischen Lehrens und Lernens" (2018) *Juristische Arbeitsblätter* 881 882.

civil law). It shows the heterogeneity in automation of legal services, which ranges from low to high degrees of automation. In the area of litigation, the best performing LT companies are able to achieve a high level of automation, whereby the assessment of claims and the estimation of compensation is done without the intervention of lawyers or other experts. In this area, automated performances proved to be more accurate than human counterparts; at the same time, however, the quality of automated systems and their performance outcomes varied substantially. Some LT products performed one task much better than another, such as autonomously assessing the plausibility of claims, but not being able to accurately estimate reasonable compensation.

Professor Elizalde argues that the drafting of legal rules determines their suitability for automation. In other words, the "technological efficiency" of law depends on standardization and objectification of legal rules. Such a rule-based system (along with the recognition of the operative facts found in cases) allows an automated system to resolve disputes by treating similarly situated cases in a consistent way. Elizalde concludes that certain types of claims allow for higher levels of automation, and the nature of the rules applicable to those claims has a fundamental impact on the degree of potential automation. In sum, automation in dispute resolution is dependent on the technological efficiency of the legal rules that apply to the merits of the dispute. When making choice-of-law decisions, thus, parties should weigh which applicable law can more easily be imputed into IT systems.

A new understanding of access to justice should exceed traditional players (fundamentally, lawyers and courts) and extend its aims to achieving fair solutions out of court, in order to avoid the costs of litigation or formal arbitration. LT companies can enable customers to achieve fair outcomes, but in some ways, they are currently restrained by legal regulations, such as the illegality of the unauthorized practice of law. The book provides a review of LT service providers, including LegalZoom (United States), LegalDutch (The Netherlands), Wenigermiete (Germany), Doctrine (France) and Demander Justice (France). The key distinction for regulatory purposes is between LT companies that offer legal information (unregulated) versus giving regulated legal advice. The complaints against LT-based legal services platforms have come from bar associations and other regulatory bodies, but the regulatory obstacles to online legal services vary greatly across countries. The United States has allowed legal services platforms to develop without the need of fitting into the regulation of legal services, while the Netherlands and Germany have placed various restrictions on such services, and France has reacted negatively to such online services. In sum, despite the high demand for modernized legal services, legal uncertainty has hindered investment and the profitability of companies operating in this area.

In Chapter 11, Martin Ebers assesses the fitness of EU law to meet the challenges of LT in the area of B2C relationships. LT applications entail both advantages and risks for consumers. On the positive side, they increase the consumer's awareness of legal problems and allow for a wider choice in pursuing claims at lower and often more transparent prices. The hope is that these benefits will increase access to justice, as consumers seek to pursue small claims otherwise abandoned due to rational apathy. However, the drawbacks of LT in increasing access to justice relate to the quality of choices, information, fairness, ability to obtain redress, and representation. The lack of IT literacy could result in exclusion of some groups. Furthermore, LT companies select the types of claims that they will service, conversely leaving other types of claims without access to justice. In respect to choice and disclosure, unregulated LT companies may fail to provide information needed to ensure the transparency of their services. The variations in the quality of LT applications raise questions concerning the accuracy of legal advice and the extent of liability for defective services. Lastly, the operation of LT companies brings about the danger of a hidden privatization of public values.

Ebers notes that EU law also distinguishes between the provision of legal information (unregulated) and legal advice that is the target of regulation. It is unclear how the services of LT companies will be classified. An inclusion of LT within legal services regulation, which is demanding, may be protective of consumer interests, but could also stifle innovation. As a result, LT companies could be over-regulated if they are treated as legal services or, instead, they could be under-regulated if consumers are left without consumer and data protections. Another issue is that current EU consumer protection laws may be insufficient, even if they do apply to LT.

In its current state, EU law is not well fitted to the issues presented by LT. Among other gaps, EU law is based on the standardized character of technology (standardized products) and is not a good fit for a digital economy that is marked by personalization. The answer to protecting consumers, while not inhibiting innovation, may be found in the concept of the regulatory sandbox. Hilary Allen defines a regulatory sandbox as allowing "startups to conduct a limited test of their products with fewer regulatory constraints, less risk of regulatory enforcement action, and ongoing guidance from regulators."[6] The development of LT would benefit from this type of liability protection. The problem is designing what types of start-ups qualify for regulatory exemptions and how to determine who deserves entry into the sandbox. Such a regulatory sandbox is found in the American proposed law entitled the Algorithmic Accountability Act of 2019;[7] this Act exempts from regulation companies and persons with annual revenues of less than $50 million dollars a year, controlling the personal information of less than one million consumers.

Another approach to regulation of LT and automated systems in general is to require the LT owner or developer to perform a benefit-cost analysis, which would also be the basis for governmental intervention. Such an approach is found in the aforementioned Algorithmic Accountability Act of 2019,[8] which requires the developer to undertake an assessment of the benefits and costs of creating an automated decision system. In performing this assessment, the developer is required to take into account a number of factors: data minimization practices, the duration for which personal information is to be stored, transparency of the information and the results produced by the automated decision system being available to consumers, the ability of consumers to correct or object to the results, and the types of users of the information. Finally, the legality of any such system and developer liability will depend on the degree of risks "posed by the automated decision system to the privacy or security of personal information of consumers and the risks that the automated decision system may result in or contribute to inaccurate, unfair, biased, or discriminatory decisions impacting consumers."[9]

LT can be used as a tool for in-house legal services of businesses involved in mass consumer relations. These include the implementation and execution of policies, as well as the internal management of consumer claims, including customer communications. Although easily categorized as business tech, Professor Tjon Tjin Tai (Chapter 12) sees the internal use of such tools as a form of LT, as they automate and implement legal decision procedures, policies, and considerations without the use of lawyers. He notes the danger of LT in B2C relations, especially when used in the under-regulated sphere of in-house matters, where underdeveloped programs

---

[6] Hilary J. Allen, "Regulatory Sandboxes" (2019) 87 *George Washington University Law Review* 579 579.
[7] See n. 3.
[8] Ibid.
[9] See US Senate Bill, OLL19293, n. 3 at section 2(2)(C).

may prove to be inadequate for interacting with consumers or actively abusing the right for a consumer to lodge a complaint. The discouraging of valid claims may be intentional or unintentional, but just as damaging. Also, the quality of an AI-guided program is dependent on the training of AI to work within a legal and ethical framework. Tjon Tjin Tai argues that to discourage unfair practices will require a mix of market pressure and legal regulation. A company should be held liable for an algorithm that leads to unfair outcomes. The liability should be benchmarked against professional due diligence in reviewing the company's testing of the LT to ensure it behaves in a lawful manner.

A similar set of concerns arises when technology (and in particular automatic decision-making) is used in the field of public administration. In Chapter 15, Antonios Kouroutakis proposes a phased implementation approach as a best practice. Such an approach would require *ex ante* checks, conducted to minimize the risk of infringement of fundamental rights and freedoms.

21.5 TECHNOLOGY AND ADR

Alternative dispute resolution (ADR) is witnessing a technological revolution. LT offers the benefits of lowering the costs of dispute resolution in general, and more specifically in the field of arbitration. From a societal perspective, this holds the potential for greater access to justice by consumers, as well as small-and medium-sized businesses. Tech-aided ADR and online dispute resolution (ODR) will allow complainants to pursue meritorious claims that were previously cost-prohibitive; an example is the use of the blockchain to verify evidence and transmit it to arbitral tribunals. AI-aided judgments or decisions through ODR for small claims have already been tested in China. In addition, the COVID-19 crisis has increased awareness of the need to explore remote modes of dispensing justice. This fundamental shift will come when established ADR providers will move to accommodate online disputes.

Arbitration is a prime example of a procedure that can be modernized and made more efficient by technology. LT can be used to select arbitrators with peer-review mechanism, so as to guarantee arbitrators' expertise and reliability, all of this within a platform that fully digitizes the flow of arbitral proceedings, complies with the existing legal frameworks for arbitration, and integrates anti-corruption measures. Traditional arbitration can focus on resolving complex disputes, where the allocation of resources cannot be automated through technologies such as smart contracts.

The book also examines the emergence of new forms of digital dispute resolution, where the enforcement of outcomes is ensured by technological means, rather than by relying on state or judicially mandated procedures (such as the procedures for the recognition and enforcement of arbitral awards). The consequence of this development is the blurring of the conceptual boundaries that lawyers traditionally use to identify and distinguish among different ADR procedures. For example, technology facilitates the creation of private adjudicative procedures that do not formally qualify as arbitration, but do nevertheless lead to enforceable decisions. Frictionless enforcement can help private parties devise cost-effective dispute resolution mechanisms, thus potentially enabling a broader range of users to access dispute resolution services. Pietro Ortolani warns, however, that the self-sufficient nature of these new digital means of dispute resolution provokes new challenges, such as the dilution of due process guarantees, the erosion of finality, and the under-enforcement of substantive law. To counteract the risk of these harms, transnational procedural minimum standards should be adopted and enforced.

21.6 LT, LEGAL EDUCATION, AND LEGAL ETHICS

Just as LT is having a disruptive effect on the practice of law, it will have a major impact on legal education and legal ethics.

21.6.1 Legal Education

Law schools have been slow to modernize their curricula to deal with the needs of future lawyers. The future lawyer will need to possess tech-related skill sets instead of the traditional mentality produced by law schools, which is increasingly becoming obsolete. Law school administrators have long needed to perform a serious assessment of legal education from the perspective of the preparation of today's law students for the expected challenges of tomorrow. A suitable strategy for imparting such knowledge would be to include a variation of computer science studies into legal education.[10] A menu of needed changes include LT as a compulsory course or courses, creation of certificate programs in LT, and creating LT master's programs. The more holistic approach, since LT is impacting more and more areas of law, is to incorporate LT in almost all courses and areas of study. Bar and certification exams should be reconstituted to test students' acumen in using LT. Currently, state exams focus mainly on legal knowledge in an array of subject areas and less so on legal practice, where LT is playing an increasingly important role.[11]

The recognition of the importance of LT in law schools and state licensing exams will allow law students to compete with non-lawyer LT providers. For the betterment of law and legal practice, lawyers should not abdicate the field of LT to technologists who do not possess an advanced understanding of the law. Instead of abdication, law schools and law firms should invest in interdisciplinarity. In a changing legal world, communication with professionals from other fields will prove essential. More interdisciplinary forums engaging lawyers and computer scientists have to be created, hybrid courses of study should be offered, and scepticism toward other professions within legal practice should be rejected. In the age of technological acceleration, lawyers can best survive, and the law can be best served, through collaborations between lawyers who are tech-savvy and technologists with a basic understanding of the conceptual nature of law.

From the law student perspective, developing tech skills while in law school should be seen as an opportunity. Many law firms have shown a preference to hire lawyers with some legal practice experience over freshly minted law graduates. However, a law student with "experience" in technical skills and using LT will be more competitive in the legal marketplace.

21.6.2 LT and Legal Ethics

LT poses a challenge to current standards of legal ethics, more specifically, how those standards apply to the issues presented by LT and its transformation of the practice of law. In the practice of law, a lawyer may delegate work to an LT system, but she cannot delegate her ethical duties. Legal ethics is a unique form of applied ethics. New standards and guidance will need to be developed to guide lawyers in the use of LT. As a result of the progress of AI, a number of ethical guidelines have been developed by the OECD and the European Commission's High-Level

---

[10] Zwickel, n. 5 at 882.
[11] M. Fries, "Staatsexamen für Roboteranwälte?" (2018) *Zeitschrift für Rechtspolitik* 161 165.

Expert Group. Möslein and Horn (Chapter 5) argue that, while the existing ethical guidelines are not binding legal instruments, they should be used by judges to fill the gaps in professional regulations, giving concrete meaning (with reference to AI) to the lawyer's general duty of due diligence. For now, the practicing lawyer must apply current professional regulations to her use of LT. The core ethical duties of lawyers are competence, due diligence, supervision, client confidentiality, and preserving the lawyer-client privilege. As they relate to LT, it is clear that lawyers must be competent in the use of LT products and supervise or manage their use. The core decisions will be determining what tasks should or should not be automated and the selection of the most suitable LT products, including an assessment of their shortcomings, the limits of their use, and the training of personnel to properly implement and monitor their use.

LT is likely to expand the ethical duties of lawyers (compliance of LT with ethical standards), but at the same time LT can help lawyers to better fulfill their ethical duties. This is most likely to occur in the area of the duty of competence. Some tasks can be performed better and more accurately by LT than lawyers. Thus, the use of LT in certain areas may no longer be a choice made by lawyers; the ethical duty of competence may require lawyers to use LT in areas involving the review of large amounts of documents, such as in e-discovery. In this way, the future has been morphed into the present: lawyers will be under a duty to implement LT and prepare for the LT of the future.

21.7 CONCLUSION

Nobel Laureate John Galsworthy once pointed out that "if you do not think about the future, you cannot have one."[12] The monopolized structure of the legal profession and the structure of law firms initially resulted in a great deal of resistance to the type of automation of jobs traditionally done by the lawyer. The basic functionality and the established working methods in legal practice are often fundamentally different from those in information technology and computer science. Law and its application are sociocultural phenomena that depend on human abilities and on solutions that are open to (human) interpretation.[13] Digital processes, conversely, are purely logic-based mathematical procedures that function according to reproducible and predeterminable sequences. Nonetheless, courts, law firms, and legal practitioners are subject to growing competition in the market for legal services, as well as the ever-increasing need for efficiency and cost reduction. For these reasons, resistance will need to give way to acceptance if law firms are to continue to flourish. As Galsworthy admonishes, lawyers must see the reality of the present and the future of lawyering. LT has already made significant inroads in the present and will be essential to lawyering in the future.

Even though the lawyers of tomorrow will not have to be computer scientists, they will be asked to display a basic understanding of the functionality of LT and AI processes, including knowledge of computer coding. This new skill set is needed for lawyers to obtain the highest benefits from LT, coordinate legal activities using different LT products, and make smart decisions in the allocation of activities to LT versus the lawyer. Being tech-savvy will allow lawyers to coordinate the human–LT interface between the law firm and its clients, to identify errors in LT systems, and to improve LT applications. In the end, the bigger question is not whether to adopt LT, but how to adopt or implement it. Numerous concerns and potential

---

[12] M. Kilian, "Die Zukunft der Juristen" (2017) *Neue Juristische Wochenschrift* 3043 3050.
[13] G. Buchholtz, "LT – Chancen und Risiken der digitalen Rechtsanwendung" (2017) *Juristische Schulung* 955 957.

liabilities need to be worked out in the areas of the costs of LT, cybersecurity and privacy protection, finding personnel with the requisite talent and skills, uncertainty of regulation and compliance, and efficient implementation.

The idea that the LT of the future (with development of superintelligence or advanced AI) will displace human lawyers is an illusion. Lawyers possess emotional, communication, strategizing, judgment, and counseling skill sets that LT cannot duplicate. In Chapter 19, Professor Jeffrey Lipshaw sees the division of labor based on System 1 and System 2 types of thinking. LT offers massive computing power that can find trends and predict outcomes (System 1), while humans offer something that cannot be duplicated by machines: "they can perceive purposes and have a will to act, characteristics that resist easy scientific explanation." LT cannot duplicate human creativity, insight, intuition, and the will to act. As such, LT has affected and will continue to affect the practice of law, but it will not replace the need for experienced lawyers. Instead, a synergy will occur with the combination of higher rationality (LT) and deliberative thinking (lawyer). The key issue becomes how lawyers and law firms can accommodate LT and create the optimum degree of synergy for themselves and their clients. Lawyers must remain in control through their management of LT; this management includes law firms discerning between fake LT, hype LT, and actual LT (see Chapter 20). The firms that will excel are those that will master the implementation of LT and successfully invest in developing their own LT solutions.[14]

---

[14] See Paw Fruerlund and Sebastian Peters, "Surviving the Digital Transformation: A Method for Lawyers to Approach Legal Tech" in this book (Chapter 20).

For EU product safety concerns, contact us at Calle de José Abascal, 56–1º,
28003 Madrid, Spain or eugpsr@cambridge.org.

www.ingramcontent.com/pod-product-compliance
Ingram Content Group UK Ltd.
Pitfield, Milton Keynes, MK11 3LW, UK
UKHW050416240426
12048UKWH00021B/1532